Mexican American Odyssey

Number two

UNIVERSITY OF HOUSTON SERIES
IN MEXICAN AMERICAN STUDIES

Sponsored by the Center for Mexican American Studies
Tatcho Mindiola, Director and General Editor

Mexican American Odyssey

FELIX TIJERINA,

ENTREPRENEUR &

CIVIC LEADER,

1905–1965

Thomas H. Kreneck

To Larry Friedman —
mentor, teacher, and friend —
Tom Kreneck
May 14, 2001

Texas A&M University Press
COLLEGE STATION

LIBRARY OF CONGRESS CATALOGING-IN-PUBLICATION DATA

Kreneck, Thomas H.
   Mexican American Odyssey: Felix Tijerina, entrepreneur and civic
leader, 1905–1965 / Thomas H. Kreneck.—1st ed.
      p. cm.—(University of Houston series in Mexican American
studies ; no. 2)
Includes bibliographical references (p.) and index.
   ISBN 0-89096-936-1 (alk. paper)
      1. Tijerina, Felix, 1905–1965. 2. Mexican Americans—Texas—
Houston—Biography. 3. Businessmen—Texas—Houson—
Biography. 4. Civil rights workers—Texas—Houston—Biography.
5. Houston (Tex.)—Biography. 6. Houston (Tex.)—
Ethnic relations. 7. Mexican Americans—Civil rights—Texas—
Houston—History—20th century. 8. League of United Latin
American Citizens—History. 9. Mexican Americans—Civil rights—
History—20th century. 9. Mexican Americans—Civil rights—
History. I. Title. II. Series.
   F394.H89 M516 2001
   305.868'073'092—dc21
                                            00-010906

*Once again, to the Houstonians of Mexican descent,
especially those of Felix Tijerina's generation*

CONTENTS

ILLUSTRATIONS

ACKNOWLEDGMENTS

This volume is a product of a twenty-year interest in the life of Felix Tijerina and a lifelong association with the ethnic population he represented. As a native of South Texas, I have had continual engagement with Texans of Mexican descent and their history. My specific interest in Tijerina, however, was a result of my twelve-year tenure (1978–90) as head of the Mexican American archival component of the Houston Metropolitan Research Center (HMRC). During that time, when HMRC began to build its research holdings on Houston's Mexican American population, Tijerina immediately emerged as a principal figure whose papers should be acquired. Though he had died more than a dozen years earlier (I never met him), Tijerina was still fresh in people's memories as an entrepreneur and civic leader, and his name seemed ever-present in the records from the 1930s to the 1960s. My fascination with him grew, and I formed the concept for a book-length biography. I felt certain that his story was critical for understanding the Bayou City's Hispanic past.

The Tijerina biography received a major boost from my appointment as Visiting Scholar in the Mexican American Studies Program at the University of Houston in 1989–90. During that academic year, I completed drafts of several chapters and conducted substantial inquiry for those remaining. The term as Visiting Scholar allowed me precious time to research, contemplate, and write and provided impetus for the additional work necessary to finish the book.

Over the course of the project, I have become indebted to many people whom I must thank profusely, for without their assistance, this biography would not have taken shape in its present form. The first group consists of individuals who knew Felix Tijerina personally and shared their remembrances with me. Foremost, I am beholden to his widow, the late Janie González Tijerina. She graciously donated the Tijerina family papers to HMRC, granted me numerous interviews, and gave me her blessing to write a balanced, factual account of her late husband's life. Mrs. Tijerina was a singular person, as I hope this volume conveys, and she will always have my gratitude. I also wish to thank Felix Tijerina, Jr., and Janie Bell Tijerina (Mr. and Mrs. Tijerina's children) for their friendship and insight, as well as their support for this study of their father. Other members of the Tijerina family who provided significant recollections include Felix's sister, the late Victoria Tijerina, and his niece, Rosie Tijerina Solíz.

Several residents of Nuevo León proved especially helpful during my memorable second research field trip in 1997 to Monterrey and General Escobedo. Francisco Peña Ayala (*compadre* of Felix Tijerina), Jesús Ayala López (former *alcalde* of General Escobedo), and Manuela Villarreal Sepúlveda de Góngora (sister of Domingo Villarreal) shared important remembrances of Tijerina and early times in General Escobedo. Born in Escobedo in 1912, 1911, and 1912, respectively, they represent true living history sources. Francisco Peña Garza (son of Sr. Peña Ayala) and Mario Góngora Villarreal (son of Sra. Sepúlveda de Góngora) and his family contributed their valuable recollections and assistance as well. Although they did not know Tijerina, Oscar Garza Guajardo (Secretario del Ayuntamiento, General Escobedo), Juan Ramón Garza Guajardo (director of the Library of Hacienda San Pedro and historian of General Escobedo), and Gerardo García Salinas (Secretario Particular del Secretario del Ayuntamiento, General Escobedo) provided me with crucial information about their town. They also arranged my oral history interviews with Sr. Peña Ayala, Sr. Ayala López, and Sra. Sepúlveda de Góngora. Myrna Martínez, secretary to Oscar Garza Guajardo, efficiently coordinated my audience with her supervisor.

My debt is immeasurable to María Villarreal Bosmans, first cousin of Felix Tijerina, who, while in her eighties, generously shared with me her memories of Felix when they were children together on the migrant trail from Robstown to Sugar Land during the 1910s. Her son, Tony Bosmans, made it possible for me to obtain his mother's valuable recollections by serving as intermediary and interpreter for our interviews. To him I likewise owe a tremendous debt. I extend my thanks also to Anselmo Villarreal, younger brother of María Villarreal Bosmans, who provided information on the family's history, which he had learned from his older brothers and his father, Aurelio Villarreal.

A special note of appreciation is due to T. C. Roselle, Herbert Shelton, and Eleno Flores (all of the Sugar Land Heritage Society and lifelong residents of that area) for their commonsense insights into that region's history. Mr. Shelton gave me an informative tour of historic Sugar Land, pointing out the places of relevance to Felix Tijerina's early life. I especially recall our visit to Sugar Land's San Isidro Cemetery. I likewise owe thanks to Blas Rodríguez, Sr., son of Juan Rodríguez, for relating to me his father's stories of Felix Tijerina as a youngster in Sugar Land. Dionicia Contreras, George Jamail, and Gloria Pina García offered much understanding of Felix's first Houston neighborhood. The late, colorful Sigmund Frucht gave a lively description of Tijerina's first work on Houston's Produce Row.

William Aguilar, Primitivo Niño, Rodrigo García, E. J. García, Ramón Fernández, Sr., Manuel Crespo, Sr., Leo Reynosa (all now deceased), and other comrades from the old days of Club México Bello and Club International told me about Felix's world during the 1920s and 1930s. Mr. and Mrs. Raúl C. Molina, Sr., and the late Mrs. Félix H. (Angelina) Morales provided specific information not only for the 1920s and 1930s, but also for other aspects of this work.

I also owe thanks to David Rodríguez (of Beaumont, Texas) and Frank Barrera (of Houston), employees of Felix Mexican Restaurants during the 1940s, for sharing their memories of what it was like to work for Tijerina. Eddie Gutiérrez, Richard Holgin, and Danny González helped me appreciate how younger men viewed Tijerina during the 1950s. Sidney Farr, the late Philip Montalbo, and the late Judge Joe M. Ingraham were of great assistance in clarifying and injecting human dimension to Tijerina's legal case over his citizenship status during the 1950s. Farr, Montalbo, and Ingraham numbered among the individuals whose recollections assisted in the considerable research necessary to gather the facts regarding Tijerina's place of birth.

In my many conversations with the men of Houston's illustrious LULAC Council No. 60, they conveyed not only factual information, but also the color and spirit for understanding their history-laden organization. Council members Sammie Alderete, Ernest Eguía, Toby Hernández, Benny Martínez, Sal García, and David Adame, as well as the late Constable Raúl C.

Martínez, Juvencio Rodríguez, Isidro García, Joe Orlando, and Moses I. Sánchez contributed their memories to my book, even if they are not specifically cited in the notes. Other LULAC veterans—Carmen Cortes, Tony Campos, Judge Felix Salazar, Daniel Sandoval, and the late Philip Montalbo—who had a special association with Tijerina, kindly responded to my inquiries on LULAC and other topics whenever called upon. Frank Pinedo, Oscar M. Laurel, and William D. Bonilla, past national LULAC presidents, likewise patiently offered important insight.

From his own particular perspective, the late John J. Herrera, Houston LULAC's most important bulwark, was crucial to my research. I hope this volume adequately conveys a sense of John Herrera's unique character. For his friendship, assistance, and instruction, I will be forever grateful.

The most important source of oral recollections, besides Mrs. Tijerina herself, was Judge Alfred J. Hernández. He candidly shared with me his considerable knowledge of Tijerina and the other people and events covered in this book. His vantage point as perhaps Felix's closest confidant greatly informed my research, especially on LULAC matters. Judge Hernández was always unselfishly available to answer my questions, from the time of our first recorded interview in 1979 until the completion of the book.

Among the more memorable interviews were those given by the learned L. DeWitt Hale (former state representative from Corpus Christi) regarding educational reform and Felix's role in that movement and the late Elizabeth Burrus, who shared her memories of the Little School of the 400. They were prime examples of the many Anglo associates and friends of Felix Tijerina who helped make his work successful. Isabel Verver, now of Norwalk, California, enthusiastically lent her recollections of her time developing the Little School. Alfonso Vázquez, keen participant-observer of Houston's Mexican American politics during the late 1950s and early 1960s, provided ongoing instruction on those events. My thanks also go to Senator Carlos F. Truan, dean of the Texas Senate, for his perceptive views on Tijerina, the Little School, and the evolution of Hispanic education.

To the other persons whose interviews are listed in the notes, I extend a blanket, though heartfelt, expression of gratitude. Like those mentioned by name, they gave life to the documents. During my research, I encountered many other people who knew Tijerina, if only casually. When I explained my writing project to them in conversation (as I did to more than cared to hear), they would often share an observation on my subject. These individuals collectively helped shape my understanding of Felix, in particular his image in the popular mind, which was an important element of his life and place in history.

Many persons not directly acquainted with Tijerina also facilitated my research. Through the efforts of Raúl Castillo and Luis Escareño, administrators with the City of Houston, I obtained a crucial leave of absence to assume the duties of Visiting Scholar at the University of Houston in 1989. People associated with the various library resources I utilized gave invaluable help as well. Chief among these individuals were Louis J. Marchiafava and his staff at the Houston Metropolitan Research Center: Nancy Hadley, Chuck Hamilton, Luciaan Blyaert, Steven Strom, the late Michael Wilson, the late Victor Borgeson, Tara Wenger, Joel Draut, Andrew Hempe, and Deborah Moore. They made materials from HMRC's Mexican American archival component fully available, responding to my sometimes rather hastily planned research visits and requests. Dr. Marchiafava, with whom I worked for fourteen years at HMRC (ten of those as his assistant director), has extended more courtesies to me than can be explained here. He also offered intellectual exchange, especially his insight into the minds of immigrant folk, thus informing my interpretation. He and the other members of HMRC's staff mentioned above hold a special place in this study. Carolyn Johnson, head of the Texas and Local History Department of Houston Public Library and her staff—Douglas Weiskopf, Ann Douglas, Will Howard, and Ellen Hanlon—were essential in accessing information I needed. In charge of one of the leading printed Texana collections in the state, they always accommodated my requests. Robert Schaadt, director and archivist of the Sam Houston Regional Library and Research Center, assisted me not only with the Price Daniel Papers under his care, but also through his considerable expertise in county records. Paul Scott, archivist for Harris County, provided assistance with Harris County and Fort Bend County records and suggested pertinent files. Margo Gutiérrez, Michael Hironymous, and other staff of the Benson Latin American History Collection at the University of Texas at Austin made the Benson's impressive LULAC holdings available. Sheri Adams, librarian for the *Houston Chronicle,* made that newspaper's clipping morgue accessible and helped in other ways.

Numerous other library professionals, including Alice Martínez of the Tyrrell Historical Library in Beaumont, Texas; Jim Leyerezapf, archivist at the Dwight D. Eisenhower Library; June Payne, reference assistant at the

John F. Kennedy Library; Robert Tissing of the Lyndon B. Johnson Library; and Frank H. Mackaman of the Dirksen Congressional Center were extremely helpful with their collections. G. Y. Rathanraj and Robert L. Reyna, administrators for the Houston Housing Authority (HHA), and their office staff made it possible for me to research Tijerina's role as a member of the HHA board of directors.

Those persons who gave me assistance with genealogy research, crucial to this undertaking, deserve separate mention. These professionals include Maxine Alcorn and her staff of the Clayton Genealogical Center of Houston Public Library, the premier genealogy resource in Texas; Margaret Rose, head of the Local History Department of Corpus Christi Public Library, who ably assisted me in finding Mexican baptismal and confirmation records; and Mira Smithwick of the Spanish American Genealogical Association (SAGA), who helped me trace Mexican birth records through her contacts with Israel Cavazos Garza of Monterrey, Nuevo León. Also of great service were the many volunteers associated with the Family History Centers of the Church of Jesus Christ of the Latter-Day Saints in Houston and Corpus Christi, who were as kind and helpful to me as they are to everyone. Mickey García, Houston genealogist, provided proficient translation of Spanish-language birth and death records. Finally, David J. Webb, friend of my youth and genealogist extraordinaire, checked source notes and methodically pursued genealogical documents that filled many blank spaces in my research.

Because of his generosity and support for the study of Houston's Hispanic history, José De La Isla provided me with and quickly taught me how to operate a personal computer that I used to write this book. Deborah A. Bauer (also a former colleague at HMRC) and Noble Enete offered stimulating intellectual dialogue and personal support during the initial stages of this project. Craig Youngblood and Ann Stangle, staff members of the late Judge Joe Ingraham, helped me gain Ingraham's valuable interview. Mayor Emeritus Luther Jones of Corpus Christi generously facilitated my meeting with Senator Carlos F. Truan, as did the senator's staff, Shelly García and Mary Helen Rodríguez.

In a class by herself, C. Elaine Cummins provided expert assistance in arranging my two research trips to Monterrey, Nuevo León, and located Tijerina's FBI files and materials on federal school programs of the mid-1960s. She also provided invaluable insight on issues raised by the data and extended many other courtesies as well. Thanks go to two of my bosses at Texas A&M University–Corpus Christi—former Library Director Richard L. O'Keeffe and current Director Abby R. Kratz, who encouraged my writing. Alva D. Neer, Grace Guajardo Charles, and Jan S. Weaver, indispensable staff members of the Special Collections and Archives Department, not only provided research assistance but assumed extra duties during the final stages of the manuscript's completion.

Among those who helped me hone my ideas for the various chapters, Marie Theresa Hernández and Nestor Rodríguez stand out for distinction. Ms. Hernández also worthily served as interpreter and advisor during my second research field trip to Monterrey and General Escobedo. Historians Roberto R. Treviño, Ignacio M. García, Alan Lessoff, and Cynthia E. Orozco were similarly instructive and encouraging during this project.

Joan T. Dusard, attorney-at-law, and Don E. Carleton, director of the Center for American History, gave me ongoing encouragement and provided insight to those parts of this book which fell within their considerable range of knowledge. These two people are my constant comrades.

For their fundamental roles, I want to thank two of my earliest associates in Mexican American studies. F. Arturo Rosales has been my close colleague since introducing me to collecting Mexican American primary sources in the late 1970s. His understanding of the Immigrant Generation and his initial observations on Felix Tijerina guided my inquiry. Second, Tatcho Mindiola, Jr., director of the Mexican American Studies Program at the University of Houston, granted me the Visiting Scholarship. He not only recognized the importance of my subject, but also displayed infinite patience while I progressed on the biography and encouraged me in many ways.

Finally and most important, Arnoldo De León, dean of Mexican American history in Texas, was a continual source of intellectual and personal support. Characteristic of his preeminence in producing and fostering Mexican American historical scholarship, he served as the sole reader for all my drafts, offered essential critiques, and made possible much of whatever merit exists in this volume. My gratitude to him cannot be adequately expressed.

Because all of the above people contributed to the production of this biography, I hope they find value—and not too many errors—in its contents.

MEXICAN AMERICAN ODYSSEY

INTRODUCTION

When Felix Tijerina died in 1965 at age sixty, he was widely viewed as the most esteemed and influential Mexican American resident of Houston, Texas.[1] Businessman, civic leader, and nationally recognized advocate of Mexican American education, Tijerina had become especially prominent in the post–World War II era. Like no one before him, he had bridged the traditional ethnic gap through his leading roles in mainstream organizations as well as in Mexican American groups. His life story was common knowledge to most Houstonians: his humble birth in 1905 (reportedly in Fort Bend County, Texas), his early days in Houston as an uneducated laborer, his rise to wealth and status as owner of a chain of Mexican food restaurants, his leadership position among Hispanics, and his many philanthropic endeavors. People knew him particularly well for his tenure as national president of the League of United Latin American Citizens (LULAC) during the late 1950s and as founder of the Little School of the 400, his internationally acclaimed program to bring English-language instruction to Spanish-speaking preschoolers. No metropolitan area prized entrepreneurial success more than Houston, the largest, most energetic city in the Lone Star state; and its residents identified Tijerina as a Latin American–style Horatio Alger character and solid citizen.[2]

Houston's respect for Tijerina prompted the Houston Independent School District in 1977 to place his name on a new elementary school. Dedicated in 1981, Felix Tijerina Elementary was the first school in the city to be named for a Houstonian of Mexican descent. As such, it both honored Tijerina and hailed the newly achieved stature of Hispanics as a demographic, economic, political, and sociocultural force in Houston.[3]

In many ways, Tijerina's life and efforts symbolized the emergence of Mexican Americans as an integral, growing segment not only within the Bayou City, but throughout much of urban America during his part of the twentieth century. This increasing significance was most evident in places such as Houston, where Mexican American communities were mainly post-1900 creations. Tijerina also had helped, by deed and by example, to give direction to Mexican American advancement.

This biography will consider, in both the local and the broad setting, the life of Felix Tijerina—his actions, aspirations, and world view—as a reflection of the wider Mexican American experience during the first seven decades of the twentieth century. At the same time, it will emphasize his contributions as a leader in shaping *la raza*'s development. Humanistic in its approach, this study aims to narrate the salient facts of Tijerina's life, while offering readers nuance for further thought about Mexican American history.[4]

The years of Tijerina's life (1905–65) included many important phenomena in twentieth-century Mexican American history which his own experiences directly mirrored. This period witnessed the century's initial wave of Mexican immigration to the United States, the movement of people just prior to, in the midst of, and immediately after the Mexican Revolution of 1910. When Tijerina was born, people of Mexican descent in the United States numbered around 500,000. By 1930, this number had been augmented by more than 10 percent of Mexico's population—as many as 1.5 million people—who came to the United States, the majority of whom arrived after 1915. Tijerina and his family were in this monumental migration.[5]

Contrary to his public image (which held him up as a Texas native), the evidence suggests that Felix Tijerina had been born in northern Mexico. In 1915, as a boy of ten and at the height of the Mexican Revolution, he came north with relatives, part of what some scholars term the Immigrant Generation. Through much travail, he and his family ultimately reached Houston.

In that era, he also began his association with mainstream U.S. society. It was the difficult beginning of his accommodation to a new world.[6]

Tijerina and his family were among the thousands who established Houston's *colonia mexicana* (Mexican colony) as a viable entity. The Tijerinas' settlement in Houston in 1922 reflected the urbanization of Mexicans and U.S.-born Mexican Americans going on in many parts of the United States. By 1930 people of Mexican descent formed enclaves in such geographically distant urban centers as Los Angeles, Saint Louis, Omaha, Detroit, Saint Paul, Chicago, Gary, Denver, San Antonio, and Houston. Although exact numbers of rural and urban Mexican Americans have yet to be fully determined by historians, at the beginning of the century the majority had lived in rural settings. The shift to the city was especially acute during the 1920s and paralleled the movement of the general U.S. population as people left the old agrarian order for the modern, urban world of the twentieth century. Tijerina would live to see the percentage of Hispanics residing in cities increase to the point that, by the beginning of the 1960s, and near the end of his life, Mexican Americans nationally were almost 80 percent urban.[7]

Tijerina's life also exemplifies the societal maturation of the sons and daughters of this Immigrant Generation. Many of these youngsters (like Tijerina) had participated in the pre-1930 migration. After their families settled them in cities, they evolved from being Mexicans to being urban Americans, integrating themselves more thoroughly into their new surroundings than did their elders. Though Tijerina retained vestiges of the earlier, more circumspect immigrant mentality, he emerged more as a part of the 1930s group, which scholars have come to call the Mexican American Generation.[8]

As one of the more important members of the 1930s generation, Tijerina illustrates that individuals who reached maturity during that decade provided much of the Mexican American leadership in the post–World War II period. Prior to the war, he already participated conspicuously in Mexican and Anglo organizations on behalf of Houston's "Latin Americans," a designation used more widely at that time than "Mexican American." As seen in Felix's life, his generation began a level of civic activism that only accelerated as a result of the war, became a political force unto itself, and influenced events from the late 1920s until the mid-1960s. Led by people like Felix Tijerina, the urban *colonias* exhibited a continuity in their development during these approximately thirty-five years and became more than passive recipients of what mainstream society dealt them.[9]

Felix Tijerina further embodies the remarkable adaptation by this important cohort of Mexican Americans. He utilized what available, socially acceptable means he had at hand to adjust to his Houston habitat, which experienced great fluidity and rapid change during this period. Felix and his contemporaries had to adapt and readapt skillfully to fit their changing environment. The portrait that emerges from Tijerina's story is one of a talented, resourceful individual who demonstrated an ability to assume different roles as his circumstances, judgment, and convictions dictated.

Significantly, too, Tijerina's biography brings into focus the relationship between the city and those Mexican people entering and living in American urban areas during his lifetime. Felix himself became an urban man in outlook and manner during the 1920s and continued to develop in this way. The adaptation by *colonia* residents in general to their new surroundings transformed them into Mexican American city people, individuals whose experiences, aspirations, and perceptions changed while they still retained parts of their Mexican heritage. They in turn altered their urban areas. Tijerina's generation would lend a Mexican American flavor to many cities where, theretofore, little Hispanic influence had been felt, thus adding their own measure to the synthesis of American society.[10]

For every immigrant who opted for the city, the transition to American urban life meant adjusting to fresh conditions and creating work skills. These immigrant folks, of necessity, could adjust quickly to some of the employment they found. Other work, such as a business venture like the one Tijerina undertook, demanded remarkable virtuosity and no little personal courage to attempt. The talent and fortitude displayed by Tijerina (and his fellow urban immigrants) were crucial in building a community's economic base and in grappling with the larger society to win the everyday battles of survival. These small victories, when tallied over a fifty-year period, accounted for the progress of Mexican Americans.[11]

The rural-to-urban demographic shift in Mexican American history highlights another important development in which Tijerina participated: specifically, increased activity by Hispanic institutions and organizations in the cities. He took a prominent part in many of the traditional as well as more modern social, cultural, civic, and political Mexican American urban groups from the 1930s forward. His work within these associations demonstrates the emergence of the small but growing Mexican American urban middle class and its style of leadership.[12]

Shortly after he began his efforts in Mexican American organizations, Tijerina also became active within mainstream Anglo groups. Such involvement was characteristic of the biculturalism that marked Mexican American urban existence, a biculturalism which will be explained below in greater detail. In Tijerina's case, his membership in the Optimist Club, Community Chest, and other such civic activity during the 1930s represented his dexterous involvement within and acceptance by the broader community; it was a logical middle-class progression in his successful accommodation to Anglo society.

Another important facet of Tijerina's personal and public life underscores the significance of Mexican American women in community history. In 1933, Tijerina married Janie González, who was, like her husband, from a working-class background. Moreover, she was a 1920s urban immigrant, though she hailed originally from rural Texas. They were linked as a team in the public eye and eventually raised two children. No mere ornament to her husband, Mrs. Felix (as she came to be known) played a lasting, active part in Tijerina's career and blossomed into a woman of property and standing. She illustrated to a large degree the place of women as both supportive of male activities and vital participants in the community and the economy in their own right. Though an exceptional person, she embodied a version of the female Mexican American experience, especially the rise to middle-class status. No biography of Felix Tijerina would be complete without understanding Mrs. Felix's role in her husband's life from the 1930s forward.[13]

Though battered by the Great Depression, Felix Tijerina exemplified how some individuals in the Mexican American community established a firm economic base beginning in the late 1930s. Launching their first successful restaurant (Felix Mexican Restaurant) in 1937, he and Mrs. Felix would increase their fortunes until together they became, after World War II, the most recognized Mexican American business success story in Houston.

Tijerina would achieve his greatest prosperity and public recognition after World War II, at the same time that the Mexican American community was coming into its own. Felix and Mexican Americans in general took an active part in the war effort, becoming even more integrated into their surroundings through their wartime participation. Afterward, they cashed in as best they could on the prosperity of the late 1940s to early 1960s. Tijerina himself reached the pinnacle of his involvement in society in numerous high-profile business, civic, and governmental endeavors in the twenty years after the war. His expansion of the Felix Mexican Restaurant chain, membership in such prestigious groups as Rotary International, and his work on administrative boards carried him ever more into the public spotlight. His most lofty civic position came when he was elected national president of LULAC. During his unprecedented four terms, from 1956 to 1960, he became one of the most visible Mexican Americans in the country, reflecting the increased visibility of the Mexican American community to mainstream society. As LULAC national president, he established the Little School of the 400. Altogether, Tijerina placed himself astride both Anglo and Mexican American cultures as no one in Houston had done before him.[14]

Additionally, Felix Tijerina proved to be the dominant LULAC national president of the 1950s. He became "Mr. LULAC" in the minds of many people across the nation. An understanding of him and his LULAC administration therefore offers important insight into the operation and nature of that significant Mexican American organization during the pre-1960s postwar period and, thus, into Mexican American activism as a whole.

Tijerina's story, like that of his entire generation, testifies to a level of self-determination that is often underemphasized in discussions of Mexican American history for this period. Such independence by Mexican American residents sprang from the resourcefulness and adaptability of individuals who, like Tijerina, worked separately as well as together with people of goodwill. Self-determination and solidarity with non-Hispanic friends were essential elements in the emergence of twentieth-century Mexican Americans; their advancement was, at one and the same time, done in spite of and made possible by close proximity to Anglo American society. For Felix and his contemporaries, there was oppression yet opportunity within the larger environment.

An understanding of how Tijerina managed to deal with both bigotry and opportunity in mainstream society helps explain the intricacies of Mexican American–Anglo American relations. A master at interacting with the Anglo mainstream, he accomplished a great deal, never allowing prejudice to force him into a state of nonachievement, overreaction, rancor, or chronic suspicion. So also did his Mexican American contemporaries carefully weigh their responses to negative situations. As a result, they were able to accomplish many things—often with the help of Anglo friends and sympathetic associates (*amigos de la raza*)—regardless of the obstacles planted in their path by others in society. During his life, Felix had Anglo employers, business colleagues, political allies, fellow civic club members, friends, and admirers who lent him assistance, and he did much for them as well. Such constructive associations demonstrate that the relationship between Mexicans and Anglos in U.S. history was not one simply characterized by conflict and victimization. As reflected in Felix's story, well-meaning members of both groups worked together toward an inclusive, equitable society, something that Tijerina saw as the most desirable goal.

As part of his dealings with Anglo society, Tijerina pursued political activism; in doing so, he reflected the wishes and efforts of other middle-class Mexican Americans wanting to fit into the mainstream. Though generally cautious and circumspect (and often crafty) in politics, Tijerina usually leaned toward the moderate wing of the Democratic Party. He developed ties with some of the loftiest public officials on the Houston and Texas scene, especially in the postwar years when he attained his greatest public stature. Though in this regard he far exceeded the majority of Mexican Americans, he also represented the political aspirations and involvement of many of their numbers during the pre-1965 period.

Much as Tijerina's biography sheds light on Mexican-Anglo relations, it also touches upon the association of Mexican Americans with other peoples of color. During the postwar period, Tijerina and his fellows had to deal with the black civil rights movement. Tijerina's own response—distancing himself and LULAC from the plight of African Americans and calling for "patience" on the part of blacks—stood at odds with the beliefs of many of his middle-class Mexican American compatriots, but reflected the position of many others. Altogether, Felix's actions showed the complexity of Mexican American views toward blacks and toward African American efforts to attain civil rights. The way that Tijerina grappled with this thorny issue (and briefly with the Puerto Rican independence struggle) reveals that Mexican Americans had a keen awareness of other minorities.[15]

Another element of Mexican American history illuminated by Felix Tijerina's life is the important psychocultural balance he and his generation adopted. Scholars have noted that throughout the nineteenth century, Tejanos developed a bicultural identity that equipped them to exist within an Anglo American–dominated environment. By 1900, Mexican Americans were accustomed to drawing behavior patterns from both Mexican and Anglo cultures. This process, termed biculturalization, was common in the Texas Mexican community by the time Felix and his generation were born. Their cohort demonstrates its twentieth century continuation.[16]

Biculturalization is predicated upon the ability of individuals to strike a personal balance between the two cultures with which they identify, dealing with each, and being a part of both. Tijerina successfully struck that balance and maintained (as nearly as can be determined) a relatively healthy psyche, though his daily existence may have had its share of troubles and anxieties. Throughout his life, he navigated successfully in both Mexican American and Anglo American society without any apparent harm to his self-image.

Tijerina lived a full life, enriched by his affiliations with both Anglos and members of his own ethnic group. He incorporated two cultures and evidenced a strong sense of personal identity, with no discernible feelings of marginality.[17] Felix adopted what he felt were the most constructive features of his new Houston milieu and advocated acculturation by other persons of Mexican descent. He successfully fit into American society on the best terms that he could negotiate. Simultaneously, he familiarized Anglo society with Mexican and Mexican American culture.

The acculturation Tijerina espoused was one which he believed to be a realistic, desirable avenue to a better life. He never envisioned abandonment or denial of his Mexican heritage, although he felt that accommodation to the mainstream involved necessary, positive change. It was an approach not without personal struggle, ambiguities, and ambivalence; however, for Felix and his generation, all of whom came up in difficult circumstances in the fields and *barrios,* life itself was realistically viewed as a proposition fraught with difficulty and contradiction.[18]

The problems and contradictions of Mexican American existence may have been most starkly manifested in Felix's life by his prolonged attempts to establish his American citizenship by "proving" his place of birth to U.S. legal authorities. This trouble emanated from conflicting claims about his nativity and lasted from 1940 until 1956. It was an episode that caused Tijerina no little personal uncertainty, chagrin, and financial expense. It no doubt affected his actions and reflected the complex position of a person of Mexican heritage in Texas society—even someone who was, by all measure, as successful as Felix Tijerina.

Tijerina's life clearly illustrates that even during the 1950s, when assimilationist impulses were prevalent, the Mexican American experience did not constitute a one-way avenue toward cultural destruction by mainstream society. Rather, there was a balance, if sometimes an uneasy one, between partaking of larger Anglo American culture and retaining ethnicity. Mexico was too close geographically, Mexican American culture too strong, and mainstream prejudices often too severe to allow obliteration of *mexicanidad* (Mexicanness), a feeling of being one of *la raza*. Felix was often impatient with Mexican residents of the United States for what he believed was their reticence to become directly involved with the larger society. He frequently criticized other members of his socioeconomic bracket, and they in turn were critical of him. This shortness with and self-criticism of *la raza*, however, should be seen for what it was: critical analysis by individuals trying to cope with real societal conditions. In their comments, they presented their views of the best way to be full, productive members of society.

Felix, like any other American entrepreneur, believed in the promise of America. He differed from many non-Hispanic businessmen because his ethnicity allowed him to see firsthand the discrepancy between the promise and the day-to-day realities of most people's lives. His fortune had been too good and he was too optimistic ever to give up on the promise, and he was too grounded in his Mexican heritage to forget that life for minorities was fraught with additional perils. He tried in his own way, with great difficulty, to reconcile the two, and he urged other members of his ethnic group to do likewise. It is to his credit that he made it look easy even though it was not. His attempt at such a reconciliation, at such a personal bicultural balance, was more than the story of one man. It was that of an entire generation of Mexican Americans who came into their own by the 1950s and to whom subsequent generations of Hispanics owe much.

A last major theme of Mexican American history which Tijerina's life reflects is the importance of regional influence. That he was identified as much as a Houston entrepreneur as he was a member of an American ethnic group testifies to the dominant role of his Houston setting. Tijerina's effectiveness as a community and national leader can be understood only within the context of his schooling as a quintessential Houston promoter—an optimistic capitalist always boosting a project and in search of success through practical means.

The many elements of twentieth-century Mexican American history that appear in the narrative of Felix Tijerina's sixty years show the development of a people that was dynamic and in constant flux, albeit featuring a certain stability as well. It should be conceded, however, that the massive numbers, urban orientation, and resulting national importance of the generation of Felix Tijerina distinguish that group's story from that of preceding Mexican Americans.[19]

Felix Tijerina contributed to the development of the twentieth-century Mexican American community in three ways. First, through his leadership role in Mexican American organizations, he fostered a civic infrastructure vital to community advancement. In this regard, his involvement with LULAC proved most stellar. As national president, Tijerina carried LULAC to national stature for the first time in its history, in particular by expanding the League into the upper Midwest and into the Northeast. Under his administration LULAC attained the status of a national organization, rather than being limited to the American Southwest.[20]

Tijerina's work with LULAC points to his second major role in the development of the Mexican American community: that of humanitarian and philanthropist. He began his efforts to help people locally during the 1930s, aiding the disadvantaged, especially Mexican Americans, on an individual basis as well as within community groups. As his financial situation improved and his public stature grew in the postwar era, his philanthropic endeavors expanded to include civic, governmental, and administrative policy-making bodies. Usually the lone Hispanic on boards and committees, Tijerina influenced public policy by providing a needed Mexican American perspective. His early presence on these bodies created a precedent for naming subsequent Mexican American appointees.

It was in LULAC after World War II, however, that Tijerina had his most important success as a philanthropist. From the bully pulpit of the LULAC presidency and afterward, he promoted Mexican American education, leading the effort to fashion, finance, and foster the Little School of the 400 and the subsequent state-sponsored program in Texas that evolved from that initial project. His Little School, which he liberally underwrote with his own money, was a preschool educational venture designed to teach a basic vocabulary of four hundred English words to Spanish-speaking children and thus to address the educational problems that plagued Mexican Americans.[21]

Between 1957 and the early 1960s, Tijerina and LULAC spread the Little School idea across Texas and publicized it as a pedagogy for Latinos throughout the nation. It was Tijerina's pride and joy, in his mind his most meaningful civic endeavor. The Little School had many long-term, positive ramifications for Mexican American education.[22]

The impressive amount of publicity for the preschool programs and their pupils that Tijerina, as humanitarian and philanthropist, managed to obtain brought the condition of Mexican Americans, especially their dire educational needs, to national attention in the late 1950s and early 1960s. The notice that he generated for *la raza* through LULAC activities and the Little School concept served as an intermediate step in the emergence of Mexican Americans into the limelight during the Chicano Movement of the late 1960s and early 1970s.

As a third major contribution to Mexican American development, Tijerina provided a highly visible, positive symbol of Mexican American character and achievement. He acquired this image in the eyes of both the Hispanic and non-Hispanic populations in his city, state, and to some extent across the country. Such an accomplishment, especially among Anglos, was remarkable at the time when negative stereotypes of Mexicans and Mexican Americans held sway in much of the mainstream popular imagination.

To be sure, Tijerina strived assiduously to establish and maintain a favorable reputation among everyone from his earliest days in Houston. But he also had crucial assistance from the major Anglo American press in the city, which followed his career closely from around 1948 until his death and repeatedly advanced his positive image. Such media coverage of a Mexican American in the state's fastest growing city was unprecedented. In Houston in those years the name Felix conjured up a distinct image in the popular mind: Felix Tijerina, the genial, business-smart, community-involved restaurateur who embodied the best of his entire ethnic group. The rags-to-riches story of his life was repeated so often that it almost became a Houston parable. As it took root in his city and spread to other regions, this positive notice of Tijerina served to counter the many reservations that mainstream society traditionally held about Hispanics.

This admiration for Tijerina was shared by Mexican Americans as well, even by those who may have opposed him on any of the issues with which he dealt. To Mexican Americans he was a source of pride. The people of Mexico who were acquainted with Tijerina held these same warm feelings. Tijerina served as an example of success, strength, civic action, and compassion for those many Hispanics who knew him personally or only by reputation. By his pathbreaking deeds, Tijerina helped to inspire Mexican Americans and to illuminate their road to greater participation in mainstream society.

To recapitulate, this biography seeks to depict a man as an individual and, in doing so, to shed light on his generation. It is an account of an accomplished, yet representative person in all his complexity, resourcefulness, resiliency, and adaptiveness who over a lifetime maintained a personal balance as a Mexican American. It describes what he did as well as what he represented, both to himself and in the eyes of others. In sum, this study attempts to recount Tijerina's personal odyssey, which was as impressive as that of the ethnic group he came to symbolize.

A couple of other observations may also be tendered about Felix Tijerina as a subject for scholarly analysis. First, the pre-1960s history of Mexican Americans may not, by and large, be the story of national leaders, but it contains an abundance of individuals like Tijerina who distinguished themselves locally or regionally or gained national attention and thus warrant biographical examination. Like Tijerina, such men and women combine elements of the illustrious and the ordinary, and they embody the story of their people. Their presence ensures that the history of Mexican Americans in the twentieth century does not have to be only the account of faceless laborers, classes, and gender as reflected in the statistics of wages, occupations, and demographics. That is not to denigrate such study, but only to suggest that biographies should always be part of the literature, so that the human dimension to Chicano history be reinforced and the individual be given proper credit, something that Felix Tijerina and his generation fully deserve.

Second, it is the goal of this volume to help incorporate biographies of Texans of Mexican descent into the literature on Texas history. Fortunately, since the 1970s, Texas historiography has been strengthened by a mounting number of excellent studies on Mexican Americans. The further addition of biographies will serve to show them not as a people apart, but as integral to the fabric of Texas society. Such inclusion was a condition for which Felix Tijerina and his generation (and those who accompanied them) vigorously strived, and to know this role is essential for all.

CHAPTER I

La Inmigración

The house at 3 Artesian Place in Houston, Texas, had known deep sorrow before the Tijerinas came there to live in 1922. Its previous occupants, Frank and Concha Orozco (a railroad worker and his wife), had lived in the wooden frame structure only briefly when, in early February of that year, their eight-month-old son Roberto came down with a severe case of influenza. Within days his illness developed into pneumonia, a wintertime scourge among the very young and old in Houston's Mexican immigrant families. A visit to a physician did no good. The infant died at three o'clock the following morning, and his parents buried him that afternoon from their residence in a hastily arranged funeral. The Orozcos soon moved across town. The house stayed empty a short time before seventeen-year-old Felix Tijerina rented it for himself, his mother, and his sisters. They had just arrived in the city looking for a better life.[1]

The Tijerinas' move to this new address had concluded an immigration trek that had started six hundred miles away and several years before. Their journey had begun out of necessity, involved both Felix's immediate family as well as members of his extended clan, and had inflicted great hardship and suffering on everyone who took part in it. This immigration experience resembled thousands of others undergone by Mexican people who came to Texas and the rest of the United States between the early 1900s and late 1920s. On an individual level, it represented a crucible in the life of Felix Tijerina.

The journey that brought the Tijerinas to Houston commenced in General Escobedo, a small *villa* (town) in northern Mexico. General Escobedo lay approximately twelve kilometers north of Monterrey, in the state of Nuevo León, near the mountains and in plain view of Cerro del Topo Chico (also known simply as Cerro Del Topo), an immense, elongated, rounded mountain that had the shape of whale lying on its belly. A modest place even by Nuevo León standards, General Escobedo stood on a rise at the edge of the steep banks overlooking the muddy Río Pesquería.[2]

Although Spanish colonizers had first settled the area in the early 1600s, the municipality itself had been created in 1868 and named in honor of General Mariano Escobedo, the Mexican patriot commander who had helped to defeat the forces of Maximilian. With a relatively stable population, General Escobedo in 1878 contained approximately eleven hundred people; in 1895, around thirteen hundred. The residents made their living mainly by farming and by raising goats, cattle, and other livestock. By the early 1900s, the heart of the town was its plaza, bounded by rows of low, one-storied *sillar* (caliche block), adobe, and stucco buildings, including, perhaps most importantly, the two-room Palacio Municipal and the ancient, stately village church, a *capilla* (chapel) called San Nicolás de Bari. Situated in a semi-arid region with scrub vegetation, the *villa* and its plaza were swept by dust from the dry terrain. One local citizen recollected that in these early days potable water had to be brought in via the railroad. In 1900–1910, the village was also decades away from having electricity. Altogether, the sturdy people of General Escobedo lived a fairly hardscrabble, agriculturally based existence.[3]

The same families had resided in General Escobedo for generations. Persons with names such as Lozano, Ayala, Saldaña, and Elizondo had headed its *ayuntamientos* (town councils). Other predominant names in the *villa* included Garza, Siller, and especially Villarreal. Many marriages had linked these families, and one such union took place in the church in General Escobedo on February 6, 1903, when Dionicia Villarreal, the daughter of Librado Villarreal and Caralampia Ayala, married Rafael Tijerina Álvarez, the son of Rafael Tijerina Elizondo and Nicolasa Álvarez. Dionicia was twenty-three years of age at the time of her marriage; Rafael was thirty.[4]

According to the civil records of General Escobedo, Rafael and Dionicia had six children, five daughters and one son. Amalia, the first girl, was born on November 13, 1903, followed by Isidra on May 15, 1907, Erinea on July 3, 1909 (she died two days after birth), María Victoria on March 23, 1911, and Trinidad on May 30, 1915.[5]

Between Amalia and Isidra, son Feliberto Tijerina Villarreal was born at the house of his parents at three o'clock in the afternoon on April 29, 1905. Rafael reported the birth to the *juez civil* (civil judge), Daniel Lozano, in the *villa* of General Escobedo on May 25; the record was witnessed by Juan L. Cavazos and Concepción Villarreal.[6] A few months later, on August 13, Reverend Toribio Cantú, a priest from the nearby town of San Nicolás de los Garza, recorded that he had that day baptized the *hijo legitimo* (legitimate son) of Rafael Tijerina and Dionicia Villarreal in the church of General Escobedo. Librado Villarreal and Rufina Góngora served as *padrinos* (godparents). Father Cantú, in slight error, recorded this baby's name as "Eriberto" and his birth as April 15.[7] When this child later came to live in Houston, Texas, he would abbreviate his name to Felix Tijerina.

Because Felix Tijerina would later staunchly maintain, at least publicly, that he was born in Sugar Land, Texas, just southwest of Houston, the biographical articles written on him after he achieved success contain no information about his birth and childhood in General Escobedo or his immigration as a youth to the United States. Necessarily, an understanding of this important period has to be gleaned from sketchy evidence.

The father, Rafael, was listed on his children's civil birth records as a *labrador* (ploughman or farmer). Most likely, Rafael tilled a small parcel of land that the Tijerinas owned east of the *villa*. Feliberto's mother centered her activities around the home and children. Their son mentioned many years later that he remembered "how hard his parents had to work." Similarly, he noted that his father taught him the maxim "Work was made for men and man was made to work," clearly the motto of a man of the fields who bore heavy family responsibilities and had limited resources.[8]

By the time Feliberto was born, economic circumstances proved extremely difficult for average Mexicans. The policies of longtime president Porfirio Díaz, which stressed modernization through the growth of urban industries, large haciendas, and other types of economic development, had severely eroded the living conditions of most working Mexicans, a situation that helped brew the great revolution that would erupt in 1910.[9]

During this last decade of the *Porfiriato,* acute problems existed in the rural and small towns of Nuevo León. In the area of General Escobedo, persistent low wages and a limited water supply offered little to hold workers to the region. In 1904, General Bernardo Reyes, Don Porfirio's hand-picked governor of Nuevo León, even sold a large portion of the land around General Escobedo to two Canadians to create a power plant and irrigated farm, in keeping with the national policy of granting concessions to foreigners. Called the Hacienda el Canadá, in honor of its proprietors, this establishment designed to "develop" the *municipio* employed only *peones* at low wages that were spent at the *tienda de raya* (company store).[10]

Similarly, the employment prospects in nearby Monterrey proved unattractive. The "better" industrial jobs were difficult if not impossible to secure by an unskilled country person recently arrived in that city. Those country folk who ventured into Monterrey found themselves relegated to the bottom of the labor hierarchy, at best desperate victims of the city's paternalistic elite who assiduously kept wages low and blocked attempts by workers to improve their condition.[11] Altogether, the economy of Nuevo León (and General Escobedo in particular), like the rest of the country, barely offered many average residents the opportunity to sustain themselves, much less get ahead.

At the same time, jobs, or more precisely, rumors of jobs, beckoned from north of the Río Bravo (Rio Grande). In Texas, the stories went, a family could make as much as five dollars a day chopping or picking in the constantly expanding cotton fields where landowners utilized large numbers of unskilled workers. If a man was lucky enough to find a job laying railroad track, he could make a daily $1.25. Though modest, the wages for such hot, back-breaking labor seemed preferable to a homeland that was barely able to provide enough to eat or give any hope for the future. In response to the conditions at home and what the new country might offer, thousands of working folks from Monterrey and the Nuevo León countryside left for Texas. One Monterrey newspaper characterized the movement in 1907 as a labor "exodus."[12]

Among the *nuevoleoneses* who moved north in this massive migration of the early twentieth century were Aurelio Villarreal, his wife Julia Lozano, and their two small sons. Residents of General Escobedo, Aurelio and Julia were the brother and sister-in-law of Dionicia Villarreal de Tijerina. Aurelio, a laborer and jack-of-all-trades, had worked for a time as a milk deliverer and as a police officer, but he had a difficult time making ends meet for his growing family. Sometime just prior to 1906, he and Julia decided to leave their home and join the expanding numbers of people then heading for South Texas in search of opportunity. Their decision to move would prove to have a watershed effect on Dionicia and her children's future lives—so much so that Feliberto's story for a time can best be understood as a tale of two families: that of his own parents and that of his *tío* Aurelio and *tía* Julia.[13]

Bidding farewell to their many kin in General Escobedo, Aurelio, Julia, and their children made the two-hundred-mile trek northeast to the international boundary at Matamoros. They crossed into Brownsville and made their way over the inhospitable South Texas countryside to the newly created farming community of Robstown in Nueces County, sixteen miles west of Corpus Christi on the flat coastal prairie. There, Aurelio managed to purchase a horse with his meager savings and went to work *desenraisando* (clearing land) for farm owners who would use the acreage for planting cotton, the crop that developed as the county's staple. Aurelio felt that here in Texas there was opportunity to make a living.[14]

The Villarreals became willing hands in a process of modernization then taking place in South Texas. After 1900, the cattle kingdom that had once stretched from the San Antonio River to the Rio Grande began to break up as land speculators and ranchers began to sell off small tracts to Anglo-American farmers. This transformation from ranching to farming utilized thousands of Mexican immigrants to remove the brush and trees with grubbing hoe and axe to prepare the ground for cotton and vegetable production. In Nueces County, extensive land clearing and its attendant farm culture sharply raised land values, facilitating further settlement of the area.[15]

Robstown was one of many new agricultural communities in South Texas that sought to revolutionize the region economically through the introduction of midwestern farmers and Mexican field hands. In 1907, not long after the Villarreals arrived, a real estate agent from Iowa took over the selling and development of Robstown lands; the following year, the town's first cotton gin opened, heralding the new age. Robstown became a prime destination for Mexican immigrants and a base of Mexican American life in Texas; indeed, it emerged as a seminal community in twentieth-century Mexican American history that many families called home at one time or another. Settled in Robstown, Aurelio and Julia regularly sent word back to General Escobedo of the new life they managed to establish.[16]

Ⅲeanwhile, back in General Escobedo, Rafael and Dionicia lived as average people whose story has been largely lost to the historical record. They seem to have ranked among a respectable class of *escobedenses* who derived at least a modest existence from the soil as *agricultores* (farmers). Oral tradition in Escobedo (more than ninety years after Feliberto's birth) identified a tall, one-storied *sillar*-and-stucco structure directly across from and facing the northwest corner of the plaza as the house of Rafael (and Feliberto) Tijerina. These recollections at least imply that the family dwelled there for some time in the heart of the *villa*, within sight of the church and Palacio Municipal.[17]

Besides the civil and church documents dealing with his birth, ecclesiastical records provide the only other contemporary glimpse of Feliberto's years in that village and indicate the central role religion played in the family's life. On February 27–28, 1911, the Catholic church of General Escobedo held one of its regular ceremonies to administer the sacrament of confirmation to a large number of its parishioners. Many persons with the name Lozano, Villarreal, Góngora, Ayala, Álvarez, Tijerina, and other related families took part, including Amalia Tijerina (daughter of Rafael and Dionicia), who served as *madrina* (sponsor) to Pilar Villarreal, the daughter of Atanacio Villarreal and Agustina Leija. Dionicia Villarreal served as *madrina* to Apolonia, another daughter of Atanacio and Agustina; Dionicia also was the sponsor of Marcela, the child of Encarnación Berlanga and Pascuala Torres. During that ceremony, Isidra Tijerina (daughter of Rafael and Dionicia) was confirmed and had María Lozano as her sponsor. Among the large group of boys, "Filiberto" (son of Rafael Tijerina and Dionicia Villarreal) also received religious confirmation during this ceremony, with Alberto Ayala as his *padrino*.[18]

By the time of this confirmation ceremony, the Mexican Revolution of 1910 had already broken out, producing increased suffering and a further exodus of the Mexican people. In 1913 and 1914, the *carrancista* rebel armies of General Pablo González waged bloody campaigns against Monterrey to dislodge the forces of Victoriano Huerta. In early 1915, violence again visited the region when first the forces of General Francisco Villa and then the opposing army of General González occupied the city. So intense and disruptive became the fighting across the breadth of Mexico (especially in the northern reaches) that food shortages existed in the entire nation during 1915.[19]

General Escobedo directly felt this turbulence. At least two major battles took place in the immediate area between the *carrancista* forces and their various foes. People of the town who remembered the period (or heard first-hand tales from their parents) all had their stories of intimidation, extortion, and pillage at the hands of revolutionary bands. The residents of Escobedo generally sympathized with the *villistas*, while the *carrancistas* gained a reputation as a particularly onerous crowd—so prone to bullying and looting that *escobedenses* used the word *acarranciar* as a colloquial verb meaning "to take" or "to steal." As the lesser revolutionary chieftains passed through the *villa*, many young men from Escobedo fled to the countryside to avoid military conscription. Some of these fellows went to Texas rather than take up arms in what seemed to them violence with little purpose. According to oral historians of the town, the economic disruption caused by local events of the revolution also sent people packing. How many persons left cannot be determined, but reportedly General Escobedo had approximately twelve hundred inhabitants by 1918, almost one hundred souls less than in 1895.[20]

Amid already meager fortunes, life took a desperate turn for the Tijerina family. In mid-July, 1915, Prisciliano Ayala, a young local businessman, reported to the civil judge in General Escobedo that his uncle Rafael Tijerina Álvarez had died at home on July 13, at 12:30 P.M. "*de cáncer y otros tumores malignos de la piel no clasificada por médico*" (of cancer and other malignant tumors of the skin not classified by physicians). The family buried him in the village cemetery. Fellow *escobedenses* would remember Rafael as a good person.[21]

The widow and her five small children (the last one, Trinidad, only a couple of months old) soon found themselves in dire straits with no provider. By 1915, both of Rafael's parents were long deceased, as was Dionicia's mother, Caralampia Ayala de Villarreal. Only Dionicia's father, an aging Librado Villarreal, survived to help his daughter with her many responsibilities. Though a kindly man—carpenter by trade and musician by avocation—he apparently proved unable to support Dionicia and her brood.

Abject poverty had begun to close around the thirty-six-year-old widow when, in 1915, she sent a letter explaining her problems to her brother in Robstown. Aurelio retraced his steps to General Escobedo where, he told his children later, he found his sister and her family living in deplorable conditions and near starvation. The decision was made that Dionicia, her children, and Librado would return with him to South Texas. As they crossed the international bridge at Brownsville, Feliberto joined the growing Mexican community in the United States and became part of the Mexican American experience.[22]

The little group entered the United States in almost total anonymity. The flimsy border restrictions on immigration that existed prior to 1917 allowed Mexican workers and their dependents to move to and from the United States with little difficulty and gave the immigrants scant reason for concern. Regulations which called for entering migrants to be of sound moral and physical health and not likely to become public charges were simply not enforced along the Rio Grande. Even the poorest were allowed to enter, providing they could walk and pay their five-cent entry fee. The four dollars per person head tax stipulated in the Immigration Act of 1907 did not apply to Mexican aliens. Nor did a literacy test exist until 1917. So great was the demand for laborers in this period that Mexicans were welcomed as an economic asset. Between 1900 and 1910, figures indicate, almost 55,000 came to Texas; by 1920, 146,000 more had made the crossing.[23]

The reunited Villarreal and Tijerina relatives were on their own in Nueces County, having to fend for themselves. No government agencies or charitable societies worked in this sparsely populated region to assist them in their need. For people like the Villarreal-Tijerina clan, only a few *mutualistas* (mutual aid societies), *la familia* (the family), and the people for whom they worked offered succor.[24]

When his elders brought Feliberto from the mountains of Nuevo León to the flatlands of Robstown, he was a rough-hewn little ten-year-old. Due to an accident in Mexico in which a pot of boiling coffee had scalded the right side of his shoulder up to near his right ear, the youngster carried scar tissue that still ached when exposed to excessively hot weather. Inside he carried the scars from the death of his father and experiences of being around the armed, unruly *revolucionarios carrancistas* who had frequented General Escobedo. By now, he was becoming inured to the painful life of poverty and deprivation.[25]

The addition of his father, sister, and her children to his household greatly increased tío Aurelio's already heavy burden. While he continued to clear land, the older children, including Feliberto, were put to work in the fields to earn what little they could. In Robstown, this meant chopping and picking cotton, a crop planted in mid-March, weeded periodically with long-handled hoe by legions of Mexican field hands during the spring and early summer, and finally harvested, again by hand, in the heat of late July and August. So synonymous was cotton with the Robstown area that a Mexican troubadour in the early part of the century composed "El corrido de Robestown," a song which dealt with cotton picking.[26]

There was no time for the children's schooling even if any facilities had been available. Before the year ended, the family had to move on because Aurelio's horse died, making it impossible for Aurelio to clear land. To worsen matters, a disease wiped out the family's chickens and, of course, the eggs they provided. It was time to move farther north and east in search of work.[27]

The region of South Texas where the Villarreal and Tijerina families sought their livelihood offered a familiar Mexican ambience, but it also had a racially charged potential for violence that kept immigrants wary. During this second decade of the twentieth century tensions between the *mexicanos* and Anglo residents in South Texas increased perilously. In 1911, a congress of *mutualista* delegates from across the region met in Laredo to condemn police brutality, lynchings, segregation, racism, and other forms of violence against Tejanos. This deplorable state of affairs was exacerbated by the violence of the Mexican Revolution just across the border and Mexican bandits who sporadically marauded north of it. Then, in early 1915, Anglos learned of the so-called Plan of San Diego—an abortive rebellion based in Duval County concocted by a few Mexican nationals to free the American Southwest from the United States. Violent retribution resulted in the killing of Mexican Texan "suspects" by local Anglo law enforcement officials and vigilantes as far east as Robstown, for the community was barely forty miles from Duval County.[28]

Departing Robstown, the Villarreal-Tijerina family made its way on foot to Bloomington, another small agricultural community seventy-five miles up the Texas coastal bend in Victoria County. There, the older family members found work in the last days of the cotton picking season. They had joined the migrant trail that began in the Robstown area and involved thousands of Mexican people who swept northward to work the crops. With both adults and children, the Villarreal-Tijerina clan by then numbered around a dozen people, and together they lived in rickety, one-room accommodations near the fields where they eked out their existence. Similar to the other Mexican field hands, the Villarreals and Tijerinas were surrounded by abysmal poverty and struggled for daily survival. Feliberto and his sisters who were old enough to work alongside the adults had by then become accustomed to the stoop labor of the cotton harvest and the blistering South Texas sun.[29]

In 1916, it was again time to move in search of work. In Bloomington tío Aurelio managed to acquire a wagon and team for the next stage of their migration. Traveling alone as a family group, they relocated to another cotton farm at the tiny agricultural community of Guadalupe less than a day's journey away. Guadalupe was just east of the county seat town of Victoria, which was founded in 1824 when Texas was part of Mexico, but which by 1916 was controlled by Anglo agriculturists.[30]

As they traveled in the Victoria environs, the Villarreals and Tijerinas could remain almost anonymous among the Mexican Texan population. In South Texas there existed a degree of cultural continuity between Texas and Mexico that allowed immigrants to mingle much of the time in a society of their own. Mexican culture had been established in this part of Texas since Spain in the eighteenth century had solidified its claim to the area with missions at Refugio, La Bahía, and San Antonio. Mexican provincial towns like Victoria and Goliad (formerly La Bahía) reinforced this Hispanic presence and contained Mexican populations that could be augmented when immigration increased after 1900. By the 1910s, the Villarreals and Tijerinas were part of a wave of laboring people that had begun to push beyond the confines of deep South Texas.[31]

This area of Texas also harbored anti-Mexican sentiment dating from the 1800s, when many Mexicans in the Goliad-Victoria region had been persecuted by Anglo newcomers after the war for Texas independence. *Mexicanos*, once pioneers of this region, were by the early twentieth century barred from public and private facilities. They were not able to patronize most businesses. Altogether, their position in society was roughly equivalent to that of blacks.[32]

Regardless of the discrimination, the Villarreals and Tijerinas managed to establish some measure of accommodation with Anglos, as many *mexicanos* did. A surviving family member recalled that the Anglo owner of the farm where they worked at Guadalupe proved to be a kind, considerate man who offered his laborers a safe haven, although he paid only subsistence wages. They stayed on the farm at Guadalupe through the summers of 1916 and 1917, when tragedy struck. The seventy-year-old Librado, with white hair and beard and stooped from many years of hard work, apparently had been ailing for some time. On August 25, 1917, as the Villarreals and Tijerinas were finishing their second season, he closed his soft grey eyes for the last time. A physician told the family that Librado had died of liver troubles. The body was wrapped, placed in a wagon, covered and taken from Guadalupe to Victoria where Aurelio bought a coffin. Only Aurelio and the *patrón* attended the burial, which took place on the following day in Victoria. There, hundreds of miles from his home, his son and his Anglo employer laid Don Librado to rest.[33]

The family decided to follow the crops farther north. With Librado gone, necessity dictated even more than before that the children work in the fields.

The youngsters had not attended school in Texas, and as they worked their way through towns like Edna and Ganado family members thought only of having shelter and enough to eat. Before 1917 ended, Aurelio, as principal provider, found employment in Sugar Land, a rather peculiar farming and manufacturing community twenty miles southwest of Houston.[34]

In Sugar Land, the family lived in what was becoming a quintessential company town, with all its limitations and at least some of its security. Located in the heart of Fort Bend County north of old Richmond and Rosenberg, Sugar Land was a settlement of several thousand people by 1917. It traced its development back to the mid-nineteenth century, when a sugarcane plantation had been established in the surrounding rich Brazos River bottomlands. The plantation owners had also started a large cane grinding mill which had given rise to a large sugar refinery in the 1890s. The town of Sugar Land itself sprouted in close proximity to the refinery.[35]

Convicts from the nearby Texas state penitentiary had once provided the labor for the plantations. Tales of cruel and inhumane conditions helped give Sugar Land the nickname "Hellhole on the Brazos" until state authorities abolished the convict leasing system in the early 1900s.[36]

After the turn of the century, a major transformation in the refinery and local farming operations took place in Sugar Land that would accommodate, and perhaps demand, Mexican immigrant labor. In 1907–1908, W. T. Eldridge and I. H. Kempner acquired ownership of, reorganized, and modernized the sugar refining plant as the Imperial Sugar Company. Simultaneously, they purchased approximately twelve thousand acres of surrounding plantation land, established a separate company known as Sugar Land Industries, and turned it into the largest farming operation in the area. With the use of convict labor terminated, the company would need a greater number of free, unskilled workers. To accommodate their companies' efforts and new work force, the owners developed Sugar Land into a rigidly controlled but well-run company town. By the late teens, this reorganization had ushered in a period of prosperity that would last until the Depression and would allow the utilization of more unskilled laborers than the local black and white populations could provide.[37]

By 1910, Mexican workers, single men and entire families drawn by word of mouth, had drifted in and were making Sugar Land their home. Some had entered the United States as early as 1900, though a few were natives of the surrounding Texas countryside. Principally Mexicans worked as sharecroppers and farmhands for Sugar Land Industries along with local whites and blacks. Less than a handful of Mexicans had gone to work in the refinery, but there was plenty to do in the fields growing and tending the cotton, corn, and extensive garden truck which were grown on the vast, fertile company acreage in the Oyster Creek basin, a stream which flowed into the Brazos River.[38]

Aurelio found employment, a place for his family to live, and the promise of enough to eat with Sugar Land Industries. The manager of the gigantic farm, "Captain" Brooks (so-called for his tenure with the penitentiary in Sugar Land) quartered the Villarreal-Tijerina family in barracks-like housing reserved for such purposes by the company near Grand Central, the focal point of the farming activities located about three miles southeast of the sugar refinery. Although Aurelio worked from six in the morning until eight o'clock in the evening, things were marginally better. The work proved steady and the family would not have to migrate, at least for a while.[39]

If Aurelio's situation resembled that of the rest of the laborers for Sugar Land Industries, he probably drew provisions with credit coupons from the company store in town for which he would exchange his wages at the end of the week; if he sharecropped, his credit would remain "on the books" until the crop came in at the end of the season. Also, the family put in a garden which, in season, provided them with beans, corn, and sweet potatoes. During these early days, no one who worked for Sugar Land Industries ever really prospered, but there was a chance of not going hungry. Sugar Land Industries even provided a plot of ground overlooking Oyster Creek not far from Grand Central for the Mexicans to bury their dead. It became known as San Isidro Cemetery and soon began to contain the graves of Mexican tenants, farm workers, and members of their families who died on the company lands.[40]

The hoped-for improvement in their living standard came too late for little Trinidad, Dionicia's youngest daughter. Barely two years of age and with the red hair and light eyes of her grandfather, she died not long after the family settled in Fort Bend County. Although no official record of her demise exists, family tradition is that the little girl perished from diarrhea; her death was part of the staggering rate of infant and early childhood mortality among transient agricultural workers of the period, a result of their poor housing, bad diets, insufficient clothing, and inadequate medical care.

Aurelio bought a plain wooden coffin for the little body, and the entire Villarreal-Tijerina family went from the farm to the place of burial (probably San Isidro Cemetery) in three mule-drawn wagons. A Villarreal cousin vividly remembered many years later that during this sad procession Feliberto said little and stared into the distance across the flat coastal farmland as they rode along in the same wagon. Within a couple of years, Aurelio and Julia would bury two of their own children at that cemetery.[41]

The life they tried to establish in this area was circumscribed by severe discrimination. The Mexicans who worked out of Grand Central generally did not frequent the stores grouped along the railroad depot of Sugar Land proper except to get their supplies. The cafes and places of entertainment were off limits, and there was always a fear of violence at the hands of local white residents or law enforcement officers. This situation was in keeping with the temper of the region because violence against people of color had a long tradition in Fort Bend County.[42]

In this general atmosphere, Aurelio and his family found it advantageous to remain at home in obscurity amid the company of other Mexican people. On the land, they turned to one another for cultural survival. Aurelio and his sons had brought more than their strong backs to Texas. Like Librado before them, they were good musicians with the accordion, violin, and guitar. They soon entertained nightly gatherings of farm workers in impromptu sessions at home and around camp fires in the cotton fields, playing tunes from northern Mexico and South Texas, a distinctive music the Tijerina children loved to hear.[43]

Sugar Land became the first place in Texas that Dionicia and her children could truly call home; they welcomed the respite from being constantly on the move. Dionicia was also grateful to her brother and sister-in-law for their help in her times of need, but she understood the added burden her presence placed upon them. Old family portraits of Dionicia Villarreal de Tijerina reveal a strong woman with a melancholy, delicate, and intelligent face, green eyes, and light-complected skin, revealing the predominance of Castilian blood that coursed the Villarreal and Tijerina veins. At five feet, four inches in height she was rather tall, humble, and handsome. Though not an assertive person, Dionicia was tenacious and devoutly Roman Catholic, to the point where, as the years wore on, it was said, she would have callouses on her knees from long hours of prayer.[44]

Although their exact whereabouts in the Sugar Land region is impossible to determine, apparently soon after settling in the quarters with the Villarreals in 1917 Dionicia and her children decided to make it on their own. Reportedly in the company of other Mexican immigrant workers, the

Tijerinas moved near Dewalt, a few miles distant, to reside on one of the large individually owned farms. With this move the Villarreals and Tijerinas would never live together again.[45]

While her older children worked the fields, Dionicia, an excellent seamstress, helped to earn their daily bread by sewing for the local Anglo and Mexican population. The Tijerinas occupied a spacious house on land where they could have chickens, hogs, and a cow. The *mexicanos* of the area abbreviated the name Dewalt to "El Dew" in honor of the Dew family, proprietors of the settlement's general store and important local land owners. During their residence there, the Tijerinas became acquainted not only with the Dews, but also with other prominent farmers, such as W. T. Eldridge, a heavy-set, massive man with a wide face whom the Mexicans appropriately called El Chato.[46]

Her many personal losses only deepened Dionicia's Catholicism, and her religiosity soon earned her a certain respect and standing among the local *mexicanos*. Since there were no priests who regularly ministered to the local Mexicans at that time, Dionicia held neighborhood prayer gatherings at their country house. With people coming to their home, Feliberto and his sisters began to come into contact with more adults, individuals who had made the perilous journey north similar to their own. Kind, generous, and altruistic, Dionicia would assist anyone in need, a trait her son would inherit. She instilled in him her spirit of even-handedness and giving. Many years later he recalled that his mother would always say, when dividing a piece of bread among him and his sisters: "O todos hijos o todos entenados" (Treat everyone equally).[47]

Also, Dionicia had turned her attention to the education of her children. Because neither she nor they knew any English, enrollment of her son or daughters even in the few "Mexican schools" run by Fort Bend County or Sugar Land Industries did not take place. But Dionicia was smart and by all accounts had received an education in Mexico. At home with her sewing, she taught Feliberto and his sisters to read and write their native Spanish.[48]

Amid the hardship and family tragedies, the bond of affection between Dionicia and her only son deepened into a mutual protectiveness. Feliberto physically resembled his mother, and drew comfort from her constant encouragement. At night, she told him that regardless of their inauspicious circumstances, he was special, destined for great achievement.[49]

Though still a boy, he was considered "the man of the house," and, like most children of Mexican immigrants in those years, Feliberto worked to help maintain his family. He keenly felt the burden of responsibility to assist his mother in supporting his three sisters; the harshness of his work steeled his youthful constitution to hard labor. There on the farms around Sugar Land, he hustled any chore that would fetch a few nickels. In addition to chopping and picking cotton, he did odd jobs and was seen peddling chickens along the road near town, always working or raising something to sell. On one occasion, a Mexican American employee of Imperial Sugar Company was so impressed by Feliberto's determination and so driven to compassion by the youngster's situation that he secured Tijerina a temporary job as a sample boy in the refinery. The lad reportedly made $2.50 a week carrying sample cans of sugar to the laboratory where the product was chemically tested for its purity. In that capacity, Feliberto would likely have heard English spoken on a regular basis.[50]

Feliberto was also able to find employment as a water boy for the Sugar Land Industries, and as such left what appears to be the only available contemporary written record of his presence in Sugar Land. While many farming operations in Texas simply placed a water keg at the turning row for the refreshment of their workers, this practice proved too inefficient for more modernized agribusiness. The management of Sugar Land Industries hired Feliberto and other youngsters to lug the water buckets down the rows to thirsty field hands to save time. Adopted from the procedures of the nearby prison farm, this policy was especially utilized during hoeing season when the gangs of black and Mexican workers were paid by the day. By the spring of 1921, the official Sugar Land Industries records list "Filiberto Tyerina" earning $1.50 per day. Less than the $2.50 daily paid to the other Mexican workers, it was probably the wages of a water boy.[51]

At that rate no one would ever get ahead, something Tijerina must have sensed. Prospects of making the extra dollar a day for regular adult field hands would have held no allure. Generally, the employee records suggest that whites earned twice the daily pay of Mexican and "colored" workers, and whites were more likely to hold the steady jobs which carried weekly or monthly salaries.[52] Avenues for personal advancement were extremely limited for a Mexican American in the Sugar Land area; Tijerina later reflected that despite the acquaintance of several helpful people (both Anglo and Mexican), he personally felt the confinements of discrimination that eventually compelled him to leave the town.[53]

The family's decision to depart the Sugar Land region was one that probably had been in the making for some time, though like much of their lives in these initial years, the exact details are unclear. Tijerina later claimed that as early as 1918, at no more than thirteen years of age, he had come to Houston, the thriving city twenty miles to the northeast of Sugar Land, to find work. A friend from these days in Sugar Land said that Tijerina ventured to Houston to sell his chickens at the Market Square located in and around the first level of Houston's downtown City Hall, where many people from the farms took their produce to get better prices. The City Market was at that time a veritable bazaar that attracted every sort of person from Houston and its surrounding areas to sell their poultry, vegetables, meats, and other wares to local shoppers before the days of supermarkets. Housewives, maids, and storekeepers browsed amid the stalls where men and women of different ethnicities and races hawked their goods. On the other hand, a cousin who was with him during the immigration north recalled that by 1920, Tijerina had secured a job selling apples and candy on a train that ran from Sugar Land to Houston.[54]

Perhaps he was introduced to Houston under all three circumstances; and while the exact date of his first coming to the city is unclear, certainly he was very young.

Houston, Texas, with a bustling population of approximately 138,000 people by 1920, was the first large Texas city Feliberto Tijerina had seen, and to be sure the most modern. Since its founding on Buffalo Bayou in late 1836, it had developed as a commercial town through which products from the interior of the state—especially lumber and cotton—passed on their way to foreign markets. The Bayou City, as it was called, had always been a place marked by constant growth; but the late 1910s and early 1920s witnessed a period of intense expansion as the city capitalized on the discovery of oil in East Texas, the opening of its deep-water port facilities in 1914, and the many railroad lines that connected it to inland regions. By the early 1920s, Houston was the commercial nexus of Southeast Texas and the coming city in the state. Tall buildings, some as high as nineteen stories, lined its downtown streets. Things seemed to be constantly in flux in Houston—a city that offered advantages that Fort Bend County could not match. Houston presented a new, cosmopolitan environment where an intelligent, adventurous youngster from the country would have felt confused, yet excited with hope and the opportunity to make a place for himself.[55]

For the thousands of young people of many ethnicities who were expanding the city's population during the 1920s, there was the lure of jobs and the possibility for advancement. By 1920, Houston was home to some six thousand people of Mexican descent, the majority of whom had come from the old country since the turn of the century. In Houston, they searched for a better life by turning to work in the vibrant railroad industry, on the ship channel, and in many other sectors of the booming economy as laborers or tradesmen. For these Mexican urban pioneers who were building the city's emerging *colonias*, these jobs presented economic possibilities that did not exist for them in places like General Escobedo, Robstown, Guadalupe, or Sugar Land. Houston's urban, ultra-capitalist ethos fostered, at least marginally, more openness to Mexicans than existed in most other parts of South and Southeast Texas. Houston offered Mexicans the hope of a better niche for themselves. At any rate, the city would draw Feliberto Tijerina and his family to their final destination in their migration northward.[56]

Knowledge that family survival depended upon economic opportunity gave a definite edge to Tijerina's attraction to Houston. By the time he entered his teens, he was no ordinary son and brother; he had for some time assumed the role of protector and principal provider for his mother and three sisters. Virtually uneducated and unskilled, he was prepared to work however many hours a day it took to make a living.[57]

Tijerina found his first steady job in Houston probably as a result of his trips to the City Market. By the late 1910s to early 1920s, a "produce row" had developed on a busy, two-block stretch of Commerce Avenue between Milam and Main Streets, not far from Market Square. The various produce houses imported fruits and vegetables for sale and distribution throughout Houston food stores. Because of the difficult nature of the work and low wages, the produce houses drew their laborers from groups of blacks and Mexicans who congregated on Commerce Avenue hoping for weekly employment.[58]

One of the young, rising stars of the Houston produce business by the early 1920s was Sigmund Frucht, a thin, fashionably dressed member of Houston's sizable Jewish community. Personable and easy to approach, Sig Frucht gave young Tijerina a job working with the other laborers in his warehouse at the 900 block of Commerce Avenue.[59]

According to Frucht's later recollections, Tijerina helped these men load a variety of produce—including poultry and eggs, vegetables, and fruit—at the nearby railroad depots, ferry the cargo to Frucht's Commerce Avenue business, and arrange it on the front-dock sidewalk for purchase by retail grocers who came to stock their stores. For this labor, Tijerina received the going rate of $1.50 a day, or $9.00 for a six-day week, wages similar to what he had apparently received from Sugar Land Industries. Tijerina's earliest extant biographical sketch recounts that "all except barest living expenses he took back to his mother each weekend," suggesting that he must have found temporary living accommodations in Houston.[60]

Exactly when Tijerina had this job or how long he stayed is unclear. By all accounts, he worked there for only a brief period. Though slender and no more than five feet, four inches in height, Tijerina was a strong, good worker. But reportedly, the manual labor he did for Frucht seriously chafed his hands, and he realized that he would have to change his situation. He did not, however, walk away from this employment empty-handed. The job allowed him to meet and observe Houstonians. He became lifelong friends with his boss, Sig Frucht, who was probably the first Houston entrepreneur and promoter that Tijerina met in a city filled with such individuals. An active booster of an industry that engaged in high-profile advertising during that era, Frucht possessed entrepreneurial talents that Tijerina would himself display in the years to come. Frucht seemed to know everyone, and many of these "personal friends" passed through the doors of his wholesale house.[61]

Situationally, Produce Row served as an introduction to city life. Trucks and automobiles continuously pulled in and out of its parking spaces to deposit or pick up merchandise. A rough set of street peddlers with horse-drawn wagons of fruits and vegetables also lined the curbs, often competing with the wholesale houses. Frucht's operation stood within sight of the south end of the Main Street Viaduct that arched Buffalo and White Oak Bayous; the viaduct served as the major thoroughfare connecting the city's north side with downtown. Houston had been founded in the immediate area, and this locale was still a center of activity. The electric streetcars that ran along Main brought passengers to the corner at Commerce Avenue, adding to the number of pedestrians. The sidewalks of Produce Row, elevated from the brick street along the entire two blocks between Main and Milam, accommodated people of all ranks and colors. Individuals with ethnic names like Desel, Boettcher, Dissen, Schoenmann, Schneider, Japhet, Kuhn, La Rocca, Levy, Liebermann, Meyers, and Morales owned the other wholesale houses on Commerce. Produce Row provided a spectrum of business people, middle-class Houstonians, and laborers. Such constant association with older men, Tijerina would tell his younger sisters, was one way by which he gained knowledge about business and life in general.[62]

Produce Row also brought Tijerina into contact with young men of Houston's Mexican community who would soon form his circle of close friends. William Aguilar, two years his junior, was on a break from his own job as a clerk in a downtown hardware store when he and Tijerina first met. He stopped by the produce house where Tijerina worked and picked up a piece of fruit for a snack. Tijerina would not allow him to pay; they began to chat, and Aguilar would return on other days as the two developed a lasting friendship. Aguilar may have been the first of his generation in Houston to experience the charm that would be Tijerina's trademark.[63]

Tijerina found a better job at a Mexican restaurant on Main Street. By the early 1920s, many young Mexican men worked as cooks, dishwashers, waiters, and busboys in Houston's hotels and cafes. Restaurant work was often the best many recent arrivals could expect, especially without speaking English fluently. Due to the underemployment among Mexican workers in the city, even during boom times, such jobs came at a premium. As a result, these men had constructed an informal network through which they placed friends and relatives in these establishments. An older friend named Doroteo Pina, whom Tijerina knew from Sugar Land, apparently worked as a waiter at the Original Mexican Restaurant at 1109 Main, and he arranged for Tijerina to secure employment there as a busboy. This move proved to be seminal in Tijerina's life.[64]

When Tijerina came to Houston he was no longer Feliberto. Somewhere in his mental move from the fields of Sugar Land Industries to the Bayou City, Feliberto Tijerina took a small but significant step on the road to urban acculturation in the United States. He had abbreviated his name to Felix.[65]

As a commercial port, Houston, Texas, in the 1920s was a place of new beginnings; most sectors of the city accommodated outsiders. Since the nineteenth century, Houston had been absorbing people of many different ethnic backgrounds—Irish, Germans, Italians, Greeks, Asians, Jews, a large black population, and numerous others. In return, it required a certain conformity. Feliberto was a name that was no doubt too foreign and cumbersome for a fast-paced English-speaking city. Even the most accepting, non-Hispanic residents in those days would have appreciated (perhaps helped to bestow) a shorter name to pronounce.

At the same time, many dominant members of Houston society were not so tolerant, and disliked or at least "suspicioned" Mexicans of the working class. The town had an anti-Mexican prejudice as a legacy from the nineteenth century and the Battle of San Jacinto, which had been fought only several miles away. In 1922, the year Felix probably brought his mother and sisters to live in the Bayou City, the Houston chapter of the newly formed organization called the Sons of the Texas Republic held what was touted as the first big celebration of San Jacinto Day in many years. By the early 1920s, the foundation of Houston society was also still distinctly American Old South. It had an active chapter of the United Confederate Veterans that still staged reunions and public affairs where the aged former soldiers paraded in their gray uniforms to commemorate the glory of the Confederacy, a government that had sought to perpetuate white supremacy. Even worse, the early 1920s witnessed the resurgence of the Ku Klux Klan. In 1922, the Sam Houston Klan No. 1 had been flourishing there for two years as the first "klavern" in Texas. The Klan was so pervasive that in mid-June, 1922, it held a barbecue off San Felipe Road to the west of town (in the direction of Fort Bend County) reportedly attended by nine thousand members. The Klan likewise published its statewide newspaper, *Colonel Mayfield's Weekly*, in Houston. While its pages did not show alarm at any Hispanic presence in the city, the newspaper stood foursquare for "white supremacy" and against the importation of "cheap labor." It vilified Catholics and saw Mexicans (especially Mexican aliens) in South and West Texas as being controlled by the papacy and in league with the anti-Klan forces. The Houston-area Klansmen, like many Houstonians, were reacting to the rapid changes brought about by what to them was the bewildering growth and transition of their city in the years immediately following World War I.[66]

Though not routinely denigrating Mexicans in print, major local newspapers like the *Houston Post,* for instance, editorialized in 1922 that urban immigrants were not desired because they congregated in particular residential areas and compounded city problems. The *Post* also deplored ignorance of the English language among many elements of the modern population in Texas; and it had no qualms about dispassionately reporting events that were patently anti-Mexican, such as a talk given in April, 1922, by a former superintendent of the Houston public schools who, when describing what he felt was the lack of religion among Mexicans, proclaimed definitively that "the Rio Grande marks the line between enlightenment and ignorance."[67] A level of intolerance thus existed side by side with opportunity and acceptance and set the stage for the often ambivalent position of Mexicans in Houston.

These mainstream Houston sentiments during the 1920s would have at best compounded the demand on a Mexican newcomer to "Americanize" if he or she wanted to live there. For young Tijerina, whose desire for success (i.e., family survival) no doubt depended upon acceptance, these circumstances necessitated that the process of adaptation and acculturation begin in earnest. Feliberto was a name that did not directly translate into an English equivalent. Felix was brief, spelled and pronounced the same in both languages. Perhaps Tijerina's first clever effort at biculturalization, "Felix" was a name better suited to his new environment. It was his big-city name and the first step in his own personal, fresh departure.

With a new restaurant job and a new name, he then needed a place to live large enough for his entire family. Felix found permanent accommodations for his mother, sisters, and himself when he rented the house at 3 Artesian Place, where the street dead-ended at the embankment that sloped into Buffalo Bayou. Located on the north side of the stream near downtown, it was an easy walk to Main Street. It was the home that Frank and Concha Orozco had left after their infant son had died earlier in 1922.[68]

Similar to the grief that had visited the Orozcos only a few months before, a string of personal sorrows and privation had led the Tijerinas ultimately to that house. Bitter hardship seemed to have dogged the path of every Mexican family that made its way to Houston in search of something better during those years.

Back in Sugar Land, the Villarreals also were packing their belongings to leave the area in 1922. They relocated to Edna, Texas, and in the following year, 1923, to another farm near Temple. In 1930, Aurelio gave up the life of a sharecropper and moved Julia and their children permanently to San Antonio, where Hispanic traditions offered *mexicano* immigrants at least cultural security, if not better economic opportunity.[69]

Houston, on the other hand, was a place where a Mexican community and culture were just becoming viable by the early 1920s. But even for Mexicans, jobs could be found, although such employment was often the most menial the city had to offer. With this economic attraction, Houston became a logical destination for immigrants, and one that people working their way through the fields of the Texas coastal bend would want to reach.

Sometime in 1922, Felix, his mother, and sisters took the train from Sugar Land to Houston, arriving at Union Station. Dionicia told her children that this was her final destination in their migration north. She was forty-three years old and tired of moving. Taking a jitney from the train station to Artesian Place, they were on their own in a new urban environment. They had come from a mountain town in Nuevo León where they were surrounded by kinfolk; in Houston they had no relatives.[70]

The Tijerinas' migration amounted to much more than a geographic movement; it formed a distinct episode in their lives during which they underwent a process of change experienced by most immigrants. They had come from a humble *villa* in Mexico to a bustling, audacious Texas city; they had lived and worked in the fields, in small communities, and in a company town. Like so many other Mexican immigrants to the United States, their family had undergone a restructuring influenced by sickness, death, economic necessity, and personal decisions. Their migration was one in which the extended family had played a significant role. It was a migration by stages, of lengthy duration and hundreds of miles; it had been motivated by the forces of modernization in northern Mexico and the United States as well as by other circumstances beyond their control, yet remarkable for the amount of self-determination and resourcefulness they managed to exercise. Along the way they had buried loved ones, made friends (both Mexican and non-Mexican), skirted prejudice, picked up work and language skills, and acculturated as best they could. In their long move from the dry mountains of General Escobedo to the humid coastland of Houston, the Tijerinas had shown a great degree of adaptability. They had joined a Mexican American community, inured to hardship, tenacious in the face of adversity. They were part of what historians identify as the Immigrant Generation, a cohort within Texas Mexican society which between 1910 and the Great Depression would make an indelible mark on the United States.

FROM *Obrero* TO ENTREPRENEUR

When Felix Tijerina settled with his mother and three sisters in Houston, he began a passage of another kind—one that other immigrants have undergone. This passage toward urban acculturation lasted from 1922 until 1929, as lengthy in duration as Tijerina's migration from Mexico; it formed a distinct phase in his life and transformed him to a greater extent than had the trek from General Escobedo.

The 1920s turned out to be an important decade for Tijerina as an individual, much as they did for most Mexican Americans. During those years, Tijerina underwent a process of urbanization reflecting a version of the general Mexican American experience. Though Houston presented a foreign and often trying environment, for Tijerina this new life proved to be less severe than the rigors he had undergone between General Escobedo and Sugar Land.

Tijerina adjusted to his Houston surroundings as he focused on the immediate concerns of city dwelling. He learned lessons and developed a bicultural outlook from close association with Houston's non-Hispanic majority as well as with its burgeoning Mexican population. This urban orientation would manifest itself in his public career, which flowered a decade later.

During the 1920s, however, Felix concentrated his energy on his job as a restaurant employee; in this manner, he achieved some level of economic stability and comfort for his family and gave himself a margin of personal advancement. In addition to the work place, Felix's life revolved around his kin, neighborhood, a small but growing number of Mexican friends, acquaintances, and organizations, and a variety of non-Hispanics and their institutions.

By 1929, Tijerina had settled upon and partly implemented a strategy to improve his condition by becoming a Houston entrepreneur, effectively breaking his way into the middle class. He had grown from an unsophisticated, seventeen-year-old *obrero* (worker) living in virtual obscurity, into a fledgling, relatively well-known restaurateur on Main Street in the largest city in Texas. Tijerina achieved this transformation as he matured in years and experience, adeptly using the means at his disposal.

İf Produce Row had offered a microcosm of Houston's ethnic make-up, the neighborhood where Felix and his family initially settled also provided a varied immigrant experience. As such, their new residential area gave them a reasonably secure environment and helped condition them to their new urban situation.

The Tijerinas' neighborhood was a small section on the west side of Houston's emerging *colonia mexicana* which, by 1922, was developing in four general locations across the city. Farthest east, an area of settlement had taken root near the turning basin of the ship channel in Magnolia Park, an adjoining independent municipality that would be annexed by Houston in 1927. Closer to downtown, the largest and oldest concentration of *mexicano* residents flourished just east of Main Street and south of Buffalo Bayou in a section of Second Ward that Mexican Houstonians referred to as Segundo Barrio. Somewhat northeast of downtown, Mexican immigrants lived in portions of the Fifth Ward. The fourth major area lay west of downtown, where Mexican families could be found living along Washington Avenue, close to jobs provided by the railroads and various manufacturing industries. The Tijerinas lived in a part of this western-most region, near the beginning of Washington Avenue.

Located in the eastern edge of the Sixth Ward, Artesian Place was part of a crowded but interesting little neighborhood comprising approximately three square blocks, with narrow, dirt streets. Its one- and two-storied frame houses were sturdy, but mostly rentals and not very well maintained by their owners. Artesian Place, where the Tijerina home stood, ran a block south of and parallel to Preston Avenue, just before Preston intersected with the lower end of Washington. Only three short blocks in length, Artesian was broken by and connected to Preston by three even tinier streets—Robinet Place, Cushman Place, and Radoff's Place—before it ended at the embankment that sloped down to Buffalo Bayou. With a few storefront businesses intermixed with the houses, the neighborhood was physically presided over by the three tall smokestacks of the city's central waterworks. Located at 27 Artesian Place, this main pumping plant helped draw water from one of the artesian wells that supplied Houston and gave the street its name. Forming a visible feature on the Houston skyline, the towers marked the neighborhood's location.[1]

Like many other areas of Houston's *colonia* during the 1920s, the Artesian Place neighborhood found itself in transition; it had originally consisted of non-Hispanics but was fast becoming an enclave of *manzanas de mexicanos* (city blocks of Mexican residents). In early 1922, just before the Tijerinas arrived, nine of its thirty households contained Mexican occupants; by the following year the number had risen to eighteen, and the trend continued. Most of the new Mexican residents were immigrants and spoke only Spanish, a trait that added to a sense of well-being among those who settled the area.[2]

At the same time, the neighborhood was multiethnic; it had what one resident later described as a "United Nations" atmosphere. It possessed enough diversity to expose the Tijerinas to the city's cultural variations without making them feel uneasy. With names like Jamail, Cacciola, Wiener, and Vianapopoulos, these neighbors represented a cross section of nationalities—Lebanese, Italians, German Jews, Greeks. Its early Mexican residents remembered these people as cordial to their new neighbors, since they too were only a generation or two removed from their immigrant origins and did not hold the mainstream Anglo Americans' view of Mexicans and Mexican Americans. Indeed, the recent Mexican arrivals actually rented their houses from these other ethnics. As one early Mexican American resident of the neighborhood succinctly put it: "The Battle of San Jacinto didn't mean a damn thing to them." By all accounts, the Mexican youngsters did not feel discrimination in the immediate neighborhood.[3]

With the people coming from or going to work, children playing in the streets, and small businesses interspersed, it was a lively area. At the time, the neighborhood's most prominent Mexican resident was Florencio Contreras, a tall, muscular man from the state of San Luis Potosí whose blacksmith shop at the corner of Cushman and Artesian served as a local gathering spot. The two youngest Tijerina sisters immediately made friends with Contreras's daughters, Dianicia and Adela, and found themselves, with many of the other children, watching the sparks fly from the blacksmith's hammer. Horses and mules were always standing next to the Contreras home, waiting to be shod. Much to the children's delight, the Greek, George Verges, peddled homemade ice cream. The adults frequented a café operated by a neighbor woman who served Mexican food in the front of her house and home brew in the rear.[4]

The first structure at the end of Artesian, the Tijerina home stood on a rise at the edge of the bayou, within sight of the Preston Avenue Bridge and the waterworks. Single-storied, it was wood frame like the others on the street. Apparently larger than the house they had occupied in the country, it had three bedrooms (one of which had previously been the dining room) and a kitchen spacious enough to double as a dining area.[5]

The Contreras sisters began to visit the Tijerinas soon after the Tijerinas arrived, mainly to play with Victoria, the youngest and closest to their age. But they were also impressed by the rest of the family, recalling that the Tijerinas kept their house "so clean you could eat off the floor."[6] Isidra, the middle sister, was around fifteen years old and did most of the housework. Called Dora for short, she always seemed to be busy scrubbing and washing and ironing clothes. Remarkably pretty and petite, she was also the beauty among the sisters. Amalia, the oldest, was friendly, but a quiet, reserved young woman, mature for her nineteen years. Their mother, Dionicia, who possessed a clear complexion that all her girls inherited, was a courteous woman, and noticeably religious. Her three daughters did everything for her around the house, treating her "like a queen."[7]

Dianicia Contreras recalled that the Tijerina sisters quickly became popular around the neighborhood. Gangly and thin with a wispy ponytail, little Victoria was soon called "skinny" by Florencio Contreras, who had the Mexican penchant for giving people descriptive nicknames. He affectionately called Dora "Mentiras" (lies) because she would spin tall tales. Dianicia Contreras also noted that the two youngest Tijerina girls were just learning English so that they could get along better with their neighborhood playmates. The Tijerina sisters, she specifically remembered, spoke very correct, but rapid Spanish, as people from Monterrey did at that time—so that Dianicia often had difficulty understanding them.[8]

As well as they knew the Tijerina sisters, Dianicia and Adela Contreras saw little of Felix because he always seemed to be at work. Their father, Florencio, told them that Felix was a solid, hard-working fellow who would "look after his family 'til the day he dies."[9]

Although Produce Row had introduced Tijerina to Houston commerce, his work at the Original Mexican Restaurant provided more important instruction on Houston business, fundamentally expanding his horizons and shaping him into a nascent Houstonian. The owners of "the Original," George E. and Bessie Caldwell, had been operating their restaurant for fifteen years on Fannin Street, but had relocated in early 1922 to 1109 Main, where they had also expanded. Originally from San Antonio, George Caldwell presumably derived his interest in Mexican food from the Alamo City, a cradle of Texas-Mexican culture. Catering to Anglo clientele, the Original Mexican Restaurant advertised "Genuine Mexican Foods Properly Prepared." [10]

While not the only Mexican restaurant in town, it was the only one on Main Street and may well have been the most popular among the Anglo residents. With its neatly arranged, cloth-covered tables, the restaurant played host to many business people as well as city and county officials, including Houston's young mayor, Oscar Holcombe (a personal friend of George Caldwell) and his retinue of political associates. This clientele as well as the restaurant's pace of operation reflected the exciting atmosphere that Felix found in Houston when he had first arrived, an excitement that only increased as the decade progressed. [11]

As busboy, Felix earned nine dollars a week and worked twelve-hour days in a restaurant that possessed a congenial atmosphere. He could immediately relate to Doroteo Pina, another man named José Aguilar, and the other young Mexicans employed there. The Caldwells proved to be considerate, and there was always food to eat at their restaurant, much like Produce Row. Moreover, the work was not as physically demanding as what he had done for Sig Frucht. [12]

Coming into close contact with Anglo Americans on a daily basis, Felix began to improve his English. While he was a busboy, an incident occurred that made a lasting impression upon him and helped to shape part of his world view. Later in life, he would tell this story almost in parable form. According to one widely-circulated version, soon after he had started his new job: "A customer asked him for some tomato catsup. Nodding, with what he hoped was a comprehending smile, he trotted back to the kitchen, repeating to himself, 'tomato catsup; tomato catsup.'

"'What, please,' he inquired in Spanish of one of the waiters, 'is tomato catsup?' The waiter pointed it out, and the busboy grabbed a bottle and rushed triumphantly to the customer." [13]

Felix would use this story to indicate how, with great difficulty and embarrassment, he learned English a word at a time; it also served to emphasize the great importance he felt the language played in everyday life in the United States for a non-English speaker. He started to read English as best he could, especially in the newspapers.

In addition to helping Felix learn the language, the restaurant allowed him to observe successful Houstonians first hand. As he told a reporter later in life, "I started watching people, how they acted and the way they talked. And I tried to copy the things I liked about their manners."[14]

In turn, Felix proved to be a steady, punctual, and trusted worker. Even when business slacked off during his first months there, his employers kept him on because of his noticeable politeness. On the advice of his employer and eager for advancement, Felix went to six months of night classes at Dow School, an elementary school in the Sixth Ward, to improve his English. This experience represented his only formal education in the United States. As a result of his efforts, before the end of his first year Tijerina became one of the waiters and got a raise. People who came in the restaurant began to take an interest in him for his gentlemanly manner.[15] The earliest known portrait of Felix Tijerina (taken by a photographer identified only as "García") probably dates from these first years at the Original Mexican Restaurant. The image reveals a slender, light-complected young man with groomed, wavy hair and clear dark eyes set in a determined countenance, and neatly dressed in coat and tie.[16]

The experience of working for the Caldwells gave Felix his start in the restaurant business.[17] Moreover, perhaps more successfully than any other Mexican Houstonian of his era, Felix took his cue from the business practices of the Anglo community.

Amalia provided a second income for the family. A seamstress like her mother, she found a job as a dressmaker for N. Schwartz and Company. Owned by local businessman Nathan Schwartz, the firm stood at 520 Preston Avenue, less than two blocks from the Tijerinas' home in an industrial area just across the bayou. The company hired young women to manufacture garments, the type of unskilled labor performed by hundreds of Mexican women in Houston. These women worked at factories as packers and labelers, in local textile mills as machinery operators, and in companies that made burlap bagging (for the cotton industry) as cutters and sewers.[18]

Like other recent Mexican arrivals in the city, the Tijerinas also took in close friends and relatives as boarders. This practice accomplished several things. First, it supplemented the family income; second, it assisted other immigrants in establishing themselves in the urban region; and third, it built community ties and contributed to a sense of personal well-being among those persons involved.

Doroteo Pina (who had obtained the job for Felix at the restaurant) knew him and his family from their days in Fort Bend County, where he and Tijerina had worked together for Sugar Land Industries. Pina was almost ten years Felix's senior, one of the older men with whom he associated. Briefly returning to Sugar Land in November, 1922, to get his wife, Petra, Pina brought her to Houston, where they rented a room from the Tijerinas. As Mexican immigrants who came in 1908 from the states of Jalisco and Nuevo León, respectively, Doroteo and Petra became very close to Dionicia, Felix, and the girls. Within a year, the Pinas moved to a rent house in the immediate neighborhood, but the friendship between the families continued.[19]

Simultaneously, Tijerina kinfolk began to make their way to Houston, underscoring the important role la familia played, not only in immigration, but also in the process of Mexican American urbanization. Pedro Villarreal, Dionicia's older brother, was apparently the first of the family to live with them on Artesian. From General Escobedo, Pedro had his own family in Nuevo León, but, reportedly, he came north twice by himself—once in 1922 and again in 1923—for only short stays before returning to his homeland.[20]

Tío Pedro's son, Luciano Villarreal, soon took his father's place. Less than a year younger than Felix, Luciano arrived in Houston from General Escobedo, moving in with the Tijerinas sometime before May, 1925, and living under their roof for several years. Similar in stature and both of light complexion, Felix and his cousin bore a close family resemblance. Felix got Luciano hired as a dishwasher at the Original Mexican Restaurant, and from that time forward he became an important member of Felix's immediate circle.[21]

These family ties to Nuevo León produced a seemingly small event in 1925 that would take on major significance. In July of that year, after his family had firmly settled in Houston, Felix took a trip to Mexico in his Model T Ford to visit his mother's relatives and remained there for approximately three weeks. Upon his return through Laredo on July 28, he was stopped at the border and denied admission to the United States by U.S. immigration authorities because he could not offer proof of U.S. citizenship. But, according to what Felix later said, in order to avoid further delay in getting back to his job, and at the suggestion of an immigration official on the scene, he signed an application for an immigration visa to enter the United States. On it, he swore that he was born in General Escobedo, Nuevo León. After obtaining the visa and paying the required eight-dollar head tax, he was allowed to cross the border and proceeded to Houston. This incident would haunt Felix Tijerina's future.[22]

Felix's shiny little Ford and his apparent prosperity must have impressed other members of the Villarreal clan in General Escobedo. During the next few years, some distant cousins, Tomás and Paula Villarreal, moved with their grown children to Houston and took up residence on Artesian, just up the street from the Tijerinas. Felix soon had their sons, Tomás, Jr., and Ernesto, working with him at the Caldwells' restaurant.

But the most important member of the family who came from General Escobedo through Felix's encouragement was his second cousin, Domingo Villarreal. "Mingo" was two years older than Felix, and, like thousands of other Mexican immigrants during the early 1920s, originally had gone north to work in a Ford plant. Finding the winters too severe for his taste, Mingo settled in Houston, where he tried unsuccessfully to get on with Ford's assembly plant on Harrisburg Boulevard. Felix soon found him employment as a cook at the Original Mexican Restaurant. As the years passed, Mingo and Felix became as close as brothers. Having helped the Villarreals move to Houston, Tijerina began to establish his reputation in General Escobedo as someone concerned about the welfare of the young people of his former hometown.[23]

In addition to work, neighborhood, and family, the most important thing in Felix's first years in Houston was the church. Historians have long viewed *la iglesia* as a crucial socializing institution in the world of Mexican immigrants in the urban United States. For the Tijerinas during the 1920s, "the church" meant Our Lady of Guadalupe Catholic Church to the east of downtown.

The nearest Catholic church to Artesian Place was actually Saint Joseph's, a monumental red brick structure just a few blocks west at the intersection of Houston Avenue and Kane Street in the Sixth Ward. But Saint Joseph's, organized for Italian immigrants in the early 1880s, did not make Mexican parishioners feel welcome during the 1910s and 1920s. Indeed, it was common knowledge among the local residents that its rectors excluded Mexican worshipers from entering, telling them pointedly that "their church" (Our Lady of Guadalupe) was across town.[24]

The Tijerinas attended Our Lady of Guadalupe Church from the time they arrived in Houston, as did the Pinas and other Spanish-speaking neighbors. By 1922, it had been Mexican Houston's most important religious institution for a decade and its only Mexican Catholic church. Located at 60 Marsh Street at Runnels, Guadalupe Church had been deliberately situated in the heart of the Second Ward, near the city's most concentrated pocket of the Mexican populace. Staffed by the missionary Oblate Fathers of Mary Immaculate (O.M.I.), the initial wooden two-storied building opened its doors in the summer of 1912 as the first formal institution serving the religious needs of Houston's *colonia*. A school, also called Our Lady of Guadalupe and run by nuns, opened later that year as part of this religious complex.[25]

Our Lady of Guadalupe had been named for the patron saint of Mexico because the majority of the congregation were Mexican immigrants and poor. Many believers attribute the apparition of Mary to the *campesino* Juan Diego in 1531 near the little village of Guadalupe as the event that prompted the conversion of the Indians and *mestizo* peoples of Mexico to Christianity. Over the centuries, the Virgin of Guadalupe became an important symbol of hope to all Mexicans, especially the dispossessed. In the early decades of the twentieth century, many towns across Texas with significant post-1900 Mexican immigrant populations had their own Our Lady of Guadalupe churches. As such, Houston's Our Lady of Guadalupe was the mother church of Mexican Houston and a quintessential urban immigrant house of worship.[26]

Our Lady of Guadalupe Church brought the Tijerinas, as a family, into close contact with the larger Houston Mexican community more than perhaps any other institution during the 1920s. On the one hand, it offered them familiar cultural surroundings, while on the other, it operated as an agent of change, exposing them to additional dimensions of the city. To get there from Artesian Place required a lengthy streetcar ride; these journeys to the church in Second Ward, past the commercial districts and other residential areas, may have been among the Tijerinas' first outings as a family.

By 1923, the congregation included individuals across the socioeconomic spectrum, from medical doctors to people of the laboring class. The Tijerinas initially attended mass in the upstairs sanctuary of the 1912 structure, probably the most impressive church they had frequented since leaving General Escobedo. For Dionicia, especially, the service had great appeal because the sermons were given in Spanish. The 1912 building, however, was already too cramped for the large numbers of Mexican faithful (four thousand by 1923), and the congregation planned to build a larger, more permanent structure.

The Tijerinas, guided by Dionicia's fervent Catholicism, became involved in the activities of the church, especially the *jamaicas* (festivals), held on the church grounds to raise money and provide fellowship. After the new, red brick church was built and dedicated in 1923, these occasions became even grander, providing opportunities for the family to mix with Mexican Houstonians from the different barrios and walks of life and to expand their horizons beyond the confines of their little neighborhood.[27]

In 1919, rectorship of the church had passed to a fiery, devout, but severe Spanish Oblate named Esteban de Anta. He had been among the missionaries who had founded Guadalupe Church, and he wanted to inject new enthusiasm into the growing congregation. De Anta and his assistant, Father Pedro Centurioni (a kindly Italian who was fluent in Spanish), built the new church and had other construction and outreach plans in the making.

Padre Esteban ran the parish with an iron hand, and at least some of his parishioners disliked him for what they perceived to be his dictatorial "Spaniard's attitude" toward Mexicans, a proclivity among Catholic clergy that had been a target of the Mexican Revolution. Though sincere in their efforts, the priests and nuns were non-Mexican and part of a religious structure that possessed a tinge of condescension toward the immigrant faithful (an attitude often present in those who "missionize").[28]

To most people at Guadalupe Church, however, Padre Esteban served as a counselor, one who worked for their best interests, and the Tijerinas counted themselves among the many who appreciated his ministry. During the decade, Amalia, Dora, Felix, and Victoria regularly served as *padrinos* (sponsors of children) in the large confirmation ceremonies, religiously binding the Tijerinas to families from various neighborhoods. Presided over by Bishop Christopher C. Byrne, these sacramental celebrations took place twice a year, involved hundreds of people, and represented a time of spiritual bonding for participants; these occasions served as reminders of other confirmations the Tijerinas had attended in General Escobedo. From their own neighborhood, Felix and Dionicia became the baptismal godparents of the baby daughter of Doroteo and Petra Pina in April, 1925, further solidifying their relationship through the important Mexican Catholic institution of the *compadrazgo*. Dora Tijerina served as the child's *madrina* at her confirmation.[29]

In the process of bringing the people together, Guadalupe Church served in its own way to alter its parishioners, becoming a "melting pot" of the different types of Mexican Houstonians. To be sure, the church promoted a shared sense of "Mexicanness" among the people, as the nuns and priests spoke Spanish, waved Mexican flags, and hung red, white, and green bunting at the little festivals. The parishioners, however, hailed from various parts of Mexico and Texas. In 1922 alone, the membership included people from more than a dozen states in Mexico and a number of Texas towns. While they were immigrants of Mexican heritage, their association and intermarriage with people from the many different locales could only lessen individual regional characteristics and make them more receptive to change on all levels. They may have retained their sense of being "Mexican," but it was of a broader, more ill-defined nature than the *mexicanidad* which they had possessed before they left their homeland, small-town, or rural Texas settings. Just as the crucible of the Mexican Revolution worked to change the regionally based identities of Mexicans from 1910 through the 1920s, forging a new, broader sense of nationality, so also did the multiple identities of Mexican refugees and immigrants to the United States become altered into something larger, albeit different than their compatriots who had remained in their traumatized homeland. In Houston, all were *mexicanos en el extranjero* (Mexicans abroad) during the church fiestas, devoid of their regional characteristics, and exhorted as *compatriotas mexicanos,* whether their place of origin had been Nuevo León or Zacatecas.[30]

Just as the Revolution served as a common experience south of the border, Mexicans in Houston shared the vicissitudes of urban life. Their attendance at Our Lady of Guadalupe brought them together and allowed them to establish bonds as no other institution did. By 1928, for instance, when the church began to publish its first parish bulletin, the priests allowed the Asamblea Mejicana, a blatantly political organization, to advertise for people to join its ranks so that they could work "*contra los atropellos y abusos de [que] son a menudo victimas*" (against the outrages and abuses of which they are often victims). Thus, Our Lady of Guadalupe Church—where the Tijerinas had to deal with foreign clergy, different neighborhoods, and Mexican Houstonians of all stripes—added another dimension to the change that they underwent in Houston.[31]

Regardless of the availability of Our Lady of Guadalupe School, Dora and Victoria went to Dow School—where their brother had attended night classes—because of its proximity to their home. They walked to school (located near Saint Joseph's Church in the Sixth Ward) with a few of the other neighborhood Mexican children. Because Dow Elementary was not a "Mexican school," they numbered among its few Hispanic students. Already seventeen when the sisters appeared in Dow's school census of 1925, Dora apparently attended for only a short time, mainly to learn English, and then returned to the household chores. Victoria, being younger when she entered Dow, quickly picked up the language and would continue her studies through Houston's public school system. As a result, she became the most acculturated of the three sisters and was the most formally educated member of the family.[32]

Although Felix had spent six months in Dow School English classes, he spoke with a thick Spanish accent (that he would retain for the rest of his life), and he read and wrote English slowly. He noted later that he came to rely on his memory because he could not write fast enough to take notes on speeches or conversations that he wanted to remember.[33]

But Tijerina displayed a respect for education. During the 1920s, a number of young Mexican students, including Primitivo Niño, enrolled in Rice Institute, Houston's foremost college. Originally from San Luis Potosí, Niño came to Houston in 1922 to study engineering after graduating from high school in Edinburg, Texas. One day, while on his way to Rice (out on South Main), he happened to enter the Original Mexican Restaurant, where Felix served him a cup of coffee and a doughnut. Finding out that Niño had little money and impressed with the fact that a young Mexican was a student in an American college, Felix gave him a meal on credit. The two became good friends, and Felix treated him to lunch on many occasions as his way of supporting Niño's education.[34]

During the 1920s, Felix explored the community, making friends in a variety of ways. He often gathered with other young working *mexicanos* in the kitchen of the Rice Hotel, where they held parties with the Mexican cooks, busboys, and dishwashers in Houston's grandest hostelry, owned by Jesse Holman Jones, the Bayou City's most powerful entrepreneur. In his search for entertainment, Tijerina ventured to Magnolia Park, where he attended dances at the Salón Juárez, the large, two-storied wooden-frame building on Navigation Boulevard built by La Sociedad Mutualista Benito Juárez, the area's foremost Mexican mutual aid society. One night (with the help of a friend), Felix had to flee the hall to avoid tangling with some of the young Magnolia Park fellows who resented Tijerina dancing with their neighborhood women. Felix also became a regular at the drugstores, barbershops, cafés, and other places of business on or near the 1800 block of Congress Avenue, the central business district of Houston's "Little Mexico." This area, on the eastern edge of downtown in the Second Ward between Main Street and the large cluster of Mexican residents near Guadalupe Church, developed during the 1920s as the lively hub of Houston's Mexican community, which by the end of the decade numbered around 14,500 people. Fed by a streetcar line that ran down Congress Avenue, this shopping area of family-owned and operated establishments ensconced itself in the one- to three-storied brick buildings previously occupied by Anglo companies and catered to people from every barrio. This *el centro mexicano* (Mexican "downtown") was representative of the adaptive Mexican business districts that emerged in large cities across the United States where Mexican immigrant communities settled during this decade. On Congress, Felix purchased Spanish-language magazines at the Librería Hispano-Americano (a bookstore) owned by José Sarabia, who was perhaps Houston's premier Mexican entrepreneur. After Sarabia opened El Teatro Azteca in 1927, Tijerina attended the performances of Spanish-speaking actors, singers, and dancers who came through Houston, or saw Spanish-language movies shown on the Azteca's large screen. Located in the middle of the block at 1809½ Congress, the Azteca may well have been the *colonia*'s secular focal point by the late 1920s. There, especially on the weekends, Tijerina could mingle with almost as many Mexican Houstonians as he did at church, for the theater's two-hundred seat auditorium hosted capacity crowds anxious for popular entertainment.[35]

Yet, these Congress Avenue businesses stood in close proximity to downtown Houston and were interspersed among many non-Mexican firms. Their Mexican clientele, therefore, had no more success than the parishioners of Our Lady of Guadalupe Church at avoiding the constant acculturating influences of the Bayou City. Even the several Spanish-language newspapers which sprouted in this commercial district during the 1920s informed their readership of local "*amigos de los mexicanos,*" such as Mayor Oscar Holcombe.[36]

Around 1927, in one of the cafés on Congress Avenue, Felix met Janie González, the woman he would marry six years later. Originally from south-central Texas, she had come to Houston the year before.

Just nineteen when she came to the Bayou City, Janie González already had a range of experiences representative of Mexican-Texan working women who populated the urban regions. Her parents, Sóstenes and

Fabiana González, had immigrated to the United States from Lagos de Moreno, Jalisco, in 1901. They settled in Sandy Fork, Texas, a small farming community in northern Gonzales County, where Sóstenes worked for a time with the railroad. There, the couple had two daughters, Frances, in 1907, and Janie, on December 20, 1908. The family moved to Pleasanton (in Atascosa County) when Janie was four. In Pleasanton, her mother took in washing while her father traveled around searching for available work. The family moved north in 1919 to the Bastrop area to join Sóstenes, who had been working in the local coal mines that hired a number of Mexican laborers.

By 1920, the family had turned to sharecropping in the immediate vicinity of Bastrop, and Janie helped her father raise cotton. They moved again in 1924 to Hills Prairie, and later near McDade, little communities in Bastrop County, where they sharecropped on different farms. Her diminutive size and high energy earned her the nickname "Peanut" from an Anglo landowner who liked her spunk. Although precocious, between the field work and the family's transiency Janie completed only three years of schooling in the various small towns where they had resided.[37]

Because a severe drought ruined their crops, in 1925 Janie walked to Austin in search of work. She found employment for a short time as a live-in companion to a Mexican American woman and in an Anglo-owned laundry near the University of Texas campus. Whatever money she had left over after paying for the barest living expenses she would send home to her family, who were by then residing in McDade.[38]

In 1926, Janie decided to move to Houston. Janie's sister Frances had married, and she and her husband, Julián Gutiérrez, had already settled in the Bayou City, where Julián, an accomplished violinist, searched for an outlet for his musical talent. At her sister's invitation, Janie and Rosa Vázquez, another young working woman from Austin who also had relatives in the Bayou City, hitchhiked the distance between the cities over a period of two days. They caught rides as they could and slept overnight under bridges. Each woman carried her simple belongings in a flour sack. By the time they entered the outskirts of Houston along Washington Avenue, Janie had only her clothing, an apple, and twelve cents to her name. She also had a tough, irrepressible personality that was already tempered by the understanding that life was hard.[39]

Janie moved in with her sister and family in the Fifth Ward and held a series of dollar-a-day jobs—first, as a clerk in a Fifth Ward grocery store owned by an Italian woman, then as a sampler at one of the large ship channel cotton compresses, as a photographic retoucher, and at a laundry—anything she could do to learn and make a living. Simultaneously, she waitressed nightly at the restaurant of Tomás Corrales at 1905 Congress, hoping to supplement her meager wages with tips.[40]

Felix was a regular customer, and Janie was bright and attractive. They talked and, over the next year or two, began to see one another on a regular basis. They would usually meet at dances held by the Roseland Steppers, perhaps the most popular young persons' club in the *colonia* during the 1920s. Commonly called the "Rolling Steppers," it was a group of fun-loving young Mexican men that came together to sponsor dances in halls from downtown Houston to Magnolia Park where young people could enjoy the music of *orquestas*. Felix and Janie would go on outings to Houston parks or often to Galveston to swim at the beach in the company of their crowd of young friends. Photographs from their dates in the late 1920s show a pretty, petit Janie with dark wavy hair. Felix looked every inch the dapper urban man, with skimmer, bow tie, white shirt, slacks, and plaid socks; he had visibly matured beyond the slender youth in the portrait by "García" a few years before and was, no doubt, a far cry from the country boy who had come to Houston to work on Produce Row. He had also become popular with hundreds of Mexican and Anglo Houstonians.[41]

Just as his experiences at Caldwell's restaurant had influenced him, the Congress Avenue area helped Felix to move beyond the confines of his working-class world. Specifically, he came into contact with Houston's Mexican business owners and professionals, a group that one local Spanish-language publication in 1928 called "*el esfuerzo mexicano en Houston*" (the Mexican initiative in Houston). These individuals, mainly in their late twenties and thirties, were represented by men like José Sarabia (originally from Guanajuato), grocer Gonzalo Mancillas (from Nuevo León), druggists Alejandro Canales and Juan José Ruíz (from San Antonio, Texas, and Veracruz, respectively), jeweler Fernando Salas A. (from Chihuahua), several young Mexican doctors from northern or western states in Mexico who had set up practice in Houston, and a host of lesser figures who worked for themselves, mainly catering to Mexican trade.

These prominent men among Houston's *mexicanos en el extranjero* (Mexicans abroad) chaired the committees that held the Mexican Independence

Day celebrations, important community events in Hispanic Houston during the 1920s. They often interceded with Anglo Houston authorities on behalf of their compatriots and were universally admired in the *colonia*.[42] As Mexicans, they reminded the members of their community to be proud of their heritage, but as entrepreneurs, they entreated other Mexicans to emulate the business practices of successful Anglo Houstonians. One 1928 editorial in Sarabia's *Gaceta mexicana* put it succinctly: "*un negocio, en manos gringas florece*" because "*el gringo se pone a trabajar como los hombres, dedicandose a el en cuerpo y alma*" (a business in Anglo hands flourishes because the Anglo works like a man possessed, as he commits himself to his work body and soul).[43]

Though not a member of this elite group, Felix, by his subsequent actions, indicated that he either listened to or shared its admonitions. By the late 1920s, he all but managed Caldwell's restaurant and, because of his competent, genial manner, received encouragement from Anglos and Mexicans alike to open a place of his own.[44]

Felix fell in with Antonio Reynaga, one of the several restaurant owners among the Congress Avenue *esfuerzo mexicano*. Reynaga owned the Iris Café and Bakery, a thriving business at 1819-21 Congress. Originally from Monterrey, he was a tall man who reportedly had business interests in Mexico and always seemed to have extra cash to invest.[45] On May 30, 1929, Reynaga and Felix signed a document of co-partnership for "establishing, running and maintaining a 'Mexican restaurant,'" and calling for each to invest fifteen hundred dollars in the venture. They agreed to call their new establishment the Mexican Inn.[46]

Reynaga's role was not only that of investor, but also as purchaser of supplies for the business, since he already operated the Iris Café and they felt he could obtain commodities more cheaply because he could buy them in quantity. From the start, they agreed that Felix would control and manage the inside operations of the Mexican Inn, such as planning the menu, supervising the employees, and overseeing all other parts of the daily operations. He also would "devote all of his time, attention, skill and energy for the purpose of promoting" the business. They were to share profits and losses equally.[47]

Shortly thereafter, they leased a location on Main Street, previously the site of the Ideal Café, and began operation in late summer. No doubt because of his popularity, Felix managed to get coverage of its opening in the *Houston Post,* one of the city's leading newspapers. Never mentioning Reynaga's role, the complete article read:

> Mexican Inn Will
> Open Doors Friday
> Announcement of the opening of the Mexican Inn, 1209 Main
> street, Friday (August 16, 1929) is made by Felix Tijerina,
> better known as "Felix" to hundreds of Houstonians. Tempting
> and spicy Mexican dishes, the best of cuisine south of the
> Rio Grande will be served patrons, Senor Tijerina said, and
> famous recipes, handed down through generations in his family
> will be used and served to add a piquant taste to the menus of
> the Mexican Inn, he stated.
>
> A seven-piece native Mexican string band will give several
> numbers during the dining hours on opening day, includ-
> ing Mexican national airs and folk music, Senor Tijerina
> announced.[48]

The Mexican Inn had one large dining room, similar to the Original Mexican Restaurant just a block north. When he began to take out ads, Felix advertised that he served "Mexican Dishes Exclusively." Also, like the Caldwells' café, Felix's food was designed for Anglo tastes and was therefore not highly spiced.[49]

Although he was influenced in many ways by Houston's Mexican entrepreneurs and by his Mexican background, Felix's Main Street location meant that, from the start, he followed the lead of George Caldwell and wanted to tap the Anglo market. Reynaga, Corrales, and others in their barrio locations would continue to deal solely with the Mexican trade. Of the more than two dozen Mexican-owned cafés in Houston, the Mexican Inn was the only one outside a *mexicano* neighborhood. When the Mexican Inn started operation, it was one of only three Mexican restaurants on Main Street; the other two included the Caldwells' and the Spanish-American Garden (in the euphemism of the time), also owned by an Anglo.[50]

Barely twenty-four, Felix had made the leap from restaurant employee to restaurant owner. Within seven years of his moving to Houston he had transcended the status of a faceless laborer to become the "Senor Tijerina" of the Houston press. He had evolved from urban *obrero* to entrepreneur, a man able to promote his efforts in a major Anglo Houston newspaper.

Felix Tijerina's personal growth had been a process of accommodation that had drawn upon his Mexican background and associations as well as upon his new, non-Mexican surroundings and had transformed him into an urban man. This transformation had witnessed the dilution of Tijerina's specific sense of Mexicanness and the emergence of a bicultural Mexican American identity geared to life in the city. Distinct from, yet deeply influenced by the 1920s' *esfuerzo mexicano* in Houston, Tijerina's efforts clearly illustrated the interconnection between the Immigrant Generation and the cohort that would come into its own during the 1930s, the group in which Felix would play a prominent role.

CHAPTER 3

EMERGENCE OF A
LATIN AMERICAN LEADER

Although part of the 1920s immigrant wave that had turned Houston's Mexican populace into a viable community, Felix Tijerina soon gained a significant place in his *colonia* during the 1930s. Young and inexperienced, Tijerina had made little impact prior to 1929. He would begin to garner influence as a restaurateur after that.

Between 1929 and 1941, Tijerina exemplified in Houston what scholars have called the Mexican American Generation—a group of leaders of Mexican descent who first emerged in the expanding southwestern barrios from the crucible of the Great Depression to lead their community in its quest for equal status in the United States. Specifically, Tijerina became representative of the middle-class, entrepreneurial element within this larger group. He was the personification of a "Latin American," the term that came to be commonly utilized from the 1930s through the early 1960s to designate people of the *colonia* who aspired to integrate themselves more fully into mainstream American society.[1]

By the time the United States entered World War II, Felix Tijerina displayed forms of behavior and had undergone seminal experiences that conform to the contours of this Mexican American (or, more precisely, Latin American) Generation. Striving for "success," he attempted to achieve and maintain middle-class status amid the economic vicissitudes of the era. He developed as a businessman and civic leader—owning two successful restaurants, belonging to local Mexican groups, and increasingly participating in Anglo organizations for personal advancement as well as societal benefit. Tijerina's actions during this period represented his first major public expression of a bicultural identity and demonstrated an approach to life that had evolved since his crossing of the Rio Grande as a boy.

Tijerina's transformation began with the opening of his Mexican restaurant, itself a bicultural statement. He had, after all, learned the Mexican food business from an Anglo entrepreneur, but he now partnered with a Mexican immigrant. Selling Mexican cuisine to Anglo as well as Mexican customers, he combined his cultural heritage with opportunities presented by his American environment.

Felix staffed the restaurant with his family. Mingo and Luciano Villarreal left the Caldwells' restaurant to help him open the Mexican Inn, to cook, and to wait on tables. A younger, single first cousin, Frank Tijerina, came up from Nuevo León to work as a general helper.[2]

Around this time, Felix also rented a better residence. By October, 1929, he and his mother and sisters had moved to a larger house at 1109 White Street, approximately a dozen blocks farther west and a block north of Washington Avenue (the principal thoroughfare of the Sixth Ward). This new address was in the midst of another old residential area where by 1930 Mexican Americans were displacing non–Spanish-speaking households in increasing numbers. Here a smattering of Mexican residents had lived for years, due to the proximity of several major railroad yards, a cotton oil company, and other industries where employment was readily available.[3]

In mid-1930, the Tijerinas found a still more spacious home just around the corner at 2008 Center Street, renting it from an Italian couple who lived on the same block. Dionicia was comfortable on Center Street because the Pina, Contreras, and other families from the Artesian Place neighborhood had also relocated there. Her sense of well-being would be further enhanced when Padre Esteban de Anta brought together the Center Street–area Mexican residents in 1932 to start a neighborhood church. Begun essentially as an alternative to the still-exclusive Saint Joseph, it consisted of a small chapel and school complex in a rented two-storied house. Dionicia proved to be one of its most enthusiastic initial members as she and her family helped to raise money, insisting that it be named Saint Stephen's, in honor of Padre Esteban. The Tijerinas were so much a part of this Sixth Ward barrio that even after Felix married in late 1933, Dionicia and her daughters remained there for many years. While living on Center Street, with encouragement from her mother and Felix, Victoria continued her schooling and graduated from Sam Houston High in the spring of 1934, the only one of the siblings to do so.[4]

Felix's home, family, and work remained closely intertwined. Frank, Mingo, and Luciano lived with Felix, his mother, and sisters during the first year or so after the Mexican Inn opened. In addition, Cecilio Villarreal (one of the distant cousins from General Escobedo) had married Amalia; the couple had a child named Carlos in 1927 and now resided in the house on Center Street as well.[5]

Even as the Tijerinas first settled on Center Street, things did not fare well at the Mexican Inn. Although Felix apparently had a fairly steady clientele at first, 1929 was an inopportune year to open a business. In October, the stock market collapsed, and by 1930 the Great Depression had gripped the nation. Though Houston in general missed the worst effects of unemployment and other economic distress experienced by most major cities, the expansion of the previous decade slowed considerably as businesses restricted their operations and county as well as city resources dwindled. The black and Mexican communities were especially hard hit, and the Mexican Inn, despite its attempts to cater to Anglo customers, felt the pinch of the times as severely as most businesses owned by members of the *colonia*.[6]

Moreover, Felix's business had already suffered from unstable partnerships. His relations with Antonio Reynaga, formally begun in May, 1929, did not survive the year. While each man had invested $975 in the fledgling restaurant, Reynaga had lent the business another $916, which was soon repaid. But in late October, with Reynaga wishing to pull out, the two men dissolved their partnership. Reynaga sold his half to an Anglo woman, Mrs. Ethyl V. Lawrence.[7]

Unfortunately, Felix's partnership with Mrs. Lawrence proved to be unsatisfactory as well. Lawrence worked for a downtown insurance agency and probably struck up a relationship with Tijerina by coming into his café. Told of his impending break with Reynaga, Lawrence bought into the business and provided operating capital. Because she would come and pick up the daily sales, Felix soon became disheartened, feeling as if he worked for her. This tenuous situation deteriorated further, and Felix turned for assistance to an Anglo couple named Durst, although he did not formally establish a partnership with them.[8]

Felix's troubles were compounded by competition from new restaurants. By early 1930, Antonio Reynaga had established the Mexico City Restaurant, which he advertised as "The Show Place of Houston." An elaborate affair located at 3916 Main Street in an Anglo business district, Reynaga's new restaurant had private rooms for banquets and competed with the Mexican Inn. Another place vied for the Anglo market when William Knorbin (a German American) opened the Old Mexico Tavern by the fall of 1933.[9]

Although financially distressed, the Mexican Inn Restaurant still placed Felix in the limelight. His location on Main Street, with its explicit attempt to garner Anglo trade, brought him into association with an important segment of Houston's Mexican community as well, especially its burgeoning number of clubs and organizations.

Reminiscences of contemporaries and newspaper articles of the day suggest that Felix utilized the restaurant to deepen his connection to Houston's *colonia* by hosting groups and contributing to community events. A member of the San Antonio acting troupe La Companía Manuel Cotera recalled many years later that when it performed in Houston Tijerina regularly invited the group to eat at the Mexican Inn. In 1932, Tijerina was one of a dozen Mexican Houston businessmen who managed to donate a few dollars to Club Chapultepec, a young women's organization that had formed the preceding year, so it could hold the *colonia's* major Cinco de Mayo celebration, an event that would attract thousands of residents to Houston's City Auditorium. This occasion was apparently one of numerous Mexican national holiday festivities that he would support as owner of the Mexican Inn. In April, 1933, the *Houston Post* noted that the Spanish Club of Rice Institute, chaired by Olivia Gonzales, planned to hold its meeting at Felix's restaurant. And, as shall be seen, other 1930s–era clubs would call the Mexican Inn their unofficial gathering place. It also served as a location where Mexican Americans from out of town would go when visiting the Bayou City.[10]

Equally important, his restaurant ensured that his already sizable circle of friends in the city's *pueblo mexicano* widened to include a group of aspiring young Mexican Houstonians who would influence the city for a generation. For example, during his earliest days at the Mexican Inn, Felix developed his close friendship with Aurelio Reynosa and Félix H. Morales. Like Tije-rina, Reynosa and Morales embodied the diverse origins and complex make-up of Houston's 1930s Mexican community, and, together, the three men rose as figures in various aspects of its Mexican American life.

Originally from Aguascalientes, Aurelio Reynosa had fought in the army of General Francisco Villa from 1914 to 1915. In the late 1910s, under-standing no English, he left Mexico and came to Houston to work for the Southern Pacific Lines. When Reynosa had first immigrated to the United States he planned to stay only a short time, but in fact, he would remain for the rest of his long life. He sojourned in the cold climates of the U.S. Mid-west but returned to Houston, where, while employed at the Ford Motor Company assembly plant, he met Felix. Their friendship developed when Reynosa stopped by the Mexican Inn during the afternoons to visit and help around the café.

The Anglos knew Reynosa as Leo, but the Mexicans called him "Chato." Handsome, dapper, and popular with everyone (Anglos and Mexicans alike), Reynosa displayed a personal warmth, generosity, and adventurous spirit, of-ten regaling his friends with stories of his exploits with Villa's army and the revolution. He and Tijerina became inseparable, true *compadres*. Their asso-ciation became such that Chato would begin to accompany Felix on his trips back to General Escobedo. Picking up pointers from his more circumspect friend at the Mexican Inn, Reynosa would have his own café by the early 1940s. He became a well-known (but not wealthy) restaurateur, who never bothered to completely master the English language.[11]

Juxtaposed against Reynosa's background and disposition was Félix Hess-brook Morales. Born in New Braunfels, Texas, in 1907, Morales moved to Houston from San Antonio in January, 1931, with his young wife, Angelina Vera. Morales was half German and all entrepreneur while Angelina proved to be a shrewd, attractive business partner and spouse. From a family of Texas funeral home owners, Morales immediately opened one in the heart of the Second Ward and its Mexican population after he and Angie gradu-ated from a Houston mortuary school. Fluent in English and Spanish and adept at dealing with the Anglo community, the couple turned their funeral parlor into a community institution, becoming advisors to many members of the *colonia*. Coming from San Antonio with its deep Texas Mexican cul-ture, Félix Morales had an abiding interest in Mexican music, a talent for playing guitar, and a desire to sing. Not long after moving to Houston, he met Tijerina at the Mexican Inn, took an instant liking to him, and soon brought Angelina to the restaurant. As the years progressed, the fortunes of Tijerina and Morales would rise simultaneously.[12]

İn March, 1933, Tijerina began to sponsor a baseball team— one of his most visible forms of business promotion and popular community involvement—and he would continue to underwrite it for several years. Appropriately called the Mexican Inn Baseball Team, it was organized and coached for two of its three seasons by Rodrigo García, a good friend of Tijerina's from the 1920s.[13]

Games between amateur clubs had been a favorite pastime for decades in Houston, and city leagues and independent teams flourished. For at least fifteen years, Mexican Americans had produced a couple of the better clubs to take to the diamond, competing successfully with Anglo organizations. Local "fast teams" such as the Mexican Eagles and Mexican Lions, along with such exceptional players as pitcher "Hokie" García, had built a reputation among Houston baseball enthusiasts. During its first season, the Mexican Inn club was one of at least a half-dozen sponsored by different Houston barrios, social clubs, or other Mexican-owned businesses.[14]

An avid sports fan, Tijerina loved his ball team and outfitted the players with handsome uniforms, complete with a large patch on the left front of the jerseys that displayed the name of his restaurant around a Mexican *charro*. The Mexican Inn squad survived for the three seasons between 1933 and 1935 and normally consisted of more than a dozen players, some of the best in the city. It was especially strong during its first year when it had pitching ace Ramón Sustaita. The Mexican Inn gave Sustaita his start in amateur ball until he went on to play for a time during the 1934 season with the Houston Buffaloes, the local farm team of the Saint Louis Cardinals. Other players such as first baseman "Black Lupe" García and pitcher Miguel "Big Foot" Zepeda were among the team's heavy-hitters. During the 1934 season, one Anglo sportswriter commented that the Mexican Inn nine were viewed as "the strongest Mexican team" in Texas.[15]

In many respects, his baseball team was just another manifestation of Tijerina's bicultural world view. By having Mexican players compete against local Anglo and Mexican clubs to the delight of mixed crowds in stadiums across Houston and out of town, the two ethnic groups came together in (usually) friendly competition, forcing Anglo fans and the media to recognize Mexican American teams as capable competitors. Upon occasion the Mexican Inn team even included a few Anglo players. Over its three seasons, it played Mexican clubs from Sugar Land, Texas City, Seguin, Beeville, and Refugio as well as Anglo teams from Tomball, Huntsville, Galveston, and other places, interacting with communities well beyond Houston. This "sports connection" gave Felix much favorable publicity, further ingratiating him with the Mexican as well as the Anglo communities, especially when his team made it one year into the statewide *Houston Post* tournament held at Buffalo Stadium. Representing Houston against out-of-town Anglo teams, the Mexican Inn squad's photograph, which included the team's sponsor, ran in the local press. Always on hand at the games, Felix became a familiar, popular figure with the players and fans who followed amateur baseball in Houston and in many small towns.[16]

In late 1933, Felix and Janie decided to get married. The wedding took place at Our Lady of Guadalupe Church early Sunday morning, December 10, 1933. Father Esteban de Anta performed the ceremony, and Fred Balderas (one of Felix's baseball players and good friend) and Refugia Roach were the official witnesses. With no money to send invitations, the couple followed the custom of the day among Mexican Americans and simply printed a public invitation in a local newspaper. A large number of family, friends, and coworkers attended. The reception was held at the Tijerina home on Center Street. The Tijerinas' wedding portrait, taken at the studio of Gregorio Cantú, Houston's premier Mexican American commercial photographer during the 1930s, showed a handsome couple: Felix in his dark, double-breasted suit and Janie in a white dress. After a brief, inexpensive wedding trip to Galveston, Felix returned to the café and Janie to her job as a saleswoman at Solo-Serve Company, a downtown retail dry goods store.[17]

Initially, the couple—along with Janie's parents (Sóstenes and Fabiana González)—rented a house on West Street in the Fifth Ward. But by 1935, Felix and Janie had moved to 2203 Center near his family, where, to cut costs, they again shared a small house with her parents, her sister Frances, and her sister's second husband Luis Zavala. Money was so tight all around that they could not afford even these meager accommodations for long, especially since Felix financially assisted his mother and sisters. To survive the Depression, Janie's parents soon moved to a farm near Sugar Land, where they grew a garden that provided them and the other family members still living in Houston with vegetables.[18]

B etween 1933 and 1935, Tijerina began his involvement in four Mexican Houston organizations, solidifying his interest in *colonia* affairs. These groups reflected the growing sophistication not only of Tijerina, but also of Houston's Spanish-speaking residents, especially an emerging, articulate middle class striving to participate within the broader Houston community. Each organization had its own particular personality that manifested a different degree of feeling toward its Mexican heritage and American present. Yet all four demonstrated a greater ease with life in the United States than that shown by the immigrant generation that preceded them. Each in its own way evidenced the transition from the Mexican to the Latin American experience that was taking place during the 1930s. Tijerina's participation in all four (reflective of much overlapping membership among the groups) indicated the broad range of his own social, cultural, civic, and political interests, that is, the complexity of his identity as a Mexican Houstonian with middle-class aspirations.

The first of the four groups and the most Mexican-oriented to claim Tijerina's membership was El Club Cultural Recreativo México Bello (or México Bello for short). México Bello had been formed in 1924 as a social and cultural club by a group of young men, the majority of whom had recently come from Mexico. They wanted to provide themselves with a recreational outlet and "*hacer un México chiquito en el extranjero*" (create a little Mexico abroad). The club's emblem was the Mexican red, white, and green, and as its motto "*Patria-Raza-Idioma*" suggested, it sought to perpetuate pride in the Mexican homeland, race, and Spanish language. Equally important, through a display of proper deportment in all its functions and endeavors, México Bello (Beautiful Mexico) wanted to improve the image of the Mexican in the minds of Anglo Houstonians. Men could join through invitation only, and by the early 1930s, membership was highly prized, as the club clearly represented the most popular organization in the *colonia,* a who's who of young, aspiring Hispanic Houston.[19]

Tijerina had entered México Bello by 1933, through the efforts of individuals such as Rodrigo García and Ramón Fernández, the latter being the club's longtime president who had been with the group almost from its beginning. Within México Bello, Felix fostered his close friendships, discovering his most lasting, favorite camaraderie. Chato Reynosa, Félix Morales, and P. L. Niño (the Rice Institute graduate whom Felix had befriended in the 1920s) were already members by the time Felix became active. A host of other like-minded young men whom he either already knew or would meet—*distinguidos* like Fernando Salas, Francisco Brett, William Aguilar (Tijerina's buddy from Produce Row days), and Isidro García—also participated in the group.[20]

In turn, these individuals saw Felix Tijerina as a young man-on-the-make who presented the greater community with the paragon of the Mexican character they desired to portray. He drank only lightly, at most a beer or two, and enjoyed friendly games of poker with Reynosa, Morales, John J. Ruíz, E. J. García, and other club members. He was a man of moderation whose only excess was work.[21]

By mid-1933, the local mainstream newspapers mentioned México Bello more than any other club in the city's *colonia* for providing activities for the "young Latin Americans of Houston" (this being one of the first examples of the term "Latin American" used in lieu of "Mexican"). Boasting sixty members, the group contained a number of committees that, consistent with its direction from the 1920s, put on dances at Houston's downtown Aragon Ballroom every two months, brought in speakers to its weekly meetings, and staged an elaborate bimonthly *velada literario musical* (literary and musical program) at Rusk Settlement House, the leading social welfare institution among Mexicans in the Second Ward. The *Houston Chronicle* reported in 1933 that "[t]he primary purpose of the organization [was] the promotion of a better understanding between Mexicans and Americans."[22]

Dora Tijerina, already known as a good amateur actress, was mentioned in association with México Bello even before her brother's name began to appear. During August, 1933, at the club's *velada* at Rusk Settlement, Dora and Lidia Lara performed a dramatic "dialogue" for the general public, one of many Spanish-language numbers designed to show Houstonians the contributions made by the Mexican colony to the literary, musical, and cultural life of the city.[23]

Beginning in the late 1920s, México Bello commissioned an annual group portrait, and Felix appeared for the first time in the one taken on January 7, 1934. At this meeting and formal dance held at the Aragon, the club installed Tijerina as a new member of its board of directors, a post he had been elected to in December of the preceding year and would again hold the following year. At this time, México Bello had also elected a different president, Francisco Chaírez, a recent graduate of Rice Institute, to replace Ramón Fernández, who had ably served ten years in that position.[24]

Under Chaírez's two-term presidency (1934 and 1935), the members of México Bello became even more visible through increased activity in Houston's civic arena, which illustrated the evolution of the club into a somewhat higher level of acculturation during the 1930s. By the fall of 1934, the club had initiated a series of benefit dinners and dances at the Rusk Settlement House to raise money for the poor of the city's Mexican community. In December, club members distributed clothes and other articles to needy children at Rusk Settlement, a response to the Depression. That fall, Mayor Oscar Holcombe attended México Bello's September dance, where he was enthusiastically made an honorary member. Like many of the club's members, Tijerina was an Oscar Holcombe supporter.[25]

Felix played his most active role in organizing the group's dances, grand occasions that always made the news. During 1934, Tijerina sat on the committees that arranged the dances and maintained order among those persons who attended. Held at the Aragon Ballroom, these dances were by invitation only, hosted several hundred people, and featured Los Rancheros, a popular Houston *orquesta* that played both Mexican and American dance music.[26]

Tijerina became even more deeply involved in México Bello by the early summer of 1934, when the club began to hold its regular meetings at the Mexican Inn, a practice that continued into the fall. These meetings were special events that consisted of dinners to honor people who had helped the Houston Mexican community. In July, the club held a "stag dinner" to make Servando Barrera Guerra, Mexico's consul in Houston, its honorary president. In August, the group feted Rodolfo Avila de la Vega, the publisher of *El tecolote* (Houston's sole Spanish-language weekly), at the Mexican Inn and presented him with an honorary membership resolution for promoting Mexican culture in the city. De la Vega eventually returned to Mexico, but during the 1930s, when not scouting for news, he spent a great deal of time at the Mexican Inn with Tijerina. México Bello also hosted a farewell dinner at Felix's restaurant in October for Demetrio Ponce, a club member who had been active in Houston's Comité Patriótico Mexicano and other local Mexican organizations. Once a general in the Mexican army, Ponce was returning to his native Chihuahua to take a job with the state government.

Available evidence indicates that Tijerina was probably more involved with México Bello during this period than with any other club. Clearly, the camaraderie he found there coincided with his affinity for Mexican culture and people. México Bello's regular meetings moved to the group's new clubhouse at 1209 Shearn Street, where Felix remained especially busy during his second term as board director in 1935.[27]

Sometime in 1935, Ramón Fernández (as a result, some say, of bruised feelings over an election within México Bello) led approximately fifteen young men in forming a new *sociedad,* which they called El Club Recreativo International. An offshoot of México Bello, this initial group included Rodrigo García, Francisco Brett, William Aguilar, Felix Tijerina, and others, many of whom numbered among the more acculturated members of the older organization. Felix was among approximately sixty members included in the group's 1935 composite photograph created by Houston commercial photographer Gregorio Cantú.[28]

With Fernández as president, the International Club greatly resembled México Bello. It sponsored regular dances, held meetings at the Rusk Settlement House, and feted such dignitaries as the Mexican consul, always paying homage to its Mexican roots. By 1936, however, it began to reflect an additional dimension, symbolic of a more modern posture. Anglo candidates for various city offices came before the group at one of its meetings at Rusk Settlement during that fall's campaign to ask for its support, an overture that hardly gives evidence of an insular, immigrant mentality on the part of the membership.[29]

By the time the International Club and México Bello became more assertive, two other organizations had emerged to give them this extra incentive. The first of these was the League of United Latin American Citizens (LULAC) which took root in Houston in 1934. As the third organization that occupied Felix's attentions at this time, LULAC's objectives moved a step beyond those of México Bello and the International Club in the civic arena. Still, Houston LULAC drew some of its membership from the two social clubs and operated as an integral part of the Bayou City's many 1930s Mexican American organizations, albeit as a pacesetter.

Much has been written about the origins, purpose, and ideology of LULAC. The league was founded in 1929 in Corpus Christi, Texas, from a union of three South Texas groups: the League of Latin American Citizens, the Order of the Sons of America, and the Order of the Knights of America. It came together that year under pro-tem chairman Ben Garza, a popular and energetic Corpus Christi community leader. (To underscore the influence of the business class, Garza was a restaurateur, like Felix Tijerina.) As a concerted attempt to break the cultural, economic, and political isolation of the Mexican American populace, LULAC sought to integrate its community into mainstream United States society. Pursuant to this goal, the organization required that its members be American citizens and stressed loyalty to the United States as a sacred duty. In its quest to identify fully with this country, LULAC adopted such things as English as its official language, began each meeting with George Washington's prayer and the pledge of allegiance to the flag of the United States, had the red, white, and blue as the organization's colors, encouraged its members to vote, and did other things to express 100 percent Americanism. For LULAC, *la patria* was the United States rather than Mexico.[30]

Even by using the term "Latin American" in its name, LULAC attempted to avoid the onus that the word "Mexican" had in the minds of Anglo Texas society and, at the same time, let Mexican Americans know that, as American citizens, they deserved the best the country had to offer. LULAC pledged to work within the system to end discrimination imposed by Anglo society and to achieve full rights as citizens for Americans of Mexican descent.[31]

From the time of its inception, LULAC placed a special emphasis on education. In its official aims and purposes, the organization stated that education was the foundation of a healthy nation and that LULAC must promote education among Mexican Americans. It likewise stressed that its members (and Mexican Americans in general) must attain middle-class status, believing that community leaders would emanate only from these ranks.[32]

At the same time, the LULAC organization officially called on its participants to respect their Mexican heritage as well as to speak the Spanish language correctly, thus acknowledging their bicultural existence and identity. This admiration for their Mexican roots, coupled with the organization's call for education, achievement, accommodation to American life, and equal rights, made it easy, especially in the political climate of the 1930s, for the more acculturated Mexican Houstonians in México Bello and El Club International to find LULAC appealing. When LULAC finally started a Houston "council" (as its chapters were called), the membership even hosted dances that featured music by the same *orquesta* (Los Rancheros) that played for the fetes put on by México Bello and other such clubs.[33]

LULAC councils immediately established themselves across South Texas, each receiving a number to designate the official sequence of its origin. Council No. 1 was in Corpus Christi, Council No. 2 was in San Antonio, Council No. 3 in Brownsville, and so forth. By March, 1933, the *LULAC News* (the league's monthly publication) listed forty-four active men's councils as the organization rapidly spread across South and West Texas. Two existed in Santa Fe and Albuquerque, New Mexico. By March, 1934, the list of men's councils had grown to fifty-five, in locations as far north in Texas as Kerrville, Victoria, and Port Lavaca.[34]

The Bayou City was a natural, proximate area for LULAC to reach as it grew out of its South Texas confines, especially since a great deal of communication took place between the Mexican American communities in Houston and San Antonio. Also, given the level of discrimination that existed along the Texas Gulf Coast and the growing number and sophistication of Mexican Houstonians, the city had the material for building a LULAC council by the early 1930s.[35]

A few men from Magnolia Park and the Second Ward came together as early as the spring of 1934 to form a LULAC group. They recruited membership for the new organization from across town, but because Magnolia Park members predominated, it was given the name Council No. 60 of Magnolia Park when the main organization conferred the charter for the Houston-area group in November, 1934.[36]

According to 1930s LULAC activists, Felix numbered among Council No. 60's earliest recruits.[37] Some of Houston's first LULAC members such as organizer Manuel Crespo (an immigrant from Spain who belonged to the International Club) and council vice president E. J. García (of México Bello) knew Tijerina well. As a prominent café owner, Felix no doubt had naturally come up as a prospective member among those who initiated the fledgling council.

By the spring and summer of 1935, local newspapers covered Council No. 60's public meetings, which took place in both Magnolia Park and downtown Houston. Houstonians learned that the group was "composed of naturalized poll-tax paying citizens of Latin extraction."[38] The council called for "Latin people" to learn about American government, vote, and be good citizens of the United States. At the top of Council No. 60's agenda was its desire to have every Mexican resident of the county file for American citizenship. True to its assertive posture, the council had a committee to launch a poll tax drive among Latinos in Harris County. From early on, the council also wanted to foster social betterment and education among all levels of local Latin American youth, calling for those in high school to receive aid to attend college.[39]

During the spring of 1935, Tijerina's Mexican Inn restaurant played an integral part in the South Texas LULAC Convention, the first major LULAC confab in the Bayou City. Hosted by Council No. 60, the convention took place on Sunday, May 13, at the Houston City Auditorium. The affair commenced at noon with a luncheon at the Mexican Inn for the LULAC officials and founding fathers, who heard a talk by Rev. William S. Jacobs, a local minister.[40]

Those present at the general assembly received welcoming remarks from Mayor Oscar Holcombe and the LULAC message from league founders and national officers such as Kingsville attorney Ramón L. Longoria, E. R. Lozano (president-general of LULAC), its secretary-general Tomás Garza, Brownsville lawyer J. T. Canales, and San Antonians Alonso S. Perales, Mauro M. Machado, and James Tafolla. That night, before a closing dance attended by some four thousand people at the auditorium, LULAC officials were treated to a banquet, again held at Tijerina's restaurant. LULAC hailed the convention as one of its most successful.[41]

Unlike México Bello and the International Club, LULAC Council No. 60 showed itself to be part of a larger, coordinated (and over the years more successful) effort to help the Spanish-speaking community and do more than just "improve relations between Mexicans and Anglos." It sought overtly to move Latinos into Houston's mainstream society by emphasizing goals consistent with those of the bicultural restaurateur on Houston's Main Street.

Tijerina's early affiliation with LULAC likewise suggests that he portrayed himself as an American citizen. The organization required its members to be native-born or naturalized. It should be added that no written proof exists (only oral tradition) that he held formal membership during the 1930s. However, his association with a fourth organization at that time strongly testifies to the idea that he claimed U.S. citizenship.[42]

Even as the LULAC conventioneers dined at the Mexican Inn, a splinter movement developed within Council No. 60 that involved Tijerina. By the summer of 1935, some young members of the local council who lived in Houston proper thought of starting another club of an even more aggressive nature in its advocacy of Latin American issues.

This new organization apparently came into existence for two reasons. First of all, the Houston men felt that Council No. 60, located in Magnolia Park, was too far removed from the center of activity in Houston. With the LULAC meetings mostly held in Magnolia Park to accommodate the majority of the membership, the Houston men found it inconvenient to attend. They felt that the organization should be centrally located in downtown.[43] Second, at least some of these men also felt that the LULACs from Magnolia

Park (always perceived as an immigrant enclave) were too reticent in their approach to the issues of the day. As part of their reservations, the Houston dissidents also believed at the time that the structure of LULAC itself limited direct political action because its constitution barred councils from taking part in electoral politics. They wanted an organization that could endorse and support candidates for public office.[44]

As a result of their qualms about Magnolia Park LULAC, these men formed the Latin American Club of Houston. Its instigators met during the summer but moved toward legal status in early October, 1935, when Leonard J. Lewis, George Deary, Felix Tijerina, and John Henry Duhig—as the club's first officers—signed for state incorporation of the club before notary public Manuel Crespo. Though Felix had the only Spanish surname of the four, the others apparently were half Anglo or Mexican Americans with non-Hispanic names. Lewis served as president, Deary as vice president, and Duhig was secretary. Felix was the club's treasurer. According to its constitution, "[a]ll officers shall be citizens of the United States and possess a poll tax receipt."[45] His position clearly indicates that Felix claimed to be a citizen, entitled to vote.

The Latin American Club resembled LULAC in many ways. Like LULAC, it reflected its founders' desires to fit into mainstream society. The club's constitution (printed in pamphlet form) made English the group's official language and red, white, and blue the organization's official colors. The American flag conspicuously appeared on the constitution's cover.[46]

But the Latin American Club struck a more strident posture than LULAC when it declared that its principal aim and purpose was "to protect Latin American Citizens of this country." Like LULAC, the Latin American Club wanted to educate Latin Americans about their United States citizenship, laws, and government. "However," according to the constitution, "in doing so we shall ever bear in mind the welfare of our Latin American people." More terse and direct in its language than LULAC's governing document, the constitution of the Latin American Club stated that "[a]ny Latin American who [was] unjustly prosecuted or . . . in need of any assistance" could "appeal for help from this organization."[47] Moreover, the club's constitution gave the group latitude for political action by allowing it to "induce the Latin American people . . . to partake in voting privileges extended to them in the Constitution of the United States and all other privileges extended to them under said Constitution."[48]

The Latin American Club of Houston soon became the most exciting

Hispanic organization in the city, albeit the most short-lived of the four to which Felix belonged. (It would disappear on the eve of World War II.) In August, 1935, the *Houston Chronicle* reported that the Latin American Club passed resolutions endorsing proposed Public Works Administration (PWA) bonds for recreational facilities and urging people to vote for the issue in the upcoming bond election. When election year rolled around in 1936, the club launched an ambitious poll tax drive to register Latin voters, exhorted *colonia* residents to get involved in the electoral process, and openly supported candidates sympathetic to *la raza*. It also received credit for ensuring that Mexicans would be classified as "white" on the newly printed Social Security application forms that appeared in Houston in the fall of 1936.[49]

Juvencio Rodríguez, a Latin American Club stalwart, recalled that Tijerina participated in many of the group's endeavors, especially during its first years. Although not a leading activist in the club's affairs, Felix concurred with its projects, particularly its endorsements of such political figures as Roy Hofheinz in his successful bid for county judge. Rodríguez noted that Felix wanted the group always to conduct itself with civility and deliberation when approaching an issue, insisting that the membership consider matters thoroughly to determine the best course of action under the circumstances and within the law. Rodríguez vividly remembered that while Tijerina wanted equity and justice for his people, he consistently advocated the use of reason with even those persons discriminating against the *colonia;* such diplomacy, Felix reasoned, might persuade them to alter their behavior.[50] This cautious approach would characterize Tijerina's actions in the years to come.

That Tijerina could belong to clubs so apparently different as México Bello and the Latin American Club testifies to the development of his versatile bicultural nature and personal needs. Both of the two basic types of clubs (the more socially oriented México Bello and El Club International on the one hand, and the civic/political LULAC and Latin American Club on the other) provided him with slightly different, but necessary forums of expression. The first kind clearly represented the residual "Mexican" side of Tijerina's cultural and ideological composition, the reminder of his Mexican roots. Such groups offered prestige, entertainment, and social interaction in a tradition that no doubt he had respected when he first came to Houston and still held dear. The latter two organizations provided vehicles for community action in the increasingly Americanized spirit of the 1930s.

At the same time, in practice, the four groups resembled one another. All consisted of young men who desired middle-class status and who wanted to better themselves and their community on a material level. Each sought improved conditions for Mexican Americans within the larger society, regardless of the degree to which its respective members embraced United States culture. And by the mid-1930s, the difference between those members who had resided in Houston or in the United States for over a decade was slight. Members of these four varied groups attended one another's dances, often spoke the same amount of Spanish in conversation, frequented the same places, and held many similar aspirations. The clubs often worked together on the same issues, especially in the drive to eradicate tuberculosis, a killer of many *colonia* residents. They had so many goals in common that by the spring of 1936, individuals within the groups attempted to confederate all the Mexican American organizations in Houston to give strength to their community efforts.[51]

The four organizations that had Tijerina as a member reflected and gave shape to his direction in Hispanic community affairs. Each wanted Houston society to accept and respect its people and culture, and Felix (principally through his restaurant on Main) was in the midst of this activity.

Pressing business concerns interfered with Tijerina's club activities. Regardless of his best efforts, the Depression caught up with him and other Mexican American restaurateurs. Of the Spanish-surnamed individuals who owned cafés when Felix had opened the Mexican Inn, few still had their establishments by the mid-1930s, indicative of the rate of business failure at the time. By 1931, the Spanish American Gardens had ceased to exist, but the Old Mexico Tavern (on Gray) and Reynaga's Mexico City Restaurant (on Main) still operated. So did the Original Mexican Restaurant, at 1109 Main, although George Caldwell, the founder and Tijerina's mentor, had died in 1934.[52] Felix held out until late 1935, but in early 1936 he had to close the doors of the Mexican Inn, a victim of the economy.[53] His former players on the Mexican Inn baseball team joined the club sponsored by Manuel Crespo's funeral home.

Felix soon went to work for a few dollars a week as a porter for Texas Old Union Company, a beer company located on Saint Joseph Street in the Second Ward. Before long, he became a driver-salesman, making fifty dollars weekly, driving a truck to deliver the company's Old Union Lager Beer around town. Turning over all his earnings to his wife, Felix kept that job for around eighteen months until he would open another restaurant.[54]

When the Mexican Inn closed, Felix and Janie moved back in with his mother and sisters at 2008 Center Street. Felix's immediate family did not wholly "approve" of Janie, with her independent-minded, working-girl background and darker complexion (they were all fair-skinned).[55] Perhaps most distressing to Dionicia and her daughters was Janie's premarital reputation as what Felix's friend Ramón Fernández described as "a runaround." According to Fernández, Dionicia had once asked him to talk to Felix so as to dissuade him from the marriage.[56] Whether fairly or unfairly, other people in the *colonia* shared this dim view of Janie's personal conduct before she married.[57]

But Janie was Felix's wife and a hard worker, and the in-laws struck an uneasy accommodation. Cramped living conditions, however, placed the household under tension that soon came to a head. In addition to the adults under one roof, Amalia had two children—Carlos and a daughter named Rosie born in 1932. Her marriage to Cecilio Villarreal had ended, and she and the little ones still lived with Dionicia and Amalia's two sisters. By 1937, Felix and Janie had moved in with Felix's good friend Chato Reynosa and his young wife Eloise, where they continued their frugal existence. Since their marriage, financial difficulties had not allowed Felix and Janie to have a place of their own except during one brief interval, forcing them to move at least every year and making their life together a strained, tumultuous experience.[58]

Felix finally went back into business under some extraordinary circumstances. From Thanksgiving Day, 1934, to the spring of 1937, Houston had a horse racetrack called Epsom Downs, one of the state's four such racing facilities that operated during the mid-1930s while Texas had legalized parimutuel betting. Named for the great track near London, England, Houston's Epsom Downs was located off the Humble Road approximately six miles north of downtown. It ran thoroughbreds from across the country to the thrill (or chagrin) of thousands of wagering Houstonians and other spectators who packed its large viewing stands each season.[59]

While Felix drove his beer truck and made plans to open another restaurant, Janie decided to take a chance. She loved to gamble (she was especially good at dice) and had played the local bookies until she had promised Felix that she would bring that practice to an end. But this time she made an exception. On a tip from her boss at Solo-Serve, she raised $450 by borrowing money against her jewelry, car, and other personal items, took off from work, went to the track, and placed the entire amount "on the nose" of a horse that paid good odds. When the horse came in the winner, she collected some $1,600. She gave the entire sum to her husband and told him that after he repaid the money she had borrowed, he could keep the rest to open another place of his own, this time without having to bring in a partner. This money, in combination with $300 that Felix had been able to save, apparently allowed him to launch his second restaurant.[60]

Tijerina found a suitable place for his restaurant at 1220 Westheimer Avenue. The building was a white, one-storied house across from the newly opened Tower Theater in a small shopping area. He rented the cottage from Zachary Mafrige for sixty-five dollars a month. Mingo quit his job at a Sixth Ward café to be the cook. With his and Janie's help, Felix scraped together tables, chairs, and other necessary items. He painted the several dining rooms and decorated the walls with *serapes,* little *sombreros,* and various Mexican curios. The tables were neatly arranged on the clean hardwood floors and draped with white tablecloths, offering the customers a pleasant, intimate atmosphere. Along a wall in the back of one of the rooms were several racks with shelves of curios which Janie had for sale—pottery, *huaraches,* and the like. In the front yard, Tijerina installed a neon sign which read "Felix Mexican Restaurant" (the new name for his enterprise) and opened for business in the fall of 1937.[61]

Felix had cleverly located his new eating establishment far from the Mexican barrios. Situated along the main thoroughfare in Houston's Anglo residential west side, it was deep in the middle-class Montrose neighborhood and immediately proximate to other affluent areas such as River Oaks (the city's most exclusive subdivision), neighborhoods from which Tijerina would draw his clientele and build his financial success. As the single Mexican restaurant on Westheimer, only Knorbin, Reynaga, and the Original Mexican Restaurant (which had moved to the 4700 block of Main after Caldwell's death) offered him any serious competition.

The new Felix Mexican Restaurant did a brisk business from the start. Because he had no money to advertise his opening (he even borrowed a few dollars from Mingo to make change that first day), Tijerina stood out in front and waved to his Anglo friends, who stopped to eat and in turn spread the word of him being back in business. Even in these relatively lean times, the residents of this area had money to spare, especially for the moderate prices he charged. When his first ads appeared in the Houston newspapers during June, 1938, they noted that his "Genuine Mexican Dishes" were "35c Up." His initial bookkeeper, Angelina Morales, recalled many years later that Felix did well, making between thirty-six and forty dollars per day, which, for the late 1930s, was very good, especially for a Mexican American Houstonian. A good business person in her own right, she noted that, even then, Tijerina was not a "social climber, like many of the old México Bello crowd," but was "a promoter and hard-headed Houston businessman" with a winning personality. She believed that the opening of his restaurant on Westheimer marked the beginning of his most important Anglo business and civic connections. Located near prosperous west-side neighborhoods whose residents would become its steady customers, the restaurant served as Tijerina's entrée into the Anglo world.[62]

But success at the restaurant carried a stiff price; the Tijerinas worked like Trojans and continued to live a Spartan existence. Felix, Mingo, and the other help opened the café just before noon and stayed open until around half past eleven at night. Janie still had her job with Solo-Serve and would help in the kitchen after six o'clock when she got off work every evening.[63]

In fact, Janie was more than a partner; the restaurant was actually in her name. She had signed as its owner when the business was registered with the Harris County clerk on February 23, 1938, claiming many years later that Felix owed too much money from his previous business failure to have the new place in his name.[64]

The couple lived in the back of the restaurant for the next ten years, first in a single ten-by-eight-foot room until Felix had more space added for their convenience. Initially, this cramped living area did not contain its own bathroom, so they made do with the restroom in the restaurant. Because customers also used these facilities during business hours, the couple had to wait until closing before they took baths.[65]

The new restaurant on Westheimer served as the means by which Felix could increase his visibility in community affairs, much as the 1929 café had done during its existence. Examples of his activities continued to reflect his bicultural consciousness, although he increasingly turned his attention to Anglo institutions. After a temporary hiatus in his activities with México Bello, by the fall of 1937, Tijerina once again was regularly attending its meetings and helping to maintain the club as a viable organization during the difficult prewar years. By late 1937, a group of approximately twenty women (mainly members' wives, including Janie Tijerina and Eloise Reynosa) organized a women's auxiliary of México Bello. Indeed, Janie played a leadership role in founding this auxiliary. In October, 1938, she worked with the group to hold a dance and *jamaica* to raise money and provisions for the poor of the neighborhood. In January, 1940, the men's club installed Felix as its newly elected treasurer. Felix and Janie (along with Félix and Angie Morales) stood in the December, 1941, wedding of México Bello friends Francisco Chaírez and Inocencia (Chencha) Pérez, the society event of the year for the club and *colonia*.[66]

As a result of continuing association with the Latin American Club, Tijerina became involved in the political arena during the 1938 campaign of Ernest Thompson, a moderate Democrat, in his race for the governorship of Texas. In mid-July of that year, the Magnolia Park barrio newspaper *El puerto* reported that the "Texas American Citizens" of Magnolia Park, or "El club T.A.C." (apparently an east-end version of the Latin American Club of Houston) held a political meeting at the Salón Juárez, home of the local *mutualista* on Navigation Boulevard. A number of Anglo candidates, including Ernest Thompson, came to ask for the Mexican American vote. Local Spanish-speaking individuals introduced and endorsed some of these candidates. Following an opening appeal by Latin American Club president John Duhig for increased political activity by Mexican Houstonians, Felix took the floor. After speaking in favor of Thompson's candidacy in "*una manera sincera*" (a sincere manner), he introduced Thompson to the crowd. As the meeting adjourned, everyone lingered for a beer.[67]

By the summer of 1938, Tijerina also became prominently involved in working with the youth of the *colonia,* a cause for which he continued to work throughout his life. He was named president of the Comité Pro-Beneficencial Juvenil (Juvenile Welfare Committee), which was organized under the auspices of the Comité Patriótico Mexicano and the Mexican consulate.[68]

Receiving attention from Houston's Anglo and Mexican newspapers, the committee announced its intentions to address the needs of underprivileged youth and combat delinquency in the various barrios. The committee vowed to investigate the conditions of sanitation, education, hygiene, morality, and recreation among these children. It sought to involve hospitals, doctors, recreational centers, employment offices, and the city and county juvenile correction departments in solving any problems it found. Its leadership maintained (no doubt hyperbolically) that the committee was "the only group of its kind in the state and probably the first in the nation." Certainly, it constituted a significant city-wide undertaking for Mexican Houstonians.[69]

The committee received a boost when México Bello announced that it would sponsor a Boy Scout troop and other such constructive activities for *colonia* youngsters as part of the larger movement. At the time, Felix chaired México Bello's committee on juvenile delinquency and Boy Scouting while simultaneously heading the club's subcommittee on the Comité Patriótico Mexicano; he was no doubt crucial in mustering this extra support.[70]

Under Tijerina's presidency, the committee cooperated with the Harris County Probation Department on social welfare matters. On one occasion, Tijerina appeared before County Judge Roy Hofheinz to deal with the matter of English-speaking Mexican Americans who were "racketeering" on non-English speakers in trouble with the law. In this case, a woman allegedly had tried to charge a Mexican girl a sum of money for her freedom. When Hofheinz learned this from the girl's mother (who spoke no English), he ordered a probation officer to bring in the person who had made the proposition. Tijerina informed Hofheinz that his organization often faced this problem of "racketeers"; that is, a small group of people who preyed upon unknowing members of the *colonia* by telling them that, for a fee, they could exert influence to resolve legal difficulties for them or their relatives. Felix also told the judge that he and his group were giving the people information on the correct sources of assistance in time of trouble, helping with such services as translation and directing people to the proper authorities.[71]

Beginning in the Depression days, Felix worked for approximately seven years as a volunteer assistant for the Harris County Probation Department. He helped investigate individual cases, distribute food to the needy, and find foster homes for distressed children. He often went to the probation and police departments late at night after closing the restaurant, to try to help Mexican American youngsters who found themselves on the wrong side of the law or to assist families in need. Felix believed that jails corrupted young people and that children needed a healthy environment, education, and rehabilitation. He frequently returned home at three or four o'clock in the morning, only to rise a few hours later to open his restaurant.[72]

By the late 1930s Felix was also active in the Houston Optimist Club, although the exact date he joined is uncertain. Part of an international organization, Houston's chapter had begun in 1924 and held its meetings every Thursday at noon at the Rice Hotel. It existed to help youth, in particular underprivileged boys. Members from the late 1930s recalled that Felix was the only Latin American in the Houston club.[73]

By the fall of 1938, Felix organized a team of Mexican Americans to solicit donations from Houston's Latin community for the seventeenth annual Community Chest campaign. Predecessor to the United Way, the Community Chest had held its first orchestrated drive for funds in Houston in 1922, and this effort had gone on to become a highly publicized yearly affair. By 1938, the campaign involved more than two thousand volunteers. The money it collected supported numerous social service agencies, including the Houston Anti-Tuberculosis League, the Houston Settlement Association (which operated Rusk Settlement House), the Neighborhood House in Magnolia Park, and the "Mexican Clinic" in the Second Ward— all organizations which helped residents of the *colonia*.[74]

A tradition of giving to the Community Chest by Houston's Mexican merchants, professionals, and laborers dated from the 1920s, but they contributed only as individuals, chipping in what they could. Felix had donated money as early as 1930. According to the newspapers, however, Tijerina's 1938 effort was "the first time that a Mexican committee ha[d] been formed for the campaign."[75] Felix told the media that his community understood the good work these agencies did for its people and that "those of us who are able to help with it feel a civic responsibility to the less fortunate members of our race."[76]

Apparently, his work in the 1938 campaign met with success because the following November Felix expanded his role. This time Tijerina headed the newly created Latin American division. Citing Felix's qualifications as leader of the Mexican Youth Committee, the general campaign chairman, Joseph H. Russell, explained that Tijerina would lead thirty civic-minded men and women in this division to raise funds from Spanish-speaking organizations and individuals. Amid the fanfare that always surrounded the nine-day event, Tijerina's division raised $545, not a great amount when compared to the almost $850,000 total, but well over the goal which had been set for his small section.[77]

Even more important for Tijerina's rising stardom was the fact that the newspapers had announced his participation both years and had also included his picture. These represented some of the first of many times the young restaurateur's portrait would appear in the press in association with community service.[78]

But perhaps the most prominent recognition of Felix's involvement as head of the Latin American division of the Community Chest came in a story in *Houston,* the monthly magazine published by the local chamber of commerce. As the self-styled "Voice of Houston," this slick publication was the most significant periodical in the city (other than the newspapers) boosting the commercial, industrial, and civic advantages of Houston and the people who made things happen. In its October, 1939 issue, *Houston* ran a feature on the upcoming Community Chest campaign and its several dozen key figures. The only person of color involved in this group's leadership, Felix Tijerina was among fifteen men (including the likes of Dr. Ralph Cooley, Walter B. Sharp, Colonel W. B. Bates, and other prominent Anglo Houstonians) whose pictures appeared near the text. Felix's portrait (the same one taken by Gregorio Cantú for the 1937 composite photograph of México Bello) appearing in this magazine amid these fourteen eminent white male Houstonians graphically illustrated the extent to which he had insinuated himself into Houston society. It represented an amazing achievement for a man who had just seventeen years before taken up residence in the city as an uneducated, teenage Mexican immigrant.[79]

This singular accomplishment resulted from Felix's considerable promotional skills and winning personality; it came through his use of his ethnicity as a Latin American, in particular as a purveyor of Mexican food to Anglo Houstonians and as one who had managed to prosper, be "accepted," and become civically involved in causes on behalf of the city's Latin community. By the late 1930s, Felix had assumed a leadership role within Latin American Houston, in the minds of both its Spanish-speaking and English-speaking communities. No doubt due to their growing prominence, Felix and Janie were guests at the newly completed San Jacinto Monument for the dedication ceremonies of the San Jacinto Museum of History in April, 1939. The Tijerinas proudly kept the lapel ribbons from the event in their scrapbook of memorable occasions.[80]

In May, Felix represented the Latin American clubs of Houston at the dedication of a new shelter building at Hennessey Park, one of a dozen recreational facilities built with the PWA-city program funds. The Latin American Club had, of course, championed the allocation of money for this structure in 1935. Located at Lyons Avenue and Maury Street, Hennessey Park was in the heart of Fifth Ward and heavily used by the surrounding Mexican American neighborhood. Speaking in Spanish, Tijerina was one of several dignitaries to address the crowd of several thousand persons gathered in the two-acre area to witness the event.[81]

In his role as an emerging spokesman, Tijerina took part in what one local Mexican American commentator at the time referred to as the "social reconstruction" of the *colonia*.[82] Tijerina and his fellows attempted to alleviate some of the social dislocation that had resulted from the Depression, especially among the youth. The work of the Comité Pro-Beneficenial Juvenil, the upgrading of park facilities, support of Rusk Settlement House, and other activities represented concrete action. Regardless of its best efforts, however, Houston's Mexican population was fighting an uphill battle during the 1930s. As Felix's own business failed by 1935, and he and Janie struggled, it was extremely difficult economically for Mexican Houstonians. For the majority in the *colonia,* federal monies brought less help to them than others, and jobs were hard to find. Most residents barely held on through this downward spiral of unemployment, business closure, poverty, and desperation. Regardless of the extreme conditions, the Houston Spanish-speaking community actually grew through in-migration and births; it strived to solidify itself through the social restructuring provided by families, friends, neighborhoods, those businesses that survived, and the developing network of organizations and institutions.[83]

Popular sentiments favoring expulsion of immigrants from the United States, which grew in force to become the "repatriation movement," added to the social trauma caused by economic problems. Between 1929 and 1939 campaigns on the local and national levels to deport undocumented immigrants or promote voluntary repatriation of legal aliens who might go on public relief or hold jobs otherwise taken by white American citizens caused approximately 500,000 Mexicans (and their American-born children) to leave the United States for Mexico. Among the states, Texas led the nation in repatriations; more than 132,000 persons left the state during the 1930s.[84]

Like other cities with a Mexican population, Houston had its own repatriation drive, which resulted in the departure of roughly two thousand persons, or around 15 percent of the *colonia's* population of 1930. Most of these repatriates went more or less "voluntarily," either on their own or as part of organized efforts by local officials, the Mexican government, and other members of the *colonia*. Most Mexican Houstonians knew the *repatriados,* the local newspapers covered the lamentable process, and people of the various neighborhoods discussed the issue.[85]

In Houston, as elsewhere, deportation pressure from U.S. immigration officials also gave impetus to these "voluntary" departures from the city. Similar to tactics employed across the nation, Immigration and Naturalization Service officers in the Houston-Galveston region raided private job sites to net undocumented Mexican laborers. The Houston INS actually expanded its office space in the early 1930s as a result of its activities. People of Mexican descent living in Houston during this time recall that INS officials used heavy-handed approaches that seemed to be aimed at pressuring people to leave. Many came to feel marked because of their Mexican ethnicity or Spanish surnames, and fear was pervasive even among legally resident Mexicans.[86]

Within this apprehensive climate, Felix had his own serious brush with the immigration authorities. His involvement with LULAC and especially his officer status in the Latin American Club of Houston (both of which required American citizenship) indicate that during the time, he had claimed, at least publicly, to be an American citizen. In March, 1940, an incident occurred that would bring his citizenship into question and show that the INS did not exempt even trusted Houston Mexican residents like Felix Tijerina from its activities. The episode likewise illustrated the lengths to which Mexican residents—in this case Tijerina—would go to preserve themselves in the troubled waters of their adopted country.

In early March, 1940, Felix and Chato Reynosa took a two-week trip to Mexico, the first time, Tijerina stated, that he had crossed the border since 1925. On March 17 or 18, they returned to the United States via Laredo. Reynosa recalled many years later that they had been to Monterrey and that on their way home the immigration officers at the international bridge were not fully satisfied with Felix's declaration of being an American citizen.[87]

At any rate, a week after Tijerina and Reynosa returned to Houston, two immigration officers (according to one account) arrested Felix because the immigration service had a record of the document in Laredo that the restaurateur had signed in the summer of 1925 admitting him to the United States as a citizen of Mexico. According to another (and probably more credible) version of the incident, the officers in Houston simply told Tijerina they were making an inquiry into his citizenship status (based on the 1925 Laredo records) and that he should "get the matter straight."[88] Immediately thereafter, Felix did what he could to "prove" that he had actually been born in Sugar Land, Texas, and, to be considered a native American citizen.

On March 25, Felix had his mother sign an affidavit in front of Albert G. Vela, a friend and notary public in Houston, which stated that she and her husband, Rafael, were both from Monterrey, Mexico, but had been residing in Sugar Land at the time of Felix's birth. The following day he went to Wharton and Fort Bend Counties. There he enlisted the assistance of one Buck Flanagan, captain of the Imperial Farm of the State Prison System, whom Felix said he had known since 1914. Flanagan took Tijerina to the home of Easter Fueler, a black woman who lived in the small town of Glenflora. Felix claimed that Fueler had acted as the midwife at his birth, later maintaining to an INS official that, at first, Fueler "did not recognize or remember me," but, after some discussion, "she remembered me well." Tijerina told this same INS officer that he had prompted Fueler's memory by naming "some of the people [he] used to know" from his Sugar Land days, including "a Mr. Felix Hasso [Jasso], a Mr. Pena [Doroteo Pina] and others." He persuaded Fueler to accompany him to the Wharton County courthouse, where she signed an affidavit (with an "X" by her name) testifying that Felix had indeed been born in Sugar Land. Based upon the sworn and notarized statements of his mother and Easter Fueler, Felix submitted a certificate of birth (a so-called "delayed birth certificate") that same day to Fort Bend county judge C. L. Dutton stating that he was born on April 29, 1905, in Sugar Land, Texas. The court accepted the document to be filed in the State Bureau of Vital Statistics (which was duly accomplished on March 27).[89]

Felix then had time enough on March 26 to go to the Houston office of William P. Autrey, acting naturalization examiner of the Immigration and Naturalization Service, where he presented his newly acquired delayed birth certificate. During this meeting, Felix stated that he had been born in Sugar Land, explained the role of Easter Fueler, and commented on other matters pertaining to his case.[90]

In response to Autrey's question about his crossing the border in the summer of 1925 as a Mexican citizen, Felix explained that he had done so because at that time he had no proof of United States citizenship and had wanted to avoid delay in returning to Houston. Tijerina stated the object of his visit with Autrey was to rectify any misinformation about his nativity. He noted that "since I was born in the United States and am an American citizen, I would like to have the records corrected at Laredo to show that I am a United States citizen instead of a citizen of Mexico, as they indicate at present."[91]

For good measure, Victoria immediately went through the same process to acquire her delayed birth certificate. Dionicia signed a sworn statement and affidavit on March 28 in front of Albert Vela that she had given birth to this daughter in Sugar Land on March 23, 1917. The following day, March 29, Easter Fueler took an oath to these facts; the birth certificate was submitted to the Fort Bend County court that same day and then filed with the state's Bureau of Vital Statistics on April 1.[92]

On April 6, Felix returned to the INS office in Houston regarding another matter and apparently spoke to naturalization examiner George F. Elsenbroich. In the course of their conversation, according to Elsenbroich, Tijerina asked about his own case. Elsenbroich told him that the INS wanted Felix to produce his baptismal certificate if at all possible before it could change its records at Laredo to show he was indeed an American citizen rather than "an alien, which seems to be the case at this time." Apparently, Felix told Elsenbroich a priest had promised to investigate the possibility of finding his baptismal record from the Sugar Land area, although he admitted no one knew where that record might be. The INS examiner responded that if this could not be located, then the authorities would accept a sworn statement by his mother as to his place of birth. In the report of his meeting with Felix, Elsenbroich concluded that indeed Dionicia had already provided such an affidavit as part of the delayed birth certificate that had been placed in his INS file. Apparently, the matter rested here; the INS office in Houston had Dionicia's testimony and Felix thought the issue was closed.[93]

In fact, the available record indicates that Felix had fabricated the evidence he used in his case, and no doubt the immigration officials suspected as much. Tijerina apparently created a story concerning his origins, and involved others in composing his tale. He and his immediate family went to their graves publicly maintaining he was born in Sugar Land, Texas.

Tijerina could have had any one of several possible motives for staging this rather elaborate deception. First of all, given the climate of uncertainty for Mexicans in Houston and across the United States during the 1930s, he may well have had a genuine fear of deportation. The entire process of repatriation and INS activity that helped define the era for Mexican Americans presented very real reasons for hiding the truth of one's Mexican origins.

Two thousand had departed Houston and hundreds of thousands left the United States under pressures which included legal expulsion. Perhaps, too, Felix had a fundamental fear of being deported that many immigrants who love their host country seem to harbor, to one degree or another, even in the best of times.[94]

And the INS had put real pressure on Tijerina during the 1940 episode. Many years later, Angelina Morales, Felix and Janie's good friend from the 1930s, recalled the incident vividly. A native Texan and counselor to her people, she often interceded on behalf of *colonia* residents (members of "her tribe" as she called them) who had difficulties with immigration authorities during the Depression. She recalled that the unpleasant affair unsettled Tijerina. She also remembered talking to Houston immigration officials on Felix's behalf and being warned not to become involved in the matter. Even though Morales could not prove that Felix was born in Texas (she herself expressed no doubt at the "fact"), it seemed to her some sort of grudge on the part of the INS officers against Tijerina. She felt as if they (especially Autrey) were determined to "get" him.[95] This zealousness by the INS toward investigating Felix's case, which Morales witnessed, seems consistent with the experience of many others during the era.

Deportation would have been disastrous to Tijerina's family and business. His mother and three sisters financially depended upon him. Had the INS deported Felix, would they too have been in peril? The restaurant was conveniently in Janie's name, but with Felix as its driving force and with the restaurant barely two years old, the business could hardly have functioned successfully without him. Perhaps his marriage to an American citizen and/or an application for "legal residency" would have ultimately blocked his expulsion, but those avenues, too, were no doubt problematic.[96]

Felix had fabricated his 1940 evidence to maintain a story of his origins that he may well have told for some time in Houston, especially to Anglo society. No one had bothered to make him an American citizen as a boy working in the fields of the Texas Coastal Bend. By the 1920s, he was residing in Houston, and few Mexican immigrants at that point showed any inclination to become citizens, and even fewer had the time. Like many Mexican Houstonians, Felix had worked hard for family survival and personal success; he had accommodated step by step to his new surroundings.

For someone as masterful at fitting in as Felix Tijerina, American citizenship was also a plus. Perhaps he had first casually told someone in Houston he was Texas-born. Perhaps he had simply not taken the time (or had been too busy) to become a citizen and, so as not to be bothered with the formality of the lengthy citizenship process, found it easier just to state that he was born in Texas, specifically where he had resided immediately before coming to Houston. Or perhaps he simply had made the claim to U.S. birth after 1929, when concerns about deportation arose among *colonia* residents, and then had to "prove" his story when INS officials called his hand.

Perhaps he had initially crafted the story of his birth more strategically. Precisely *because* of his adeptness at fitting in, he might have made an earlier, conscious effort to claim Texas birth. He may have felt it necessary or at least more advantageous (as he developed in Houston) to alter the story of his origins deliberately—a very minor thing to do—to create a fable of his immigration to the Bayou City; such is a practice common to most immigrant folk making their way in a new land where conformity is a must. In the process of creating such a story, the person forgets particular facts and alters others.[97]

Certainly, it seemed more acceptable within Anglo Houston society for a person to have been born in Texas rather than in Mexico, a country whose leader and army (as Texas history lessons in the schools, at each San Jacinto Day celebration, and elsewhere constantly reminded everyone) had killed "freedom-loving Texans" at the Alamo and Goliad and had perpetrated other foul deeds. Anglos in Houston did not generally portray Mexico, and its people's character, in positive terms. Indeed, it should be remembered that the organizations to which Felix belonged—México Bello, the International Club, the Latin American Club, and LULAC—worked to overcome these negative images. It obviously would have been much better *not* to have been born in Mexico; it would have been much smarter to have been Texas-born regardless of how personally comfortable Felix was with his Mexican ethnicity. Better at fitting in than perhaps any of his contemporaries in *la colonia,* more clever than them all, and one whose fond memories of *la patria* were probably mixed with recollections of childhood deprivation and the death of his father, Felix could well have changed the place of his birth to accommodate his new environment, almost as innocently as he had altered his first name when he had come to Houston. He had figuratively shaken the dust of Mexico from his shoes and had fully embraced what for him had proven to be a better place to live.

In addition, Felix Tijerina no doubt justifiably took pride in his growing reputation and leadership within both the Mexican and Anglo communities in Houston. He had worked eighteen years in Houston to build an honest, honorable name. Possibly his pride or the fear of being shamed prevented him from officially admitting in 1940 that he had misled people (whether casually or deliberately) about his birthplace all along, even if the INS would have allowed him to "get the matter straight." Rather than native-born as he had held himself out to be, Felix Tijerina, a man of integrity and rising Latin American leader, would have had to admit that he had not been telling the truth. Moreover, such an admission would have allowed INS officers like Autrey and Elsenbroich to categorize him as "an alien"—much like the pathetic *repatriados* who had recently made their way back to Mexico in beat-up Model A trucks; Felix Tijerina would have been transformed into just another "Mexican" to be handled by arrogant immigration authorities. Such a fate would have been humiliating for a proud man.

Regardless of his story's origins, circumstances in 1940 necessitated that Tijerina fabricate documents to give it validity. While interpreting his motives may call for a good deal of conjecture, the matter of Felix's citizenship was definitely not put to rest with his delayed birth certificate in 1940. Indeed, it became a dark spot in his life, a nagging issue which would be resurrected one more time, fourteen years later in a legal showdown.

On a larger scale, the affair represented Tijerina's personal dilemma concerning the placement of people of Mexican descent in Texas; that is, regardless of how mightily and successfully he strived to "fit in," mainstream society (at least an important element of it) viewed him as somewhat of an outsider (an "alien") whose very presence was subject to question. Houston society had accepted him, but with limitations. Even as Tijerina called himself "Latin American," someone, in this case the INS, pushed for exclusion. Regardless of the number of speeches he gave, the variety of organizations to which he belonged, his popularity in many circles, the amount of money he made, the good he did for the community, or even how much he may have tried to share in the patriotic fervor at the San Jacinto Monument, he was, after all, still a "Mexican"—a term that had long since been embedded in the traditional Anglo-Texan psyche as a deviant worthy of exclusion.

But other things beside his citizenship status (more positive ones, at that) arose to occupy Tijerina's attention. Business was good on Westheimer. By 1940, Felix for the first time increased the size of his advertisement in the telephone directory. In 1941, he publicized his restaurant in *The Woman's Building of Houston Directory,* the only Mexican American to be listed in this exclusive business publication and a step indicative of how he cultivated the Anglo market.[98]

In the meanwhile, Janie had left her sales job and, with her husband's encouragement, opened a small Mexican curio store (called Felix Mexican Curio Shop) in the arcade of the Iris Theatre on Travis Street. Felix had bought her thirty-eight dollars' worth of curios in Mexico and told her either to quit her job or go into business for herself. She did well and by early 1940 moved the store to 811 Capitol Avenue in the Uptown Center next to the Uptown Theater between Milam and Travis. To maintain her inventory, Janie began to travel to Mexico on buying trips that soon began to familiarize her with many regions of that country.[99]

By 1941, Felix had prospered and possessed enough confidence to expand his restaurant operations. He opened his second Felix Mexican Restaurant, this one in Beaumont, some seventy miles east of Houston. According to Mrs. Felix Tijerina, her husband had monied friends from Beaumont who urged him to plant a business there. Certainly, the choice made sense. The county seat of Jefferson County, Beaumont had a growing population of approximately sixty thousand people and was in many ways a smaller version of Houston. A port city located on the deep-water Sabine-Neches Canal and near the seminal Spindletop oil field, by 1940 it was cashing in on coastal and foreign trade, oil-related industries, and recent national defense industry programs that gave the town a good potential for growth. Specifically, Beaumont presented an open market for a quality Mexican restaurant. Only the Aztec Inn, owned and operated by Ramiro Ramírez and his wife Inez, offered any viable competition at the time.[100]

Tijerina rented a small house at 1716 Calder Avenue, a main street near the middle of town. Calder ran through Beaumont's choicest area of prosperous white residential neighborhoods that would produce a good clientele. Similar to his Houston location, he converted the cottage into a café that would seat eighty-five customers and opened for business in August, 1941. In mid-December, he moved his cousin, Luciano Villarreal, there to be its manager. Luciano had worked for Felix since the latter had opened his first place on Main Street. He would run the Beaumont location until his death more than a dozen years later. When Felix announced in the *Beaumont Journal* the arrival of Luciano as the new manager, the notice called him Louis Villarreal, an abbreviation reminiscent of what Felix had done to his own first name years before. Open from eleven to eleven, Felix's Beaumont restaurant immediately became popular with the locals (including customers from nearby Port Arthur), and would remain a community landmark long after Luciano and Felix died.[101]

In December, the United States entered World War II, and Tijerina's civilian life would be partially interrupted. But between 1929 and 1941, Felix had established the contours of his private and public self, as married man, entrepreneur, community activist, and survivor. During the crucial decade of the 1930s, he had carved his niche as a well-known restaurant owner, member of Mexican American and Anglo organizations, and broker for the *colonia* with the Anglo Houston community, basically establishing his approach to life. Within the context of his personal struggles and the community's travail during the Great Depression, he had emerged as a representative and leading member of Houston's Latin American Generation. He would expand, refine, and filigree this role during the Second World War and immediate postwar period, a role with activities and an essential dilemma to be amplified in the 1940s and early 1950s.

CHAPTER 4

HORATIO ALGER SUCCESS STORY

D uring and immediately following the Second World War, Felix Tijerina maintained the direction and pace he had established in the 1930s as a businessman, public figure, and private citizen. Scarcely hampered by almost twenty-one months of wartime military service at an army airfield near Houston, he demonstrated his ability and drive as an entrepreneur by continuing to operate his restaurants in Houston and Beaumont, and by beginning three new ones—in 1948, 1952, and 1956—which proved to be his most lucrative ventures. Tijerina launched these establishments with highly successful grand openings, revealing his mastery of promotion in the Houston tradition. These businesses allowed him to prosper far beyond his prewar days.

Expanding his economic interests even further, Tijerina had started a small loan company by 1955 and, of more significance, he joined with local Anglo entrepreneurs to establish the Montrose National Bank, serving as a member of its initial board of directors. These endeavors marked a new departure for him as a Houston capitalist.

Tijerina likewise remained prominently connected to several prewar Mexican American organizations, although he had curtailed his activity with these groups by the late 1940s. He increasingly established ties with important mainstream Anglo organizations that offered him avenues of civic involvement, often as their foremost (or only) Hispanic member. In 1948, he joined the Houston Rotary Club, a move that proved to be his most lasting and personally advantageous Anglo civic affiliation. During these hectic but productive years, Felix and his wife also adopted two children—a son in 1948 whom they named Felix, Jr., and a daughter, Janie Bell, in 1952.

As he pursued these various activities, Felix became a subject of regular media attention, a phenomenon unprecedented for Mexican Americans in Houston. In the local press and elsewhere, he was identified as no less than the Bayou City's Latin American Horatio Alger character, renowned in the public eye as the embodiment of the self-made man and solid citizen. This developing image—a response to Tijerina's behavior—acclaimed Felix as a Mexican American leader who sought to bring his people and Anglos together. His image identified him as a native-born Texan, a modest, frugal, polite, popular figure, active clubman, and by-the-bootstraps capitalist imbued with the work ethic; it extolled Felix Mexican Restaurants as the places to go for good Mexican food and Tijerina as the city's expert in Mexican cuisine. Significantly, too, he was publicly hailed as a responsible father who, with a thrifty, supportive, hardworking wife at his side, raised his son the middle-class American way. Altogether, by the early 1950s he had evolved as Houston's archetype of the ideal postwar "Latin American," one striving diligently, courteously, and cautiously to fit into mainstream society, an example for others to follow.

As such, Tijerina embodied a personal balance, internally as well as externally, between his Mexican roots and Houston environment. These wartime and immediate postwar years reveal a man in the full stride of action, striking a psychocultural "Latin American" posture which had resulted from a complex outgrowth of his immigration and postimmigration experiences, from his own desires, responsibilities, and innate character, as well as from the options presented by wartime and postwar Houston.

On October 3, 1942, Felix enlisted in the United States Army Air Corps and served his time at Ellington Field, an air base approximately twenty miles southeast of Houston along Galveston Road. Ellington Field had been established in 1917 to train pilots and bombardiers for the First World War and had remained in operation until the late 1920s. Reactivated in 1940, just before the United States entered World War II, Ellington was used as a training facility for navigators and flexible gunnery as well as bombardiers and pilots. During the Second World War, the base encompassed almost two thousand acres and housed a population of more than seventeen thousand people.[1]

Felix's military records stated that, at the time of enlistment, he was thirty-seven and a half years of age, with brown eyes, black hair, ruddy complexion, that he stood five feet, three inches in height, and that he was born in Sugar Land, Texas. He identified his occupation as a restaurant owner, and the army made him a cook, assigning him to a mess hall where he helped to prepare three meals a day for approximately fifteen hundred cadets. He made corporal on June 1, 1943, and was promoted to sergeant only ten days later, becoming mess sergeant for the officers. While at Ellington, he was with a number of other distinguished Houston cafémen, including Bill Williams and Luther Allbritton. Both men remembered Felix as a good comrade in service. By the end of his enlistment (with the 2517th AAF Base Unit, Section A, Platoon 3), the army concluded that his character was "excellent."[2]

Consistent with his deportment as a civilian, Felix received the good conduct ribbon at Ellington Field on November 11, 1943. On July 15, 1944, he was honorably discharged probably because of his age, which was nearly forty. Tijerina had performed one year, eight months, and twenty-three days "of honest and faithful service to his country."[3]

During most of his stay at Ellington, Felix commuted between base and town. The terms under which he enlisted obligated him to be on duty for twenty-four hours and off for forty-eight. During his first months in service, Janie picked him up at the end of each shift and ferried him home. Though he oversaw the operation of the restaurant as best as he could, he had the help of Mingo and Janie in his absence. Janie found herself taking on more and more responsibility, regularly driving their truck across town to pick up food supplies made scarce by wartime rationing.[4]

The restaurant did a brisk business amid Houston's wartime prosperity. In April, 1943, playing on the "home front" spirit, Felix ran a large advertisement in the *Houston Chronicle* which featured Janie as a veritable "Rosie the Riveter" of the Mexican restaurant business. It exclaimed that "MRS. FELIX CARRIES ON!" while "Felix is with the armed forces." Explaining that their table service was "not up to the old Felix standard" because of "the shortage of experienced employees," this promotion alluded to wartime scarcity by promising to serve delicious Mexican dishes "Just As Long As GOOD FOOD Is Available!" An accompanying photograph showed the restaurant's main dining area crowded with happy, well-attired customers. Likewise, a smaller portrait of Janie in the advertisement showed a strong, attractive woman in her mid-thirties who presented a positive image to the Anglo clientele. She was actually listed in the *Houston City Directory* for 1943–44 as the restaurant's manager. "Mrs. Felix" had clearly emerged as an integral part of her husband's image and success.[5]

Neither his wartime service nor his efforts within the Anglo restaurant market carried Felix too far away, at least in spirit, from Houston's Mexican community and his *amigos* during the war years. Memorably, for example, he helped his much-beloved *compadre* Leo "Chato" Reynosa (and wife Eloise) in their business affairs. With Tijerina's advice and assistance, the couple relocated to the Anglo west side where they purchased a Mexican restaurant in 1944 on South Shepherd Drive, which eventually became Leo's, a favorite Tex-Mex spot. Also in 1944, Tijerina helped sponsor the Cinco de Mayo program being hosted at Jefferson Davis High School by his old friend Ramón Fernández and the Federación de Sociedades Mexicanas y Latino-Americanas, an umbrella organization that had been trying since the 1930s to unify the various Hispanic groups in the Houston region. In February of that same year, "Sgt. Felix Tijerina, United States Army" and "Señora Felix Tijerina" purchased a half-page worth of advertising space for the restaurant and curio shop in a commemorative brochure produced by the Sociedad "Unión Fraternal," a Mexican-oriented burial association comprised generally of common folk of the *colonia*. The Sociedad was marking its fourth anniversary, and, tellingly, the celebration highlighted fifty-six young club members who were serving in the armed forces. All young men from the Houston barrio, they were pointed to with pride as "*Hombres Mexicanos que están sirviendo y honorando a la Patria.*" But the *patria* that these young men of the *colonia* served and honored was now the United States and not Mexico. It was a primary loyalty that individuals like Felix Tijerina had long since come to hold, and had even more solidly confirmed by their service in World War II.[6]

Felix entered and emerged from the army with his association with LULAC and México Bello intact. While LULAC across the Southwest had suffered during the war from the lack of young men available to fill its ranks, Council No. 60 had managed to coalesce. The split that had occurred during the mid-1930s between the LULACs from Magnolia Park and the young men of the Latin American Club of Houston had healed, and so the council moved into Houston proper and effectively recruited members from across the city. It stayed reasonably active throughout the war due to the presence of men like Fernando Salas, Dr. John J. Ruíz, John J. Herrera, and others who for various reasons did not join the military.

Tijerina was in the LULAC fold when, in mid-January, 1942, just after the United States entered the war, Council No. 60 identified him as the "100% LULAC" who underwrote the printing of a program for a LULAC banquet at the Texas State Hotel in downtown Houston. Honoring LULAC's president general, George I. Sánchez, and attorney Manuel C. González, the affair was attended by a number of other LULAC dignitaries from Houston and San Antonio who spoke on the Latin Americans' role in defense of the nation and on their condition in the Houston area. Speakers admonished everyone to "Remember Pearl Harbor."[7]

The extent of Felix's actual participation in LULAC during his military service is difficult to gauge due to the dearth of official records from that period. Having to juggle commitments to the restaurants, family, and Ellington Field, he probably found scant time to devote to organizational affairs. For example, he apparently did not contribute to or take part in the LULAC regional state convention held at Houston's Arabia Temple in late August, 1943. But he was listed among the approximately fifty names on the only surviving Council No. 60 membership roster which appears to date from the war years.[8]

When the war ended, the local LULAC council was clearly the most important voice for Mexican American affairs in the Bayou City. In 1945, it held its meetings every Thursday evening on the second floor of the Old Court House Building in downtown, and, though a bevy of other Latino groups existed in Houston, most people looked to this small band of brothers as the articulators of Latin American concerns in the Bayou City. With his old friends Fernando Salas and John Ruíz as council president and treasurer, respectively, Felix remained a member and, in his own way, a supporter of its efforts. In addition, the council's nucleus included Isidro García, Juan Serrano, John J. Herrera, and other associates from Felix's prewar days as well as younger, newer faces such as Alfred J. Hernández, who represented the generation fresh from military service and anxious to move their people forward, especially in the struggle against discrimination and for civil rights.

Touting his membership in the organization and ready to help with his pocketbook, Tijerina purchased the largest and most prominent advertisement (for his restaurants and Janie's curio shop) in the October, 1945, issue of the monthly *LULAC News,* which was sponsored by the Houston council. This edition, though published in Laredo where then–President General Arnulfo A. Zamora resided and where LULAC was headquartered, brought Council No. 60 once again to the attention of the entire national organization. The *News* announced that the Houston council would host the 1946 national convention, doubly reinforcing No. 60's presence within LULAC.[9]

Felix and Janie were also two of the largest individual contributors to the "Pro-Macario García Committee," a group established under the auspices of Council No. 60 in November, 1945. The committee intended to raise funds for the legal defense of Sergeant Macario García, the Medal of Honor winner who had recently been indicted for assault when he violently resisted being denied service in a café in Richmond, a little town just south of Houston near Sugar Land in Fort Bend County. While a majority of the more than fifteen hundred dollars in donations made by hundreds of Mexican Americans from all across the state averaged from fifty cents to five dollars per person, Felix and Janie separately donated twenty-five dollars each; their employees even gathered a few dollars among themselves to help in the cause. By this gesture, Mexican Americans expressed their dismay that many establishments in Texas still refused service to people of Mexican descent.[10]

As a regular member, Felix attended Council No. 60 meetings during 1946 when he could. He supported a motion to have a special committee investigate a charge of discrimination when a local dance hall allegedly refused admittance to a group of Latin Americans, took special interest in the poll tax drive initiated by the council, and, always a social person, helped to plan the LULAC dances. Felix served as cochair of the entertainment committee for the 1946 national convention and on at least one occasion he hosted the meeting of the convention planners at his restaurant on Westheimer.[11]

In 1946, a controversy existed in LULAC over the membership status of Mexican citizens. The LULAC constitution, it should be recalled, required its members to be naturalized or native-born Americans; however, Council No. 60 operated at variance from this policy as several of its members were noncitizens. While most Council No. 60 members came down on the side of allowing Mexican citizens to participate as fully as possible, a small faction (including, at one point, Tijerina) insisted that the constitution's rule be strictly enforced. In a more inclusive spirit, however, Felix reconsidered his position and asked the council to take to the upcoming national convention a formal resolution calling for the cessation of all discrimination against Mexican citizens within the organization. The group did not act upon his request because some members felt that Council No. 60 already allowed Mexicans to be involved in a de facto manner; that is, in Council No. 60 noncitizens could belong and vote, but not hold office, reflecting the general practice in LULAC that each local council could exercise its own discretion on the matter. (The status of Mexican citizens in LULAC remained an issue until 1950, when the constitution was amended so that they could become "Participating Members" with rights similar to what Council No. 60 had allowed in 1946; this move codified what had no doubt been the tradition among many, perhaps most, LULAC groups.)[12]

In mid-1946, Tijerina became embroiled in an incident that not only revealed the bickering that sometimes transpired within Council No. 60, but also illustrated another side of Felix's temperament. In planning Council No. 60's annual Cinco de Mayo dance, a misunderstanding arose over the manner in which Tijerina and another member, Jesús Gómez, handled the concession stand. After he failed to attend a few meetings subsequent to the event, the council sent Tijerina a letter giving him thirty days to clarify the matter or "forfeit your rights and privileges to any present or future membership in this organization." Flaring at this perceived affront, according to the council minutes, Tijerina and Gómez came to a July meeting "showing resentment" and engaged those present in a "heated discussion." Before any conclusion could be reached and as the hour was late, the meeting adjourned. No official record remains of how the membership finally resolved the trouble, but, according to Alfred Hernández, the council secretary who had penned the missive, Felix felt that the letter questioned his honesty. Hernández recalled that when Tijerina entered the meeting, he produced a large roll of one-thousand-dollar bills (that by this time he regularly carried in his pocket), and angrily announced that "he could buy and sell the whole damned bunch of them" and that he would pay the few dollars they felt he owed. Still agitated, Felix finished by telling those in the room that he did not need them or their organization.[13]

Aggravated or not, Felix remained on the LULAC roster throughout 1947 as one of the council's thirty-seven active members. More important, he received the nomination in December, 1947, along with Hernández, for council president. The younger man edged Felix out in the balloting; however, the membership elected Tijerina as its vice president by acclamation.

This arrangement seemed to work satisfactorily because Tijerina and Hernández would develop a close friendship over the years. Indeed, Hernández would become the older man's loyal lieutenant in LULAC—in many respects, Tijerina's advisor and protégé. But the role of Alfred Hernández will be examined in greater depth later.[14]

Planned by Tijerina, the installation banquet for the 1948 Council No. 60 officers proved to be a telling occasion. Several LULAC dignitaries, including President General José Maldonado (a physician from Santa Fe, New Mexico), Gus C. García (the eloquent civil rights attorney from San Antonio), and Texas regional governor Raúl A. Cortez, attended, which illustrated the concern LULAC gave to its postwar rebuilding efforts as well as the importance it placed on Houston as a growing stronghold of the organization.[15]

Dr. Maldonado administered the oath of office en masse to Hernández, Tijerina, and the other incoming council officials. He told them that LULAC members must "fight with a missionary zeal for their rights and especially the rights of their children." Gus García spoke to the issue of Mexican American education by informing the group that of the 250,000 Latin American children in Texas, less than half of them attended school. At this time, García was the principal counsel in a federal court case in Austin to stop school segregation of Mexican American children. Picking up on García's words, Raúl Cortez declared that these children must have the same opportunity as everyone to prepare themselves for leadership in business and the professions.[16]

Tijerina took to heart these messages on the need for protection and education of Latin American youth. During this gathering, the *Houston Chronicle* reported, Felix recalled that he had left his "native Sugar Land [as a boy] because of the prejudice against those of Mexican parentage." The *Chronicle* article also included a photograph of the LULAC officers taking their oath, indicating a greater level of attention given to local Mexican American affairs by the community in general.[17]

The year 1947 also witnessed a high point for Felix in México Bello. Paralleling his work with LULAC, Tijerina had stayed active in this older social club so that in December, 1946, he was elected its president, a position he would hold for several terms.[18] Under the auspices of México Bello Felix immediately staged a major event designed to build bridges of goodwill between Mexico and the United States.

On behalf of the club, Felix invited Mayor Félix González Salinas of Monterrey, Nuevo León, in late December, to be the guest of honor at México Bello's annual banquet on February 1, 1948. González Salinas readily accepted, as he and a Monterrey delegation would be in transit at that time to represent his nation at the Mayors' Conference in Washington, D.C. After receiving the good news, Felix, Phil Montalbo, John J. Ruíz, and several other México Bello stalwarts (most, of course, members of LULAC as well) planned extensively for the occasion. It would be the group's first attempt at entertaining such a high-level Mexican official. Completely bicultural in approach, Tijerina's many letters of invitation were in English to the Anglos and in Spanish to the Mexicans. He and the club membership hoped, in keeping with the prevailing spirit of pan-Americanism, to make the banquet a vehicle for bringing attention to U.S.–Mexico relations, to further the work of the Texas Good Neighbor Commission, and to build commercial ties between Houston and Monterrey, two cities in close proximity and with similar development patterns.[19]

The affair took place without a hitch and amid much fanfare. Felix went to Monterrey and accompanied González Salinas, his wife, daughter, and their party (which consisted of two Monterrey city commissioners, the city attorney, and their wives) to Houston. They arrived by automobile on Friday, January 31, and stayed at the Rice Hotel until Monday morning. The local press noted that Janie Tijerina and Mrs. John J. Ruíz extended the club's greetings to the visitors. By pre-arrangement, on Saturday morning, Mayor Pro-Tem Phil Hamburger (Mayor Holcombe was out of town) and the Houston City Council grandly received González Salinas and company, presented the mayor with the key to the city, and held a special council session for the guests' benefit. At a luncheon sponsored by Tijerina, Mayor González Salinas spoke on the mutual concerns of the two nations (such as Mexico's difficulty with hoof-and-mouth disease among its cattle) and urban problems. At Tijerina's invitation, wealthy Houstonian R. E. "Bob" Smith, as chairman of the Texas Good Neighbor Commission, and Hamburger attended the luncheon where Tijerina and Montalbo presented the mayor with a gray, Texas-style Stetson hat. In his remarks, Tijerina noted that "the many thousands of Houstonians of Latin American extraction are perhaps a bit more conscious than our non-Latin neighbors of the nearness of Monterrey and of the parallel to be found between the two cities." México Bello held its formal banquet and dance that evening at the Rice. This likewise proved to be successful, attended by club members and their guests, including the mayor pro-tem and several other prominent Houston Anglos. During his weekend stay, the mayor (a rancher in Nuevo León) even attended the Houston Fat Stock Show and Rodeo as well as visited several close relatives who made Houston their home. A tall, husky man, Felix González Salinas heartily thanked everyone for the elaborate feting, especially thanking Tijerina for the manner in which he and his club had arranged it.[20]

The Houston newspapers widely covered the mayor's stay, noting the prominent role Tijerina and México Bello played as "the leading element of Houston's Latin-American colony." The newspapers identified Tijerina as a "prominent Houstonian and leader of Latin Americans here." The visit and publicity surrounding it no doubt represented a heady, memorable occasion for Felix Tijerina. He had wined and dined the mayor of the important northern Mexican city near which he had once resided as a child of a humble family. The episode brought him public notice as an unofficial ambassador to Mexico for the city, a role he would foster in the upcoming years. As he told the Mexican consul, he had worked hard on this event *"para atraer la simpatia del pueblo americano hacia nuestra raza"* (to attract the positive attention of the Anglos toward our people, i.e., Mexicans *and* Mexican Americans). At the same time he told Anglos that "in order to bring about a closer relationship and understanding between two peoples, one of the most effective [methods] is to get better acquainted." Trying to bring the two groups together in harmony represented the essence of Felix's non-confrontational approach, and he wanted the club to sponsor other such events.[21]

Subsequently, however, the club did not meet Tijerina's expectations as president. By March, 1948, in his second term, he complained that he found little cooperation or help for his projects from the members outside the same small circle. Although the group apparently reelected him to a third term for 1949, Felix submitted his letter of resignation from the office on February 4, effective immediately, because he felt it was impossible to have any new projects or advance the organization due to what he perceived as inactivity among the general membership. He expressed his belief that México Bello, because of such inertia, was losing its prestige in *el pueblo*. With this, Tijerina returned to the status of a regular member.[22]

In these postwar years, Felix still enjoyed belonging to México Bello, because it was where he associated with his closest friends, such as Chato Reynosa, Félix Morales, Francisco Chaírez, Ramón Fernández, Isidro

García, John Ruíz, and others, as well as many newer members like Phil Montalbo and Alfred Hernández. At their meetings and functions, he could express that still-important Mexican side of himself through the Spanish language, traditional customs, and familiar, male fraternity. México Bello continued to represent an ingredient in Felix's psychocultural balance as a Mexican American.

Tijerina's connection with his *mexicanidad* also still extended to his roots in General Escobedo. In 1948, the year he and México Bello hosted Monterrey mayor Felix González Salinas, Tijerina reportedly donated one hundred dollars (a considerable sum in Mexico at the time) to a local committee for construction of an important new road to Escobedo. Although dates for other specific interaction are probably impossible to determine, Felix apparently had always maintained contact with the *villa*. Often with friends like Chato Reynosa, with Janie, or later with México Bello or LULAC buddies such as Phil Montalbo, Felix's stops in General Escobedo likely took place in conjunction with his numerous trips to Monterrey. Tijerina's many acts of generosity to *escobedenses* ranged from buying bread to distribute among family and loved ones (including Mingo's sisters, who resided there) to making financial contributions to help local teachers educate the town youths. People from the *villa* respected Tijerina not only for his largess, but also for the success he had achieved in Texas. Never turning his back on his kin or his kind, Felix would always be known as Feliberto in General Escobedo.[23] Clearly, however, Tijerina did not intend that his relationship to Escobedo be public knowledge within mainstream Houston.

No doubt linked to his leadership role in Club México Bello and his sincere feelings for his native land, Tijerina served in 1948 as president and chairman of the city's Comité Patriótico Mexicano. Very Mexican in its orientation, this group celebrated the national holidays of Cinco de Mayo and Dies y Seis and could trace its origins back to the first decade of the twentieth century as perhaps the oldest institution in the city's *colonia*. Felix's name on its stationery lent the organization prestige. The group, as was the custom, included the Mexican consul (Álvaro G. Domínguez), the vice consul (Luis G. Zorrilla), and a number of working men who were grassroots leaders in the barrios.

Besides lending his name, Felix was the largest individual financial contributor to the group's endeavors, listed as giving $150 to the May 5 celebration that drew a crowd of more than two thousand people to the Houston City Auditorium. The September 16 festivities, also staged at the City

Auditorium, took place over two evenings. Though equally impressive, this event was somewhat marred when a knife fight broke out between two young Latin American men in the balcony; one stabbed the other to death before the police could intervene.[24]

Felix's tenure as head of the Comité, however, hardly outlived his México Bello presidency because in May of 1949, his name had been stricken from the group's stationery.[25] By then, too, he had withdrawn from active membership in LULAC.

Although the exact date is impossible to determine, sometime during 1948 Felix cooled toward Council No. 60. It should be remembered that the group had elected him as its vice president for that year, but the meeting minutes reveal scant mention of Tijerina other than his interest in helping with the annual poll tax drive and some involvement on a council committee that went to the grand jury over alleged cases of police brutality.[26]

In all probability, the council's direction at this time and the simultaneous emergence of another individual within the group at least in part account for Felix's withdrawal from participation. While the council involved itself in many activities—from giving scholarships to starting new LULAC councils in the area—its mission by 1948 centered around the fight against segregation and discrimination in the Houston region, a trend that, again, reflected the route taken during these years by the young Latino men of the World War II G.I. Generation across the Southwest. In 1948 alone, Council No. 60 was involved with the Latin American PTA of Pearland (a community southeast of Houston) in a struggle LULAC had waged for several years against discrimination within that school district. The council likewise dealt with the segregation of Mexican children in the schools of Alvin, another town in the vicinity. It investigated discrimination against Latins in such local labor unions as the International Longshoremen and in an array of public business establishments as well as cases of police brutality. The legal battles by Gus García in San Antonio were topics of discussion at the meetings, and the council's efforts "to collect funds to fight discrimination" became a recurring theme in its minutes.[27]

One of the leaders (perhaps the personification) of this ongoing struggle and more aggressive posture of Council No. 60 was John J. Herrera. Between the early 1940s and 1952, John Herrera was emerging as "Mr. LULAC" in Houston. And, by 1948, Herrera—the man and his style as much as the issues he articulated—most likely rubbed Felix the wrong way, to the point of irritation.

Indeed, much about John Herrera annoyed Tijerina, and vice versa. But one cannot write about Felix Tijerina, the League of United Latin American Citizens, or Mexican American development in Houston, especially during the 1940s and 1950s, without discussing Herrera and his adversarial relationship with Tijerina. From the 1940s until Tijerina's death (Herrera would outlive him by more than twenty years), people who understood the community viewed them as rival leaders of Houston's Latin American population. And their rivalry placed in stark contrast two different approaches to the issues faced by the postwar Mexican American community, two different methods which essentially sought the same end—that is, full participation by Mexican Americans in United States society.[28]

Any generalization about these two men and the contrasts their relationship embodied would be oversimplification because they were complex individuals who also shared many similar characteristics. However, John Herrera personified the more confrontational approach in dealing with the numerous manifestations of discrimination faced by Mexican Americans. His career in LULAC would become a metaphor for that line of action within the organization during the 1940s and early 1950s. On the other hand, Tijerina, as events would show, represented a more accommodating, education-oriented style. His method subscribed more to another strain that had likewise always been present within the LULAC philosophy and would become ascendant when Felix actively put his ideas into practice during his national presidency in the late 1950s. Each man felt that his particular emphasis would be the most effective avenue for the level of participation in American society that his people sought.[29] A brief survey of the commonalities and differences in their backgrounds, personalities, and work can show to some degree not only what brought these two interesting characters into the same arena, but also what accounted for their contrasting approaches which so sharply crystallized by the late 1940s.

Born in Cravens, Louisiana, on April 12, 1910, while his parents were temporarily away from their native San Antonio, John James Herrera could trace his ancestry in the Alamo City to the early eighteenth century. Unlike Felix, Herrera was secure in his native-born status. Herrera's parents moved the family back to San Antonio for a time, and his mother died there in the influenza epidemic of 1918. Like Tijerina, he had lost a parent at a tender age. Thereafter, again similar to Felix's experiences, the Herrera family had to be transient to survive. They briefly lived in Galveston and for a time worked the migrant trail as far north as Michigan until, in the mid-1920s,

Herrera's father brought them to Houston in search of employment. Johnny Herrera arrived in Houston with his family just after Tijerina came with his, and it was from that point on that their careers intertwined.[30]

It so happened that the Herreras settled on Artesian Place, up the street from the Tijerinas. Like the Tijerina girls who were more his age, Johnny attended Dow School. As a citizen of the United States and more acculturated than Felix, Herrera by this time spoke fluent English that would eventually betray no Spanish accent. He was also five years Tijerina's junior and, though he shined shoes around the Rice Hotel to make money, at least during the 1920s Herrera had a father who earned a basic living for the family. As a consequence, with his native intelligence and personal drive, John obtained as good an education as Houston schools provided Mexican American children at the time, an advantage Felix lacked. John went to Sam Houston High while working as a newspaper boy, dropped out for a time, but ultimately graduated with Victoria Tijerina in the spring class of 1934. During his freshman year at Sam Houston, he had been inspired by Lyndon B. Johnson, who taught speech there at the time.[31]

To an even greater extent than Tijerina, Herrera came of age in the Bayou City during the crucible of the Depression. He entered the South Texas School of Law in 1934, before rules for admission to law school required more than just a high school diploma. Herrera worked his way through by holding various daytime jobs. While a laborer with other local Mexican Americans in the Houston City Water Department, he became involved in the Latin American Club (which, of course, Tijerina had helped to found) and tested his mettle first in several of the more daring controversies that the group met head on during the late 1930s. After Felix fell away from prominent activity with the club, Johnny Herrera held several high-profile offices and apparently served as its last president before the group dissolved. As a working law student, young John showed himself to be in solidarity with his proletarian Spanish-speaking friends. He was assertive, outspoken, and, when necessary, confrontational with Houston's Anglo authorities—characteristics which seemed to be imbedded in his nature. As Alfred J. Hernández put it, John "had a heart as big as Texas and more guts than ten guys."[32]

Because he worked and had a wife and growing family, Herrera did not complete law school until 1940. After multiple attempts, he passed the bar exam in 1943 and became one of Houston's few practicing Latin American attorneys.[33]

Herrera had gained a reputation among *la gente* of Houston for his courage, or what some called his brashness. As impetuous as Tijerina was cautious, Herrera was truly one of a kind. Tall, handsome, flamboyant, dynamic, often emotional and controversial, most times likable but sometimes abrasive, he was a complicated person, one of the two most interesting and important Mexican Americans ever to walk across the stage of Houston history. Felix Tijerina was the other. The two men were emerging as peers by the 1940s, and, again, as things developed, they would soon be arch-rivals.

During the war, Herrera was a principal figure in keeping the LULAC flame burning in the Bayou City. He numbered among those in the Latin American Club who had integrated themselves with the reformed local LULAC council at the end of the 1930s. By 1942, Herrera was president of Council No. 60, an office he would hold several times during that decade. That office was the beginning of his ascent within LULAC, which would culminate with his being elected national president in 1952. The father of three children by 1943, he was deferred from military service, but like his LULAC brothers he was a superpatriot. Beginning in the war years, he led a LULAC delegation in laying a wreath at the San Jacinto Monument during the yearly celebration, commemorating Tejano participation in Sam Houston's battle against Santa Anna. Herrera likewise served as an advisor to the local draft board and named his second son Douglas MacArthur Herrera because the child had been born on the day it was announced that the general had successfully eluded capture in the Philippines and reached safety in Australia.[34]

Herrera and LULAC were on the front lines of trying to end what he called the "un-American" practice of discrimination against hiring and promoting Mexican Americans in the local defense industries and other Houston companies. In that effort, Herrera (a lifelong "yellow dog" Democrat) worked closely with Carlos E. Castañeda, the University of Texas professor and scholar who served as assistant to the chairman of the President's Committee on Fair Employment Practice during the war. In 1944, Herrera, Fernando Salas, and the rest of Council No. 60 became involved in the struggle against the segregation of Mexican American children in Pearland. Like all Mexican Texans, Herrera despised the segregated "Mexican Schools," a Texas institution that he and Council No. 60 worked to abolish.[35]

In other words, Herrera and LULAC battled the manifestations of prejudice that Latin Americans had traditionally encountered in Houston and its environs. This domestic struggle was in keeping with that waged by other LULAC councils and Latin American groups across the Southwest. It represented an outgrowth of Mexican American participation in the war to uphold democratic principles fought for by the Allies in Europe and the Pacific.

As the war ended, the overt fight against discrimination still prevailed, and Herrera helped to shape the local LULAC agenda in these ongoing battles. He chaired the local arrangements for the 1946 convention and in 1948 was elected as the Texas regional governor of LULAC.[36] Though Tijerina was still, of course, supportive of LULAC efforts and associated with Herrera in many meetings and events, by 1948 a natural antagonism between the two men was beginning to surface.

A LULAC confidant of both men suggests that the animosity between the two men first erupted when Felix criticized Herrera's ability as an attorney after the latter unsuccessfully handled the case of a mutual acquaintance. Felix felt that John was an opportunist who sought publicity for the sake of getting clients for his law practice.[37]

All of their associates (in and out of LULAC) agree, however, that a clash between the two men was inevitable. In important areas, Tijerina and Herrera were two different kinds of men. By nature, Felix was more circumspect, no doubt in part because he was a restaurant owner who catered to Anglo clientele and could not afford to alienate his source of income. Such dependence would reinforce his natural desire to be liked by the mainstream community and to avoid confrontation with its structure. Felix seems to have retained at least some measure of the natural inclination to keep a low profile harbored by many immigrants (in his case, one who also hid the fact that he was foreign born). But Felix was also personally, by nature, more subdued, exactly the opposite of John Herrera.

Though not unattractive, Felix was short in stature, not physically commanding. On the other hand, Herrera stood over six feet tall, was handsome, and had a "presence" that dominated a room when he entered. (He was even a good ballroom dancer.) As a lawyer with Mexican Americans as his primary clients, Herrera found the roles of advocate and adversary to be elements of his profession as well as part of his personality. Secure in his status as essentially a seventh-generation Texan, Herrera possessed none of the innate caution (or insecurity) of an immigrant and few fears that he would alienate potential sources of his livelihood. As Raúl Martínez, a longtime friend to both, remarked: "They had two different styles, two different approaches. John J. hammered at things like a defense attorney while Felix approached situations as a more reserved businessman. They were both very good men."[38]

As important as the differences between these two individuals were, the men also shared a similarity that would help drive them apart. David Adame, a kind-spirited young LULAC member during the late 1940s, said it as well as anyone: "Felix and John each had to have things *his* way." In short, the two men possessed abundant egos that clashed within Latin American organizations and allowed little room for compromising with one another. Felix and John each felt a sense of his own importance and, as longtime LULAC brother Ernest Eguía recalled, they were both strong willed. Being fundamentally committed individuals, each was equally convinced that *his* direction would be best for the community and could be forceful in the implementation of his approach. In sum, their natures and styles formed what one mutual friend described as a "collision course" with one another by 1948.[39]

Felix's final comment recorded in the Council No. 60 minutes in 1948 probably indicated his attitude toward Herrera and the group's militant posture. At the April 22 meeting, following another update by Herrera on the situation in Pearland, the recording secretary noted that "Mr. Tijerina [who was presiding] tell[s] us, the less talk about discrimination, the sooner we forget it." Janie Tijerina recalled years later that her husband's reservations about Herrera in part sprang from the latter always "yelling segregation."[40] Clearly, Herrera and the confrontational approach he represented, with its focus on prejudice and segregation, had worn thin with Tijerina and ran counter to his methods. Thereafter, references to Felix Tijerina at the council meetings disappear.

Herrera, of course, did not let up. He loved LULAC intensely, probably more than any other man of his generation in Houston and as fervently as anyone in the group's history. While other men served the organization well, for Herrera it was a passion and a key part of his identity. Though he had his critics inside Council No. 60, Herrera led its delegates to the LULAC national convention held in Austin in mid-June, 1948. The Houstonians carried with them a proposed resolution in which they called for LULAC involvement in "politics as self defense."[41] The resolution stated:

> Whereas: The constitution of LULAC deprives LULAC Councils as such to openly participate actively in politics. Be it therefore resolved that the League of United Latin American

> Citizens at national convention assembled change our consti-
> tution so that all LULAC Councils have the right to openly
> engage in politics and to endorse or refrain from endorsing
> any candidate which the League or the Council will deem of
> mutual good for our people.[42]

Although they failed to get the resolution passed, Herrera and the others clearly tried to shape LULAC into a version of the Latin American Club of the 1930s. In keeping with this approach, the council minutes noted with pride that all the Council No. 60 delegates to the LULAC regional convention of 1949—a delegation that included Alfred J. Hernández, Ben Canales, Raúl Palacios, Felix Salazar, Jr., and Henry González—were law students. Ready to confront issues, these young Turks received much of their lead from Herrera. He had been a member of the pro bono defense team for Macario García in 1946, as well as an initial attorney with Gus García in the case of *Delgado v. Bastrop Independent School District,* which, in 1948, would at least legally end segregation of Mexican Texans in the state's public schools. That year, as Texas regional governor for LULAC, Herrera broadened his influence within the organization on the road to his 1952–53 term as national president.[43] Therefore, the climate within LULAC Council No. 60 by 1948 had reached a point for Felix Tijerina to look elsewhere for civic involvement more suitable to his liking.

B y mid-June 1948, Felix seems to have moved in other directions, but he was also unusually preoccupied with personal and business matters. First of all, in mid–March, 1948, after over fourteen years of childlessness, the Tijerinas went to Monterrey, Nuevo León, where, through the help of Mayor González Salinas, they adopted a baby boy recently born to two of Janie's distant relatives. Upon adoption, they named the infant Felix Tijerina, Jr., and brought him back to Houston.[44]

Shortly thereafter, Tijerina opened a new, expanded version of Felix Mexican Restaurant and closed the café in the little cottage that he had successfully operated for a decade. Located at 904 Westheimer, the new place was three blocks closer into town and was a grand affair. For this restaurant, he had purchased and remodeled a building on the northwest corner of Westheimer Avenue and Grant Street that apparently had for several years housed Irene's Tea Room. The new structure "was designed throughout" by architect Allen H. Caldwell, son of Felix's late boss George Caldwell of the Original Mexican Restaurant. J. O. Jones, general contractor, did the remodeling and construction work.[45]

Far larger and more impressive than Tijerina's previous place, this new, $125,000 restaurant was wholly Mexican in style. Its exterior was bright white stucco with dark, ornate wrought-iron trim. Heavy, carved double front doors of ebony (which opened onto the corner where the sidewalks along Westheimer and Grant met) were set into the arched entrance of a large turret. The turret rose above the restaurant's façade and had a rounded, red tile roof. Alternating blue-and-white and green-and-white Mexican tiles decorated the step to the entrance, and tiles of similar blue-and-white design framed the lower part of this walkway on each side of the double doors. The restaurant had six large arched windows—three of them evenly spaced along each of the two wings of the building that faced the streets. Above these windows on both wings, a red metallic sign illuminated by yellow-gold neon spelled "Felix Mexican Restaurant" in cursive letters. On the corner turret just above the double doors, the name "Felix" was identically written, but in bolder red metal and yellow-gold neon. For added color, a thin green neon light circled the turret just under its roof. Barely noticeable from the street, a spacious seven-room apartment (where the Tijerinas now resided) sat atop the new restaurant.[46]

The interior of the restaurant was as impressive as its outside. The front doors opened into a rotunda that held artistically carved wooden display cases filled with Janie's Mexican jewelry and curios. Beyond this room lay an L-shaped main dining area with a linoleum tile floor, adobe-type, buff-colored walls, huge wooden beams running across the ceiling, and large wrought-iron chandeliers with inlaid colored glass. The tables and chairs, painted in bright, festive colors, came from across the border. Two Mexican-tiled steps led to a smaller, elevated dining alcove beyond the main space.

On the Grant Street side, there was also a separate, white stucco and red-tile roofed banquet room for private parties of up to 125 people. Containing delicate hand-painted interior beams, this banquet room had its public entrance through the small garden area next to the main restaurant. The combined dining areas could accommodate 375 customers and made an attractive, exciting addition to Houston's restaurant scene.[47]

Felix was extremely proud of this new establishment. In fact, he bubbled with joy. With faithful Mingo at his side as head chef, he stood for a formal photograph with his staff of more than a dozen waiters, busboys, cooks, and kitchen helpers. He widely announced the grand opening, which took place on Wednesday evening, June 23. This opening was his biggest fanfare yet, and it illustrated how he had mastered the art of promotion so typical of the boosterism in Houston. A full-page advertisement in the *Houston Press* stated that the "dazzling splendor of Mexico has been embraced in the colorful setting for the New Felix Mexican Restaurant." It was no less than "America's Newest and Finest Mexican Restaurant." Again targeting Anglo customers, the ad stressed that the food had "the delicate flavor of Mexico modified to suit the American taste." [48]

In its reports on the opening, the media focused on Tijerina as a central attraction. Featuring his "Latin" charm, the *Houston Post* pictured Felix courteously opening the establishment's front door and noted that the restaurateur had "served Mexican food to three generations of Houstonians." [49]

By locating the restaurant a little east of the busy corner of Westheimer and Montrose Boulevard, Felix had chosen an even better spot than his previous place, once again showing his solid, conservative business acumen. With an established clientele, loyal employees, and essentially the same menu, he would now build success upon success. He now drew even more patrons from the flourishing postwar Anglo neighborhoods with their wide green lawns. As Bill Roberts (society writer for the *Houston Press*) recalled, people identified Felix's as the place to get good basic Mexican food at moderate prices. The regular "Felix Mexican Dinner" cost 50¢; the most expensive plate—the "Felix De Luxe Dinner"—was $1.25. These items included various portions of tamales, enchiladas, frijoles, sopa de arroz, chile con carne, tortillas, and other basic Tex-Mex cuisine. Felix had one rather peculiar specialty that came with several of his plates: "spaghetti con chile," an item he included apparently because he personally liked it. One could also get a bowl of chile con carne for 30¢, an order of tamales for a quarter, huevos rancheros for 50¢, and other familiar dishes at similar prices. Most important, his customers felt that his food had that distinctive "Felix" taste that never varied. [50]

The opening ceremony included H. Merlyn Christie, Bob Smith, and Councilman J. S. Griffith (representing Mayor Holcombe). Mrs. Abe Zindler, a Felix regular for many years, officially cut the silk ribbon at six o'clock to let in the first of hundreds of friends and customers who came that evening. Felix received a flurry of telegrams from people—including Mayor González Salinas of Monterrey—who, while not able to attend, wanted to send their congratulations and wishes for continued good fortune. One reporter noted that Tijerina's "dream of three decades was realized with [this] opening."[51]

By 1950, the *Houston Chronicle* noted that the new Felix's was becoming "a 'must' for out-of-town tourists." With handsome decor and inexpensive Mexican dishes, it had "developed into one of the show places of Houston."[52] People continued to appreciate the consistent quality of the food, the restaurant's architecture, the courteous, longtime waiters, linen tablecloths and napkins, and many other small, but important touches that made it a landmark. In the words of more than one of its customers, Felix Mexican Restaurant at 904 Westheimer was something that "never changed."[53]

As Felix expanded his operations with other locations, 904 Westheimer remained his flagship. The restaurant's basic design—white stucco, ironwork, red trimming, arched windows, and distinctive Felix signs—became the architectural motif for his subsequent smaller locations around town. This restaurant also represented the cornerstone of Felix Tijerina's image as Houston's premier Latin American entrepreneur in the postwar era.

Located on the Anglo west side, the new restaurant also expressly excluded blacks, as had the one up the street before it. This policy was the custom of mainstream Houston eating places at the time; to do business in Houston's white society, Tijerina could hardly have done otherwise. A written policy entitled "NEGROES" was typed on the restaurant's distinctive new stationery and posted where presumably only the staff could see it. The notice stated that it was "against the policy of Felix Mexican Restaurant to serve Negroes. If a Negro enters the Felix Mex. Restaurant, the proper thing to say is, 'I'm sorry, we cannot serve you.'" It detailed at length the process by which a black interloper should be evicted, including calling the police and having "the Negro" arrested for disturbing the peace if he or she became "noisy or demonstrative" and tried to stay. The black person in question might also be arrested for trespassing if he or she simply refused to leave. This policy statement concluded by informing the restaurant employees that they should explain to the police that "according to the law, we have the right to select our customers."[54]

Tijerina's new business carried him further into the light of favorable Anglo public opinion and activities. Even before 1948, however, he had engaged in numerous mainstream endeavors, maintaining his balance between Mexican and Anglo American affairs much as he had during his prewar days. In February, 1946, for example, he served on the Harris County grand jury, less than two years after his friend Fernando Salas was empaneled as the first Mexican American grand juryman in Houston. This was the first of several grand jury terms Tijerina served. Within the Houston Optimist Club, Felix had become especially active by 1947 in its efforts to raise funds to establish a boys' home on Galveston Bay at La Porte. This project resulted in the Optimists converting the former mansion of ex-governor Ross Sterling, its grounds, and two hundred acres of surrounding area into Boys' Harbor, a privately funded residence for neglected or homeless boys. But his attendance at the Optimist Club meetings would not last much longer.[55]

In early 1948, Felix joined Houston's Rotary Club, an exclusive, more prestigious Anglo male civic group that contained numerous prominent businessmen, executives, professionals, and civic leaders. With membership in Rotary coming through invitation only, Felix was its only Hispanic member except for a couple of local consuls from Latin American countries. Tijerina enthusiastically embraced Rotary. Since the Rotarians and Optimists both met at noon on Thursdays, he fell away from the latter group as he became one of the Rotary Club's most lasting, energetic members. Within a year, he was part of Houston's official delegation that traveled to the International Rotary convention held in New York City, broadening his horizons even more. From this new association, Tijerina's public profile received a major boost.[56]

As a Rotarian, Felix further solidified his friendship with R. E. "Bob" Smith, the multimillionaire head of the Texas Good Neighbor Commission and Houston Rotary vice president at the time Felix joined. The club performed many service projects, but it also ranked "making the acquaintance of men you ought to know" at the top of the "Benefits of Rotary," the group's official list of perquisites that came with being a member.[57] In ultra-capitalist Houston that meant business contacts and self-promotion.

Sure enough, in August, 1948, as a so-called "baby Rotarian" (first-year member) the first major biographical article on Felix Tijerina appeared. Published a few months after Felix opened his new restaurant, the piece was written by Silas B. Ragsdale (a fellow Houston Rotarian) for *The Log,* the club's local bulletin. However, it also ran under the title of "Mother—Wife—Friends Form Real Keystone of Felix's Success Story" in the *Houston Press* on August 26, thus receiving much greater circulation. A biographical feature on a Mexican American was something which had seldom, if ever, appeared in mainstream Houston periodicals.[58]

This article may well have been the most significant attention given to Tijerina's rising star in business and civic affairs since the *Houston* magazine published his portrait in 1939. The piece dealt with his success in Mexican restaurants and his work in various Anglo organizations, and it set the tone for much of the publicity that would focus on him in the postwar years.

The article put into print the fable of Tijerina's origins by stating that he was born in Sugar Land, Texas—the author no doubt accepting Felix's version of his life as he wanted Anglo Houston to know him. Ragsdale dealt mainly with Tijerina's struggle for success, beginning Felix's story at the time of his father's death when he "started out in the 'cruel world'" as an "eight year old, doing what chores he could pick up . . . on the farms around Sugar Land" so that he could "support his mother and five sisters." The author recounted how Felix came to Houston, where he labored at a fruit company and as a busboy; how he attended night classes at Dow School; how he devoted his attention to family and friends; and how he went broke in his first café during the Depression. The article emphasized that through thriftiness, hard work, and sacrifice Felix and Mrs. Felix had endured until finally hitting it big in the late 1930s and 1940s. Now, according to Ragsdale, with a new business that was "so much bigger and better" than what he had earlier, Tijerina thought "he might be dreaming." The article mentioned his involvement in the Community Chest, probation department, the YMCA, and other civic work, but failed to note his Mexican ethnicity or activities in Latin American clubs. All the while, Ragsdale stressed, Felix was a modest man who had saved his first job in Houston by "'yes ma[a]ming' the proprietor's wife." As an adult, Tijerina avoided "high falutin airs" and simply tried "to do the things that are expected of good citizens."[59]

Perhaps most significant was the article's major thesis. The author concluded that "[i]f ever there was an example of how America is the land of opportunity for people with the right sort of stuff in them, it is the case of Mr. and Mrs. Felix." In an added preface to the article when it appeared in the *Houston Press,* the newspaper's editor drove the point home by labeling Tijerina one of the best "Horatio Alger success stories" in Houston, a place that was "replete" with such tales. Felix must have been proud of Ragsdale's piece because he kept several copies of it from the *Press.*[60]

By 1948, the locals certainly identified Felix Tijerina as their own Latin

American version of the Horatio Alger story, probably the first Mexican Houstonian so honored. This belief in the self-made man represented an integral part of the collective mentality of Houston, Texas. It was a depiction which, in Tijerina's case, had a basis in fact. Felix himself had outlined and fostered his image (with at least one important alteration of reality), and he would carry it with him for the rest of his life. It was a view that the print media as well as speeches by friends, associates, and admirers would adamantly sound in the early and mid-1950s. In this vein, a March, 1951, story by Carrie Jones Wingfield, women's editor for the *Houston Chronicle,* featured Tijerina as a "man of Mexican ancestry" who was living proof of the "maxim that this is the 'land of opportunity' for the fellow who is willing to work." Under a photo of him snappily clad in a double-breasted suit and bow tie, she noted that Felix "believe[d] that the only real requisite for attaining success in a chosen field is the ability and desire to work hard." Another article on Tijerina, this one in 1953 by staff writer Louis Alexander of the *Chronicle,* repeated this theme of the rising restaurateur. The column (part of the paper's "Neighbors of Note" series) began by recounting Tijerina's rags-to-riches, by-the-bootstraps personal history of a poor "8-year-old" boy who had gone from "the head of the family" upon his father's death to prominent Houstonian and caféman.[61]

During this immediate postwar era, Felix clearly became *the* Latin American darling of the Houston media, and his image had several aspects. In addition to the qualities ascribed by Ragsdale and the others, Tijerina was singled out as Houston's specialist in Mexican food. Articles of this nature, long and short, plaster his family scrapbooks. In 1950, for instance, editorial writer George Fuermann mentioned Felix's preferred style of enchiladas in his "favorite dishes of Houston restaurateurs"—along with items prepared by the likes of "Masterfoodman" Henry Barbour of the Houston Club and George Kelley of Kelley's. Carrie Wingfield's piece had him reveal the recipe for his chile con queso, "[o]ne of his most popular dishes." The *Houston Post* in the summer of 1953 featured him in its "Post Kitchen" section, clad in a bright plaid jacket, whipping up a Mexican summer buffet of chile con queso, enchiladas, and pineapple dessert. The *Chronicle* showed him making Mexican food favorites for the Smith College Club's International Cooking School that took place in February, 1954. In covering that event, Ann Valentine, of the *Press,* called Felix one of "Houston's top culinary artists." She included him as one of "the local 'Big three'" along with Hans, head chef at the Petroleum Club, and Camille Bermont, owner of Maxim's. Through these articles and other venues, this period became Felix's heyday as Houston's purveyor extraordinaire of Mexican cuisine.[62]

Even the Felix waiters became minor celebrities and news items. One of the more endearing of these men, Henry Canales, achieved a special popularity for his memory. George Fuermann noted in his *Houston Post* column in January, 1954, that Henry was "the fellow who has amazed you at Felix's Mexican Restaurant on Westheimer" because he "never, *never,* NEVER writes up an order." Henry would repeat each order after the customer placed it, "keeping everything straight" in his mind, "even when there [were] 18 diners at one table." Having amazed the regulars for twelve years with this practice by 1954, Henry never made an error. Whether it was Henry, Frank Barrera, or another of the longtime waiters, every Felix devotee had his or her favorite whose constant presence added an extra touch to the magic of Felix, the Mexican food restaurateur.[63]

Tijerina's fame was even more enhanced when he opened another Felix Mexican Restaurant in Houston in the spring of 1952. Located at 5821 Kirby Drive (at Kirby and Dunstan Road) at one end of a shopping strip within a larger commercial district known as the Village, it was likewise set amid middle- and upper-middle class Anglo neighborhoods, including the subdivisions around Rice Institute (to the east) and the incorporated satellite communities of West University Place, South Side Place, and Bellaire (to the west). Running south to north, Kirby Drive was a main artery that connected the southwest Houston suburbs with River Oaks, and, ultimately, downtown. This choice of location again reflected Felix's keen observation of the growth patterns of affluent Anglo Houston neighborhoods to the southwest in the postwar period.

He had begun construction on the Kirby location in November of the previous year. It contained three thousand square feet of floor space that would seat 150 customers. Although it was a rented section of a small shopping strip and not nearly as large as his 1948 restaurant, this branch location resembled his flagship with its white plastered façade, two large arched windows along each side (facing Kirby and Dunstan), and its entrance doors at the corner. The "Felix" name, written in cursive on red metal signs with yellow-gold neon, hung over the front doors and windows in similar fashion to the design on Westheimer. Exterior iron trim and interior walls finished in "soft buff," Mexican wrought-iron chandeliers, and painted wooden south-of-the-border furniture completed the resemblance to his main location.[64]

The formal opening of the Kirby restaurant, which took place at 5 P.M., Thursday, April 3, 1952, was another successful promotion announced by all three major Houston newspapers. Mayor Hal E. Terry of West University Place, Mayor Everal West of Bellaire, Houston's Mayor Pro Tem Harry Holmes, and Felix's good friend Bob Smith took part in the ceremony. With his son at his side, Felix veritably beamed with joy as he shook hands with these dignitaries. Smith's young daughters, Mimi and Bobby Sue, cut the ribbon. The newspapers made much of the fact that four-year-old Felix, Jr., served the Smith girls as the restaurant's first official customers and performed the duties of busboy. The articles focused on how the lad was following in his father's footsteps. When the doors opened, Felix made his way through the crowd of Anglo customers who packed the premises, seeing to their comfort. Like his main location, his restaurant on Kirby Drive became popular, helping to increase his fortune.[65]

Exactly how much money Tijerina earned is difficult to determine. But he did well, no doubt far beyond the expectations of his early years. Friend and LULAC associate David Adame recalled that around 1953 Felix showed him a day's receipts from the two restaurants that totaled three thousand dollars—a great deal of money for the time, especially considering the modest prices of his food.[66]

This income apparently did not even include his profits from the Beaumont location, which continued to prosper. Luciano, who lived next door to the restaurant in Beaumont, proved to be a popular, reliable, and diligent manager; his presence ensured that things fared well, as the place cultivated its clientele from among the most socially prominent people in the city. Felix routinely motored there once a week to meet with Luciano and the employees; he was inspiring to the restaurant's young workers and admired by the people of Beaumont, just as he was in Houston.[67]

Within a few years, Tijerina's increased postwar prosperity led him into finance and banking. By the summer of 1955, he started Fidelity Financial Corporation with a capital stock of five thousand dollars. Located at 2434 Navigation Boulevard in Houston's east-side Mexican American community, the company advertised itself as "[a] Texas Lending Institution for the Working Family." Felix, Janie, and Felix's attorney friend Philip J. Montalbo were listed with the Texas secretary of state as its incorporators. The company opened with Felix as its president and Montalbo as its treasurer and general counsel.[68]

More significantly, Tijerina helped to initiate the Montrose National

Bank. In the summer of 1955, a group of twenty-five Houston businessmen applied for its charter. Although Tijerina was not part of this organizing committee, when the bank opened its doors on June 2, 1956, Tijerina served on its initial board of nineteen directors, the bank's stock having been offered for sale to Montrose area businessmen. Located at 3400 Montrose, it filled a need for a bank in the Montrose–Tower Center area where Felix's Westheimer restaurant operated. Opening day ceremonies included Mayor Oscar Holcombe cutting the ceremonial ribbon at the bank's main entrance, with Tijerina and the other directors and officers looking on. With a capital structure of one million dollars, it was Houston's thirtieth bank and ninth national bank. Participation on its board (which consisted of George F. Bellows, George W. Butler, L. E. Cowling, Hyman E. Finger, N. D. Jamail, Sam H. White, and other such prominent business leaders) represented another impressive milestone in Tijerina's development as a capitalist. His name being listed in the newspaper advertisements for the bank's grand opening in the company of these elites could only have made him proud and raised the level of public recognition for his accomplishments as a self-made man. This achievement became even sweeter as the bank quickly prospered with soaring deposits of over five million dollars during its first year.[69]

Capping his postwar business expansion, Tijerina formally opened his third Houston-area restaurant in late November, 1956, the fourth in his chain. He strategically located this new Felix Mexican Restaurant at 5208 Richmond Road in a shopping area called "the Circle" in Bellaire, a satellite community on Houston's far southwest side. Although founded in 1911 as an independent municipality, by the mid-1950s Bellaire had become part of the postwar expansion of Houston's Anglo subdivisions. Again carefully noting Houston's growth patterns, Tijerina purposefully placed this new establishment a few miles beyond his Kirby Drive restaurant, in close proximity to his burgeoning pool of customers.[70]

Comprising approximately thirty-five hundred square feet of space, the restaurant had been built at a total cost of approximately fifty thousand dollars. Although similar in exterior design to his other locations with Spanish-style arched windows, "Felix Mexican Restaurant" neon signs, and a simple "Felix" neon sign above the front door, the Bellaire restaurant, unlike the others, had a brownish brick veneer and an irregular, somewhat triangular shape, with its front façade significantly narrower than the rear of the building. Its interior dining space consisted of a single room that seated approximately 150 patrons and looked identical to the Westheimer and Kirby restaurants, with a Mexican multicolored linoleum tile floor, stucco walls of colorful "Indian hues" with a series of framed Mexican landscape paintings, dark ceiling beams, heavy chandeliers, brightly painted Mexican chairs, and cloth-covered tables. The facility employed a staff of between fifteen and twenty people.[71]

The formal opening ceremony took place at 6 P.M. on Friday, November 30, 1956, amid a throng of customers and well-wishers. Effectively promoting this new expansion in the Houston newspapers, Felix invited Bellaire mayor Harry Reed who cut the ribbon. Sharply attired in business suits, Felix and Janie mingled with the capacity crowd as two Mexican musicians serenaded and Felix's distinctive, white-jacketed waiters saw to everyone's needs. Felix promised "the same type food and service . . . featured at his other restaurants" and "the same friendly service and a gracious South-of-the-Border atmosphere." For the opening, he told the *Houston Post* that "[t]he People of Houston have been very good to me through the years, . . . and I am very grateful."[72]

Charlie Evans, social columnist of the *Chronicle,* featured the opening in his regular article. The *Houston Press* ran an even more generous report, complete with a clever picture of head chef Manuel Gutiérrez ("a Felix employee for 20 years") serving his boss a "taste test" from a large ladle. Readers were informed that the new place had regular serving hours from 11:30 A.M. to 10 P.M., seven days a week. Following the lead of the other two Houston Felix locations, the Bellaire restaurant quickly became a popular dining spot for local residents.[73]

Shortly after opening the restaurant on Kirby Drive, the Tijerinas had adopted a baby girl who had been born in Houston on July 10, 1952. They located the infant through a local agency and picked her up on August 7. Naming her Janie Bell, they took the infant to Laredo to be baptized by the elderly Reverend Esteban de Anta, the longtime pastor of Our Lady of Guadalupe Church in Houston who had married the couple in 1933. In May, 1953, the court formally approved Janie Bell's adoption. And like most other things Felix did during these years, the newspapers reported the event when Charlie Evans noted in his May 13 column, amid other society happenings, that "Felix Tijerina, and the Mrs., operators of Felix Mexican Restaurants, this week adopted their second child."[74]

His role as father to two adopted children began to be highlighted by the press during these years as another dimension of Tijerina's public image. When, for example, in February, 1951, it had come time for Felix, Jr.'s adoption under U.S. law (which legally had to be at least two years after he had been adopted in Mexico), the *Houston Post* saw fit to carry a story on "3-Year-Old Felix a Lad of Distinction." Complete with an eye-catching photo of father helping his cute little son aim his toy pistol, the piece emphasized Felix's position as a prominent restaurateur and stated that Tijerina "hoped the boy would carry on his business but that he will choose his own future." Indicative of Felix's sensitive nature, especially when it came to his children, the *Post* quoted him saying that "[y]ou never know when you raise children what they are going to want to do when they grow up. . . . If he wants to be a bum, I want him to be a good bum. If he wants to be a lawyer, I want him to be a good lawyer."[75]

The article on the adoption likewise stressed the restaurateur's bicultural nature, but with a desire to "Americanize" being dominant, again, much in the spirit of Tijerina's developing image during these years. The piece made public the private nature and direction of his household, situated outside the barrio atop the restaurant on Westheimer. While noting that the little boy was born in Mexico, "had the distinction of being adopted both north and south of the border," and especially liked Mexican music, it also observed that he spoke "a little Spanish but not much. Otherwise, he is like any other American boy. Hopalong Cassidy is his present hero."[76] Few could miss this clear media message on the upbringing of the perfect postwar Houston Latin American child. In a similar vein, an article during the same period by *Chronicle* society writer Maurine Parkhurst (in her column "Gadabout") noted: "Felix Tijerina (pronounced Te-ha-rina), who is best known for his Felix Mexican restaurants, is making certain that his little son, Felix, acquires first an excellent command of the English language. He feels that Spanish should and will come later. But the Spanish speaking waiters and other domestic help are seeing to it that 'the young man' express[es] himself in Spanish also with correct enunciation."[77]

This lesson on Americanization in the raising of his son was, again, more complex for Felix than simple, unmitigated assimilation. Felix never advocated denial of his heritage even in Junior's upbringing. With Janie well versed on Mexico and in the Mexican import business, and Felix making his fortune from Mexican food, the lad was exposed to things Mexican. Ever the practical man, however (and with genuine feelings for his adopted country), Felix's policy of making his son "like any other American boy" no doubt reflected what he felt was the best way for the youngster to fit into his contemporary Houston environment, much as he had conducted his own life. As his wife recalled, Felix wanted his children to learn English first because "their country was this country [and] this is where they had to make a living."[78] Indeed, Felix and Janie spoke English to their son (and later to Janie Bell) at home. Felix's policy embraced biculturalism, but the elements of integration and Americanization clearly predominated for the next generation of his family. And the Houston mainstream newspapers were quick to point out this approach approvingly. (Living on Westheimer, away from the barrio, the children would not be exposed consistently to peer group Mexican American culture, and this would naturally lessen further their connection to *Mexicanidad*.)

It should be added that the article on the adoption proceeding in February, 1951, noted that this court action prepared the way for Felix, Jr., to become "a full-fledged American citizen," no doubt a cause for joy in the Tijerina home. However, when the time for the citizenship application came in two years, it would bring chagrin to the family. But that story will be considered in greater detail later.

While the manner in which he and Janie raised their children provided more positive notice for Felix Tijerina, it helped that his adopted son also happened to be an exceptionally attractive, photogenic child. The February, 1951, article was one of the first of many local news items showing the Tijerinas' endearing little boy. The *Houston Press* coverage of the inauguration of the restaurant on Kirby Drive in April, 1952, included a photo which showed the youngster preciously attired as a miniature Mexican bullfighter, complete with toy *estoque* (sword) and standing on one of the Mexican-style chairs at the restaurant as his father smiled in approval.[79] These notices on Felix Tijerina the father portrayed another laudable side of a man who seemingly could do no wrong, especially in the eyes of much of Houston's mainstream society.

During this period, family grief did touch Felix's life. By 1949, his mother had become ill. She still shared the house on Center Street with Amalia and Victoria. (Dora had married in the early 1940s, but she lived nearby with her husband, Antonio Quintero.) Dionicia had never enjoyed what could be called good health, but now her malady grew severe and was diagnosed as cancer. For about a year Felix's wife and sisters took her to Saint Joseph's Hospital for periodic treatments until finally she was admitted for good. Janie and her mother-in-law had long since overcome any initial reservations they may have had about one another and had forged a strong relationship. At the end, Dionicia had Janie summon Petra Pina, her friend and neighbor for many years. When Pina arrived, the elder woman shed a tear and closed her eyes. Although Dionicia was too ill to speak, her *comadre* felt that the ailing woman's thoughts were of her children. At approximately seven o'clock on the evening of July 20, 1950, after much suffering, Dionicia Villarreal Tijerina died, just a few months past her sixty-sixth birthday and approximately thirty-five years after leaving General Escobedo.

Dionicia was interred in the first grave of the plot that Felix had purchased in 1945 for his family in the Garden of Gethsemane part of Forest Park, a mammoth cemetery on Lawndale Street in Houston's east side. The Garden of Gethsemane (Forest Park's Roman Catholic section) contained the graves of Houstonians of Italian, Czech, Mexican, and other ethnic backgrounds, a "United Nations" area reminiscent of the Tijerina's first neighborhood on Artesian.

In 1952, Felix had a tall, spare, grey granite monument placed at the foot of his mother's grave memorializing the family's Mexican roots. According to his wife, Felix and Dionicia together had agreed on its design.[80] It simply bore the name Tijerina and an oval bas-relief of La Virgen de Guadalupe, patron saint of Mexico, clearly a statement of the feelings of *mexicanidad* which Felix harbored even at a time when, in other areas of his life, he blazed a trail of Americanization as he strived to "make it" within Houston mainstream society. Regardless of his public claims of nativity or his recipe for Mexican American accommodation, in his heart he never denied his Mexicanness.

Felix and Dionicia had shared an unusually close bond. As many accomplishments, friends, and family members as Felix had, Janie recalled that her husband—a man of great sentiment—never completely recovered from the passing of his mother.

Tijerina suffered another acute personal loss during this period when, on July 1, 1954, Luciano Villarreal unexpectedly died of a heart attack in Beaumont. He had first come to live and work with Tijerina in the 1920s and had been in charge of the Beaumont location since it opened in 1941. Cousin Luciano had been more like Felix's younger brother. Only forty-eight years of age, his demise greatly affected Tijerina. According to Mrs. Felix, her husband attended a rosary for the deceased but shut himself in his room during the funeral to grieve while the family buried Luciano alongside Dionicia.[81]

But in his quest for success, these postwar years were crucial, and personal hardships notwithstanding, Felix Tijerina hardly missed a beat. He had clearly emerged as Houston's Latin American Horatio Alger ideal. Felix's image, however, included another important element, specifically that of a man of civic participation. The nature, level, and public perception of his many civic activities during the early to mid-1950s will be examined in the next two chapters.

CHAPTER 5

"ALWAYS DOING SOMETHING NICE"

FELIX TIJERINA AND ANGLO AMERICAN GROUPS, 1948–1956

A lthough the biographical article by Silas Ragsdale had at least touched on Tijerina's community endeavors, his reputation for civic involvement grew to grand proportions between 1948 and 1956. Felix's activities—mostly with Anglo clubs during this specific period, but with some important Latin American ones as well—intertwined with the other parts of his positive image. Chief among those people identifying Tijerina as a civic leader were representatives of the Houston media who regularly publicized his many humanitarian acts within a plethora of organizations and agencies, mainly to benefit both Anglo and Mexican American youths. With his name and face regularly in the news, these years firmly established Felix Tijerina in the public mind as Houston's leading Latin American resident, the culmination of his work begun in the 1930s.

From the late 1940s through the mid-1950s, Felix maintained such a hectic pace of simultaneous civic activities that it would probably be impossible even to mention them all. Nonetheless, an analysis of the most significant of these projects reveals that Tijerina, in his own cautious, nonconfrontational manner, had a broad, multifaceted, bicultural civic life that brought Mexican American social issues into the mainstream agenda. Though he simultaneously invested himself in Anglo and Latin American organizations and institutions (usually bringing the two peoples together), this chapter will focus on Tijerina's pathbreaking efforts in the Anglo arena. It will also feature the crucial role assumed by Mrs. Felix in this aspect of her husband's stellar image.

THE HOUSTON JUNIOR FORUM

Around the time he opened his Westheimer restaurant in 1948, Tijerina became active with the Houston Junior Forum. A civic association of young, upper-middle-class Anglo women, the Junior Forum had begun two years before on the city's west side as an offshoot of another club called the Woman's Forum and became an independent volunteer organization in 1947. In the fall of that same year, it started a welfare department that immediately targeted the needy among Houston's Mexican Americans; in particular, in 1947 this department established a library at the old Rusk Settlement House, which still served El Segundo Barrio and people from Fifth Ward. A delegation from the forum soon enlisted the help of Felix and Janie Tijerina (Felix was already deeply involved with fostering the work of old Rusk Settlement). The women of the forum believed that Felix's stature in Latin civic affairs and as the well-known owner of their favorite Mexican restaurant made him the logical person to ask. Because of the resulting level of his assistance, forum women recall, the group soon came to look to Felix as its "patron saint." [1]

To support its efforts among local Mexicans, in June, 1948, the forum held its first "fiesta" to raise funds. The club staged this initial affair at Houston's prestigious Junior League building. The Tijerinas were its principal benefactors, donating three hundred dinners and the decorations and providing the costumes for the orchestra that played for the occasion; the Tijerinas would continue to assist with this annual fund raiser, to one degree or another, throughout the 1950s and beyond. Over the years, these benefits were held at different locations, including a nightclub called the Plantation, the Sam Houston Coliseum, and the popular Shamrock Hilton Hotel. For the earliest fiestas, it was advertised that all proceeds would go toward welfare work for Latin Americans. Always, the Tijerinas were in the thick of the preparations. [2]

In 1952, the Junior Forum purchased and remodeled a house on Avenue H in Magnolia Park, where it established a day nursery for children of working Latin American mothers. By then one of the directors of this day nursery, Felix was pictured in the *Houston Post* in May, 1952, working to restore the facility for use, along with fellow board members Mrs. Blanche Largent and W. W. Sullivan. Clubs for adults and teenagers, classes on various topics, and a health program for the nursery children soon commenced in this building, which went by the name of the Community House.[3]

Perhaps most important, the Community House nursery school became a special favorite of Felix Tijerina. It provided English instruction combined with day care for preschoolers.[4]

From the beginning of the Junior Forum's efforts at Rusk Settlement in 1947 (and at a student library the group started at Anson Jones Elementary School in 1949), the club officially emphasized that "[t]eaching English to Latin children became our battle cry."[5] Such a mission was something that Felix believed in and would assume an even larger role in his life in the upcoming years, much as he first saw it pursued by the Junior Forum.

By 1953, Tijerina had risen to president of the Community House's board of trustees, which still consisted mainly of Anglos (one of whom was his friend Bob Smith). But the board also included T. C. López, A. D. Salazar (a well-known printer from Magnolia Park), and Sammie J. Alderete (a young construction contractor and LULAC member) as representatives from the Latin population. The trustees held their monthly meetings in Felix's banquet room.[6]

Much ado was made in the local newspapers when the debt for the Community House was paid off in 1953, and the Junior Forum held a formal ceremony in November at which Tijerina, Mrs. H. M. Qualtrough (forum president), W. W. Sullivan, and Albino Torres (the famous Houston orchestra leader who provided the music for the annual fiestas) publicly burned the mortgage. Tijerina had been instrumental in raising the several thousand dollars to repay the money owed on the Community House.

Indicative of Felix's growing reputation for such philanthropic endeavors was a note sent to him by Houston demolition and lumber yard magnate Emmanuel "Wrecker" Olshan. Along with the newspaper photo clipping showing Tijerina and the others burning the Community House mortgage, Olshan had attached one of his large business cards upon which he had simply scribbled: "You're always doing something nice, Felix!"[7]

The Tijerinas' assistance with these efforts remained such that in April, 1958, the forum's Community House Board would pass a resolution making Felix and Janie honorary life members.[8]

Tijerina's philanthropy with the Junior Forum's Community House paralleled his involvement with the Burnett-Bayland Home, an institution located in Bellaire that cared for dependent and neglected children. Operated by Harris County, the home had received its name in 1952 after the Bayland Home for Boys in Clear Lake had been moved and combined with the Mary Burnett School for Girls in Bellaire. The Rotary Club of Houston had been assisting the girls' school since the 1910s. Felix had, of course, been a diligent Rotarian since 1948, a member of the club's Service Committee in 1950, and had represented Houston at Rotary meetings in Mexico on his many trips to Monterrey and Mexico City during these years. But it was on the Rotary's Burnett School committee that Felix demonstrated his best efforts.[9]

The committee's work with the home had apparently been confined mostly to the Christmas season; it had been sponsoring a Christmas party for the children since 1919. But in 1952, the committee was asked to expand its efforts to provide the kids with year-round recreational events. In 1952–53, Felix (as committee vice chairman) and chairman Rowland Manatt spearheaded the effort to hold a major function for the youngsters every few months. Among the major recreational events that the Rotary Club held for the more than one hundred boys and girls of the home was an outdoor barbecue at Bob Smith's ranch (which Felix, not surprisingly, worked with Smith to stage) and an annual Mexican dinner that Tijerina began for the youths at his restaurant. *The Log,* the Houston Rotary Club's weekly publication, noted in July, 1954, how these deprived children especially enjoyed their dinner outing at Felix's Westheimer Restaurant—almost as much as Tijerina enjoyed providing it for them. Felix became the chairman of the committee for the 1954–55 term and kept up its tradition of financial support of the home by actively raising money so that at the Christmas party in December, 1954, he was able to present its superintendent with an eighteen-hundred-dollar contribution from the Rotary membership.[10]

During preparation for the 1954 Burnett-Bayland Home Christmas party, Felix came into public view in the usual fashion. Fellow Rotarian and *Houston Press* editor George Carmack went on at length in his regular column in late November to let his readership know about "one of the best speeches [he had] ever heard—certainly one of the most moving." Explaining that Felix Tijerina—"known to all of you as the Felix of Felix's restaurants"—was this year's Christmas party chairman, Carmack praised the speech that Tijerina had given at the most recent Rotary Club meeting to generate interest in the yuletide event. "Told with an apologetic air and almost in an undertone," the story Felix related was of a poverty-stricken widow and her small children who received food and a bit of cash at Christmas time from a poor, elderly stranger who appeared at their humble abode. Carmack insightfully interpreted that "one of those children" in the story may well have been Felix "and that he has repaid that Christmas charity many thousand fold." Carmack reminded Houstonians that "[f]or whatever is good in Houston—there you find Felix and Mrs. Tijerina working for it. It would be hard to find two better people—people with kinder hearts and more willing hands." [11]

THE VARIETY CLUB AND CANTINFLAS

By 1952, Tijerina also sat on the board of trustees of the Houston Variety Boys Club, which was sponsored by the Variety Club of Houston. The local branch of an international organization that had been founded in the late 1920s to help youngsters, Houston's Variety Club chapter—Tent No. 34— had begun in the 1940s and had opened its first boys club facility in May, 1952. As a board member, Felix helped to stage a highly publicized extravaganza in late 1952 that combined his Anglo club work and love of Mexican culture. That year, he played a crucial role in bringing Mario Moreno, better known as "Cantinflas," Mexico's most famous comedian, to do his celebrated act in Houston. Himself a prominent member of Mexico City's Variety Boys Club and a friend of the poor, Cantinflas agreed to appear free of charge on the condition, Tijerina told the local press, that "every penny" of the money raised would be donated to the Variety Boys Club. In particular, the funds were slated for the construction of a Variety Boys Club in a neighborhood of Houston where 90 percent of the residents were Mexican American. [12]

Reportedly, this Houston show was to be the legendary comedian's first appearance in the United States. Houston newspapers noted that he had already passed up other, lucrative offers to perform in this country. [13]

The upcoming performance was promoted in true Houston fashion with a great deal of fanfare by the Houston Variety Club—especially by the event's ringleaders, "chief barker" L. C. Kirby, event coordinator Mack Howard, and ticket sales cochairmen Bob Smith, George Strake, Mitchell Lewis, and Felix Tijerina. In late October, the *Houston Press* society writer Bill Roberts (alias "Town Crier") dropped it in his column, along with other "Celebritems," that "Variety Clubbers Mack Howard, Bob Smith and Felix Tijerina off to Mexico to book a big act for Big Town." The mainstream newspapers carried articles on this coming attraction, stories which not only extensively focused on Moreno's unique comic genius (the Charlie Chaplin of Mexico, they called him), but on his personal rags-to-riches story as well as his reputation for helping the poor. Charlie Evans of the *Houston Chronicle* noted in his regular column on happenings around the city that Felix had even shown a film on Cantinflas at his restaurant for the other club members, to let them know what to expect.[14]

The performance, which took place at the Houston Coliseum on the evening of Wednesday, December 17, 1952, was an overwhelming success. Approximately, nine thousand people attended, a sizable number of whom were Mexican American. A parade of acts, including Mexican dancers, singers, and other musicians, opened the show. Seven professional matadors and their assistants who had come as part of the Cantinflas Production also warmed the crowd by fighting three bulls in the special ring that had been constructed in the Coliseum.

But the audience most wildly cheered the famous bullfight routine of Cantinflas himself. The lengthy review of the show by Winston Bode in the *Houston Press* entitled "Cantinflas Leaves Bulls and Crowd Dizzy" described Moreno's daring antics and remarkable ability as an entertainer. Dressed in the costume of the *peladito,* the traditional sloppy vagabond of Mexican comedy, Cantinflas stunned the audience by maneuvering the dangerous animal with expert cape work, and then, just as handily, made people laugh by performing daredevil comic hijinks, alternately waltzing, mamboing, or doing the rumba past the bull's horns, clinging to its tail, and barely escaping its charge.[15]

At an accompanying public ceremony in the Coliseum, Variety Club dignitaries Tijerina, Smith, Howard, and master of ceremonies Fred Nahas watched as George Strake, a wealthy oilman and a member of the Texas Good Neighbor Commission, made Cantinflas an honorary Texan on behalf of Governor Allan Shivers. The *Houston Press* especially noted that Felix and Mack Howard had "worked hard to make the Cantinflas Production possible."[16]

During Cantinflas's stay in Houston, Felix helped entertain him. The two men even went to the offices of KLVL, Houston's recently opened Spanish language radio station where they met with its owner and Tijerina's long-time friend, Félix H. Morales. Morales's son Joe, a Houston media personality in his own right, had been at the Coliseum ceremony to help Tijerina publicize the affair in the Latin American community.[17]

Cantinflas's appearance earned fifty thousand dollars for the project that, when combined with forty-two thousand dollars in matching funds donated by Bob Smith, amounted to a major part of the financing needed to construct the new Boys Club building. When Felix and fellow members of Houston's Variety Club participated in the organization's seventeenth annual international convention held in Mexico City during May, 1953, "the now famous . . . first U.S. appearance of Mario Moreno 'Cantinflas'" and its positive results received a great deal of praise from the Mexican press. The Houston delegation visited with Moreno at a barbecue he gave at his ranch, El Tapatío, and feted him with a banquet in his honor at the Hotel Prado. Again, Tijerina and his Anglo colleagues thanked the Mexican film star for helping them spread international goodwill. From these occasions, Tijerina and Moreno became fast friends; Tijerina rarely missed an opportunity thereafter to visit him when in Mexico City.[18]

By having Mario Moreno and his Cantinflas Production in Houston, Tijerina's exposure of Mexican culture and himself to the local Anglo and Mexican communities had reached another plateau that would be hard to best. It had been an event in the tradition of the visit of Mayor González Salinas and the opening of Felix's two booming restaurants. It etched in the public mind another victory for Felix Tijerina, a further example of a civic reputation being enhanced at every turn.

But Tijerina did not limit his activity in the Variety Club to the appearance by Cantinflas. He made the news in January, 1955, as a representative of associate members. The *Houston Chronicle* reported in May that a movie crew under the direction of Columbia Studios' Ralph Staub "breezed in to the city" to film the Houston sequences of a documentary being put together by the Variety Clubs International. Entitled *The Heart of Show Business,* the film would recount the origins and spread of the Variety Clubs. The *Chronicle* concluded: "On hand . . . to watch and participate in the filming were such local notables as [actress] Hedy Lamar[r], Robert E. [Bob] Smith, Fred Nahas, W. Stewart Boyle, Felix Tijerina, and [local Variety's "Chief Barker" Mack] Howard."[19]

During this period, perhaps the most important governing position that
Tijerina held was as a member of the Houston Housing Authority's Board
of Commissioners, the mayoral-appointed body that oversaw the operation
of the city's five low-income housing projects scattered around town. Felix
became commissioner as a result of Roy Hofheinz's election as mayor in the
fall of 1952. The forty-year-old, reform-minded Hofheinz inherited a mess
in the housing authority; a scandal centering around alleged financial and
personal improprieties had produced the dismissal of its executive director.
These troubles in the Housing Authority had been bantered about in the
local media. When Hofheinz took office in January, 1953, all but one
member of the five-person board resigned, and the new mayor picked
Lewis Cutrer (former city attorney), Leo Linbeck (a contractor), Fred Lucas (secretary of the AFL Carpenters Union Local 213), and Tijerina to fill the
vacancies.[20]

Although Felix was the first Mexican American appointed to the HHA
board since its inception in 1940 (when the city of Houston initially went
into the business of public housing), apparently no one gave it any special
notice. The announcement of Felix's appointment was made in the media
along with the other members—all Anglo males.[21]

Like the mayor who appointed them, these new commissioners saw
themselves very much as a reform board. On April 16, 1953, amid much
publicity, Hofheinz swore them in at the authority's office at No. 1 San Felipe Courts, Houston's oldest public housing project, and they held their first
meeting shortly after the ceremony. With Linbeck as their chairman, the
commissioners declared to the press that from then on "[e]very transaction
will be as clean as a hound's tooth." And, apparently, Linbeck and his fellow
board members proved good to their word. Within the week, again amid
much press coverage, the new commissioners made an inspection tour of the
public housing projects under their care.[22]

From the start, Felix was a conscientious member of the board, especially
prone to support the efforts of Commissioner Cutrer, who assumed a leadership role in these efforts. Cutrer would, in fact, be elected Houston's
mayor within a few years.

In their efforts to continue improving the image of the Authority, the
commissioners crossed with its executive director, E. A. Eversberg, who had

taken over during the preceding year. He, in turn, resigned in early May amid much acrimony, publicly denouncing the commissioners as a "green board." On the heels of Eversberg's resignation, C. M. Redfield (the lone Holcombe board holdover) likewise quit. Now firmly in control, the new board members soon replaced Eversberg with Thomas F. Booker, who would remain in that position for a number of years.

As part of this highly publicized controversy, Ernest Villarreal (Felix's distant cousin who owned a funeral home in the Second Ward and was active in East End affairs) became a de facto spokesman for a movement among some of the public housing's Latin American tenants who petitioned the commissioners to retain the services of Eversberg. The Eversberg incident was fully aired in the local newspapers, and the Tijerinas kept a small file of clippings on its course and outcome—the board's actions, Eversberg's heated response, and Villarreal's role—which at least indicates that Felix found it of more than passing interest.[23]

Although the efforts of Villarreal and the tenants came to naught, a couple of individuals disgruntled by the developments within the Houston Housing Authority immediately tried to make serious trouble for Tijerina. According to FBI records, on May 25 (later in the same month that Eversberg and Redfield resigned), two men personally contacted the FBI office in Houston to question Tijerina's citizenship status. Due to privacy considerations, these released records do not disclose their names, thus making conclusive identification impossible; however, one of them, the file reveals, had been "recently released from his position" (apparently with the HHA) while the other had "recently resigned" from some capacity with "one of the housing projects administered by the Houston Housing Authority."[24]

The two individuals (described by the reporting agent as "rather bitter" over the recent HHA fracas) alleged to the Houston FBI that Tijerina was not a citizen of the United States and "stated they had made personal inquiries into the matter" that revealed the facts of Tijerina's birth. "These gentlemen," the reporting agent noted, questioned the veracity of Tijerina's 1940 certificate of birth on file in Fort Bend County. One of them had contacted an employee of Imperial Sugar Company, "who informed him that Tijerina's family came to Sugarland, Texas about 1917" when Felix "was approximately 12 years of age" and that "the father did not accompany the family." He also contacted a former Sugar Land resident (by then living on Westheimer Road in Houston) who stated that "the Tijerina family had resided at the home of his family at Sugarland after coming to the United

States from Monterrey, Mexico, and that Felix Tijerina was approximately 12 years of age at that time."[25]

The agent reported the above information directly to FBI director J. Edgar Hoover, noting that apparently the two men wanted an investigation made of Tijerina, "who is a rather prominent restaurant owner in Houston, in view of the fact that Tijerina was recently appointed to the Board of Directors of the Houston Housing Authority by Mayor Hofheinz." In response, Hoover wired the Houston office to present these facts to the United States attorney for possible "prosecutive action" regarding a violation of the law for falsely claiming citizenship.[26]

The Houston office presented the case to the assistant United States attorney, William R. Eckhardt, who advised that prosecution be declined. It did not appear to Eckhardt that a violation of the law had occurred because the recording of a birth certificate did not constitute sufficient evidence to warrant prosecution. With that, the Houston office closed the case and wired Hoover on June 16, 1953, of this disposition, concluding to the director that "no further investigation is contemplated in this matter by this office."[27]

But the issue of Tijerina's citizenship status did not end with the decision by Eckhardt and the local FBI office to drop the matter. As shall be suggested in the next chapter, the information gathered by the "rather bitter" former employees' "personal inquiries" apparently also made its way to the local Houston office of the United States Immigration and Naturalization Service and provoked Tijerina's final bout—between 1953 and 1956—with the controversy over the place of his birth.

Whether aware or unaware of this back-door assault, Tijerina remained productive on the HHA. As Houston's initial Mexican American housing commissioner, he was understandably attentive to the Susan V. Clayton Homes, the most recent addition to the holdings of the authority and probably one of the reasons for appointing a Latin American to the board. The Clayton Homes, a 348-unit project, had just been completed—Houston's first housing project constructed since World War II. Located on the south bank of Buffalo Bayou immediately east of downtown near Our Lady of Guadalupe Church, it had replaced a slum called Schrimpf Alley, a particularly squalid area in the Mexican American Second Ward that had been a byword for poverty, crime, vice, and violence since Felix had first come to Houston. The new project was slated specifically for Latin American residents. At the formal opening of Clayton Homes on March 22, 1953,

Tijerina and John Herrera (the latter representing LULAC) had been the only two featured speakers from the Latin American community to address the four hundred persons who attended. Now on the HHA, Tijerina had to help guide the project's upkeep.[28]

As usual, Felix had the help of his wife in working with Clayton Homes. As president of the Clayton Homes Women's Club and chair of its program committee, for example, Janie and the group staged a "family fiesta" at the project in June, 1953. In addition, Felix endorsed the hiring of Luis Rodríguez (whom he had known since 1940) as manager of Clayton Homes. In a liberalizing move obviously aimed at this housing project, the board approved a recommendation by Booker and Rodríguez that if any responsible member of a family was an American citizen (in particular the wife) then "an alien" could be allowed housing. Apparently, previous policy had been to deny housing if the head of the household was a noncitizen. The commissioners agreed that families who had been turned away in the past for this reason should be contacted and their applications for housing revived. But these people were to be encouraged to attend the citizenship classes conducted at Clayton Homes or at nearby Rusk Settlement. By the fall of 1953, Clayton Homes had reached almost full occupancy for the first time since it had opened.[29]

Tijerina also solicited financial support from the Houston Junior Forum to expand the authority's day nursery at San Felipe Courts. Designed to help working mothers, this nursery offered services resembling those available at the Magnolia Community House.

Felix was so diligent in his attendance at the board's monthly meetings and in its endeavors that he was soon chosen to be the prime signer of checks and loans for the HHA. In April, 1954, the board elected him as its vice chairman; in March, 1955, he was elevated to the chairmanship. Felix served in that position until May, 1956, when, after Oscar Holcombe beat Roy Hofheinz for a third term as mayor, he resigned from the board and Fred Lucas became the new board chairman.[30]

Felix's exit from the Houston Housing Authority was set in motion by a series of political events that began the year before when, in the first week of June, 1955, Mayor Hofheinz appointed him as the only Latin American on the so-called Citizens' Charter Committee. This sixteen-person panel consisted of pro-Hofheinz women and men representing

Houston's business, academic, religious, and civic-action communities. Hofheinz charged the group with the responsibility to study and recommend changes to the city's charter—alterations along the lines that the young mayor wanted. Hofheinz had initiated the committee as a rival to a similar body simultaneously put together by the Houston City Council to push its own changes in the city charter, and, as such, was controversial from the start. These rival panels were just another part of an ongoing struggle between the headstrong Roy Hofheinz and the recalcitrant council, a struggle that marked Hofheinz's three-year tenure as mayor.[31]

Hofheinz's Citizens' Charter Committee did what was expected. After two weeks of public meetings in which the theatrical, loquacious Hofheinz played the prominent role, it drew up charter recommendations that, among other things, called for new elections to be held in November, 1955, for city council and mayor, allowed future city elections to be held in odd-numbered years, and permitted a group of candidates for mayor and council to run as a team or ticket. Hofheinz's proposals came to be embodied in "Amendment 19," so-called because the council members' group had rammed-rodded eighteen other recommended changes of its own. Houston voters were to express their wishes on these amendments in a special election held in mid-August.[32]

The council's proposed eighteen amendments went down in defeat, but Amendment 19 passed by a margin of approximately fifteen hundred votes. This effort established Houston's tradition of holding municipal elections during odd years.[33]

Ironically, however, the victory of Amendment 19 ultimately spelled defeat for Hofheinz and resulted in Felix Tijerina's departure from the Houston Housing Authority. The mayoral campaign was gearing up by late October when the pro-Hofheinz group called the United Citizens Association (headed by staunch Hofheinz/Amendment 19 supporter Bob Smith) announced its field of candidates for mayor and city council with, of course, Roy Hofheinz heading the ticket. These candidates had been named by a UCA "secret nominating committee" comprised of people hand picked by Smith. Wherever Bob Smith (and Hofheinz for that matter) went in these days, Felix would not be far away, and so the only Latin American member on the UCA nominating committee was Alfred J. Hernández, by late 1955 among Tijerina's closest confidants and no doubt his recommendation to Smith for such an assignment.[34]

Unfortunately for the UCA people, in the hotly contested November election Hofheinz (and his slate) went down in defeat to Oscar Holcombe, who had been hurriedly brought out of retirement to sweep the "Boy Wonder" from City Hall. Although Felix always played his political cards close to his vest (often financially contributing to both sides in a race and seldom speaking openly for a candidate), he had been conspicuous as a member of the Citizens' Charter Committee, had lent his name in support of the committee's recommendations, and had shown himself to be a Hofheinz man, being close to Bob Smith on just about everything. With Hofheinz ousted, Felix would soon vacate his position with the HHA. Along with two other Hofheinz appointees, Tijerina had resigned by April, 1956, early in Holcombe's first year back in office. Alfred Hernández speculated that Tijerina (even though he had always gotten along with Holcombe) stepped aside because he felt that his ties with Hofheinz would make his role as HHA chairman untenable under the new mayor. Holcombe subsequently appointed three new commissioners. One of these fresh faces was David Casas (owner of Santa Anita Mexican Restaurant), the only Latin American appointee, thus continuing the practice of naming a Hispanic on the board.[35] Undoubtedly, the entire episode during 1955 acted to reinforce Tijerina's normal policy of caution when dealing with Anglo society.

Felix's absence from the HHA board did not last long, however. He would be reappointed to the authority in 1958, after his friend and former board colleague Lewis Cutrer defeated Holcombe for mayor. A year later, Tijerina would once again become its chairman and serve in different positions on the board until his death; this second tenure will be recounted later.[36]

DEFENDER OF THE ESTABLISHMENT / DEFENDER OF HIS PEOPLE

In the midst of his successful mainstream activity, Tijerina became engaged in a public tiff with his nemesis, John J. Herrera, when the latter called into question certain actions of the Houston Police Department. During the early 1950s, Houston was upset over a rash of incidents of juvenile delinquency, some of which were perpetrated by Latin American youth gangs. One of the most notorious of these outrages occurred on Monday morning, March 2, 1953, when four young toughs abducted a twenty-seven-year-old Mexican American woman on her way to church in Houston's east side just off Harrisburg Road; they took her to Milby Park, where they held her for two and a half hours while criminally assaulting her in a most vicious manner. By the following day it was front-page news. Within a few days, Officer Raúl (Roy) Martínez (who, with the help of Herrera, Tijerina, and others, had become one of Houston's first Mexican American uniformed police officers in 1950) had located and, along with Officer Rufus L. Ramírez, arrested two of the culprits through a tip from a local barrio informant. Both were fifteen-year-old Latin Americans from Magnolia Park. They confessed to their part and named their two older accomplices, who were ultimately apprehended. This pair, aged seventeen and twenty, were likewise Magnolia Park residents and Mexican American. All four were positively identified by their victim and went to prison for their foul deed.[37]

While the search for the culprits had proceeded, however, the Houston Police had, according to the *Houston Post,* "arrested a good many youths for questioning" in a general "roundup." Many years later, Raúl Martínez remembered the overreaction by the police department as scores of "suspects" were brought in and lined up for interrogation, literally packing the jail to its limits.[38]

John Herrera was extremely dismayed by the way officers had acted during the affair. He wrote Anglo civic leaders, decrying the fact that the police had "arrest[ed] without charge or reason scores of youngsters and [kept] them in jail . . . and then dismiss[ed] them without even an apology." Amid the public uproar, Herrera also presented a nineteen-year-old youth named Rodrigo Bermea before Acting Assistant Chief George Seber. Bermea had been one of the many "suspects" hauled in by the police during the investigation; he alleged that, while in custody, two officers had beaten him with their fists and a flashlight. Bermea further claimed that two detectives then took him to a wooded area off Clinton Drive, where they shocked him with wires attached to their automobile battery. Herrera stated that while he was not representing Bermea nor would he represent the youths charged with the assault, he was there as a concerned private citizen. According to the *Houston Press,* Herrera insisted "that police have mistreated Latin American youths questioned" about the culprits.[39]

Felix immediately responded by blasting Herrera in the press. Two days after the newspapers reported Herrera's actions on behalf of Bermea, a letter to the editor from Tijerina appeared in the *Houston Post* under the heading "Felix Defends Police Department." In it, he expressed his "disappointment that a self-styled representative of the Mexican people would accuse the police department of inefficiency, hysteria and brutality." After explaining that it had been his experience that the police department exercised "intelligence, patience and understanding" with people in its custody, Tijerina accused Herrera of exposing the Latin American people to "shame and ridicule by giving the matter [of the assault] undue publicity" and by taking "advantage of the weaknesses of the Mexican people to seek publicity for himself." Felix congratulated the police department for doing "a splendid job" with the case. Again condemning Herrera for bringing "unnecessary publicity" to the affair, he concluded by stating that "I know that that individual does not represent the Mexican group and does not voice their feelings or opinions on any matter."[40] The *Chronicle* likewise had received a copy of Felix's letter criticizing Herrera and, on the previous day, had incorporated pertinent parts of it in a front-page story on the juvenile delinquency issue.[41]

In many ways, of course, Tijerina's criticisms of Herrera in this case were misguided. For one thing, he erred when he said that Herrera did not represent the Mexican American community. John was LULAC national president at the time. And while not every Mexican American in Houston may have "liked" Johnny Herrera or backed his position publicly, the overwhelming majority would have been aware (probably from first-hand experience) of the heavy-handedness of many police officers toward people of color. Furthermore, most observant Mexican Americans probably admired Herrera's courage in the affair and at least quietly agreed with him. Herrera was well known among Houston Latins for the "force" of his presence and respected for his efforts in the struggle for civil rights just as they recognized and admired Felix's influence and diplomacy. Also, it was no "weakness" of the Mexican character to want fair treatment from law enforcement officials. To be sure, Herrera could showboat as well as anyone, but, as this period of his life demonstrates, Felix also utilized press coverage and understood publicity as a legitimate means of promoting one's cause.

But Felix's cautious approach in dealing with the problems confronting Mexicans in white society (i.e., his accentuating positive aspects while trying to avoid negative attention), his growing stature, and his knee-jerk animosity toward Herrera were all readily apparent in his letter defending the police. Moreover, it was the police force of Mayor Roy Hofheinz, Tijerina's friend and patron, and this increased Felix's adverse reaction to anyone—especially John Herrera—who would publicly criticize that department's policies. Certainly, his letter to the press lost Felix no support with Hofheinz and his other Anglo associates (as his advancement to the HHA board would soon illustrate).

Altogether, Tijerina's behavior in this affair represented the low-key "Latin American" approach that had taken root by the early 1950s and would define the era. Indeed, as Tijerina was writing his letter, the Houston LULAC members were planning a community meeting in which they would try to calm tensions, working with police officials, and loudly condemning the hoodlums who had perpetrated the heinous assault. Felix was scheduled to be a member of the panel at this initial gathering that would take place at the Civil Court Building the evening his letter appeared, although it is not clear whether he attended. But Herrera was there, and he confronted the chief of police about overgeneralizations the chief had recently made about Latin youths encountering trouble with the law. Herrera also spoke at a large East End community meeting on the issue (held at Mason Park), and, according to one Anglo Houstonian who attended, gave the most "common sense" talk of the evening.[42]

While he denounced Herrera for his efforts and defended the Houston police, Tijerina did not abandon young Latin Americans to the negative stereotypes that many non–Hispanics held in the 1950s. In his letter to the newspapers, Tijerina had even referred to the culprits in the Milby Park assault case as "misguided youths." Approximately two months later, Louis Alexander's "Neighbors of Note" feature on Felix (May 18, 1953) appeared. Entitled "Cafeman Tijerina Likes to Help Boys," the article pointed out his hard-earned reputation for helping disadvantaged youngsters, noting that "[w]hat Mr. Tijerina has done to help Latin Americans, and many non-Spanish-speaking peoples of the Houston community[,] is impressive." It also stated his views on delinquency, quoting the empathetic restaurateur: "I know what it feels like. . . . I understand how a boy can feel almost ready to be a delinquent. I don't think any boys are bad. You just have to get them into the right background of church and home."[43]

Tijerina's public pronouncements always called for Hispanics to assume individual responsibility, but he characteristically defended deprived, struggling Mexican Americans by relating their behavior to his own life's experiences. As he told a *Houston Post* reporter around this time: "I know what it's like to be hungry. . . . [A] stomach is not going to be a good American if it is hungry. It isn't interested in anything but food."[44] Felix translated his feelings into action at the grassroots level by helping Mexican American individuals overcome the struggles of their daily lives;

his role as counselor to his people will be treated in more depth in the following chapter.

AND MANY MORE

Felix by no means limited his activities to the groups noted above. Snippets from the Tijerina family archives reveal a range of additional civic endeavors during the early 1950s that at least deserve mention. For example, the public was constantly reminded of Felix's part in the Community Chest (soon-to-be United Fund) campaigns, a carry-over from his prewar activities. His picture repeatedly appeared in the Houston press, often with his children, as he gave a handsome contribution to the yearly effort. A signature donor by 1954, Tijerina had been elected to Houston's United Fund board of trustees as the only Latin American among three dozen men, including Roy Hofheinz, Herman Brown, Simon Sakowitz, Leopold Meyer, and other civic heavyweights. He remained a highly visible force in the annual campaign thereafter.[45] For another example, *Houston Chronicle* writer Charlie Evans noted in early November, 1952, that "Mexican Restaurant Owner Felix Tijerina" deserved a bouquet for serving the forty-two election workers at Precinct 34 with free meals on election day. In February, 1953, the *Houston Legionnaire,* the official publication of the American Legion Central Council, carried a front-page photograph showing Houston Post 52 commander Dan Brown presenting a life membership in the post to Medal of Honor holder Macario García, while Tijerina and Post Adjutant Dudley Davidson looked on approvingly. All four men donned their American Legion caps. Standing next to the recipient, Felix was identified in the caption not only as a Post 52 member, but also as a lifelong friend of García. With this ceremony (also attended by the Mexican consul and a large crowd), Tijerina helped once again to bring Latins and non-Latins together in the public eye to honor a bona fide war hero and share a common American experience as brothers in arms.[46]

By the mid-1950s, Felix likewise received kudos from fellow restaurant owner and army buddy Bill Williams for his years of hard work with the "Capon Dinner." Williams and company annually staged the well-known event, which raised thousands of dollars for charity. In 1953, Felix was the only Hispanic among fifty-four prestigious sponsors of the Southwest Scholarship Dinner held under the aegis of the Institute of International Education and organized by a steering committee that included such illustrious Houstonians as Bob Smith, Jesse H. Jones, and Lamar Fleming.[47]

As one final example of his civic activities, Tijerina served during August and September, 1955, as the chairman of the first city-wide fund drive of the Houston Youth Symphony. Felix would head a force of 124 volunteers during the twelve-day campaign. At the center of this community endeavor, Tijerina found himself yet again recognized in the media for his position as "restaurateur and civic leader."[48]

"MRS. FELIX"

As the many previous mentions of his wife suggest, Janie had become an important, inseparable part of Tijerina's public image. She was a complex person, perhaps even more complicated than her husband. On the one hand, Janie was an interesting, intelligent, capable, energetic, mercurial, and highly independent woman and could well merit her own biography. However, true to the temper of the times, she was also an extension of and an asset to Felix, whether dealing with home, work, or community. Certainly, she necessitates separate examination for an understanding of her husband's life, especially during these years.

Known as "Mrs. Felix," she maintained a high profile in her own business and civic affairs as well as being closely identified with many of Felix's activities. While he served at Ellington Field, she had been the one who, according to the advertisement, "carried on" with the restaurant. In his 1948 article on Tijerina, Silas Ragsdale mentioned her curio stores. At that time she operated one at 906 Texas Avenue across from the Rice Hotel and a much larger "Felix Mexican Curio Shop" at 1404 Main, which stocked all sorts of imported items from south of the border.

Always a hard worker in her shops or at the restaurants, in the public eye Janie was linked with Felix as a team. The Ragsdale article mentioned Janie being side by side with him; it noted that the new restaurant was " [t]heir business," and that "Mr. and Mrs. Felix" were "an example of how America is the land of opportunity for people with the right sort of stuff in them."[49]

Although born and raised Mexican American and poor, Janie had adapted to her Houston surroundings as adeptly as had Felix. By 1948, she was forty years old and had maintained her trim good looks and dressed stylishly. She had transcended her deprived background and flowered into a refined, cosmopolitan individual. Over the years she carefully observed and emulated what she felt were the better elements of her environment; that is, she had learned how to conduct herself in the manner of Anglo upper-middle-class society. When asked many years later to explain how she managed this metamorphosis, she stated simply that "[n]ecessity is the success of life."[50]

In covering most of Felix's community activities, the press often featured Janie's presence as well. The photos of her that appeared in the newspapers when she took part in such events as the visit by Monterrey mayor González Salinas in 1947 or various benefit fund raisers show a pretty, dignified woman. Often clad in well-tailored, conservative business suits and furs, she was recognized for her correct, courteous manner by the Anglo customers who flocked to the Felix restaurants. She received wide exposure as the wife of the successful, amiable restaurateur and was respected by her husband's Anglo associates for her polite demeanor and hard work. She and Felix made a handsome couple when they attended lavish functions to which other Mexican Americans were usually not invited.[51]

Mrs. Felix also shared her husband's concern for education. For example, she was the featured speaker at the first gathering of Mexican American mothers of the Saint Patrick's School PTA (in the Fifth Ward) in October, 1946. In her address to the group she dealt with the necessity of their involvement with the PTA. She exhorted them to give the teachers their support, respect, and absolute cooperation in order to mold their children into the pride of their church, society, and state.[52]

By the late 1940s and early 1950s, Janie had developed a bicultural approach to life and maintained her independent nature. Indeed, in the fall of 1950, the *Houston Post* ran a feature article on Janie, the first of at least three to appear in the local newspapers during the early part of the decade. This initial sketch featured her as "Mrs. Felix Tijerina" but also as a businessperson in her own right and a "Mexican American citizen." The article likewise revealed her as one whose world view often defied categorization and that she could be extremely plainspoken if the mood struck her.[53]

The writer (a *Post* columnist named Barbara Liggett) noted that because of Mrs. Tijerina's frequent, lengthy trips south of the border to purchase items for her stores, she knew Mexico possibly "better than many Mexicans." Entitled "American Behavior Distresses Her," the article focused upon Mrs. Tijerina's concern with "[t]he way the average American acts in Mexico," especially the arrogance and misbehavior of tourists. As a result,

Mrs. Felix felt, Mexicans have adopted "a rather obstinate attitude." The average Mexican, "Mrs. Tijerina explain[ed], . . . loves his country too well to 'give it away' to boorish Americans by being too nice to them."[54]

According to Liggett, Mrs. Tijerina stated that one source of this "slight hostility" was the difference in the two people's attitudes toward women. North American women, Mrs. Felix said, conducted themselves poorly, by "wearing slacks, shorts, going about at night unescorted, drinking too much in public, giving too much freedom to strangers." Such practices disgusted Mexican men and women. Mexican men then blamed their American counterparts for exercising so little control over their women—ergo Mexican male contempt for Americans generally.[55]

The article went on to relate that Mrs. Tijerina harbored a special sympathy for the poorer classes of Mexico and that she herself claimed to be "pure Indian with no Spanish blood." This assertion amounted to Mrs. Felix's personal statement of *indianismo* at a time when it was more opportune to be "white" and wealthy. Janie also stated that her interest in Mexico came straight from her heart, an interest which was "in her bones."[56]

While she ran Mexican curio stores and kept an interest in the affairs of the Mexican American community, Mrs. Tijerina fit into mainstream society, becoming involved with Anglo women's clubs, a parallel to the activities of her husband. She became popular in middle- and upper-middle class women's circles, proved to be a charming, energetic participant, and was often included as a club's only Hispanic member. Like her husband, Mrs. Felix crossed over as no female Houstonian of Mexican heritage had previously done, in a sense becoming a trailblazer of interethnic association in the Bayou City. Also like Mr. Felix, she genuinely enjoyed her friends, contacts, and status within affluent Anglo society and, in her own way, strived to keep things Mexican visible to the Houston public in a myriad of ways.

Even before the adoption of Felix, Jr., Janie had been recruited into the Pilot Club International, an organization of executive and professional women who wanted to improve the local social, civic, and business climate. The organization demanded much of her time because it met weekly at various locations around town and plunged her into numerous activities. In these endeavors, Mrs. Felix often used the restaurant as a vehicle for service; in mid-July, 1952, for instance, the Houston newspapers covered her (as clearly the group's lone Hispanic) hosting a benefit Mexican dinner for the Pilot Club on the upstairs, outdoor terrace. Local society writer Maurine

Parkhurst (in her column "Gadabout") noted that the evening had "a foreign flavor" and was designed to raise funds for the club's charity work. "Mrs. Janie Tijerina (Mrs. Felix)," Parkhurst let it be known, was "picking up the food check." Those guests who purchased an admission ticket were entertained with a "Mexican atmosphere," complete with "strolling musicians . . . sing[ing] songs from 'South of the Border.'"[57] Although inclement weather somewhat dampened the event, the *Houston Chronicle* afterward pronounced the dinner a success, running a captioned photo showing a smiling Mrs. Felix strumming a guitar while standing between club officers Geneva Kerlin and Sonia Marvins. They were, the newspapers reported (in the words of a popular contemporary movie), "singing in the rain" from happiness over the public's response.[58]

Mrs. Felix continued to host benefit suppers for the Pilot Club at the Westheimer restaurant during the early and mid-1950s, often in the banquet room. Like her husband, she remained clearly identified with her Mexican roots in these public affairs. By 1953, she chaired the club's international relations committee. In May, 1956, the *Chronicle* again reported a Saturday night dinner given by the Pilot Club at the restaurant in honor of 125 exchange students from all over the world. Mrs. Felix, in her capacity as committee head (and no doubt because of her "Latin" background) was pictured in the *Chronicle's* features section with a young woman from Tokyo named Tashiko Nagatani to emphasize the "international aspect" of the event. The caption to the news photo stated that Nagatani and Tijerina were "international symbols." At this affair, Janie and her club awarded educational scholarships to worthy students and promoted goodwill among the different nationalities.[59]

Janie likewise became active in the predominantly Anglo Women of Rotary (also known as the "Rotary Anns")—the wives' auxiliary of Felix's downtown Rotary Club. A reflection of the men's group, the Women of Rotary was civic and philanthropic in nature. Janie first shows up on the roster in 1948, with her address listed as 1220 Westheimer, no doubt joining when Felix entered Rotary.[60]

For the 1948–49 year, with Janie as its only Mexican American participant, the Women of Rotary met every third Friday at noon at the River Oaks Country Club, the most prestigious location in town. An active member from the start, by 1952 (after the group had moved its meeting place to Pine Forest Country Club) Janie became one of the club's half-dozen directors and served on its nominating and social committees.[61]

In May, 1952, Mrs. Felix and other women Rotarians attended a Rotary convention in Mexico City in the company of their husbands. There she and Winnie Davis Mauk, wife of the president of Houston Rotary, were quoted favorably by a local newspaper. Identified as "*una simpática texana, hija de padres mexicanos*" (a genial Texan, daughter of Mexican parents), Janie told the newspaper with great gusto that while she herself was born in Texas, she adored Mexico and felt herself to be more Mexican than anything else. The reporter noted that "Juanita" traveled to their country at least three times a year and was on each occasion astonished at Mexico's continuing progress. Expressing her great affection for Mexico which sprang from her ancestry, Mrs. Felix served as the Rotary women's de facto ambassador of goodwill and bridge between the two peoples.[62]

Janie's role with the Women of Rotary continued to expand in the following years as she became active on its finance committee, which raised funds for numerous worthy causes. During the mid-1950s, she received much favorable public attention for being co-chair of its annual "games party," an event held at the Shamrock Hilton Hotel to raise money for local charity hospitals, the Rusk and Lubbock schools, Ripley House, and other welfare agencies. By 1954, Janie was the club's corresponding secretary, and she subsequently rose in office, becoming treasurer, vice president, and (for 1961–62), its president, thus capping a stellar record of service.[63]

In addition to her work with Pilot and Rotary, Janie was involved in a flurry of other civic enterprises by the early and mid-1950s, some well publicized, others not, most dealing with Mexican American issues. In 1952, for example, she was active with the March of Dimes against polio in Houston, particularly directing her efforts toward the Latino community. In April of that year, she served as cochair with Ernest Eguía (who represented LULAC Council No. 60) in staging a highly successful dance at the Pan American Night Club on North Main for the antipolio campaign. Mrs. Felix and Eguía not only marshaled the efforts of Council No. 60, but also received help for the affair from the Ladies LULAC Council No. 22, the Club International, Club Familias Unidas, Club Verde Mar, México Bello, and the Magnolia Park Mothers' Club. Some fifteen hundred people attended, danced to the music of the orchestras of Benny Flores and Claro Galván, and were entertained by a floor show of dancers from a local studio. The event raised approximately two thousand dollars for the fight against the dread disease. Mrs. Felix happily reported to the press (if perhaps a bit hyperbolically), that the occasion was the first time the "entire Latin American civic and charitable organizations of Houston have banded together, and I hope it's not the last."[64]

During these years, Janie continued to be in charge of collections from the Latin American community for the Mother's March on Polio (March of Dimes). As such, she coordinated efforts among her ethnic group much like Felix had done for the Community Chest during the late 1930s.[65]

By mid-1953, she was hard at work raising funds for other charities (some of which were separate from her husband's), including the Oblate Mothers Club, the Ladies Club of Clayton Homes, the Rusk Settlement (where she was on the board), and the Optimist Club. Along with her husband, Mrs. Felix was also known for helping Latin American boys and girls on an individual basis.[66]

On the cultural front and amid much fanfare, in October, 1953, she sponsored, publicized, and chaperoned a non-profit nine-day "Good Neighbor Tour" to Mexico, "at the request of friends." She escorted a group of forty-two Houstonians to Mexico City, Puebla, Cholula, Cuernavaca, Taxco, and Xochimilco. She designed the trip to show people the "scenic places around the Mexican capital and to explain . . . a little of the cultural past of her forefathers' country." She told one newspaper correspondent: "'I want our people to know the real Mexico . . . —not the Mexico for tourists.'"[67]

Whether planning the tour of Mexico or raising funds for her favorite causes, as the *Houston Chronicle* noted in *two* biographical articles on her in 1953, Mrs. Felix was a "born promoter" and someone who constantly worked to foster the "Good Neighbor" policy between the peoples north and south of the Rio Grande. Indeed, one of these articles (a piece written by Margaret Webb Dreyer entitled "Two Countries 'Unite' in Family") had as its theme Janie's penchant for developing such cordial relations. Dreyer contended that the "Good Neighbor" spirit was so ingrained in Mrs. Tijerina that she and Felix had, in adopting their two children, selected one from Mexico and one from the United States. The large photo that accompanied the article showed Mrs. Felix holding five-and-a-half-year-old Felix, Jr., and fifteen-month-old Janie Bell and called the trio "a living example of the 'Good Neighbor' policy." The piece insisted that the children were "being brought up in the American way and at the same time [were] benefiting from the Latin-American heritage of their parents, both native Texans." Dreyer even noted that Janie Bell, though still a baby, was bilingual, "answering questions—one syllable—in Spanish or English, as the mood dictates."[68]

Not content with simply helping her own children, Dreyer went on, Mrs. Felix recently brought a fourteen-year-old daughter of a friend from Monterrey to live in the Tijerina home and attend Houston public schools. Actually the child (named Lupita García) was a blood relative of Felix, Jr., and Mrs. Tijerina. Mrs. Felix explained to Pat Manley (author of the other 1953 *Chronicle* feature) that because she herself had to quit school early and Felix had been able to receive his education only in night school, they "enjoy[ed] giving students a chance we would [like] to have had."[69]

Even Mrs. Felix's parents served during these immediate postwar years to educate the public at large on Mexican and Mexican American culture. In early September, 1953, the *Houston Press* ran a touching article on Sóstenes and Fabiana González, whose daughter, the writer noted, was "Mrs. Felix Tijerina, beautiful wife of the Houston restaurant man."[70]

The article related how, a year previous, Mrs. González had prayed to the image of the Virgin of San Juan for the recovery of her husband as he lay near death, paralyzed and unconscious in Hermann Hospital. According to the article, doctors gave no hope of recovery but after twenty-four hours of uninterrupted prayer, Mrs. González received the good news from Janie that her husband had revived, could move his legs, and would live. The article announced that Mr. and Mrs. González, in the company of their daughter and Felix, Jr., were to make a pilgrimage to San Juan de los Lagos in Mexico, "their native land." There, at the shrine of the Virgin of San Juan, they would offer thanks for the miracle. The lengthy, sensitive piece on Mexican Catholic beliefs and practices included a photograph of the elderly, serene González couple, with Sóstenes holding an image of the Virgin of San Juan while Fabiana clutched a rosary.[71]

Often pictured by the press in the company of Anglos, Mrs. Felix seemingly received as much coverage for her activities as did her husband during these years. In a typical instance, in November, 1954, the *Houston Chronicle* ran a large photo of her sipping coffee with Dick Kruger and Mrs. Honore Nicholson at a benefit planning session for Houston's Sacred Heart Dominican College. "Mrs. Tijerina," the photo caption noted, was "chairman of ticket sales for the show."[72] Much as he sought to report on idiosyncrasies of many of Houston's prominent people (in these years, mainly Anglos), the *Post*'s George Fuermann stated in his popular column "Post Card" in April, 1955, that "Mrs. Felix Tijerina, wife of the owner of the Felix Mexican Restaurants, is extremely fond of Mexican food. Having an allergy, however, she can't touch a bit of it."[73] In June of that same year, the *Chronicle* ran a large front-page photo of a "Graduation and Good-By" supper that Mrs. Felix held at the Westheimer restaurant for Lupita García, the relative who had come to live with the Tijerinas in 1953. The caption noted that Lupita, by then sixteen years of age, had completed two years of study at Woodrow Wilson Elementary School and was being feted in preparation for her return to her hometown (Villa de Juárez) near Monterrey. The photograph showed Mrs. Felix, Wilson School principal Mildred Smith, and a smiling Lupita, who, the paper emphasized, "now . . . speaks, reads and writes . . . [English] . . . like a native," clearly the reason for her having come to school under the Tijerinas' auspices.[74]

While she publicized her Mexican roots and extended herself in many ways to Houston's Mexican Americans, friction often existed between Janie and members of that community. Most local Latin Americans admired Felix for his humility, humanity, and good works and acknowledged his wife's assistance; however, some of them felt that when Janie involved herself with Hispanic organizations she seemed to want things run exactly as she wanted them to be, with little room for compromise. They remember her frequently proving difficult to deal with, short-tempered, and sharp-tongued in her criticism of their efforts. Often, they recall, she chided them for "segregating themselves" from the rest of society within their own organizations. Other times, they felt her to be overly picky and moody when dealing with their views. It seemed to more than a few of them that Janie acted as if she were "better" than other Latinos, that she had "risen above" the others and now rubbed elbows with important people in the Anglo world. For them, her demeanor and behavior stood in contrast to Felix's humble nature, and, when her prickly moods became blatant, proved embarrassing to Felix, or so some of his close friends recall. She, on her part, felt that certain members of Mexican American society—especially from its middle and "upper" classes whom she derisively called "*españoles*"—could be two-faced, insincere, snobbish, envious, and prone to slight people whom (like she in her younger years) they viewed as their "inferiors." Caught in one of her more critical moments, Mrs. Felix could even be known to tell intimates that she did not particularly like Mexican Americans, although her many worthy efforts on their behalf and her multitude of Latino friends belied such occasional exaggeration. In short, Janie and a portion of the community held strong reservations about the other. As we shall see, Mrs. Felix was especially harsh in her views of LULAC after her husband reemerged as a leader of that group in 1954.[75]

The conflicts notwithstanding, Mrs. Felix, a most complex woman, maintained a high civic profile with her many activities during this period, which brought even more positive attention to Felix. She recalled that she and her husband found themselves so busy with their various organizations and causes that they barely had time to greet one another.[76]

During these immediate postwar years Felix Tijerina—with his wife playing an indispensable role in his advancement—had immersed himself in a host of Anglo civic activities as well as demonstrated himself as a quintessential Houston entrepreneur and family man. These humanitarian endeavors portrayed him (and, by inference, Mexican character) in extremely positive terms and placed issues facing Mexican Americans in front of mainstream society. His example of participation with Anglos was there for everyone to see. His name and image seemed to be constantly in the public eye as Houston's most renowned Latin American, someone who, in the words of his friend "Wrecker" Olshan, was "always doing something nice." Tijerina's stellar public involvement with Anglo organizations went hand in hand with his simultaneous activity within the Latin American community and its groups, which is the focus of the following chapter.

FIGURE I. The one-storied *sillar* and stucco structure directly across from the *plaza* of General Escobedo, Nuevo León, identified by local oral tradition as the house of Rafael (and Feliberto) Tijerina. The slope of the immense *Cerro Del Topo Chico* in the left background. Photo by author, 1999

FIGURE 2. Felix Tijerina, ca. 1920s. This earliest known portrait of Tijerina probably dates from his time as a waiter at the Original Mexican Restaurant. Courtesy Tijerina Papers, Houston Metropolitan Research Center, Houston Public Library. Photo by García

FIGURE 3. Felix Tijerina and Janie González on a date at Hermann Park, Houston, Texas, ca. late 1920s. Courtesy Tijerina Papers, Houston Metropolitan Research Center, Houston Public Library

FIGURE 4. Felix Tijerina standing on the front porch of his first Felix Mexican Restaurant, 1220 Westheimer, Houston, Texas, ca. late 1937. Courtesy Tijerina Papers, Houston Metropolitan Research Center, Houston Public Library

FIGURE 5. Private Felix Tijerina, U.S. Army Air Corps, ca. 1942–43. Courtesy Tijerina Papers, Houston Metropolitan Research Center, Houston Public Library

FIGURE 6. Five friends in *Club México Bello,* ca. late 1940s.
Left to right: Ramón Fernández, Leo "Chato" Reynosa, Phil Montalbo,
Félix H. Morales, and Felix Tijerina. Courtesy Tijerina Papers,
Houston Metropolitan Research Center, Houston Public Library

FIGURE 7. Felix Tijerina and Houston dignitaries fete Mayor Félix González Salinas of Monterrey at the Rice Hotel, 1947. *Left to right:* two unidentified men, Houston Mayor Pro-Tem Phil Hamburger, Mayor Salinas, Tijerina, and R. E. "Bob" Smith, chair of the Texas Good Neighbor Commission and Tijerina's fellow Rotarian. Courtesy Tijerina Papers, Houston Metropolitan Research Center, Houston Public Library

FIGURE 8. Felix Mexican Restaurant, 904 Westheimer, Houston, Texas, 1948. Courtesy Tijerina Papers, Houston Metropolitan Research Center, Houston Public Library

FIGURE 9. Felix Tijerina and faithful Mingo Villarreal around the opening of Felix Mexican Restaurant, 904 Westheimer, Houston, Texas, 1948. Courtesy Tijerina Papers, Houston Metropolitan Research Center, Houston Public Library

FIGURE 10. Felix Mexican Restaurant, 5821 Kirby Drive (at Kirby and Dunstan Road) in the Village, Houston, Texas, 1952. Courtesy Tijerina Papers, Houston Metropolitan Research Center, Houston Public Library

FIGURE 11. Felix and Janie Tijerina greet customers on opening day of their Felix Mexican Restaurant, 5208 Richmond Road in Bellaire, Texas, late November, 1956. Longtime employee Geneva Harper is leaning over table at far right. Courtesy Tijerina Papers, Houston Metropolitan Research Center, Houston Public Library

FIGURE 12. Felix and Janie Tijerina with Dr. Logan H. Wilson, president of the University of Texas, at the 1955 Alba Club Award ceremony naming Felix as the state's Outstanding Latin American for 1954. Courtesy Tijerina Papers, Houston Metropolitan Research Center, Houston Public Library

FIGURE 13. Janie Tijerina *(center)* as she appeared "singing in the rain" in the *Houston Chronicle* with fellow Pilot Club members Geneva Kerlin *(left)* and Sonia Marvins *(right)* at the group's July, 1952, benefit fund raiser. Courtesy Tijerina Papers, Houston Metropolitan Research Center, Houston Public Library

FIGURE 14. Felix Tijerina with his children, Felix Tijerina, Jr., and Janie Bell Tijerina, ca. late 1950s. Courtesy Tijerina Papers, Houston Metropolitan Research Center, Houston Public Library

FiGURE 15. Federal District Judge Joe Ingraham in 1954, who presided over Felix Tijerina's suit for a declaratory judgment. Courtesy *Houston Press* Collection, Houston Metropolitan Research Center, Houston Public Library

FIGURE 16.
John J.
Herrera,
Houston
attorney,
LULAC leader,
and Tijerina
rival, ca. 1950s.
Houston's
Mayor Oscar
Holcombe is
seated behind
Herrera.
Courtesy
Herrera
Papers,
Houston
Metropolitan
Research
Center,
Houston
Public Library

FIGURE 17. Trustees of the LULAC Council No. 60 clubhouse.
Standing, left to right: Gabriel Ramírez, Philip Montalbo, Felix Tijerina,
Sammie Alderete, Ernest Eguía, and Arnold Quintero. *Seated, left to right:*
Alfred J. Hernández and Gilbert Gómez, 1955. Courtesy Tijerina Papers,
Houston Metropolitan Research Center, Houston Public Library

FIGURE 18. Senator Lyndon B. Johnson and Felix Tijerina with Alfredo G. Garza and Police Sergeant José Davila *(front seat, left to right)* in front of the Hamilton Hotel at the LULAC National Convention in Laredo, June 28, 1958. Courtesy Lyndon B. Johnson Library

FIGURE 19. Felix Tijerina meets with Chicago LULACs at Chicago
Midway Airport, August 22, 1958. *Left to right:* Sal García, Tijerina,
Tacho Alderete, and LULAC's energetic national organizer Val
Hernández. Courtesy Tijerina Papers, Houston Metropolitan
Research Center, Houston Public Library

FIGURE 20. Governor Price Daniel signs an official proclamation for
LULAC week, ca. late 1950s. *Left to right:* Tony Campos, Governor Daniel,
Felix Tijerina, and Felix Salazar, Jr. Courtesy Tijerina Papers, Houston
Metropolitan Research Center, Houston Public Library

Figure 21. Officers and Directors of Surety Savings Association, Houston, Texas, June, 1965. Vice President Felix Tijerina seated fifth from left. This photograph appeared in the *Houston Post* and may have been the final image of Tijerina in the media during his lifetime. Courtesy Gittings and Felix Tijerina, Jr.

Figure 22. Felix Tijerina, genial restaurateur, optimistic capitalist, and civic leader, as many of his friends and admirers would have remembered him, 1961. Courtesy *Houston Press* Collection, Houston Metropolitan Research Center, Houston Public Library

CHAPTER 6

SIEMPRE HACIENDO POR LA RAZA

FELIX TIJERINA AND LATIN

AMERICAN GROUPS, 1950−1956

Even as he hobnobbed with his prominent Anglo friends at the restaurant's Banquet Room, in Rotary, the Variety Boys Club, in the Housing Authority, and in other endeavors, Felix Tijerina illustrated his ongoing balance between Anglo and Latin ventures by participating in Mexican American organizations. He continued to work with El Club Cultural Recreativo México Bello, his most lasting, perhaps favorite, "Mexican" organization. In addition, he helped to direct a newly formed group called the Emergency Relief Committee for Cancer Patients' Aid. Most significantly, he rejoined the League of United Latin American Citizens in 1954. His subsequent activities within LULAC carried his name beyond the confines of Houston, across Texas, and to many other parts of the United States as well. Tijerina also spearheaded an apparently futile attempt during these years to unify the various Latin organizations in the city, thus trying his hand at something that remained an elusive goal among Mexican Houstonians over the decades. Moreover, on an individual basis Tijerina counseled and provided personal assistance to many Latin Americans young and old in his never-ending quest to better the condition of *la raza*.

CLUB MÉXICO BELLO

After Felix had resigned from the presidency of México Bello in 1949, he remained true to his promise of returning to the ranks of regular membership and served on the club's festivities committee. In the fall of 1952, Felix made mainstream news with México Bello when the club announced that it had initiated a plan to build "a casino and Mexican cultural center" that would "serve the city's Latin-American population and their non-Latin friends." As contemplated, the center would cost approximately fifty thousand dollars. A México Bello arrangements committee chaired by Phil Montalbo and consisting of Tijerina, Chato Reynosa, and Félix H. Morales scheduled an initial fund-raising event for building the facility. The committee planned to bring to Houston the "International Review" of Eduardo Martínez of San Antonio, a troupe that featured musicians, dancers, and singers from the various regions in Mexico. A photograph in the *Houston Chronicle* accompanying the September announcement of these plans showed Tijerina and Montalbo clad "in Mexican festive costumes" (and both wearing large, ornate *sombreros*), enthusiastically discussing their plans at a meeting of the committee. The show took place on Sunday evening, October 12, at the City Auditorium, but the event received little media coverage. Apparently, the club's plans for building the casino and cultural center fizzled and its intention to contribute something tangible came to naught.[1]

Although it continued to be an elegant reminder of the Mexican presence in the Bayou City during these years, México Bello (no doubt in Tijerina's mind) still suffered from the problems he had complained about in the late 1940s. Its program of events for 1953 (planned at a meeting at Felix's restaurant), for example, was mainly social in nature, consisting of a benefit supper, a *velada literaria* (literary program), and five dances.[2] Although Tijerina enjoyed these affairs, their social focus did little to provide for the well-being of the community at large. As a businessman who wanted his efforts to produce more accomplishments, he turned to Anglo organizations with better resources to aid the Hispanic population. The contrast between the results of México Bello's October 12 event and the Cantinflas Production by the Variety Boys Club two months later testified to the difference.

Regardless of México Bello's limited impact, Felix remained an active member along with his best, oldest friends. He could not attend its meetings as regularly as he may have wanted, but he continued to support the group financially and always enjoyed its dances and social functions.[3]

As an essential sidebar to the above discussion, it was through one of his most enduring México Bello buddies—Félix Morales—that Tijerina met

Benito Flores, a Monterrey businessman who would rank among Tijerina's closest friends south of the border. A colleague of Morales in the mortuary industry, Flores co-owned and directed Funerales Modernos, a prominent Monterrey funeral home. Morales had introduced the two men during one of his and Tijerina's regular trips to that city, and the Tijerinas quickly became close to Flores and his wife Isabel. Emblematic of this relationship, in May, 1951, amid much Monterrey press coverage, Felix and Janie were the official padrinos at a ceremony "baptizing" a new, luxurious hearse obtained by Flores and his business. Captured by a feature photo and article in the society pages of Monterrey's newspaper *El porvenir,* Janie cracked an obligatory bottle of champagne on the shiny Cadillac's front grille, as her husband, Benito and Isabel Flores, and an impressive crowd looked on in good cheer. Like México Bello, this friendship with Flores (which lasted until Tijerina died) represented yet another plank in Felix's internal bridge to Mexico and an expression of his almost seamless bicultural posture.[4]

EMERGENCY RELIEF COMMITTEE
FOR CANCER PATIENTS' AID

Much as they did in the Houston Junior Forum's Community House, Tijerina and Albino Torres teamed up during the early and mid-1950s in another major effort to bring succor to Latin Americans, but, in this case, it was in the field of health care. By at least 1951, Torres served as chairman and Tijerina vice chairman of the board of directors of the Emergency Relief Committee for Cancer Patients' Aid. The committee was designed to assist cancer patients who were not hospitalized and financially unable to help themselves.

To raise money, the committee held a very successful benefit dance, Mexican buffet supper, and floor show at the Crystal Ballroom of the Rice Hotel in late September, 1951 (probably its first major fund raiser). Fellow Rotarian and local radio personality Fred Nahas served as the evening's master of ceremonies. Of course, Albino Torres's Orchestra provided the music. Janie Tijerina was in the middle of its preparations. The *Houston Post* noted that she was one of the people "who worked to make the affair a success." The *Houston Chronicle* pointed out that "Mr. Tijerina met most of the expenses (for the event) personally," a role that Felix often played in the work of this and other organizations.[5]

The committee came to operate La Posada (The Inn), a convalescent home that was free of charge for Mexican American outpatients receiving cancer treatment at M. D. Anderson Hospital, Houston's emerging cancer treatment facility. In addition to Tijerina and Torres, by 1954, the committee's directors and its executive board included Mrs. John J. (Liz) Ruíz and Mrs. William (Emma) Knorbin as well as prominent Anglo women and social workers, a mixture of talent and charitable types similar to those who ran the Community House.

La Posada was a two-storied frame house in the Fourth Ward designed to provide a comfortable environment for the sufferers and their families. The committee apparently received operating funds for the facility from various sources (including Tijerina). The committee's annual benefit fiesta, which it called "An Evening in Mexico," was publicized around town. Felix was always recognized for his involvement in promoting this event and support for the committee and its guest house.[6]

AN ATTEMPT AT UNITY AMONG
LATIN AMERICAN ORGANIZATIONS

Simultaneous with their tenure on the Emergency Relief Committee for Cancer Patients' Aid, Tijerina and Albino Torres called together a series of meetings among Houston's Latin American groups. Held during the spring and summer of 1954 at Felix's banquet room, these gatherings initially explored "what the various clubs, in a cooperative manner, [could] do to improve certain social problems . . . facing the community." By the third meeting (held in mid-May), each organization was asked to send three representatives to take part in the discussions, present ideas, and establish a program for the public good.[7]

Unfortunately, as the meetings progressed that summer, attendance was poor and included participants from only seven organizations—LULAC Council No. 60, Ladies LULAC Council No. 22, the Emergency Relief Committee, the American G.I. Forum (a veterans' organization begun in Corpus Christi in 1948), Club Verde Mar, Sociedad Familias Unidas (the last two being social clubs), and Bosque Xochilt #2019 (a Masonic lodge). This *junta* represented only a portion of the several dozen groups that existed in the city at that time.

Apparently, this "umbrella organization" had run its course by the end of the summer. Such an outcome must have again reminded Felix (as if he needed a reminder) of the difficulties that Houston Mexican American groups had in mustering resources sufficient to address the problems of their community. However, these gatherings added to the growing reputation, at least in the minds of many Anglos, that Felix's banquet room served as a center of Mexican American "politics," a place where Latin American activists discussed and promoted their community's welfare.[8]

By then, too, Tijerina had been convinced to pick up the cudgel in the other Latin American organization that had, to one degree or another, attracted his attention for many years. By early 1954, he would add participation in it to his crowded schedule and image as civic leader. In turn, he would help shape that group's direction for the remainder of the decade.

BACK IN LULAC

By late 1953 and early 1954, Felix had returned to the LULAC fold, ending his six-year hiatus, and he did so by going straight to higher office. In truth, his heart had never been far from the organization; even though Tijerina had dropped out in the late 1940s, he helped Council No. 60 whenever he could. Regardless, Tijerina had to be persuaded to reenter LULAC by some of its younger adherents.

As much as anything, the partial eclipse of John J. Herrera helped to pave the way for Felix's return. Herrera had made it to the top of the organization by 1952, having been elected national president. He had worked hard during his term and spent a great deal of his own money in pursuit of making LULAC a more visible organization. But when he ran for reelection to the national presidency at the 1953 annual convention in Santa Fe, he was defeated by Albert Armendariz of El Paso. Though Herrera remained a force in the organization (and active in Council No. 60), his time in the national presidency had passed. For all the good he did, Herrera—a complex individual—could also rub people the wrong way. Besides that, LULAC had a way of ignoring, even slighting, its past national presidents, especially if they had lost the election to their successor. This tendency to be ignored by subsequent leadership in the organization extended to other past national officers as well. As one important LULAC member commented at the time: "There [was] nothing as dead as a has-been in National LULAC."[9]

Meanwhile, younger Houston LULAC stalwarts such as Sammie Alderete and Alfred J. Hernández had been working on Felix to rekindle his interest in the league. Sammie Alderete knew Tijerina from their work together with the Junior Forum; though much younger than Felix, Alderete saw the good the restaurateur had done in that program and others. He had sat at his table many times in the banquet room during the Community House board meetings where Felix fed them as they discussed juvenile delinquency problems and other difficulties faced by Latins.

Sammie's conversations with Felix at the restaurant invariably centered on how much Sammie felt they needed Felix in LULAC. Felix would speculate on LULAC's potential; if the organization could just have a million members paying dues of one dollar per month, he reasoned aloud to Alderete, the money would work wonders within the Latin community—initiating educational programs, hiring lobbyists in state capitals and Washington, D.C., and so forth. But to do this, he told his young friend, LULAC needed a well-promoted, aggressive expansion program.[10]

No doubt Alderete was among several individuals who helped to coax Tijerina. But the man who played the most crucial role in getting him back in LULAC and shaping his future role in the organization was Alfred J. Hernández.[11]

There seemed to have been an affinity—a natural chemistry—between Tijerina and Hernández which sprang from many similarities and a mutual identification. Like his relationship with John J. Herrera, Felix cannot be properly understood without examining Alfred Hernández and the nature of their association.

Born in 1917 in Mexico City, Alfredo José Hernández had immigrated north as a small child with his parents during the early 1920s, fleeing the turmoil of the revolution. The family lived for a short while among kinfolk in Monterrey; within months, however, they continued north via Laredo to Houston (again to join relatives) in 1921, settling in the Fifth Ward, a neighborhood that consisted of Italians, Germans, Mexicans, and other ethnic nationalities. His father, a tradesman, opened a shop to repair watches and shoes.[12]

Displaying a keen intelligence, Hernández went through Houston public schools and graduated from Jeff Davis High School in 1935. Along the way he became well known around the Mexican neighborhoods as an assertive, vocal, and handsome young man. During his high school days of the 1930s, he organized local Hispanic teenagers into a group called El Club Tenochtitlán through which these young people tried to show Houston the beauty of Mexican culture with its songs, dances, and other traditions. Thoroughly bicultural, Hernández—through tutoring by a supportive, local Anglo voice teacher—studiously perfected his English to the point where he displayed no Spanish accent. He likewise continued to develop the Spanish he had learned at home so that he was an impressive public speaker in both languages. He became so fluent and well presented that he landed a part-time job as a radio announcer.[13]

After graduating from high school, Hernández married and established his own family watch repair shop. With the outbreak of World War II, he was drafted into the United States Army and, though he was still a Mexican citizen, served as an infantryman and interpreter in North Africa and rose in rank to sergeant. The military made him an American citizen while he was stationed in Sicily. After four years in the service (including a stint in France), Hernández rotated back to the United States, where he was mustered out in San Antonio in 1947.[14]

Back in Houston, Hernández resumed his work as a watchmaker and again did radio announcing, hosting a program that played Mexican music and featured live Spanish-language talent. Through continual encouragement from his mentor Dr. John J. Ruíz, Hernández attended the University of Houston and the South Texas College of Law, from which he graduated in 1953, becoming one of Houston's few Mexican American attorneys.[15]

Alfred Hernández had first met Tijerina during the 1930s but had become associated with him in LULAC during the late 1940s when he returned from Europe and joined the organization. Indeed, Hernández had been the corresponding secretary who had penned the letter that offended Felix in 1946. He had also served as council president when Felix was vice president and had remained active after the older man fell away from the group. But it was beginning with Felix's reentry into the organization in late 1953 that Hernández became one of Tijerina's best friends and his closest confidant in LULAC. Their similar Mexican backgrounds, immigrant experiences, desire for respectable achievement, rootedness in Houston, and enjoyment of their camaraderie seemed to bind them together. Besides that, Hernández had been schooled by his elders to show deference to someone older and as distinguished as Tijerina. At the same time, Felix respected Hernández's educational achievement, his refinement, dignified bearing, ease at public speaking, and prudent judgment. The two men became so close that Tijerina and Mrs. Felix became the *padrinos* to one of Hernández's sons.[16] Perhaps in this younger man, Felix saw something that he himself might have been had he only had the opportunity for a formal education. As his own career peaked in the 1950s and 1960s, Hernández in many respects would become the third most recognizable leader among Houston's Mexican American community, behind only Tijerina and John J. Herrera.

Over a period of a few months, Hernández frequently visited the restaurant on Westheimer in the evening after closing his law office, and he implored Felix to rejoin LULAC, insisting that the organization needed him but that, in turn, he needed LULAC. Hernández especially stressed the good that Tijerina could do in the field of Latin American education with LULAC as his base. With Tijerina's financial resources and contacts with influential members of the Anglo community, Hernández told his friend, they could work wonders. He also stated that their plan would be to run Felix immediately for Texas regional governor and elevate him to the national presidency as soon as they could.

Hernández also interceded with John Herrera. The latter was fresh from his clash with Tijerina over the juvenile delinquency episode as well as his own defeat for LULAC national president, but Herrera always had the good of the organization at heart, and Hernández (a fellow attorney) helped to persuade him not to oppose Felix's reentry and bid for high office. Besides, John never disliked Felix to the extent that Felix disliked John.[17]

By the end of 1953 Hernández and the others were well on their way to having Tijerina's active participation in the council's efforts. At the December 3, 1953, meeting of Council No. 60, Hernández reported that "Felix Tijerina, the well known restaurater [sic] who is very much interested in the education of our young Latin-American and Anglo-American Students," had met with the committee that was planning the group's annual fund-raising fiesta and had offered a new automobile to be given away at the affair. Hernández related that Tijerina also suggested that LULAC team with the Variety Boys Club to cosponsor a big event called the Noche Mexicana, the expenses of which Tijerina planned to underwrite to the tune of seven thousand dollars.[18]

Felix was soon reinstated as a member in the organization because on January 15–17, 1954, he became one of eight delegates from Council No. 60 to attend the LULAC regional (i.e., state) convention held in Fort Worth. With Hernández heading the delegation and managing a strenuous campaign by the Houston delegates, Tijerina was unanimously elected as the LULAC regional governor for Texas (to succeed Austin attorney Frank Pinedo). His term was to begin in June.[19]

Now that he had committed himself to the organization once again, Tijerina became a conspicuously active state leader as well as a participant in local council affairs. The February, 1954, issue of the LULAC News, the group's official organ, commemorated the organization's silver anniversary. Among other items, it carried a feature article entitled "An Outstanding LULAC: Felix Tijerina," which introduced him to members everywhere. Probably written before he was elected regional governor and designed to promote him to office, the story spotlighted Felix as someone who "has led the Lulacs and his friends in the fight against oppression and exploitation of the underprivileged minority groups." Noting that he was "as generous as he is practical," it described Felix as a self-made businessman and gave his credo for success: "Work hard, help yourself, help others, be a good citizen, take an active part in community affairs, and attend a church of your choice regularly." Most important, the story drove home his conviction that mastering English and universal education represented the way for Latin Americans "to take their place in the community as leaders." This belief, so eagerly expressed by the article, would become the guiding tenet for one of Tijerina's two major contributions within LULAC in the coming years.[20]

Reporting on the twenty-fifth year festivities that took place in the Bayou City during February, the Houston Chronicle and the LULAC News ran identical photographs of Felix (as governor-elect) with other LULAC dignitaries attending Council No. 60's celebratory formal dance at the Crystal Ballroom of the Rice Hotel. By June, when Felix assumed office, the News noted his enthusiasm "when he talks of the plans for making his tenure of office . . . something to be remembered. Brother Tijerina is bursting at the seams with ideas of organization and promotion." That same issue (which was sponsored by the Houston council) featured him not only as regional governor-elect, but also as "an outstanding philanthropist" by running another photo of him contributing one hundred dollars to the Council No. 60 scholarship fund.[21]

Before Felix could firmly set a course in his new position, however, an issue arose involving LULAC that must have caused him no little concern. Beginning in June, 1954 (in the California-Arizona region), Attorney General Herbert Brownell, Jr., and the United States Immigration and Naturalization Service (INS) launched "Operation Wetback," an effort to rid the nation of the many undocumented Mexican workers who had entered the country since World War II. A stringent enforcement of immigration laws already in place, Operation Wetback was highly publicized for a short time in advance so as to encourage Mexican workers to leave. In July, amid fanfare, the operation began in Texas. A dragnet and massive deportations across the nation lasted through the year, resulting in the removal of more than one million people to Mexico. In many respects the program resembled the repatriation efforts of the Great Depression.[22]

In early July, INS officials in Texas notified such groups as the American G.I. Forum and LULAC of the impending drive and earnestly sought their help, on the grounds that "wetbacks" hurt Mexican Americans economically. The American G.I. Forum, in conjunction with the Texas State Federation of Labor, had already expressed its opposition to "wetbackism" and responded favorably to this overture. LULAC, through its national president, Frank Pinedo, also firmly endorsed Operation Wetback. In a column entitled "Wetback Round-up Needs Support of LULAC," the LULAC News of July, 1954, "whole-heartedly" supported the drive. Pinedo had just assumed the presidency and echoed the organization's stated opposition to undocumented labor. A conscientious young Austin attorney and also general counsel for the American G.I. Forum, he articulated LULAC's position when he noted that "wetback" laborers in Texas "created a health problem in the valley" and lowered wages for resident farm workers. LULAC likewise launched a "vigorous campaign" in favor of two "anti-wetback" bills introduced in June in the United States Senate, one of which would have penalized employers for hiring "aliens."

But LULAC's position on the issue of "illegal" residency of Mexicans in the United States was, as might be expected, more complex than its endorsement of "Operation Wetback" suggests. Through a resolution introduced by Albert Armendariz of El Paso, Pete Tijerina of San Antonio, and Phil Montalbo of Houston (the latter Felix's close associate), the LULAC national convention in June condemned the "[w]holesale importation of Wetback laborers in that wetback laborers are a amenace [sic] to the social, economic and educational well being of American born citizens of Mexican descent"; it also restated LULAC's standing opposition to the McCarran Immigration Law of 1952. The resolution condemned the law as "oppressive and unjust" because it allowed the deportation of people who, although they may have "entered the country illegally, . . . have established residence." In particular, the resolution condemned "the deportation of parents of American born children and parents of members of the Armed forces." The resolution proposed revision of the McCarran Act to exclude from deportation and allow for the legal residence of those "aliens" who entered the country after 1924 but had established themselves through marriage to "an American wife," had American-born children, were law-abiding, or had maintained steady employment.[23]

In its feature editorial in the August, 1954, issue, the LULAC *News* again voiced the group's staunch support of Operation Wetback, stating that its position sought to avoid exploitation of the undocumented as well as to upgrade the wages of Mexican American workers. The editorial concluded: "We can only respect the courageous spirit of men who leave their own country to tackle hardships and uncertainties in the hope that they may improve the material lot of their families. . . . But we do feel that their struggle will always be a losing one by its very nature."[24]

Clearly, Felix personified the difference between Mexicans whom LULAC considered to be "wetbacks" and those who had "established residence." Yet, he and his presence within the organization also silently pointed out an inherent degree of contradiction in LULAC's position on those undocumented who were targets of Operation Wetback, people who, after all, shared ethnicity with LULAC membership. While supporting the forceful exclusion of a class of "aliens" in their midst, LULAC unknowingly (at least to most) had someone as its Texas regional governor who, by some people's yardstick, could be viewed as an "illegal." While he fit LULAC's definition of the person who had "established" himself, Tijerina's early life, if honestly revealed, had resembled that of the undocumented worker. His younger years represented a version of the "hardships and uncertainties" of someone who had come from Mexico (though publicly he claimed otherwise) and did not have United States citizenship. Though herculean, his "struggle" had been anything but "a losing one," and he had not been a burden to society.

The contradiction of Felix's place in the organization was further manifested when one recalls that LULAC stressed the American citizenship of its regular membership, with noncitizens allowed to be only "Participating Members." The whole intent of LULAC's use of the term "Latin American"—which reached its peak in these postwar years—had always been to differentiate themselves from "Mexicans." (At the January, 1955, LULAC state convention, the delegates, apparently with Felix presiding, would adopt a resolution which "condemn[ed] state officials who identif[ied] Spanish-Speaking Texans as 'Mexicans' on state forms.")[25]

In fact, with Felix's legal status far from settled, in March of 1954, just a few months before Operation Wetback commenced, he had filed suit in federal court to establish his American citizenship through a declaratory judgment. When the INS program was in full swing and with LULAC falling into line, Tijerina was engaged in a legal battle to have himself declared a native-born American by the court—his final attempt to disguise the true facts of his nativity. Although his lawsuit arose from events not directly related to Operation Wetback and will be the subject of the next chapter, as we shall see in great detail Felix's citizenship troubles between 1954 and 1956 were highly publicized, at least in Houston.

As of June, 1954, Felix may well have felt a personal dilemma over LULAC's support of Operation Wetback, which not only transpired at a time when he was trying to "settle" his own citizenship status but also resembled one he had escaped in 1940. It was part of an internal dilemma of a Mexican American trying to make it in the Anglo world.

Perhaps any reservations Felix may have had about Operation Wetback were assuaged by LULAC's position on the presence of other Mexicans who had long-term "established residence" in the United States, something he could legitimately have claimed. For LULAC, and perhaps for Felix, that would have made him different from the thousands who would be rounded up and sent back to Mexico.

Apparently, Tijerina responded to Operation Wetback with silence. Neither Frank Pinedo nor Alfred Hernández could later recall him voicing an opinion on the program one way or another. Felix always refrained from criticizing the federal government even if he had been disposed to question its actions. Perhaps his pending lawsuit in a Houston federal court at the time reinforced this silence. On the other hand, vocal support of the operation by someone whose "legal status" was being adjudicated might have appeared unseemly. Regardless of his motives, Tijerina apparently made no comment.[26] As was his usual policy, Tijerina would use his position as a LULAC official to address other important issues, ones of a less controversial nature.

Felix's tenure as Texas regional governor for LULAC lasted from June, 1954, until June, 1956. (He was reelected for his second term at the state convention in San Antonio in January, 1955.) During his two terms, Felix mainly emphasized expansion of the organization and education, although initially he also pushed for social welfare efforts among Latins. As regional governor-elect in early 1954, he tried (apparently unsuccessfully) to persuade the district convention meeting in Baytown to assess members an extra seventy-five cents monthly to fund more student scholarships and to help pay for eight social workers who would be stationed around the state to help Latinos. Tijerina had to report to Council No. 60 that his idea received thumbs down by local councils from Edna, San Antonio, and Corpus Christi, but, he added, he would work to convince these opponents that social workers' services would greatly benefit their people. At the national convention in Austin, Texas, in June of that year, however, he succeeded in having the delegates adopt the so-called Felix Tijerina Amendment, which provided for the various regions (states) of LULAC to establish special educational "funds" for students not already provided for by LULAC scholarship monies. These proposed special educational funds apparently were to be raised by donations from outside sources and by an optional dues increase of seventy-five cents a month, if the various LULAC regions chose to do so. This Tijerina Amendment went nowhere. It failed to be ratified by the required number of local councils, apparently because of the reticence among rank-and-file LULACs to raise their dues. Still, it represented Tijerina's first attempt to have LULAC be more systematic in underwriting education, and it won widespread recognition for Felix within the organization as a man focused upon education.[27]

Felix's view of education as central to the LULAC mission was evident from the start of his governorship—specifically, education designed to ensure that Mexican Americans fit into American society. The article "An Outstanding LULAC: Felix Tijerina" in the February, 1954, *LULAC News* emphasized that he believed in education as "the weapon against ignorance and discrimination." Somewhat nebulous in its message, however, this feature carefully avoided placing the blame on mainstream society for these ills. It conveyed the idea that Felix believed that the need for "[u]niversal education" among people of "Latin extraction" meant that they must "master the English language."[28]

By at least mid-1955, not long after being reelected Texas regional governor, Felix toured the state in the company of brother LULACs Alfred Hernández, Phil Montalbo, and others to explain his educational plan. In Laredo a newspaper reported that Tijerina and his entourage met with the local LULAC council and national president Oscar Laurel (a Laredoan and the man whom Felix and Council No. 60 had supported to defeat Frank Pinedo that summer). Felix told them that "now that the fight against segregation and discrimination has been won," LULAC should "encourage and promote assimilation through a huge education program." Like many of their generation,

Felix, Al Hernández, and their LULAC lieutenants continued to be alarmed with the low level of Mexican American education. Specifically, Felix and his fellow LULAC members were concerned that Spanish-speaking students often had to repeat initial grades because of their difficulty with English. Repeating grades put these students behind the mainstream in education, and being held back heavily contributed to their staggering drop-out rate.[29]

Felix's concern for some sort of LULAC-sponsored educational program was aired in an August 8, 1955, front-page story. Written by Marie Moore for the *Houston Post,* the article was reprinted in the September issue of *LULAC News* as its "Personality of the Month" feature. In this lengthy, important biographical article, Moore noted Tijerina's belief that "English is the national language" of the United States, and when Mexican American children started school "they must understand English, or they will not be able to keep up with the other children, . . . will be embarrassed, and they will drop out of school; and unless they work very hard by themselves, they will grow up to be farm hands instead of business or professional men." For Felix, the solution was clear: "We need to see that the young children learn English before they start to school, so they can keep up with the other children and go on through high school." In a process that would "Anglicize" them, these kids, he hoped, would become professionals. (It should be added that by 1955 Felix's suit in federal court to establish his American citizenship had yet to be decided, and this situation, as we shall see in the following chapter, may well have added an intensity to his call for Mexican American assimilation through education. But the lawsuit's existence would only have added extra emphasis to his message; Tijerina had long since come to believe in preschool English training.) Felix concluded that "education is the thing. I have a dream, and . . . LULAC is working hard on it."[30]

Although in 1955 the exact nature of LULAC's proposed education program still seemed to be in flux, Tijerina advocated that the group finance it through "a road talent show" brought to each city for a special educational fund. As visualized, the "road show" would originate in San Antonio and perform in each town where a LULAC council existed. Apparently a "road show and a dance" took place in Austin and Houston, but like the Tijerina Amendment of the preceding year, the idea for a mobile talent review accomplished little or nothing toward raising money.[31]

The ideas of Tijerina and his circle for preschool English education germinated during 1955 in their conversations while traveling, at LULAC meetings, and at the restaurant; these plans would ultimately take shape as the

"Little School of the 400." But Tijerina and his fellows were not alone in advocating such programs; the push for preschool language instruction seemed to be in the air. Indeed, one such program already operated in Freeport, Texas (a town only sixty miles from Houston on the Gulf Coast), which caught their attention. In his monthly "Message from the National President" printed in the LULAC News, September, 1955, Oscar Laurel reported on a visit he and another LULAC official made to Freeport, where local educators ran a project known as La Escuelita (the little school). The Freeporters' "little school," Laurel informed his LULAC readership, sought to familiarize Spanish-speaking preschoolers with the English language, a project that the national president ringingly endorsed: "[A] more laudable project cannot be undertaken by any organization or one which aims to serve a more useful purpose." Echoing Felix's concerns, Laurel noted "the urgent need of having our young boys and girls get their feet wet, linguistically, so to speak, in order that they may be able to start school with less of a language handicap than the other school children." Laurel likewise urged the initiation of similar La Escuelita projects wherever a LULAC council existed. Stating that LULAC was the logical organization to implement such a program, Laurel promised to contact the presidents of individual councils about the feasibility of instituting such an experiment in each locale.[32]

Felix and his LULAC associates certainly knew of this effort in Freeport since the town was so near Houston.[33] They presumably saw Laurel's message on La Escuelita, as it appeared in the same issue of the LULAC News that reprinted Marie Moore's article on Felix from the Houston Post. (Alfred Hernández was Laurel's national legal advisor at the time.) Furthermore, as we shall see, the Freeport authorities who ran La Escuelita later charged that Tijerina himself had paid a call to their town along with Laurel and other LULAC officials in 1955 and had received "a thorough explanation of the program"; that visit, they claimed, had prompted Laurel's later comments and LULAC's interest in such a preschool effort. To be sure, as things played out over the four years of Tijerina's national presidency, from 1956 to 1960, Felix and his circle picked up on the spirit of Freeport's escuelita and Laurel's admonition in his LULAC News article (even naming their effort the "little school") but pushed the ideas to fruition as no one before them had.[34]

Felix's desire to spread LULAC as an organization was inseparable from his push for education. In his first message as Texas regional governor in September, 1954, Felix promised "to engage, at my own expense, a qualified man as a special organizer to cover the entire state," forming councils where none existed, and "helping our people to help themselves." At the 1955 state convention, Felix publicly pledged three thousand dollars of his own money to hire three organizers for LULAC expansion in Texas. While it is not clear how many people he employed at this time to perform this service, in early 1955 Felix brought onto his restaurant payroll full time a young LULAC activist and Baylor-educated teacher from Baytown named Tony Campos. He was hired to help Tijerina with business-related duties as well as with LULAC affairs. In many ways, Campos became his "right hand man" in LULAC, at an annual salary substantially more than the three thousand dollars Felix had promised the organization. At the national convention in mid-1955, Felix praised Campos's efforts in the Texas Panhandle, where the latter traveled to Lubbock and Levelland promoting local membership drives among adults and LULAC-sponsored "Back to School" programs for youngsters. Most important, Campos helped Tijerina, Hernández, and the others begin to formulate their plans about educating preschool Hispanic children.[35]

At this time, competition existed between LULAC and the American G.I. Forum in their organizing efforts across Texas and elsewhere. The two groups vied with one another for prospective members and over many of the same issues. In Houston and its surrounding area, this rivalry truly became no contest at all because of Felix's presence. In April, 1955, Alfredo M. Cárdenas, chairman of Houston's struggling G.I. Forum chapter, wrote Ed Idar, Jr. (the forum's executive director in Austin), that Felix Tijerina's aggressive expansion of LULAC in the Texas Gulf Coast neutralized attempts by the forum to penetrate the region. "This man Tijerina," Cárdenas informed Idar, had allegedly put another organizer (named Gonzalo González Moya) on a salary, given him an expense account, and provided him with "a new 1955 Mercury" to work the local area. Regardless of the Houston Forumeers' hard work and energetic state leadership (such as Dr. Hector P. García and Ed Idar), Council No. 60's longstanding presence in Houston and the efforts of Tijerina, Hernández, and Herrera prevented the American G.I. Forum from ever gaining more than a toehold in the Bayou City. Cárdenas lamented that while all three of the above fellows were "very very good friends" of his and treated him "just perfectly," they had "the money and the time and us guys don't have either," making it difficult for the Houston-area forum "to stay alive."[36]

Tijerina himself traveled extensively, visiting councils around the state in such places as Harlingen in the Rio Grande Valley and Brazosport on the Gulf Coast to be present when groups installed their new officers. At a Council No. 60 meeting in February, 1955, he had even commended John Herrera for his organizing efforts in Refugio, Victoria, Freeport, and Beaumont. On February 1, Felix was one of a three-man delegation that met with Texas governor Allan Shivers in Austin when Shivers officially designated February 13–20 as "LULAC Week," thus enlisting the state's chief executive in spreading the organization's good name. As Felix told the LULAC Supreme Council (the group's national governing body) at a meeting in Pecos in September, 1955, the duty of all the members was "to sleep, talk, and preach LULAC."[37]

On a local level, Regional Governor Tijerina was active in an array of issues as a member of Council No. 60. Not oblivious to continuing discrimination (his public pronouncements notwithstanding), Felix served on a four-man committee in May, 1954—along with Mike Zepeda, Gilbert Gómez, the Reverend James Novarro, and J. G. Medellín—that persuaded a local swimming pool operator on South Main to discontinue his practice of excluding Mexican American youngsters. In March, 1955, Felix had the council establish "a permanent investigating committee" to examine all local charges of discrimination against Latin Americans, this move coming in response to an allegation that a Houston skating rink had denied entry to a couple "because they were of Mexican extraction." Typical of Felix's approach to things, as the meeting minutes state, "[t]his committee would be strictly private and all information will be kept confidential." Felix, Phil Montalbo, and Al Hernández subsequently volunteered to look into the skating rink incident.[38]

Felix likewise remained conspicuous in helping with LULAC charity functions and educational scholarship drives in Houston. In November, 1954, the colorful Houston Press columnist Andy Anderson told his readership that Felix Tijerina—"A Swell Guy"—totally underwrote LULAC Council No. 60's second annual Christmas Basket Fiesta and Dance to the tune of one thousand dollars. The gala event, held at the Houston Coliseum, featured the popular mambo bands of Henry Tovar and Eloy Pérez. It proved to be a "huge success"—with Tijerina at the microphone telling a Christmas story to the two thousand people attending—and helped to raise money for needy Latin Americans. In February, 1955, the *Houston Chronicle* ran a captioned photo showing him with Petra Cisneros, a Houstonian and national president of the Junior LULACs, "filled with enthusiasm over the 1955 goal of nine college scholarships for worthy Latin-American boys and girls." The effort had been announced at the annual LULAC anniversary banquet held that year at Felix's Westheimer restaurant.[39]

Perhaps Tijerina's most lasting material contribution to the local LULAC presence during this 1954–56 period resulted from his role in the acquisition of a permanent Council No. 60 clubhouse, something the group had never owned before. When Felix had reentered LULAC, the council still held its meetings at the Harris County Court House. With the crucial help of a $5,000 loan from Tijerina, Council No. 60 purchased (at a total price of $10,500) a two-storied stucco house at 3004 Bagby, on the southern edge of downtown. Tijerina, regional governor and the group's financial "angel," was named as one of the initial seven trustees of the new LULAC building, along with Council No. 60 stalwarts Gabe Ramírez, Gilbert Gómez, Ernest Eguía, Alfred Hernández, Sammie Alderete, and Arnold Quintero. Phil Montalbo, Tijerina's LULAC legal advisor, apparently would soon be added to this select group. Under construction contractor Alderete's direction, through fund raising and volunteer labor by Council No. 60 members, as well as with additional monetary assistance from Felix, the council handsomely remodeled the structure to include a meeting room, bar, and other facilities.[40]

On December 17, 1955, the council held the building's grand opening. Attended by LULAC national president Oscar Laurel, numerous city and county officials, and a host of area LULACs, including Tijerina and past national president John Herrera, this gala event was the first of many gatherings that would make the clubhouse a center of Mexican American civic activity in Houston. Having a clubhouse of its own represented a milestone in the development of the group, adding even more enthusiasm to its quest to have LULAC and Latin American issues more visible in Houston. Given the educational and employment programs that would soon emanate from Council No. 60, the new headquarters became one of the most historic buildings for the city's Hispanic population.

The December 17 ceremony and the entire story of the "New Houston Council Home" was reported as the cover article written by Houston LULAC Richard Ante in the January, 1956, *LULAC News*. The account touted the Houston council's role in the organization and its "can-do" spirit.

Important as well, it praised Felix Tijerina once again as a "philanthropist and humanitarian who from humble beginnings pulled himself up by his own bootstraps to become one of the outstanding businessmen of Houston"; he was a man, the article noted, who, "with a wave of his hand," could get things done.[41]

By then, Tijerina's growing publicity in LULAC had also included his claim to have been born in Texas. Although the biographical sketches and other comments on Tijerina written exclusively for the *LULAC News* had not mentioned his birthplace, Marie Moore's *Houston Post* article, which ran in the September, 1955, issue of the *LULAC News,* had broken that silence. In addition to stating Tijerina's prescription for Hispanics to fit into mainstream society through Anglicization, Moore repeated Felix's fable of being born in Sugar Land, Texas. This "fact" meant that Felix spoke with the authority of a native-born citizen, which gave further legitimacy to the archetype of Felix Tijerina as the perfect postwar Latin American. He had become a standard for aspiring Hispanics wherever the *LULAC News* circulated.[42]

Despite his high profile, Felix would not be reelected regional governor after his second term. At the convention in Corpus Christi in February, 1956, he withdrew his name from nomination when he, Hernández, and their fellow Houstonians realized that his opponent, Pete Tijerina, a popular young attorney from San Antonio, would win in the balloting. According to Alfred Hernández, Felix withdrew so magnanimously—throwing his support behind the San Antonian so as to prevent dissension—that it gained him increased stature within the organization. This move would stand Felix in good stead with LULAC delegates when he ran for national president in June of that same year.[43]

His defeat notwithstanding, Felix Tijerina had made a mark in LULAC between 1954 and 1956 as a champion of education and expansion. He had also established his image across the breadth of the organization. He would be back in an even greater leadership capacity within a matter of months.

COUNSELOR TO HIS PEOPLE

The stories that survive in Houston's Mexican American community from these years of Felix's personal, heartfelt intervention into the lives of Mexican Americans, especially young men, are too numerous to recount. Many fellows in trouble with the law sought his help; in some cases, youthful offenders worked at one of his restaurants as part of the stipulations of their parole or probation. By the mid-1950s, he was on the Rotary Club's rehabilitation committee to counsel those being released from prison. He also gave personal counseling to men who did not pay their child support, in hopes of shaping their future compliance with their obligations. Tijerina would often encounter individuals on the street whose lives he had helped to set on the right path through such efforts.[44]

Many young Mexican Americans (and older folks, too) just trying to make their way in Houston society sought Mr. Felix out for advice, something he willingly gave along with personal loans (which he always insisted they repay for a sense of responsibility), jobs, and/or help in finding employment. People from Mexico who came to Houston seeking advancement likewise got a helping hand from Felix. Some worked for him in the restaurants, where they learned under his wing. Tijerina also readily provided young people with encouragement and financial assistance to advance their education. Recollections portray him as firm, practical, kind-hearted (in a tough-minded sort of way) and sincere, often given to delivering stern commonsense lectures on getting ahead by living up to individual potential rather than being satisfied with something less. Latin Americans saw him as someone to model themselves after; many a young man expressed a desire "to be just like Mr. Tijerina," inspired by his message to go to school and/or start a business of their own.[45]

Among the more exceptional people whose progress Felix fostered in a more commercial manner was an industrious young couple named Tommy and Ninfa Laurenzo. The Laurenzos had come to Houston in 1948 and immediately established a small tortilla factory on Navigation Boulevard. Within a year (and through a local jobber), their fledgling business began to provide all the tortillas for the Felix Mexican Restaurants. Felix proved to be one of the Laurenzos' more lucrative, sustaining accounts, growing as Tijerina expanded his restaurant chain. Moreover, the Laurenzos and Tijerinas became social friends, with Tommy and Felix developing an especially tight bond. Like many young Houstonians just starting out, the Laurenzos looked up to the older man as an established Hispanic entrepreneur whom they considered to be "an excellent human being." (After Felix and Tommy died, Ninfa Laurenzo would develop Ninfa's, a celebrated chain of Mexican restaurants that in many ways became for the

1970s through 1990s what Felix Mexican Restaurants were during their heyday.)[46]

Tijerina reached out on a personal level to groups of youngsters, beyond simply supporting agencies and programs. In the postwar years, he would enlist the aid of younger acquaintances (who had risen from the local barrios to become successful professionals) into accompanying him around town to various schools that Mexican American pupils attended. Felix would address the budding scholars, using his companions as examples of what young people could be if they would not drop out, a tendency of epidemic proportions among Hispanic youngsters during that era. Tijerina confided to one of these young college-educated friends as they sped from school to school in his Cadillac that he hesitated to use himself as a role model to students because, while he was wealthy, he possessed little formal book learning and felt himself to be unpolished—in his own spicy language among men, "an uneducated son-of-a-bitch."[47]

A man of the public arena, Felix understood that money was a source of power and influence and an important ingredient for being "well connected," and he conveyed some of these life lessons to his younger associates. Alfred Hernández recalled how Tijerina attuned him early on to the wisdom of making noticeable financial contributions to the national Democratic Party, thereby obtaining recognition by political elites and invitations to important party functions. Even Felix's regular practice of carrying on his person a roll of thousand-dollar bills (as many as thirty or forty), Hernández felt, "gave him a feeling of being able to do things that ordinary people would not."[48]

Tijerina's acts of monetary aid to the working poor abounded. In one unsung case he paid a youngster's train fare to a Denver tuberculosis hospital. On another occasion he purchased an artificial leg for a needy man. Always wanting to allow folks their dignity, he gave a sizable loan to a paralyzed fellow who paid it back at fifty cents a week.[49]

More than a few people in the community who knew him in these days recalled that they felt strengthened and more secure by the thought that there was such a man as Felix Tijerina in their midst. He was a generous, concerned Latin American who had the ability to place calls on behalf of the *raza* to men like Bob Smith, Roy Hofheinz, or other representatives of the power structure.[50]

Felix's efforts to have a positive impact on the lives of young people and, for that matter, on the existence of his people as a whole, was as earnest as was his defense of the "Establishment," a paradox to be sure, but one, given his abiding faith in the system that was rewarding him handsomely, he apparently could not discern. If he did notice the contradictions, he avoided trying to deal with or resolve them publicly. Just as individuals often fail to perceive the contradictions in a structure that, in the name of opportunity and freedom, exploits the labor of many while making it possible for a few to advance beyond their wildest dreams, so Felix firmly believed that everyone could drive a Cadillac if they just went to school, worked hard, stayed straight, and did not complain too loudly. Like many middle-class Mexican Americans of his period, he was as much a captive of the chimera of America the Promised Land as his image suggested, and he held faith that everyone could share in it as he had.

"OUTSTANDING LATIN AMERICAN OF THE YEAR"

As his activity within LULAC carried Felix beyond the confines of his city, his many efforts attracted statewide acclaim during these years. In the spring of 1955, the Alba Club (*alba* being Spanish for "dawn"), an organization of Latin American students at the University of Texas at Austin, named Tijerina the outstanding Latin American in the state for 1954, "for his encouragement of the movement to advance . . . the Latin American people through education."[51]

The club, cosponsored by UT professors George I. Sánchez and Carlos E. Castañeda, held its annual banquet on April 30, 1955, at the Driskill Hotel in Austin, where the membership presented Tijerina with the award. It was a grand occasion and, in keeping with the course of his life since 1948, took place amid much publicity and fanfare. A large delegation of friends from Houston—including his sister Victoria, Alfred Hernández, Phil Montalbo, Francisco and Chencha Chaírez, District Judge Edmund Duggan and his wife, Tommy and Ninfa Laurenzo, and others—accompanied the Tijerinas to the gala affair.[52]

Judge Duggan introduced Felix to the approximately 120 people in attendance; he lauded his old friend as a warm human being who "never forgot his humble beginning or those of his extraction." Duggan's introduction echoed the well-established theme of Felix Tijerina, the Mexican American Horatio Alger ideal, successful businessman, and philanthropist. The judge reiterated at length the established message that Tijerina, born in Sugar Land, Texas, and fatherless at an early age, came up from nothing by being endowed with "a special heritage," personal "spirit," "lady fortune," and "a desire to work" (Alger's veritable Latin American Ragged Dick with pluck, luck, and work ethic). With Mrs. Tijerina holding the ladder of success as he ascended, Duggan explained, Felix had prospered because they "never lost faith" that "in this great country of ours, humble men have reached great heights." Furthermore, Felix was someone who helped his people with money, time, and effort to proselytize "the ideals of Americanism" among them so that they recognize that "in this great Country of ours" there are "opportunities that await all who have the determination, the faith and the willingness to work hard for the realization of a dream." Clearly, Duggan's speech drove the message home that by emulating Felix Tijerina, an "Outstanding Latin American"—that is, by being self-reliant, aspiring, frugal, capitalistic, married (to a supportive wife), middle class, patriotic, optimistic, regimented, and desiring to fit in and work within the structure as it existed—Mexican Americans could be part of Texas society.[53]

In his response, Felix told the young Latin American students and other guests that he disliked the words "segregation" and "discrimination" because they could be "eliminated through education." Applying his personal, cautious approach as the way for all Texas Mexicans to live, Tijerina explained: "We must ask for our rights and privileges, but we must ask for them intelligently. We must make ourselves worthy of being American, rather than just Latin-Americans."[54]

Duggan and Felix each received a standing ovation. Felix Tijerina had indeed become a symbol and paradigm of proper Latin American behavior for a significant number of people, Mexican and Anglo, during the postwar era.

During the ceremony, Mrs. Tijerina presented their gift of five hundred dollars for scholarships for outstanding Alba Club students. The newspapers in Houston, Austin, and perhaps elsewhere ran photographs of the occasion showing a beaming Felix and Janie receiving a congratulatory handshake from Dr. Logan H. Wilson, the distinguished-looking president of the university.[55] Such broader recognition and influence as a Latin American role model represented, in many respects, a culmination of this period of Felix's development and a portent of things to come.

F elix's many endeavors in the Latin American community rounded out his profile as a civic man, a generous, practical person always working for the public good. In all his civic activities he continued to display the art of public promotion, an ability that would serve him well in the important work that lay ahead for LULAC and Mexican American education.

While Tijerina was an accomplished, sincere man of many virtues worthy of emulation, he also had a problem. For he spoke from the perspective of an immigrant concealing his background, rather than as one who truly was a native-born citizen. His secret made the paradigm of Felix Tijerina as the ideal postwar Latin American less than totally genuine regardless of the efficacy of his many good works. His citizenship status (which had even come to the attention of the FBI in the mid-1950s) could only have served as another factor reinforcing his reticence to confront some of the issues with which Mexican Americans dealt. But in addition to his numerous other involvements, he waged a successful legal battle between 1953 and 1956 to "resolve" the question of his nativity, in effect keeping his image as a native-born American intact. The next chapter recounts the details of this court case.

CHAPTER 7

"IN EXILE FROM HIS NATIVE LAND"

Felix Tijerina v. Herbert Brownell, Jr.

Between September, 1953, and May, 1956, Felix's citizenship status became the subject of a series of official inquiries and court actions which finally put the matter of his nativity to rest, at least legally. Regrettably, the complete case file on Tijerina compiled by the Immigration and Naturalization Service is unavailable at this time, thereby making a full understanding of this important episode impossible. Enough is known, however, to sketch most of the events and their significance. The time and chagrin involved in Felix's legal maneuvering during these years to "prove" his native-born status made his uninterrupted schedule of other activities seem even more remarkable.

This ordeal—lasting well over two and a half years—represented an important chapter in Tijerina's life. It proved to be a continuation of the problem he had encountered with the INS in 1940, the trouble that had prompted him to obtain his delayed birth certificate. His course of action in 1953–56, however, carried his efforts to a more serious level because Tijerina ultimately resorted to the federal court system. In the end, the affair demonstrated how firmly entrenched he was in his adopted Houston surroundings, illustrated his ability to utilize the system to maintain his place in Houston society, as well as revealed the extent to which his supporters (especially his friends and admirers in the Anglo power structure) would avail themselves to protect the Bayou City's most valued Latin American citizen. It showed that people of goodwill appreciated Felix Tijerina's constructive works and his efforts to accommodate to the mainstream. Nevertheless, the incident proved to be tedious for Felix personally. It became one of the most difficult obstacles that he would hurdle in his struggle to fit in and construct his life's balance as a Mexican American.

Tijerina's final bout over this issue grew out of his attempt in 1953 to gain citizenship for his son, Felix, Jr. By law, Felix and Janie had been required to wait two years after adopting the child in Mexico (in 1948) before qualifying for adoption under Texas law; then, they had to wait another two years to apply for his American citizenship. As stipulated by law, Felix and Janie in May of 1953 apparently filed their request with the INS for permission to petition to naturalize the boy. On September 24, 1953, the Tijerinas filed the naturalization petition itself with the United States District Court in Houston.[1] The court set a naturalization hearing on Felix, Jr., for January 21, 1954, and referred the case to INS hearing examiner George Elsenbroich, apparently the same officer associated with Felix's incident in 1940.[2]

In September, 1953 (presumably at the filing of the naturalization petition), Elsenbroich questioned Felix, Sr.'s citizenship by presenting him with two crucial documents. First of all, Elsenbroich produced the application for the immigration visa that Tijerina had signed in 1925 to enter the United States; on this visa, it should be remembered from the 1940 incident, Tijerina stated that he had been born in General Escobedo, Nuevo León, on April 29, 1905. Second, Elsenbroich had a certified copy of a document which purported to be the record of the birth of a son named Feliberto Tijerina to Rafael Tijerina and Dionicia Villareal Tijerina (the same names as Felix's parents). This birth certificate further stated that the child had been born in the village of General Escobedo, Nuevo León, on April 29, 1905.[3]

Elsenbroich and the INS had possessed the 1925 document since 1940. Now, they also had obtained a copy of Felix's (*né* Feliberto) civil birth record.

Although Tijerina told Elsenbroich that he had explained the circumstances of the former document to the satisfaction of INS officer Autrey in 1940, and he stoutly denied that the birth certificate was his, Elsenbroich would not recognize that Felix, Sr., was an American citizen and declined to approve the petition to naturalize his adopted son. Instead, at the naturalization hearing on January 21, Elsenbroich recommended to the court that it continue with Felix, Jr.'s case for the purpose of making a more thorough investigation into the place of Felix, Sr.'s birth. The hearing was then reset for May 20, 1954.[4]

Even before the January hearing, INS inspector E. L. Brimberry had been assigned to investigate Felix's citizenship status. By Tijerina's account, Brimberry told him at the January 21 hearing that he did not believe that Felix was in fact a U.S. citizen, and he warned him that in the event that he left the country he would be prevented from reentering. Apparently, too, Brimberry advised (indeed urged) Tijerina to file for a petition of naturalization for himself.[5]

Disturbed by this resurrection of his citizenship problem, Felix counseled with Phil Montalbo, his lawyer for Felix, Jr.'s naturalization procedure (in addition to being his friend in LULAC and other organizations). Montalbo, a bilingual attorney, had experience with immigration and residency matters. Montalbo spoke to the INS officials, who told him that they had what they considered to be evidence showing the place where Felix was born in Mexico. When exactly they had obtained this 1905 document, or from whom, is not certain. Available INS records dealing with Felix's 1940 citizenship affair do not indicate that the agency possessed it during that earlier episode, so presumably the INS had obtained the birth record sometime later. Montalbo believed that the INS officers had actually traveled to the Monterrey region, where they had secured a typewritten copy.[6]

Evidence strongly suggests, however, that the INS officials had at least been informed of the possible existence of this 1905 document by outside sources. One can reasonably envision that the information provided to the Houston FBI office by the two "rather bitter" individuals on May 25, 1953, relative to Felix's Mexican birth, had made its way to the INS, either directly from the FBI (via interagency communication) or more likely from the two self-appointed "investigators" themselves. It seems logical to assume that in their attempt to make trouble for Tijerina, these two unnamed persons would not have stopped with the FBI, especially since Assistant U.S. Attorney William Eckhardt had made no effort to prosecute. The INS would have seemed a logical, primary agency to inform of the results of their "personal inquiries." Certainly, the timing of Felix, Jr.'s September 24 petition filing, coming as it did on the heels of the Houston Housing Authority squabble/tip to the FBI, would suggest a connection.

Community scuttlebutt named one of the possible "informants" or at least someone who supposedly supplied evidence on Tijerina's nativity. Many years later, Montalbo claimed that he suspected someone who was jealous of Felix's success (specifically, Ernest Villarreal) had told the INS of the birth record, thus providing the agency with evidence that officials could not ignore. Montalbo's assertion echoed what Janie Tijerina maintained in her recollections of the incident, namely, that Ernest Villarreal, the funeral home owner and distant cousin whom Felix had helped in the early years, had been a prime mover in this effort to embarrass her husband. She contended that the move arose because Felix had received the prestigious appointment to the Houston Housing Authority.[7]

Ernest Villarreal was well known around town, having first come to work with Felix in the 1920s. For a time he belonged to LULAC Council No. 60 and was a community activist in his own right. Apparently, he frequented the Farmers Barber Shop, a popular place among local Mexican Americans during the early 1950s. Operated by Ernest Olivares, the shop came to be more commonly called the "Pitch In" because patrons customarily contributed money to buy a bottle of liquor to share. Located at 529 Preston Avenue across from the Farmers Market, the "Pitch In" became a place where men (Felix Tijerina included) got together for conversation. There, according to one credible individual, Villarreal (in Felix's absence) related that he had known Felix in Mexico when they were boys and laughed that his cousin came from a family of *marraneros* (pig farmers) near Monterrey. This same source maintained that word in the community at the time held that Villarreal had "snitched" on his cousin, again presumably out of petty jealousy.[8]

The timing of the controversies and Ernest Villarreal's involvement against the HHA board tend to support these claims (especially Mrs. Tijerina's) linking Villarreal to the resurrection of Felix's troubles, although Villarreal's identity as a player remains based on oral reminiscences, circumstantial evidence, and inference. Whether "jealousy" or simply HHA politics played a role in this murky, sordid affair will likewise remain subject to speculation, as will the names of any conceivable informants.

Regardless of the possibility of third parties touching off Tijerina's citizenship problems in 1953, it should be added that the 1925 visa application stated the place and date of Felix's birth in Mexico. INS officers, with no outside informant, could have traced his birth to the civil records in Mexico had they chosen to do so.

At any rate, the 1905 birth record in the INS file represented a startling piece of information. As Phil Montalbo later commented, although the INS officers displayed no particular rudeness, they thought they had Felix's case "in the bag with the birth certificate."[9]

Montalbo advised Felix not to avail himself of the opportunity to naturalize himself as the immigration officials had suggested because such an action would be admitting that his mother had not told the truth when, in 1940, she had sworn that she had given birth to her son in Sugar Land. Of course, Tijerina was not disposed to make such an admission even without the advice of his friend.

Here, again, the exact sequence of events remains unclear. But in order to settle the issue, Montalbo (the lawyer claimed) traveled to the little village in Mexico, located the civil birth record of Feliberto Tijerina, and had it taken to Monterrey, where he had a photostatic copy made.

Montalbo then accompanied Felix to a meeting with the immigration officials in Houston, where, according to Montalbo's recollections, he showed that the photostatic copy varied enough from the wording of the certified typewritten copy held by the INS to have the matter dropped. In Montalbo's estimation, the issue of Tijerina's citizenship was taken care of, and he advised Tijerina that it was not necessary to pursue the matter any further.[10]

But Felix did not let the matter rest. No doubt, some of the motives that had prompted his behavior in 1940 once again moved him to action. Perhaps he suspected (or knew, as Mrs. Felix contended) that disgruntled former HHA figures had informed on him; perhaps he felt that he would be vulnerable as long as his citizenship remained open to question. He apparently had had enough of this issue and wanted it terminated.

Felix subsequently contracted the services of William J. Knight, a prominent Houston civil attorney. Tijerina knew Bill Knight well because Knight and his family, residents of River Oaks, ate at Felix's restaurant on their maid's weekly night off. From this acquaintance and for a substantial fee, Knight initiated and pleaded the case of *Felix Tijerina, Plaintiff, v. Herbert Brownell, Jr., Attorney General of the United States, et al., Defendants,* a "Complaint for Declaratory Judgment to Establish Citizenship" of his client. Filed in federal district court for the Southern District of Texas in Houston on March 25, 1954, the complaint stated that Tijerina was a native-born citizen of the United States and that his rights and privileges as such were being denied by immigration officers through the ongoing issue of his alleged citizenship status. It called on the court to grant him "a declaratory judgment establishing his citizenship and removing the uncertainty and unsecurity" that the matter fomented in his life. The eight-page legal document outlined the controversy according to Felix Tijerina—how it had prevented the granting of citizenship to his adopted son and the inconvenience and embarrassment it would cause him by not being allowed to leave and reenter the country. The plaintiff alleged that INS officers "threatened" that they would not readmit him into the United States on the grounds "that he was an alien," thus potentially keeping him "in exile from his native land." [11]

In support of Tijerina's claim, the complaint gave a full recounting of his story of the controversy in 1940, including the testimony of his mother and Easter Fueler regarding his birth in Fort Bend County as well as other salient facts in obtaining the delayed birth certificate. Furthermore, it noted how during his life the plaintiff had always in good conscience held himself out as a native-born citizen and that he had served in the military as such. It noted that Tijerina enjoyed a good reputation for his work in numerous civic organizations and institutions, for his business enterprises, and for many other accomplishments. Regardless of all this, the document concluded, the plaintiff's legal rights would remain in doubt without the declaratory judgment. In short, the suit was designed to terminate once and for all the question of his status by getting the federal court to declare that he was indeed a citizen of the United States and, in effect, acknowledge that he was a native-born American. Phil Montalbo, as Felix's regular attorney, would assist Knight in the effort. [12]

This action clearly indicated how exasperated Tijerina was with the lingering problem—in particular with immigration agents questioning his nativity—and how determined he was to bring the controversy to an end. It may also have been designed to make the INS move on granting naturalization to Felix, Jr.

On the evening that the complaint was filed and on the following day, the Houston newspapers reported that Felix Tijerina, "Houston restaurant man" and "a leader in Latin-American civic activities," was suing to establish his citizenship. The coverage made public the details of the suit, especially Tijerina's claim to having been born in Fort Bend County, his 1940 delayed birth certificate, the precipitating incident in which the immigration officials had declined to naturalize his son, and his many contributions to the community. The articles also mentioned that the federal immigration chief in Houston, L. D. Crossman (named as a defendant along with Brownell), commented that he knew little about the case. [13] But, clearly, from the time of its initiation, the suit drew publicity, and Felix's reputation rode on its outcome.

The case sat in federal court from late March until late May. This period represented almost the entire sixty days that the defendants had, under the law, to answer.

In the meantime, on April 28, a hearing took place before Elsenbroich on the naturalization of Felix, Jr. Apparently, that session fully aired the matter of Felix, Sr.'s citizenship. The INS formally introduced the 1925 visa application and the 1905 Mexican birth record into evidence, over the objections of Tijerina's counsel. Perhaps it was at this hearing that Montalbo compared his copy of the birth record of Feliberto Tijerina with the one in the possession of the INS. Felix's 1940 delayed birth certificate was likewise introduced. Various witnesses, including Tijerina, testified on his behalf regarding his place of birth and citizenship. Tijerina's suit later alleged that during a recess at that hearing INS inspector Brimberry again told him, off the record, that regardless of the outcome of Felix, Jr.'s case Tijerina would still have to establish his own citizenship before an INS board of inquiry. The suit also alleged that he "threatened" Felix once again with possible arrest if he left the country and tried to return. The government claimed that Brimberry's remarks had been "not so much threats as friendly (if mistaken) advice" that the best and easiest solution to the problem was for Tijerina to file for naturalization.[14]

Regardless of Brimberry's alleged remarks, on May 20, Elsenbroich formally recommended to the U.S. District Court that the petition for Felix, Jr.'s naturalization be granted. On that same day, the federal judge accepted the INS recommendation and signed the petition, making the boy an American citizen.[15]

The following day, the *Houston Chronicle* ran an article stating that "[h]andsome little Felix Tijerina, Jr." had been duly naturalized. Much in the theme of his parents as Latin American favorites of the press, the photo that accompanied the article showed a precious, smiling six-year-old little Felix clad in an embroidered Mexican *charro* suit, complete with a matching *sombrero*. The article noted that his mother was born in Gonzales County, and his father was "a native of Sugar Land."[16]

Of course, the issue of Tijerina's nativity had not gone away. The declaratory judgment case was still pending. Because the question of Felix, Sr.'s birth was not the central issue ruled upon in the naturalization proceedings for Felix, Jr., but merely evidence considered, no official ruling on the citizenship status of the elder Tijerina had been rendered as a result of the April 28 and May 20 actions.

On May 26, Carlos Watson, Jr., the assistant United States attorney who handled Tijerina's suit on behalf of the government, requested and received a sixty-day extension to answer the initial complaint filed by William Knight. Watson claimed that he needed more time to examine the information presented at Felix, Jr.'s May 20 hearing.[17]

The issue of Felix's citizenship heated up that summer when he and the INS had a squabble at Houston's Municipal Airport. In June, 1954, Tijerina had obtained what appears to have been a temporary U.S. passport which was valid for a period of six months. In early July, Felix made a several-day business trip to Mexico. Over the years since 1940, he had journeyed to Monterrey and Mexico City numerous times for business, pleasure, and club work, and had never encountered any difficulty. This time proved to be different. On Saturday, July 10, Felix returned to Houston via Pan American Airways. Apparently, when he came through immigration, Officer Brimberry was on hand and refused to acknowledge the birth certificate or the passport that Felix had in his possession. Brimberry briefly held Tijerina in custody before releasing him under parole with the requirement that he report to the Houston INS office at 9 A.M. Monday. This detention greatly embarrassed Tijerina, especially since Brimberry had questioned his right to enter the country in the presence of other passengers and told the airline that it would be subject to a one-thousand-dollar fine if Tijerina failed to show Monday morning. Even the government would later admit that the airport dispute had wounded Tijerina's sensibilities.[18]

This incident vividly demonstrated the authority that INS agents had, including the ability to detain, question, or bar entry of a person into the country, at their discretion.[19] They had the legal power to make life uncertain for anyone whom they suspected, even a person with the stature of Felix Tijerina.

On Monday morning, Tijerina presented himself at the INS office and was released, still under parole pending a final hearing on his admissibility to the United States as a citizen. The immigration officials claimed that, because of Tijerina's federal lawsuit to confirm his citizenship, they had no choice but to keep him under parole. Recognizing his documents and allowing him to enter uncontested would have amounted to the government confirming his status as an American citizen.[20]

This action made the news as the Houston press reported that the restaurateur was in Houston "on parole." The reports also mentioned, once again, that Felix claimed to have been born in Sugar Land. Since these articles noted that Tijerina was at this time being considered for the honor of being a member of the Harris County grand jury for August, the level of possible embarrassment (if he lost his case) increased. By then, even such luminaries as Senator Price Daniel had taken special note of Tijerina's citizenship troubles.[21]

Within a week, the affair resurfaced in the news when on July 20, Felix's attorneys used the occasion of the airport detention "as a further denial of his rights and privileges" as a citizen to file in court an amended complaint for the declaratory judgment. This amended complaint named not only Brownell, but INS office chief T. C. Carpenter (who had become head of the Houston INS office) and Brimberry as defendants.[22]

On August 20, the special INS inquiry that the airport incident had prompted was terminated without an official ruling. Felix was released from parole and formally admitted into the United States. But his citizenship status remained uncertain.[23]

Felix's suit remained in federal court for the rest of 1954 and into the next year. Apparently, Knight and Montalbo suspected that the parole termination had been caused by a ruling on Felix's citizenship by the INS general counsel that had not been communicated to their client. Accordingly, the two attorneys filed a "Second Amended Complaint" for the declaratory judgment in June of 1955. During that summer, Assistant U.S. Attorney Carlos Watson (who was still handling the case) successfully petitioned the court to dismiss INS officers Crossman, Carpenter, and Brimberry as defendants; this action removed the three men as targets of Tijerina's suit and from all possible civil liability. Watson was not successful, however, in having the suit dismissed against U.S. Attorney General Herbert Brownell.[24] Tijerina's move to be declared a citizen, thus, remained active.

Positive public sentiment toward Felix, plain luck, and maybe shrewd foresight by Bill Knight played the most crucial part in Tijerina's effort to find relief from his citizenship troubles. When first initiated, his suit (apparently assigned at random to one of the three federal district judges in Houston) went before eighty-year-old Judge Thomas M. Kennerly. Judge Kennerly, a twenty-three-year veteran of the bench, was also a member of the

Downtown Rotary Club and no doubt knew Felix, his good works, and reputation. In February, 1954, however, a month before Knight initiated the suit, Kennerly had asked President Eisenhower to make effective his retirement as soon as a successor could be sworn in. In May, a longtime rumor was confirmed when the White House announced the nomination of fifty-year-old Houston attorney Joe Ingraham as Kennerly's replacement. In early August, 1954, Ingraham received confirmation by the Senate and was soon sworn in. This turn of events, as was Felix's usual good fortune in these days, provided a perhaps even more sympathetic judge to the plaintiff and his attorneys.

Originally from Pawnee County, Oklahoma, Joe McDonald Ingraham had come to Texas in the late 1920s, after earning his law degree in Washington, D.C. After seven years in Fort Worth, he had settled in Houston in 1935 where he practiced law before and after serving as an officer in the Army Air Corps during World War II. More important, he had been Harris County Republican Party chairman for seven years after the war; in 1952, he served as co-leader of the local Eisenhower movement and received a good deal of public recognition for his role in helping to obtain the presidential nomination for the general. He became President Eisenhower's first judicial appointment in Texas.[25]

Although conservative, Joe Ingraham was no extremist. Indeed, the "Minute Women," a rabidly right-wing Houston group, had lobbied hard against his appointment. At the time of his nomination the newspapers described him as "soft-spoken and pleasant." Unpretentious by nature, he publicly described himself in May, 1954, as a "Red River wetback" for his Oklahoma roots. Years later, he referred to himself as "a native Texan who happened to be born away from home," a comment that may well have given further indication of his attitude toward nativity. (Felix could certainly have identified with Ingraham's latter self-description.) An attorney who operated in Ingraham's court during his earliest days on the bench characterized him as down-to-earth, practical, and compassionate. At the time of his death in 1990, a colleague called him "an ideal judge" because of his patience and common sense.[26]

A bachelor resident of the elegant Riverside subdivision immediately adjacent to the Montrose area, Ingraham ate at Felix Mexican Restaurant during the early 1950s. He knew Felix by sight, having spoken to the popular restaurateur upon occasion while dining. Indeed, Tijerina had himself been conspicuous in the Democrats for Eisenhower-Nixon organization during the 1952 election—so much so that he had received a letter of appreciation from Eisenhower after his victory. Departing from his traditional Democratic affiliation, Tijerina had crossed party lines to vote for the popular Republican nominee, as did the majority of Texans who went to the polls that year. Close associate Alfred Hernández (also an Eisenhower Democrat) recalled that Felix's support for Ike (in both presidential campaigns) was well known and ranked among the few times that the cautious restaurateur vocally backed a political candidate during these flush times.[27]

Moreover, Ingraham and Knight were friends and close associates. For five years just prior to his being appointed to the federal bench, Ingraham had shared an office suite with Bill Knight and one other attorney in the Texas Commerce Bank building; he had come to know and respect Knight as "a thorough, competent lawyer." They were near the same age and had similar backgrounds, both having been born and raised in Oklahoma Indian country.[28]

Knight had initiated Tijerina's suit barely a month after Thomas Kennerly announced his retirement. Such timing seems to have been more than mere coincidence. Rumors no doubt circulated about Ingraham's nomination, and perhaps Knight's insight into how the likely nominee would preside over Tijerina's case served as another initial element in his strategy of going for a declaratory judgment. To be sure, Ingraham's appointment and Tijerina's good standing guaranteed that the plaintiff would have a wonderfully favorable judge inheriting his case.

Judge Ingraham's attitude toward the plaintiff could only have been enhanced when, not long after Knight and Montalbo filed their "Second Amended Complaint" for the declaratory judgment, the *Houston Post* ran Marie Moore's August 8, 1955, feature article on Felix. This was the lengthiest, most glowing biographical article that had ever appeared on the life, work, and world view of Felix Tijerina. The article ran on the front page as part of the newspaper's "Titled Texan" series, complete with a large photo of Felix at home in his easy chair reading a newspaper. Headlined "The Cap Still Fits: When Felix Tijerina Feels Like a Big Shot, He Thinks of Beer Truck," the piece, much in the spirit of the 1948 article by Silas B. Ragsdale, played the theme of Tijerina as a generous, but modest Latin American Horatio Alger character.[29] Felix's ultimate triumph in his push for a declaratory judgment can only be fully appreciated in light of this timely biographical sketch and the favorable impact it would have had on the court of Houston public opinion, including Judge Ingraham and those persons directly involved with the court proceedings.

Moore covered Felix's life from birth, categorically stating that he was "a native of Sugar Land, a fact he proved to the satisfaction of immigration authorities."[30] This was no doubt a reference to Felix, Jr.'s naturalization and/or the INS dropping the elder Tijerina's parole status in August of the previous year. In fact, Tijerina's complaint for a declaratory judgment was still pending in federal court.

Commencing her article with the story of Felix's boyhood struggle, Moore described (apparently for the first time in print) how as a busboy in Houston he had known so little English that he had to have a waiter explain the meaning of "tomato catsup." She recounted Tijerina's life from his early years as a farm worker after his father's death to his ultimate success as a restaurateur. Moore also stressed that Felix Tijerina was a family man— good husband and father. Every Sunday, "starting right after church," readers were informed, the Tijerinas spent the day on a fifty-acre ranch they owned "at Sugar Land, very close to the place where Mr. Tijerina was born."[31]

The article especially emphasized the many charitable and philanthropic works Tijerina participated in for the Latin American and Anglo communities. Regarding Felix's personal demeanor, Moore portrayed him as "a stickler for politeness," who would fire one of his employees "sooner for failing to say 'Yes, Ma'am' to a lady than I would for cussing me out." The headline's reference to the cap that still fit was his old Union Brewery deliveryman's cap that Felix kept in his closet and donned periodically, so as to humble himself, whenever he thought he was "a big shot."[32]

But it was in revealing Felix's view of society—in particular the plight of Mexican Americans—wherein the Moore article surpassed the one written seven years before by Ragsdale. Moore gave Tijerina a forum to speak his mind, and he clearly seized the opportunity; what came out were opinions acceptable to Anglo Houston society at a time when Tijerina needed favorable public attention more than ever.

Marie Moore noted that "his view-point on most matters is more 'Anglo' . . . than it is Latin," stressing that for Felix, integration and assimilation were the prescription for the problems of people of Mexican heritage in American society. Placing the responsibility mainly on the shoulders of the Latin American, Tijerina was "impatient with American citizens of

Mexican ancestry who stick too close to their own clans and continue speaking Spanish in their homes." He "severely" admonished his fellow Latin Americans that "[y]ou are American citizens and English is the national language." For Tijerina, Spanish should not be forgotten; however, English was to be emphasized for success in life. In his own home, his children learned English first, Spanish later, so that "they won't speak [English] with an accent" as he did.[33]

Believing that Mexicans should "'Anglicize' themselves," Felix explained that "[t]here are natives of this country who still think of themselves as 'Mexicans' instead of 'Americans.' That is not right; if they are going to live here, they must become Americans just like the English and the Swedes and French and Italians who have come to this country." As he put it: "If a man comes into my restaurant, I don't think of him as a gringo; he's an American, just like I am." And, in Felix's inclusive view of things, Latins were to incorporate themselves into society through education to attain a middle-class lifestyle; they "must not live so much to themselves." In other words, the Latin American had to fit in. "My children," he noted, "will always feel like Americans." Felix, Jr., he continued, "knows the American flag is his flag, and he recites the Pledge of Allegiance every time he sees it."[34]

Even the accompanying photo of the Tijerinas around their dining table at home with their two children visually portrayed Felix and Janie as veritable Latin American versions of Ozzie and Harriet Nelson, whose popular television program of the day portrayed the quintessential white American middle-class nuclear family (who also had the *de rigueur* two kids). It was a message that mainstream Anglo Houston society during the mid-1950s would have wanted to hear—and one that Mexican Houstonians could not have missed.

Tijerina's vision of hard work would also warm the hearts of those in postwar Houston caught up in veneration of the self-made man. Education had to be for a practical purpose; there should be no "educated fools" who were not willing to get their hands dirty. According to Felix, "[e]verybody has to work; this country doesn't owe anyone a living."[35]

Yet, through Moore, Felix pointed out the problems of the Latin American community. The article expressed his empathy with fellow Mexican Americans who found themselves suffering from poverty and marginality. Though he exonerated Anglo society for these ills, Tijerina informed the readership that such deprivation prevented people from being good citizens.

For Felix, however, rectification of these problems did not lie in finger pointing; the solution had to come from Latin American self-help and through organizations such as LULAC—a do-it-yourself, by-the-bootstraps action within the system. Felix noted that people had to "work hard and save their money, instead of spending it in beer joints." He likewise mentioned the proposed LULAC effort to teach English to Spanish-speaking children before they began school so that they could graduate from high school. Through education, he reasoned, "the children of the next generation [could] begin living like real Americans."[36]

In his discussion of such systematic language instruction—his "dream"—Felix said absolutely nothing about government involvement, an omission that most white Houstonians during the 1950s would have endorsed. Nor, incidentally, did he mention the possibility of concerted political action by Latin Americans to alleviate their troubles.

Through Marie Moore, Felix articulated his convictions at an opportune time. Predisposed to such beliefs in the postwar years, his situation as of August, 1955—an acutely stressful phase in his life as a Mexican American—would only have prompted him to tout them louder. It was a philosophy that would help his own cause as well as assist his people. It was a philosophy tailored to prevent Latin Americans from being, in his own words in the article, "outsiders"—a condition he had personally struggled all his life to avoid and now fought through his suit against the INS to prevent from being designated as "an alien from his native land."[37] (It should be recalled that the LULAC News reprinted Marie Moore's article in its September, 1955, issue. This was Felix's message, shaped to some degree by local and secretly personal circumstances, that also went out to LULAC members everywhere.)

Felix's personal struggle as of August, 1955, stood against the backdrop of at least two persisting overall realities. One involved Anglo Houston's longstanding view of Mexican Americans in general. On the same front page with the Moore article, the *Houston Post* ran a more typical report about a Mexican American with *five* children who was stabbed to death in a tavern brawl by someone with whom he "had been drinking beer."[38] The juxtaposition with the life of Felix Tijerina, while perhaps accidental in its physical placement on the page, symbolized both the Anglo stereotype that Felix, as a leader of *la raza,* had to live down as well as the esteem that the Anglo community wanted him to maintain.

Second, Tijerina's assimilationist message represented what Anglo Houstonians liked. Felix no doubt gave Moore the material she probably needed and/or found agreeable to include. The prevailing temper on the local and national levels during the postwar era was conformity, something that the Eisenhower presidency came to symbolize. The growth of suburbs and middle-class prosperity marked this era as one of societal and political homogeneity. The American people's basic uneasiness with the rapid changes of the postwar era as well as pervasive fears from the Cold War strengthened their desire for conformity as they saw enemies abroad and within, fears most poignantly stated by the phenomenon of the Red Scare and its most notorious proponent, the United States senator from Wisconsin, Joe McCarthy. And Felix preached homogeneity, not diversity.[39]

During the 1950s, the *Houston Post* was owned and personally operated by William Pettus Hobby and his wife, Olveta Culp Hobby. With W. P. Hobby being a former governor of Texas and Olveta as national chair of "Democrats for Eisenhower" (among their many other positions), they were two of the city's entrepreneurial power elite. At a time when a small group of conservative power brokers—of which the Hobbys were an integral part—determined just about every major development in the Bayou City, the *Post* generally reflected the prevailing opinion of this ruling class. No one could have failed to understand that Houston's "establishment" smiled on Felix Tijerina and his efforts.[40]

It certainly would have been difficult for Judge Joe Ingraham to miss the message of the *Post* article on Tijerina. Only a year earlier, in May, 1954, just after his nomination to the bench and no doubt to promote a fellow Ike supporter through the Senate confirmation process, the *Post* had featured Ingraham in its "Titled Texan" series.[41] The article of August, 1955, making "Titled Texan" Felix Tijerina *the* Houston Latin American role model would have been an embarrassment to all concerned if the declaratory judgment suit had somehow gone against him.

Tijerina's press coverage notwithstanding, his legal action still had to succeed in the court system. During 1954 and 1955, U.S. Assistant Attorney Carlos Watson followed a routine defense against Tijerina's suit. Rather than mounting any sort of spirited effort, Watson simply filed motions to get the case dismissed based on the contention that the court lacked jurisdiction.[42]

Nor did Felix inherit a vigorous adversary when in late 1955 or early 1956, a young federal attorney named Sidney Farr took over the defense from Watson. Sensitive and reflective by nature, Farr was one of those Anglos in the 1950s who held sympathy for Mexican Americans. His feelings were largely out of gratitude. A native of Louisiana, Farr had come to Texas after serving in World War II in order to finish law school at Southern Methodist University. Upon graduation, he found work in Corpus Christi with a Mexican American attorney named Hector De Peña, who, Farr reminisced, "was kind enough to have pity on me . . . and he took me in." Farr subsequently practiced law for several years in Edinburg, near the border. From there he came to work in Houston for the U.S. Attorney's office in December, 1955.[43]

When Farr began his tenure with the federal government, Felix's suit was one of about a dozen or so pending citizenship cases that he inherited. He did not know Tijerina personally, but, not surprisingly, ate at his restaurant on Westheimer and knew of Felix's good reputation in the community.[44]

Although energetic, Farr did not have his heart in the Tijerina case. He stated years later that had it been solely his decision, he probably would not have prosecuted any of the immigration cases; he had little respect for INS inspectors because of what he felt was their impersonal police mentality, which prevented them from taking into consideration the more human aspects of the individual cases. More important, Farr wondered, what did the exact status of Tijerina's citizenship matter when the restaurateur was such a solid member of the community? Not that Farr was fooled. Based upon the evidence the INS had at the time, Farr would recall, it seemed that Felix had been born in Mexico; still, privately, he felt that Tijerina's place of birth should cause no one any alarm.[45]

In early February, Farr submitted the defendant's answer to Tijerina's complaint for declaratory judgment. Like Watson before him, he did not contest Felix's citizenship; rather, his position strictly held that the court did not have jurisdiction to grant the judgment, that the plaintiff was not being denied his rights, and that the court should dismiss the suit or not give the plaintiff the judgment requested. Regardless of the evidence he and the INS possessed on Felix's nativity, Farr never alleged that the plaintiff was Mexican-born. While denying that the 1940 inquiry had firmly established Felix's place of birth, Farr's position held that the government could neither concede nor deny that Tijerina was born in the United States.[46] Again, Farr's legal response seemed essentially to be a conscientious defense, but one that did not "go after" Tijerina as truly having been born in Mexico.

Still, the government's exhibits submitted into evidence before Judge Ingraham for the upcoming hearing included the visa application Felix had made in 1925 and the 1905 birth record of Feliberto Tijerina. Also, both sides acknowledged that Felix's older sister Amalia (who would testify on her brother's behalf) was born in the same village, General Escobedo, where the record of this infant Feliberto originated.[47] Taken together, these three items would have led anyone to conclude that Feliberto was in fact Felix, especially someone as astute as Joe Ingraham.

On February 15, 1956, the formal hearing took place. Apparently because neither side requested a jury trial, Judge Ingraham alone would make the final ruling. All three major Houston newspapers (the *Post, Chronicle,* and *Press*) followed the proceedings, once again placing Tijerina's fate in front of the public. Felix took the stand and was questioned by Bill Knight. Under oath, Tijerina gave his usual story about how he had obtained the Mexican passport in 1925 and his version of the 1940 controversy and delayed birth certificate, and he reasserted that he was born in Sugar Land. Former Fort Bend County judge C. L. Dutton also testified on Felix's behalf, saying that he had known the plaintiff since 1920 and that in 1940 he had taken affidavits, heard sworn witnesses, and signed Tijerina's delayed birth certificate. Finally, Amalia testified that it was "family history" that her brother was born in Sugar Land. The plaintiff's case also included exhibits that Dora and Victoria were likewise ready to take the stand to say that they had always understood that Felix was Sugar Land–born and that he had never been known by any other name than Felix. Court documents reveal that Dora and Victoria gave Robstown and Sugar Land, respectively, as their places of birth.[48]

Farr called no one to testify. He did, however, recall and question Felix, but even while he had the restaurateur on the stand, Farr made no effort to contradict Tijerina's contention that he was born in the United States. Farr recalled that his attention in the courtroom quickly focused on Bill Knight, who came to the proceedings dressed in his usual well-tailored suit and Stetson hat, looking and acting more like a Texas oil man than the Harvard-trained lawyer he was, and full of righteous indignation over the government putting upon Felix Tijerina, business man, civic leader, and good citizen. Amused by Knight's demeanor but respectful of his stature, Farr had no inclination to counter his protestations.[49]

By the end of the day-long hearing, things looked good for Tijerina. At its conclusion, Ingraham let it be known that although he would not announce a formal ruling until both sides turned in formal briefs, he felt that the plaintiff had established a case that the government had not overcome. In late February and early March, both sides would submit several briefs to the court reiterating their cases.[50]

A few days after the hearing, George Carmack, editor of the *Press* (and constant admirer of the genial restaurateur), wrote that it "would be hard to name a better American—a better Texan—a better Houstonian than Felix Tijerina. No one can ever know the good that man and his fine wife do." He concluded by stating that "Felix has now gone into court to settle for once and all the question of his U.S. citizenship. All who know Felix are at his side in this matter."[51]

Indeed, most people probably favored Felix's case, although their words contained a degree of irony, even as they expressed support. Carmack offered as proof of Felix's citizenship simply the fact that he was a good member of the community. One of Janie's many Anglo friends wrote her that she hoped that it would be settled in Felix's favor: "I am sure he is indeed a real American citizen thru and thru, a martter [sic] of formality. You evidently have the press on your side!" The friend lamented that Felix "has had such a hard time trying to do the one thing he wishes so much," that is, to prove he was "a real American."[52] She could not have known the profound truth that her words conveyed, especially in her tone about the *true nature* of his status. Felix had indeed strived all his life through great adaptation and conformity to survive, fit in, and prosper. Yet, the question of his citizenship had always hovered in the background as if to question, to one degree or another, if he truly belonged.

Although there was certainly no conscious collusion among all the principals involved, in hindsight the outcome could hardly have been in question. With Ingraham on the bench making the final determination, his friend the eminent William J. Knight as Felix's spokesman, Sidney Farr doing his job while sympathizing with the other side, the press calling for "justice" for a great American, and the plaintiff as everybody's Latin American Horatio Alger ideal, Tijerina stood on friendly ground. Still, he was probably nervous enough. The photo that accompanied the *Houston Press* article on the hearing showed Felix taking a long puff from a cigarette.[53]

By 1954–56, Felix Tijerina had gone beyond his innocuous claims that presented him as an American citizen during the 1930s, beyond his fabrication of documents for the INS in 1940, and beyond the altered story of his origins for the press that started in earnest with the 1948 article by Silas Ragsdale. In 1956, Tijerina found it necessary to "prove" his story in a well-publicized proceeding in federal court, and, with the assistance of his lawyers, he did so seemingly without reservation.

And he won. On Friday, May 25, 1956, Judge Ingraham filed the "Opinion of the Court" wherein, after a lengthy recapitulation of the facts of the case, he found that the controversy engendered between the INS (as part of the Department of Justice) and the plaintiff was a denial of Tijerina's rights and privileges as an American citizen, and thus granted Felix Tijerina the declaratory judgment stating he was "a native-born citizen of the United States."[54]

After addressing the controversy between Felix and the INS that had been going on since at least 1940, and all relevant judicial precedent, Judge Ingraham denied Farr's motion to dismiss the case and asserted the court's jurisdiction to enter the declaratory judgment. But Ingraham's ruling rested on his belief that "a preponderance of the evidence" showed that Felix Tijerina "was born at Sugarland [sic], in Fort Bend County, State of Texas, on April 29, 1905, the son of Rafael Tijerina and Dionicia Villareal Tijerina." He based this conclusion essentially upon Felix's testimony (and Farr's refusal to object), Amalia's statements, the readiness of Dora and Victoria to testify, and the delayed birth certificate. Furthermore, he accepted Felix's story that he had applied for the 1925 immigration visa out of "expediency."[55] Thus, with Judge Joe Ingraham's ruling the fable of Felix Tijerina's origins became a legal reality.

Although Ingraham mentioned in his opinion the existence of the 1905 birth record of Feliberto Tijerina (and made reference to Rafael Tijerina and Dionicia Villareal Tijerina), he did not attempt to explain it, apparently giving it little weight in his decision. It is impossible to determine whether he knew of the "personal inquiries" that had probably informed the INS and ultimately prompted the court proceedings (and perhaps even revealed the 1905 document). Clearly, the straight-laced Ingraham would have frowned on such shenanigans. When asked in an interview about that seemingly irrefutable piece of evidence some twenty-five years after his decision, the venerable jurist acted slightly perturbed but replied: "I don't know how many Mexicans may be named Felix Tijerina." Understanding how much his declaratory ruling meant to Felix and stating that he believed that Tijerina had felt harassed over the years by the INS, Judge Ingraham added solemnly that "Felix is dead and gone now; but he died a citizen of the United States."[56] Ingraham's May, 1956, decision buried Feliberto Tijerina Villarreal beyond future resurrection by the INS.

For his part, Sidney Farr commented to Ingraham off the record after the verdict that he felt the correct outcome had been achieved. He also chose not to appeal the decision to a higher court.[57] Farr's determination was fortunate for all concerned.

The judge's ruling made the weekend news in Houston and caused much celebration within the Tijerina family and circle of friends and associates. On May 26, a Saturday, the sympathetic *Houston Post* reported on its front page that Felix had won his citizenship case. After detailing the outcome of the battle that he had waged since 1940, the newspaper article quoted Felix saying: "I'm very happy. It's wonderful to be born in a country where every man has a voice." That same day, the *Houston Press* carried a photo of a beaming Felix, Sr., with Felix, Jr., stating that they had their "Troubles Over." After noting that all his years of worry about citizenship were behind him, it reported that both father and son said: "It's good to be Americans — at last."[58] The Tijerinas were so happy over this turn of events, that the family saved several dozen copies of the articles. For its part, the *Houston Chronicle* noted that by his ruling Judge Ingraham "told the Immigration and Naturalization Service to stop bothering the Houston civic leader." A close Anglo friend from Pasadena jubilantly wrote Felix that "I followed your battle for years and it gives me great joy to see that the immigration authorities have at last accepted your proof of American Citizenship." General Maurice Hirsch, one of Houston's most distinguished residents, jotted him a note which simply stated "congratulations to a splendid citizen!" Local banker A. Pat Daniels wrote to say that he "was extremely happy to see a wonderful guy's record cleared."[59]

The judge's ruling had indeed "cleared" several things. It ended years of uncertainty, insulated Tijerina from continued personal humiliation, and preserved his image as the preeminent Latin American role model in Houston. It made him as much an "insider" as he — as a Mexican American — could ever become. Although many people in the local Mexican American community apparently knew the truth of Felix's origins, the declaratory judgment maintained Tijerina's secret and sealed his dark spot behind a legal wall. As is often the case with life's many moral ambiguities, it could be said that the outcome of *Felix Tijerina v. Herbert Brownell, Jr.*, served justice rather than the truth. Perhaps most significantly, by releasing Tijerina from this nagging problem, Judge Ingraham's ruling may well have smoothed the way for Felix to venture into higher office in LULAC and accomplish his "dream" for Mexican American education.

How did Houston's Mexican American community respond to Felix's victory? Any answer has to be purely impressionistic since Tijerina's nativity was privately discussed among Mexican Americans rather than publicly debated; there apparently exists no written record by local Hispanics on the subject. Recollections of contemporaries, however, overwhelmingly suggest that the Mexican American populace was pleased that he had won his case. Of course, at the new LULAC clubhouse on Bagby Street, the news caused great jubilation; those members who had only second-hand knowledge of the proceedings had seen no reason for him to have gone through the ordeal in the first place. Moreover, most of *la raza* liked Felix and viewed him as a symbol of Latin American achievement. He even had the grudging respect of those individuals who, like John Herrera, may have seen him in less than a totally favorable light. Mexican Americans sensed that tarnishing Tijerina's image would have reflected poorly on their community, hindering its progress at a crucial time of struggle. As a consequence, even those who knew (or suspected) that Felix had come from Mexico were relieved that he had been able to utilize the system and win at his own personal "politics as self defense."[60]

If people had hoped the victory would save Felix's stature and maintain his momentum, their hopes were realized. In the May, 1956, issue of the *LULAC News,* Tijerina formally placed his name in the ring for national president of the organization.[61] He would be elected to that position at the LULAC convention that summer and begin a lengthy, productive tenure as head of the league. Tijerina would serve four consecutive terms as president and lead the organization in establishing one of the era's most significant projects, an educational enterprise that benefited thousands of Spanish-speaking youngsters. He and his program would bring national attention to LULAC as well as to the condition of Hispanic education in the United States. Beginning with 1956, Felix Tijerina—newly declared "native-born citizen of the United States"—would become synonymous with LULAC and Mexican American education and would become one of the nation's most recognized "Latin American" leaders.

CHAPTER 8

THE LULAC NATIONAL
PRESIDENCY, PART I

1956–1958

From June, 1956, through June, 1960, Felix Tijerina served four consecutive terms as the national president of LULAC, a tenure unprecedented in the history of the organization. The most consequential civic position that Tijerina ever held, it dominated his time and energies and brought him into contact with people across the nation. During those four years, he continued to pursue the two goals which he had established as LULAC regional governor—expansion and education, aims consistent with his nonconfrontational nature. As national president, however, his efforts proved to be more successful and made a universally recognized impact.

Tijerina's national LULAC presidency is best covered in two chapters: one addressing the organization's expansion into the Midwest and the genesis of Tijerina's Little School of the 400 project, and the other studying LULAC's more limited inroads into the Northeast and the institutionalization of the preschool project as a Texas state-funded educational program with national influence. The present chapter examines his initial two terms, from June, 1956, to June, 1958, when the organization moved into six Midwestern states: Illinois, Wisconsin, Indiana, Iowa, Michigan, and Minnesota. By planting the LULAC banner in these northern reaches, Tijerina ensured the organization's nascent national cast. Chapter 8 will also describe how Tijerina and his colleagues developed their preschool educational concept into a modest pilot project. It relates how, finally, during the summer of 1958, Tijerina and his fellow LULACs turned it into a privately financed program that they expanded to nine Texas communities. It will also examine the countervailing opinions within LULAC and how these opposing beliefs buffeted Tijerina and his efforts. Chapter 9 will review Tijerina's LULAC presidency from June, 1958, through June, 1960, consider the group's thrust into the Northeast, its laborious efforts to establish the Little School approach as a state-sponsored program, and the final struggles Tijerina and his stalwarts waged within the organization as they brought the Tijerina era in LULAC to a close.

ASSUMING THE PRESIDENCY

At the twenty-seventh annual LULAC national convention, which took place at the Hilton Hotel in El Paso on June 21–24, 1956, Tijerina, Al Hernández, Phil Montalbo, and the other delegates from Council No. 60 threw themselves into Felix's campaign for president. Reportedly, some fifteen hundred LULAC members gathered, representing the five states—Texas, New Mexico, Arizona, California, and Colorado—that made up the organization. Indicative of the mainstream tone of LULAC, Judge Harold R. Medina was the featured speaker at the main banquet, during which the organization made him an honorary member. The Brooklyn-born Medina, as state district judge in New York in 1949, had gained much notoriety when he presided with a heavy hand over the nine-month-long trial of eleven leaders of the American Communist Party for allegedly advocating the forceful overthrow of the United States government. Highly admired by the LULACs, Judge Medina was of Mexican extraction on his father's side.[1]

During the convention, Tijerina (still the outgoing Texas regional governor) wore a flashy sharkskin suit and seemed at his gregarious best as he mingled with those in attendance. At fifty-one years of age, Felix was near the peak of his physical and mental energy. Even John J. Herrera, as a fellow Houstonian, laid aside their differences, went to El Paso, and spoke on Tijerina's behalf.[2]

Felix's candidacy was immeasurably aided by the fact that everyone knew he was wealthy. Many reasoned that his financial wherewithal and contacts in the business world would allow him to do great things for LULAC, a boost certainly welcomed by an organization chronically short of money. Outgoing president Oscar Laurel, who had decided to run for the state legislature rather than stand for reelection as the head of LULAC, threw his full support behind his friend Tijerina; Laurel reported glowingly to the convention delegates that not only was "Don Felix" a successful regional governor, but also that he had "at no time . . . submitted an expense account or a single bill to the National Office," a practice that had helped to keep LULAC financially solvent. With such an endorsement, Tijerina won the election on Sunday, the final day of the meeting, when his opponent, Joe Trujillo of Los Alamos, New Mexico, withdrew his name and asked the assembly to elect Felix unanimously.[3]

Shortly after the convention, Tijerina, Hernández, and Felix Salazar, Jr., (a young Council No. 60 stalwart and Tijerina man) visited Oscar Laurel in Laredo to discuss moving the national office to Houston. In this meeting, Laurel also turned over three thousand dollars in the treasury to the new administration. Laurel, his three predecessors, and indeed most of the men who had held the office had served only one year each, but Tijerina, the organization's twenty-fifth president, would break this single-term tradition with a vengeance.[4]

In his first official message (which appeared in the July, 1956, issue of the *LULAC News*), Felix set the course for his presidency by reasserting his desire to make education and expansion the twin foci of his administration. In education, he wanted to continue the LULAC tradition of scholarships, but he also specifically mentioned that the organization must address the problem of educating the children of migrant farm workers. Regarding expansion, he reminded members that people of their ethnicity had settled in such states as New York, Ohio, Kansas, Illinois, and Michigan, and he stated his intention to establish councils in those northern reaches, thus making LULAC "a truly National Institution."[5]

Continuing a method he had begun as Texas regional governor when he hired Tony Campos, the new president also called for paid workers to avoid relying exclusively on voluntary effort, which inevitably, he felt, led to stagnation. Paid workers, he noted, would be hired from money raised through a special campaign for such a purpose. Reflective of the way he always operated, Felix vowed he would run LULAC economically, like "a business enterprise."[6]

The June convention had elected national officers who were mainly from Texas, indicative of the fact that LULAC was still mainly a Texas-based organization. Luciano Santoscoy of El Paso became first national vice president; Aurora González of Las Vegas, New Mexico, won as second national vice president; Dr. Francisco Licón from El Paso was reelected as national director of health; and Richard Moya of Austin earned the position of national director of youth activities.[7]

With input from Alfred J. Hernández, Felix quickly appointed the other officers to his first administration as prescribed by the LULAC constitution. These were mostly Houstonians and included Hernández as national secretary; Gilbert Gómez as national treasurer; Phil Montalbo as national legal counsel; Ernest Eguía as national director of publicity; and Carmen Cortes as Felix's national executive secretary, his only woman appointee.[8]

Like Hernández and Montalbo, Gómez and Eguía were dedicated Council No. 60 members who had worked with Tijerina for several years. Gómez, a successful jeweler, was a young but popular figure in LULAC. Eguía, a decorated combat soldier in World War II, had returned from the service determined to make things better through his activity with the league. Carmen Cortes had been active in Houston women's organizations from the 1930s, was a close LULAC associate of Hernández, and had been a driving force in Houston's Ladies LULAC Council No. 22 since the late 1940s. She had also led Council No. 22 in its support of Tijerina for president. The only non-Houston appointee was the chaplain, Guadalupe C. Martínez, a founder of the LULAC movement in Galveston.[9]

Soon, Tijerina also named another Council No. 60 member, Gabe Ramírez, as his manager of publicity to help Eguía with the burdensome duties of producing the monthly *LULAC News*. The Houston appointees, along with a few other individuals like Tony Campos and Felix Salazar, formed Tijerina's inner LULAC circle. Quintessential postwar LULACs, these comrades were of the Mexican American middle class and had deep roots in and knowledge of their community. With no little personal sacrifice of time and money, they would do much to promote the goals of their national president, the interests of the league, and the cause of Mexican Americans.[10]

THE PASSIVE MEMBERSHIP PLAN
AND INITIAL EXPANSION

Ever the promoter, Tijerina initiated the so-called "Passive Membership Plan" as his first project. The plan was adopted by the LULAC Supreme Council meeting in mid-August, subject to approval by the next national convention. It established the category of "passive" (or associate) member for those persons sympathetic to LULAC goals and willing to contribute to the organization (financially and through other types of help), but who would not hold full-fledged membership or have a vote or direct voice in the league's business. Much like the proposed "Tijerina Amendment" that he had pushed as regional governor to raise revenue, the "Passive [or Associate] Membership Plan" was designed to generate funds for expansion and development of the proposed education programs.[11]

Tijerina appointed Tony Campos (who still worked for him) to coordinate the passive membership effort, but despite the enthusiasm of both men, the program encountered difficulties from the outset. By the end of Tijerina's first administration in 1957, the plan had yielded few results, and Felix complained that opposition from many of the LULAC councils had caused its lack of success.[12]

As he had promised, Felix quickly expanded LULAC through the establishment of councils in previously untapped areas, in particular the upper Midwest. This expansion initially came through the efforts of longtime Council No. 60 member J. B. Casas, the brother-in-law of Alfred Hernández. Casas, an insurance agent, personally knew several transplanted Houstonians living in the Chicago area and traveled there (with Tijerina paying his expenses) to organize the first group in the Midwest.[13]

By October, 1956, Felix reported that three new states—Illinois, Wisconsin, and Indiana—had been added to the LULAC roster. Accompanied by Alfred Hernández, Oscar Laurel, and the LULAC governors for these three areas, Tijerina attended and addressed a "banquet and ball" on September 30 at the Hotel Shoreline, where the officers of Chicago's newly formed Council No. 288 were installed. (This group became known as the "Pioneer Council of the Middlewest.") Felix made quite an impression, Oscar Laurel recalled, by paying for the entire installation banquet from his ever-ready roll of thousand-dollar bills, a characteristic Tijerina gesture during his efforts to move the organization into these new territories. *Noticias,* a weekly magaine for *la raza* in the Midwest published in Chicago, ran a front-page report of Tijerina's several-day visit. Proclaiming that the inauguration of this first LULAC chapter amounted to one of the most significant events in the history of Chicago's Latin American *colonia,* the story carried a large, formal portrait of the national president, thus introducing Tijerina to the Spanish-speaking population of the Windy City.[14]

By mid-October, Charles Toribio, recently appointed regional governor of Illinois LULAC, sent Tijerina a letter exuding hopes for expansion. Telling Felix that his presence and that of his fellow Texans at the Chicago installation had had a powerful impact on those who had been there, Toribio announced initiation of "Operation New Horizons," an effort to establish LULAC councils in Iowa, Missouri, and Kansas. In Topeka, for example, Toribio noted, "there exist[ed] a Mexican population of three thousand," from which LULAC membership could be recruited. He also speculated that a council might be mustered from the seventy-five hundred to eight thousand Mexicans estimated to live in Kansas City, Kansas/Missouri. Most propitious for the future of LULAC growth over the next four years was Toribio's appointment of Valeriano (Val) Hernández, a fellow member of Council No. 288, to help with "Operation New Horizons."[15]

The initial LULAC presence in Wisconsin came with the formation of Council No. 289 in Racine, shortly after Chicago entered the fold. On December 8, 1956, Alfred Hernández (on Felix's behalf) and Oscar Laurel attended the joint formal installation ceremony for the three Indiana councils—Indiana Harbor (East Chicago) Council No. 290, Indiana Harbor (East Chicago) Ladies Council No. 294, and Gary Council No. 295—at the Hotel Gary in Gary.[16]

Just a few days before the ceremonies in Gary, on December 2, the fourth midwestern state came into the league when Illinois regional governor Toribio and Val Hernández (by then Illinois district 1 governor) helped initiate a new council in Fort Madison, Iowa, 265 miles southwest of Chicago. People of Mexican descent had taken up residence there and worked at such places as the Santa Fe Railway, the Shaeffer Pen Company, the state penitentiary system, and a nearby federal ordnance plant. Probably typical of LULAC's relatively small numerical presence in these new areas, the Fort Madison members initially consisted of five men and two women from a total Mexican American population of around twenty-one hundred in the town and surrounding rural region. Regardless, by the end of 1956 LULAC had a foothold in states outside the Southwest for the first time in its twenty-seven year existence. The regional governor of Indiana, Angelo Machuca (one of the men Tijerina had met in Chicago) proclaimed in early 1957 that since Felix's visit to the Midwest, the area LULAC groups had been "growing by leaps and bounds." Through such things as "LULAC Week" proclamations and associated newspaper coverage, the organization made mainstream politicos and society aware of the Latino presence in these midwestern urban regions.[17]

The initiation of the Fort Madison, Iowa, council further marked the emergence of Chicagoan Val Hernández as a LULAC organizer. For the remainder of Tijerina's tenure, the energetic Hernández would shine as perhaps the most productive LULAC proselytizer in the organization's history and the key person on the scene for its expansion in the Midwest.[18]

By June, 1957, Felix claimed proudly that a total of twenty-one new councils had come into the league during his first administration (similar to the number of councils that had been started under previous presidents such as John Herrera in 1952–53 and Oscar Laurel in 1955–56). Much excitement was generated, for example, when sixty-one students at the University of Texas at Austin came together in December, 1956, to charter the first LULAC council on a university campus. In California, where LULAC was yet to be strongly represented, a council had formed in San Diego by the spring of 1957.[19]

Felix also traveled a great deal, almost a prerequisite for a LULAC national president. When Oscar Laurel ended his term in 1956, he stated that he had personally covered twenty-five thousand miles visiting LULAC councils across the Southwest. At the end of his first term in 1957, Tijerina claimed that he and Alfred Hernández had traveled more than fifty thousand miles on behalf of the organization, most of those miles on trips they had taken together. Felix had visited New Mexico, Arizona, California, Illinois, Indiana, Wisconsin, and Iowa, as well as many towns in Texas. He had always paid his own way, and, except for Hernández (who paid his share), Felix had picked up the expenses of the LULAC members who often accompanied him. Almost every issue of the *LULAC News* mentioned Felix being on the road at a regional convention, council installation, or Supreme Council meeting. Reflecting upon these times, Carmen Cortes believed that Felix's freedom to travel at his own expense, especially to foster expansion of the league, made him indispensable to the organization's postwar development.[20]

From the outset of his presidential tenure, Tijerina constantly cajoled the councils to recruit new individual members. In August, 1956, he urged each local council to have a member present at the graduation of all citizenship classes in its area "to welcome the new citizens and to invite them to join LULAC."[21]

TIJERINA'S FIRST EDUCATION PROPOSAL:
THE "ESCUELITA DEL AIRE"

By early 1957, Tijerina and his LULAC cohorts began to deliver on the other half of Tijerina's promise for his national presidency by initiating an education program, a program that would ultimately keep Felix in office for three more terms. Attempting to break the language barrier in school, Tijerina's administration by February had initiated plans to teach English to preschool Spanish-speaking children in Texas over the radio. To spread the word and gather support, Tijerina traveled extensively, the written record of which no doubt only hints at the number of places he and his entourage visited. For instance, he, Hernández, and Gib Devine (a public relations man) appeared before the February 9 meeting of the Texas Good Neighbor Commission in Dallas, where they received the commission's unqualified endorsement. In March, Tijerina, Hernández, and Tony Campos took their emerging proposal to Laredo, where Oscar Laurel publicly urged Tijerina to carry his "wonderful program" to completion. The threesome even drove to Monterrey and stayed at the luxurious Hotel Ancira; the local newspaper *El tiempo* published a glowing report of its interview with the LULAC president who expounded on his plans for teaching English (via radio broadcasts) to Spanish-speaking children so that they might obtain *"una educación superior."*[22]

This initial proposal was officially announced to the organization in an article by a University of Texas at Austin LULAC member named Leo Cárdenas in the May issue of the *LULAC News.* This "big package" was called the Escuelita del Aire (Little School of the Airwaves). Still in the planning stage, the *escuelita* was to be a statewide program that would carry two fifteen-minute English lessons daily on radio stations with Spanish-language programming. The entire course of study would cover thirty-nine weeks. These lessons were designed to teach children from ages three to six four hundred basic words of English before they entered the first grade. Although initially focusing upon Texas, LULAC envisioned that the program would soon spread to other states.[23]

The radio lessons would feature an on-the-air "mother" and three children. The mother would appeal to Mexican American women at home to involve themselves and their children in learning English. The program also planned to utilize three illustrated textbooks containing a total of 390 lessons, to use in conjunction with the broadcasts. The textbooks would illustrate a vocabulary of actions and objects constructed for children from homes where predominantly Spanish was spoken. Mrs. Carlos Calderón, a public school teacher in Austin, had developed the vocabulary; the illustrations were to be done by art specialist Jo Ann Roth.[24]

Clearly, the four hundred basic words of English to be used by the *escuelita* had already been established. Carlos I. Calderón, an Austin junior high school English teacher and presumably Mrs. Calderón's husband, had assembled and published this list in the July, 1956, issue of the *Texas Outlook,* the official publication of the Texas State Teachers Association. According to Calderón's article, entitled "The Fewest Words to Open the Widest Doors," these four hundred words represented a minimum English vocabulary for Spanish-speaking youngsters to master before they entered school—a vocabulary, Calderón hoped, that other teachers could use as their point of departure in compiling their own. Calderón's list was his synthesis of "several recognized minimum vocabulary lists" for teaching spoken English to Spanish-speaking children. Established by educators from Texas, New Mexico, and California over the preceding decade, it reflected the growing concern of Hispanic leaders that Mexican American children learn to communicate in English before they began formal instruction.[25]

Leo Cárdenas concluded his May announcement of the Escuelita del Aire by noting that a public relations firm in Austin specializing in Spanish-language marketing would handle the program. As planned, the *escuelita* would initially be carried by radio stations in Austin, Victoria, San Antonio, San Angelo, Fort Stockton, El Paso, Houston, El Campo, Edinburg, Del Rio, Corpus Christi, Brownsville, and Laredo.[26]

Along with State Senator Henry B. González of San Antonio and Oscar Laurel (by then a state representative from Laredo), Tijerina had already met with Texas governor Price Daniel to discuss the plan. Daniel pledged his cooperation with the effort, which was to be privately financed. Tijerina had likewise solicited and received the verbal support of the heads of the Texas Good Neighbor Commission, the Texas Department of Public Safety, the Railroad Commission of Texas, the Texas Health Commission, and the Texas Commission of Education.[27]

In the midst of this genesis of the Escuelita del Aire, Felix planned to run for reelection as LULAC national president. In March, 1957, the *LULAC News* announced that Council No. 60 had "drafted" him for a second term; the Laredo council and Oscar Laurel also unanimously pledged their support, citing his efforts at league expansion as well as his ambitious education project.[28]

ISABEL VERVER AND THE PILOT PROJECT

Shortly after Tijerina and LULAC made public their education plans, a young woman came into the picture who would fundamentally alter the approach of the project. The exact details of what initially transpired cannot be clearly determined, so much do the different accounts vary. According to the earliest written evidence, however, a seventeen-year-old high school sophomore from Ganado, Texas, named Isabel Verver, while reading in the waiting room of her dentist's office in April, 1957, saw an announcement of LULAC's proposed Escuelita del Aire that appeared in the *Texas Outlook*. The article also quoted Tijerina as saying that the program would bridge the "language barrier" of thousands of Spanish-speaking children in Texas before they entered school, a goal that reflected Verver's thinking.[29]

Verver had personally experienced many of the same language problems that other Mexican American youngsters had during their first years in school. She had vivid memories of her own frustration and embarrassment when, as a first grader who knew only Spanish, she could not communicate with her English-speaking teacher. She remembered being placed in segregated classrooms where, with great difficulty, she and her classmates had struggled for the first few years to master English; in the process, she had seen many children quit school after the third grade. One of her two brothers had dropped out after repeating the fourth grade several times; another brother left school after failing the seventh grade twice. Isabel had continued on, hoping to become a teacher.[30]

As convinced as Tijerina that this early "language barrier" precluded Mexican American success in school and excited that LULAC was taking the initiative, Verver telephoned Felix at his office and discussed with him her similar desire to teach children English. Impressed with the young woman's sincerity and spunk, Tijerina drove to Ganado in his Cadillac with Tony Campos, where they met with Verver and devised a strategy to put her ideas into practice. According to one of the more widely circulated stories of what transpired, Tijerina offered to pay her twenty-five dollars a week of his own money if she would organize a summer class for preschoolers in Ganado and teach them enough English so that they could understand their teachers when they began first grade in the fall.[31]

Enthused by Tijerina's personal support, Verver persuaded Ganado High School principal Pat Ozment to provide her with classroom space. She walked her neighborhood, inviting reluctant mothers to send their five- and six-year-olds to her "school." There is some question over just when she began her first class; according to the first report on her efforts, which appeared in the *LULAC News*, Verver's class began on June 10, although later LULAC literature claimed May 26 as the starting date. Because of the reticence of local Mexican American parents, this initial class commenced with only three or four children.[32]

By the time Verver's class began, Felix had obtained for her a list of approximately four hundred basic English words from Elizabeth Burrus, a Baytown elementary school teacher whom he had met through Tony Campos. Burrus had long experience with Mexican American children, first while growing up on her father's ranch in Knox County in northwest Texas, then as a teacher for eight years in the same area during the 1930s. She had taught Mexican Americans at Zavala Elementary in Baytown for a dozen years, further increasing her acquaintance with their educational needs. Practical in her approach to teaching, Burrus had always stressed vocabulary training among her students. Indeed, the list that she gave Felix, she noted, was compiled "as the result of [her] experiences through the years" and was then being utilized at Baytown's Zavala School. Burrus believed that children had to obtain a speaking vocabulary before they began to read, that they ought to be encouraged to speak English among themselves, and that they "must learn to think in English." Taking an immediate liking to Felix and his goal, Burrus vowed to help him in any way she could.[33]

As it was finally printed in pamphlet form (in 1958), Burrus's list contained word categories which resembled those of the vocabulary published by Carlos I. Calderón in the *Texas Outlook* two years before. Both lists contained categories on such topics as school environment, home and family, the body, and cleanliness. They indicated the shared, common conclusions held by educators seeking to teach basic English to preschoolers.[34]

Armed with Burrus's list and through repetition, Verver taught her students no fewer than five new words each day. According to one journalist, Verver began every day with a review of the previous day's lesson. Being bilingual, she could revert to Spanish if a child did not understand. Her techniques for holding the children's attention ranged from mothering to scolding—anything she could think of to get them to learn English.[35]

According to this same source as well as Verver's later recollections, her class soon took on the name "Little School of the 400" because of its diminutive size and the number of words in the vocabulary. Clearly, however, the name could be traced back to previous *escuelita* ideas and the concept of the 400-word list publicized by the Calderóns. Indeed, as it was finally printed, Burrus's list actually contained some 477 words, including the numbers one through ten. Regardless of what after-the-fact articles and other sources later reported, the actual name "Little School of the 400" does not appear to have been used until the summer of 1958.[36]

At the end of the first few weeks, Verver had the children demonstrate their progress to the local Mexican American mothers, many of whom had been skeptical of Verver's efforts. After this demonstration, her class enrollment swelled from the initial handful to more than 40 students, ranging in age from four to fourteen, most of whom had never attended school, while others had already failed a grade. Before long, Verver began another class of 35 students in the nearby town of Edna. That summer, according to the earliest newspaper report of her pilot projects, Verver would teach vocabulary to a total of 151 children.[37]

Felix visited the Ganado class at least every other week to pay Verver, offer fatherly encouragement, and see the results of her work, often giving fruit and candy to the children as rewards for responding correctly to his questions in English. He also spoke to the local parents, cajoling them to support Verver's efforts and to become involved with the local schools, especially in the activities of the PTA. For all Felix Tijerina did to launch this education project, Isabel Verver would forty years later emphatically describe him as "an angel sent from heaven."[38]

CRITICISM SURFACES

Even as his preschool plans gelled, Felix began to receive volleys of criticism from John J. Herrera, which reflected a broader strain of anti-Tijerina sentiment in LULAC. Their cooperation at the El Paso convention notwithstanding, the two men became embroiled in a partisan political brouhaha in October, 1956, when Felix responded to an article written by columnist Drew Pearson. Apparently, Tijerina saw an October 9 column by Pearson in the *El Paso Times* stating that LULAC had spread the word among its membership to vote against Vice President Richard Nixon because of Nixon's record on civil rights. While in Weslaco, Texas, attending the installation of local council officers, Felix told the Associated Press that Pearson's comments were "untrue and malicious"; he noted that at no time did the LULAC national office make any statements relative to the presidential campaign. Tijerina concluded that such comments—if they had been made—could be seen only as the personal opinion of individuals since the organization "cannot participate . . . in political activity.'" The AP story as it appeared in the *Houston Post* on October 15 (where apparently Herrera read it) went on to note that Felix, sporting an "Ike" campaign button on his lapel, later told journalists that he personally endorsed Eisenhower-Nixon and would vote for that ticket in November.[39]

A week later, a letter to the editor from Herrera appeared in the *Post* attacking Felix's criticism of Pearson. Noting that minority groups in California and across the Southwest considered "Dickie" Nixon to be "reactionary and unsympathetic," Herrera blasted the Republican Party in general. Ever the Democrat, Herrera added that the vast majority of Latinos did not share Tijerina's enthusiasm for the Republican administration, but rather supported the Democratic Party nominees, Adlai Stevenson and Estes Kefauver.[40]

In addition, Herrera wrote Drew Pearson, informing him of Tijerina's objection to Pearson's column; he identified Felix as "a recent member to Lulac who infiltrated into the organization for political purposes." Stating that Tijerina was "now subject to censor and impeachment proceedings" for partisan politics, Herrera called him "a White Man's Mexican."[41]

Determined to take his case to the membership, Herrera photocopied on one sheet of paper his letter to the editor, the *Post* article on Tijerina, and an October 23 telegram from Danny Olivas, immediate past LULAC regional governor for California, which denounced the vice president; he apparently sent this collage to other LULACs as a mailer entitled "The Truth about Richard Nixon!" Herrera especially resented Tijerina wearing an Eisenhower campaign button while acting as national president. Any earlier rapprochement between the two nemeses had dissipated with the fall election.[42]

In early 1957, Herrera again angrily responded to comments Felix made to the Monterrey newspaper *El norte* regarding the plight of Mexican Americans. Tijerina allegedly had told the newspaper that 85 percent of Mexicans in the United States earned no more than thirty-two dollars a week and that only 4 percent went beyond the third grade, no doubt emphasizing their disadvantaged status. He supposedly added that what discrimination existed toward Mexicans resulted to some extent from their own behavior.[43]

Writing the newspaper in Spanish, an infuriated Herrera asserted that Tijerina had lied. He explained at length that many Mexican Americans commanded better wages and enjoyed a relatively decent standard of living, except those who worked at "certain places like Mr. Tijerina's restaurants that employ Mexicans recently arrived from Mexico, and by their bad luck have to accept wages of $20 per week, with the privilege of completing their salary with tips." Herrera noted that educationally the present generation fared better as well, with 85 percent finishing their high school studies, and many hoped to become professionals. Regarding Felix's comments on discrimination, Herrera explained that discrimination still existed in many places in the United States, especially in Texas, because of historic racial prejudice, not because of the deportment of the Mexican people. He invited Tijerina and his "millionaire friends" to visit some of the establishments near Houston that still refused to serve Mexicans. "[W]e can only lament," Herrera went on, "that a man like Felix Tijerina is at the head of . . . LULAC . . . due to his money, not for his ideological convictions." Tijerina would do best, Herrera concluded, "to complete his elementary education . . . and leave in peace *la raza mexicana* living in the United States, who do not need semi-literate leaders."[44]

A third public spat between the two men soon followed. In late May, 1957, national legal advisor Phil Montalbo wrote an open letter to Tijerina in which he counseled against LULAC joining forces with the National Association for the Advancement of Colored People (NAACP), State Senator Henry B. González, and State Senator Abraham Kazen, Jr., in their opposition to House Bill 231, a measure then being considered by the Texas state legislature and one which, allegedly, had the tacit approval of Governor Daniel. H.B. 231 would have allowed local school superintendents to place students in whatever schools that they, as administrators, considered appropriate; the NAACP, González, and Kazen believed that such a law was designed to subvert the 1954 Supreme Court decision to end school segregation. To express their opposition, González and Kazen mounted a filibuster against the bill on May 2, which lasted thirty-six hours, reportedly the longest in Texas history.[45]

As one of his political confidants remembered, Tijerina was never happy with the NAACP and shunned any alliance with the black community for fear of a possible white backlash. But even more specifically, by May, Felix was busy gaining support for his preschool project among the Austin establishment, especially with Price Daniel, whom many perceived as a moderate on matters of race. Felix, always the practical man, would hardly have been disposed to make waves with political allies. The prospect of an English language program, with the support of a sympathetic governor, would have no doubt seemed much more important to Tijerina than opposing the bills before the Texas senate. Even more cautious than Tijerina, Montalbo advised his national president that to link arms with the NAACP would "tend to admit to our anglo-american friends that we [Mexican Americans] considered ourselves separate . . . from the majority of American citizens" and that if segregation should occur as a result of the bill's passage, it would be "our problem to be worked out with the help of our anglo-american friends and not with the help of the NAACP."[46]

On June 1, at a LULAC installation banquet at the Menger Hotel in San Antonio, with such distinguished members present as Alonso S. Perales, M. C. González, Mauro Machado, Jake Rodríguez, and John Solíz, Herrera delivered a searing speech against H.B. 231 and the LULAC national administration's lack of opposition to the measure. While paying homage to Senators González and Kazen—who were also in the audience and being honored for their filibuster—Herrera noted that H.B. 231 struck "at the very heart of the Delgado Decision," the 1948 court ruling which had abolished the hated "Mexican schools." He ridiculed the national LULAC administration for not taking a stand against the bill even though González and Kazen received support from Mexican Americans across Texas.[47]

Herrera followed up this speech with an equally angry open letter to Montalbo, mimeographed copies of which he sent far and wide. Penned in early June, just before the LULAC national convention, Herrera's letter took Montalbo and Tijerina to task for their lack of solidarity with the progressive forces against H.B. 231. He castigated the two men for their fear of "controversial" issues and stated that the proposed bill, though "ostensibly aimed at Negro children," might well be applied by traditionally biased school districts to segregate Mexican American students.[48]

Herrera went on to remind Montalbo that Felix had not shied from courting "controversy" when he identified himself during the 1956 election as an Eisenhower supporter, even to the point of wearing an "Ike" button, the memory of which continued to irritate Herrera. Such conduct, along with this recent failure to support the NAACP, led Herrera to conclude that "Felix has been weighed in the scales of Lulac opinion and has been found sadly wanting." Noting that he was "ashamed and embarrassed at the way Felix has conducted himself as . . . National President," Herrera lamented that he had personally supported Tijerina's first election. Herrera even blamed Felix for what he perceived as the recent dearth of successful projects by Houston Councils No. 60 and No. 22. Spicing his letter with Spanish proverbs, Herrera passed judgment on Tijerina's leadership in his home city and across the organization by noting that "el que no es rey de su casa no puede ser rey del mundo" (he who is not king of his own house cannot be king of the world). Herrera concluded that Felix "should and must be repudiated" by LULAC, referring to Tijerina's upcoming bid for reelection.[49]

On behalf of Tijerina and Council No. 60, Felix Salazar, the council secretary, issued an open letter of his own to Herrera, refuting the latter's accusations about Houston LULAC's poor showing over the preceding year. He not only informed the past national president that LULAC in the Bayou City was "very much alive and active," but he also noted that over the past eighteen months Herrera had attended only four council meetings—three of these times to ask for the privilege of representing the council at some outside function. Noting that such conduct hardly enabled Herrera to belittle the efforts of his fellow LULACs and irritated at Herrera's penchant for quoting Spanish maxims, Salazar closed with one of his own: "No más oyen el Gallo cantar y no saben para donde queda El Rancho" (loosely translated: Some folks only hear what the problems are, but don't know where the work gets done).[50]

Though Salazar may have been correct about Herrera's lack of activity with Council No. 60, Tijerina and Montalbo had shown no sympathy for ethnic solidarity in their stance on H.B. 231. By choosing to side with their "anglo-american friends" rather than with the NAACP and its Mexican American legislative allies, Tijerina definitively communicated that blacks could not look to him, as LULAC national president, for support. Felix had, as always, chosen the practical route. Indeed, regarding his opposition to González on the segregation issue, Tijerina later told the *Houston Chronicle*: "Let the Negro fight his own battles. His problems are not mine. I don't want to ally with him."[51]

Herrera's opposition to Tijerina fueled other criticism of the national administration. Prompted by what he had heard from Herrera, national chaplain Guadalupe C. Martínez had circulated a couple of self-styled "news letters" to the LULAC membership just prior to the June convention. Though vague in his accusations, Martínez complained that the LULAC Supreme Council was now controlled by "a click [sic], centered around Council No. 60," which considers itself "unique and absolute." Echoing Herrera's sentiments, Martínez expressed a desire "for responsible and qualified leadership" in LULAC, leadership rooted in educational attainment "and not money."[52] Just as he responded to Herrera's accusations, Felix Salazar (by now a lightning rod for Tijerina) wrote Martínez that his state-

ment about the Council No. 60 clique was both "asinine and wholly without foundation."[53]

THE ANAHEIM CONVENTION

Regardless of the reservations held by members such as Herrera and
Martínez, Felix handily won reelection to his second term as LULAC president at the twenty-eighth national convention held June 27–30, 1957, at the
Disneyland Hotel in Anaheim, California. Alfred Hernández would later report at the clubhouse on Bagby that Council No. 60 and the Tijerina forces
"had complete control" of the proceedings. For the first time in the organization's history, areas from outside the Southwest were represented at the
national gathering. The front cover of the convention issue of the *LULAC
News* boasted of councils attending from nine states: Texas, Colorado, Arizona, New Mexico, California, Indiana, Illinois, Iowa, and Wisconsin. Together, they presented LULAC as a national organization for the first time.[54]

Hosted by the Placentia Council, the Anaheim convention featured the
usual flurry of activities of a LULAC national gathering: business meetings,
seminars on such topics as education and local government, reports by the
various LULAC regional governors and national officers on the activities
within their jurisdictions, a dance, and even a special program at Disneyland, which had opened the year before. At the banquet and presidential
ball on Saturday evening, Los Angeles city councilman Edward R. Roybal
and California assemblyman Richard T. Hanna addressed those assembled,
while United States congressman D. S. Saund delivered the keynote speech.
Roybal especially impressed Tijerina when he referred to Mexican Americans as the "sleeping giant" of United States society. On the following afternoon, June 30, the delegates elected Tijerina to his second term as national president, a ringing endorsement of his role as "guide and prophet"
of the largest Hispanic organization in the United States.[55]

Mrs. Felix and her children had gone to California during the convention but had stayed in Los Angeles. Mrs. Felix made no secret of her dislike
for LULAC or her husband's involvement as national president. Her over-
arching objection was that it took up too much of Felix's energy and
finances, as well as taking him away from his business and family, particularly since they had two young children. She particularly found the conventions distasteful, occasions that she felt were filled with "dirty politics" and

people "hungry for prestige." (Nor was she fond of the rumored womanizing alleged to have transpired at the annual LULAC meetings.) But on the final day of the Anaheim proceedings, she personally attended to lobby for Felix's reelection so that he could carry out his dream of an education program for Mexican American children.[56]

During their visit to Disneyland, Janie Bell and Felix, Jr., had posed for a souvenir photograph with wax mannequins of popular Disney characters Davy Crockett and Georgie Russell (i.e., likenesses of actors Fess Parker and Buddy Ebsen). The photo of the two Tijerina children with their coonskin caps and toy rifles was a quintessential statement of mid-1950s American mainstream culture.[57]

The 1957 LULAC convention delegates also passed their usual number of constitutional amendments and resolutions. Reflecting Herrera's earlier criticisms, the assembly passed a resolution, promoted by Texas regional governor Pete Tijerina and San Antonio Council No. 2, "emphatically condemning and protesting" Texas H.B. 231, an action which amounted to a repudiation of Montalbo's timid advice from the previous month. Although the resolution affirmed LULAC's belief that "the decision of the Supreme Court of the United States . . . should be abided by . . . all . . . Citizens," it made no reference to the NAACP or African Americans; rather, it stated that H.B. 231 would nullify "all the accomplishments of our organizations in the Delgado case, the Salvatierra case, and the Driscoll case," court decisions that directly helped Mexican Americans.[58]

The anti–H.B. 231 resolution obviously reflected a sentiment within the organization against Felix's direction. Immediately after the Anaheim gathering, Pete Tijerina wrote Johnny Herrera (who had refused to attend) "that there were times when our convention seemed more like a White Citizens' Council meeting than a LULAC convention." Noting that a split brewed, the San Antonian concluded that "we [the opposition] came out with a strong united group that is going to battle the Houston-Laredo coalition."[59]

Following his election to a second term as national president, Felix made some adjustments in the appointed offices of his administration. Montalbo moved out and the loyal Felix Salazar took his place as his new national legal advisor. Tijerina also replaced Guadalupe C. Martínez with David Adame as national chaplain, no doubt in response to Martínez's earlier barbs. Daniel Sandoval, a Tijerina confidant from the Baytown council, replaced Gilbert Gómez as national treasurer. Val Hernández, of Chicago LULAC, was appointed to the newly established position of national organizer, a job designed to continue Tijerina's expansion of the league and one that Hernández had all but forged for himself with his energetic style. Angelo Machuca of East Chicago, Indiana, was designated as special organizer for the Midwest. Tony Campos was Tijerina's national coordinator, a position in which he had already been serving. Ernest Eguía relinquished the editorship of the LULAC News, and that chore shifted to Paul Garza, Jr., of the Laredo council. Although the LULAC News was often viewed as an albatross, Eguía had produced a distinctive run of the monthly publications, ones that chronicled the doings of the league as well as any in its history. Felix's two mainstays, Alfred Hernández and Carmen Cortes, remained in their respective positions as national secretary and national executive secretary. Tijerina made other appointments of lesser prominence, one being Isabel Verver as chair of the Committee on Citizenship.[60]

ABANDONMENT OF THE "ESCUELITA DEL AIRE"

In the meantime, the "Escuelita del Aire" had not materialized, and never would. Indeed, the May announcement had amounted to a false start. Although Felix had already invested a good deal of his own money in the initial planning and development of the preschool program, by late May his and LULAC's inability to raise the necessary funding from other sponsors had stalled its implementation. According to the best recollections of participants, the radio project, as designed in Austin, carried too much initial cost.[61]

As of June, 1957, Felix remained vague in his monthly presidential messages about the exact nature of his proposed education program, except to say that LULAC had initiated a project in Texas to teach English to preschoolers, that it was still "in its first stages," and that his administration "sincerely hope[d] to realize this dream in the very near future." Though plans seemed still to be in flux, Felix's main concern by July, 1957, remained the same: for him the overriding fact was that "in Texas alone, the average . . . education for our Latin children is 3.6 years of schooling," and he wanted to do something for the preschooler to turn this deplorable condition around.[62]

Tijerina had come to see something that he really liked in Isabel Verver's direct, hands-on instruction. Although he and his LULAC circle had done much planning during his first term, it was in his second year as LULAC national president that his "dream" of a preschool education program would take definite shape with Verver's approach serving as the model.

During the summer (probably after the Anaheim convention), Tijerina obtained the services of Bill Taylor and Jack Zilker, fellow Rotarians and owners of Photographic Laboratories in Houston, to produce a film for LULAC that featured the efforts of Isabel Verver and promoted the need for preschool language instruction. Written by Warren Ferguson and narrated by Alfred Hernández, this fifteen-minute, black-and-white production was entitled *Forgotten Minds* and produced at a cost of twenty-five hundred dollars, borne totally by Taylor and Zilker. *Forgotten Minds* pointed out the desperately low educational level of most Mexican Americans and the resulting marginality among many in that population, and squarely blamed the language barrier (i.e., the inability of Mexican American children to speak English) for these societal ills.[63]

In addition to noting Verver's example, *Forgotten Minds* suggested the possibility of teaching English to Mexican American families over the radio as well as through such language classes as those operated by the Junior Forum in Houston—anything to get Mexican American children to be fluent in English. The film did not explain Verver's teaching methodology, made no mention of her use of any word list, nor any help she may have received from Tijerina. Nor did it use the name "Little School of the 400." It did conclude with the idea that the average child beginning school needed a four-hundred-word vocabulary in order to succeed, and it urged people to become involved in any way they could to destroy the language barrier. Completed by early August, *Forgotten Minds* was slated to be viewed the following month at the first Supreme Council meeting of Tijerina's second term.[64]

RELAUNCHING THE PRESCHOOL PROGRAM

In what amounted to a new departure from the stillborn Escuelita del Aire, Tijerina announced his plans for a preschool program in grand style at the LULAC Supreme Council meeting held at Houston's Shamrock Hilton on September 14–15, 1957. With Mrs. Felix and Elizabeth Burrus present, Felix formally unveiled this program on the evening of the fourteenth at a banquet in the Shamrock's Castillian Room. A host of LULACs and other dignitaries were on hand, including Governor Price Daniel, Bob Smith,

Senator Kazen, District Judge Fidencio Guerra of McAllen, Texas Education Commissioner J. W. Edgar, state representatives Eligio "Kika" de la Garza of McAllen and Oscar Laurel, and Judge Albert Treviño of San Antonio. Fred Nahas—Tijerina's fellow Rotarian, president of Houston's KXYZ radio, and someone who would play an active role in promoting the preschool program—emceed the gala event. In addition to screening *Forgotten Minds,* Tijerina told those in attendance that LULAC planned to establish Verver-style classes in or near the fifty towns in Texas that contained active LULAC councils. These classes, he noted, would teach preschool Mexican American children the four hundred basic words.[65]

Tijerina also told the audience that the project would entail great expense, citing costs for teachers' salaries and radio time. (The plan still envisioned a radio component.) He estimated the program's total price to be $146,000. To stress its necessity, Felix recounted his own childhood difficulties with the language barrier, relating that as a young uneducated waiter he had struggled along in the days when he knew little more than "Thank you; come and see us again."[66]

When his time to speak came, Governor Daniel, himself an honorary member of the San Antonio LULAC council, reiterated his support for the project, stating that such a program would allow Latin Americans to "render even greater service to the nation in the future." A history enthusiast and descendant of nineteenth-century Texas colonists, Daniel expressed his admiration for those Latin Americans who "fought side by side with Anglos in the Texas War for Independence." Tijerina and the LULACs viewed Daniel as *simpático,* noting his appointment of several Mexican Americans to governmental positions.[67]

Governor Daniel also announced at the banquet that he had named Tijerina as one of his six appointments to the prestigious Hale-Aikin Committee of Twenty-four. This body of two dozen influential Texans had been recently established by the state legislature to study the Texas public school system. Felix's triumph was complete when, at its business meeting on the following day, the LULAC Supreme Council unanimously endorsed his preschool program. The *LULAC News* "acclaimed" the effort to be "one of the most inspirational projects ever attempted by Lulac."[68]

As expected, the Houston newspapers gave good play to the story, noting that Tijerina and LULAC, with the full endorsement of their guest of honor, Governor Price Daniel, had "started an all-out drive to teach all preschool Latin American children in Texas the 400 basic words of English." As

Felix explained through the *Houston Post,* by allowing Mexican American children to begin school on an equal footing with Anglo students, the program "would keep them from getting inferiority complexes because of a language barrier." [69]

THE LULAC EDUCATIONAL FUND, INC.

During the September meeting of the LULAC Supreme Council, Tijerina and his cohorts also established a nonprofit corporation called the LULAC Educational Fund to serve as a vehicle to finance and direct the proposed preschool program. Filed with the state of Texas on October 14, 1957, by Tijerina, Alfred Hernández, and Oscar Laurel, the LULAC Educational Fund, Inc., existed for two stated purposes: first, to teach the four hundred basic English words to preschool Mexican American children through classroom instruction as well as through "the media of radio and television," and second, to award scholarships to deserving students to attend institutions of higher learning. As created, the fund had nine directors, including Tijerina, Hernández, Laurel, Bob Smith, Judge Fidencio Guerra, Fred Nahas, J. W. Edgar, G. A. "Pop" Mabry (of Humble Oil Company), and J. O. Webb, assistant superintendent of the Houston public schools. Through this agency, Tijerina would soon begin to solicit financial contributions to put his program into action. [70]

Immediately following the September Supreme Council meeting, Felix encouraged the general membership, through the *LULAC News,* to become involved in his new education program. He challenged its "self-styled leaders who brag of their doings" and those who kept "living on their past glory" (no doubt Herrera et al.), to admit that the organization was not fully succeeding in bettering the lives of less fortunate Mexican Americans— "those they profess to represent." Felix firmly told the organization that if Roybal's Mexican American "sleeping giant" was to ever awaken, it would have to be through LULAC efforts to instruct Mexican Americans on their responsibilities as citizens; after that they could assert their civil rights. While some in the organization may have felt Felix's strategy was overly cautious, like so many other views Tijerina held, it was perfectly in keeping with the letter of the "LULAC Code" which, from the beginning of the organization's existence, decreed that one must "[l]earn how to discharge your duties before you learn how to assert your rights." [71]

Nevertheless, criticism quickly sprang from within the organization. On November 9, Tijerina held a mass meeting in San Antonio of the forty-five LULAC Texas district governors to explain the project and enlist their assistance. Following this confab, in early December, Jake Rodríguez, a longtime LULAC associate from the Alamo City who had been in the organization since 1931, wrote Felix Salazar (and sent a copy to Tijerina) that: "Confidentially, IT STINKS!" The "kindergarten school film" and proposal, Rodríguez maintained, represented an "utter denial and refutation of LULAC's twenty-eight year stand" on Mexican American education; that is, it suggested that the presence of Mexican American children in public schools "retarded" the development of their classmates, an argument Anglos had historically used to perpetuate separate facilities. Rodríguez added that another prominent member at the San Antonio affair had also spoken derisively about Tijerina's beloved project, commenting that it would "never get to first base!"[72]

Salazar responded in kind, taking Rodríguez to task for his silence and "demeanor . . . of . . . apathy and boredom" at the San Antonio meeting when it had been time for comments from the audience. More important, Salazar stated, the program did not intend to suggest that Latin children "retarded" anyone; rather, it simply meant to familiarize children with English before they began regular school instruction. He urged Rodríguez not to discourage LULACs from assisting their effort, even though he and others might disagree.[73]

But Rodríguez was not finished. In a follow-up letter he told Salazar (and Tijerina) that what had been mistaken for "apathy or boredom" had been "just pure disgust." He continued: "But you boys reminded me so much of a bunch of kids playing with a new toy, that I just didn't have the heart to bust it right in your face." To make his point about school segregation remaining a concern for Mexican Americans, Rodríguez also enclosed a recent news clipping reporting that Governor Daniel had just signed into law three segregation-type bills. No doubt reacting to Tijerina's traditional aversion to airing the segregation issue publicly, Rodríguez drew an arrow to the word "Segregation" in the title of the article and noted: "Here's that UGLY word we CAN'T EVEN BREATHE!"[74]

Rodríguez's comments may well have had merit, but only to a point. While Felix and his cadre understood that discrimination existed, they insisted on handling such matters discreetly and on a local, case-by-case basis. In fact, during the summer of 1957 a committee composed of Tijerina,

Alfred Hernández, and Moses M. Sánchez (a young Council No. 60 Korean War Marine Corps veteran) effectively investigated an alleged case of discrimination at Houston's Gateway Crystal Pool, after a World War II widow reported that she and her young son had been refused entry to that local swimming spot.[75]

Rather than public protests or court action, the Tijerina approach entailed private, but firm negotiations. Rightly or wrongly, as Felix Salazar later reflected, Tijerina believed that reasoning with people and increased education would ultimately eliminate discrimination.[76]

Regardless of any opposition from skeptical LULACs, Tijerina pushed his education program forward. For one thing, the children who had been in Verver's 1957 summer classes were proving the efficacy of her teaching methods.

During the 1957 fall term, the Ganado Elementary School principal and four of the school's first grade teachers quickly agreed that Verver's students progressed much better than youngsters who had not attended her classes. (By the end of the school year and much to Tijerina's delight, the overwhelming majority would pass the first grade.)[77]

Felix used every occasion to solicit support for the LULAC Educational Fund and prepare for implementing an expanded preschool program for the summer of 1958. In his capacity as national president, he visited Latin American communities in various Texas towns to convince the local LULAC councils to begin a class in their area. Felix promised that if fifteen parents in a locale would enroll their children, he would hire a teacher for a summer class. He also sought the help of ministers and priests to announce the program to their congregations.[78]

Tijerina's hectic traveling and solicitation efforts consumed his time. In early January, 1958, he was in El Paso to confer with LULAC power broker Paul Andow; on February 8, Felix hosted Council No. 60's annual officers' installation dinner at his Westheimer restaurant. The toastmaster for that occasion was Gus García, the legendary LULAC lawyer whom Felix had heard back in 1947 explain the appalling statistics of Mexican American education. In mid-February, Tijerina flew to Milwaukee, Wisconsin, to preside over the Supreme Council meeting held there to help solidify that region within the organization; on February 22, he traveled to Laredo with Price Daniel and Oscar Laurel to be at the annual LULAC Noche Mexicana celebration held by Council No. 12 (an event Governor Daniel always enjoyed); and on March 21–23, Tijerina attended the Texas state LULAC convention in Waco, where he saw Alfred Hernández elected Texas regional governor and met Judge Sarah T. Hughes of Dallas, the convention's principal speaker. At each event, Tijerina spoke on "our beloved project," the LULAC Educational Fund, Inc.[79]

Felix anxiously sought media coverage to promote the fund and its mission, and, as usual, he found it. On March 12, what was probably the first of the many major newspaper articles publicizing these efforts appeared in the *Houston Press*. Written by Marie Dauplaise, the story featured Isabel Verver, Felix, and their "simple dream" of teaching four hundred basic words of English to Mexican American children. The article noted that Felix and the board of directors of the LULAC Educational Fund, Inc., were contacting some three thousand Latin American businessmen to contribute $18.45 each, the estimated cost of preparing a child to speak English before entering school. Through Dauplaise, Felix reminded the readers that the "hard, cold facts" were that Latin Americans lagged far behind in educational attainment and that learning English was the key so that, as Felix noted, they would be on equal footing when they "go to schools geared to the Anglo children." Noting that the program was revving up for the coming summer, the article included Tijerina's plea for help: "We need kindergarten books, pencils, anything for school. Of course we need money gifts too." Indicative of the response that the program would always get from the Anglo media, a concurrent *Press* editorial called it "a magnificent undertaking—one that deserves the full support of . . . Texas." These favorable articles came just as LULAC was holding a banquet at Felix's Westheimer restaurant to raise funds.[80]

Dauplaise's story soon garnered some important national recognition when it caught the eye of Ralph Yarborough, Texas' junior United States senator. Impressed by what he read, Yarborough had the article reprinted in the *Congressional Record* on March 18, 1958, and noted that "leaders in the League of United Latin American Citizens recently took an important step for education in Texas." Noting that the project was "being spearheaded by Mr. Felix Tijerina, prominent Houston restaurant operator" and LULAC national president, Senator Yarborough went on to say that this "is the beginning of broader educational opportunities for the 1,600,000 Latin American citizens in Texas." Yarborough's action likely represented the first national mainstream publicity for Tijerina's preschool program and probably the initial time it came to the attention of the federal government.[81]

While most applauded, some LULACs continued to question. On March 20, Albert Armendariz, past national president from El Paso, sent a five-page memo to "All Members of Lulac" blasting Tijerina and the Supreme Council for creating the LULAC Educational Fund, Inc., as a separate entity from LULAC. In Armendariz's opinion, Felix and the Supreme Council had taken it upon themselves without obtaining authority from the national assembly or having their actions ratified by the required number of councils, "to divide our League into two separate and distinct entities," that is, LULAC itself and the Educational Fund. He argued that because the corporation's board had a majority of non-LULACs, it was "a self-controlled corporation completely divorced from the League." In short, he felt that the Educational Fund violated LULAC organizational rules.[82]

By making themselves officers on the Educational Fund board, Armendariz charged, Tijerina, Hernández, and Laurel had "perpetuated themselves . . . by their own vote." He suggested that while the Educational Fund might be retained as established, it had to include directors from states other than Texas, allow only LULAC members on the board (including the treasurer), and present itself to the next national assembly for approval—in the form of a constitutional amendment. Until then, he concluded, councils should hold any funds they had collected for the program or send them to the national treasurer.[83]

Subsequently, in a missive to Alfred Hernández, Armendariz complained that his objections to the LULAC Educational Fund had not been addressed. He lamented that the "dictatorial attitude of our leadership" will doom an otherwise good project "to only partial support of the league." In a flourish characteristic of many LULACs during that era, Armendariz concluded that he would "choose to fight, with what little power I may possess, for the defeat of the present form of the Lulac Educational Fund, Inc."[84]

Other LULAC members quickly came to the defense of Felix and the Educational Fund. Dr. Francisco Licón, LULAC national health director and fellow El Pasoan, sent out his own "To All Members of Lulacs" memo in mid-April in which he refuted the "Albert Armendariz Manifesto" with his own interpretation of the LULAC constitution. Val Hernández, Felix's energetic organizer, sent a letter on June 18 to Tijerina that was meant for public dissemination. Writing under the title of "Illinois Chairman of the Tijerina Campaign Committee," Hernández dismissed the "Armendariz Manifesto" as propaganda designed "to provoke . . . the membership against your administration" in order to advance someone else for the top office. He asked Felix to run for a third term as national president so that the league could continue to expand. He assured "Don Felix" that the "new LULAC" most needed him at its helm as a role model: "Your success in life is in the all American, Horatio Alger tradition and it is [a] symbol and example to the rest of us American-Mexicans in the United States of what can be accomplished in this wonderful land of opportunity."[85]

The squabble initiated by Armendariz over the Educational Fund would be settled that summer. The board of directors elected Tijerina as its president by acclamation at its June 22, 1958, meeting and expanded its membership only to include the Texas regional governor. On June 29, at its national convention in Laredo, the LULAC membership would formally adopt the Educational Fund through a constitutional amendment as a separate, subsidiary corporation. In addition, the national LULAC treasurer was officially relieved from all responsibility for the monies collected.[86]

OPENING THE LITTLE SCHOOL OF THE 400

Felix and his cohorts had hoped to establish classes in approximately fifty Texas cities and towns during the summer of 1958, but they fell short of their goal. By the first week in June, they had started seven, which Felix personally underwrote to the tune of $175 a week—a $25 weekly salary for each teacher. Two more were soon added, giving them a total of nine schools that the Educational Fund would officially operate that summer. These locations included Sugar Land, Aldine, Ganado, Edna, Brookshire, Rosenberg, Vanderbilt, Wharton, and Fort Stockton. All but Fort Stockton in far West Texas were in the Houston area.[87]

LULAC members had recommended candidates for paid positions as instructors; Felix had conducted the final interviews and hired them. Although he initially paid their salaries, he planned to have the money collected by the LULAC Educational Fund cover these expenses after the first week in June. Theretofore, Felix and his cohorts had actively sought assistance from only Mexican Americans; however, by early June they had sent out three thousand letters to Anglos seeking their financial support as well.[88]

The teachers who came on board that first summer included Margie García (Sugar Land), Mrs. Nat Espitia (Aldine), Mrs. Toney Zarate (Ganado), Geneva Santellana (Edna), Mrs. Terry Barrera (Fort Stockton),

Josephine Salazar (Brookshire), Mrs. Blas Rodríguez (Rosenberg), Rachel Garza (Vanderbilt), and Teresa Hernández (Wharton). Unfortunately, Isabel Verver was not among them. After her summer teaching, she found it necessary to leave school and find employment to help her family. She soon married John González, the oldest brother of one of her former students. By the time Marie Dauplaise interviewed Verver, she and her husband had moved to Houston, where she worked in the tailor shop of Sakowitz's Gulfgate store. She hoped to return to Ganado to develop another preschool class, but her plans never fully materialized. She would eventually move to Corpus Christi, where by 1961 she had become assistant manager of a women's clothing store. Though she never became a teacher, the irrepressible Isabel Verver later made her way to California, where she continued to educate herself and became seriously involved in grassroots unionism, electoral politics, LULAC, and other forms of meaningful community activism.[89]

In late June, after the schools had been operating for several weeks, the preschool program for the 1958 summer was officially inaugurated in Felix's usual grand style, and it was for this dedication ceremony that the classes were first specifically referred to, at least in the written record, as the "Little School of the 400," rather than simply as the "LULAC Educational Program."[90]

After much planning and advance publicity, this formal dedication took place on Monday, June 23, 1958, in Sugar Land, where the first class for that summer had opened. The day—which proved to be another high point in Tijerina's life—began at 9 A.M. with a reception for Felix at the Sugar Land Shopping Center. Hosted by W. H. Louviere, president of the Imperial Sugar Company, it also included Governor Price Daniel, his wife and thirteen-year-old son Houston, Bob Smith, and other dignitaries.[91]

At 10 A.M. the dedication ceremony took place at 2610 Ash Street, at the small frame building which served as the site of the Sugar Land Little School of the 400. The building, situated on the campus of the Sugar Land public schools in the Mexican American section of town, was draped in red, white, and blue bunting as was the large open-sided tent in front that contained a temporary platform where the speakers and other distinguished guests were seated. A crowd of two hundred people, including representatives and teachers from the other eight Little Schools, had assembled. As part of the opening ceremonies, forty-five Latin American children from the Sugar

Land Little School recited the pledge of allegiance in English, which they had learned during their previous few weeks of class.[92]

With great solemnity as a band played "God Bless America," representatives from the American Legion presented Tijerina with an American flag. Master of ceremonies and publicist for the event Fred Nahas explained how the Little School took its name from the basic list of words to be taught there. He then introduced Felix, who told the crowd how, as a youth, he had been handicapped by the language barrier until he began his study of English with the words "tomato ketchup." He noted: "I pledged to myself and my God that if I could help my fellow Latin Americans to speak English I would do so." He added that he still studied English an hour each day. At the conclusion of his remarks, Felix introduced Governor Daniel, the principal speaker, as "the best governor Texas ever had."[93]

In his speech, Daniel praised the program as "one of the truly great privately financed educational projects in our State" and its formal dedication as "the most important event in the recent history of Texas." Reiterating his support for the effort, Daniel also hailed LULAC as an organization whose "primary goal . . . has been the strengthening of citizenship and patriotism," especially through its emphasis upon education, as well as being "among the staunch supporters of law and order in th[e] fight for decency and moral behavior."[94]

The governor told the audience that the "Latin Americans in Texas have contributed much in building our State," that it was "this strong Latin influence in Texas which long ago sealed the bond of friendship between the Lone Star State . . . and . . . Mexico." He likewise reminded listeners of the emerging numbers: that there were "more people of Mexican descent in Texas than in . . . Tamaulipas, Chihuahua, and Nuevo León combined." As always, Daniel mentioned that "Mexicans fought side by side with Anglos in the Texas War for Independence."[95]

He reserved a full third of his laudatory comments, however, for Felix Tijerina personally. There, near where Felix had once labored in the fields of Sugarland Industries, the governor of Texas heaped golden praise upon the erstwhile *obrero,* telling the audience and media representatives that the Little School of the 400 represented "the fulfillment of an American dream by a boy who was born in poverty and ha[d] risen to become one of Texas' most distinguished citizens." Noting that the restaurateur and LULAC national president "was born here in Sugar Land," Daniel reminded listeners that Felix had mastered the English language "the hard way." Daniel stressed his admiration and affection for Felix, someone who, through the Little School, had "set in motion a plan to give . . . children more opportunity than he had as a boy." [96]

Upon completion of the governor's talk, the band played the "Eyes of Texas" as Daniel presented Tijerina with a Texas flag. Five-year-old Dolores Zepeda, one of the Little Schoolers, presented Governor and Mrs. Daniel with a bouquet of flowers. They posed for the many photographers on hand to capture the various parts of the auspicious occasion. The photographs that feature Felix during the event show him justifiably filled with pride and satisfaction. [97]

The entire ceremony dedicating the Little School of the 400, including Daniel's speech, was broadcast live over Houston-based KXYZ radio and was covered by local newspapers, the United Press International, as well as by television news, including Houston's KGUL-TV. It was a media coup that projected the accomplishments of LULAC and Felix Tijerina as embodiments of the best efforts of the Latin American people. Moreover, it spread the word on Mexican American education as probably never before, informing thousands of residents that Latin Americans, with the support of well-meaning Anglos (including the governor of Texas), were working at self-determination in an area that had long proved problematic for their community but could no longer be ignored. [98]

The day concluded with a luncheon for Governor Daniel and his family at the Castillian Room of the Shamrock Hotel. Back in Austin, Daniel sent Felix a letter again congratulating him on the "splendid" education program that he had started; the governor also extended his appreciation for his many kindnesses at the dedication, especially "your kind introduction of me." The dedication ceremony sealed an already close friendship between the two men. [99]

TIJERINA AND HENRY B. GONZÁLEZ

While Tijerina further solidified his relationship with Price Daniel at the Little School dedication, the event marked a downturn in his association with Henry B. González. Although the governor's dedication-day speech had been billed in the media as "non-political," he was at that time in the midst of the primary campaign, and Felix was essentially playing a role for Daniel by providing a visible link to the emerging Latino vote. [100]

Felix was, of course, a publicly acknowledged Price Daniel partisan and had financially contributed to his political campaigns. He had been featured with Daniel in an April *Houston Chronicle* article on election year activities. It reported that Felix had caballed with the governor, Mrs. Lloyd M. Bentsen, Jr., and others at the local Democratic Party headquarters to field a slate of moderate Democratic precinct committee members for the July primary.[101]

By June, Daniel had three opponents in the primary, including W. Lee "Pappy" O'Daniel, Dallas insurance man Joe Irwin, and, of more importance to Mexican American history, State Senator Henry B. González from San Antonio. González, the son of educated, middle-class Mexican immigrants, was the rising star of Texas Mexican politicians in the state. Although financially strapped—he was married with a growing family—he had served as San Antonio city councilman from 1953 to 1956 and thereafter as the first Mexican American state senator from Bexar County during the twentieth century. In 1958, González offered himself to the liberal wing of the Democratic Party as an alternative candidate to Price Daniel.[102]

Although the liberal Democrats did not officially endorse him, by June, González was in the midst of what he and his enthusiastic supporters called their "Poor Boys" campaign—a candidacy that had no chance of victory, but the first truly viable gubernatorial bid made by a Mexican Texan. He had many supporters, mainly Mexican Americans in South Texas, but his backers also came from wherever Mexican Americans resided, including Houston, Felix's hometown. There, a group of ardent González admirers formed, calling itself the Civic Action Committee and raising money for González's campaign.[103]

Felix and Henry B. knew one another and had worked together. Indeed, there seemed to be some initial affinity between the two men, although González was ten years Tijerina's junior. According to Felix Salazar, Tijerina recognized potential in the younger man and wanted to promote his budding career. The *LULAC News* in September, 1956, had carried a picture of González, clearly for campaign purposes, posed with LULAC national president Tijerina when the former was the Democratic nominee for state senator. As senator, González had accompanied Felix during visits to Austin and elsewhere to foster the latter's preschool program, but a divide between the two men soon developed.[104]

In 1957, González and Tijerina had already evidenced their divergent views over H.B. 231: González had militantly filibustered to support African

Americans against segregation, while Tijerina had distanced himself from the cause of blacks and stressed education, particularly English-language training. Fresh from his filibustering in the state senate and other political tiffs with Price Daniel, González capitalized during the 1958 primary on his more confrontational approach to the issues facing people of color. Tijerina, on the other hand, had clearly hitched his LULAC education program to the prestige gained by his association with the governor. By having Daniel on the podium in Sugar Land and openly endorsing him, Tijerina had, as one newspaper article on the election later noted, "left Gonzalez out in the cold."[105]

Felix's actions on behalf of Daniel in 1958 extended well beyond the Sugar Land invitation. Tijerina, through Tony Campos as LULAC's national director of publicity, lent the Daniel campaign the KGUL-TV newsreel of the governor's appearance at the dedication, a clip from which Daniel's people used in a statewide television broadcast the evening prior to election day. The Tijerina administration simultaneously distributed the July, 1958, issue of the LULAC News, which featured on its cover a benevolent Price Daniel and his wife (side-by-side with Felix, Bob Smith, and others) greeting Mexican American pupils at the Sugar Land Little School. George Christian, Daniel's administrative assistant, wrote Campos shortly after the election, expressing the governor's sincere appreciation for "the support you and Mr. Tijerina gave him during the campaign." Grateful for use of the newsreel, Christian added that "the widespread distribution of [the] LULAC News helped immeasurably but regret the furor which arose." The "furor" no doubt referred to the reaction of other LULACs and González supporters to such brazen partisanship; these actions by Felix and his lieutenants once again illustrated that LULAC functioned as a de facto political organization, Tijerina's protestations to the contrary notwithstanding.[106]

For his part, González stated shortly after the election that Tijerina had "incurred the wrath of many Latin Americans" by supporting Daniel. Furthermore, González noted, he did not "give a hoot" what Tijerina did politically, as he "owed me nothing." When asked about endorsing Daniel over González, Felix told the same reporter that he backed the candidate who did "the best job for all the people." During the election campaign, observers familiar with the Mexican American scene came to see González and Felix as the embodiments of the two main strains of political thought in the Mexican American community: Felix with his stress on language and the nonconfrontational approach versus Henry B. González, who felt the Mexican Americans were "a minority group militantly fighting for its rights."[107]

In many ways, Henry B. González came to represent the same contrast with Tijerina as John J. Herrera had.

According to Tijerina confidants, however, the rift between Tijerina and González in 1958 was more complex than politics or political ideology. These stories relate that sometime just prior to the primary, Tijerina made a substantial loan to González specifically to alleviate the latter's continuing personal financial woes. According to these sources, González accepted the money but then announced for governor against Tijerina ally Price Daniel, something that irritated Tijerina to no end. Furthermore, Felix felt that González had used at least some of the loan to pay his filing fee, a belief that compounded Tijerina's aggravation.[108]

Regardless of the exact details of what transpired, with the Sugar Land ceremony and primary election of 1958, the relationship between the two men permanently cooled.[109] And it was a distancing that probably was as inevitable as that which had taken place between Tijerina and John Herrera, especially given González's own strong, independent spirit.

As Council No. 60 prepared to support him in his bid to run again for the LULAC national presidency, Tijerina could take stock of his accomplishments during his first two terms in office with no little satisfaction. He had moved LULAC forward by concentrating his resources and efforts on two principal goals. Although the passive membership drive had fizzled and he constantly prodded councils to submit their delinquent dues, the expansion of the organization that he had promised had certainly continued apace. By March, 1958, Felix had proudly reported that a LULAC council had begun in Detroit, the first in Michigan. This council (Council No. 329) would begin with approximately eighteen members. By the summer, a council of twenty-two members (Council No. 328) started in Saint Paul, Minnesota. As a result, by early June, 1958, Felix could boast that LULAC was active in eleven states and had the possibility of an annual revenue of fifteen thousand to eighteen thousand dollars. As he told Council No. 60: "LULAC is not a two bit organization anymore."[110]

The criticisms from within LULAC notwithstanding, the Little School of the 400 had been established. The project had developed in two years from a concept to the point that by the summer of 1958 classes had opened in nine Texas towns, attended by a great deal of positive public recognition and attempts to raise funds to finance their operation. While the various components for the Little School had originated from prior sources, Felix and his LULAC circle had put them together as a coherent program and pushed the project to fruition. It had been a difficult, lengthy process; Tijerina had personally prompted, guided, and promoted its development, so heavily investing himself in its existence that he and the Little School of the 400 were synonymous in the public eye. In the process, Tijerina had called upon many individuals to help in its establishment, including the governor and other Anglo officials of Texas. To remain in the good graces of these Anglo friends, Felix had seen fit to distance himself and the LULAC national presidency from blacks in their struggle against segregation, a strategy of keeping close to the mainstream that he had always followed.

Tijerina's advocacy of his preschool program would become even more intense during the final two years of his LULAC national presidency. He would successfully lobby to have the Little School of the 400 approach adopted by the state. The program and its founder would receive an unprecedented level of acclaim, focusing national attention on Mexican American education. Tijerina's strenuous efforts to develop his education project as well as his less productive attempts to expand LULAC into more states during the last half of his presidency will be the subjects of the next chapter.

CHAPTER 9

THE LULAC NATIONAL
PRESIDENCY, PART II

1958–1960

The initial two years of Felix Tijerina's LULAC national presidency laid the groundwork for the accomplishments of the last half of his tenure in office. Although expansion of the league would not be as spectacular during his final two terms, LULAC would claim two more states—New Jersey and New York—by early 1959. This new spurt established the organization's presence in the Northeast and brought the closing tally of states in LULAC during the Tijerina era to thirteen. Felix continued to travel the country, doing his best to bind the organization together; as he noted, for the first time in its history LULAC stretched from border to border and from coast to coast. Under Tijerina's gavel, LULAC would hold its first national convention outside the Southwest when its delegates convened in Chicago in June, 1959. The first time that Mexican Americans had ever held such a comprehensive meeting in the Windy City, the Chicago convention ranked among the earliest expressions of Mexican American national identity.

Between June, 1958, and June, 1960, Felix Tijerina and his LULAC allies carried the Little School of the 400 from being a privately funded project to having its basic concept adopted by the state of Texas as a program called the Preschool Instructional Classes for Non-English Speaking Children. Tijerina tirelessly devoted himself to bringing about this transition. He worked assiduously within the Hale-Aikin Committee of Twenty-four, the state-level education reform body, to bring the idea for preschool English-language training to the attention of public officials. He then lobbied the state legislature for passage of a bill that contained that particular committee recommendation. The resulting state-sponsored program enrolled more than fifteen thousand Spanish-speaking preschoolers by the beginning of the summer of 1960, just as he left office.

As Tijerina, LULAC, and many others institutionalized the Little School concept within the Texas public education system, it became something of national acclaim, gaining Felix even broader recognition as a leader and symbol of the 1950s "Latin American" community. His efforts between 1958 and 1960 thrust him and Mexican American educational concerns into the national limelight as never before.

THE LAREDO CONVENTION

Tijerina moved into his third year as national president in grand style. In the wake of the Little School dedication ceremony, he traveled in triumph to the 1958 LULAC national convention. Amid much local publicity and hosted by Council No. 12, the convention was held at the Hamilton Hotel in downtown Laredo from June 26 to 29. It proved to be an exciting, memorable occasion (like most LULAC conventions of this era) and one that crackled with organizational and electoral politics.[1]

Tijerina had already decided to seek reelection for an unprecedented third term. In addition to his success with establishing the Little School, he could boast of having expanded LULAC into Michigan and Minnesota and beginning twenty-seven new councils during his second term. Earlier that month the Council No. 60 membership had not only charged its four delegates—Joe González, Moses M. Sánchez, Louis Hernández, and their chairman, Sammie Alderete—with fostering Tijerina's reelection, but had also instructed them "to make any deals possible to reach [the council's] goal."[2]

Felix and several members of his national staff arrived in Laredo on Wednesday, June 25, two days after the Little School dedication ceremony at Sugar Land. Along with the other early arrivals they attended the Thursday evening reception at the "LULAC Home," at 1208 Houston Street, headquarters of Laredo Council No. 12, immediately across from the Hamilton. The next morning, Tijerina presided over the convention's opening session, during which he and the assembly heard welcoming remarks from Mayor Joe C. Martin, Jr., a leader of the Independent Club, the local political party that ran the "Gateway City." That afternoon and the following day, the various regional governors delivered their reports to the delegates. In these presentations, Tijerina later complained, many of the governors criticized his national LULAC administration. Although he tried to remain stoic, this criticism profoundly wounded his feelings. Resentment even developed against Tijerina and his group for the way they conducted the convention; at least one Texas district governor felt that he had been "denied the right to speak in the order of the day." Felix drew great support, however, from the complement of delegates from Chicago and other Midwest councils whose presence once again added a national air to the proceedings.[3]

The highlight of the convention for Tijerina took place on Saturday, June 28. At 2:30 P.M., Lyndon B. Johnson, majority leader in the U.S. Senate, arrived by automobile from his ranch near Austin. Johnson had accepted LULAC's invitation to be the featured speaker at the convention's main banquet that evening. Looking tanned and fit, Johnson was met by LULAC delegates and convoyed to the Hamilton, parade-style, in an open convertible. As national president, Tijerina sat next to the senator in the rear seat, while Laredo LULAC and convention chairman Alfredo G. Garza sat in the front with a local traffic sergeant who chauffeured. (Johnson and Tijerina were already acquainted; Tijerina had successfully lobbied Johnson earlier that year to obtain a Senate page post for the son of a prominent LULAC member.) Johnson and Tijerina chatted freely and were all smiles as the senator—extremely popular in Laredo and recognized as the most powerful Democratic Party leader in the nation—took time to shake hands with those who approached the car along the downtown parade route.[4]

That same day, the LULAC Ladies Councils hosted a luncheon at the Pan American Room of Laredo's Plaza Hotel. Mrs. Felix and Mrs. Lyndon Johnson were the honored guests.[5]

Senator Johnson spent approximately ten hours in Webb County during his visit, a stop that was highly charged for everyone, not only because of his stature, but also due to election-year activities in Laredo. Although he used the trip to maintain political support, Johnson studiously avoided becoming embroiled in local political bickering. He met in his third-floor Hamilton Hotel suite with Mexican American Democratic delegations from various South Texas counties; however, he declined to attend a dinner arranged by Laredo's Independent Club in order to sidestep the running political feud between that group and its local rival, the Reform Party. Reportedly,

Johnson had even asked beforehand that no one associated with local politics (including Mayor Martin) ride with him in the LULAC parade. According to later recollections, the senator wanted only Felix with him on his way to the Hamilton. When asked by the press what he thought about a Latin American (i.e., Henry B. González) running for governor, Johnson replied: "I don't worry about any race except my own."[6]

Regardless of the senator's public declaration that he wanted to remain outside the fray of local politics, Mrs. Felix recalled many years later that prior to the convention, LBJ had telephoned her husband and talked to him about trying to heal the widening rift in the Laredo Democratic Party. She remembered that these political concerns underpinned Johnson's motives for attending the Laredo convention and that, behind the scenes, the senator sought Felix's (and others') help in settling those troubles.[7]

That evening, Oscar Laurel emceed the main banquet, which took place at the Laredo Boys' Club Gymnasium. At about 10 P.M., Tijerina warmly introduced Senator Johnson to the fifteen hundred people in attendance. Although the LULAC News would report that the steak dinner was "tantalizing" and the senator delivered "a very inspiring message" on the importance of commerce and trade with Latin America, apparently the hot Laredo summer made things almost unbearable for everyone in the gym, which had no air conditioning. As a consequence of the heat and the good spirit of the occasion, some recall, Senator Johnson had much to drink. The dinner was followed by a dance in the adjoining hall, and Johnson left Laredo around midnight.[8]

To complicate matters at the convention even further, Henry B. González showed up to promote his gubernatorial candidacy. González had many supporters in Laredo, including Oscar Laurel, from the different political factions as well as among the LULAC delegates. Always a showman, González arrived at the Hamilton Hotel on Saturday with a guitar player and an accordionist at his side, along with two of his sons. In addition to appearing on Laredo television that evening, González, dressed in his trademark white suit, later came to the LULAC banquet. Although not invited to sit at the head table, he received the largest ovation of the night when introduced to the crowd. González left Laredo for Corpus Christi, his next campaign stop, around 3 A.M. Tijerina took note of González's presence, with no little sense of irritation.[9]

On Sunday morning, the final day of the convention, the delegates passed the enabling act that made the LULAC Educational Fund part of the organization's constitution. Elizabeth Burrus had gone to the Laredo convention as Tijerina's guest, and, in recognition of her work with the preschool program, she had sat next to Felix at the head table of the main banquet. According to her best recollections, it was by the time of this convention that Tijerina had published her vocabulary in pamphlet form (complete with her photograph and an introduction she had written) and was distributing them to people at the gathering to promote the Little School. This little booklet—entitled *Beginner's Speaking Vocabulary*—not only saw wide usage, but also became a document from that era of Mexican American education and a treasured memento for those persons who participated in the program's development. Among the bevy of other amendments and resolutions adopted by the assembly on Sunday, one (pushed by Hector De Peña of Corpus Christi—the same attorney who had once employed Sidney Farr—and Pete Tijerina of San Antonio) called on the governor and state legislature to repeal House Bill 231, the segregation bill which Felix had failed to oppose.[10]

Later that morning, the delegates unanimously reelected Tijerina to a precedent-breaking third term over William Bonilla, an energetic young attorney from Corpus Christi. Tijerina's campaign slogan had been "Go with Felix in 1958 to make LULAC Great." Except for Raúl Cortez and Dr. George J. Garza (who had each held the position for two years), the previous twenty-four presidents in LULAC's twenty-nine year history had served only single terms.[11]

After he and the other officers were sworn in for the coming year, Tijerina adjourned the convention. The day concluded with a festive farewell barbecue at the Laredo Waterworks picnic grounds.[12]

During the convention, Felix had, as usual, relied heavily on the assistance of his inner circle of LULAC associates. And he soon reappointed them to their positions in his new administration, including Felix Salazar as national legal advisor, Carmen Cortes as national secretary, and Daniel Sandoval as national treasurer. (Before long, the reliable Danny Sandoval would go to work for Felix as his assistant manager and bookkeeper/accountant for the restaurants.) Tony Campos, his trusted friend who had helped him with his correspondence and monthly "President's Message" in the *LULAC News* during the previous year, became national director of publicity. Alfred J. Hernández had become Texas regional governor and no longer served as national executive secretary, but he, as always, remained one of Tijerina's top aides. Tijerina named Val Hernández to be national organizer for the Midwest, so grateful was he for Hernández's hard work as well as for his support at the Laredo convention against some of the harsher critics. The loyal Dr. Francisco Licón of El Paso was reelected national director of health. In tight with Felix once àgain, Guadalupe C. Martínez of Galveston was appointed national chairman for the Committee on Expansion. Giving further strength to the coming year of his administration, Tijerina brought in Moses M. Sánchez to be the editor of the *LULAC News*.[13]

The other new major appointments to Tijerina's LULAC administration for 1958–59 included Houstonian Agustín L. Hernández as national executive secretary; Reverend Adrian Kempker, a Catholic priest from What Cheer, Iowa, as national chaplain; Joe O'Campo of Santa Ana, California, as national organizer for the West Coast; and William Rocha of West Des Moines, Iowa, as deputy national organizer. Hector Godínez of Santa Ana, California, had been elected first national vice president; Susana Pavón, a native of Fort Madison, Iowa, had been elected second vice president; and Anne Alvarez of Chicago, Illinois, had been elected national director of youth activities. These fresh faces again reflected the more national character of LULAC that emerged during Tijerina's tenure in the late 1950s.[14]

As a postscript to the doings of the convention, from Washington, D.C., Lyndon Johnson sent Tijerina a letter of appreciation for his time in Laredo. Reiterating his gratitude for Tijerina's "wonderful introduction" at the main banquet, Johnson sounded a familiar theme when he noted: "You are the epitome of the American dream of success and an excellent example of the wonderful things that can happen in this country." By now some of the highest political officials in the land knew what Felix Tijerina represented and the education program he championed.[15]

THE LITTLE SCHOOL OF THE 400,
SUMMER, 1958

True to the promise of the June 23 dedication in Sugar Land, the Little School of the 400 operated effectively throughout the summer of 1958. The teachers of the nine Little Schools (in Sugar Land, Aldine, Ganado, Edna, Fort Stockton, Brookshire, Rosenberg, Vanderbilt, and Wharton) employed the techniques that Isabel Verver had used during her 1957 summer classes.

With Burrus's list as their basic vocabulary, as one observer noted, they "relied on the age-old teaching method of demonstration and repetition of new words, until the children mastered them. Spanish was spoken in class, but sparingly," suggesting a type of bilingual approach, at least in practice. Tijerina visited these classes regularly, as he had during the previous summer.[16]

In late September, Tijerina, as president of the LULAC Educational Fund, Inc., issued a report to its board of directors detailing the successful operation of the Little School for the summer as well as plans for the program's future. His report noted that during their first three months of operation the classes taught the "400 Basic Word Vocabulary" to 402 children. Also, at the time of the report, six of the Little Schools remained in operation, with an enrollment of 222 students for the coming three-month period. (This second session extended to December 15 and also produced excellent results.)[17]

The report detailed that during the first three months of the summer the fund had spent $3,518.45 in teachers' salaries, office rent, secretarial services, and other miscellaneous expenses, or $8.75 per child. Always stressing the bottom line, Tijerina noted that the program would thus substantially save money for the Texas public schools if one considered that without preschool language preparation, most of these children would have to repeat the first grade.[18]

Tijerina further averred that school authorities had observed a significant difference between the children who had received the vocabulary instruction and those who had not. In this manner, he hoped to raise the average educational level of Latin Americans from 3.5 years to 7.6. In Tijerina's estimation, the Little School would prevent Latin American children from having an "inferiority complex" when they began public school since they would "no longer have to be separated in order to learn the basic English words."[19]

Including promotional costs, the report stated, the LULAC Educational Fund, Inc., had spent a total of $4,925.33 on the 1958 summer program. After all their efforts for contributions, public donations had amounted to only $2,477.16. Tijerina personally had given $2,448.17 to cover the deficit.[20]

By this time, Tijerina had come to see state financing as the surest method to fund his project. He was working through the Hale-Aikin Committee (of which he had been a member since late 1957) to see such a subsidy come to fruition. He concluded his September 23 report by stating that he had reported the costs of the Little School program to the committee. The Hale-Aikin Committee, he proudly added, had "unanimously endorsed" the pre-school project and "will prepare it for presentation to the Texas Legislature for approval during the coming year." He added that the financial donations to support the program "were exhausted long ago," and he solicited the board's suggestions for how to keep the Little School classes operating until the legislature acted.[21]

Although more will be said later regarding the operation of the Hale-Aikin Committee (and Felix's fundamental role in it), by September, 1958, the committee envisioned an extensive, state-funded plan for teaching English to Mexican American children. It would be modeled largely after the Little School.

PROMOTING LULAC, AUGUST–OCTOBER, 1958

In the meantime, Tijerina was on the road for LULAC from the upper Midwest to the West Coast. During late August, in the company of Alfred J. Hernández, Tijerina flew to Saint Paul, Minnesota, to attend a joint installation banquet. Along the way, the two men made a half-hour stop at Midway Airport in Chicago on August 22, where they met with a large group of Illinois LULACs, including David Cerda, chairman of the upcoming national convention, organizer Val Hernández, Tacho Alderete, and Sal Garcia (the last two being former Houstonians). Upon arrival in Saint Paul, Tijerina and Hernández were greeted at the airport by the city's mayor and a large Minnesota LULAC delegation. On Saturday evening, August 23, they attended the banquet at Saint Paul's Lowery Hotel, during which they installed the newly elected officers of two local councils. On their return, Tijerina and Hernández stopped off in Kansas City, where they met with a group interested in forming a LULAC chapter in Kansas.[22]

On September 27, Tijerina and Hernández attended a dual installation of officers for LULAC Councils No. 2 and No. 187 at DeWinne's Belgium Inn in San Antonio. The ubiquitous Henry B. González was also present, and, in the words of the LULAC News reporter, he "again inspired the membership with his timely remarks and oratory."[23]

On October 12, Tijerina attended a LULAC area meeting in Placentia, California. He was particularly interested in the progress the organization in that state had made through the efforts of Hector Godínez, first national vice president. The meeting was well attended, and the host council treated Tijerina and the various LULAC representatives to a reception immediately afterward.[24]

These travels, which involved speaking engagements, meetings, banquets, and conferences, were representative of the rigorous schedule Tijerina maintained on behalf of the organization. In this manner, he sought to kindle unity and enthusiasm among the membership of the various regions. In his own words, he was determined to "continue to sell LULAC and promote the ideals and beliefs of a true American and a true LULAC." As usual, selling and promoting remained Tijerina's *modus operandi*.[25]

Tijerina rejoiced when, on October 4, 1958, LULAC officially admitted a council from Elizabeth, New Jersey, into its ranks; this addition represented the seventh state brought into LULAC during his presidential tenure. The Elizabeth Council No. 339 came together through Val Hernández and his "Expansion Team" working with an enthusiastic group of some dozen local men and women, including Bernardo Escandón (attorney and native of New Jersey), Anthony Pazos (realtor and insurance agent), and Hilda Vázquez (former Houstonian and Council No. 22 member). Inspired by what she had learned in Houston, Vázquez played a missionary role in forming this new group. A photograph of the fourteen well-attired New Jersey LULACs ran in the November issue of the *LULAC News* in commemoration of this achievement. Below that one, another photo of the council officers appeared in which they held a shield emblazoned with the words "Eastern LULAC Salutes 'Don' Felix."[26]

For Tijerina, the admittance of New Jersey was the "[c]ornerstone of LULAC . . . laid in the East." This new addition represented for him a milestone in LULAC history, since, as the league's initial inroad into the Northeast, it culminated his "dreams of a Greater LULAC . . . a National Organization truly representative of our Latin-American people throughout the United States, from coast to coast and border to border." He reported to the membership of Council No. 60 during a regular meeting later that same month that LULAC had 3,363 members nationally, with 1,763 in Texas alone. He was especially gratified to note that this would amount to nine thousand dollars more in annual dues than the previous year.[27]

On his return trip from Placentia, California, Tijerina stopped in Austin for the final meeting of the Hale-Aikin Committee of Twenty-four on October 15, 1958. This body had proved crucial for the future of the LULAC pre-school program.[28]

During the past year, the Hale-Aikin Committee, composed of two dozen distinguished Texans and led by its legislative sponsors Representative L. DeWitt Hale of Corpus Christi (as vice chairman) and Senator A. M. Aikin, Jr., of Paris (as chairman), had undertaken a comprehensive study of the needs of the Texas public school system through input from local committees in all 254 counties. In an attempt to update the state's educational legislation initiated ten years earlier by the Gilmer-Aikin Committee, Hale-Aikin had been charged with formulating recommendations which would be submitted to the upcoming fifty-sixth legislature in 1959.[29]

As one of the governor's six appointees, Tijerina was the only Mexican American among the twenty-four members; he was also one of only two Houstonians (oil company executive and Houston Independent School District trustee Stone Wells being the other). The meetings of the Hale-Aikin Committee, beginning on October 16, 1957, had figured prominently in Felix's regular visits to Austin.[30]

The Hale-Aikin Committee contained four subcommittees. Tijerina was a member of the important six-person School Program Subcommittee, which, as its name suggests, evaluated the instructional programs offered by the public schools. By July, 1958, the subcommittee had compiled a summary of the reports it had received from the numerous county-level committees. This document called for the state to provide "a summer school for non-English speaking children." From the start of the subcommittee's deliberations, Felix specifically focused on English training for Hispanic youngsters and initiated the idea. By mid-July, through Tijerina's guidance, the School Program Subcommittee had adopted the concept of the Little School into its recommendations. The tentative draft of proposals developed by the School Program Subcommittee included a proposed plan, "based on data reported by Mr. Felix Tijerina," to provide "Pre-School Experiences for Non-English Speaking Children." This plan had a projected cost of $1.35 million to reach seventy-five thousand pupils through one thousand bilingual instructors at an average salary of $1,350 per year. Each teacher, the plan mandated, would instruct twenty-five pupils for approximately four months and would "graduate" around seventy-five students a year. In August, the subcommittee honed this recommendation into final form, which called for "[s]pecial pre-school instructional units for non-English speaking children" who were at least five years old and eligible to enter the first grade the year following enrollment in the language training classes. These pre-school instructional units would be established through "a plan to be developed by the State Board of Education with the . . . assistance of the Commissioner of Education." It retained the estimated number of instructors, children to be served, and expenditures, but added the rationale that such a program would save the state money, rather than be an added cost. At a meeting in early September, the plan (as a part of the School Program Subcommittee report) was "unanimously endorsed" by the full Hale-Aikin Committee. Tijerina was so proud that Hale-Aikin had embraced the idea that he included its full, rather grand details in his already-mentioned September 23 report to the LULAC Educational Fund board of directors.[31]

Tijerina's recommendations were being enthusiastically received by influential Anglos. This reception (and the sentiment behind it) was no doubt best expressed by the *Corpus Christi Caller* in a September 3, 1958, editorial assessing the Hale-Aikin proposals. Describing the "vital importance" of the School Program Subcommittee's recommendation that $1.35 million be set aside for the summer preschool English program, the editorial noted that "educators throughout the state" agreed that "the No. 1 problem in Texas education at this time" was the non-English speaking student. "Of the many groups in Texas," it explained, "Latin Americans present[ed] the chief problem." The Nueces County Hale-Aikin committee had made the need for special preschool classes "one of its major recommendations" to the state body.[32]

At its October 15, 1958, meeting, the Hale-Aikin Committee formally approved the recommendations formulated by all four subcommittees. Among many other things, it simply called for state statutes to require each public school system to provide "Pre-school orientation in basic English for non-English speaking children." Trimmed down from the earlier version, and not mentioning dollar amounts or other specifics, the amended proposal simply read:

> Research has shown that many children who enter school
> without a speaking knowledge of the English language are re-

quired to repeat a grade one or more times during their school career. A solution to this problem has been attempted in many local districts by providing, through local funds, special preschool work for non-English speaking children. The State makes no provision for this type of special instruction, although it is needed both to prevent drop-outs from school and to avoid the unnecessary repetition of grades because of a language barrier.[33]

This exact wording appeared in the Hale-Aikin's final report entitled "Proposals to Improve Public Education in Texas," which was published in December, 1958, and distributed across the State.[34]

Tijerina's presence on the committee had clearly borne fruit for LULAC's language program. He personified the push for preschool English instruction in the minds of the other twenty-three influential Texans—people from every part of the state—who participated. His sincerity and good humor, willingness and diligence at the Hale-Aikin deliberations had made many friends for the cause of Mexican American preschool education; he had intelligently brought English-language instruction to center stage, focusing state government's attention on it and successfully recommending that a state law address the issue. As we shall see, this preschool language proposal would result in one of the only successful pieces of legislation to emerge from the many recommendations made by the Hale-Aikin Committee of Twenty-four.[35]

FALTERING FINANCES

It was fortunate that the Hale-Aikin Committee moved forward in its call for public funding of the preschool instruction because despite the fervent pleas of Tijerina and other LULACs, private contributions were proving inadequate to the task of financially supporting the Little School program. This predicament was, of course, poignantly demonstrated when Felix had to personally supply half the money for the first three-month period of operation that summer. He visited the meetings of various organizations and continued to send letters of appeal for financial assistance, even some written in Spanish, to local mutual aid societies asking for help so that children could learn English.[36]

Extant evidence indicates Tijerina's limited success in fund raising during this time. His best results came from donors closest to home. For example, in November, Council No. 22 held its annual Charity Autumn Ball at the Crystal Ballroom of the Rice Hotel to raise money for the fund. During the intermission of this successful affair, representatives of the Galveston LULAC council presented Felix with a check for $500. Baytown Council No. 227 donated $150 in December, raising its total contribution to $470. Others, farther away, like Council No. 1 of Corpus Christi, may have been more typical. Although the council "whole-heartedly endorsed the LULAC educational fund project," it could only manage to forward $24 in late October. In a similar vein, the men's Council No. 290 of East Chicago, Indiana, donated $25 in December. In addition to simple financial constraints and lack of direct involvement, distant councils might have been reticent to send money because their own local areas had similar experimental educational efforts in operation. For instance, Council No. 1 may well have been influenced by the fact that Corpus Christi public schools, under local language teacher and prominent LULAC member Edmundo E. Mireles, had had a functioning English vocabulary program for preschoolers since at least 1956, completely separate from Tijerina's LULAC Educational Fund, Inc.[37]

At any rate, official financial statements indicate that the fund raised just over $2,700 between the time of the September 23, 1958, report and the end of the year, money which was used to support the 437 students who attended the Little Schools operating in December. These figures certainly did not live up to the grandiose plans for the "$146,000 program" envisioned when the program was unveiled at the Shamrock Hilton Hotel in September of the previous year. But such contributions were the best Tijerina and LULAC could muster.[38]

FROM CHICAGO TO MEXICO CITY

While the report of the Hale-Aikin Committee went to press, Tijerina continued to travel for LULAC. On November 8–9, 1958, he flew to Chicago, this time to attend a Supreme Council meeting held at the Midwest Hotel. LULAC national officers and the regional governors from all eleven states met to discuss the progress and expansion of the organization. As part of the occasion, Tijerina attended a gala LULAC banquet and dance, where he crowned the winner of the local LULAC queen contest and helped conduct a "mass installation" of Illinois LULAC councils. He also conferred with the committee planning the league's 1959 national convention to be held in Chicago.[39]

Back in Houston, Tijerina, as LULAC national president, was appointed on November 26 by Mayor Lewis Cutrer to be the city's Ambassador of Goodwill and official emissary to the inauguration of Adolfo López Mateos, president-elect of Mexico. (Longtime admirers of one another, Cutrer already had reappointed Tijerina to the Houston Housing Authority Board in February, a position in which he had served with Cutrer during the Roy Hofheinz administration.) Governor Price Daniel also named Felix as one of the state's representatives to the inauguration.[40]

Tijerina arrived in Mexico City via Pan American Airlines on November 28, and *Excelsior,* a leading local newspaper, photographed him as he deplaned. In being interviewed for the favorable article that accompanied this photograph, Tijerina took the opportunity to inform *Excelsior'*s readership about LULAC and the plans afoot in the Texas legislature to fund a massive project to teach English to Mexican children living in that state. He explained that two million Mexican Americans resided in Texas and eleven million in the United States. Realizing his audience, Felix told the newspaper: "The majority of them should learn English, without forgetting their own language, so that they may obtain the same social and economic level of other young people."[41]

Tijerina had a splendid time at the inaugural festivities. In the company of Bill Daniel (the governor's brother), Raymond Telles, Jr. (mayor of El Paso), and the two men's wives, he attended one of the receptions in honor of the new president. At the inauguration itself, he spoke with John Foster Dulles (Eisenhower's imperious secretary of state) and Senator Ralph Yarborough, and made sure that these individuals "knew that LULAC existed." Always the promoter, he reported to the national membership upon his return that he felt gratified that through his presence in Mexico City "the representatives from all over the world knew that LULAC was there."[42]

As he boosted LULAC from New Jersey to California and from Chicago to Mexico City in his role as national president, Tijerina did no more than remain true to the ideology he had developed over the years since he had first come to Houston. Firmly aware of his Mexican heritage, he projected the qualities of a positive-thinking entrepreneurial capitalist promoter imbued with virtues of middle-class American society, always with the objective of fitting in.

TIJERINA AND A COMMUNITY "DISCOVERED"

Tijerina returned to Houston from Mexico City in time to see himself prominently featured in an eleven-part, front-page series of newspaper articles in the *Houston Chronicle*. Running from December 1 through 11, this watershed series proclaimed the presence of the Bayou City's emergent postwar Mexican American community like no previous media coverage. Entitled "Houston's Latin American" and written by Marie Dauplaise, the series focused the popular imagination upon Houston's fifty-thousand-strong Mexican American population, with all its problems and possibilities.[43]

Overall, Dauplaise noted the "paradox" of Mexican American life in Houston: that a wide discrepancy in living conditions existed among Mexican Americans—a spectrum that stretched from the wretched poverty of many within the Latino slums near Buffalo Bayou to the comfortable life led by successful Mexican American inhabitants of the suburban upper-middle class.[44]

Dauplaise emphasized that although a portion of Houston's Mexican Americans had "made it" socially and economically, most had not. Despite the great progress made since the 1930s and 1940s, a myriad of "challenges" yet remained for them as a people, and, thus, for the city as a whole.[45]

Moreover, the series set Houston's fifty thousand Latins within the context of the larger statewide Latin American population, which likely numbered somewhere between 1.5 million and 2 million persons, according to the best estimates at the time. As "the fastest growing ethnic group in Texas," Dauplaise noted, it was beset by the same problems plaguing its Houston cohort.[46]

Dauplaise highlighted Tijerina as LULAC national president and, most important, as one of the few persons trying to address these problems plaguing his community. Indeed, the series mentioned no other prominent Mexican American Houstonian by name, marking him, at least in the eyes of the mainstream media, as *the* leader of Houston's Latin American population and at the zenith of his civic career. No stranger to the restaurateur's many endeavors, Dauplaise devoted an entire article (and parts of others) to Tijerina,

LULAC, and their work trying to crash the "language barrier" with the Little School of the 400.[47]

It was Dauplaise who, in this series, juxtaposed Tijerina and Henry B. González as community leaders who represented the two philosophies struggling over how to define and solve the "Latin American problem" in Texas: Tijerina with his belief that Latins had their rights but needed education to use them, versus González and his stance that Mexican Americans, like blacks, were victims of discrimination and should consider themselves "a minority group militantly fighting for [their] rights." The larger community, perhaps for the first time, was realizing the coming of age of Mexican American politics.[48]

Indeed, the Dauplaise series of December, 1958, marked a point of departure for Houston Latin Americans in the popular mind. It not only heralded, as never before, the emergence of Houston's postwar Mexican American community, it also recognized Felix Tijerina as its key figure and his contributions and cautious approach at high tide. In many ways, the series demonstrated that he had come to represent more than local leadership or LULAC as an organization; for many, he had become a symbol of his entire ethnic group.

"THE BIG STORY"

By the middle of his third term (probably even earlier), the LULAC national presidency had taken its toll on Felix, a result of the internal criticism and bickering, as well as the hectic pace demanded by the office. In its February issue, the LULAC News reported "The Big Story": after a lengthy meeting with Tony Campos and Alfred J. Hernández prior to the Texas regional convention in Houston, Tijerina announced that he would "definitely not run for re-election as national president." In spite of Council No. 60's entreaty that he seek a fourth term, he felt that "more energetic leadership" should arise from the ranks "to guide the destinies of our beloved LULAC."[49]

LULAC now seethed with internal politics and speculation mushroomed about who would succeed Tijerina. A survey of the membership conducted by the LULAC News revealed that at least five hopefuls had emerged by March, including Hector Godínez of Santa Ana, California; Gilbert Maes of Los Alamos, New Mexico; Alfred Hernández of Houston; Guadalupe C.

Martínez from Galveston; and Val Hernández from Chicago. Indeed, three months before the Chicago gathering, jockeying for the position by various contenders was in full swing.[50]

Tijerina's decision not to seek another term did not slacken his work for the organization. In late January, he, Campos, and Alfred Hernández had been in Austin to stand with Price Daniel as the governor proclaimed "LULAC Week in Texas." Felix spoke to the delegates at the well-attended though rain-drenched, Texas Regional (State) Convention at Houston's Rice Hotel, where he proudly read a telegram he had solicited from President Eisenhower congratulating LULAC on three decades of leadership in education, citizenship, and social welfare. In late February, he traveled to Waco, attended the local LULAC's annual George Washington Birthday Ball, crowned yet another LULAC queen, and, by his presence, helped the council raise seven hundred dollars for its scholarship fund. He also peppered Senator Lyndon Johnson with letters in March reporting the good work of LULAC, as well as his high regard for Robert Kennedy and the activities of Senator John McClellan's Rackets Investigating Committee in their fight against "hooliganism." In late February, Felix had heard (and no doubt met) Kennedy when the committee's young chief counsel had spoken on racketeering in labor-management relations at the Houston Rotary Club. Tijerina was especially concerned that Johnson support a bill before Congress that would appropriate a half million dollars to underwrite the Third Pan American Games to be held in Chicago that summer.[51]

As an extension of his work on Hale-Aikin and the Little School, Tijerina was appointed to the 126-member Texas Committee to Plan for the 1960 White House Conference on Children and Youth, which held its first meeting in Austin on March 14. Governor Daniel delivered the welcome and emphasized the need for the committee to help address the needs of young people. Felix was the only Mexican American participant from Houston and expressed his concern for educating "the 150,000 immigrants who have this language barrier, especially [the] children."[52]

Felix's expansion of LULAC claimed one more new area. In the April, 1959, issue of the LULAC News, Tijerina announced that the "State of New York has joined our ranks. We are 13 states in this our beloved LULAC." This addition occurred when, on Easter Sunday, March 29, a council had been established in the town of Lackawanna, a satellite community of Buffalo in the western part of the state on Lake Erie. Situated near the Canadian border, Lackawanna had developed a *colonia mexicana* beginning in the 1920s, when Bethlehem Steel Corporation started to recruit Mexican workers for its local plant.[53]

Once again, LULAC's national organizer Val Hernández had facilitated this growth. On Saturday, March 28, he and a delegation of midwestern officers had traveled to Lackawanna, where they met with members of the Centro Social Mexicano Club, Inc., and its president, Francisco Rivera. Rivera and Joe Gradeda, another Lackawanna LULAC inductee, treated the visiting dignitaries to a tour of the city, including a visit to Niagara Falls, just a few miles north of Buffalo. That evening, local residents were invited to a dinner and dance in honor of the Midwest LULACs who, in turn, showed films on the progress of their organization.[54]

Rivera was immediately selected LULAC regional governor for the Empire State and sworn in by Val Hernández. A native of Tampico, Rivera had first come to New York during World War II as one of many contracted by the government to work on the railroads. Featuring a photograph of Rivera and his staff and another of thirteen men and women charter members of this "Pioneer Council" (with each group holding a shield that read "New York Salutes 'Don Felix'"), the LULAC News reported that "Lackawanna, New York, is in LULAC to stay." The photos showed the New York LULACs in a hall standing beneath images of George Washington and Miguel Hidalgo, symbolic of the Mexican American culture which, by 1959, had spread so far from its Southwest beginnings.[55]

With the addition of New York, the expansion of LULAC under Tijerina had reached its geographical limits. Although Val Hernández would continue to try to organize in Ohio, Nebraska, and Kansas, LULAC territory remained at thirteen states for the rest of Don Felix's tenure.[56]

While he was thrilled with LULAC's expansion, Tijerina had definitely concluded that the organization would not financially support the preschool program even though it continued to show success; according to LULAC's figures, at the end of four months of regular school in the fall of 1958, only 2 percent of the children who had been in that summer's preschool program failed their first grade work. Felix and the Little School also continued to receive good press, including a lengthy article by Jim Bowman that was disseminated by the Associated Press. Nonetheless, in the April,

1959, *LULAC News,* he noted that contributions from the membership for the preschool project had been very disappointing. He complained that "[v]ery few councils have participated in this program and very few have contributed towards its progress." (Treasurer Danny Sandoval even lamented that many councils failed, as usual, to keep current on their constitutionally mandated quarterly dues to the national organization.) As for the preschool program, his "only hope now," Tijerina reported in despair, was that the Texas state legislature would come through with support.[57] In the meantime, he had been working with the legislature to foster a bill that would perpetuate the Little School concept.[58]

H.B. 51

The bill that Felix had been working on was H.B. 51, a direct result of the Hale-Aikin Committee's recommendation that a state law provide special preschool language training for non-English-speaking children. It was one of eleven pieces of proposed Hale-Aikin legislation introduced in the fifty-sixth legislative session (which convened on January 13, 1959), attempting to implement the committee's range of proposals.

H.B. 51 was authored and introduced by Representative Malcolm McGregor, a liberal Democrat from El Paso. McGregor wanted the legislation passed because English-language training would profoundly impact his district and because he had served with Tijerina on Hale-Aikin's School Program Subcommittee. McGregor was joined in cosponsorship by DeWitt Hale of Corpus Christi, who had similar reasons for coauthoring it: the law would benefit the large numbers of Spanish-speaking children in his district and he had played a primary role in the committee. Both McGregor and Hale had a personal dedication to the bill. In the state senate, the measure was introduced by Abraham Kazen of Laredo as S.B. 62 and cosponsored by Senator Aikin, and both men were also eager to see it pass.[59]

Filed in the House of Representatives on January 23, H.B. 51 was referred to the Committee on Education a few days later. Tijerina, Hernández, and other LULACs registered as lobbyists and worked diligently to influence a favorable outcome. According to one popular magazine article, during that legislative session Felix made no fewer than twenty trips to Austin to buttonhole virtually every senator and representative. In addition to telling leg-

islators of the accomplishments of the Little School, Tijerina gave the legis-
lators information on similar projects that had independently emerged in day
nurseries and school districts in such places as McAllen, Victoria, and
Laredo. Results from the English-language, preschool summer program in
the Corpus Christi School District (coordinated by E. E. Mireles) were also
used to show political figures the practicality of such projects.[60]

According to another contemporary journalist, Speaker of the Texas
House Waggoner Carr accompanied Tijerina at some point to Little School
classes to gain first-hand knowledge of the project in operation. So impressed was he by this demonstration, Carr promised to help get the legislation enacted. Representatives McGregor and Hale, both energetic legisla-
tors, proved to be especially active in their sponsorship of the bill and key to
its passage.[61]

At every occasion, Tijerina let it be known that he and his fellow supporters did not envision this bill as being directed only at Mexican Americans; this strategy sought to blunt criticism from some non-Hispanics that
the measure would "discriminate" against other ethnic groups. He told all
who would listen, especially the press, that it was LULAC's purpose that the
proposed legislation "would accommodate Polish, German, French, or any
other children who do not speak English at first grade age and therefore are
handicapped at the very beginning of their educational lives." Although the
bill was primarily intended toward Spanish-speaking children, neither its
title nor its wording mentioned any ethnicity by name.[62]

On March 9, Tijerina appeared before the House Education Committee
to speak on behalf of the bill and show its members the film *Forgotten Minds*.
The reel reportedly had a dramatic impact. Supporting Tijerina were Representatives McGregor and Hale and L. P. Sturgeon of the Texas State
Teachers Association, who spoke eloquently for passage. After postponing
the measure for a week, the committee reported the bill favorably to the
House on March 16.[63]

Needless to say, Price Daniel gave it his full support. He wrote Felix on
April 3 that "[y]ou were the one who showed me the value of the preschool
program for Spanish speaking children, and I think that legislative enactment
of this program would be one of the finest accomplishments in many
years."[64]

With such backing, on April 20, H.B. 51 passed the House by a vote of
118 to 27. On May 11, with its own minor amendments, the Senate ap-

proved the measure 26 to 1; Henry B. González was, of course, among those senators who voted in its favor. The House concurred with the Senate amendments the following day. Having cleared both bodies, the bill advanced to the governor for his signature.[65]

Tijerina's gratitude knew no bounds. He told the LULAC membership that passage of the act "stirred me to the depths." According to one magazine account, "Felix addressed the State Senate after the bill was passed. For once, he was at a loss for words in either tongue. Near tears, he said simply: 'Thank you gentlemen, for what you have done. May God bless you.'" On May 14, he wrote the bill's sponsors, blessing them for their "tremendous accomplishment" and prophesying that neighboring states with large Latin American populations would no doubt follow Texas' example and establish similar programs.[66]

And it represented quite an accomplishment. Of the eleven bills introduced embodying the Hale-Aikin recommendations, the regular session of the fifty-sixth legislature enacted only H.B. 51 and one other, H.B. 30 (permitting retired teachers to serve as substitutes). The parsimonious state legislature refused to pass the others, largely due to the costs they would have incurred.[67]

On June 1, 1959, surrounded by Senators Aikin and Kazen, Representative Hale, Oscar Laurel, and Felix Tijerina, Governor Daniel gladly signed the bill into law. LULAC hailed it as "The Most Momentous Occasion"; Tijerina looked jubilant in the picture taken by the capitol photographer.[68]

The bill authorized "a pre-school instructional program for non-English speaking children" to be developed by the Central Education Agency. The program would "prepare such children for entry into the first grade . . . with a command of essential English words which will afford them a better opportunity to complete successfully the work assigned them." It stipulated that the program would cover a three-month period and that it would be open to "[a]ny non-English speaking child at least five (5) years old and who would be eligible to enter the first grade the ensuing school year." The state and individual participating school districts would bear the costs of the program. Teachers were to be paid no more than two hundred dollars' monthly salary; a program could be set up and paid for in any district which had a minimum of fifteen participating children. The act was to take effect for the 1959–60 school year. (As events transpired, the preschool classes would actually begin during the summer of 1960.)[69]

Undoubtedly, H.B. 51 had received its backing from people for a wide variety of motives. Its overwhelming support from many within the frugal Texas legislature sprang from reasons which Tijerina and LULAC had persuasively championed. Individuals such as DeWitt Hale, a moderate Democrat from Nueces County who had emerged as the House expert on education, staunchly argued that the preschool program made sense for two important reasons: first, to relieve the suffering and embarrassment experienced by Latin American children because of their inability to understand English when they entered school, and second, because it would save Texas money by not having students repeat the first grade. Shrewd in the ways of the legislature, Hale had a real commitment to education. Moreover, he and Felix had become good friends on the Hale-Aikin Committee and were of a like mind on helping Hispanic youngsters. Hale was one of many who saw *Forgotten Minds,* a movie, he noted, whose "heart-rending" message made him want to "sit there and cry to watch those poor kids" struggle with a language difficulty. Like LULAC, Hale and people with his level of genuine compassion wanted to prevent the high rate of Mexican American dropouts.[70]

Support for the measure among others within broader Texas society likely sprang from similar motives, as many were caught up in the spirit of the times calling for teaching English to Spanish-speaking children. While reasons of humanity and cost effectiveness may have guided this thinking as well, a hard edge of cultural and racial bias also underpinned at least some of the support for the bill. Rather than viewing the use of Spanish by Mexican American children simply as a "language barrier," many saw it as a "handicap" that made Hispanics trouble for the local schools. Individuals with such a mind-set would likely believe that the Spanish language needed to be expunged. Corpus Christi public schools, for example, fostered an English-only rule on playgrounds as well as in classrooms. Many school districts across Texas during the period followed this practice and administered punishment to students who reverted to Spanish among their playmates. Parents were likewise admonished to speak English at home.[71]

The ability to speak Spanish, especially in areas away from the border, was hardly prized in Texas (unless to address one's laborers or maid), just as having a Mexican or Spanish accent was considered an impediment, humorous, or at best quaint. Under pressure to conform, many Mexican American youngsters worked long and hard (under the tutelage of well-intentioned teachers) to "overcome" their "handicap" through torturous voice exercises designed to obliterate their accent.[72]

Although great strides had been made in the condition of and attitudes toward Mexican Americans by the late 1950s, a level of racial prejudice also still prevailed in most areas across the state. De facto classroom segregation of Mexican American children based on skin color continued in many Texas schools, and the vocabulary of many non-Hispanic Texans included such pejorative words as "spic," "greaser," "pepper belly," and "meskin." For many non-Hispanics in Texas society during the 1950s, the support for the drive to teach children English was as much a part of an effort to "de-Mexicanize" the Spanish-speaking (to the extent to which they felt that any "Mexican" could be made "white") as it was to get them to excel in education. For many, suppression of Spanish and the drive to "teach 'em English" were integral parts of the anti-Mexican discrimination of the times. With all these reasons in the mixture, the status of Mexican Americans, as ever, remained a dicey one.[73]

Regardless of society's varied motives, Tijerina and his LULAC adherents took their support from wherever they could get it, always choosing to view mainstream society's attitudes toward them as half positive rather than half negative. As usual, Tijerina and LULAC were treading waters that included people who ranged from genuine *amigos* to hard-core bigots.

In their struggle to get H.B. 51 passed, Tijerina and his co-horts, as always, managed to maintain their bicultural balance and hold on to a pride in their heritage, regardless of how "conservative" they may have been viewed by other Mexican Americans in or out of LULAC. In the May, 1959, *LULAC News,* for instance, the council from McAllen, Texas, formally proposed an amendment to the LULAC constitution which would have changed the organization's name to the League of United Loyal American Citizens. As an expression of the Cold War atmosphere, the amendment argued that retaining the word "Latin" discouraged prospective members from joining because it "segregated" the membership from the rest of society at a time when "our country is . . . demanding the loyalty" of its citizens and "is . . . being challenged . . . by a country where the principles of democracy are unknown."[74]

In the same issue of the *LULAC News,* Felix stated in his monthly message that it should be a goal of the organization to keep communism "from our doors." On the preceding page, however, Tony Campos (a principal Tijerina spokesman) came out against the McAllen proposal because "[m]any of us are of Mexican descent and are proud to be identified as Latin Americans" and because "we are proud of our heritage and are likewise proud to belong to a Latin American organization whether we were born in America or whether our parents came from Mexico." With this sentiment ascendant in national LULAC, the amendment never passed.[75]

THE CHICAGO CONVENTION

Around the beginning of June, 1959, Felix changed his mind about running for a fourth term as LULAC national president when he bowed to "a definite and spontaneous movement" to draft him for reelection. Passage of H.B. 51 and his single-minded desire to carry its provisions to fruition no doubt fueled Tijerina's decision to run again. He was likewise cajoled to place his hat in the ring by members, including his regional and district governors, who feared that some of the newly established councils, especially those in the Midwest, might shrivel with him out of office. Councils becoming "inactive" posed a constant problem for LULAC. The June *LULAC News* (just prior to the Chicago convention) raised the drumbeat for his reelection. This issue (produced, of course, by Tony Campos and other Tijerinistas) boasted a formal portrait of "Don Felix" on its front cover, proclaiming him "Mr. LULAC." An inside editorial by Guadalupe C. Martínez noted that never in the history of LULAC had it owed so much to one individual, particularly in regard to education and growth. During his third term alone, the issue informed, New Jersey, New York, and fifteen new councils had been added. In an open letter to the membership, Alfred Hernández not surprisingly withdrew his own candidacy and threw himself behind this effort to elect Tijerina "for a fourth and glorious term as our National President." For Hernández, another term for Don Felix would be "the culmination of an era never to be forgotten" in the history of the league. Perhaps most illustrative of his followers' view of their national president, the back page of the June issue carried an almost ludicrous drawing of Mount Rushmore which, in addition to the images of Washington, Jefferson, Theodore Roosevelt, and Lincoln, included a bust of Felix Tijerina, with a caption reading: "Among the Greatest." This heavy-handed, partisan issue obscurely announced that Alfredo G. Garza, of Laredo Council No. 12, had filed as a candidate for the national presidency.[76]

The 1959 LULAC national convention took place at Chicago's massive Hotel Sherman, June 25–28, and was the organization's first national meeting outside the Southwest. Reportedly, this was the first time any Latin American organization had ever convened such a gathering in the Windy City. Although the confab was well planned and successfully executed by host Council No. 288, it did not pack the outward political punch of the previous year's convention at Laredo. Mayor Richard Daley and Governor Price Daniel of Texas were scheduled to address the delegates; however, two of Daley's administrative assistants stood in for their boss, while Bill Daniel spoke in his brother's stead. Even the *Chicago Tribune,* the city's major newspaper, failed to give the convention any coverage.[77]

Unaccompanied by his wife, Tijerina flew to the convention with Alfred Hernández to preside over the proceedings. Other members of his usual LULAC coterie made their way to Chicago in their own manner. Felix was, of course, a favorite among the councils from the states that had entered the league under his administration, especially those in the Midwest. His Chicago LULAC hosts hailed him as "the Latin American counter-part" of "the traditional Horatio Alger type of American achievement." At the presidential banquet and ball in the hotel's Grand Ballroom on Saturday evening, his admirers presented him with a LULAC lapel pin that contained diamonds for the three years he had held the national presidency. At election time on the following day, a delegate from Des Moines successfully moved to nominate Don Felix for his fourth term, a draft which, of course, had been building since the beginning of the month. Felix readily accepted.[78]

But Tijerina had his detractors from back home. And not even all his friends fell into line behind the call for his reelection. Laredo's Alfredo Garza had long since declared himself as a candidate for president. At election time on the final day of the convention, Oscar Laurel formally placed Garza's name in nomination; Albert Armendariz of El Paso, a longtime Tijerina opponent, gave Garza's nominating speech. Though Tijerina won his fourth and precedent-setting term by "an overwhelming majority," the vote was 94 to 42, unlike the unanimous reelections from previous years.[79]

In addition, the assembly had passed an amendment to the LULAC constitution the day before, stating that "No person may be elected to the post of National President if he or she has previously held such position for *more* than one full term, unless said person shall receive the unanimous vote of the delegates at a National Convention." Submitted by Laredo Council No. 12 and moved for adoption by a representative from San Antonio Council No. 2, the measure was clearly anti–Felix Tijerina, although, according to some observers, the movement would have gathered the support of the majority from a general sentiment against any one person continually holding the office.[80] The amendment would take effect by the next convention. For all intents and purposes, this would help bring Tijerina's presidential tenure to an end.

Despite these distractions, the Chicago convention was well attended and helped to solidify LULAC as a national organization. According to Alfred Hernández, the meeting reinforced the expansion which the group had accomplished in the Midwest. The gathering augmented LULAC national consciousness, especially among the assertive, middle class that Felix Tijerina personified. Felix met and conversed with LULACs from different parts of the country as people sought him out for advice and inspiration. Importantly, the Chicago convention helped to connect *Mexico americanos* of the Southwest with their compatriots in the North. LULAC territory consisted of two distinct regions: the original five LULAC states along the Mexican border and the eight newcomers clustered around the Great Lakes. The front of the 1959 convention program carried a map graphically illustrating this peculiar geography. Felix's efforts to "unify" his people took a step forward as delegates from these separate parts of the country attended the various sessions, talked together, listened to the music of Mariachi Jalisco and the orchestra of Miguelito Hernández, and generally mingled under the LULAC shield. All of this, in a fashion, added to a national sense of Mexican American solidarity and identity.[81]

These "connections" could be seen in the common experiences of the participants from the two LULAC regions. The convention's printed program, for example, saluted sixty-nine-year-old Vicente F. Garza, "the Dean of the Latin American Businessmen in the Midwest." In many ways, Garza embodied the Mexican American entrepreneurial class (and the community it served) which had been developing in the North since Mexicans had first settled there in the post–World War I era. According to the program, Garza and his wife had first migrated to East Chicago, Indiana, from Monterrey, Nuevo León, in 1923. They opened a plant to manufacture chocolate and package spices in 1928 and expanded as the Mexican population of the area grew. By 1959, the program further informed, his chocolate's trade name, "El Popular," had gained an "unmatched" reputation with more than a "generation and a half of Mexican Americans." Notably, the profile concluded, Garza was "an ardent booster of . . . LULAC" and "very proud of his great friendship for Don Felix Tijerina whom he admires and esteems deeply." Though Garza was older than Tijerina, their association illustrated a remarkable similarity of Mexican American experiences coming together under the auspices of LULAC after years of growth in different parts of their adopted country. Tijerina must have certainly recognized Vicente Garza as a compatriot, someone from the same part of Mexico, a successful 1920s urban immigrant, and a man well connected to *el esfuerzo mexicano* of the Immigrant Generation, which had been such a big influence during his own formative years. For other LULACs from the Bayou City who attended the 1959 convention, Chicago seemed to be "Houston duplicated," as they saw how *mexicanos* had coalesced there into a similarly vibrant community.[82]

Coming out of the Chicago convention, Tijerina's 1959–60 roster of national officers boasted the usual faces: Felix Salazar retained his place as national legal advisor; Tony Campos shifted to the position of executive director; Houstonian Virginia Ochoa (who had been helping Campos with the always-troubled *LULAC News*) became director of publicity; Carmen Cortes remained national secretary; Daniel Sandoval stayed as national treasurer; and Father Adrian Kempker of What Cheer, Iowa, was reconfirmed as chaplain. The convention had reelected Hector Godínez of Santa Ana, California, as first national vice president; Hilda Vázquez of Elizabeth, New Jersey, became second national vice president; Raúl Casas of Southgate, California, was elevated to director of youth activities; and Dr. Armando Durán of Lubbock, Texas, received assignment as director of health.[83]

THE STATE–SPONSORED
PRESCHOOL PROGRAM EMERGES

Back in Houston, Tijerina resumed work on the preschool educational effort, now underwritten by the state of Texas. Implementing this program consumed his last year as LULAC national president, to the exclusion of even expanding the league into more states.

On July 6, 1959, the State Board of Education approved the appointment of an advisory commission consisting of R. L. Williams of Corpus Christi, Henry Otto of Austin, Felix Tijerina, Mr. and Mrs. A. X. Benavides of Brownsville, and Elizabeth Scrivener of Eagle Pass. This commission was to help the Texas Education Agency develop policies for the forthcoming Preschool Instructional Program for Non-English Speaking Children created by H.B. 51. V. J. Kennedy, director of curriculum development for the Texas Education Agency, had the task of formulating guidelines for the state-sponsored preschool program. To do this, he worked closely with the commission and traveled extensively gathering information. Beginning in mid-July, the TEA contacted school districts around the state by mail, notifying them of the upcoming guidelines and supplying them with forms to complete if they planned to apply for one or more of the instructional units. These activities would begin the process which culminated in the classes actually beginning full operation in the summer of 1960.[84]

In addition to receiving crucial input from Tijerina and LULAC, Kennedy inspected projects that would help his planning. For example, in August, he visited Corpus Christi, where the district had preschool English-language classes in ten of its schools. These classes were instructing 680 pupils in a vocabulary of approximately five hundred words. Six weeks in duration and directed by E. E. Mireles (one of Kennedy's advisors), these summer classes were in their fourth year of operation and hailed by the Corpus Christi newspapers as "a pattern for the rest of the state." It was one of the programs that had provided Tijerina with some of the data he used in promoting the concept, and one which he closely monitored.[85]

With the passage of H.B. 51, Tijerina's "official" Little Schools withered, since their mission had been fulfilled. The expenditures on teacher salaries reflected in the financial statements of the LULAC Educational Fund, Inc., indicate that of the original nine Little School locations, only one instructor, Mrs. Nat Espitia of Aldine, remained on the payroll into the summer of 1959, apparently operating the only class still underwritten by the LULAC Educational Fund. As late as January, 1960, Mrs. Espitia held her Little School class in a small church on Houston's Market Street Road.[86]

Although numbers are extremely imprecise, the Educational Fund later estimated that approximately one thousand children had been served by the privately funded Little School of the 400 since LULAC began operating it in 1957. The Little School had served its purpose by illustrating that the English vocabulary needs of Spanish-speaking preschoolers could be effectively addressed.[87]

While the local school districts were being notified by the TEA of the upcoming instructional units and guidelines, the state legislature had not provided money for publicizing the program within the general population. This omission concerned Tijerina and LULAC members who wanted the tutoring to reach everyone, especially the more isolated Mexican American families it sought to affect. Also, because the classes were optional, Tijerina and LULAC felt pressure to encourage reluctant parents to enroll their children.[88]

Tijerina pushed ahead for implementation of H.B. 51 in the way he knew best: through promotion. For one, he continued to score with the media. In addition to local coverage that he always managed to obtain, Felix received significant national recognition when the education section in the August 17, 1959, issue of *Time* magazine carried a two-column story on him and his efforts for Spanish-speaking preschoolers in Texas. Entitled "A Four-Hundred-Word Start," the article focused on Felix's rags-to-riches life, recounted his efforts with the Little Schools, and told of his successful bid (with "strong support" from Price Daniel) to get the state legislature to underwrite the establishment of "Tijerina-style schools throughout Texas." Mistakenly, the article claimed that past segregation of Mexican Americans in Texas schools had been based on language (rather than skin color); however, it brought to national attention the plight of the estimated 200,000 Texas preschoolers who could not speak English, and how this "language barrier" eventually led to an alarming level of school dropouts. *Time* portrayed lack of English-language skills as *the* impediment to Mexican American educational advancement; it also carefully noted that "Tijerina pointed the finger [of responsibility] squarely at his own people, who refuse to speak English at home." Felix and his efforts seemed to be a peaceful, conservative counterbalance to the concurrent events in Little Rock, Arkansas, which *Time* covered on the same page. There, a separate article reported, the struggle still went on over integration of blacks into the high schools.[89]

Upbeat in its characterization of what Latin Americans were doing for themselves, *Time* stated that "70 Texas communities were ready to start Tijerina schools . . . in a grand attack aimed at smashing the language barrier forever." It concluded that Latin Americans in New York City, Buffalo, and Elizabeth, New Jersey, hoped to begin similar classes.[90]

Complete with a photo of Tijerina instructing a group of Mexican American preschoolers on their numbers and ABCs, the story was the media coup of Felix's life up to that point, as it fixed the national spotlight on Mexican American education, albeit on only one of the problems Hispanics faced in the school system. Understandably, he was extremely proud of this article. The *LULAC News* reproduced it in its November, 1959, issue, triumphantly proclaiming that "[o]ur national President Felix Tijerina makes news in *Time* Magazine."[91]

As positive as the *Time* magazine coverage may have seemed, even that rose had a thorn of criticism under it. A month after it appeared, Council No. 60 member Rudy Rodríguez reported to a regular council meeting that Paul Weber, head of the Freeport preschool language training, "was very disgusted" because the article had not mentioned his program, since Freeport's example, Weber felt, had helped inspire Tijerina's Little Schools. Weber said that the Freeport program had successfully operated for five years, and that he had sent a letter to *Time* expressing his chagrin at being left out. Weber also claimed, Rodriguez further alleged, that the LULAC national administration had become interested in such an effort only after Tijerina and other LULAC officials had visited Freeport in 1955 and received a thorough explanation of the local program. Weber had reminded Rodríguez of then–national president Oscar Laurel's comments on this visit in the *LULAC News*. To cap things off, again according to Rodríguez, Weber complained that Felix "had failed to respond" to Freeport officials' calls for assistance.[92]

In sympathy with these grievances, Rodríguez went on to claim that Tijerina had "expropriated" the preschool program from the Freeport people and had used it "for self prestige and politics." Accusing Tijerina of having done "a very poor job in Austin," he concluded that Council No. 60 should take the program on itself. Though Felix was not present to hear these allegations, Alfred Hernández was and no doubt reported Rodríguez's comments to his mentor. At a subsequent meeting, Tijerina called Rodríguez "a punk" who, rather than promoting the preschool program as he should have, "went out to investigate him" and criticized Felix for his work. Tijerina also upbraided Council No. 60 for not doing more. Though nothing came of Rodríguez's suggestion, the incident represented a typical "hassle" in the process.[93]

Regardless of Tijerina's aggravation with Rodríguez, the *Time* article had great effect. A Spanish-language version circulated throughout Latin America. The international edition of *Impacto,* a major magazine of photojournalism produced in Mexico City, published it in abbreviated form in its January 20, 1960, issue, which focused primarily on President Adolfo López Mateos. Entitled "Las Escuelas Tijerina, en Texas," Felix's story as seen in *Impacto* was not only read in Mexico, but also in Puerto Rico, the Dominican Republic, and sixteen nations in Central and South America where the magazine had distributors.[94]

Another spin-off from the publicity in *Time* came when a writer for *Reader's Digest* contacted Tijerina in August to do an article on his work with Spanish-speaking children. The piece was due to appear in the December, 1960, issue; however, for some reason, the story apparently never saw print, greatly disappointing Tijerina.[95]

Meanwhile, on October 1, 1959, Felix appointed Jake Rodríguez of San Antonio as his "personal representative" to help develop and promote the preschool program statewide. He charged Rodríguez with establishing local units (of what he and LULAC still referred to as the Little School of the 400) wherever Latin American children in Texas were in need. By now a convert to the concept that he had once condemned, Rodríguez enthusiastically wrote the LULAC membership that their first objective was "a full-scale publicity campaign." Rodríguez was just the man for such a task, regardless of his earlier criticism of the project. A seasoned LULAC member, Jake Rodríguez was a sincere, eloquent speaker in both languages and thoroughly devoted to Felix and the program. Echoing Tijerina, he admonished the organization that "the responsibility to promote it amongst our people [is] squarely on our shoulders." With Rodríguez as lead person, the LULAC national office initiated its own public information program regarding the English-language classes, which were due to begin in the summer of 1960. Rodríguez solicited every Texas council to establish a committee to disseminate information to Mexican Americans with children eligible to attend the schools. (By December, Felix had made Rodríguez executive director of the LULAC Educational Fund, Inc., with full authority to solicit funds.)[96]

Tijerina and his office also directly contacted school districts across the state, paralleling and reinforcing the efforts of the TEA. In January, 1960, he sent information on the program to all Texas LULAC councils, exhorting them—on the distinctive Little School of the 400 stationery—to promote the state-sponsored classes to their local school authorities. Around the same time, the LULAC Educational Fund, Inc. (under Rodríguez's direction) hired several district supervisors to do the necessary "leg work" to advertise the upcoming program among residents, school superintendents, and local organizations in "target" communities. By June, 1960, six of these promotional agents had been employed, including Homer Sifuentes of Corpus Christi, M. L. Ramírez of Kenedy, O. B. Garza and Reynaldo de la Garza of San Antonio, David Adame of Houston, and Andrés T. Juárez of Laredo. Like Tijerina, these men were absolutely committed to the idea of English-language training. All LULAC members, they literally went house to house in the urban and rural areas, trying to convince the often-reticent Mexican American heads of households to enroll their children in the upcoming program. David Adame, for example, encountered recalcitrant parents (especially fathers) who, when approached, told the Little School proselytizer to "mind his own business" and let others tend to the raising of their children. Such reaction notwithstanding, the promotional agents also did what they could to determine the number of youngsters eligible in each area they covered and contacted local school officials to apply for the state-funded project.[97]

To underwrite all these activities, Tijerina and the Educational Fund, Inc., tried to raise funds, with dismal results. First of all, they sought financial aid from LULAC by asking LULAC members to contribute ten cents a week for a year (or five dollars annually) to "get this program rolling." He hoped to enlist one thousand subscribers, but by early November, 1959, only 137 members had signed up, once again disappointing the national president. This "dues" scheme, like all the others he had proposed before, fell short.[98]

As much lip service as everyone gave to the preschool effort, between June, 1959, and June, 1960, the fund only managed to raise around $3,000 in public contributions from individuals, businesses, and LULAC members and councils. The largest donation came from Houston's prestigious Brown Foundation, which managed to come up with only $150. Tijerina was, to say the least, dejected by these results, especially in the lack of help from LULAC and its leaders.[99]

In May, 1960, Tijerina made an unsuccessful overture to the Ford Foundation. He spoke to a representative who had come to Houston to address his Rotary Club and pursued the issue by mail. Not only did the foundation reject his request for funding, it even returned the materials Tijerina had sent.[100]

The most gratifying results for Tijerina during this promotion campaign emanated from his association with Gulf Oil Corporation. In late March, 1960, amid much press coverage, Gulf Oil executives Robert L. Boggs and Madison Farnsworth announced that their firm would contribute several thousand dollars to publicize the Little School of the 400. The company extended this support after Tijerina had explained his funding troubles to Farnsworth, Gulf's marketing general manager in Houston and a man with whom Felix had forged a close relationship. On March 27, the Houston newspapers carried stories on the corporation's pledge to underwrite the promotion; the articles included photos of Mr. and Mrs. Tijerina with the two executives, as Boggs, Gulf Oil vice president, handed over an initial check. Eager to spread the word of its efforts, Gulf Oil sent news releases of the announcement to the Associated Press, United Press International, and to more than ninety other newspapers and periodicals.[101]

Along with money came use of the *Gulfstar,* Gulf Oil's company airplane, for a one-day, whirlwind trip around the state—a sally that the LULACs called Operation Little Schools—to advertise the preschool program. At seven o'clock in the morning on Saturday, April 16, the *Gulfstar* took off from Houston's Hobby Airport with Tijerina, Farnsworth, Tony Campos, Lawrence Hood (a Houston Boy Scout executive), and James Golaz (Gulf Oil district manager) on board. The plane also carried thousands of posters and circulars, the printing of which had been donated by Gulf Oil, "to inform the Latin American people of Texas of the opening of a statewide program of 'Little Schools of the 400' officially known and adopted by the Texas Public School System as Pre-School Instructional Classes for Non-English Speaking Children." These posters and circulars (which carried the eye-catching Little School logo of a Mexican American mother clutching her crying daughter) became keepsakes of the event. Headlined "Special Notice!" the bulletins told in English and Spanish the particulars of the upcoming program: when, where, why, who could participate, and what the parents must do to enroll their children. They also informed the public that the school was free to all.[102]

The trip was another media event in the Felix Tijerina tradition. The twin-engine *Gulfstar,* piloted by Floyd Stark and Roy Young, took its cargo of people and printed material to Corpus Christi, McAllen, Laredo, El Paso, and San Antonio—this final destination reached well after four in the afternoon. In each city, local Boy Scouts were on hand at the airport to receive a quantity of the advertisements to distribute to businesses and Spanish-speaking households. In addition to this local Scout contingent, the mayors of the various cities—Ellry King of Corpus Christi, Philip Boeye of McAllen, Raymond Telles of El Paso, and J. E. Kuykendall of San Antonio—along with other local officials and LULAC members were present to receive the flight and laud the program. Dressed in a dark suit, Tijerina was in his element as publicity photos were snapped and the local dignitaries praised the Little School. At the McAllen airport, Mayor Boeye, state representative Eligio "Kika" de la Garza, Texas LULAC director Robert Ornelas, Felix, Farnsworth, and the rest of the delegation donned Mexican sombreros and over-the-shoulder *serapes* for the occasion. In Laredo, the local newspaper photographed Tijerina handing leaflets to the Boy Scouts. In El Paso, Mayor Telles and Felix reviewed a line of eager Scouts, like generals inspecting an army. While it is difficult to measure the actual number of pupils that it actually recruited into the program, the day-long Operation Little Schools plane trip was a spectacular (though tiring) event, with kudos for everyone involved.[103]

Although he spent most of his time proselytizing to the public about the preschool program, Felix tried to be mindful of regular organizational affairs. It was clear, however, that his tenure as LULAC national president was on the downslide. Publication of the *LULAC News,* always a burden, seems to have been intermittent at best. He traveled out-of-state on LULAC business, though apparently not as extensively as during previous terms. In an attempt to keep the regions of LULAC stitched together, he attended the Supreme Council meeting in Santa Fe, New Mexico, on December 6, 1959, in the company of Danny Sandoval; he and Tony Campos went together to the final Supreme Council gathering of his tenure in far-off Albert Lea, Minnesota, on April 24, 1960.[104]

But even at the Supreme Council meetings, his thoughts were almost exclusively on his preschool efforts, and he spent most of his time talking up the Educational Fund and the Little School. At least some of the LULAC officials in attendance from across the country spoke to other issues, ranging from scholarships to the appalling sanitation/health conditions that still existed in many Mexican American communities, to LULAC membership service on city and state commissions, and to discrimination. At the Santa Fe confab, Arcenio Gonzales, New Mexico's past regional director, even told Tijerina and the others that LULAC was out of touch with the change taking place in the nation with respect to minority groups. Gonzales felt that LULAC "should discard our conservatism" and help other minorities, especially blacks. "When [the] NAACP invited LULAC to join them in their fight," he reminded them, "we did not accept and this perhaps was a mistake." Tijerina made no response. (For that matter, no one at the Santa Fe Supreme Council meeting seconded Gonzales's comments.) Felix consistently encouraged his fellow LULAC members to participate in civic affairs, but he had no inclination to take LULAC in any of the directions suggested by Gonzales.[105]

At the Santa Fe meeting, Tijerina expressed his belief that while LULAC fared well on the East Coast, "the league was too young" to tackle further expansion in New York because of "the Puerto Rican problems." (Like everyone else, Felix had followed the reports of the armed assault on Congress by Puerto Rican nationalists in March, 1954. He had seen the reports in the *Houston Chronicle* speculating that the Spanish-surnamed assailants were part of a possible "Commie Plot"; he had especially noted that his friend and local congressman, Albert Thomas, remarked at the time that he thought the shots had been fired by a group of "crazy Mexicans" angered by a Mexican labor bill under discussion.) Tijerina simply felt that Puerto Ricans did not carry an "image" suitable to the work of LULAC, nor did they understand the problems of Mexican Americans. Like his position on blacks, Tijerina distanced himself from these other Hispanics.[106]

At the April, 1960, Albert Lea gathering, super-organizer Val Hernández let it be known that his efforts in Ohio, Nebraska, and Kansas were pretty much at a standstill "due to the financial condition of the National Organizer's office." Clearly, the Tijerina/Val Hernández era of LULAC expansion had ended.[107]

Felix had one more opportunity while LULAC national president to align himself with blacks on the civil rights issue. But consistent with his past stance, Tijerina sided with the Anglo American establishment, in this case playing to his hometown audience. The issue arose in the spring of 1960 — during some of Tijerina's most intensive work for the Little School — when blacks in Houston sought to integrate the city's lunch counters. A direct reflection of the actions which began in February at lunch counters in Greensboro, North Carolina, some seventeen students from Texas Southern University (Houston's historically black institution of higher learning) staged a "sit-in" at the segregated lunch counter of a local Weingarten's grocery store. Similar sit-ins soon spread to other parts of the city, including downtown locations and the City Hall cafeteria.[108]

To ease political pressures and avoid possible violence, Mayor Lewis Cutrer established a forty-two-member biracial committee to review the issues and submit recommendations. Not only did he appoint Felix to that body, but Tijerina became a member of its executive committee. Simultaneously, Cutrer called for a voluntary moratorium on the demonstrations so that the biracial committee could pursue its duties, a hiatus that the majority of Houston's black leadership supported. The city avoided violence, although dissenting members of the student youth staged a successful (and peaceful) sit-in that desegregated the local Greyhound bus station cafeteria in late April.[109]

Amid this air of tension, Felix stepped forward with a major statement totally in keeping with his beliefs. In mid-May, he wrote and circulated among the biracial committee a page-and-a-half-long letter that called for patience on the part of Houston's blacks in dealing with desegregation. Noting that he too was "a member of . . . a minority group" that had likewise been on the receiving end of "much bias," Tijerina explained that his success in dealing with prejudice had involved "years of patient and carefully planned work" which was designed to make friends and gain the support of "other fair-minded citizens." Adding that he personally had "much sympathy for their [the black community's] position," he counseled them to avoid tactics that "will alienate the friendship of the white people." Instead, they should realize that their betterment must be gradual, climbing the ladder of progress "one step at a time." Stating that "[t]he Negro must remember that his best friend has been the white man of good will," Felix wrote that sit-ins and other such tactics, while "melodramatic," will "irritate . . . [and] antagonize" and would cause "more harm than good." He warned blacks that their use of "pressure" might prompt employers to "get along without Negro help in their businesses and homes," a consequence that would be "a catastrophe for every Negro in Houston and in the South." He concluded with the idea that "for my part, I am convinced none of these . . . aims [i.e., black advancement] will be achieved with pressure, threats, demonstrations or picketing and I for one will not agree to give in to such methods."[110]

Tijerina's comments were reported by the Houston press under the title "Latin Leader Urges Negroes to Be Patient." Naturally, he struck a responsive chord with most white readers. Reflecting this sentiment, James J. Braniff, Jr., a local insurance executive, sent Felix a copy of one of the newspaper articles stapled to a congratulatory, one-line personal note that read: "Your words are like pearls of wisdom."[111]

THE STATE-SPONSORED PRESCHOOL PROGRAM COMMENCES, SUMMER, 1960

The work which Tijerina and his cohorts had put into the education program came to grand fruition in the summer of 1960. By the spring, V. J. Kennedy and the TEA had produced their curricular guide describing the materials and instruction procedures that had proven effective in teaching English to children who did not speak the language. This guide had emerged approximately nine months after the appointment of the advisory commission upon which Felix served.[112]

The guide had incorporated input from many sources. For example, it based its methods on eight principles of teaching a second language developed by Faye Burrpass, a faculty member of Texas Technological College. The guide's recommended list of words for the classroom came from the vocabulary used by the Little School as well as from lists in textbooks of various school districts, including, most probably, Corpus Christi, since the TEA's list included five hundred words.[113]

The curricular guide also evidenced a level of sensitivity for the pupils. Echoing Elizabeth Burrus's earlier admonition, it stated that only those instructors who truly had "a sympathetic understanding of the children involved" be hired, a polite way of eliminating bigots. Also, the guide noted that if instructors overheard children speaking their native tongue, they were not to be reprimanded. On the other hand, it did not require hiring bilingual teachers; while it conceded that knowledge of the students' native language was "sometimes useful," ability to converse in that foreign tongue was not seen as "necessarily essential" for effective instruction. According to the guidelines, the summer classes were to last between forty and sixty days, with no less than 2 hours of instruction per day so that students would receive at least 120 hours of lessons.[114]

With the curricular guide in hand, the state-sponsored program began in a massive way. By June 1, 614 units of the Preschool Instructional Program for Non-English Speaking Children (with as many teachers) had opened their doors for the summer to more than 15,000 students. A total of 135 Texas school districts in eighty-one counties participated. Most of the units were in South Texas or along the border; however, some were farther north, in places like Austin, Waco, Abilene, Temple, Dallas, and other localities with Mexican populations. As mentioned above, the classes would teach the children five hundred basic words.[115]

END OF THE TIJERINA ERA

By the time of the 1960 LULAC national convention in San Antonio, Tijerina had decided not to run for another term. As the home of Pete Tijerina and host Council No. 2, the Alamo City was unfriendly ground for Felix and his Houston faction. Val Hernández, Tony Campos, and Carmen Cortes even suspected that "young punks" within Council No. 60 had been working since the beginning of the year trying "to discredit the old man," "afraid he might pull something out of the bag" by convention time. With all this antagonism, there probably would have been little hope for Felix to be unanimously reelected, as the anti-reelection amendment to the LULAC constitution required, even had he chosen to run.[116]

But the main consideration driving his decision was the fact that he was simply tired of the office, with all the traveling, personal expense, criticism, and other "hassles." Though much of his work had been rewarding, Tijerina, like all LULAC national presidents, had found the office to be a tiresome job and the organization to be a bottomless pit of financial need. By

1960, he felt that he had given enough and wanted to devote more time to his businesses, family, and other civic activities. Altogether, those closest to him recall, Felix was relieved to be leaving office. To no one's surprise, Mrs. Felix was even happier.[117]

The convention met at San Antonio's Hilton Hotel, June 30 through July 3, 1960, the final occasion in which Tijerina would preside over such a gathering. Because of his status as outgoing president, however, he played a more passive role in the proceedings. As usual, local political figures addressed the assembly. After welcoming the delegates at the opening ceremony, San Antonio mayor J. Edwin Kuykendall presented Felix with a proclamation making him honorary "Alcalde of La Villita." Emblematic of the area's strong Hispanic clout, Bexar County commissioner Albert Peña and City Councilman Joe Olivares also greeted the delegates that first day. San Antonian Gus García spoke to the convention on the history of LULAC and "the various stages that the league has gone through." Like everyone else, Tijerina publicly lamented the recent death of his "very close friend" and LULAC founder Alonso S. Perales, another of the organization's first generation that was passing from the scene.[118]

To underscore LULAC's pride in Hispanics in higher education, the convention planners had invited two distinguished academicians. Dr. Américo Paredes, literature and folklore professor at the University of Texas at Austin, gave a talk on southwestern culture at the Friday luncheon. On Saturday evening at the traditional Presidential Ball, Dr. Arthur L. Campa, folklorist and chairman of the University of Denver's Department of Modern Languages, delivered the keynote speech.[119]

No doubt making the most of its home field advantage, the San Antonio/Corpus Christi faction pushed through a number of more assertive resolutions at the business sessions. Among other things, these resolutions called for the federal government to increase federal aid to public school construction; pass the so-called Forand Bill to provide federal assistance for medical care of the needy elderly; establish a federal institution, similar to West Point and Annapolis, to train personnel for the foreign service; increase federal aid to higher education; and protect agricultural workers by provisions of the Minimum Wage and Hour Act. Each resolution directed that copies of these documents be sent to all senators and representatives from every state that had sent delegates to the convention. On its own, San Antonio Council No. 2 promoted and had passed a resolution "urging the creation of a commission to investigate and recommend improvement of present or existing FEPC (Fair Employment Practice Committee) Legislation on [the] National, State, and Local Level" for the purpose of fighting employment discrimination "against people of Mexican descent." [120]

As national president, Tijerina was obliged to sign each of these resolutions, but he passively did so. As his closest associates recall, he hardly approved of such active federal aid, being an Eisenhower Democrat and "by the bootstraps" in outlook. Typical of the ongoing friction between the established LULAC factions, the San Antonio council accusingly passed another directive that questioned the league for not having "followed through" on such measures taken at previous meetings. The resolution further instructed the national secretary to keep them "informed of the action and status of all resolutions approved at this and future National Conventions." [121]

Such contentiousness aside, the assembly passed many other resolutions, one of them submitted, not surprisingly, by Council No. 60 delegates David Adame and Ernest Eguía. It called on the convention to recognize the "brilliant accomplishments" of Felix Tijerina as "one of the most outstanding presidents in the history of LULAC" by giving him a standing ovation and by writing it into the minutes of the gathering. [122]

Felix and his cohorts, for their part, made the convention a showplace for their educational efforts, complete with an opening day workshop on the Little School of the 400. They also mounted a large display showing the number and location of participating counties, districts, classes, and students in the summer state-sponsored program. The LULAC Educational Fund, Inc., had printed a handsome illustrated brochure for distribution, rather cumbersomely entitled *LULAC in Action—Human Values, Unlimited: A Report on the "Little School of the 400," A Heart-Warming Project of the League of United Latin American Citizens.* A crisp, black-and-white publication with a cover photo of one of the classrooms in action, the booklet became an immediate souvenir of the Little School program. A group of convention delegates took tours of San Antonio public schools holding the preschool classes. They saw teachers with their eager pupils going through their vocabulary routines. The local newspapers, as usual, carried items on Felix and his efforts during the convention to raise money for even more promotion. [123]

After a noon barbecue at La Villita on Sunday, the last day of the convention, the delegates reconvened at the hotel and elected Hector Godínez of California, Tijerina's first national vice president, to succeed Felix as the new national president. Though, like all retiring LULAC national presidents,

Tijerina was somewhat bitter from past sniping, he wished the members and the organization well. Following the election of the other officers for the coming year, the convention adjourned at 5:45 P.M., bringing to a close Felix Tijerina's tenure in office.[124]

PRACTICAL ACTIVIST

As LULAC national president, Felix had focused his attentions between 1956 and 1960 on expansion and education, and in the final analysis he and his LULAC followers could point to noteworthy results. After four years, the organization had moved into eight new states and could for the first time claim the status of a national organization, even if its presence in some of the northern states was only a toehold. Felix Salazar later characterized this growth as nothing less than "the renaissance of LULAC." This expansion had been greatly facilitated, perhaps made possible, by Tijerina's penchant for promotion and his financial ability to travel as well as to pay the expenses of others who traveled with him or on his behalf. As to education, the Little School of the 400 had brought Mexican Americans to national attention, been institutionalized in the state of Texas, and served as an example for early English vocabulary training in other regions of the country. To accomplish these things, Tijerina had brought to bear great enthusiasm, optimism, and resources, which included having on his business payroll what amounted to a paid LULAC staff (i.e., Tony Campos and to a lesser extent Danny Sandoval). He had likewise paid the salaries of the initial Little School teachers, and he and his comrades had initiated the LULAC Educational Fund, Inc., which in turn had hired individuals like Jake Rodríguez and others to do a more effective job than volunteers ever could. Tijerina understood the power of money, and he invested it in those issues to which he dedicated himself. As seasoned observer L. DeWitt Hale succinctly commented: "Felix's pocketbook followed his mouth."[125]

Tijerina seems to have been an indispensable figure for LULAC during this time in the organization's development. During the late 1950s, his approach and message of education rang true with the Latin American community, especially its middle class. These folks saw merit in the wealthy entrepreneur's approach to life, which called for education as the hope for succeeding generations. During these same years, the American G.I. Forum, the veterans' group founded in 1948 by Dr. Hector P. García in Corpus

Christi, experienced similar geographic growth. As LULAC's biggest rival for membership in this period, the American G.I. Forum also emerged as a national organization; it reportedly formed chapters in twenty states during the 1950s, in part due to its own motto: "Education is our Freedom, and Freedom should be Everybody's Business."[126]

Felix's presence gave vigor to LULAC, just as the expansion of the American G.I. Forum in the 1950s came, in large measure, as a result of Hector García. Tijerina's promotional instincts, zeal, money, and freedom to travel, and García's boundless energy, powers of oratory, finances, and charisma provided the essential ingredients for their respective organizations, thus making the role of individuals important in this transitional decade of Mexican American history. With Felix's departure, LULAC would not resume the geographic growth he had given it. To some extent this hiatus had set in during his last year in office and would continue with the coming of the liberalism/radicalism of the 1960s, which passed LULAC by. Additionally, Val Hernández, a force unto himself, would die prematurely of a heart attack in 1961. But the halt in LULAC's growth undoubtedly had to do with Felix's leaving the presidency. His successor, Hector Godínez, fretted even before taking office that the organization would be in dire straits when Felix stepped down and took his checkbook with him. It is little wonder that when LULAC had its 1966 national convention in Houston (the year after Tijerina passed away), the organization consisted of the same thirteen states that it had when Felix left office. As the following chapter will note, after Tijerina's death, the zeal for the Little School concept likewise diminished in part due to his passing, though there were other factors as well.[127]

Of course, Tijerina had his critics all along, and any assessment of his work as national president begs for a discussion of his shortcomings as well as his successes. As already noted, even the Little School of the 400 came in for criticism. Toward the end of Felix's presidency, John Herrera expressed this longstanding complaint by calling Tijerina's beloved project a "big step backward" because it, in effect, "segregated" the Latin-American child. Herrera and others argued LULAC's traditional belief that anything less than full integration hurt Mexican Americans. The weakness with this argument against the Little School stems from the fact that the program specifically aimed to fit Mexican American children into the public school system, only in what Tijerina (and like-minded people) felt was a more effective manner. Anyone who knew Felix understood that fitting into mainstream society was always his prime objective.[128]

The facts are that the Little School and the subsequent Texas state program had overwhelming support from all sectors of society, including (perhaps especially) Mexican Americans. Hardly originating with Felix Tijerina, English vocabulary training was the pedagogy of the day. It was the way people felt they could make a better life for the next generation. The program's appeal, its advocates argued, was a principal reason why LULAC expanded as it did, so attracted were Mexican Americans to the initiative. Without doubt, Felix Tijerina and his Little School helped to make Houston and Council No. 60 a focal point of national LULAC. The program's critics were for this period relegated to a minority within the organization. When LULAC published its fiftieth anniversary history in 1979, it would rank the Little School of the 400 at the top of the list of its historic accomplishments, and many of the program's originators continued to believe it was superior to later developments such as bilingual education.[129]

Although not articulated at the time, one substantive criticism of the program may well have been that it was not extensive enough. According to most figures, it failed to reach thousands of needy Texas preschoolers, and Tijerina did not directly influence other state legislatures. One might also question, as many did as the 1960s unfolded, whether the relatively brief language course adequately addressed the child's language deficiency. For example, educator H. T. Manuel argued in 1965 that not only were five hundred basic words insufficient, but a partial summer's instruction could hardly redress the child's previous six years of English language deficiency. He also pointed out that the program wrongly ignored use of the child's native language and thus essentially lacked the finesse and effectiveness of bilingual education.[130]

In terms of general critics, Tijerina had many within LULAC during his tenure, as this chapter has noted. For those like Herrera, he could do little, if anything, right. Herrera, for example, tersely passed overall judgment some years later on Felix's presidency by stating the restaurateur had "[u]sed LULAC. Perpetuated Himself in LULAC. Was going to make LULAC Rich. Left us broke." Such sentiments failed to acknowledge that while Tijerina may not have made LULAC "rich," he did expend a considerable amount of his own wealth on the organization.[131]

Skeptics also pointed out that Tijerina, by setting the national LULAC agenda on only two issues, failed to attack the spectrum of problems facing the Mexican American community. Even contemporary Anglo journalists noted that Mexican American reality included a myriad of troubles in the late 1950s: in employment, in housing, in neighborhood school facilities, in health, in income, and in crime rates. Mexican Americans also faced subtle as well as virulent forms of racial prejudice that worked to exclude them from the better things in life. Discrimination because of skin color and their generalized "fear of rebuff" prevented them from full participation in society. When one considers all these areas that could have been attacked, it would be easy to believe that Felix's approach as LULAC national president seemed evasive, at best too simplistic.[132]

Furthermore, many of Tijerina's opponents felt that under him, LULAC had "mellowed" from its origins as a crusading organization that had filed federal lawsuits against segregation, fought to abolish the poll tax, and waged other protests similar to those of the NAACP. As national president, Tijerina had admonished the African American "to fight his own battles," and many LULAC members, like John Herrera, believed that his focus was "a far cry from former LULAC interests." In short, Felix's adversaries within his own organization called him nothing more than an "appeaser."[133]

In Tijerina's defense, perhaps it was his very focus that brought LULAC the success it had during his presidential years. LULAC was not a strong organization in those times and, as some scholars argue, the zeal that its membership had in the immediate postwar years seems to have waned by the time Felix took the helm.[134] Tijerina had found that, regardless of his best efforts, the economic resources (or the will of LULAC members to allocate them) simply did not exist to deal with more than one or two issues. It should be recalled, for example, that as Texas regional governor he had tried to raise money within LULAC to hire social workers among needy Mexican Americans around the state, an endeavor which did not even receive the endorsement of the Texas membership. Even his attempts to raise funds for the Little School met with disappointing results; much of the money used to pay for the Little School was his own. Lack of funds also precluded expansion into other states. Attacking too many problems may well have overextended already scant resources and would hardly have had positive outcomes.

Also, Tijerina continually called for Mexican Americans to do for themselves and develop leadership within their own ranks, especially within LULAC. In most of his monthly messages in the *LULAC News,* he "pep-talked" the membership to take the initiative in their respective communities. Even during his national presidency, he himself managed to squeeze in service on such bodies as the Houston Housing Authority and other agencies that sought to address many of the problems of the Latin American populace.[135]

While he had gone about his work for LULAC with zeal, Tijerina certainly was no *provocateur,* as some wanted him to be. On most issues, he was a moderate Price Daniel Democrat at best, much more conservative than John Herrera, Pete Tijerina, the emerging Henry B. González, and their kind, and these individuals were impatient with him. But he was neither an attorney nor a politician with a Mexican American constituency.

To the contrary, Felix was a Houston establishment entrepreneur who would not risk estranging his Anglo customers or financial colleagues. Moreover, like other generous Houston businessmen, Tijerina enjoyed the prestige and sense of belonging associated with his philanthropy, and he was someone whose citizenship status had only recently been "resolved," a factor that no doubt also played a role in guiding his approach to dealing with Anglo society. He was grateful to the mainstream that had embraced him. He always said that he was "just paying a little back" to society in return for his success.[136] Tijerina could no more bring himself to criticize Price Daniel's Texas or Dwight Eisenhower's America than he could to question the Houston of Roy Hofheinz and Lewis Cutrer. Like most Americans whose livelihood and identity (not to mention mere presence) are predicated on being part of the structure, Tijerina's freedom of action and expression was effectively circumscribed by a subtle, but potent degree of social control. Though an activist, Felix, as always, took a positive, accommodationist approach to the established order. He had never been confrontational with larger society; for him to have been otherwise as LULAC national president, especially when trying to develop a massive education program with the help of the establishment, would have been a reversal of his entire life's course.

Furthermore, times had changed since the 1930s. If LULAC had ever been the strident group that some of its members nostalgically remembered, the temper of the 1950s called for the more gradual approach that Tijerina's educational thrust represented. To be sure, his refusal to ally with blacks and Puerto Ricans showed a pronounced lack of solidarity with other oppressed minorities. But Tijerina, true to LULAC tradition, considered "Latin Americans" to have (or at least should strive to have) more in common with the mainstream and would not have wanted to associate his people with any group whose members marched in protest or shot up the U.S. Congress; he behaved accordingly, if with less boldness and sensitivity to the plight of other people of color than one would have hoped.

As far as accusations of Felix being an "appeaser," he did carefully work to get along with mainstream society. However, terms like "appeaser" are relative, often meaningless. LULAC and all its leaders prior to 1960 strived to "fit in" to middle-class society, and in doing so naturally "accommodated" to the structure to one degree or another.

His shortcomings notwithstanding, Felix at least tried to do something to get at what he saw as the root of the longstanding problems his community faced. He had an abiding faith that education was the "key" to a better to-morrow; to the end of his life he felt that crashing the language barrier would be his greatest legacy because it would give Mexican American kids more of a chance and foster societal harmony. Like many people who appreciate but do not fully understand the true meaning of education, he could only relate it to his own life's experiences, which caused him logically to conclude that had he been better educated, in particular had he known English, his own road would have been smoother. This personal identification with the problem, his genuine compassion, as well as a desire to fit Mexican Americans into the mainstream society that he so much wanted to placate and be a part of himself, prompted him to push for preschool English-language training.

Although preschool language instruction did not originate with Felix Tijerina, his program was a direct reflection of his mind-set. He was not a man trained for or disposed to theorizing. He simply saw the Little School of the 400 (and the state-sponsored Preschool Instruction Program) as a workable solution to a vexing problem. He tackled the mission of LULAC much as he ran his businesses or did his other club work. He increased the number of LULAC councils much like he expanded his chain of restaurants. A pragmatic, practical activist, he identified the "Latin American problem" as best he could, located an "acceptable" solution, and promoted his remedy until he had a finished product. As it emerged through his high-profile promotion, Felix's solution, the Little School of the 400, became synonymous with his name. He put his heart and soul (as well as his money) into its development; it was considered his "brain child," "Tijerina's schools," an identification which obscured the role of many others who often independently had struggled to bring English vocabulary training to the Spanish speaking.

Regardless of any reservations, Tijerina's four terms as LULAC national president constituted a successful tenure, not only for the organizational expansion and educational program he spearheaded, but by the mere example he set of getting out and accomplishing something. Through his activist example as "Mr. LULAC," he showed other Mexican Americans a level of self-determination that had reached beyond the barrio; his actions represented a logical extension of the process his generation had begun in the 1930s: to reach out beyond the confines of their traditional ethnic enclaves and work with larger society, even the highest circles of power.[137]

He was in fact living up to the dream of his generation. He had achieved wealth and status in the American environment, effectively bargained with Anglo society, and in the process had not turned his back on *la raza* or its culture. Indeed, as his cohort had always hoped, he raised the profile of LULAC as an organization and Mexican Americans as a people, successfully working to bring Mexicans and Anglos together in harmony.

One of the Mexican American Generation's own, Tijerina was respected (though sometimes grudgingly) by its other members. As the four-term leader of LULAC, his contemporaries' quintessential organization, Tijerina was an embodiment of the "Latin American" and proof that the decade of the 1950s was an active period in Mexican American development, regardless of the criticism its participants would receive in subsequent years.

Though no longer its president, Tijerina would keep his hand in LULAC affairs, in particular the preschool program he had been so instrumental in creating. The following chapter will consider this involvement and his many other activities during the last five years of his life.

CHAPTER 10

CITIZEN FELIX

THE FINAL YEARS, 1960—1965

After he left the LULAC national presidency, Felix Tijerina never broke his stride of societal involvement as he continued to busy himself in civic, business, and personal matters. Seldom one to seek repose, even as his health declined before his untimely death, he maintained the stressful level of commitments that had always been his fare.

Most of his activities during these last five years of life were carryovers from his previous endeavors, many of which he somehow continued during his hectic days as LULAC's chief executive; other efforts represented new, albeit logical, outgrowths of prior involvements. During the fall of 1960, for example, Tijerina made his one bid for mainstream elective office by mounting an impressive though unsuccessful race for a seat on the Houston Independent School District Board of Trustees; this foray represented another step in his crusade for education and a manifestation of the growing possibilities for Mexican Americans in Houston politics.

Tijerina also maintained a steady pace in LULAC affairs, particularly in the position of past national president and as chairman of the LULAC Educational Fund, Inc. In these offices, he proselytized for expansion of the Preschool Instructional Classes for Non-English Speaking Children (his Little School program). In large part because of Tijerina's resolve, this Texas program not only served thousands of children, but also gave impetus to some of the federal preschool efforts developed during President Lyndon B. Johnson's administration.

In the civic arena, too, Tijerina emerged as an even more prominent member of Rotary, the group that had held his attention since 1948. Rotary provided Felix with a concomitant vehicle for spreading the word about education and his other charitable works. Mrs. Felix likewise remained part of Rotary, facilitating her husband's endeavors and, in her own right, serving as a leader of the women's group. Tijerina also continued his principal role on the Houston Housing Authority and on an array of other bodies to which he had been appointed.

During his last years, Felix Tijerina, the seasoned civic man, reaped unprecedented accolades for his accomplishments, public kudos that came regularly and almost expectedly. He remained a community favorite and sweet subject of the local media. Significantly, the attention that had been given to his educational efforts by printed media during the late 1950s multiplied with the appearance of national publicity on radio and television and in other periodical literature in the United States and Mexico. Such praise generated increased interest across the nation in Tijerina-style English-language training and for the cause of Mexican American education. Felix received much acclaim from individuals and groups on both sides of the border. Though he had little time for reflection amid the swirl of daily affairs, Tijerina, in the latter years of his relatively short life, reaped no little gratification for what he so abundantly had sown.

In his business affairs Felix seemed to make up for the time he had lost while LULAC national president. He opened three new restaurants between 1961 and 1965, which raised the number of Felix Mexican Restaurants to seven. In American entrepreneurial style, he opened his final one just before he died, living out what he had told a reporter over a decade before: "[Y]ou never have it made in business until you die or retire." On other fronts, he expanded his economic interests into the savings and loan industry, reaching another level of maturity in the financial world.

Regarding his family, Felix had always been a loving, attentive father, and his children—Felix, Jr., and Janie Bell—felt his presence even more so in the 1960s. Tijerina used every occasion to foster that relationship, leaving them a legacy of care and respectability that he had sought in every aspect of his life.

Altogether, an understanding of his last five years provides a comprehensive view of Felix Tijerina as an active, balanced, mature public and private man. This period represented the culmination of three decades of personal development as he engaged himself in those commitments he found most meaningful. He had established a complex network of endeavors, constructed over a lifetime, that reflected his own impressive level of energy, sophistication, and individual achievement and that mirrored the growing involvement of Mexican Americans in larger society.

Tijerina continued to make his crowded schedule look easy. To the outside world, he seemed to manage things effortlessly, but the difficult process of balancing the many aspects of his life no doubt took its toll. Nonetheless, Felix Tijerina's image as the perfect postwar Latin American remained intact to the end, a leader of the Mexican American community respected by all, someone who had begun in obscurity and finished with as much recognition as anyone could have ever hoped to attain, especially a competitor who had started so far back in the hunt.

THE POLITICS OF 1960 – 1961

By the summer of 1960, the nation's political atmosphere was becoming electrified. The presidential race between Senator John F. Kennedy and Vice President Richard Nixon became a watershed event, especially for Mexican Americans. Initially, Tijerina supported Lyndon B. Johnson's unsuccessful bid for the nomination and made a substantial contribution to his candidacy. After the Democratic convention in July, he predictably threw his support to the Kennedy-Johnson ticket, as did other Texas Democrats, from Price Daniel to Henry B. González. Felix liked Kennedy as a man, charmed, as many were, by his charisma and abilities as a public speaker.[1]

Though he heartily endorsed the Democratic standard-bearers, Tijerina was not active in the Viva Kennedy-Johnson Clubs that sprang from the Mexican American community's captivation with Senator Kennedy. Co-chaired in Texas by the likes of Albert Peña, Henry González and Dr. Hector P. García, the Viva Kennedy-Johnson Club in Houston comprised men and women of the Civic Action Committee who had pushed González's 1958 gubernatorial bid, individuals who had little political association with Tijerina. As a wealthy man with "connections" to state leaders like Price Daniel, Tijerina operated at a higher level than the rank-and-file Mexican Houstonians who threw themselves into the 1960 effort. These differences notwithstanding, Felix so supported and contributed to JFK-LBJ (and the Democratic National Committee) that after the victory he received an invitation to the inauguration in Washington, D.C., though apparently he did not attend.[2]

Mrs. Felix, never one to fall in line, had supported the Republican candidate, Richard Nixon.[3]

Tijerina's political efforts during the fall of 1960 were actually more directed at a local campaign: namely, his own. In early September, Felix Salazar reported to a meeting of Council No. 60 that "many local citizens" had urged Tijerina to run for the Houston Independent School District Board of Trustees because of his background and interest in education. In response, Council No. 60 put together a committee to approach him about this prospect. On October 7, the final day for filing, Tijerina announced for Position 2 on the ballot, hoping "to repay the community for many, many things people have done for me." This effort represented his first and only time to run for any publicly elected office. Assuming a low-key, enlightened business approach, he told the *Houston Post* that he would serve with the purpose of securing a better education for children and a "careful spending of our tax dollars." He also pledged that he would "not be a part of any faction or any group."[4]

Tijerina's latter promise—not being a member of any "faction"—spoke to the tumultuous condition of Houston school politics of that era. During the 1950s, the Houston school board had been marred by continuing friction between conservatives and liberals. Since 1952, the conservative forces had coalesced during each election in a quasi-political party called the Committee for Sound American Education (CSAE). The liberals, that same year, had formed the so-called Parents' Council, which, in 1957, transformed itself into the Houston Association for Better Schools. Beginning in 1952, each group fielded its slate of candidates in what proved to be the most hotly contested, polarized, and publicized races on the city's political landscape, many of them manifesting Houston's own version of the 1950s Red Scare. With the conservative elements mainly in control and utilizing McCarthyite tactics, school board meetings themselves became petty political circuses, what one scholar of the era called "one of the city's top entertainment attractions."[5]

Though the doctrinaire Red Scare–style politics on the school board had largely dissipated by 1960, animosity and strife between the conservatives and liberals still existed, and into this divisive situation Tijerina offered himself as a polite alternative. Four positions out of a total of seven on the board came up for election, and a record number of candidates (twenty-seven) ran. Stone Wells, the conservative CSAE incumbent in Position 2, announced that he would not seek another term; Tijerina and seven others filed for his spot.[6]

Tijerina's chief opponents for Position 2 turned out to be Mrs. James Street Fulton and Robert (Bob) Eckels. Fulton was the wife of a philosophy professor at Rice University and was endorsed by the Houston Association for Better Schools; Eckels, a thirty-one-year-old former schoolteacher turned branch manager of an insurance company, was the CSAE standard-bearer. To win this four-year, non-paying post, the victor had only to receive a simple plurality (i.e., the most votes), as there was no run-off. All positions were at-large, chosen by the city's entire registered electorate.[7]

Everyone knew of Tijerina's good intentions and his keen desire to serve on the school board. This campaign represented his best opportunity ever to be elected. With all his civic and business endeavors, he was on his loftiest perch in Houston's public eye as a philanthropist and manager of finances. People had long known of his commitment to helping youth; his name was synonymous with education.[8] And Council No. 60's interest in his candidacy reflected the atmosphere of political possibility among Mexican Americans generated by the 1960 presidential campaign, especially for the election of someone like Tijerina who had the goodwill of the majority community.

Not only was the school board race hotly contested, but the district itself was big business. HISD, in 1960, was the sixth-largest school district in the nation, with 168,262 students and more than 6,000 teachers. Its annual operating expenses totaled $52.5 million. Tijerina, like many Houstonians, followed HISD doings and no doubt fancied running for the position long before he announced.[9]

Campaigning began quickly with Tijerina appearing on a number of rostrums across town. Setting the tone for the race, twenty-three of the school board candidates (including Felix) attended and spoke at a rancorous rally held on the evening of Tuesday, October 11, 1960, by the Houston Association for Better Schools at the MacGregor Elementary School auditorium. Thereafter, every couple of days (sometimes, every day), the candidates would address packed-house gatherings that numbered as high as 350 people at various places across town, including schools, churches, and synagogues.[10]

Emotions ran high at every public assembly, with the conservatives and liberals denouncing each other and their platforms. By the time it concluded, the campaign was characterized as one of "the hottest in recent years."[11]

A whole range of issues came in for heated discussion, including factionalism on the board, teachers' pay, wasteful spending, and the question of federal aid. Generally, the liberal slate advocated the use of federal commodities and milk for school lunches, higher teacher pay, and the need to emphasize "world knowledge." The conservatives rejected federal aid, supported increasing the teacher salaries only if such pay hikes could be accomplished without raising taxes, and decried the "one-worldism" which they felt the liberals pushed.[12]

But at the heart of the discord were differences over desegregation of the Houston schools. HISD was under court order to implement the so-called "Twelve Year Plan," which desegregated the schools one grade per year. The liberals felt the plan was too slow, and they pledged to bring about fuller, more rapid integration. By and large, the CSAE conservatives wanted to stick closely to the gradual approach. And the CSAE candidates were not the most right-wing on the ballot. One independent candidate vying for Position 2, Mrs. John R. Barnett, was an avowed segregationist, who claimed that the Houston schools had become "a sounding board for socialist propaganda."[13]

By mid-October, Reverend James Novarro, a Baptist minister, Council No. 60 member, and the only other Mexican American running for the school board (Position 1), spearheaded the formation of a third slate of candidates who called themselves the "Independent Moderates" and ran as an alternative to the conservatives and liberals. Tijerina, for his part, shunned this effort and made it clear early on that he, as "an independent, free-thinking candidate not encumbered by liberal, conservative or middle-of-the-road labels," would align himself with no group of candidates. From the start, the media portrayed Felix as the leading independent candidate.[14]

Never one to seek conflict, Tijerina took his turn to speak at every rally and generally tried to remain above the fray. Reports of what he said at the meetings indicate that he tried to skirt specific issues by running on a simple noncontroversial platform of improving public education, saving the taxpayers' money, and, like the other independents, wanting to help "see an end of bickering on the board." He felt that the liberal and conservative candidates unfortunately were "committed to vote a certain way on an issue before the issue even arises," a problem which struck a responsive chord among many fair-minded Houstonians.[15]

Regarding specifics, Tijerina made it clear in his printed platform that he favored raising salaries "to attract and hold teachers of the highest quality." He also emphasized that "under no circumstances can I go along with those who seem to have as their objective the replacement of the present Superintendent of Schools," Dr. John McFarland, a conservative (but self-described "middle-of-the-roader") who was then under attack by ultra-rightists.[16]

At one gathering, Tijerina chided Bob Eckels for running on a slate "picked by a handful of people." When, at an assembly at Saint Michael's Episcopal Church, Mrs. Fulton expressed the opinion that Houston schools overemphasized the teaching of Texas history and called for more world history and geography, Tijerina told the audience that she was incorrect. Pointing out that Fulton came "from New York and has been here only five years," he noted that while "we do talk about Texas," the curriculum already included world history.[17]

During the give-and-take of such assemblies, Tijerina had at least one embarrassing moment when, at Red Elementary School (in front of 350 people), he had to admit that both his children attended parochial school, but he responded: "If that exempts me from paying taxes, then I'm not qualified for the school board."[18]

Not surprisingly, Felix enjoyed some vocal supporters, many of whom were as tired as he was of the ideologically based tussling on the board. The more independent-minded *Houston Press*, under the editorship of fellow Rotarian and longtime friend George Carmack, recommended to the voters during the last week in October that they elect Tijerina as part of its "ticket against tickets." Indeed, the newspaper called him "outstanding among the 27 candidates" making the race. On November 1, the *Press* ran a powerful editorial (no doubt penned personally by Carmack) entitled "Why We Are Strong for Felix Tijerina." The editorial noted that Tijerina, unencumbered by slate affiliation, would be able to consider each problem that came before the board on its own merits—"without prejudice"— because he "would be able to think and act independently," just as he had in his other civic services and in building his restaurant chain.[19]

Tijerina's cautious stance on the main issues—federal aid and desegregation—as well as the goodwill he enjoyed among mainstream conservatives was illustrated during the week before the election when he also received the endorsement of Dr. Henry A. Peterson. Described by the *Houston Chronicle* as a "venerable physician," Dr. Peterson had served twenty-two years on the school board, two of those terms as the head of the conservative slate, and was at the time school board president; he had played a major role in the McCarthyite mischief that had marred the board's operation during the 1950s. Like Stone Wells, however, Peterson had decided not to run again. In 1958, he had squabbled with other conservative members of the board and allied himself with liberal members to hire Superintendent McFarland. By 1960, Peterson had irrevocably split with the CSAE leadership and was a man without a party. On November 3, on the grounds that he was opposed to all slates, Peterson announced to the media that he was voting for Felix Tijerina, the independent. He no doubt appreciated Tijerina's support of McFarland, but he also stated that he would not have endorsed anyone who favored federal aid or rapid integration.[20]

The appreciation for Felix demonstrated by the *Press* and Peterson was shared by many of his fellow candidates as well. In a secret poll conducted by the *Houston Post* among twenty of the candidates appearing at a rally less than a week before the election, Felix received eight votes, more than any of the others. Tom English, the independent candidate who suggested the poll (and who garnered only two votes), commented that the balloting represented the most informed understanding of the convictions, character, objectives, and personality of those persons in the race; they had picked the person whom the *Post* chose to call the "Candidates' Candidate."[21]

To bolster his chances, Tijerina had taken on the loyal Alfred J. Hernández as his campaign manager. Together, they printed push cards and bumper stickers and mailed postcards, signed by Hernández, which implored voters to cast their ballot for Tijerina, "an outstanding American" who would deliver "better schools and sound education." They also had television and radio advertisements. In the local newspapers they ran variations of an ad entitled "This Is What I Believe," which stressed Felix's many qualifications, his basic positions, and his refusal to play politics. He asked for the black vote (as even the CSAE candidates did) by running ads in *The Informer,* Houston's respected African American newspaper.[22]

When the results came in on election day, November 8, it was politics as usual, with the CSAE candidates winning all four slots by wide margins, thus maintaining conservative control of the school board. The liberal Houston Association for Better Schools hopefuls came in poor seconds, by margins of almost two to one. These results undoubtedly reflected many things, including the fact that Harris County experienced an overwhelming voter turnout that went decisively for the Republican presidential ticket. The so-called Independent Moderate school board slate (including Reverend Novarro) lost miserably, none of them pulling over four-figure totals.[23]

Tijerina was the only independent candidate who made a credible showing. Eckels, described by the media as one of the "big guns of the campaign," received more than 75,000 votes to Mrs. Fulton's 43,380 and Tijerina's 40,312. The other three remaining candidates for Position 2 (two had dropped out) each garnered more than 7,000 votes apiece. That Tijerina did so well spoke to the respect he commanded among the general population.[24]

As a Mexican American and independent candidate, Tijerina never stood much of a chance of winning, even though he had run a good campaign.[25] His candidacy, however, did illustrate for the first time in Houston that a Mexican American could mount a serious effort for a city-wide office.

His race also demonstrated, in a rather cruel way, that Tijerina's fixation on teaching Spanish-speaking children to "speak English" was not misplaced. Many Mexican Houstonians who recalled the race felt that, though Tijerina had much support, his heavy accent and poor English diction on his radio and television ads left a poor impression on voters and damaged his chances.[26]

Undaunted by his loss, Tijerina placed a gentlemanly closure on his campaign within a week after the election. On November 15, the *Houston Press* printed a letter to the editor from Felix that congratulated the winners and urged everyone "to forget politics and all pitch in behind the new school board, elected by the majority, and work for the best interests of our children and school system."[27]

Predictably, however, people did not "forget politics"; the conservative and liberal forces on the Houston school board continued to be at odds. With Bob Eckels and other CSAE candidates elected in 1960 taking the lead, the conservatives maintained a strained political atmosphere similar to that of the 1950s: promoting rabidly anticommunist programs in the Houston schools, chastising educators with liberal political views, and requiring people to sign a loyalty oath before they could use school facilities. The school board remained the "best show in town," and perhaps better for him, Tijerina stayed on the sidelines.[28]

Пot long after the school board race concluded, Tijerina's name was promoted by LULAC admirers for a federal appointment, forming a postscript to the 1960 election season. In late December, Tony Campos, as executive director of LULAC, sent lengthy telegrams to Governor Price Daniel and Lyndon Johnson urging that Tijerina be appointed ambassador to Mexico. Campos asked them to contact the proper parties to effect this, so that the Latin Americans of the United States would know that the White House had confidence in their abilities and that the nation could combat any impending "communist campaign" against Mexican president Adolfo López Mateos and the people of Mexico who were accused of being on close terms with alleged "Yankee aggressors." In their replies, both elected officials expressed their high regard for Felix: Daniel said that he would do what he could to assist and Johnson promised to pass the suggestion along to Kennedy and his staff, as Felix was "one of [his] favorite people." But each stated that he had no direct connection with making such appointments, and if either promoted Felix's candidacy, no written evidence exists. At the same time, Campos telegrammed president-elect Kennedy, telling him that LULAC believed that Tijerina should be considered for the post and that Tijerina's friends, Lyndon Johnson and Price Daniel, "would be more than willing to endorse this appointment."[29]

Campos and his LULAC circle apparently solicited the support of others on Tijerina's behalf. On December 29, two days after Campos's telegram to Kennedy, Mayor Lewis Cutrer sent one of his own to the president-elect stating that it "ha[d] been brought to [his] attention" that Tijerina was interested in the ambassadorship and urging Kennedy to consider Felix for this high position.[30]

According to Tony Campos's best recollections, Felix was enthusiastic about the possibility of the appointment. In early 1961, Tijerina took note of an Associated Press story reporting the remarks of John A. Flores, a Californian and "executive national director of 'Americanos con Kennedy and Johnson.'" Flores was in Washington where he urged the newly installed Kennedy administration to recognize U.S. citizens of Mexican background in the distribution of federal patronage. Expressing his disappointment in the results thus far, Flores noted that while there had been "some five or more top level Negro appointments" not a single Spanish-speaking person had been named to represent the seven million to eight million Hispanic voters in the West and Southwest. Among those individuals he suggested for high government positions were Mayor Raymond Telles of El Paso and Felix

Tijerina of Houston. Flores had been involved in California LULAC and no doubt knew Telles and Tijerina from their work in that organization.[31]

It is not clear exactly how widespread (or connected) these efforts were to promote Tijerina's name. Felix did, however, notice the announcement in mid-February that the Kennedy administration appointed his friend Raymond Telles as ambassador to Costa Rica; according to a report by the *New York Times,* this was the highest post ever offered to a Mexican American. Telles clearly possessed attractive, more fitting credentials: he was college educated, had been an air force officer during World War II, had served as an aide to Presidents Eisenhower and Truman on visits to Mexico, had seen duty in Korea in 1952, and then in 1954 acted as a liaison officer to the chief of the Mexican air force. Perhaps more important, he was a faithful Democrat, having worked in the 1956 campaign of Adlai Stevenson, where he first met Senator Kennedy. A veteran officeholder, Telles had served two terms as mayor of El Paso and was in the midst of his race for a third term when he received word of his appointment.[32]

Shortly after this announcement, Special Assistant Lawrence O'Brien sent courteous but brief replies to Campos, Cutrer, and probably others who had recommended Tijerina, stating that their suggestion would be "weighed in considering the matter." Two weeks later, on March 31, the Kennedy administration announced that it would appoint a career diplomat, Assistant Secretary of State for Inter-American Affairs Thomas C. Mann as ambassador to Mexico, indicating the high priority placed on that position. As the first Texan in nearly fifty years to be in that post, Mann had been raised on the border and spoke flawless Spanish with a Mexican accent.[33]

It is impossible to determine if the Kennedy administration took seriously the idea of Felix representing the United States in Mexico City; Mrs. Felix steadfastly claimed that two or three men, presumably from the government but unknown to her, came to their home and spoke with her husband about the appointment. For his part, Tony Campos recalled that Felix's name was at least "tossed around," but he also felt that, lamentably, Felix's lack of formal education and ability to express himself in a polished manner hindered his candidacy.[34]

Politically, Tijerina remained a moderate, establishment Democrat. In the special U.S. Senate election that came as a result of Lyndon Johnson's election as vice president, he supported William A. (Bill) Blakley, who had been appointed to fill Johnson's vacated seat and was making his bid for the rest of that unexpired term. Along with Tony Campos, Felix attended a Latin American Press Association (LAPA) conference held in Harlingen during March, 1961, where he publicly sported a Blakley campaign button on his lapel and joined LAPA in its endorsement of the senator, who was on hand to seek their votes in his ultimately unsuccessful bid to defeat the Republican aspirant, John Tower. Their endorsement of Blakley ran counter to Texas LULAC, which, at its February, 1961, convention under the influence of such men as Roberto Ornelas and William Bonilla in always politically charged Corpus Christi, voted to back Henry B. González for that post, a man the young Turks of LULAC called "one of the greatest living Americans."[35]

LULAC AND THE PRESCHOOL INSTRUCTIONAL PROGRAM, 1960–1962

From July, 1960, to July, 1961, Tijerina held the position of immediate past national president of LULAC, which, though not nearly as taxing as holding the presidency itself, required time and effort. After July, 1961, he became simply a past national president when Frank M. Valdez, San Antonio architect and a LULAC district director, succeeded Hector G. Godínez, the Californian, who served only one term in office.[36]

From mid-1960 through 1961, Felix convened only one board meeting of the LULAC Educational Fund, Inc. (in September, 1960), as little transpired to warrant its attention. The board's main charge was, as before, to promote the state's program, and especially to raise funds for that purpose. Best of intentions notwithstanding, the money-raising events staged by Tijerina, Campos, and their supporters were a bust. On July 16, the fund held a local benefit baseball game between the Houston Buffs and the Saint Paul Saints at Busch Stadium. The affair resulted in a net loss of $193.25. More disastrously, during the fall of 1960, the fund sponsored a raffle which lost $3,173.94, due to poor follow-through on ticket sales by the LULAC members around the state. Felix constantly complained that the pronouncements of support made by LULAC members across Texas, especially by some of the leaders, were never backed up with cash. Some funds did trickle in: fifty dollars here, five dollars there, but mainly from individual LULAC councils and Felix's local Anglo friends.[37]

But what Tijerina lacked in financial support for promotional activities, he more than made up for in media coverage. Indeed, recognition of the LULAC-brokered preschool program reached its height during the summer of 1961, expanding Tijerina's and the program's name beyond even the considerable limits they had already achieved. In late June and early July, Felix, Phil Montalbo, and Alfred Hernández attended the LULAC national convention in Phoenix. At this gathering, Tijerina spoke at a special seminar on the Little School of the 400 and conferred with officials of the Arizona Department of Education.[38]

One sour note did sound when members of Jake Rodríguez's San Antonio council submitted a resolution before the assembly to bestow upon Felix the honorary title of "President Emeritus." The effort failed when, in the typical LULAC fashion of dealing with former national presidents, certain members questioned Tijerina's actions on behalf of the organization and succeeded in getting the resolution turned down, a move denounced by Jake Rodríguez as a "silly display of . . . rancor and petty envy" and which clearly embarrassed and chagrined Rodríguez, Tijerina, Hector Godínez, and others. For Felix, it represented simply another display by those LULAC members who "continue to criticize my every step."[39]

In a letter to Hector Godínez a week after the convention, Felix (through Tony Campos, who typed the message) eloquently summed up his feelings about this affair, LULAC, its leadership, and his preschool effort:

> You will find that in LULAC we have fakes and hypocrites. . . .
> Long after a LULAC leader has done great work, those who
> are disappointed or envious continue to cry out that it could
> not be done. The leader is assailed because he is a leader, and
> the effort to equal him is merely added proof of that leader-
> ship. When a man's work sets a standard for the whole League,
> it will go forward at a continuous stride regardless of the ob-
> stacles that are frequently thrown in front.
>
> Because of the "Little Schools of the 400," LULAC will
> truly hold its laurels through the ages. "For that which de-
> serves to live . . . lives."[40]

Meanwhile, the Phoenix media had seized on Felix's presence at the convention. The *Arizona Republic,* the state's leading newspaper, ran a feature article highlighting Tijerina's educational efforts and philosophy, one of several stories the newspaper would publish touting him as a role model. Detailing Felix's rise from a ten-year-old cotton picker to his success as a Mexican restaurant owner, this article stressed his views on the high rate of Latin American dropouts. Like most folks, the Arizonans took to him and his program because of his powers of empathy; as he told the columnist: "I know what those little kids face. I was one of them." Throughout his trip to the Southwest, which included a stop in New Mexico, Felix explained the project's success in Texas and urged people to adopt his ideas for their own school systems.[41]

The July, 1961, issue of *Coronet,* a national magazine written for younger readers, carried an article entitled "Now Juanito Can Read" by Keith Elliott. Complete with a benevolent caricature of Tijerina surrounded by Mexican American boys with books in their hands and eager to learn, the story lauded him as a "field hand turned tycoon" who had given "Mexican-American kids in Texas the precious gift of English language." It was a chatty rendition of the familiar rags-to-riches/Little School themes and was clearly the biggest media hit for Tijerina since the *Time* magazine article in 1959. So impressed was U.S. Senator Ralph Yarborough that in early August, he had the *Coronet* article (along with a similar write-up on Tijerina and his efforts from a June issue of the *Houston Press*) included in the *Congressional Record.* This gesture by Yarborough was at least the second time that Washington leadership had Felix's and LULAC's educational work for Spanish-speaking preschoolers brandished before them by the Texas senator.[42]

As nice as the *Coronet* article was, something even bigger happened on its heels. A feature article on Tijerina and his endeavors appeared in the August, 1961, issue of the *Saturday Evening Post.* Written by Louis Alexander (a Houston journalist who had profiled the restaurateur before), this four-page spread was entitled "Texas Helps Her Little Latins" and represented the best single piece of national publicity Felix ever received for himself or his program. In addition to the oft-told, Horatio Alger story of Felix's life and the most complete telling of the history of the Little School, the article carried photos of Elizabeth Burrus as well as of Isabel Verver and Tijerina with former students of the original Little School class in Ganado. Though it told of the traditional Anglo indifference toward Mexican American education, its message related the encouraging strides being made now that people—Anglos and Mexican Americans—had begun to work together. It also reported that Felix had personally spent to date around twenty-five thousand dollars of his own money on these labors.[43]

Because the *Saturday Evening Post* was more ubiquitous in homes across the nation than even *Time,* few people—especially anyone interested in preschool instruction—would have failed to see this feature. It brought the Little School and the issue of Mexican American education to mass American attention and represented the pinnacle of acclaim given to Felix Tijerina.[44]

To herald the appearance of "Texas Helps Her Little Latins," Gerald Davenport, district manager of the Curtis Circulation Co. (Curtis Publishing produced the magazine), presented Felix with a handsomely bound copy of the August 5 issue. Even this occasion was picked up by the Houston newspapers. And on Houston's KHOU-TV, Dan Rather, then director of news and public affairs, shortly thereafter interviewed Felix on the air—a dialogue that aired nationally—concerning Alexander's magazine article. To garner more mileage for the piece, Gulf Oil Corporation, apparently on its own, had immediately reprinted Alexander's story in *The Orange Disc,* its national company publication. In late November, John Chancellor and NBC radio did a nationally broadcast news program on the work of Tijerina, LULAC, and the Little School. Felix's delight with these favorable commentaries was manifest, as he drew great personal meaning from what the program had achieved.[45]

Immediately following this publicity in the United States, Monterrey, Mexico's *Magazine reportaje del norte* (in its September-October, 1961, issue) carried a full-page story on "La pequeña escuela de los 400" and the dramatic results it was having on the Texas educational scene for "los ciudadanos norteamericanos de procedencia mexicana." LULAC, the Texas state government, and naturally Felix came in for their share of the credit, as the story was obviously written using the program's promotional literature.[46]

These endorsements were clearly shared by the Mexican American community. *La prensa* of San Antonio, the most widely read Texas Mexican newspaper, reprinted in a six-part series the contents of an important pamphlet entitled *What Price Education?,* the official report on the Little School of the 400 published in 1962 by the LULAC Educational Fund, Inc. This report, written and produced by Jake Rodríguez for Tijerina as the fund's chairman—and the verbatim reprinting of it in *La prensa* (a series that began in August, 1962) recounted the Little School's development through the summer of that year and assessed the progress of the Texas preschool efforts in overcoming what the report emphatically identified as the "language and scholastic retardation" of Spanish-speaking children. The pamphlet urged its readership to support the program and the Educational Fund's efforts for the project so that the thousands of potential students could learn the "official language" of the nation. Sounding the refrain which had guided Felix's life and work, the report concluded that completing an education "*from a good sound start* enables the recipient to fit better into the general scheme of things in his society—to produce more, to earn more; to help society more as a humane, enlightened, social being."[47]

What Price Education? itself—a fourteen-page bound document—was broadly distributed by the LULAC Educational Fund. This publication became yet another icon of Tijerina/LULAC-generated literature about their historic endeavor.

Within the Mexican American community, *La prensa* was by no means alone in its public endorsement of the approach that Felix and the preschool program had taken. Writer Frank Trejo of the *San Antonio Light,* in August, 1962 (when *What Price Education?* came out), hailed the program's progress as an "inroad to full, happy lives." At the same time, no less a Mexican American establishment voice than the San Antonio Mexican Chamber of Commerce bulletin called attention to the appearance of the report and congratulated "Messrs. Tijerina, Rodriguez and all concerned . . . for their splendid work." In another story in July, 1963, M. Ruíz Ibañez of the *San Antonio News* lauded Tijerina and company for shattering the "language barrier" with their efforts, a barrier that, as Ruíz Ibañez explained, "once handicapped tens of thousands of Latin American children" in San Antonio alone. Indeed, the Preschool Instructional Program had taken strong root in the Alamo City.[48]

As a result of all the publicity, Tijerina received a multitude of letters, many congratulatory, others inquiring about the program. The articles in *Coronet* and the *Saturday Evening Post,* quite naturally, fetched the most correspondence. Friends, public officials, and admirers sent expressions of their respect for Tijerina and his school. One fresh face on the political scene, newly elected U.S. Senator John Tower of Texas, stressed his admiration for Tijerina's "sense of individual responsibility and personal initiative." People wrote from as far away as Florida, Chicago, and California, offering their heartfelt best. School officials, teachers, and clergy who dealt with educating Spanish-speaking youngsters (and looking for assistance) in places like Brentwood, New York; Memphis, Tennessee; Paola, Kansas; Grants, New Mexico; Glendale and Tempe, Arizona; Nampa, Idaho; Roosevelt, Puerto Rico; and points in between requested materials, especially "the list of the 400 'Magic Words.'" Even the special education coordinator from Balboa

Heights in the Panama Canal Zone wrote Felix asking to purchase manuals on the project so that they might teach English to the youngsters of Puerto Rican servicemen. M. J. Senter, director of education for the government of American Samoa (in Pago Pago), solicited information on the Little School so that he might apply the techniques to his locale. After reading Elliot's article in *Coronet,* Beatrice Griffith, author of the classic *American Me* (1948), wrote Tijerina for material to include in the revision of her book. Felix sent literature to these correspondents when he could and referred others to the Texas Department of Education. It was difficult for him to keep up with all the inquiries, especially after the summer of 1961, when Tony Campos, his loyal assistant and amanuensis, left his employ to pursue his career in public education.[49]

In the wake of this acclaim, Felix continued to be hailed as the LULAC chief by his many admirers within the league, in particular his Houston cohort. J. B. Casas, by then residing in Compton, California, summed it up when he wrote Tijerina that through the *Coronet* and *Saturday Evening Post* articles, he "had really put LULAC in the public eye nationally." In late November, 1961, Council No. 60 held a testimonial banquet in Felix's honor in the Grand Ballroom of the Rice Hotel, pleasant and familiar turf.[50]

Simultaneously, however, other LULAC officials around the state wanted to know what was going on with the fund, particularly after the national publicity began to appear. Concerned that the Educational Fund, Inc., was "a LULAC program" and feeling that LULAC officers were not kept adequately informed, national executive director Jim Silva of San Antonio, for one, wrote Tijerina in late 1961 for reports on the fund's activities and chided him for not responding to his and others' letters. Felix, no doubt still smarting from the Phoenix convention embarrassment and annoyed with Silva's entreaties, referred him to fellow San Antonian Jake Rodríguez and the multitude of newspaper and magazine articles for the information he requested, pointedly noting that his pleas for money from LULAC to support the fund's endeavors had met with poor results. After Silva continued to press his inquiries, an exasperated Tijerina wrote Frank Valdez in early 1962 that "this man" Silva was "either misinformed or . . . digging at me" and that the fund had no cash (except for money from his friends). He reiterated his complaint that it had received little financial help from LULAC.[51]

Regardless of Tijerina's explanations that there was actually nothing of substance to report, the 1962 Texas state LULAC convention in Austin passed a resolution, offered by Roberto Ornelas of McAllen and Manuel V. López of San Antonio's Council No. 2, requesting that the LULAC state director from Texas be made a member of the fund's board of directors. (The state director had always held an advisory position on the board.) Felix had attended that convention, and when William Bonilla (then state director) forwarded a copy of the resolution to him in Houston, he took no issue with it; Tijerina promised to hold a board meeting in March where the resolution would be considered. The board of directors met on March 23 at the Westheimer restaurant and voted unanimously to make the state director a member, which, along with written financial reports for those attending, helped to calm the criticism.[52]

To that March meeting with Tijerina and the other directors, William Bonilla had sent Carlos Truan, a twenty-six-year-old LULAC activist from Corpus Christi, to represent him (Bonilla) as state director. Truan would be elected to the Texas legislature in 1968 where, during a long, distinguished career both in the House and Senate, he would have a profound impact on Mexican American education in the Lone Star state. The knowledge he gained from Tijerina's work, as well as from his familiarity with the activities of E. E. Mireles in his home city, would help inform Truan's actions in the years to come, much as these early efforts would help to motivate future Hispanic leaders. Universally credited as the state legislator most responsible for bringing bilingual education to Texas during the late 1960s and 1970s, Truan attributed his later actions in large measure to his association with LULAC, Tijerina, and the Little School. In Truan's considered opinion, Felix's project served as an inspiring step on the road to addressing the needs of Hispanic students and helped lay the foundation for bilingual education.[53]

In the spring of 1962, Tijerina, Rodríguez, and company launched a solicitation drive for funds, hoping to raise sixty thousand dollars; the Rodríguez-authored *What Price Education?* was a part of this push, and these efforts continued into the following year. Though some money came in from LULAC councils, businesses, and individuals, the results were, as in the past, far less than satisfactory. At the same time, Tijerina's name went out on letters to Texas newspapers, radio, and television stations, asking them to publicize to their local school districts that the opportunity now existed for their non-English-speaking children to be properly trained in the "official language of our country" and "the democratic processes which have made our country the greatest in the world today."[54]

During these years, Felix worked into his busy schedule as many regular speaking engagements about the preschool program as he could handle. These occasions ranged from talks to area civic groups such as a meeting of the Huntsville Texas Woman's Forum to more expansive gatherings like the regional conference of the Texas Social Welfare Association. The latter, which met in Harlingen in May, 1962, featured Tijerina at its noon luncheon. He, of course, continued to visit and encourage state officials in Austin about the program on a person-to-person basis, including administrators within the Texas Education Agency. In late November, 1963, he had a meeting with the new Texas governor, John B. Connally, who had ousted Felix's good friend Price Daniel in the Democratic Party primary and taken over the executive office that year. In addition to discussing the preschool classes, Felix brought up another proposal with Connally: a follow-up program that would encourage students to remain in school throughout high school and possibly go on to college and other institutions of higher learning. Tijerina expressed his concern that guidance needed to be given to students in the higher grades so that the dropout problem could be further alleviated. (Felix was national chairman of LULAC's anti-dropout program.) The following year, Tijerina proudly wrote the recently elected LULAC national president William Bonilla that his visit to the governor had "produced eight well qualified men to work all over the state" for the promotion of a school dropout project. He no doubt was referring to the "Stay-in-School" Program that had emerged under the TEA during the 1963–64 academic year. Developed by such TEA staffers as Dr. George J. Garza, this endeavor had implemented special projects for dropouts and migrant children in many of the South Texas areas serviced by the preschool English classes and represented the type of effort Tijerina and LULAC had long favored.[55]

Meanwhile, the Texas preschool program showed substantial progress. According to the Texas Education Agency counts, 130 school districts in 1960 were participating in the venture, sponsoring a total of 614 classes that reached 15,805 children; in 1961, 143 districts took part, holding 708 classes and teaching 17,301 children; 1962 saw an increase to 155 participating districts, 810 classes, and 18,965 pupils addressed. (During 1963, the figures would remain constant at 166 districts, 811 classes, and 18,791 students; but in 1964 and 1965, as will be noted below, the numbers were substantially greater.) Though Tijerina had reason to feel by 1962 that his "dream" was moving forward, he and his cohorts also realized that since those participating districts represented approximately 10 percent of the state's total, they were "barely scratching the surface" of the problem. Regardless of the accolades they received in the post-1960 period, Tijerina and his LULAC colleagues knew that thousands more children remained in need.[56]

"A GREAT ROTARIAN"

Tijerina maintained his intimate association with Rotary International, as it continued to serve as a principal touchstone of his mainstream status. Indeed, it was within the Houston Rotary Club that he did his most effective networking. Still meeting at noon every Thursday at the Rice Hotel's Grand Ballroom, the downtown club had elected him in March, 1959, to a regular two-year term (1959–61) on its prestigious nine-man board of directors. He told his fellow Rotarians that this honor constituted "the biggest thrill of [his] lifetime" up to then.[57]

Rotary was a major vehicle to showcase Tijerina's many interrelated civic activities. The downtown Rotarians constantly touted his work with LULAC, Governor Price Daniel, the Little School of the 400, and other projects to improve the education, health, living standards, and "civic responsibility" among Latin Americans. As the club's publication (The Log) noted in a profile of Tijerina in October, 1959, he was "[a] great citizen, a great Rotarian . . . FELIX." During their observance of "Brotherhood Week" in February, 1961, the Pasadena Rotary Club honored Felix, W. H. Avery, and Albert Gee (the latter Tijerina's counterpart in Houston's Chinese community), "for putting brotherhood in their everyday lives." By this time, the Pasadena Rotarians (and the front-page coverage given to the honorees by the Pasadena Daily Citizen) congratulated Tijerina for his long list of civic activities, including participation in three new posts: as a director of the Texas Literacy Council, membership on the International Good Neighbor Council on Education, and membership on the Texas Committee on Migrant Farm Workers.[58]

As before, Tijerina remained visible in Rotary's educational, humanitarian, and Pan American affairs. Ever ready to promote Spanish among non-Spanish speakers, he was pictured by the Houston Press in a September, 1960, layout that advertised the Houston Rotary Club's program to teach its members to speak Spanish. *Houston Press* photographers showed Felix tutoring fellow Rotarians E. A. Vaubel and Wendell Phillips at their regular Thursday luncheon where, it was reported, more than sixty-five club members vowed to practice their Spanish thirty minutes each meeting. Though one may question how much Spanish the participants could learn from such scanty exposure, the newspaper reported that the well-intentioned Rotarians wanted to be able "to extend the 'good neighbor' policy" as individuals and that their president, James Stillwell, had written to some of the fifty-five Rotary Clubs then operating in fifteen Latin American countries, telling them of this "Houston innovation."[59]

Felix was without question Houston's special connection to the Rotary Clubs of Mexico, and he enjoyed this role immensely, reveling in the associations that developed. In December, 1960, the Houston Rotary *Log* spotlighted his efforts in the cooperative effort between the Rotary Clubs of Hermosillo, Sonora, and Houston to bring a boy to Houston from that Mexican city for heart surgery. The youngster, José Ramón Bustamante, and his mother and father had been sent north with money raised by the Hermosillo Rotarians. Many from Houston's Rotary helped, but Felix, Janie, and Tony Campos "kept a constant vigil" with the boy and his parents during their five-day stay. The lad died, however, and Felix flew the parents and the body back to Mexico for burial. From this endeavor, in February, 1961, Felix helped guide Houston Rotary's "first experience in international Rotary relations" when he and James Stillwell led a small group of Houston Rotarians to Hermosillo, where they attended a Rotary banquet as invited guests. There, Tijerina and the other Houstonians met many distinguished Mexican Rotarians, including Don Ignacio Soto, former governor of Sonora.[60]

In September, the *Houston Post* noted, Felix took his good friend Ramón Salcido, president of the Mexico City Real Estate Board, to lunch with Charley Bell (of the Houston Real Estate Board), when Salcido visited the Bayou City. Salcido was also one of the founders and first president of the Better Business Bureau of Mexico City. Fellow Rotarians, Tijerina and Salcido had first met a few years before at a Houston Rotary luncheon, after which Felix had driven him around town promoting Houston, especially its booming Sharpstown subdivision.[61]

Of course, Felix and Mrs. Felix had many friends and contacts in Monterrey, both inside and outside of Rotary, who were long since acquainted with his (and her) numerous accomplishments in *relaciones latinoamericanas* and looked for every occasion to extend their appreciation. In December, 1961 (not long after the great publicity on the Little School in *Magazine reportaje del norte*), Felix attended a luncheon of the Monterrey Rotary Club Obispado as its special guest, where he spoke on the preschool educational campaign in Texas. Monterrey's *El norte* and *El porvenir* ran lengthy articles on Felix's speech and the homage which the club paid him for his efforts to provide English-language training to Mexican children in Texas and the United States. As was his practice, Tijerina not only explained his own endeavors but also lauded the Texas state government for funding the gigantic program; he described how knowledge of English in the United States allowed children to encounter fewer problems in their occupations and prevented them from feeling fragmented from society. *El norte* identified Felix as the only Rotary member (among seventy) in Houston who was Mexican and stated that he "belonged to a family of the mountainous region around Monterrey[;] his parents went to the United States when he was very young."[62]

In Houston, in April, 1962, the downtown Rotary Club held an impressive Pan American Day banquet and program in which Felix was one of a number of representatives from the United States and twelve Latin American countries who were, in the words of the *Houston Press,* featured "for their efforts to create a new and greater unity in the hemisphere." Tijerina, "founder of the famed Little School of the 400," sat at the head table, which also included the Houston-based consuls from Mexico, Central and South America, Houstonians such as George Carmack, Howard Tellepsen, Félix Morales, Dr. Frank M. Tiller, Lewis Cutrer (mayor of the "crossroads city of the Americas"), and Medal of Honor recipient Macario García, as well as out-of-towners such as Price Daniel and Rodolfo De La Vega (the former Houston newspaperman then living in his native Mexico). Tijerina reveled in his distinguished place alongside his men friends, as the five hundred persons gathered in the high-ceilinged ballroom of the Rice Hotel heard Ambassador Raymond Telles speak on President Kennedy's newly created Alliance for Progress foreign aid program designed, in Telles's words, "to meet the challenge of Communism" and help "the people of Latin America . . . have [a] more abundant life." Mrs. Felix was also pictured at the accompanying cocktail reception, as she chatted with the spouse of the consul of Mexico. Labeled in the photograph caption as "consul's wife, businessman's wife," respectively, the two women were characterized as "Ladies of Americas," fitting into the spirit of hemispheric "solidarity" which "filled every heart."[63]

But the pinnacle of Tijerina's Pan American Rotary recognition during these years (indeed, during his lifetime) and its appreciation of his work in Mexican American education came later that month in Mexico City. Because of Felix's "international eminence" and many personal contacts, the Mexico City Rotary Club hosted him and a delegation of Houston Rotarians consisting of Gail Whitcomb, Virgil Lee, Dick Proctor, and Bob Ives specifically to honor the Houston restaurateur. The Anglo Houstonians were overwhelmed with what turned out to be a "three-day experience in Latin American hospitality." According to Ives, the delegation was received at the Mexico City airport by a welcoming committee—"all friends of Felix"—and had a grand time meeting with key Mexican business leaders, staying at the Hotel Del Prado, and engaging in "good Rotary discussion." Altogether, it was an "adventure filled with Pan American friendship."[64]

The focus of their visit, however, was the luncheon on April 24, instigated by Ramón Salcido (then Mexico City Rotary Club secretary), which paid homage to Tijerina for his educational efforts on behalf of children of Mexican descent in Texas. According to Ives, Felix's speech was impressive—vintage Felix Tijerina—and its reception by the two hundred people in attendance even more so. "Beginning in his slow quiet way," Ives later reported to the Houston membership, "Felix carried them through the [vicissitudes] of his early life, his ambitions, and from whence he drew his strength. As the story unfolded," Ives continued, "the attention of all the room became fixed on every word said." When Tijerina concluded his remarks by recounting LULAC's success with the Little School of the 400, "the entire room swept to its feet in an enthusiasm of acclaim" that lasted for several minutes. Dr. Jaime Torres Bodet, Mexico's secretary of public education, then presented Felix with a gold medal of merit.[65]

The prominent Mexico City newspaper *Novedades* had announced the affair with relish. Its April 22 issue recounted Tijerina's assault on "LA BARRERA DEL IDIOMA" ("the language barrier") through his Little Schools and told of the Mexican Rotary's plans to pay tribute to the Houston restaurateur. *Novedades* concluded with the idea that such a gesture by Rotary was commendable because many people in Mexico were not aware of Felix Tijerina's altruism on behalf of those Mexicans who had made their home in the United States.[66]

Back in Houston, the honor bestowed on Tijerina in Mexico City made all the newspapers. As usual, friends—especially from the Anglo community—sent him clippings, congratulating him on yet another accolade, this time from the Mexican government, and commenting how proud Houston was of his efforts. More important, however, because of their association with Felix Tijerina, the Anglos who had accompanied him returned to Houston with an appreciation of Mexico as "a worthy neighbor, aggressive and independent," "represented by a highly sensitive and responsive group of Rotarians, who speak our language by and large" and "eagerly welcome our hand of friendship."[67]

Tijerina continued to interact with Mexican Rotarians on behalf of his city. In late October, 1962, a delegation from the Mexico City club consisting of men involved in the April visit came to Houston as they had earlier agreed so that some of the many kindnesses they had extended could be reciprocated and the lines of communication could be maintained. This represented the first joint meeting of the two clubs in Houston. Felix naturally played a central role in arranging and escorting the group around town. As "chairman of the day," he introduced the Mexican club's president, Ernesto Maurer, at the Rice Hotel luncheon held in the delegation's honor; his good friend Mayor Cutrer attended to present Maurer with an "Honorary Citizenship Certificate" and made him a Goodwill Ambassador to the City of Houston.[68]

Felix's concern for his Mexican Rotary brothers extended well beyond club business. During the mid-1960s, he assisted many of their children in coming to study in the United States, and numerous of his Mexican acquaintances looked to him for advice about this country.[69]

While Felix operated as a Rotary director, Janie reached her highwater mark in the Women of Rotary during these years as well, more than dutifully paralleling and complimenting the actions of her husband. She, like Mr. Felix, was a Rotarian in full sail and held in much esteem by the membership. She had already held positions within the women's group during the mid-1950s, including the positions of director, corresponding secretary, and treasurer, and she continued to ascend the ladder of office with aplomb: director once again by 1958, then second vice president and general chair for the annual charity fund raiser in 1959, first vice president in 1960, and in May, 1961, in recognition of her commitment and ability, election to president for the year, 1961–62.[70]

Still the sole Mexican American in this upper middle-class Anglo women's group, she was by this time a seasoned Rotary veteran and a leader of the club. Constantly being pictured in the major newspapers with her Anglo Rotary sisters for this or that occasion, she seemed to be everywhere, sometimes seriously reviewing donations for a fund raiser while at other times arm-in-arm with smiling Rotary women. In the role of "proper" Rotary spouse, she assisted Felix in every way and went with him to most of his club's formal functions. She had, for example, played a crucial role in making the Bustamante family's stay in Houston as comfortable as possible when Rotary had arranged heart surgery for their son. In the press coverage of the luncheon for Ernesto Maurer, she was shown dressed immaculately and seated strategically next to Maurer's wife. Mrs. Felix also played a crucial role in helping the women's group do things on their own; at ease in her various roles, she worked diligently in each of her assignments and helped to bring attention to the group's endeavors. Most impressively, she made the pages of the *River Oaks Times,* the prestigious Houston society periodical, when she appeared in a photograph and in an accompanying article covering the preparations for the Rotary Women's "fall games party" fund raiser for their pet project: dental care for needy children at Burnett Bayland, Faith Home, and Ripley House.[71]

Mrs. Felix's tenure as president of Women's Rotary (1961–62) was a model of hard work and productivity. She efficiently presided over the monthly board and general membership meetings, the latter held at the Houston Club, and she worked especially close with the other Rotary officers to bring about a successful year of fund raising and charity work. In addition to helping the local Tuberculosis Association and the Children's Ward at Jeff Davis Hospital, the group paid for dental supplies for more than three thousand youngsters. As she retired from office, she received many letters of praise from her sister Rotarians for an outstanding year. One wrote, typically, that she "never knew a President who worked longer hours or who was more dedicated to her position." Another noted: "Janie, you have devoted so much of yourself to Women of Rotary, it will be difficult for anyone to follow you." Yet another member fretted that she could not "conceive of the organization without you as an officer." Perhaps most important, Mrs. Felix was always viewed by her Anglo sisters as a team with her husband. Rotarian Margaret Coleman concluded in her laudatory missive that "[y]ou and Felix do so much for the community and are admired and respected by all who know you."[72]

Even after she left office, Janie remained productive as a past club president. She appeared in the society news columns with regularity on behalf of the Women of Rotary, always doing for Rotary that which was appropriate.[73]

TO FOSTER THE PUBLIC GOOD

Continuing his usual range of public service, Tijerina sat on various appointed bodies in the post-1960 period and also played a role as spokesman in the media for worthwhile community projects. He was, for example, a participating member of the Harris County Voluntary Parole Board, which was charged with helping to rehabilitate parolees under its supervision. Felix had actually been named to this position back in September, 1956, by then-Governor Allan Shivers, when Tijerina had first assumed the LULAC national presidency. As was common in those years, Tijerina was the lone Mexican American on the Harris County board. He had, during his LULAC presidential tenure, worked through the Texas Board of Pardons and Paroles (a state-level agency) for his fellow Latin Americans. Undoubtedly because of his experience with the probation department dating from 1930s, Tijerina believed that youths who got into trouble were often further corrupted by their time in jail. He felt that it was society's duty to see that opportunity be given any individual offender willing to make a fresh start. With this attitude, he often interceded with the Board of Pardons and Paroles to assist Mexican Americans who had appealed to him on behalf of a family member and made himself the responsible party for the parolee. It should be added, however, that Tijerina was no soft touch; at least one of these young men who received a second chance by going to work for Don Felix remembered that "the old man," while fair and concerned about his welfare, could be as tough a taskmaster as a jailhouse guard.[74]

Nor did he limit himself to individual intercessions, for he readily worked with inmates as a group. In July, 1962, for instance, Tijerina gave a talk at the state prison in Huntsville in which he tried to inspire his captive audience about succeeding in life on the outside. In September, 1963, he participated in the Pre-Release Program at the Harlem Pre-Release Center in Richmond, Texas. There he spoke to groups of inmates on the topic "Keeping Your Job" and answered their questions. The Harlem Unit was part of the prison farm complex near Sugar Land. During these years, Tijerina often reflected to an old friend from his Sugar Land days that it now took him barely thirty minutes to cover these miles to Houston in his Cadillac, a distance that had once taken him half a day to walk along the railroad track. After his talk at the Harlem Unit, perhaps he contemplated those earlier times as he drove home past the fields where he had labored as a youth.[75]

While he counseled those men getting out of jail, he also helped to judge those who were headed for prison. He served another term on the Harris County grand jury in the spring of 1961. Again harkening to his earliest years, Tijerina sat on this grand jury with Sig Frucht, his old boss (and longtime friend) from Houston's Produce Row, and with other notables such as local banker Marcella D. Perry.[76]

Even during the busiest days of his LULAC presidency, Felix had made room for his work as a commissioner of the Houston Housing Authority. Lewis Cutrer had, of course, reappointed him in February, 1958; Tijerina would remain on the board until he died. During this second part of his tenure, the HHA oversaw the same five housing projects that it had during his first stint in the position. All federally built and subsidized, these units included San Felipe Courts, Irvington Courts, Cuney Homes, Kelly Courts, and Clayton Homes. And, as before, board members served without pay.[77]

Tijerina was one of three new appointments the reform-minded Cutrer made in his 1958 "shake-up" of the board that had served under his predecessor, Mayor Oscar Holcombe. These three appointments replaced all the Holcombe men, and the new board swiftly brought about administrative changes. In this case, it seems to have been payback time, especially for commissioners Leon Green and Fred W. Lucas, both holdovers from the days of Roy Hofheinz. Since 1956, Green and Lucas had boycotted the HHA board meetings because the Holcombe majority had fired Thomas F. Booker as executive director and replaced him with Jim R. Langan. Tijerina, a Hofheinz man himself and former board colleague of Green and Lucas when they hired Booker, immediately became a party to their efforts. In March, 1958, they dismissed a total of four Holcombe-era officials. Most important, with Tijerina voting in a three-to-two majority with Green and Lucas, they fired Langan. Within a month, through nomination by Tijerina, the new board unanimously re-hired Booker. At the same time that they ousted Langan, Tijerina, Green, and Lucas terminated the employment of Albert G. Vela as attorney for the authority and soon replaced him with someone else. Curiously, Vela was apparently the same person who had helped Felix obtain his delayed birth certificate in 1940.[78]

For the next seven and a half years, Tijerina was a steady, conscientious member of the HHA board, which, once the initial changes occurred, was consensus-oriented and congenial in its deliberations. Felix served on a number of committees, including Family and Child Welfare, Conditions of Rentals, and Recreation Centers. He served a year as board chairman in 1959–60, was reappointed to the board for another two-year term by Mayor Cutrer in January, 1960, and again in February, 1962. With more time to spare by the early 1960s, he was elected as the board's vice chairman in 1962–63, and was thereafter reelected to that position every year, apparently uncontested, for the remainder of his tenure. The newly elected mayor and Tijerina admirer, Louie Welch, would reappoint him in March, 1964, for yet another term, which would prove to be his last.[79]

Felix's attendance at the board meetings (about one per month) was exemplary; from 1958 through 1965, he missed only eight. Active in the board's deliberations, Tijerina expressed compassion toward the residents of the five housing projects, voicing his concerns that rents be set at a level which would allow them to have money for groceries. And although he was concerned about expenditures, he strongly supported Booker and his management of the properties. As vice chair, Felix presided admirably over the meetings in the absence of the chairman on many occasions and was held in high esteem by his fellow board members.[80]

Felix's stature was also used, especially by the media, to endorse community programs. In September, 1961, the *Houston Post*—an avid champion of the restaurateur since it had first introduced him with the opening of his Mexican Inn in 1929—had him promote its "Learn-a-Language Spanish Course." One of seven languages that could be learned from 33⅓ R.P.M. records and easy-to-read booklets offered by the newspaper, this course was billed as a quick and easy way for non-native speakers to grasp Spanish. The front-page article featured Tijerina, "one of Houston's leading Latin American citizens," as its spokesman; the course, he noted in the story, was "the best method I have seen to learn Spanish during spare time at home." In his advocacy of the lessons, Tijerina went on at length to advocate learning Spanish: "We're going to have to realize that we don't live alone in the world. Most Americans can speak only English." He added that "[l]earning their language is one way of showing the people [of Latin American countries] we're interested in them as individuals," so as to dispel "the idea that we're big rich neighbors lavishing big gifts that seldom improve the lot of the average farmer or laborer."[81]

In another step in the public effort during this era to stamp out polio, the *Post* utilized Tijerina in a September, 1962, endorsement of the Sabin vaccine program. The *Post* reported that some 1.68 million doses of Sabin oral poliomyelitis vaccine had just been flown into Houston from Philadelphia for the Harris County Medical Society's "Victory over Polio" campaign. In a related front-page article, Tijerina urged "all Latin American people—and everyone else" to visit their neighborhood school clinics and take the vaccine. His face gazing benevolently from the page, Tijerina told the public: "This campaign is a wonderful thing," and "[m]y family is looking forward to taking the second dose of the Sabin Vaccine Sunday," concluding "[a]ll you and I have to do is eat a cube of sugar." As usual, Houston had turned to him to foster the public good and societal unity.[82]

EXPANDING BUSINESS INTERESTS

The restaurants remained Tijerina's principal means of livelihood and community identification, and in these years he expanded into new areas around Houston. Even while serving as LULAC national president, however, he had remained attentive to their welfare. In 1958, he had completely redecorated his flagship restaurant at 904 Westheimer, ten years after its initial construction, and held a well-advertised reopening. It was his practice to shut down periodically (usually for a week), repaint, and generally spruce up his establishments. In December, 1959, he had put in place a management structure that helped him better control the operation of all three lucrative Houston locations: he appointed his faithful Mingo Villarreal as general manager; Daniel Sandoval as his and Mingo's assistant; longtime employee Florine La Rue as supervisor of the Westheimer restaurant; Geneva Harper as supervisor of the Kirby and Bellaire restaurants; and Joe González, Jesse González, and Manuel González, as head chefs of the Westheimer, Kirby, and Bellaire restaurants, respectively. (Joe and Jesse were Mrs. Felix's first cousins, while Manuel was her nephew.) Although these and other employees saw to many of the details of daily operations, Felix still maintained an important, even-handed level of personal oversight, and everyone remembered him as a good boss. Often in the company of Leo Reynosa, he continued to make his weekly trips to Beaumont to ensure the proper running of the restaurant in that location. Felix's lasting success with the restaurants—as in the other parts of his life—stemmed from his ability to deal effectively with people.[83]

In the operation of the restaurants, Mingo was especially important. Felix and Mingo were as close as always. More than a general manager, Mingo was Felix's "watchdog," a loyal and trustworthy supervisor; by now, he sat out front and made sure things ran smoothly and served as the commodities buyer for all the restaurant locations.[84]

On July 27, 1961, Tijerina opened a new restaurant, his fifth, at 719 Telephone Road. The property (which he purchased) included a pre-existing structure that he remodeled to suit his purpose. Though somewhat smaller than the Kirby store, this new restaurant was a substantial, rectangular red brick building upon which he installed architectural motifs similar to those of his other locations: a white stucco façade, two arched windows flanking the double entrance doors, red roofing tiles, and an identical, free-standing red, white, and green sign, highlighted by neon, with the distinctive "Felix" signature and a Mexican *campesino* in a characteristic seated position against a giant desert cactus. It was Tijerina's first new location since the Bellaire restaurant opened in 1956. Also, situated on a major thoroughfare east of downtown, it was his effort to "serve our many friends who live and work in the great East Side area." As such, it represented the first of his chain in Houston to be placed away from the southwestern subdivisions.[85]

Fanfare once again accompanied the grand opening, as the ribbon was cut by Winston A. McKenzie, the great-grandson of Mrs. A. S. Foote, one of Felix's customers who had been eating regularly at his cafés since his earliest days in business. To illustrate what a fixture in Houston society Felix and his restaurants had become, the *Houston Chronicle* ran a captioned photograph of Tijerina on opening day, dressed in a waiter's white jacket, personally serving Mrs. Foote, her daughter (Mrs. Maxwell Taylor), granddaughter (Mrs. Winston McKenzie), and little Winston—four generations of River Oaks people who were Felix Mexican Restaurant devotees.[86]

The Telephone Road restaurant had the same complete menu as the other restaurants, the same reasonable prices, the same "South-of-the-border atmosphere," and the same unmistakably Felix taste, which never varied. Also like the others, this location proved successful, especially its lunch business. As an opening promotion, Felix offered two-for-one coupons for his all-time favorite "Felix Special $1.00 Dinners." Before long, he was running ads thanking the people of the "Great Eastside Area" for their "wonderful patronage."[87]

In November, 1962, the city took special notice of the tenth year of operation of the Felix Mexican Restaurant on Kirby Drive, in the "Village" area. The media reports described Felix as a "sincere citizen"; he seemed to be as big an attraction as the place itself. Supervised by the loyal Geneva Harper, the Kirby Drive store had long since become a tradition for many of the residents of the Rice University/West University area, a "regular spot" in their weekly dining.[88]

In 1963, Tijerina opened his sixth Felix Mexican Restaurant, this one at 616 Main Street, in a sense returning to the place of his business beginnings. This establishment was not like his others, as it was a small cafeteria that Felix designed to sell "fast food" to the downtown lunch crowd. The chili, beans, rice, and such were actually cooked every morning at the 904 Westheimer location and ferried over by nine o'clock in the morning. Because the new place had just a steam table, only the enchiladas, tacos, and tostados were prepared on site. It closed its doors every day around three or four after business slacked off.[89]

A typical rented storefront in a row of Main Street businesses, the new restaurant had a façade of chrome, glass, and veneer, bearing no resemblance architecturally to the other Felix locations except for the familiar "Felix Mexican Restaurant" sign over the door. Inside, its festively colored space was smaller than his other establishments, long and narrow, with limited seating. Customers sat at booths and small tables on either side of a middle entryway, and unlike every other restaurant Tijerina operated, this eatery served food on plastic platters and had no tablecloths. But like the others, the new location was successful, attracting a steady stream of hungry noontime patrons from the time it opened.[90]

Tijerina had served as a director of the Montrose National Bank since its founding in the mid-1950s. The only Mexican American among more than a dozen and a half directors, Tijerina sat on the board with George Butler, Hyman E. Finger, Morris Lee, Shearn Moody, Jr., Sam White, and other men of finance and influence. In 1959, however, significant interest in the bank was purchased by Kenneth L. Schnitzer, a thirty-three-year-old developer who was beginning to make his mark on the Houston scene. Schnitzer was soon responsible for the bank moving downtown to the impressive thirteen-storied 2100 Travis Building that he was constructing. By the time the bank reopened in November, 1961, it had changed its name to the Central National Bank, and its new home was accordingly renamed the Central National Bank Building. Felix and the other directors, as well as the bank officers, remained in their positions of authority as the institution continued to prosper. By then, its resources totaled approximately thirteen million dollars, with Schnitzer as chairman of the board.[91]

Felix's associations continued to evolve in the Central National Bank as, before long, new faces began to appear. Controlling interest of the bank passed to the Gulf Interstate Company when this Houston-based gas transmission firm bought out a substantial part of Schnitzer's share in mid-1963; with this purchase, Hy Byrd, president of Gulf Interstate, became the new board chairman. In January, 1964, John N. Hunt and another group of Houston business leaders acquired majority interest in Central. Hunt became the bank's new president, and men like oil operator Jack S. Josey and attorneys Joe Jamail, Jr. and Harry Holmes, Jr. joined the board, widening Felix's direct contact with some of the most energetic movers and shakers in the Bayou City.[92]

Simultaneously, Tijerina branched out into the savings and loan industry, marking his continued maturation as a Houston capitalist and entrepreneur. In 1961, he helped lead a group of more than 230 local business and professional people to organize the Surety Savings and Loan Association. In March, 1962, Surety opened in the Americana Building at 1142 Travis at Dallas Avenue in downtown Houston, with Tijerina as a director and vice president. His closest associates in this venture included Charles E. Lambert (president), Clark L. Brandon (treasurer), Julian A. Kirk (secretary), and a dozen other directors. Surety Savings soon had a brisk stream of depositors. As it prospered, its officers and directors also contemplated their first branch location, which would be established, predictably, on Houston's west side near the association's growing number of suburban patrons.[93]

By 1963, as the owner of six restaurants, a director of two financial institutions, and a subscriber to the *Wall Street Journal,* Tijerina was more firmly entrenched in the Houston business scene than ever before. Although Tijerina's financial statements from these years do not exist, Daniel Sandoval (who worked as his bookkeeper/accountant for the last seven years of Felix's life) felt certain that Tijerina was Houston's first Mexican American millionaire. Felix Tijerina had, by all measure, "made it" in the world of business, though, like most of his capitalist peers, he never let up in his quest for success.[94]

FAMILY TIES

Felix, Jr., and Janie Bell always received affection and attention from their father, as he was devoted to their well-being and happiness. In turn, they loved and enjoyed their daddy immensely. Around his children, any vestiges of Felix's tough-minded business exterior vanished. He, in fact, tended to shelter them.[95]

For the lower grades, both were sent to Saint Anne's Catholic school to be taught by nuns. Anglo and rather exclusive, Saint Anne's was located at Westheimer and Shepherd, not far from their home. The children were raised as strict Catholics. Though Tijerina had become lax in his own church attendance, when Felix, Jr. (at age four), balked at accompanying Mrs. Felix to mass because his daddy stayed home, Felix, Sr., immediately began to go with them every Sunday to provide his son (and later his daughter) with a proper example.[96]

Because his children needed room, Tijerina had purchased a one-story brick house at 2703 Grant Street, conveniently located just across the street from his Westheimer restaurant. The first house he had ever owned, Tijerina had moved his family in by 1958, leaving the penthouse apartment above the restaurant, rich in *ambiente,* to serve as his business offices. The house on Grant was simple in design, sturdy and comfortable, and, after Felix's initial remodeling, had three bedrooms and a good deal of yard space for the children. It would be the Tijerinas' home from then on.[97]

The Tijerinas had long employed housekeepers, but with their new residence such employees became even more crucial to the household. Of these individuals, perhaps the most important was Marie Jenkins, an African American Houstonian who came to work for them when the children were small and the family was still living over the restaurant. After they moved to the Grant Street house, Jenkins became even more central. Ever present, she helped raise the Tijerina kids and became so close to the family that after she married, Felix, Sr., helped her and her husband purchase a home. By the time Felix, Jr., entered Saint Thomas High School in 1962, Marie was firmly ensconced as a "special lady" in their lives and would remain so.[98]

Being the children of prominent parents, Felix, Jr., and Janie Bell were well known and received a share of media attention, to some extent growing up in the public eye as part of Houston's unofficial Hispanic First Family. Yet, living on the west side and enrolled in private Catholic schools with predominantly Anglo student bodies, Felix, Jr., and Janie Bell had few, if any, Mexican American friends and no particular feel for the barrio. Nor did either of them learn to speak Spanish growing up, as their parents insisted that the family speak English at home.[99]

Perhaps the children's "celebrity status" in part led their parents, especially Felix, to shelter them more than most kids their age. Their father's success—and wealth—led to fears (and apparently some threats) of kidnapping. More important, however, Felix simply did not want his own children to have to work as hard as he had when he was young, and this feeling doubtless led him to protect them all the more.[100]

Because he was a traditional father in the norms of that era, with a full schedule of business and civic affairs, Felix found himself away from home a great deal, and Mrs. Felix was the children's principal caretaker. She arranged most things the children did, whether it was a family affair or school-related function. Mrs. Felix also had the role of disciplinarian, while Felix was more lenient and generous, never demanding of his son and always paying special attention to his daughter.[101]

The family, particularly Mrs. Felix and the children, made numerous automobile trips to Mexico, to such places as Monterrey, Mexico City, and Acapulco, where Felix would often join them. A baseball lover all his life, Tijerina regularly took Mrs. Felix and the children to Colt Stadium on South Main to watch the Colt .45s, Houston's first major league baseball team, after it began playing in 1962. He also enjoyed taking Felix, Jr., and Janie Bell to the wrestling matches at the City Auditorium. There, on one occasion, he and his two children were introduced (to the kids' delight) on live television by his good friend Paul Boesch, Houston's longtime wrestling empresario and announcer. And the children would later fondly remember hearing Mexican accordion music—*música ranchera* (their father's favorite)—playing on his car radio as they accompanied him to different destinations around town.[102]

At home, the family watched television together, something Felix enjoyed. All was not picture perfect, however. The Tijerinas had their share of family spats. Like most people, they had their good times and bad times.[103]

Felix impressed upon his children the importance of education, as it was central to his philosophy of life. They also knew that he had worked hard, that it was important to him to do well, and that he was extremely talented at what he did. A true entrepreneur, Felix told his son on more than one occasion: "It's better to have people work for you than to work for them"; he emphasized to Felix, Jr., that it was best to "be the boss." But the children likewise grew up knowing that their father felt that people were important. In their eyes, he seemed to know everyone and easily conversed with others. Felix, Jr., and Janie Bell saw in him a sensitive and easily touched heart, as generous to the less advantaged as he was to his own family, capable and kind, someone to emulate. Felix Tijerina made an indelible imprint on his children, but they would not have him much longer, not nearly long enough.[104]

LULAC LEGACIES

In late 1964, Felix learned that the summer Preschool Program for Non-English Speaking Children had had another banner year. The Texas Education Agency notified him and Jake Rodríguez in December that approximately 182 school districts (12.7 percent of the state's total), more than 20,000 children (20,786), and 900 teachers had participated. Earlier, Tijerina had informed LULAC national president William Bonilla that during the preceding year the LULAC Educational Fund had not expended any money "promoting the little schools because we felt enough people were aware of it and we would leave it up to the Texas Educational Agency to measure its success."[105]

In early 1965, Tijerina took note of two important developments in President Lyndon Johnson's War on Poverty. These two federal initiatives—the Elementary and Secondary Education Act of 1965, and a specific program called Project Head Start—reminded Felix and others of his work for disadvantaged preschoolers in Texas.

In February, Tijerina saw in the Houston newspapers that Johnson's massive, $1.2 billion education bill was winding its way through Congress. In the article he read, he circled in red ink the part which noted that, among many other things, its funds (under its Title I) could be used to provide preschool programs and English instruction for non-English speaking children.

In March, Tijerina also noticed in the local newspapers that the community relations committee of the Houston Independent School District had invited a local social agency to submit a plan for participation in the federally funded Project Head Start. (Ironically, the committee that had extended the invitation was composed of the board's four-member conservative majority, which by now had softened its stance on accepting federal money.) The plan that the committee requested was to give preschool education during the summer to at least five thousand "culturally deprived" children in Houston's poverty-stricken north side, much of which was Mexican American. This invitation included the committee's offer for the agency to use district school buildings and curriculum consultants.[106]

With Title I of the ESEA in 1965 and Project Head Start the same year, the basic concept of preschool programs for disadvantaged children—to prevent school dropouts, break the cycle of poverty, and preclude societal exclusion (the basic approach Tijerina and many others across the country had championed and publicized)—was adopted and massively funded at the federal level. Indeed, the extensive material presented to the Senate subcommittee hearings by LBJ's Commissioner of Education Francis Keppel in late January, 1965, on the proposed ESEA specifically included a description of the Preschool Educational Program for Non-English Speaking Children operating in El Paso as an example of what the nation's schools would do with the resources made available under Title I. When Project Head Start began to be implemented in the Houston Housing Authority projects during the summer of 1965, Tijerina's fellow HHA commissioners commented (no doubt representative of what many people thought) that this federally supported summer program was "very similar to the Little School of the Four Hundred project which was originated and sponsored by Mr. Tijerina beginning in 1960." Also perceiving this similarity, LULAC members especially felt that their beloved Little School served as the primary model for Project Head Start. Whether it was *the* model for this federal program is doubtful; however, the Little School had played its role. No less authorities on education than L. DeWitt Hale and Carlos F. Truan reflected that Tijerina's Little School of the 400 was a definite forerunner of Head Start, helping to pave the way for the implementation of this national-level effort.[107]

Indeed, any comparison of the preschool efforts in Texas with those that emanated from Johnson's War on Poverty reveals that Tijerina, the Little School, and the state-funded program anticipated and helped to prompt the

1965 federal efforts. The Little School of the 400 and the Preschool Instructional Classes, with all their attendant publicity from the late 1950s through the mid-1960s, helped establish a climate conducive for implementing the bold actions that transpired during the latter half of the 1960s. People across the nation had come to know about his program through the articles in *Time, Coronet,* the *Saturday Evening Post,* as well as other publications and media. National television and radio had spotlighted his endeavors. Anyone interested in preschool efforts would have noticed such publicity. Felix had personally touched such players in the 1965 events as Lyndon Johnson and Senator Ralph Yarborough and had impressed them with his preschool efforts. Indeed, Yarborough was a cosponsor of the 1965 education act and an influential member of the Senate committee that reported it out. (It should be recalled, too, that Senator Yarborough had articles about Tijerina's preschool efforts printed in the *Congressional Record,* which had been read far and wide.) Along with other preschool advocates across the nation at the time, Felix had played a role in moving the idea of such programs for the disadvantaged from the local communities to the national arena; his efforts in Texas and in the other states where he promoted the idea for similar Little Schools served as an intermediate step between those which had taken place in towns like Freeport, Texas, and that which Lyndon Johnson, Sargent Shriver (LBJ's head of the War on Poverty), and their cohorts put into operation nationally. According to Alfred Hernández, Felix took a good deal of satisfaction in seeing that the federal government had picked up on and now financed programs that put into practice the basic ideas he had fostered. Tijerina and his fellow Texans had made an impact.[108]

During the summer of 1965, the Preschool Instructional Classes for Non-English Speaking Children continued to flourish, although their numbers were down slightly from the previous year. In 1965, 177 school districts participated, with a total of 893 classes that reached 20,149 pupils. This decline would continue thereafter, scholars speculate, because of the existence of such competing programs as Title I and Project Head Start. Felix still had ample opportunity to tout the program, as local clubs and schools regularly invited him to speak on his Little School. He had every reason to be honored; since its start as a state-funded effort in 1960, the program had instructed a reported 91,648 Texas children, and would handle the additional 20,000 plus during 1965.[109]

That summer, too, Felix took great pleasure in seeing Alfred Hernández elected LULAC national president, becoming the third and last member from Council No. 60 (along with Herrera and Tijerina) to attain that lofty office. He had encouraged his younger friend to seek the position, although Felix himself did not attend the convention. Thus elevated, Hernández became a member of an unofficial triumvirate that represented Council No. 60's most historic and colorful generation.[110]

PART OF THE MAINSTREAM, 1964–1965

When Kennedy was assassinated in November, 1963, Felix wept at the dinner table, a reaction shared by many—both Hispanic and non-Hispanic—who had emotionally invested in the young president. John Herrera, in a similar response across town, had to be led away weeping from his office when news of that national tragedy broke. The death of the president had a special poignancy for Houston Mexican Americans because he and Jackie, along with Vice President Johnson, Lady Bird, and their entourage had spent part of Kennedy's last evening at a LULAC banquet at the Rice Hotel, a function orchestrated and emceed by Herrera, and one which Felix did not attend.[111]

Like other Texas Democrats, Felix expressed immediate support for Lyndon Johnson as he assumed the office of president. Tijerina sent him a telegram expressing his deepest condolence on President Kennedy's demise. "Being a Texan like you," he noted, "I feel regret that this monstrous occurrence had to happen but more so that it happened here."[112]

The Civil Rights Act of 1964, which President Johnson pushed through Congress after the assassination, outlawed discrimination in all places of accommodation, such as theaters, hotels, and restaurants. This act brought further along in Houston what the sit-in demonstrators had begun in 1960, when they had provoked Felix's letter to the Houston media. On July 3, 1964, however, the day after the Civil Rights Act passed and was signed by Johnson, a new notice to the staff, signed by Felix himself, went up on walls of the Felix Mexican Restaurants. It informed all hostesses, cashiers, and waiters that the Civil Rights Bill had been signed into law by the president. "And being good Americans we must obey this law. Beginning today Negro citizens will be served in all our restaurants[;] they are to be given the same service as any other patron."[113]

Because the 1964 Civil Rights Act also outlawed discrimination in publicly owned facilities and federally aided programs, it had a direct impact on Felix in his role with the Houston Housing Authority. By the spring of the following year, twenty-eight black families had moved into Allen Parkway Village (formerly San Felipe Courts), which had previously been for whites only. Felix and the other board members were especially gratified that under Thomas Booker's directorship this integration was "continuing without trouble."[114]

Also indicative of the changes overtaking U.S. society by 1964, Tijerina was interviewed in April by a sociologist named Joan W. Moore, then involved in an inquiry about Mexican Americans that was more far-reaching than anything Felix (or anyone else for that matter) had ever been associated with relative to that community. Moore was associate director of the Mexican American Study Project at the University of California, Los Angeles. The project was an ambitious interdisciplinary effort to study the socioeconomic position of Mexican Americans in selected urban areas across five Southwestern states. Made possible by a grant from the Ford Foundation, it represented the first time a national foundation had given funds for a major research effort on this particular minority group and was part of what the principal investigators called "the current discovery of Mexican Americans in the United States."[115]

Coming to Houston on April 20–21, Moore met with Felix as one of two hundred "key persons" in the Southwest and Chicago that she and many other project workers interviewed to begin their investigation and to savor "the enormous diversity" of the population under consideration. The resulting hefty volume by Leo Grebler, Joan W. Moore, Ralph C. Guzman, et al., was entitled *The Mexican-American People: The Nation's Second Largest Minority*. It would be a massive, landmark study, helping to establish in the scholarly literature the importance of Mexican Americans within the national fabric. Estimating their population by 1970 at more than five million, the project highlighted the rise to national prominence of the Mexican American community during the 1960s. Tijerina would receive credit in this opus for his participation, along with the two hundred other old and new players across the nation; in many respects, his meeting with Joan Moore symbolized how he had lived to be part of a community that had finally been "discovered" on the national scene.[116]

Among the other activities that crowded his life, in May, 1964, Tijerina had done another term on the Harris County grand jury. A few weeks later, he paid for the funeral of Jesús González, Mrs. Felix's cousin. Called Jessie, he had been working as the chef at the Bellaire location. In June, Felix was named Father of the Year for 1964 by radio station KLVL's Latin American Baptist program, which was directed by Rev. James Novarro. The program's executive committee had unanimously picked Felix because he was "*un padre modelo*" (a model father). *La voz,* the local Spanish-language newspaper, featured this honor in a front-page story, complete with an imposing photograph of Tijerina seated reassuringly in his easy chair at home, surrounded by Mrs. Felix, Felix, Jr., and Janie Bell. Around this time, too, Felix took a stressful, emergency trip to Monterrey where Mingo Villarreal, during a personal visit to the area, had unexpectedly been hospitalized for a severe internal ailment. Friends and family in Monterrey and General Escobedo marveled that by the morning after receiving word of Mingo's illness, Felix was at his cousin's bedside, took charge of the situation, and ensured that his life-long companion received the extra medical care he needed to recover.[117]

In the fall, Tijerina supported Lyndon Johnson for the presidency, like most Mexican American voters and other Texas Democrats. Felix appreciated Johnson's attention to his work in LULAC, and as LULAC president he had been a guest at the LBJ ranch. Though a Johnson man, he predictably did not join in with the Viva Johnson-Humphrey Clubs, the barrio groups consisting of individuals who had been active in the old Civic Action Committee and during JFK's 1960 race, and were now trying to rekindle the enthusiasm of that previous campaign.[118]

Mrs. Felix, true to form, went for the Republican contender, Senator Barry Goldwater.[119]

Felix's heart and his time were, as always, in the Houston Rotary Club. He continued to travel to Mexico on Rotary business with friends like Dick Proctor. The Thursday Rotary meetings at the Rice Hotel reflected the pace of Houston's development. Most exemplary, on March 25, 1965, the program was chaired by R. E. "Bob" Smith and featured Roy Hofheinz, whose topic was "The Astrodome Story." The Astrodome would open within three weeks amid great international fanfare as the first domed sports stadium in the nation. Smith and Hofheinz had been key figures in bringing the stadium into existence, and Tijerina's long relationship with both men underscored his integration into the city's fabric. Few men, by this moment in Tijerina's life, could have claimed to be more part of Houston. On April 29, he celebrated his sixtieth birthday.[120]

In late June, the officials of Surety Savings Association ran an impressive advertisement in the *Houston Post* thanking the "many thousands of people" who had deposited money in their institution and announcing that it had doubled its office space to accommodate such a positive response from the community. Inviting people to come see their newly decorated offices, the advertisement carried a group portrait of the association's fourteen officers and directors. This formal photograph, taken by Gittings (Houston's most prestigious portrait studio) was telling. Felix Tijerina, vice president, sat in the front row, indistinguishable from the thirteen others (all older, graying, balding white men in dark business suits) against the studio's luxurious backdrop of dark oak paneling and book-lined shelves. This portrait—what may well have been the final image of Tijerina in the media during his lifetime—graphically illustrated the degree to which he had fit himself into mainstream Houston, something for which he had always strived. It represented an appropriate punctuation mark for his life and career and foretold, in the mid-1960s, the manner in which large numbers of Hispanics would integrate themselves into U.S. society in the decades to come.[121]

DEATH OF AN ENTREPRENEUR

The dark cloud on Felix's horizon was his health, which, since the late 1950s, had not been good. His legs gave him trouble from circulation problems, affecting his ability to walk for sustained periods. More important, he had high blood pressure and a heart ailment. His physicians had prescribed more exercise, and he took daily naps at home to deal with fatigue. Mrs. Felix and friends like Leo Reynosa (with whom he lunched regularly) often drove him where he needed to go during spells when he felt especially bad. He went to the hospital for regular medical checkups and for rest, and he took a great deal of medication. In the fall of 1964, he had spent a week at the hospital for a general exam. Of this visit, he wrote Jake Rodríguez that "[o]ld folks, as you know, have to maintain constant contact with the doctor to keep from deteriorating further." He concluded his letter to Rodríguez with the statement: "I am supposedly in 'A-1 condition.'" Health problems or not, he kept on going and tried not to let his ailments show.[122]

On August 4, 1965, Tijerina opened a new Felix Mexican Restaurant at 105 West Bird in Pasadena, the Bayou City's major satellite community, which was southeast of town along the Houston Ship Channel. Situated near the intersection of Southmore and South Shaver in the heart of Pasadena, this new place extended Felix's chain eastward, well beyond his Telephone Road location. It was a small, store-front building that he leased from a friend. Felix had it attractively remodeled to resemble his other restaurants: a white stucco façade, two large arched windows (one on either side of the dark wood double front doors), and a modest red-tiled awning over the entrance. The establishment accommodated about 110 people. The successful grand opening was attended by Pasadena city officials and business leaders.[123]

But even with this warm reception, as well as the Felix reputation for good food, business was not as constant there as it was at the other locations. That particular area of Pasadena was "dry"; no beer could be served to complement the Mexican cuisine. Also, Pasadena residents simply proved less receptive than the traditional Felix customers on Houston's west side.[124]

There was really no burning reason for Tijerina to open the Pasadena location, but it was his idea in life to keep expanding his restaurant business and he was not to be dissuaded, even, in this instance, by the cautionary advice of Mrs. Felix. (Always pushing forward, he likewise made plans to remodel the Beaumont location.) The Pasadena restaurant brought the total number Tijerina owned to seven, with well over a hundred people on his payroll at any one time.[125]

But preparing the new restaurant that summer had been physically hard on Tijerina. He had especially suffered from the oppressive heat. Moreover, the new restaurant was a long distance from Westheimer. Returning in the car one day, Felix, Jr., noticed that his father seemed physically ill.[126]

Felix entered the hospital soon after the Pasadena restaurant's grand opening and underwent extensive tests for his heart, blood pressure, and circulation. Mrs. Felix saw to his needs and, in between, helped keep the new restaurant going as best she could.[127]

On September 3, he was released from the hospital to go home for the Labor Day weekend; he seemed to feel fine. September 3 being a Friday, Felix, Jr., went out for the evening with friends. Late that night, Felix, Sr., retired to his bedroom; experiencing some sort of trouble, however, he sat down on a cot that Mrs. Felix had earlier placed near his bed where she could sleep and easily attend to him. Mrs. Felix and Janie Bell came to his side, trying to give whatever assistance they could. After a while, he suddenly had a heart attack, convulsed, and died immediately. Mrs. Felix ran to the bathroom, brought a towel dampened with cold water, and tried mightily to revive him. Janie Bell called an ambulance, pleading with them to hurry. By then, too, Felix, Jr., had come home and tried to help. Of course, their efforts proved futile. The death certificate listed the time of death to be approximately 1 A.M., Saturday, September 4. With his wife and children near him, Felix Tijerina, entrepreneur and remarkable citizen, was dead at age sixty.[128]

As word spread, the Tijerina home and lawn began to fill with people. Dr. Robert Crouch, Felix's physician, came as quickly as he could in response to Mrs. Felix's telephone call. Felix's three sisters, Mingo (who was in a daze), Lewis and Katherine Cutrer, Geneva Harper, Florine La Rue, fellow Rotarians, and many others came and held vigil during most of that sorrowful night.[129]

The following day, the Houston media was filled with notices of Felix's death. The newspapers—the *Chronicle* and *Post*—that had followed his career so closely ran front-page stories reserved only for the most respected citizens. Rather unpoetically, George Carmack's *Houston Press* could not herald his passing as the *Press* had gone out of business the year before.[130]

The funeral, held at Saint Anne's Catholic Church on Monday, was standing room only, from the most humble citizen to the highest city officials. Friends from Monterrey drove all night to attend. Many of those from Houston who came to pay their respects were past recipients of Tijerina's various unsung acts of charity. To many of these folks, Felix Tijerina had seemed indestructible and far too young to die, and for that his death stunned them all the more.[131]

Alfred J. Hernández, along with Felix, Jr., made the funeral arrangements and named the pall bearers, who included Richard Ante, Benito Flores, Joe González, Alfred Hernández, Tommy Laurenzo, Raúl Martínez, Leo Reynosa, and Felix Salazar, a mixture of LULAC associates, family, and longtime friends. Father Walter B. Sullivan performed the high mass and delivered the sermon, which was brief and to the point. He did not dwell, as many would have, on the Horatio Alger thread in Felix's life, but rather on the fact that although he encountered prejudice in his life, Felix had not responded with violence, but rather with "a desire to do something positive to help his fellow man." His Little School of the 400, the priest concluded, "will be his memorial." Though he did not directly say so, Sullivan held up Felix as a reminder of a peaceful, inclusive way in a time of American societal strife.[132]

The lengthy funeral procession took a long while to make the drive across town from Saint Anne's to Forest Park Cemetery. The cortege traveled down Westheimer, carrying Tijerina's remains past his great white restaurant, almost as a tribute to his presence in Houston. At the gravesite, in the hot, humid Houston afternoon, Father Sullivan gave the last blessings over the casket; Council No. 60 member, Baptist minister, and former school board candidate James Novarro made a moving speech to Felix's memory. There in the family plot near the graves of his mother, his cousin Luciano Villarreal, and Janie's relative, Jessie González, under the gray granite likeness of Our Lady of Guadalupe, Felix Tijerina was buried.[133]

Numerous memorials and tributes immediately followed. Sympathies for the family poured in from people of all ranks. The personal letter of condolence to Mrs. Felix from former vice president Richard Nixon, then residing in New York, noted that "[m]en with the . . . feeling for others that he possessed are all [too] few in our times." As expected, the civic and professional organizations that he touched made much of his demise. His Rotary brothers, from Houston to Mexico City, were deeply moved. Ramón Salcido wrote an editorial, "Ha muerto un grán Rotario!" in the *México Rotario,* the group's national bulletin, which recounted Felix's life, many achievements, contributions to Texas Mexicans, and recognition he received from Mexico itself. Needless to say, LULAC members across the country took sad note of his death. John J. Herrera, now back in the top echelons of the organization as Alfred Hernández's national executive director, for one example, penned a long memorial to his former rival. In this tribute, one of his characteristically expansive gestures, Herrera displayed not a trace of animosity and noted at length that Tijerina's life had been a symbol of hope. The *Chuck Wagon,* the magazine of the Texas Restaurant Association, ran an article representative of business's view of Felix Tijerina, embodiment of the American dream, which recounted his "rags-to-riches life." Many newspaper editorials across the state played on the theme of Felix as a Horatio Alger figure and founder of the Little School of the 400. The *Houston Post* editorial section, however, best summed it up by noting that the honor and respect Tijerina received came from the fact that he was "A GOOD CITIZEN," someone "moved by a deep and genuine interest in the welfare of all his fellow men. The imprint he left upon the community will long endure."[134]

With the death of Felix Tijerina, Houston's most prominent Latin American resident and the embodiment of an era in the Mexican American experience passed into memory. His death might be seen as marking an important moment in the evolution of his city, his nation, and his ethnic group. The same issue of the newspapers that told of his demise also contained reports on the recently opened Astrodome and the escalating conflict in Vietnam, the former a badge of Houston as metropolis, the latter a major flash point of civil strife in the 1960s that would tear at the fabric of American society.[135] To be sure, Felix's death came on the threshold of some of the most profound incidents of civil and racial turmoil in American history. He died just before the beginning of what came to be called the Chicano Movement, when many elements within the Mexican American population began their own brand of civil rights agitation, paralleling that of the African American community.

All told, Tijerina reflected and, as a leader, played a significant part in twentieth-century Mexican American development. His story symbolized that of a people who moved from the immigrant facelessness of the 1910s into the limelight of the 1960s. Tijerina and his generation did much to put names and faces on an ethnic group that was an important part of the American scene, help determine its future, and blend that populace into American society. He and his fellows handed down a legacy of dignity, respect, self-confidence, and an ability to work with others that would well serve subsequent generations of Hispanics.

Felix Tijerina was, in the end, a decent man who had lived a full, productive life. He had ventured a long way from the dusty plaza of General Escobedo to the green lawns of Houston. In the process, he dealt resourcefully with the many vicissitudes he encountered and tried to promote social harmony. He believed in the promise that his constantly evolving society offered. A man of ambition, Tijerina pursued his dreams vigorously and with no apologies for the drive he possessed; but he also did more than his share to make that promise attainable for others.

NOTES

INTRODUCTION

1. I have chosen not to place an accent on the *e* in Felix Tijerina's first name because he personally did not use an accent. Conforming to the rules of Spanish orthography, however, all other Spanish names in the text of this volume will contain accents in the appropriate places, although in most cases Tijerina's Mexican American contemporaries, especially his Houston associates, did not use accents in their names, either.

2. *Houston Chronicle,* Sept. 4, 1965, p. 1; *Houston Post,* Sept. 5, 1965, pp. 1, 4; Francisco A. Rosáles, "Mexicans in Houston: The Struggle to Survive," *Houston Review* 3, no. 2 (summer, 1981): 241; *Houston Press,* Aug. 26, 1948, p. 9.

3. Approval of Name for New School in the Franklin-Burnet Area, 6-27-77, Records of the Houston Independent School District Board of Education; *Semanario el méxica* (Houston), June 30, 1977, p. 1; Invitation to Dedication, Felix Tijerina Elementary, Folder 18, Box 4, Mr. and Mrs. Felix Tijerina, Sr., Papers, Houston Metropolitan Research Center, Houston Public Library (collection cited hereafter as Tijerina Papers; archive cited hereafter as HMRC); Richard Holgin, interview by author, Houston, Tex., Sept. 25, 1983; Thomas H. Kreneck, *Del Pueblo: A Pictorial History of Houston's Hispanic Community,* p. 200.

4. While *la raza* literally translates as "the race," it is used in the colloquial sense in this volume to connote the Mexican or Mexican American people as an ethnic group (i.e., "peoplehood").

5. Oscar Martínez, "On the Size of the Chicano Population: New Estimates, 1850–1900," *Aztlán: International Journal of Chicano Studies Research* 6, no. 1 (spring, 1975): 56; Mark Reisler, *By the Sweat of Their Brow: Mexican Immigrant Labor in the United States, 1900–1940,* p. ix; Ricardo Romo, "The Urbanization of Southwestern Chicanos in the Early Twentieth Century," *New Scholar* 6 (1977): 194.

6. Silas B. Ragsdale, "Biography: Felix Tijerina," *The Log: Weekly Bulletin of the Rotary Club of Houston* 36, Aug. 19, 1948, p. 4; *Houston Chronicle,* Sept. 4, 1965, p. 1; *Houston Post,* Sept. 5, 1965, pp. 1, 4; General Escobedo Municipio, Nuevo León, Mexico, Civil Registration, Nacimientos, 1896–1910, Acta 17, pp. 6–7, Genealogical

Department, Church of Jesus Christ of Latter-Day Saints, Salt Lake City, Utah (microfilm) (hereafter cited as Genealogical Dept., LDS); Acta de Nacimiento, Filiberto Tijerina Villarreal, 29 de abril de 1905, Escobedo, Nuevo León, birth certificate issued by the Gobierno del estado Nuevo León, dirección del Registro Civil, Sept. 28, 1990, in author's possession; Bautismo de hijos legitimos, Bautismo de hijos naturales, 1899–1908, vol. 5, no. 63, p. 127, Archivo de la parroquia de San Nicolás Tolentino en San Nicolás de los Garza, estado de Nuevo León (microfilm), Local History Department, Corpus Christi Public Library, Corpus Christi, Tex. (hereafter cited as Archivo de San Nicolás, CCPL); Confirmaciones, 1869–1911, vol. 1, p. 53, Archivo de San Nicolás, CCPL; General Escobedo Municipio, Nuevo León, Mexico, Civil Registration, Defunciones, 1868–1916, p. 10, Genealogical Dept., LDS; telephone interviews: María Villarreal Bosmans and Tony Bosmans, by author, Feb. 10, 1985; Tony Bosmans, by author, May 19, 1986, Oct. 1, 1989; Anselmo Villarreal, interview by author, San Antonio, Tex., Feb. 5, 1985.

7. Francisco A. Rosales, "The Mexican Immigrant Experience in Chicago, Houston, and Tucson: Comparisons And Contrasts," in Francisco A. Rosales and Barry J. Kaplan, eds., *Houston: A Twentieth Century Urban Frontier*, pp. 58–64; Matt S. Meier and Feliciano Rivera, *The Chicanos: A History of Mexican Americans*, pp. 130–33; Emilio Zamora, *The World of the Mexican Worker in Texas*, pp. 11–14, 211; Arnoldo De León, *The Tejano Community, 1836–1900*, pp. 22, 87, 114; Romo, "Urbanization of Southwestern Chicanos," pp. 183–85, 193–94, 201; Victoria Tijerina, interviews by author, Houston, Tex., Sept. 17, 1980 (telephone), Mar. 1, 1981, June 26, 1985 (telephone); Arnoldo De León, *Ethnicity in the Sunbelt: A History of Mexican Americans in Houston*, pp. 10–18.

8. Mario T. García, *Mexican Americans: Leadership, Ideology, and Identity, 1930-1960*, pp. 1–22, provides the seminal statement on the Mexican American Generation and its leadership that largely informs this biography's conceptual framework. Also see Mario T. García, "Mexican Americans and the Politics of Citizenship: The Case of El Paso, 1936," *New Mexico Historical Review* 59 (Apr., 1984): 187–204; Mario T. García, "Americans All: The Mexican-American Generation and the Politics of Wartime Los Angeles, 1941–45," *Social Science Quarterly* 65 (June, 1984): 278–89; Rosales, "Mexicans in Houston," pp. 227–32; Kreneck, *Del Pueblo*, pp. 42–43.

9. Rosales, "Mexicans in Houston," pp. 241–44; De León, *Ethnicity in the Sunbelt*, pp. 45–143; Kreneck, *Del Pueblo*, pp. 80–83, 116; M. T. García, *Mexican Americans*, pp. 16–20.

10. De León, *Ethnicity in the Sunbelt*, pp. ix–xi, 60–90.

11. Ibid., pp. 10–16, 31–39; Rosales, "Mexicans in Houston," pp. 226–27, 235–37; Kreneck, *Del Pueblo*, pp. 30–31.

12. "An Outstanding Lulac: Felix Tijerina," *LULAC News*, Feb., 1954, p. 49, LULAC Council No. 60 Records, HMRC (hereafter cited as LULAC Records, HMRC); M. T. García, *Mexican Americans*, pp. 16, 19, 31–38; De León, *Ethnicity in the Sunbelt*, pp. 133–35.

13. *Houston Press*, Aug. 26, 1948, p. 9; Mrs. Felix Tijerina, Sr., interviews by author, Houston, Tex., Oct. 16, 1978 (Oral History Collection, HMRC), Sept. 13, 1980, Jan. 20, 1990; Barbara Liggett, "American Behavior Distresses Her," *Houston Post*, ca. fall, 1950, Clippings, Tijerina Papers; Margaret Webb Dreyer, "Two Countries 'Unite' in Family,"

Houston Chronicle, ca. 1953, Clippings, Tijerina Papers; Pat Manley, "Mrs. Felix Is Kept Busy Aiding Others, Planning Tour," *Houston Chronicle*, July 31, 1953, sec. D, p. 2.

14. De León, *Ethnicity in the Sunbelt*, pp. 134–37; Rosales, "Mexicans in Houston" p. 241; Louis Alexander, "Texas Helps Her Little Latins," *Saturday Evening Post*, Aug. 5, 1961, pp. 30-31, 54-55.

15. *Houston Chronicle*, Dec. 8, 1958, sec. A, p. 4; "Latin Leader Urges Negroes to Be Patient," ca. May, 1960, Clippings, Tijerina Papers; Alfred J. Hernández, telephone interview by author, Houston, Tex., Aug. 11, 1993.

16. De León, *The Tejano Community*, pp. xii–xix.

17. Ernesto Galarza, *Barrio Boy: The Story of a Boy's Acculturation*, pp. 1–2.

18. M. T. García, *Mexican Americans*, p. 20.

19. Ibid., pp. 17–18.

20. De León, *Ethnicity in the Sunbelt*, pp. 134–36; *LULAC News*, Feb., 1959, p. 1, Alfred J. Hernández Papers, HMRC; *LULAC News*, Apr., 1959, p. 3, LULAC Records, HMRC; *LULAC News*, June, 1959, p. 2, Carmen Cortes Papers, HMRC.

21. Keith Elliott, "Now Juanito Can Read," *Coronet*, July, 1961, pp. 132–36; Alexander, "Texas Helps Her Little Latins," pp. 30–31, 54–55; Guadalupe Campos Quintanilla, "The 'Little School of the 400' and Its Impact on Education for the Spanish Dominant Bilingual Children of Texas" (Ed.D. diss., University of Houston, 1976), pp. 129, 134, 136–37; Guadalupe San Miguel, Jr., *"Let All of Them Take Heed": Mexican Americans and the Campaign for Educational Equality in Texas, 1910-1981*, pp. 141–47.

22. Elliott, "Now Juanito Can Read," pp. 132–36; Quintanilla, "The 'Little School of the 400,'" pp. 129, 134, 136–37; Alfred J. Hernández, "The Little School of the 400," in *LULAC: Fifty Years of Serving Hispanics, Golden Anniversary, 1929–1979*; M. T. García, *Mexican Americans*, p. 59.

CHAPTER I. *LA INMIGRACIÓN*

1. *Houston Post*, Feb. 11, 1922, p. 3; Standard Certificate of Death for Robert Orosco [*sic*], Feb. 10, 1922, Texas State Board of Health, Bureau of Vital Statistics, City of Houston, Tex.; *Houston City Directory, 1920–21*, p. 1037; *Houston City Directory, 1922*, p. 1057; *Houston City Directory, 1923–24*, p. 1151; Victoria Tijerina, interview by author, Houston, Tex., Feb. 1, 1985.

2. I gained an understanding of General Escobedo and its surrounding area from two memorable research field trips there: the first in early August, 1993, and the second in late September, 1997. See also Daniel Sifuentes Espinoza, "De un rancho a otro: haciendas congregaciones y poblados en Nuevo León, siglo XIX," *Bitacora: revista trimestral de la hacienda San Pedro* (May, 1997, No. 1), p. 29; Juan Ramón Garza Guajardo, *Municipio de General Escobedo, N.L.: historia de sus ayuntamientos (1868–1997)*, photo captioned "Hermosa postal del 'Cerro del Topo, símbolo de nuestro municipio,' Anexo fotográfico."

3. *Los municipios de Nuevo León (Colección: Enciclopedia de los Municipios de México)*,

p. 164; Santiago Roel, *Nuevo León: apuntes historicos,* 2:58; Francisco Javier Alvarado Segovia, Rogelio Velázquez de León, and Sandra Lara Esquivel, *Historias de nuestros barrios,* pp. 283–84; Censo del estado de Nuevo León, Oct. 20, 1895, p. 78, Local History Department, CCPL; Garza Guajardo, *Municipio de General Escobedo,* p. 34; interviews: Juan Ramón Garza Guajardo, by author with assistance of Marie Theresa Hernández, General Escobedo, N.L., Sept. 26, 1997; Jesús Ayala López by author with assistance of Marie Theresa Hernández, General Escobedo, N.L., Sept. 26, 1997; Juan Ramón Garza Guajardo, by Marie Theresa Hernández for author, Monterrey, N.L., Oct. 21, 1997 (telephone).

The area of the *municipio* of General Escobedo experienced various name changes prior to 1868. During the early 1600s, the region initially consisted of La Hacienda del Topo de los Ayala. The hacienda's owner, José de Ayala, soon bestowed another new name on his land holding: San Nicolás del Topo de los Ayala (known also as La Hacienda de los Ayala). On the opposite (southwestern) slope of the mountain known as Cerro del Topo Chico was La Hacienda de los González. Eventually—to differentiate between the two hacienda settlements—La Hacienda de los González came to be called Topo Chico, and La Hacienda de los Ayala took on the popular name Topo Grande, which is still often used to designate the *villa* of General Escobedo. Thus, the close relationship between the names Cerro del Topo Chico, Topo Chico, Topo Grande, and General Escobedo might cause some confusion among those unfamiliar with the area. See Juan Ramón Garza Guajardo, *La estación del Topo Grande de General Escobedo, N.L.,* pp. 15–16; interviews: Oscar Garza Guajardo, by author with assistance from Gerardo García Salinas, General Escobedo, N.L., Sept. 25, 1997; Juan Ramón Garza Guajardo by author with assistance from Marie Theresa Hernández, General Escobedo, N.L., Sept. 27, 1997; *Los municipios de Nuevo León,* p. 164.

4. *Los municipios de Nuevo León,* p. 170; Alvarado Segovia et al., *Historias de nuestros barrios,* p. 283; General Escobedo Municipio, Civil Registration, Matrimonios, 1868–1910, Acta 1, Folio 2 (microfilm), Genealogical Dept., LDS. In the written record, Dionicia Villarreal's first name is often spelled Dionisia. For consistency, the former spelling is used in this text.

5. General Escobedo Municipio, Civil Registration: Nacimientos, 1896–1910, Acta 43, p. 17; Acta 23, p. 7; Acta 35, p. 20; Defunciones, 1868–1916, Acta 23, p. 13; Nacimientos, 1911–1930, Acta 14, p. 6; Acta 27, p. 10, all in Genealogical Dept., LDS.

6. General Escobedo Municipio, Civil Registration, Nacimientos, 1896–1910, Acta 17, pp. 6–7; Acta de Nacimiento, Feliberto Tijerina Villarreal, 29 de abril de 1905, Escobedo, Nuevo León, Birth Certificate Issued by the Gobierno del Estado Nuevo León, Dirección del Registro Civil, Sept. 28, 1990, in my possession.

7. Archivo de la parroquia de San Nicolás Tolentino en San Nicolás de los Garza, Estado de Nuevo León, vol. 5, 1899–1908, Bautismo de hijos legitimos, bautismo de hijos naturales, no. 63, Eriberto de Escobedo el 13 de agosto, 1905 (microfilm), CCPL. During this period, the records of baptisms and other sacraments for General Escobedo were maintained at the church of San Nicolás de los Garza, a town approximately fifteen kilometers east of General Escobedo. The church of San Nicolás de los Garza was the seat of

the parish of San Nicolás Tolentino, of which the General Escobedo church was a part. Because Escobedo's San Nicolás de Bari was only a *capilla* (chapel), it had no resident priest and was served by the clerics from San Nicolás de los Garza. The recorded baptismal entry for "Eriberto" noted that this child was born on Apr. 15, 1905. It listed the baby's parents as Rafael Tijerina and Dionisia Villarreal and his grandparents as Rafael Tijerina and Nicolasa Alvares and Librado Villarreal and Caralampia Ayala, matching the civil record of Feliberto's birth. The discrepancy over the name "Eriberto" rather than Feliberto can perhaps be accounted for by a misunderstanding in pronunciation of the child's name by the priest or by the priest misremembering the name between the time he administered the sacrament in General Escobedo and when he recorded the event in the registry at San Nicolás de los Garza. The discrepancy over the date of birth (Apr. 15 rather than Apr. 29) might also be explained by the lapse of time between the April birth and the baptism in mid-August. Genealogists often encounter such errors in handwritten documentation. Altogether, one can reasonably conclude that the Feliberto born in April, 1905, in General Escobedo and the "Eriberto" baptized less than four months later were the same person. I would like to acknowledge Margaret Rose, head of Corpus Christi Public Library's Local History Department, for assistance with these records.

Constructed in 1826, San Nicolás de Bari finally became a full-fledged parish by 1972. The original building was expanded in 1985–86 through the addition of a wing on both sides of the original façade, giving the structure its present appearance. See Juan Ramón Garza Guajardo, *Capilla de San Nicolás de Bari*, pp. 31–32, 41; Juan Ramón Garza Guajardo interview, Sept. 26, 1997; and Oscar Garza Guajardo interview, Sept. 25, 1997.

8. For Rafael Tijerina's status as a *labrador* see General Escobedo Municipio, Civil Registration, Nacimientos, 1896–1910, Acta 43, p. 17; Acta 23, p. 7; Acta 35, p. 20; Defunciones, 1868–1916, Acta 23, p. 13; Nacimientos, 1911–30, Acta 14, p. 6; Acta 27, p. 10; Nacimientos, 1896–1910, Acta 17, pp. 6–7 (microfilm), all in Genealogical Dept., LDS; Jesus Ayala López interview, Sept. 26, 1997; Fred Nahas, "A Salute to Felix Tijerina—and His 'Little Schools of the 400,'" *Houston Press*, June 19, 1958, p. 14, Unprocessed Clippings, Tijerina Papers; *LULAC in Action—Human Values, Unlimited: A Report on the "Little School of the 400," A Heart-Warming Project of the LEAGUE OF UNITED LATIN AMERICAN CITIZENS 1960*, Folder 13, Box 2, Tijerina Papers.

Available evidence indicates that members of the Tijerina family had once owned considerable acreage in the General Escobedo region and had been people of economic importance. According to genealogical research, during the 1600s Don Gregorio Fernández de Tijerina established his own hacienda, known as Los Tijerina, in the locality of La Hacienda de los Ayala, today General Escobedo. By the late 1800s, one Jesús María Tijerina, a descendant of the earlier Tijerina *hacendado*, owned the Hacienda Jesús María, the only hacienda in the *municipio* of General Escobedo at that time. Reportedly, this latter holding contained substantial acreage and La Presa Tijerina, a well-known lake used for diverting river water for irrigation. Local historians believe, however, that by the time Feliberto was born in 1905 even this latter hacienda had dwindled to nothing; the land had either been significantly divided among heirs, sold to other individuals, or otherwise removed from Tijerina family ownership. What association, if any, that Rafael may have had with the remnants of the hacienda properties is undetermined. See Ernesto

Tijerina Cantú, *Apuntes genealogicos familia Tijerina, China, Gral. Bravo, y Los Herreras,* p. 14; Sifuentes Espinoza, "De un rancho a otra," p. 41; interviews: Juan Ramón Garza Guajardo, Sept. 26, 1997, by Marie Theresa Hernández for author, Nov. 5, 1997 (telephone); Jesús Ayala López, Sept. 26, 1997; Francisco Peña Ayala and Francisco Peña Garza by author with assistance of Marie Theresa Hernández, Monterrey, N.L., Sept. 26, 1997.

9. Reisler, *By the Sweat of Their Brow,* p. 14; Rodolfo Acuña, *Occupied America: A History of Chicanos,* pp. 146–48; Ramón Eduardo Ruiz, *The Great Rebellion: Mexico, 1905–1924,* pp. 9–23, 59–64, 75–78.

10. Juan Mora-Torres, "The Transformation of a Peripheral Society: A Social History of Nuevo León, 1848–1920" (Ph.D. diss., University of Chicago, 1991), pp. 91–94, 247–48, 263–66; *Los municipios de Nuevo León,* p. 164; Gustavo Garza Guajardo, *Testimonios de ciudad General Escobedo, N.L.,* p. 9; interviews: Juan Ramón Garza Guajardo, Sept. 26, 1997; Gerardo García Salinas by author, General Escobedo, N.L., Sept. 25, 1997.

11. Alex M. Saragoza, *The Monterrey Elite and the Mexican State, 1880-1940,* pp. 89–92; Mora-Torres, "Transformation of a Peripheral Society," pp. 135–38.

12. Reisler, *By the Sweat of Their Brow,* pp. 13–14; "Se necesitan doscientos hombres mexicanos para trabajar en la linea del ferrocaril MK&T," para Oklahoma, Oct. 5, 1905 (photocopy of original flyer from Mexican consular office), Centro de Información de Historica Regional, Hacienda San Pedro, Zuazua, Nuevo León; Saragoza, *Monterrey Elite,* p. 90.

13. Matrimonios, Aurelio Villarreal con Julia Lozano, Sept. 27, 1902, vol. 1, 1857–1906, p. 353 (microfilm), Archivo de la parroquia de San Nicolás, CCPL; interviews: Anselmo Villarreal, Feb. 5, 1985; María Villarreal Bosmans and Tony Bosmans by author, Redmond, Wash., telephone Feb. 10, 1985 (María Villarreal Bosmans is a daughter of Aurelio and Julia Villarreal. Born in 1906 in Robstown, Tex., she [through her son Tony Bosmans, who served as interpreter and go-between] provided me with especially important information for this chapter); Jesús Ayala López by author, General Escobedo, N.L., Aug. 7, 1993.

14. Interviews: Victoria Tijerina, Feb. 1, 1985; María Villarreal Bosmans and Tony Bosmans, Feb. 10, 1985; Tony Bosmans, Oct. 1, 1989; *Texas Almanac and State Industrial Guide, 1911,* p. 281.

15. David Montejano, *Anglos and Mexicans in the Making of Texas,* pp. 103–109, 114; Nueces County Historical Society, *The History of Nueces County,* pp. 94–95; Paul Schuster Taylor, *An American-Mexican Frontier: Nueces County,* p. 83.

16. Walter Prescott Webb, ed., *The Handbook of Texas,* 1:519; 2:491–92; Nueces County Historical Society, *History of Nueces County,* pp. 94–95; W. D. Doughty, "History of Robstown" (manuscript), pp. 1–2, Kilgore Collection, Special Collections and Archives Department, Bell Library, Texas A&M University–Corpus Christi (archive location cited hereafter as TAMU-CC); *Houston Chronicle,* July 17, 1960, Robstown File, *Houston Chronicle* microfiche, Texas and Local History Department, Houston Public Library (hereafter cited as Texas and Local History, HPL); María Villarreal Bosmans and Tony Bosmans interview, Feb. 10, 1985.

17. My search for the houses where Felix Tijerina was born and/or spent his child-hood in General Escobedo bore partial fruit. The particular structure identified by oral tradition as the house of Rafael and Feliberto Tijerina stands on the southwest corner of the intersection of present-day Lic. Raúl Caballero E. and Hidalgo Streets. Constructed of massive *sillar* blocks plastered with stucco, the house is taller than the surrounding buildings, although it too has only one story. Its construction date is estimated to be ca. 1890–1900. At the time of this writing, Jesús Ayala López owned the building, and it served as the public archives and library. Oral tradition also holds that the Tijerinas moved to another house farther west of the plaza and near the railroad tracks that ran to Laredo, although the house in question was never specifically identified. See interviews: Oscar Garza Guajardo, Sept. 25, 1997; Juan Ramón Garza Guajardo, Sept. 26, 1997; Jesús Ayala López, Sept. 26, 1997; Francisco Peña Ayala, by author with assistance of Marie Theresa Hernández and Juan Ramón Garza Guajardo, Monterrey, N.L., Sept. 27, 1997; and Mario Góngora Villarreal, by author with assistance of Marie Theresa Hernández and Juan Ramón Garza Guajardo, General Escobedo, N.L., Sept. 27, 1997. I was un-able to find any records indicating that Feliberto Tijerina attended school in General Escobedo.

18. Confirmaciones, vol. 1, 1869–1911, pp. 41, 43–44, 51, 53–54 (microfilm), Archivo de de la parroquia San Nicolás, CCPL.

19. Charles C. Cumberland, *Mexican Revolution: The Constitutionalist Years,* pp. 47–49, 114–15, 119–20, 209–10; Alan Knight, *The Mexican Revolution,* 2:131–32; Israel Cavazos, *Nuevo León: montes jovenes sobre la antigua llanura,* pp. 149–56.

20. Interviews: Francisco Peña Ayala, Sept. 27, 1997; Manuela Villarreal Sepúlveda de Góngora and Mario Góngora Villarreal, by author with assistance of Marie Theresa Hernández and Juan Ramón Garza Guajardo, General Escobedo, N.L., Sept. 27, 1997; Jesús Ayala López, Sept. 26, 1997; Oscar Garza Guajardo, Sept. 25, 1997; Juan Ramón Garza Guajardo, Sept. 26, Oct. 21, 1997; Juan Ramón Garza Guajardo, by Marie Theresa Hernández for author, Nov. 5, 1997 (telephone); Garza Guajardo, *Municipio de General Escobedo,* p. 34.

21. General Escobedo Municipio, Civil Registration, Defunciones, 1868–1916, De-funcion del adulto Rafael Tijerina, p. 10 for 1915 (microfilm), Genealogical Dept., LDS; Jesús Ayala López interview, Sept. 26, 1997.

22. General Escobedo Municipio, Civil Registration, Nacimientos, 1896–1910, Acta 17, pp. 6–7; interviews: Victoria Tijerina, Feb. 1, 1985; María Villarreal Bosmans and Tony Bosmans, Feb. 10, 1985, Oct. 1, 1989; Anselmo Villarreal, Feb. 5, 1985.

23. Reisler, *By the Sweat of Their Brow,* pp. 12–13.

24. Ibid., p. 8.

25. María Villarreal Bosmans and Tony Bosmans interview, Feb. 10, 1985; Permit of Local Board for Registrant to Depart from the United States, Aug. 1, 1945, Federal Dis-charge Records, vol. 8, pp. 676–77, Office of County Clerk, Harris County, Tex.

26. María Villarreal Bosmans and Tony Bosmans interview, Feb. 10, 1985; Taylor, *American-Mexican Frontier,* pp. 98–99, 143–45.

27. María Villarreal Bosmans and Tony Bosmans interview, Feb. 10, 1985.

28. Montejano, *Anglos and Mexicans,* pp. 116–19.

29. María Villarreal Bosmans and Tony Bosmans interview, Feb. 10, 1985.

30. Ibid.; Webb, ed., *Handbook of Texas*, 2:839; *Texas Almanac and State Industrial Guide, 1911*, p. 357; Roy Grimes, ed., *Three Hundred Years in Victoria County*, pp. 448, 490–93; Montejano, *Anglos and Mexicans*, pp. 26–27.

31. De León, *The Tejano Community*, pp. 1, 7, 15; Webb, ed., *Handbook of Texas*, 1:699, 2:456, 2:839. An examination of the 1910 federal census for Victoria County, Tex., indicates that a sizable Mexican population of "day laborers" was in residence in Victoria and its environs and had, like the Villarreal-Tijerina family, entered the United States after 1900. See U.S. Bureau of the Census, Thirteenth Federal Census, 1910, Victoria County (microfilm), Texas and Local History, HPL.

32. De León, *The Tejano Community*, pp. 14–15, 18–19; Webb, ed., *Handbook of Texas*, 1:699; Montejano, *Anglos and Mexicans*, pp. 26–27, 29; María Villarreal Bosmans and Tony Bosmans interview, Feb. 10, 1985.

33. María Villarreal Bosmans and Tony Bosmans interview, Feb. 10, 1985, Tony Bosmans interview, May 19, 1986; An Index to Death Records, Texas, 1903–1940 (microfilm), Vol. 46, File No. 23588, Clayton Genealogical Library, Houston Public Library; Death Certificate of Librado Villarreal, Office of City Secretary, Victoria, Tex.

34. María Villarreal Bosmans and Tony Bosmans interview, Feb. 10, 1985.

35. Eric Walls, "Texas's 'Sugar Bowl' Heaps Three Million Pounds of Sugar Daily," *Texas Historian* 34, no. 2 (Nov., 1973): 2–7.

36. Ibid.; U.S. Bureau of the Census, Thirteenth Federal Census, 1910, Fort Bend County, Tex. (microfilm), pp. 112–19, Texas and Local History, HPL; William R. Johnson, *A Short History of the Sugar Industry in Texas*, p. 58; S. A. McMillan, *The Book of Fort Bend County Texas*, pp. 151–53.

37. Johnson, *A Short History of the Sugar Industry*, 66–71; T. C. Roselle and Herbert Shelton, interview by author, Sugar Land, Tex., Apr. 11, 1984; T. C. Roselle, telephone interview by author, Feb. 4, 1985; *Houston Post*, Nov. 12, 1922, p. 37.

38. Thirteenth Census, 1910, Fort Bend County, Tex.; interviews: Roselle and Shelton, Apr. 11, 1984; Tomasa De León, by author, Houston, Tex., June 20, 1980, Oral History Collection, HMRC.

39. Interviews: Herbert Shelton by author, Sugar Land, Tex., Apr. 11, 1984; Roselle and Shelton, Apr. 11, 1984; T. C. Roselle, by telephone by author, Feb. 12, 1985; María Villarreal Bosmans and Tony Bosmans, Feb. 10, 1985.

40. Interviews: Eleno Flores, by telephone by author, Jan. 12, Jan. 19, 1985; María Villarreal Bosmans and Tony Bosmans, Feb. 10, 1985; Roselle and Shelton, Apr. 11, 1984; Shelton, Apr. 11, 1984; Blas Rodríguez, Sr., by author, Sugar Land, Tex., Jan. 12, 1985.

41. Interviews: Victoria Tijerina, Mar. 1, 1981, Dec. 1, 1982; María Villarreal Bosmans and Tony Bosmans, Feb. 10, 1985; Tony Bosmans, May 19, 1986, Oct. 1, 1989 (telephone).

42. Shelton interview, Apr. 11, 1984; Flores interview, Jan. 12, 1985; Blas Rodríguez, Sr., interview, Jan. 12, 1985; Robert V. Haynes, *A Night of Violence: The Houston Riot of 1917*, p. 93.

43. Interviews: Victoria Tijerina, Feb. 1, 1985; Tony Bosmans, Oct. 1, 1989; Anselmo Villarreal, Feb. 5, 1985.

44. Portrait of Dionicia Villarreal Tijerina in possession of Victoria Tijerina as of February, 1985; interviews: Victoria Tijerina, Mar. 1, 1981, Feb. 1, 1985; Angelina Morales by author, Houston, Tex., Feb. 12, 1981; Mrs. Felix Tijerina, Sr., by author, Houston, Tex., Sept. 13, 1980, Sept. 4, 1982 (all subsequent interviews with Mrs. Felix Tijerina, Sr., conducted in Houston, Tex.).

45. María Villarreal Bosmans and Tony Bosmans interview, Feb. 10, 1985.

46. Interviews: Victoria Tijerina, Mar. 1, 1981; Eleno Flores, Jan. 19, 1985, June 21, 1985 (telephone); Mrs. Felix Tijerina, Sr., Sept. 13, 1980; "The Story and the Realization of a Dream," *LULAC in Action-Human Values, Unlimited,* Tijerina Papers.

47. Interviews: Mrs. Felix Tijerina, Sr., Sept. 13, 1980; Victoria Tijerina, Mar. 1, 1981, Feb. 1, 1985; *LULAC News,* Sept., 1958, p. 3, Alfred J. Hernández Papers, HMRC; Francisco Peña Ayala and Francisco Peña Garza interview, Sept. 26, 1997.

48. Interviews: Victoria Tijerina, Mar. 1, 1981, Feb. 1, 1985; Mrs. Felix Tijerina, Sr., Sept. 13, 1980; *LULAC News,* Sept., 1957, p. 4, Hernández Papers; "A Four-Hundred-Word Start," *Time,* Aug. 17, 1959, p. 56.

49. Interviews: Mrs. Felix Tijerina, Sr., Sept. 13, 1980; Victoria Tijerina, Mar. 1, 1981; "Felix Tijerina," speech delivered by Judge Edmund Duggan at presentation of "Man of the Year" award to Felix Tijerina, 1955, p. 2, "Speech Delivered . . . " Folder, Tijerina Papers.

50. "The Story and the Realization of a Dream," *LULAC in Action;* Ragsdale, "Biography: Felix Tijerina," p. 4; interviews: Mrs. Felix Tijerina, Sr., Sept. 13, 1980; Blas Rodríguez, Sr., Jan. 12, 1985. Blas Rodríguez, Sr.'s father, Juan Rodríguez, was a longtime employee of Imperial Sugar Company. Known to all as "Mexican Johnny," Rodríguez was hired in 1909 as the first Mexican American employee of the company. A friend of young Tijerina from his days in Sugar Land, Juan Rodríguez related to his son how he had secured the youngster the job as sample boy.

51. Roselle and Shelton interview, Apr. 11, 1984; "Sugarland Industries, Employees Numerical Register—From 1/1/21. To December 31, 1925. No. 1 to 4789 inclusive" (ledger), p. 18, Employee #648, Box 4, Imperial Sugar Company Records, HMRC. The identity of this "Filiberto Tyerina" as being one and the same as the subject of this biography is further confirmed by the fact that two friends of his named Doroteo Pina and a Felix Jasso (both of whom, as we shall see, he knew from Sugar Land in these days) also appear in close proximity to his name in this official ledger: "Doroteo Pena" (employee #662) appears on p. 18 with Filiberto and "Felix Joso" (employee #567), on p. 16. Pina is likewise found in the Fourteenth Federal Census, 1920, Fort Bend County, Tex., p. 121A (microfilm), Clayton Genealogical Library, Houston Public Library. According to the 1920 Census, Pina (age twenty-four) and his wife Petra (age eighteen) lived on the Dew brothers' plantation on Stafford Thompson Road in Fort Bend County. Examination of the 1920 Census failed to reveal the Tijerinas.

52. "Sugarland Industries, Employees Numerical Register—From 1/1/21. To December 31, 1925. No. 1 to 4789 inclusive" (ledger), p. 1–11, 20–50, Imperial Sugar Company Records, HMRC. His sister Victoria especially stressed that Felix did not like field work. (Victoria Tijerina interview, March 1, 1981.)

53. *Houston Chronicle,* Dec. 29, 1947, Clippings, Tijerina and LULAC 1940s Folder, Tijerina Papers.

54. Ragsdale, "Biography: Felix Tijerina," p. 4; District Court of the United States, Southern District of Texas, Houston Division, *Felix Tijerina, Plaintiff v. Herbert Brownell, Jr., Attorney General of the United States, et al.,* Civil Action No. 8113 (hereafter cited as *Tijerina v. Brownell*), "Complaint for Declaratory Judgment to Establish Citizenship," Mar. 25, 1954, p. 6; *Houston Post,* Aug. 8, 1955, pp. 1, 11; Blas Rodríguez, Sr., interview, Jan. 12, 1985; *Houston Post,* Sept. 3, 1922, p. 7; María Villarreal Bosmans and Tony Bosmans interview, Feb. 10, 1985.

55. Don E. Carleton and Thomas H. Kreneck, *Houston: Back Where We Started,* pp. 1–22; Don E. Carleton, *Red Scare!: Right- wing Hysteria, Fifties Fanaticism, and Their Legacy in Texas,* pp. 6–9; David G. McComb, *Houston: A History,* pp. 68–69, 77–81, 97–98; "The Story and the Realization of a Dream," *LULAC in Action.*

56. De León, *Ethnicity in the Sunbelt,* pp. 8–18; Kreneck, *Del Pueblo,* pp. 41–49; Rosales, "Mexicans in Houston," pp. 227–37.

57. Interviews: Victoria Tijerina, Feb. 1, 1985; María Villarreal Bosmans and Tony Bosmans, Feb. 10, 1985; Flores, Jan. 19, 1985; "The Story and the Realization of a Dream," *LULAC in Action.*

58. Interviews by author: Sigmund Frucht, Houston, Tex., Sept. 18 (telephone), 19, 1980; William Aguilar, Houston, Tex., Nov. 11, 1980.

59. Frucht interviews, Sept. 18, 19, 1980; Ragsdale, "Biography: Felix Tijerina," p. 4.

60. Frucht interviews, Sept. 18, 19, 1980; Ragsdale, "Biography: Felix Tijerina," p. 4.

61. Frucht interviews, Sept. 18, 19, 1980; Open House Guest Book, Feb. 1, 1959, Sig Frucht Papers, HMRC; Mrs. Felix Tijerina, Sr., interview, Sept. 13, 1980; John Jones, *This Is The Way It Was: The Reminiscences of Sig Frucht,* unnumbered section entitled "Friends," pp. 3–29; *Houston Post,* Jan. 14, Mar. 26, 1922. Tijerina's time in Houston without his family must have been intermittent or not have lasted for long. His sister Victoria could not recall being separated from him during these early years except when he came to Houston long enough to scout the area, find a job, and rent a house before bringing the family (Victoria Tijerina interviews, Sept. 17, 1980, Mar. 1, 1981, Feb. 1, 1985).

62. William Aguilar interview, Nov. 11, 1980; Jones, *This Is The Way It Was,* pp. 22–27; *Houston City Directory, 1922,* pp. 1854–55, 1923–24, 2060; Victoria Tijerina interview, Sept. 17, 1980.

63. William Aguilar interview, Nov. 11, 1980.

64. Interviews: Frucht, Sept. 19, 1980; Raúl Molina, Sr., by author, Houston, Tex., Dec. 12, 1984; Mrs. Felix Tijerina, Sr., Sept. 13, 1980, Dec. 5, 1989; Gloria Pina García by telephone with author, Houston, Tex., Dec. 11, 1989; Ragsdale, "Biography: Felix Tijerina," p. 4; Louis Alexander, "Cafeman Tijerina Likes to Help Boys," *Houston Chronicle,* May 18, 1953, Unprocessed Clippings, Tijerina Papers. Although printed accounts vary concerning the time and exact circumstances of Tijerina's earliest jobs in Houston, most all agree that he began at the Original Mexican Restaurant as a busboy.

65. María Villarreal Bosmans and Tony Bosmans interview, Feb. 10, 1985. The first

extant record of "Felix" Tijerina appears in *Houston City Directory, 1923–24*, pp. 1427, 1573. In his interviews of Sept. 18 and 19, 1980, Sig Frucht claimed that when he first met Tijerina in the early 1920s, he went by the name Felix and already "could speak pretty good English." Frucht stated that he had known Tijerina by no other first name than Felix.

66. De León, *Ethnicity in the Sunbelt*, pp. 4–5; Kreneck, *Del Pueblo*, pp. 19–22; Carleton, *Red Scare!*, pp. 9–10; Kenneth T. Jackson, *The Ku Klux Klan in the City, 1915–1930*, pp. 83–84; *Houston Post*, Apr. 21, 1922, p. 5; June 18, 1922, p. 1; *Colonel Mayfield's Weekly*, Jan. 7, 1922, p. 6; Mar. 25, 1922, p. 1; Apr. 8, 1922, p. 1; Apr. 15, 1922, p. 5; May 6, 1922, p. 1; Dec. 3, 1921, p. 3; Dec. 17, 1921, p. 1; Dec. 31, 1921, pp. 2, 4 (microfilm), Texas and Local History, HPL.

67. *Houston Post*, Mar. 13, 1922, p. 6; Apr. 8, 1922, p. 6; Apr. 13, 1922, p. 1; Apr. 14, 1922, pp. 1, 6; Apr. 16, 1922, p. 16; Apr. 17, 1922, p. 7; Apr. 21, 1922, p. 6; Apr. 22, 1922, p. 1; June 18, 1922, p. 1.

68. Ragsdale, "Biography: Felix Tijerina," p. 4; Victoria Tijerina interviews, Sept. 17, 1980, Mar. 1, 1981, Feb. 1, 1985.

69. Anselmo Villarreal interview; María Villarreal Bosmans and Tony Bosmans interview, Feb. 10, 1985.

70. Victoria Tijerina interviews, Sept. 17, 1980, Mar. 1, 1981, June 26, 1985.

CHAPTER 2. FROM *OBRERO* TO ENTREPRENEUR

1. Telephone Interviews by author, Houston, Tex.: Dianicia Contreras, Jan. 19, 1985, Dec. 7, 1989; George Jamail, Apr. 6, 1983; *Map of Houston, Harris Co., Texas,* by P. Whitty, Civil Engineer and Land Surveyor, 1900, Texas and Local History, HPL; *1923 Street Map of the City of Houston* by Texas Map and Blue Printing Co., Texas and Local History, HPL; *Houston Post,* Oct. 22, 1922, p. 35.

2. Contreras interview, Jan. 19, 1985; *Houston City Directory, 1922,* pp. 1440, 1495, 1625, 1630; *Houston City Directory, 1923–24,* pp. 1573, 1642, 1798, 1803.

3. *Houston City Directory, 1923–24,* pp. 1573, 1642, 1798, 1803; Jamail interview, Apr. 6, 1983; John J. Herrera, interviews by author, Houston, Tex., May 22, May 25, 1981, John J. Herrera Papers, HMRC (hereafter cited as Herrera Papers).

4. Interviews: Jamail, Apr. 6, 1983; Contreras, Jan. 19, 1985.

5. Contreras interview, Jan. 19, 1985; Victoria Tijerina interviews, Mar. 1, 1981, Dec. 1, 1982.

6. Contreras interview, Jan. 19, 1985.

7. Ibid.; Anselmo Villarreal interview, Feb. 5, 1985.

8. Contreras interview, Jan. 19, 1985.

9. Ibid., Dec. 7, 1989.

10. *Houston Post,* Jan. 28, 1922; *Houston City Directory, 1908–1909,* p. 108; *Houston City Directory, 1922,* p. 1056.

11. William A. Bernrieder, interview by author, Houston, Tex., Dec. 7, 1982; *Houston Post,* Sept. 4, 1934, p. 6.

12. Mrs. Felix Tijerina, Sr., interview, Dec. 8, 1989; *Houston Post,* Aug. 8, 1955, p. 11; Bernrieder interview, Dec. 7, 1982.

13. *Houston Post,* Aug. 8, 1955, p. 11; "A 400-Word Start," p. 56.

14. *Houston Post,* Aug. 8, 1955, p. 11.

15. *Houston Post,* Sept. 4, 1934, p. 6; Ragsdale, "Biography: Felix Tijerina," p. 4; *Houston Post,* Aug. 8, 1955, p. 11; Marie Dauplaise, "They Have a Simple Dream, 400 English Words for Every Child," *Houston Press,* Mar. 12, 1958; Elliott, "Now Juanito Can Read," p. 134.

16. Portrait of Felix Tijerina, ca. mid-1920s, Tijerina Papers.

17. Ragsdale, "Biography: Felix Tijerina," p. 4.

18. *Houston City Directory, 1923–24,* pp. 1300, 1427, 1793.

19. Ibid., p. 1190; *Houston City Directory, 1925,* p. 1303; Gloria Pina García interviews, Dec. 11, 1989, Jan. 5, 1990 (telephone); "Sugarland Industries, Employees Numerical Register," Employee #662, p. 18, Imperial Sugar Company Records, HMRC; Fourteenth Federal Census, 1920, Fort Bend County, p. 121A.

20. María Villarreal Bosmans and Tony Bosmans interview, Feb. 10, 1985; Tony Bosmans interview, Oct. 1, 1989; *Houston City Directory, 1923–24,* p. 1458.

21. *Houston City Directory, 1925,* p. 1594; Victoria Tijerina interview, Mar. 1, 1981; David Rodríguez, telephone interview by author, Beaumont, Tex., June 14, 1993.

22. *Tijerina v. Brownell,* Mar. 25, 1954, pp. 4–5, and Feb. 15, 1956, Plaintiff's Exhibit 8, "Statement of Felix Tijerina made at Houston, Texas, before Acting Naturalization Examiner William P. Autrey on Mar. 26, 1940, in the English language," p. 2; "Felix Tijerina Offers Proof of U.S. Birth," *Houston Press,* Feb. 15, 1956, p. 10.

23. *Houston City Directory, 1926,* p. 1684; *1927,* pp. 1814–15; *1928,* pp. 1762–63; interviews: Mrs. Felix Tijerina, Sr., Dec. 8, 1989; Victoria Tijerina, Mar. 1, 1981; Jesús Ayala López, Sept. 26, 1997.

24. Interviews: Herrera, May 25, 1981; Contreras, Jan. 5, 1990 (telephone); Robert C. Giles, *125th Anniversary: Diocese of Galveston- Houston, 1847-1972,* pp. 100–101.

25. Interviews: Victoria Tijerina, Mar. 1, 1981; Gloria Pina García, Dec. 11, 1989; Sister Mary Paul Valdez, M.C.D.P., *The History of the Missionary Catechists of Divine Providence,* pp. 1–6.

26. Valdez, *The History of the Missionary Catechists,* p. 3; Kathleen E. Houston, "Our Lady of Guadalupe Church to Celebrate Anniversary Today," *Houston Post,* Dec. 12, 1937.

27. Valdez, *The History of the Missionary Catechists,* pp. 11–12; Victoria Tijerina interview, Dec. 1, 1982.

28. Valdez, *The History of the Missionary Catechists,* pp. 3–4, 11; interviews: Herrera, May 25, 1981; Rev. Anton Frank by author, Houston, Tex., Feb. 1, 1981.

29. Mary Villagómez, telephone interview by author, Houston, Tex., Jan. 9, 1990; Our Lady of Guadalupe Church, Confirmation Register, pp. 18, 24, 30, 43, 46, 55, 89, 237, 246 (microfilm), Genealogical Dept., LDS; Our Lady of Guadalupe Church, *Bap-*

tismorum Registrum Ecclesiae, vol. 4, May 16, 1924–Jan., 1926, p. 54 (microfilm), Genealogical Dept., LDS; Gloria Pina García interview, Dec. 11, 1989.

30. Our Lady of Guadalupe Church, *Liber Matrimoniorum in Ecclesia,* pp. 35–40 (microfilm), Genealogical Dept., LDS.

31. *Boletín parroquial,* Our Lady of Guadalupe bulletin, Apr., 1928 (vol. 1, no. 1), inside cover, Juan Rodríguez Family Collection, HMRC.

32. Interviews: Victoria Tijerina, Mar. 1, 1981; Contreras, Jan. 19, 1985, Dec. 7, 1989; Dow School Census, 1925, Dow School, Houston, Texas. The only school in Houston at this time exclusively for children of Mexican parentage was located far east of downtown in Magnolia Park. Founded in 1920 and called the Mexican School, it changed its name to Lorenzo de Zavala Elementary in 1928. See Lynne W. Denison and L. L. Pugh, "Houston Public School Buildings: Their History and Location" (typescript, 1936), p. 87, Texas and Local History, HPL.

33. *Houston Post,* Aug. 8, 1955, p. 11; Judge Felix Salazar, Jr., telephone interview by author, Houston, Tex., Apr. 21, 1997.

34. Primitivo L. Niño, interview by author, Mar. 16, 1979, Oral History Collection, HMRC.

35. Interviews: E. J. García by author, Houston, Tex., Dec. 12, 1981; Leo Reynosa by author, Houston, Tex., Mar. 25, 1983; Salazar, Apr. 21, 1997; McComb, *Houston,* p. 98; Alfredo Sarabia and Socorro Sarabia, interview by author, Houston, Tex., Aug. 28, 1980, Oral History Collection, HMRC; Mrs. Raúl Molina, Sr., telephone interview by author, Houston, Tex., Dec. 14, 1989.

36. *Gaceta mexicana: revista quincenal* (Houston), Sept. 15, 1928 (microfilm), HMRC.

37. Mrs. Felix Tijerina, Sr., interviews, Oct. 16, 1978, Sept. 13, 1980, Jan. 12, 1990 (telephone).

38. Ibid., Jan. 12, 1990.

39. Ibid., Oct. 16, 1978, Jan. 12, 1990, Aug. 8, 1992.

40. Ibid.

41. Ibid., Sept. 13, 1980; William Aguilar interview, Nov. 11, 1980; *El anunciador* (Houston), Feb. 21, 1925; Photograph Box, Tijerina Papers.

42. *Gaceta mexicana,* Sept. 15, 1928.

43. Ibid., p. 45.

44. Interviews: Ramón Fernández by author, Houston, Tex., Sept. 24, 1982; Gloria Pina García, Dec. 11, 1989; William Aguilar, Nov. 11, 1980.

45. *Gaceta mexicana,* Sept. 17, 1928, p. 2; *Houston City Directory, 1928,* p. 1040; interviews: Mrs. Raúl Molina, Sr., Dec. 12, 1984, Dec. 14, 1989; Manuel Crespo, Sr., by author, Houston, Tex., Apr. 1, 1981; Augustine Gabino by author, Houston, Tex., Feb. 8, 1983.

46. A. Reynaga with Felix Tijerina, Co-Partnership Agreement, No. 429052, Partnership Records, vol. 3, pp. 168–69, Harris County, Tex., Records.

47. Ibid.

48. *Houston Post,* Aug. 15, 1929, p. 12.

49. Mrs. Felix Tijerina, Sr., interview, Sept. 13, 1980; *Houston Classified Telephone Directory,* Oct., 1929 (Southwestern Bell Telephone Company, 1929), p. 156; *Telephone*

Directory for Houston, Apr., 1929 (Southwestern Bell Telephone Company, 1929), p. 84; Assumed Name Certificate, 5247, "Mexican Inn," July 16, 1929, Harris County, Tex., Records.

50. *Houston City Directory, 1929-30,* pp. 2562–66; *Houston Classified Telephone Directory,* Oct., 1929, p. 157.

CHAPTER 3. EMERGENCE OF A
LATIN AMERICAN LEADER

1. García, *Mexican Americans,* pp. 1–22.

2. *Houston City Directory, 1929–30,* pp. 1743, 1783; *1931–32,* p. 1759; Victoria Tijerina interviews, Mar. 1, 1981, Dec. 1, 1982.

3. *Telephone Directory for Houston,* Oct., 1929, p. 162; *Houston City Directory, 1928,* p. 2296; *1929–30,* p. 2367; Victoria Tijerina interview, Mar. 1, 1981; *Map of Houston, 1928* (River Oaks Corporation), Texas and Local History, HPL.

4. *Telephone Directory for Houston, Apr., 1930,* p. 166; *Sept., 1930,* p. 164; interviews: Victoria Tijerina, Mar. 1, 1981; Gloria Pina García, Dec. 11, 1989; Contreras, Jan. 19, 1985; *Houston City Directory, 1931–32,* p. 1735; *125th Anniversary: Diocese of Galveston-Houston,* p. 101; interviews: Mrs. Felix Tijerina, Sr., Sept. 13, 1980; Herrera, May 22, 1981; "Sam Houston Graduates from 1879 through 1939" (Binder), Spring Term— 1934, Sam Houston High School Records, HMRC.

5. *Houston City Directory, 1928–30,* pp. 1743, 1783; Victoria Tijerina interview, Feb. 1, 1985.

6. Interviews: William Aguilar, Nov. 11, 1980; Mrs. Felix Tijerina, Sr., Sept. 13, 1980; McComb, *Houston,* pp. 115–16; James M. Sorelle, "'An de Po Cullud Man Is in de Wuss Fix uv Awl': Black Occupational Status in Houston, Texas, 1920–1940," *Houston Review* 1, no. 1 (spring, 1979), pp. 15–26; Marilyn D. Rhinehart and Thomas H. Kreneck, "'In the Shadow of Uncertainty': Texas Mexicans and Repatriation in Houston During the Great Depression," *Houston Review* 10, no. 1 (spring, 1988): 21–33.

7. No. 432393, A. Reynaga with Felix Tijernia [*sic*], Dissolution of Partnership, Partnership Records, vol. 3, p. 170, Harris County, Tex.

8. *Houston City Directory, 1929–30,* p. 1145; Mrs. Felix Tijerina, Sr., interviews, Sept. 13, 1980, Mar. 1, 1990 (telephone).

9. *Houston Classified Telephone Directory, Apr., 1930,* p. 155; Nov., 1933, p. 98.

10. Diego Arturo Pino, interview by author, Houston, Tex., Feb. 26, 1986, Oral History Collection, HMRC; *El tecolote* (Houston), May, 1932, Scrapbook Clipping, Melecio Gómez Family Collection, HMRC; *Houston Post,* Apr. 2, 1933, p. 7; interviews: Mrs. Felix Tijerina, Sr., Mar. 1, 1990; Frank Brett by telephone with author, Houston, Tex., Jan. 19, 1985.

11. Leo Reynosa, interview by author, Houston, Tex., May 13, 1981; Barbara Karkabi, "Riding with Pancho Villa Is Lasting Memory for Restaurateur," *Houston Chronicle,* Sept. 21, 1986, sec. 7, p. 6; Francisco Peña Ayala interview, Sept. 26, 1997.

12. Angelina Morales, telephone interview by author, Houston, Tex., Apr. 10, 1990.

13. *Houston Post,* Mar. 22, 1933, p. 8, col. 1; Rodrigo García, telephone interview by author, Houston, Tex., Dec. 1, 1982.

14. *Houston Chronicle,* Mar. 29, 1915, p. 10; Kreneck, *Del Pueblo,* p. 46; *Houston Post,* Mar. 6, 1934, p. 10, col. 8; Mar. 12, 1933, p. 5, col. 3; Apr. 5, 1933, p. 8, col. 7; Apr. 24, 1933, p. 6; May 4, p. 11, col. 1.

15. Rodrigo García interview, Dec. 1, 1982; Photograph of the Mexican Inn Baseball Team, Houston, Tex., Apr., 1934, Mr. and Mrs. Lupe García Collection, Mexican American Small Collections, HMRC; *Houston Post,* Aug. 3, 1934, p. 8, col. 1; Mar. 30, 1934, p. 9, col. 1; Mar. 31, 1934, p. 9, col. 1; and Apr. 1, 1934, p. 6, col. 1. The sports pages of the *Houston Post* reveal continuous existence of the team from Mar. 17, 1933, through at least September, 1935.

16. Undated newspaper clipping (Houston), ca. mid-1930s, Tijerina Papers; Juvencio Rodríguez, interview by author, Houston, Tex., Nov. 25, 1980; *Houston Post,* May 14, 1933, p. 18, col. 4; May 23, 1933, p. 11, col. 6; Aug. 8, 1933, p. 9, col. 2; Aug. 30, 1933, p. 15, col. 3; May 9, 1934, p. 12, col. 7; May 3, 1935, p. 11, col. 8; July 14, 1935, p. 12, col. 7; Aug. 30, 1935, p. 9, col. 4.

17. *Matrimoniorum Registrum Ecclesiae,* Jan. 3, 1925–Nov. 23, 1940, p. 66, Our Lady of Guadalupe Church Records (microfilm), Houston, Tex., Microfilm Order 0025193, Genealogical Dept., LDS; Mrs. Felix Tijerina, Sr., interviews, Sept. 13, 1980, Mar. 1, 1990; Wedding Portrait, Photograph Box, Tijerina Papers.

18. Mrs. Felix Tijerina, Sr., interviews, Sept. 13, 1980, Apr. 27, 1991; *Houston City Directory, 1934,* pp. 642, 1438; *1935,* pp. 1489, 1738. Mrs. Tijerina stated that although the 1934 *Houston City Directory* listed a Felipa Tijerina with the family on West Street, no such person existed.

19. "Baile de Gala Blanco y Negro, Club México Bello, 1965" (program, Houston, 1965), "Historia," p. 1, Folder 13, Box 3, Club México Bello Records; De León, *Ethnicity in the Sunbelt,* pp. 33–34.

20. Interviews: Rodrigo García, Dec. 1, 1982; Mrs. Felix Tijerina, Sr., Feb. 22, 1981; "Club Cultural Recreativo México Bello, enero 7, 1934, Houston, Texas," Photograph Mss. 330-10, Isidro García Collection, HMRC; *El tecolote,* Scrapbook, Chaírez Family Collection, HMRC (hereafter cited as Chaírez Collection).

21. Interviews by author: Leo Reynosa and Mrs. Felix Tijerina, Sr., Houston, Tex., May 13, 1981; Morales, Feb. 12, 1981, Apr. 10, 1990; E. J. García, Nov. 21, 1980.

22. *Houston Chronicle,* May 27, July 9, 1933, Scrapbook, Chaírez Collection.

23. *Houston Post,* Aug. 12, 1933; *Houston Chronicle,* Aug. 12, 1933, Scrapbook, Chaírez Collection; Estella Gómez Reyes, interview by author, Houston, Tex., Oct. 5, 1989.

24. "Club Cultural Recreativo México Bello," Photograph Mss 330-10, Isidro García Collection; *El tecolote,* Jan. 7, 1934, Feb. 25, 1934; *Houston Chronicle,* Dec. 14, 1934, both in Scrapbook, Chaírez Collection.

25. *El tecolote,* Sept., 1934, Nov. 16, 1934, Dec. 22, 1934, Mar. 20, 1935, Apr. 6, 1935; *Houston Post,* Nov. 16, 1934, Apr. 5, 1935; *La patria* (clipping), Nov. 30, 1934, all in Scrapbook, Chaírez Collection; *Houston Chronicle,* Feb. 12, 1933, p. 12; Bernrieder interview, Dec. 7, 1982.

26. *El tecolote,* Feb. 25, 1934, Nov. 16, 1934; *La prensa* (San Antonio), Feb. 25, 1934, Nov. 25, 1934, Dec. 2, 1934; *Houston Post,* Apr. 22, 1934, Scrapbook, Chaírez Collection.

27. *Houston Chronicle,* 1934; *El tecolote,* July, 1934, Aug., 1934, Sept., 1934, Oct. 18, 1934, Nov. 5, 1935; *Houston Post,* Oct. 18, 1934, Scrapbook, Chaírez Collection; Fred Nahas, telephone interview by author, Houston, Tex., Dec. 2, 1982.

28. Interviews: William Aguilar, Nov. 11, 1980; Rodrigo García, Dec. 1, 1982; Rebecca Aguilar by telephone with author, Houston, Tex., Mar. 14, 1990; "Club Recreativo Internacional, Houston, Texas, 1935," Photograph by Cantú Studio, Mexican-American Photograph Collection, HMRC.

29. *El puerto* (Magnolia Park, Houston), Nov. 8, 1935, p. 1, HMRC; *Houston Post,* Oct. 29, 1936, p. 3; Sept. 10, 1937, p. 5, col. 7.

30. García, *Mexican Americans,* pp. 25–31, 34; "Founding and History of LULAC," by George J. Garza, in *LULAC: Fifty Years of Serving Hispanics.* Ben Garza owned and operated the Metropolitan Cafe in Corpus Christi. See *Corpus Christi City Directory,* vol. 6, 1929, p. 214.

31. García, *Mexican Americans,* pp. 31, 35, 46–47.

32. Ibid., pp. 30, 37, 53; "Aims and Purposes" (of LULAC) and "Founding and History of LULAC," in *LULAC: Fifty Years of Serving Hispanics.*

33. García, *Mexican Americans,* pp. 31–32, 42–46; *Houston Chronicle,* June 13, 1935, p. 5.

34. *LULAC News,* Mar., 1933, inside front cover, LULAC Records, HMRC; *LULAC News,* Mar. 1934, p. 3, LULAC Folder, E. E. Mireles and Jovita González de Mireles Papers, Special Collections and Archives, Bell Library, TAMU-CC (hereafter cited as Mireles Papers).

35. De León, *Ethnicity in the Sunbelt,* pp. 82–83.

36. Manuel Crespo, Sr., interview by author, Houston, Tex., Jan. 30, 1984.

37. Interviews: Crespo, Apr. 1, 1981; Juvencio Rodríguez, Nov. 25, 1980 (telephone).

38. *Houston Chronicle,* Apr. 9, 1935, p. 25.

39. Ibid., Mar. 13, 1935, p. 12; Apr. 9, 1935, p. 25; June 9, 1935, p. 20; June 26, 1935, p. 19; July 3, 1935, p. 14.

40. Ibid., May 12, 1935, sec. 1, p. 14; May 13, 1935, sec. 1, p. 3.; *Houston City Directory, 1935,* p. 826; *Houston Press,* May 13, 1935, sec. 1, p. 11.

41. *Houston Press,* May 13, 1935, sec. 1, p. 11; *Houston Chronicle,* May 13, 1935, p. 12.

42. A check of the marriage books of Our Lady of Guadalupe Church in Houston (*Matrimoniorum Registrum Ecclesiae,* Jan. 3, 1925–Nov. 23, 1940, p. 66, Our Lady of Guadalupe Church Records [microfilm], Houston, Tex., Microfilm Order 0025193) revealed that the spaces for the *dies e locus baptismi* (date and location of the baptism of the persons being married) for Felix and Janie's marriage, no. 644, p. 66, were left blank. These church records list more than fifteen hundred marriages from 1911 through 1940. The vast majority of the marriages entered have the space for the baptism information completed (and most were from Mexico). This omission suggests that Felix may have deliberately avoided committing to record his Mexican origins since, according to Mexican church records cited in chapter 1, his baptism was in General Escobedo. This theory

is rendered inconclusive, however, by that fact that six of the other nine couples listed on the same page with Felix and Janie also left the space for baptism information unfilled, an unusually high number for these records.

43. Interviews: Herrera, Nov. 5, 1983; Crespo, Apr. 1, 1981, Jan. 30, 1984.

44. Interviews: Juvencio Rodríguez, Nov. 25, 1980; Herrera, Nov. 5, 1983; García, *Mexican Americans,* p. 40.

45. Juvencio Rodríguez interview, Nov. 25, 1980; *Houston Chronicle,* Aug. 2, 1935, p. 10; Constitution of the Latin American Club, Houston, Tex., Harris County, pp. 1–2, Juvencio Rodríguez Collection, HMRC.

46. Constitution of the Latin American Club, cover, p. 3.

47. Ibid., p. 4.

48. Ibid.

49. *Houston Chronicle,* Aug. 22, 1935, p. 10; unidentified clippings, ca. 1936: "Latin Americans Drive for 10,000 qualified voters," "Mann Addresses Club on Campaign," "Monteith Endorsed for Judge's Office," "U.S. Security Board Replies To Club Here"; Latin American Club, Committee to Honorable Joe H. Eagle (memorandum), Social Security board to Honorable Joe H. Eagle, Nov. 28, 1936 (Western Union telegram), all in Juvencio Rodríguez Collection; Juvencio Rodríguez, interview by author, Houston, Tex., Nov. 23, 1980.

50. Juvencio Rodríguez interviews, Nov. 23, 25, 1980.

51. *El puerto,* Aug. 12, 1938, p. 1, HMRC; "Latin-American Health Week Is To Be Observed" (clipping, ca. May, 1938), Juvencio Rodríguez Collection; Minutes of Meetings, Apr. 9, 1936, Club México Bello Records, all in HMRC.

52. *Houston, Texas Classified Telephone Directory, June, 1936,* pp. 122–23; *Houston Chronicle,* Sept. 3, 1934, p. 1. In 1943, Raúl Molina, Sr., purchased the Mexico City Restaurant on Main Street. He subsequently renamed the establishment Molina's Mexico City Restaurant and would, along with his family, expand Molina's into a popular Houston restaurant chain. See narrative history (1997) of restaurant on the menu of Molina's Mexican Restaurant. Apparently, after selling the restaurant to Molina in 1943, Antonio Renaga moved back to Monterrey. Molina interview, Dec. 14, 1989.

53. Ragsdale, "Biography: Felix Tijerina," p. 11. The final listing in the Houston telephone directory for the Mexican Inn Restaurant appeared in the November, 1935 issue; in the next issue, June, 1936, there is no listing.

54. *Houston Post,* Mar. 15, 1936, p. 18, col. 1; Ragsdale, "Biography: Felix Tijerina," p. 4; *Houston Post,* Aug. 8, 1955, p. 11; *Houston City Directory, 1936,* pp. 1405, 1421.

55. Mrs. Felix Tijerina, Sr., interviews, May 31, 1983, Apr. 20, 1990 (telephone).

56. Fernández interview, Sept. 24, 1982.

57. A number of people I interviewed made negative comments about Janie's premarital behavior, but all asked not to be identified.

58. *Houston City Directory, 1937–1938,* pp. 1318, 1581, 2122; interviews: Fernández, Sept. 24, 1982; Mrs. Felix Tijerina, Sr., Sept. 13, 1980; Rosie Tijerina Solíz by telephone with author, Dec. 28, 1990.

59. Mrs. Felix Tijerina, Sr., interview, Mar. 1, 1990; clippings: Bob Tutt, "Bet was a hot meal ticket," *Houston Chronicle,* Mar. 18, 1990, sec. C, p. 7; *Houston Post,* Apr. 21,

1934, June 7, 1974; *Houston Chronicle,* "Watchem," Dec. 15, 1976, sec. 4, p. 3, all in "Horseracing" Vertical File, Texas and Local History, HPL.

60. *Houston Chronicle,* Mar. 18, 1990, sec. C, p. 7; Mrs. Felix Tijerina, Sr., interviews, June 17, 1982, Mar. 1, 1990; *Houston Post,* Aug. 8, 1955, p. 11; Sammie Alderete, interview by author, Houston, Tex., Mar. 14, 1983.

61. Mrs. Felix Tijerina, Sr., interview, June 17, 1982; Ragsdale, "Biography: Felix Tijerina," p. 4; Photographs of "Felix Mexican Restaurant," ca. 1938, Photograph Box, Tijerina Papers.

62. Ragsdale, "Biography: Felix Tijerina," p. 4; *Houston Chronicle,* June 1, 1938, sec. 2, p. 19; interviews: Daniel Sandoval by telephone with author, Baytown, Tex., June 12, 1997; Mrs. Felix Tijerina, Sr., Sept. 13, 1980; Morales, Feb. 12, 1981; Richard Holgin, interview by author, Corpus Christi, Tex., Aug. 13, 1997.

63. Mrs. Felix Tijerina, Sr., interviews, Sept. 13, 1980, June 17, 1882.

64. Certificate Operation Under Assumed Name, No. 13327, Records of County Clerk, Harris County, Tex.; Mrs. Felix Tijerina, Sr., interview, May 1, 1990.

65. Mrs. Felix Tijerina, Sr., interviews, Sept. 13, 1980, June 17, 1882; Ragsdale, "Biography: Felix Tijerina," p. 4.

66. Meeting Notes and Attendance Rolls for Club México Bello, 1937–1940, Folder 2, Box 1, and Club México Bello Dance Program, 1940, Folder 11, Box 1, both in Club México Bello Records; *Houston Post,* Nov. 24, 1937, sec. 8, p. 8; *El puerto* (Magnolia Park, Houston), July 22, 1938, p. 3; Oct. 7, 1938, p. 5, HMRC; Photograph of Chaírez Wedding Party, 1941, taken by Gregorio Cantú, in Mr. and Mrs. Félix H. Morales Papers, HMRC.

67. *El puerto,* July 15, 1938, p. 3, HMRC; "Tempest Abates After San Jacinto Day 'Joke,'" May 12, 1938, Clippings, Juvencio Rodríguez Collection.

68. *El puerto,* Aug. 12, 1938, p. 1; Aug. 26, 1938, p. 1, HMRC; "Mexico Club to Push Program for Juveniles," ca. late 1930s, Clippings, Tijerina Papers.

69. *El puerto,* Aug. 26, 1938, p. 1, HMRC; "Work Started by Group on Aiding Mexican Youths," ca. late 1930s, Clippings, Tijerina Papers.

70. "Mexico Club to Push Program for Juveniles."

71. "Judge Scores Those Preying upon Helpless," ca. late 1930s, Clippings, Tijerina Papers.

72. *Houston Chronicle,* May 18, 1953, Clippings, Tijerina Papers; *Houston Post,* Aug. 8, 1955, sec. 1, p. 11; Mrs. Felix Tijerina, Sr., interview, Sept. 13, 1980; *LULAC News,* Nov., 1959, p. 3, Cortes Papers.

73. Verle Witham, telephone interviews by author, Houston, Tex., Feb. 1, 16, 1992.

74. "Tijerina Organizes Mexican Team to Aid Chest Campaign," and "Mexican Team to Aid Chest," ca. 1938, Clippings, Tijerina Papers; *Houston Chronicle,* Nov. 1, 1938, sec. A, p. 8; Nov. 9, 1938, sec. A, pp. 1, 9; *The Houston Community Chest and Its Agencies: Campaign for 1937* (pamphlet), Texas and Local History, HPL.

75. *The Houston Community Chest: A Description of Nine Months' Working, with a Statement of Accounts and a List of Subscribers, with Amounts Pledged, 1925; 1927; 1928; 1930* (pamphlets), p. 44 , all in Texas and Local History, HPL; "Tijerina Organizes Mexican Team to Aid Chest Campaign."

76. "Tijerina Organizes Mexican Team to Aid Chest Campaign."

77. "Felix Tijerina Heads Latin-American Drive for Chest" and "Mexican Boys' Group Leader to Aid Chest," ca. 1939, Clippings, Tijerina Papers; *Houston Post,* Nov. 15, 1939, sec. 1, pp. 1, 3.

78. "Tijerina Organizes Mexican Team to Aid Chest Campaign"; "Mexican Boys' Group Leader to Aid Chest."

79. *Houston,* Oct., 1939, pp. 10−11, Texas and Local History, HPL.

80. Guest Dedication (name tag ribbons), San Jacinto Museum of History, Apr. 20−21, 1939, Tijerina Papers.

81. *Houston Chronicle,* May 29, 1939, Clipping, Juan Rodríguez Family Collection.

82. *El puerto,* Sept. 2, 1938, p. 2, HMRC.

83. De León, *Ethnicity in the Sunbelt,* pp. 45−47, 49−51, 54−55; Kreneck, *Del Pueblo,* pp. 72−83, 86−109.

84. Rhinehart and Kreneck, "'In the Shadow of Uncertainty,'" pp. 21−22.

85. Ibid., pp. 21−33.

86. Ibid, pp. 25−26; *El puerto,* July 29, Aug. 5, Aug. 12, Aug. 26, 1938, HMRC; Morales interview, Apr. 10, 1990.

87. Statement of Felix Tijerina made at Houston, Tex., before Acting Naturalization Examiner William P. Autrey on Mar. 26, 1940, in the English Language, p. 2 (hereafter cited as Statement of Felix Tijerina, Mar. 26, 1940), Exhibits, Civil Action No. 8113, *Tijerina v. Brownell,* Feb. 15, 1956 (hereafter cited as *Tijerina v. Brownell* Exhibits, Feb. 15, 1956); Reynosa interview, May 13, 1981.

88. "Felix Tijerina Offers Proof of U.S. Birth," *Houston Press,* Feb. 15, 1956, p. 10; "Restaurateur Continues Fight on Citizenship," *Houston Chronicle,* Feb. 15, 1956, sec. B, p. 9.

89. Statement of Felix Tijerina, Mar. 26, 1940, pp. 1−2; Certificate of Birth, No. 14963, for Felix Tijerina, Filed Mar. 27, 1940, Bureau of Vital Statistics, Texas Department of Health, County of Travis. (*Tijerina v. Brownell* Exhibits, Feb. 15, 1956). The 1920 federal census for Fort Bend County lists a Robert Flanagan, age forty-one, whose occupation was captain at the state prison farm. Presumably, this individiual was Buck Flanagan. See Fourteenth Federal Census, 1920, Fort Bend County, p. 162A. The last name of the African American midwife appears in various documents as Fueler, Fueller, and Fuller. I chose to use Fueler because it appears as such on her 1940 affidavit.

90. Statement of Felix Tijerina, Mar. 26, 1940, pp. 1−3.

91. Ibid.

92. Certificate of Birth for Victoria Tijerina, No. 15357, Filed Apr. 1, 1940, Bureau of Vital Statistics, Texas Department of Health, Austin, Tex.

93. George F. Elsenbroich, Naturalization Examiner (Report of Apr. 6, 1940, Conversation with Felix Tijerina), Apr. 11, 1940, *Tijerina v. Brownell* Exhibits, Feb. 15, 1956.

94. Dr. Louis J. Marchiafava, interview by author, Houston, Tex., Dec. 20, 1982.

95. Morales interviews, Feb. 12, 1981, Apr. 10, 1990.

96. According to legal advice printed in a local Houston *colonia* newspaper during the late 1930s, "illegal aliens" could have "legalize[d] their residency" (through a formal application process with the INS) if they had entered the United States before mid-1921.

Though Tijerina could have met this initial requirement, the naturalization process was lengthy and had no guarantee of a successful resolution for the applicant. See *El puerto,* July 29, 1938, p. 1, HMRC.

97. Marchiafava interview, Dec. 20, 1982.

98. *Houston, Texas, Classified Telephone Directory, Aug., 1940,* p. 205; *The Woman's Building of Houston Directory* (Houston, 1941), in Tijerina Papers.

99. Ragsdale, "Biography: Felix Tijerina," p. 4; "3er Baile Blanco, Club Social Terpsicore" (program, May, 1940), Folder 11, Box 1, Club México Bello Records; Pat Manley, "Mrs. Felix Is Kept Busy Aiding Others, Planning Tour," *Houston Chronicle,* July 31, 1953, sec. D, p. 2; *Houston City Directory, 1941,* pp. 358, 1216; Mrs. Felix Tijerina, Sr., interview, May 1, 1990.

100. Mrs. Felix Tijerina, Sr., interviews, May 11, 1981, June 17, 1982; *Houston Post,* Aug. 8, 1955, p. 11; *Beaumont, Texas, Telephone Directory, Apr., 1942* (Southwestern Bell Telephone Company, 1942), p. 26; *Texas Almanac, 1939–40,* p. 103, foldout Texas map; *Texas Almanac, 1941–42,* p. 466; David Rodríguez interview, June 14, 1993; *Beaumont City Directory, 1941* (Morrison & Fourmy Directory Co., 1941), pp. 530, 550–51. A search by the county clerk's office of Jefferson County on May 4, 1990, failed to reveal the original registration document for the Felix Mexican Restaurant in Beaumont. The first year it appears in their assumed names file is 1944.

101. Mrs. Felix Tijerina, Sr., interviews, May 11, 1981, June 17, 1982; David Rodríguez interview, June 14, 1993; Gary Smith, telephone interview by author, Beaumont, Tex., Jan. 29, 1997; *Beaumont Journal,* Aug. 23, 1967, p. 10; Dec. 17, 1941, p. 14; Dec. 23, 1941, p. 16.

CHAPTER 4. HORATIO ALGER SUCCESS STORY

1. Federal Discharge Records, vol. 8, pp. 676–77; Webb, ed., *Handbook of Texas,* 1:556.

2. Federal Discharge Records, vol. 8, pp. 676–77; telephone interviews by author, Houston, Tex.: Bill Williams, Nov. 18, 1982; Luther E. Allbritton, Apr. 9, 1990.

3. Federal Discharge Records, vol. 8, pp. 676–77.

4. Interviews: Victoria Tijerina, Mar. 1, 1981; Morales, Feb. 12, 1981; Mrs. Felix Tijerina, Sr., Mar. 1, 1990; Allbritton, Apr. 9, 1990; *Houston Post,* Aug. 8, 1955, p. 11.

5. *Houston Chronicle,* Apr. 25, 1943, p. 10.

6. Reynosa interview, Feb. 6, 1979, Oral History Collection, HMRC; Mrs. Felix Tijerina, Sr., telephone interview, Feb. 14, 1995; Certificate No. 26042, June 14, 1944, and Certificate No. 63595, Aug. 1, 1951, Assumed Name Index, Records of Harris County Clerk, Harris County, Houston, Tex.; "Leo's faces difficult move," *Houston Chronicle,* July 11, 1989, sec. D, pp. 1, 10; "Sociedad 'Unión Fraternal' Quarto Aniversario" (brochure, Houston, 1944), pp. 1–2, 7,; and "5 de Mayo de 1944" (program), both in Juvencio Rodríguez Collection.

7. De León, *Ethnicity in the Sunbelt,* pp. 89–93; LULAC Banquet Program, Jan. 18, 1942, Folder 1, Box 5, Herrera Papers.

8. Program of the Regional State Convention of the League of United Latin American Citizens, Arabia Temple, Aug. 29, 1943, Rudy Vara Folder, Box 3, Small Collections, HMRC; Membership Rosters, 1940s–1950s Folder, LULAC Records, HMRC.

9. De León, *Ethnicity in the Sunbelt,* pp. 126–30; *LULAC News,* Oct., 1945, Folder 4, Box 5, Herrera Papers, HMRC.

10. Fernando Salas A. to Alfred Hernández, Incoming Correspondence, 1947, Box 5, LULAC Records, HMRC; *LULAC News,* Oct., 1945, pp. 13, 15, Folder 4, Box 5, Herrera Papers.

11. Minute Book, Jan. 17, 1946–July 18, 1946, Minutes Folder, Box 5, LULAC Records, HMRC (hereafter cited as LULAC Minutes, with date of meeting).

12. LULAC Minutes, Jan. 10, 1946, Apr. 18, 1946; Constitution and By-Laws of the League of United Latin American Citizens, 1952, p. 4, LULAC Constitution and By-Laws Folder, Tijerina Papers.

13. LULAC Minutes, May 9, June 28, and July 18, 1946; Letter marked "Tijerina," Outgoing Correspondence, 1946 Folder, LULAC Records, HMRC; Alfred J. Hernández, interviews by author, Houston, Tex., Apr. 5, 1979 (Oral History Collection, HMRC), Oct. 26, 1983.

14. LULAC Minutes, Dec. 18, 1947, Meetings and Membership Lists, 1947 Folder, Box 5, LULAC Records, HMRC; Hernández interview, Apr. 5, 1979.

15. LULAC Minutes, Dec. 18, 1947; *Houston Chronicle,* Dec. 29, 1947, sec. A, p. 7.

16. *Houston Chronicle,* Dec. 29, 1947, sec. A, p. 7.

17. Ibid.

18. E. J. García to Estimado Consocio (ca. 1946–1947), Inter-Club Correspondence, Folder 9, Box 1, Club México Bello Records, HMRC.

19. Felix Tijerina to Felix González Salinas, Dec. 21, 1946, Folder 12; Felix González Salinas to Felix Tijerina, Jan. 11, 1947, Folder 10; Felix Tijerina to Oscar Holcombe, Jan. 23, 1947, Folder 10; Felix Tijerina to R. E. Smith, Feb. 10, 1947, Folder 12, all in Box 1, Club México Bello Records.

20. Manuel Coello to Felix Tijerina, telegram, Jan. 30, 1947, Folder 9; "Monterrey City Officials to Be Entertained Here," *Houston Chronicle,* Jan. 29, 1947, both in Box 1, Club México Bello Records; "Monterrey Mayor Discounts Hoof-Mouth Disease Danger," Clipping, Feb., 1947; Photographs of González Salinas and Party Visit to Houston; Félix González Salinas to Felix Tijerina, Jan. 11, 1947, Folder 10, all in Tijerina Papers; Felix Tijerina to the City Editor of the *Houston Chronicle,* Feb. 10, 1947, Folder 12; Felix Tijerina to Phil Hamburger; Félix González Salinas to Felix Tijerina, Feb. 4, 1947, Folder 10; *Houston Post,* Feb. 2, 1947, p. 15, all in Club México Bello Records.

21. "Monterrey City Officials to Be Entertained Here"; *Houston Post,* Feb. 2, 1947, p. 15; Felix Tijerina to Alvaro G. Domínguez, Jan. 24, 1947, Folder 12; Felix Tijerina to Phil Hamburger, Feb. 10, 1947; Felix Tijerina to Fisher Dorsey, Feb. 10, 1947, all in Box 1, Club México Bello Records.

22. Felix Tijerina and Francisco Chaírez to Membership (ca. Mar., 1948), Folder 9; Felix Tijerina to Isidro García, Feb. 4, 1949, Folder 12, both in Box 1, Club México Bello Records.

23. Francisco Peña Ayala interview, Sept. 27, 1997; Manuela Villarreal Sepúlveda de Góngora and Mario Góngora Villarreal interview, Sept. 27, 1997 (Peña noted that Tijerina donated money to María E. Villarreal, a prominent teacher whose career in the Escobedo schools lasted from the late 1920s until the early 1960s); Juan Ramón Garza Guajardo interview, Oct. 21, 1997.

24. Luis G. Zorrilla to Council No. 60, Apr. 28, Aug. 5, 1948, including "Corte de Caja del Comité Patriótico Mexicano de Houston, Texas, Desde Su Fundación, el Día 10 de noviembre de 1947 Hasta el Día 6 de mayo de 1948," Incoming Correspondence, 1948, Folder, LULAC Records, HMRC; "Spirit of Democracy Reigns at Cinco de Mayo Festival," *Houston Chronicle,* May 6, 1948, p. 1; *Houston Chronicle,* Sept. 16, 1948, sec. C, p. 11; Sept. 17, 1948, sec. A, p. 11.

25. Luis Zorrilla to Club Cultural México Bello, May 24, 1949, Correspondence from Other Clubs to México Bello, 1940, 1947, 1949, Folder 10, Box 1, Club México Bello Records.

26. J. A. Álvarez to Daniel T. Valdés, Jan. 14, 1948, and Regular Meeting, Jan. 15, 1948; LULAC Minutes, May 19, 1948; Associated Newspaper Clippings Folder; Constitution of the Pan American Political Council, 1948, all in LULAC Records, HMRC.

27. LULAC Minutes, Mar. 18, Apr. 1, May 19, May 27, June 9, June 17, July 1, July 22, Aug. 19, Sept. 2, 1948, all in LULAC Records, HMRC.

28. De León, *Ethnicity in the Sunbelt,* pp. 130–42, offers the first scholarly analysis of Tijerina and Herrera as a case study of contrasts in leadership styles, especially during the 1950s.

29. Ibid.

30. Herrera, interviews by author, May 22, 1981, Oct. 29, 1981, Feb. 2, 1984, Herrera Papers.

31. Ibid.; "Sam Houston Graduates from 1879 through 1939" (Binder) Spring Term— 1934, Sam Houston High School Records, HMRC; Herrera interview, May 22, 1981.

32. Herrera interviews, May 22, 1981, Oct. 29, 1981, Feb. 2, 1984; Juvencio Rodríguez interview, Nov. 25, 1980; "'Starkey's Remarks Unjust,' City Employee Says," J. J. Herrera to Editor of the *Houston Press,* Juvencio Rodríguez Collection; Hernández telephone interview, Nov. 16, 1990.

33. Herrera interviews, May 22, 1981, Oct. 29, 1981, Feb. 2, 1984; Biographical Article on John J. Herrera, ca. 1940s, Folder 3, Box 1, Herrera Papers.

34. LULAC Banquet Program, Jan. 18, 1942; Herrera interviews, May 22, 1981, Oct. 29, 1981, Feb. 2, 1984; Résumés of John J. Herrera, Folder 3, Box 1, Herrera Papers; Biographical Article on John H. Herrera.

35. Herrera interviews, May 22, 1981, Oct. 29, 1981, Feb. 2, 1984; Biographical Article on John J. Herrera; LULAC: Speeches by John J. Herrera, 1970s, Folder 1, Box 7, Herrera Papers.

36. LULAC Minutes, Mar. 28, Apr. 4, June 13, 1946; LULAC Minutes, July 22, Sept. 2, Oct. 7, 1948, and Dec. 5, 1948 (meeting held in San Antonio), all in LULAC Records, HMRC.

37. Interviews: Hernández, Mar. 10, 1981, Nov. 11, 1983, Nov. 16, 1990; Salazar, Apr. 21, 1997.

38. Interviews by author, Houston, Tex.: Ernest Eguía, July 7, 1990; Raúl C. Martínez, Sept. 13, 1989.

39. Interviews: David Adame by author, Houston, Tex., May 30, 1990; Eguía, July 7, 1990; Salazar, Apr. 21, 1997.

40. LULAC Minutes, Apr. 22, 1948, LULAC Records, HMRC; Mrs. Felix Tijerina, Sr., interview, June 17, 1982.

41. LULAC Minutes, June 3, 1948, LULAC Records, HMRC.

42. "To the League of United Latin American Citizens in Convention Assembled at Austin, Texas," June 11, 1948.

43. LULAC Minutes, Dec. 16, 1948; Fernando Salas A. to Alfred Hernández, Incoming Correspondence, 1947 Folder, Box 5, both in LULAC Records, HMRC; Résumés of John J. Herrera, Folder 3, Box 1, Herrera Papers; Richard Vara, "John J. Herrera Remembers When," *Houston Post,* Aug. 22, 1976, sec. D, p. 8; Fernando Salas A. to Alfred Hernández, Incoming Correspondence, 1947 Folder, Box 5, LULAC Records, HMRC; San Miguel, Jr., "*Let All of Them Take Heed,*" pp. 123–25.

44. Philip Montalbo, telephone interview by author, Houston, Tex., May 15, 1990; *Houston Chronicle,* May 21, 1954, Clippings; *Houston Post,* undated clipping, both in Tijerina Papers; Mrs. Felix Tijerina, Sr., interview, June 17, 1982.

45. Mrs. Felix Tijerina, Sr., telephone interview, Dec. 9, 1989; *Houston City Directory, 1945,* p. 1611; *1946–47,* p. 1763; "New Mexican Restaurant to Open Tonight," *Houston Post,* June 23, 1948, p. 7. Tijerina purchased the property in his own name on Jan. 31, 1946, from J. E. Burkhart, Sr., for $12,500. According to Harris County records, Tijerina gave Burkhart $10 in hand and a promissory note of $12,500 at 5 percent interest to be paid off in quarterly installments of $300 commencing on May 1, 1946 (Harris County Deed Records, vol. 1421, pp. 485–86, Harris County Clerk's Office, Houston, Tex.).

46. Ragsdale, "Biography: Felix Tijerina," p. 4; Photograph of Felix Mexican Restaurant, 904 Westheimer, ca. 1948, Photograph Box; "Announcing Grand Opening of Tonight, Felix Mexican Restaurant," *Houston Press,* June 23, 1948, n.p., Clippings, both in Tijerina Papers.

47. Photograph of Interior of Felix Mexican Restaurant, ca. late 1940s, Photograph Box; *Houston Press,* June 23, 1948, n.p.; Menu, "Felix Mexican Restaurant," ca. 1948, all in Tijerina Papers.

48. Mrs. Felix Tijerina, Sr., interview, Dec. 9, 1989; Photograph of Tijerina and staff, ca. 1948, Photograph Box; *Houston Press,* June 23, 1948, n.p., both in Tijerina Papers.

49. *Houston Post,* June 23, 1948, sec. 2, p. 7.

50. Interviews by author, Houston, Tex.: M. E. Lee, telephone, Dec. 12, 1980; Bill Roberts, Apr. 6, 1982; Menu, "Felix Mexican Restaurant," ca. 1948; Mrs. Felix Tijerina, Sr., interview, Dec. 9, 1989; Linda Ellerbee, "Losing Favor: Bush and the Black Olives," *Houston Chronicle,* Sept. 27, 1992, sec. G, p. 12.

51. *Houston Press,* June 24, 1948, p. 24; Telegrams of Congratulations for Opening of Restaurant and Other Messages, 1948 Folder, Tijerina Papers; "New Mexican Restaurant to Open Tonight," *Houston Post,* June 24, 1948, p. 7.

52. *Houston Chronicle,* Jan. 16, 1950, p. 15.

53. Kathyrn Howe, interview by author, Houston, Tex., Aug. 16, 1990. Anglos who

have been regular customers at the 1948 location (some for fifty years) always note the consistency in the taste of the food, for them a positive feature in a city marked by constant change. See *Houston Chronicle,* Mar. 5, 1999, sec. J, pp. 1, 4.

54. "Negroes" (typescript), Folder 4, Box 1, Tijerina Papers.

55. "Harris County Grand Jury, Feb. 1946," photograph caption, Photograph Box, Tijerina Papers; Fernando Salas to Dr. J. J. Ruíz, Jan. 23, 1947, Incoming Correspondence, 1947 Folder, Box 5, LULAC Records, HMRC; "Boys' Harbor," Vertical Files, Texas and Local History, HPL.

56. "Delegates to New York," *The Log,* June 16, 1949, p. 1, Texas and Local History, HPL.

57. *50th Anniversary, 1912–1962, Rotary Club of Houston,* pp. 29, 42, 141; *The Log,* June 17, 1948, p. 1; Nov. 16, 1950, p. 2.

58. Ragsdale, "Biography: Felix Tijerina," p. 4; *Houston Press,* Aug. 26, 1948, p. 9.

59. Ibid.

60. Ibid. For the earliest identification in scholarly literature of Tijerina as the Horatio Alger ideal, see Rosales, "Mexicans in Houston," p. 241.

61. *Houston Chronicle,* Mar. 9, 1951, sec. B, p. 4; Louis Alexander, "Cafeman Tijerina Likes to Help Boys," *Houston Chronicle,* May 18, 1953.

62. *Houston Post,* Aug. 24, 1950, sec. 2, p. 1; *Houston Chronicle,* Mar. 9, 1951, sec. B, p. 4; *Houston Post,* July 18, 1952; *Houston Chronicle,* Jan. 31, 1954, sec. I, p. 1; *Houston Press,* Feb. 3, 1954, p. 9.

63. *Houston Post,* Jan. 12, 1954, sec. 3, p. 1, Unprocessed Clippings, Tijerina Papers.

64. Photographs of Felix Mexican Restaurant on Kirby Drive, 1952 Opening, Photograph Box, Tijerina Papers; *Houston Press,* Apr. 3, 1952, p. 7.

65. "Three Cities Welcome Felix," *Houston Post,* Apr. 4, 1952, Clippings; "Felix Opens 3rd Mexican Restaurant," *Houston Chronicle,* Apr. 3, 1952; "Felix Jr., 4, Turns 'Busboy' for Opening of Dad's 3rd Cafe," *Houston Press,* p. 7; Photographs of Felix Mexican Restaurant on Kirby Drive, all in Tijerina Papers.

66. Adame interview, May 30, 1990.

67. David Rodríguez interview, June 14, 1993; *Beaumont City Directory, 1953,* p. 42.

68. "Many Charters Issued to Harris County Concerns," undated clipping, Tijerina Papers; *Houston City Directory, 1955,* p. 410.

69. Montrose National Bank, *Houston Chronicle* microfiche, June 19, 1955, June 1, 1956, Apr. 14, 1957, Texas and Local History, HPL.

70. *Houston Post,* Nov. 30, 1956, sec. 3, p. 7; McComb, *Houston,* p. 98.

71. *Houston Post,* Nov. 30, 1956, sec. 3, p. 7; Photograph of Opening of Bellaire Felix Mexican Restaurant, Photograph Box, Tijerina Papers.

72. Photograph of Opening of Bellaire Felix Mexican Restaurant; *Houston Post,* Nov. 30, 1956, sec. 3, p. 7.

73. *Houston Chronicle,* Nov. 30, 1956, sec. B, p. 6; *Houston Press,* Dec. 4, 1956, p. 8; *Houston* (chamber of commerce magazine), Feb., 1958, p. 35.

74. Mrs. Felix Tijerina, Sr., interview, June 17, 1982; *Houston Chronicle,* May 13, 1953, sec. D, p. 9.

75. *Houston Post,* Feb. 18, 1951, sec. 1, p. 11.

76. Ibid.

77. Maurine Parkhurst, "Gadabout," *Houston Chronicle,* undated clipping, ca. early 1950s, Tijerina Papers.

78. Mrs. Felix Tijerina, Sr., interview, Oct. 16, 1978.

79. *Houston Press,* Apr. 3, 1952, p. 7.

80. *Houston City Directory, 1949,* p. 1045; *1951,* p. 829; Copies of documents relative to purchase of family cemetery plot and the family monument, Tijerina Papers; Mrs. Felix Tijerina, Sr., interview by author, June 6, 1990; Tombstone inscription from grave of Dionicia Tijerina, Forest Park Cemetery, Houston, Tex.; *Houston Post,* July 21, 1950, sec. 1, p. 14; Gloria Pina García interview, Dec. 11, 1989.

81. Mrs. Felix Tijerina, Sr., interview, June 25, 1990; Tombstone inscription from the grave of Luciano Villarreal, Forest Park Cemetery, Houston, Tex.

CHAPTER 5. "ALWAYS DOING SOMETHING NICE":
FELIX TIJERINA AND ANGLO AMERICAN GROUPS,
1948–1956

1. *Houston Junior Forum: Thirty-fifth Anniversary, 1946–1981* (Houston, 1981), pamphlet, pp. 1, 6–7, 10–11, Houston Junior Forum Activities and Felix Tijerina Involvement (1940s–1970s) Folder, Tijerina Papers; interviews by author, Houston, Tex.: Mrs. Robert Simonds, Apr. 6, 1990; Dr. June Holley, July 18, 1990.

2. *Houston Junior Forum,* pp. 7–9; "Annual Benefit of the Houston Junior Forum" (programs, 1951, 1953); "Fiesta de Cohetes" (program, 1959), all in Houston Junior Forum Activities and Felix Tijerina Involvement (1940s–1970s) Folder, Tijerina Papers.

3. *Houston Post,* May 4, 1952, sec. 5, p. 1, Clippings Folder; "Junior Forum Will Celebrate Debt Payment," clipping, ca. 1953, Houston Junior Forum Activities and Felix Tijerina Involvement (1940s–1970s) Folder; "The Houston Junior Forum Welfare Program" (brochure, ca. 1950s), all in Tijerina Papers; Mrs. Robert Simonds interview, Apr. 6, 1990; *Houston Junior Forum,* p. 11.

4. *Houston Post,* Aug. 8, 1955, sec. 1, p. 11; "The Houston Junior Forum Welfare Program."

5. "The Houston Junior Forum Welfare Program"; *Houston Junior Forum,* p. 11.

6. *Houston Junior Forum,* p. 12; *Houston Chronicle,* Feb. 8, 1953, sec. G, p. 3; Mrs. Robert Simonds interview, Apr. 6, 1990.

7. *Houston Chronicle,* Nov. 9, 1953, sec. 2, p. 2, Unprocessed Clippings, Tijerina Papers; "Wrecker" Olshan to Felix Tijerina, Houston Junior Forum Activities and Felix Tijerina Involvement (1940s–1970s) Folder, both in Tijerina Papers.

8. Corrinne S. Tsanoff, *Neighborhood Doorways,* p. 122.

9. Robert Waller, telephone interview by author, Houston, Tex., July 19, 1990; *The Log,* July 6, 1950, p. 3; May 3, 1951, p. 2; June 19, 1951, p. 4; July 19, 1951, p. 2; Oct. 4, 1951, p. 2.

10. Rowland Manatt to Dear Rotarian, July 21, 1952; Rowland Manatt to the Members of the Mary Burnett School Committee, Aug. 7, 1952; Rowland Manatt to Silas B.

Ragsdale, Mar. 28, 1953; Mary Burnett School Committee List; Otto U. Wymer to Editor, *The Log,* July 1, 1953; "Memorandum for O. U. W. Re Mary Burnett Bayland School," all in Burnett-Bayland Home and Felix Tijerina (1950s–1960s) Folder, Tijerina Papers; *The Log,* July 8, 1954, p. 1; Dec. 16, 1954, p. 4.

11. *Houston Press,* Nov. 20, 1954, p. 4, Clippings, Tijerina Papers.

12. Ibid., Dec. 18, 1952, p. 10; Variety Club, *Houston Chronicle* (microfiche), Texas and Local History, HPL.

13. *Houston Press,* Dec. 18, 1952, p. 10; "Variety Clubs International" (program of 17th annual convention, May 18-21, 1953, Mexico City), p. 114, Variety Clubs International Folder, Tijerina Papers.

14. "Bull Ring Comedian Coming," *Houston Chronicle,* Nov. 23, 1952, sec. C, p. 6; "Town Crier by Bill Roberts," *Houston Press,* Oct. 21, 1952; *Houston Chronicle,* Nov. 18, 1952, sec. C, p. 7; Virginia Snow, "The Mexican Parade," undated clipping; *Houston Chronicle,* Dec. 14, 1952, sec. 2, p. 2, all in Clippings, Tijerina Papers.

15. *Houston Press,* Dec. 18, 1952, p. 10.

16. Ibid.

17. Photograph of Morales, Tijerina, and Cantinflas at KLVL, ca. 1952, Morales Papers, HMRC; "Variety Clubs International" program, p. 114.

18. "Variety Clubs International" program p. 114; *The News* (Mexico City, Special Variety Convention Special), May 21, 1953; Clippings and "Variety Club International" program, Mexico City, May, 1953, Folder, all in Tijerina Papers; Tony Campos, telephone interview by author, Houston, Tex., July 25, 1994.

19. Variety Club, *Houston Chronicle* (microfiche), Texas and Local History, HPL.

20. *Houston Chronicle,* Apr. 17, 1953, sec. A, p. 15; Housing Authority of the City of Houston Minutes, Nos. 287-305: 1952, pp. 1569, 1582, 1585, Houston Housing Authority Office, Houston, Tex. (hereafter cited as Housing Authority Minutes).

21. *Houston Chronicle,* Apr. 17, 1953, sec. A, p. 15.

22. Ibid.; *Houston Post,* Apr. 24, 1953, sec. 3, p. 2.

23. Housing Authority Minutes, Nos. 306–17: 1953, pp. 1612, 1626, 1629–38, 1665; "Colonel Blasts Board for Dealing Him 'Low Blow,'" clipping, ca. May, 1953; "Eversberg Backing Increases"; "Petition HHA to Keep Eversberg," all in Clippings re Felix Tijerina on Houston Housing Authority Board Folder, Tijerina Papers.

24. Memorandum to Director, FBI, from SAC, Houston, Subject: Felix Tijerina Falsely Claiming Citizenship, Date: 5/27/53, File: Felix Tijerina, 39-2521, Records of the U.S. Department of Justice, Federal Bureau of Investigation (hereafter cited as FBI Records), Washington, D.C. I obtained Tijerina's FBI records through the Freedom of Information–Privacy Acts Section, Information Resources Division.

25. Ibid.

26. Ibid.; AIRTEL, Hoover to SAC, Houston, June 5, 1953, FBI Records.

27. Memorandum to Director, FBI, from SAC, Houston, Subject: Felix Tijerina Falsely Claiming Citizenship, Date: June 16, 1953, FBI Records. For the local FBI office summary of the incident see Form No. 1, Title: Felix Tijerina, Character of Case: Falsely Claiming Citizenship, Date When Made: 7/7/53, Period for which Made: 6/5/53, FBI Records.

28. *Houston Chronicle,* Mar. 23, 1952, Clayton Homes File, *Houston Chronicle* (microfiche), Texas and Local History, HPL; *Houston Post,* Mar. 23, 1952, sec. 2, p. 1.

29. Housing Authority Minutes, Nos. 306–17: 1953, pp. 1676, 1687–88, 1705–1707, 1718.

30. Ibid., pp. 1711, 1722; Nos. 318–29: 1954, p. 1783; Nos. 343–56: 1956, pp. 2035, 2043; *Houston Post,* Mar. 18, 1959, sec. 4, p. 6; *Houston Press,* ca. April, 1956, vol. 41, 1956, Scrapbook, Oscar Holcombe Papers, HMRC.

31. *Houston Chronicle,* June 3, sec. B, p. 1; June 4, 1953, p. 1; Kraus Earhart to Dear Fellow-Citizen, June 25, 1955, Small Collections, HMRC; Edgar W. Ray, *The Grand Huckster: Houston's Judge Roy Hofheinz, Genius of the Astrodome,* pp. 185, 224–30.

32. Kraus Earhart to Dear Fellow-Citizen, June 25, 1955, with attached "You Can Help End the Deadlock at City Hall!" Small Collections, HMRC; *Houston Chronicle,* June 9, 1956, sec. D, p. 1; Aug. 15, 1955, p. 1; Ray, *The Grand Huckster,* pp. 224–25.

33. Ray, *The Grand Huckster,* p. 229; *Houston Chronicle,* Aug. 17, 1955, p. 1.

34. *Houston Post,* Oct. 20, 1956, p. 1; Ray, *The Grand Huckster,* pp. 231–32; Hernández interview, Aug. 7, 1990.

35. Ray, *The Grand Huckster,* pp. 230–36; Kraus Earhart to Dear Fellow-Citizen, June 25, 1955; Hernández interview, Aug. 7, 1990; *Houston Press,* Apr. 26, 1956, vol. 41, 1956, Scrapbook, Holcombe Papers.

36. "Cutrer Names Three to City Housing Board," clipping, ca. 1958, Clippings Re Felix Tijerina on the Houston Housing Authority Board Folder, Tijerina Papers; *Houston Post,* Mar. 18, 1959, sec. 4, p. 6.

37. *Houston Post,* Mar. 3, 1953, pp. 1, 6; Mar. 5, 1953, p. 1; Mar. 6, 1953, pp. 1, 5; Mar. 15, 1953, p. 15.

38. Ibid., Mar. 4, 1953, pp. 1, 9; Raúl C. Martínez, interview by author, Houston, Tex., Mar. 22, 1989, Oral History Collection, HMRC.

39. John J. Herrera to Fred Nahas, Mar. 5, 1953, LULAC: John J. Herrera Correspondence and Documents as National President, Jan.-Mar., 1953, Folder, Herrera Papers; *Houston Post,* Mar. 10, 1953, pp. 1, 6; *Houston Press,* Mar. 10, 1953, p. 1.

40. *Houston Post,* Mar. 12, 1953, sec. 4, p. 2.

41. *Houston Chronicle,* Mar. 11, 1953, p. 1.

42. Ibid.; *Houston Post,* Mar. 17, 1953, sec. 1, p. 8.

43. *Houston Chronicle,* May 18, 1953, sec. A, p. 11.

44. *Houston Post,* Aug. 8, 1955, sec. 1, pp. 1, 11.

45. *Houston Chronicle,* Oct. 24, 1950, sec. A, p. 10; "No Holdup," *Houston Chronicle,* Oct. 23, 1952, Sports-Radio Section; *Houston Post,* Nov. 8, 1954, sec. 3, p. 1; "Need Leadership, U.F. Workers Told," *Houston Chronicle,* clipping, ca. 1954; *Houston Post,* Nov. 8, 1954, sec. 3, p. 1, all in Unprocessed Clippings, Tijerina Papers; *Houston Chronicle,* July 11, 1954, United Fund File, *Houston Chronicle* (microfiche), Texas and Local History, HPL.

46. *Houston Chronicle,* Nov. 11, 1952, sec. C, p. 7, Unprocessed Clippings; *Houston Legionnaire,* Feb., 1953, p. 1, Folder 12, Box 1, both in Tijerina Papers.

47. Al Parker and Bill Williams to Felix Tijerina, May 23, 1956, Unprocessed Correspondence, Tijerina Papers; Variety Club, *Houston Chronicle* (microfiche), Texas and

Local History, HPL; "Southwest Scholarship Dinner of the Institute of International Education" (program, Dec. 3, 1953), Unprocessed Papers, Tijerina Papers.

48. *Houston Chronicle,* Aug. 14, 1955, sec. C, p. 1, Unprocessed Clippings, Tijerina Papers.

49. *Houston Press,* Aug. 26, 1948, p. 9 (my emphases in quotation).

50. Mrs. Felix Tijerina, Sr., interview, Nov. 26, 1990.

51. Photographs of Janie Tijerina dancing with Mayor Felix González Salinas and of Mr. and Mrs. Felix Tijerina with Mayor and Mrs. Neal Pickett, Photograph Box, Tijerina Papers; *Houston Post,* Sept. 30, 1951, sec. 1, p. 16; Mrs. Felix Tijerina, Sr., interview, Sept. 13, 1980.

52. "St. Patrick School, Houston, Texas, Oct. 29, 1946" (summary of address by Mrs. Felix Tijerina), Folder, Tijerina Papers.

53. Barbara Liggett, "American Behavior Distresses Her," *Houston Post,* clipping, ca. fall, 1950, Tijerina Papers.

54. Ibid.

55. Ibid.

56. Ibid.

57. Mrs. Felix Tijerina, Sr., interview, Nov. 3, 1990; *Houston Chronicle,* July 15, 1952, sec. C, p. 1.

58. *Houston Chronicle,* July 18, 1952, sec. D, p. 1.

59. *Houston Post,* Monday, Feb. 20, 1956, Editorials, Fashions, Clippings, Tijerina Papers; *Houston Chronicle,* July 31, 1953, sec. D, p. 2; May 18, 1956, sec. D, p. 6.

60. *Women of Rotary Club of Houston, 1948–1949* (ca. 1948), p. 30, Women of Rotary Club of Houston Membership Booklets Folder, Tijerina Papers.

61. Mrs. Felix Tijerina, Sr., interview, Apr. 29, 1983; *Women of Rotary Club of Houston, 1948–1949,* p. 1; *1952–1953,* fly leaf and pp. 3, 5, 11.

62. *La prensa* (Mexico City), May 24, 1952, p. 21, Unprocessed Clippings; "Lo que Dicen las Rotarias Visitantes," undated clipping, ca. May, 1952, both in Tijerina Papers.

63. *Houston Chronicle,* July 31, 1953, sec. D, p. 2; *Houston Press,* Oct. 30, 1956, p. 13; Mrs. Felix Tijerina to Jake Oshman, Nov. 10, 1954, Women of Rotary Folder, Tijerina Papers; Women of Rotary Club Minute Book, 1961–62, both in Tijerina Papers; *Women of Rotary Club of Houston, 1954–1955* (ca. 1954), p. 5; *1957–1958* (ca. 1957), p. 8; *1959–1960* (ca. 1959), p. 8; *1961–1962* (ca. 1961), p. 8.

64. *Houston Chronicle,* Apr. 4, 1952, sec. 4, p. 7; Ernest Eguía, interview by author, Houston, Tex., Nov. 9, 1990.

65. "Hope Marches with Mothers against Polio," *Houston Press,* undated clipping, ca. 1952, Tijerina Papers; Mrs. Felix Tijerina to José De La Isla, Feb. 14, 1956, Club México Bello Records.

66. *Houston Chronicle,* July 31, 1953, sec. D, p. 2, Unprocessed Clippings, Tijerina Papers.

67. Ibid.; "Good Neighbor Tour to Mexico Will Leave Oct. 11," clipping, Sept. 27, 1953; *Houston Chronicle,* Oct. 25, 1953, sec. H, p. 1; Margaret Webb Dreyer, "Two Countries 'Unite' in Family," *Houston Chronicle,* clipping, ca. 1953, all in Unprocessed Clippings, Tijerina Papers.

68. *Houston Chronicle,* July 31, 1953, sec. D, p. 2; Dreyer, "Two Countries 'Unite' in Family."

69. Dreyer, "Two Countries 'Unite' in Family"; Felix Tijerina, Jr., telephone interview by author, Houston, Tex., Nov. 5, 1997; *Houston Chronicle,* July 31, 1953, sec. D, p. 2.

70. *Houston Press,* Sept. 3, 1953, p. 17, Clippings, Tijerina Papers.

71. Ibid.

72. *Houston Chronicle,* Nov. 10, 1954, sec. D, p. 1, Clippings, Tijerina Papers.

73. *Houston Post,* Apr. 6, 1955, sec. 3, p. 1, Clippings, Tijerina Papers.

74. *Houston Chronicle,* June 2, 1955, p. 1, Clippings, Tijerina Papers.

75. Anonymous interviews by author, 1979–1990; Mrs. Felix Tijerina, Sr., interviews, July 17, 1982, Feb. 14, 1995.

76. Mrs. Felix Tijerina, Sr., interview, Nov. 26, 1990.

CHAPTER 6. SIEMPRE HACIENDO POR LA RAZA:
FELIX TIJERINA AND LATIN AMERICAN GROUPS,
1950–1956

1. J. Cruz López to Estimado Consocio, June 9, 1950, Treasury Reports, 1950s, Folder 13, Box 1, Club México Bello Records; *Houston Chronicle,* Sept. 28, 1952, sec. F, p. 3; *Houston Post,* Oct. 12, 1952, sec. 1, p. 13.

2. "Junta de directiva en el lugar del Sr. Felix Tijerina," Feb. 6, 1953, Treasury Reports, 1950s, Folder 13, Box 1, Club México Bello Records.

3. *Libro de asistencia, Houston, Texas,* Box 2; *Mexico Bello Girls' Auxiliary* (pamphlet, 1954), Oversize Scrapbook, Box 5, both in Club México Bello Records.

4. Mrs. Felix Tijerina, Sr., interview, June 17, 1982; *El porvenir* (Monterrey), May 13, 1951, p. 18, Folder 9, Box 1, Tijerina Papers.

5. *Houston Chronicle,* Sept. 28, 1951, p. 1; Sept. 30, 1951, sec. A, p. 11; *Houston Post,* Sept. 30, 1951, sec. 1, p. 16.

6. Rosa Bradbury to Club México Bello, May 22, 1954, Correspondence from Other Organizations to Club México Bello, Folder 17, Box 1; Albino Torres to Club México Bello, ca. 1955, Correspondence from Other Organizations to Club México Bello, 1955, Folder 20, Box 1; México Bello Scrapbook, 1950s, Box 5, all in Club México Bello Records; Mrs. Felix Tijerina, Sr., interview, June 17, 1982; *The Log,* Sept. 23, 1954, p. 3.

7. Virginia Ochoa to Club México Bello, ca. May, 1954, Correspondence from Other Organizations to Club México Bello, 1954, Folder 17, Box 1, Club México Bello Records.

8. Virginia Ochoa to Dear Members, July 13 and July 22, 1954, Correspondence from Other Organizations to Club México Bello, 1954, Folder 17, Box 1, Club México Bello Records; Roberts interview, Apr. 6, 1982.

9. Sammie Alderete, interview by author, Houston, Tex., July 21, 1990; Carmen Cortes to Val Hernández, ca. 1950s, Folder 4, Box 2, Cortes Papers.

10. Alderete interview, July 21, 1990.

11. Interviews: Eguía, July 7, 1990; David Adame, by telephone with author, Houston, Tex., Mar. 10, 1997.

12. Hernández interviews, Jan. 15, 1979, Nov. 16, 1990.

13. Ibid. Some of my more subjective observations in this biographical sketch of Hernández are based on our twenty-year personal acquaintance.

14. Hernández interview, Nov. 16, 1990.

15. Ibid.

16. Ibid., Apr. 5, 1979, Nov. 16, 1990, Aug. 31, 1991.

17. Ibid., Nov. 16, 1990, Aug. 31, 1991; Salazar interview, Apr. 21, 1997.

18. LULAC Minutes, Dec. 3, 1953, LULAC Records, HMRC.

19. Hernández interview, Nov. 16, 1990; *LULAC News,* Feb., 1954, pp. 29, 63, LULAC Records, HMRC; Adame interview, Mar. 10, 1997.

20. *LULAC News,* Feb., 1954, p. 49, LULAC Records, HMRC.

21. *Houston Chronicle,* Feb. 18, 1954, sec. B, p. 1; *LULAC News,* June, 1954, n.p., pp. 1, 3, LULAC Records, HMRC.

22. Matt S. Meier and Feliciano Rivera, *Dictionary of Mexican American History,* p. 264; Juan Ramón García, *Operation Wetback: The Mass Deportation of Mexican Undocumented Workers in 1954,* pp. 169–234.

23. *LULAC News,* July, 1954, pp. 4, 12–13, Hernández Papers; *LULAC News,* Dec., 1954, p. 12, Rare Books Room, Benson Latin American Collection, University of Texas at Austin (location cited hereafter as Benson Collection); García, *Operation Wetback,* pp. 206–10.

24. *LULAC News,* Aug., 1954, pp. 1–2, LULAC Records, HMRC.

25. Ibid., Mar. 1955, p. 12, LULAC Records, HMRC.

26. Hernández interview, Aug. 31, 1991 (telephone); Frank Pinedo, interview by author, Houston, Tex., Sept. 5, 1991 (telephone).

27. *LULAC News,* Mar., 1955, p. 12; LULAC Minutes, Jan. 27, 1955; May 27, 1954, and undated (ca. early 1954), all in LULAC Records, HMRC; *LULAC News,* July, 1954, p. 14; Feb., 1955, pp. 8–9, Benson Collection; Hernández interview, Aug. 31, 1991.

28. *LULAC News,* Feb., 1954, p. 49, LULAC Records, HMRC.

29. "Lulac Governor Explains Big Educational Program," clipping, ca. mid-1955, Tijerina Papers; interviews: Hernández, Nov. 16, 1990, Aug. 31, 1991; Pinedo, Sept. 5, 1991.

30. *Houston Post,* Aug. 8, 1955, pp. 1, 11; *LULAC News,* Sept., 1955, pp. 3–4, LULAC Records, HMRC.

31. "Lulac Governor Explains Big Educational Program"; *LULAC News,* Jan., 1956, p. 10, Hernández Papers; *LULAC News,* Feb., 1955, pp. 8–9, Benson Collection; Hernández interview, Aug. 31, 1991; *Houston Post,* Aug. 8, 1955, pp. 1, 11.

32. *LULAC News,* Sept. 1955, pp. 2–4, LULAC Records, HMRC.

33. Alfred J. Hernández, telephone interview by author, Houston, Tex., Oct. 2, 1991.

34. *LULAC News,* Sept., 1955, pp. 2–4, 6; LULAC Minutes, Sept. 17, 1959, both in LULAC Records, HMRC.

35. *LULAC News,* Sept., 1954, Benson Collection; *LULAC News,* Mar., 1955, LULAC Records, HMRC; Tony Campos, telephone interviews by author, Houston, Tex., Sept. 8, 1991, Jan. 19, 1992; *LULAC News,* Sept., 1955, pp. 7–8, LULAC Records, HMRC.

36. Alfredo M. Cárdenas to Ed Idar, Apr. 2, 1955, Folder 141.15; Ed Idar to Dear Fellow Officers, Aug. 8, 1955, Folder 146.2, both in Dr. Hector P. García Papers, Special Collections and Archives, Bell Library, TAMU-CC (hereafter cited as García Papers).

37. *Valley Morning Star* (Harlingen, Tex.), Mar. 20, 1955, sec. B, p. 12; *LULAC News,* Sept., 1955, pp. 7–8, and April, 1956, p. 3, both in Hernández Papers; LULAC Minutes, Feb. 23, 1955, LULAC Records, HMRC; *LULAC News,* Feb., 1955, p. 5, Benson Collection.

38. LULAC Minutes, May 20, May 27, July 15, 1954; LULAC Minutes, May 10, 1955, both in LULAC Records, HMRC.

39. Andy Anderson, "LULAC Dance Festival Saturday in Coliseum Aids Christmas Fund," *Houston Press,* Nov. 24, 1954, p. 18; Andy Anderson, "Christmas Basket Fiesta Huge Success," *Houston Press,* Nov. 30, 1954, no page shown; *Houston Chronicle,* Feb. 17, 1955, all in Clippings, Tijerina Papers.

40. *LULAC News,* Jan., 1956, cover, pp. 12–13, Hernández Papers; LULAC Minutes, Jan. 6, 1955, Jan. 13, 1955, LULAC Records, HMRC; Ernest Eguía, telephone interview by author, Houston, Tex., Sept. 15, 1991.

41. *LULAC News,* Jan. 1956, cover, pp. 12–13, Hernández Papers; LULAC Minutes, Mar. 17, 1955, Dec. 15, 1955, Dec. 22, 1955, all in LULAC Records, HMRC.

42. *Houston Post,* Aug. 8, 1955, pp. 1, 11; *LULAC News,* Sept. 1955, pp. 3–4, LULAC Records, HMRC.

43. Hernández interview, Aug. 31, 1991; LULAC Minutes, Feb. 23, 1956, LULAC Records, HMRC.

44. *Houston Post,* Aug. 8, 1955, sec. 1, p. 11; Francisco Peña Garza interview, Sept. 26, 1997.

45. *Houston Post,* Aug. 8, 1955, sec. 1, p. 11; interviews: Francisco Peña Garza, Sept. 26, 1997; Eddie Gutiérrez by author, Houston, Tex., Dec. 29, 1982; Richard Holgin by author, Houston, Tex., June 8, 1990; Dr. Tatcho Mindiola, Jr., by author, Houston, Tex., Aug. 9, 1990; David Rodríguez, June 14, 1993; Félix Martínez by author, Houston, Tex., Feb. 19, 1982.

46. Ninfa Laurenzo, telephone interview by author, Houston, Tex., Mar. 12, 1997; *Houston City Magazine,* May, 1981, pp. 35–36; *Houston City Directory, 1949,* p. 1082.

47. Danny González, interview by author, Houston, Tex., Feb. 26, 1983.

48. Hernández interview, Apr. 5, 1979.

49. *Houston Post,* Aug. 8, 1955, sec. 1, p. 11.

50. Antonio Arias, interview by author, Houston, Tex., May 13, 1983; Hernández interview, Apr. 5, 1979.

51. *Houston Chronicle,* Apr. 11, 1955, sec. B, p. 2; "Scholarship Awards Highlight Alba Banquet," clipping, ca. May, 1955; "U.T. Club Honors Felix Tijerina," *Houston Chronicle,* May 1, 1955, all in Clippings Re Alba Club Award Folder, Tijerina Papers.

52. "U.T. Club Honors Felix Tijerina," *Houston Chronicle,* May 1, 1955; "Scholarship Awards Highlight Alba Banquet," clipping, ca. May, 1955.

53. "Scholarship Awards Highlight Alba Banquet," clipping, ca. May, 1955; "Felix Tijerina," Speech by Edmund Duggan, Apr. 30, 1955, "Speech Delivered . . . "Folder, Tijerina Papers.

54. "Scholarship Awards Highlight Alba Banquet."

55. Ibid.; "Houstonian Honored," clipping, ca. May, 1955; Photographs of Logan Wilson Shaking Hands with Felix and Janie Tijerina, Apr. 30, 1955, Photograph Box, Tijerina Papers.

CHAPTER 7. "IN EXILE FROM HIS NATIVE LAND": FELIX TIJERINA V. HERBERT BROWNELL, JR.

1. "Opinion of the Court," May 25, 1956, p. 4; "Notice of Continued Preliminary Naturalization Hearing," Sept. 24, 1953, Plaintiff's Exhibit 10, both in *Tijerina v. Brownell; Houston Chronicle,* May 21, 1954, sec. B, p. 12; "Complaint for Declaratory Judgment to Establish Citizenship," Mar. 25, 1954, p. 2, *Tijerina v. Brownell.* (I would like to thank attorneys Joan T. Dusard and Gary Endelman for their valuable help with this chapter.)

2. "Answer," Feb. 6, 1956, p. 2; "Brief of the Plaintiff on Right to Recover Judgment," Feb. 25, 1956, p. 8, both in *Tijerina v. Brownell.*

3. "Pre-Trial Stipulation of Facts," Feb. 14, 1956, p. 3; "Brief of the Plaintiff," Feb. 25, 1956, p. 8, both in *Tijerina v. Brownell.* Although Dionicia's maiden name (Villarreal) was normally spelled with two "r"'s, the court documents spell it with one "r."

4. "Complaint for Declaratory Judgment," Mar. 25, 1954, pp. 2–3; "Brief of the Plaintiff," Feb. 25, 1956, p. 9; "Pre-Trial Stipulation of Facts," Feb. 14, 1956, p. 3, all in *Tijerina v. Brownell.*

5. "Brief of the Plaintiff," Feb. 25, 1956, pp. 9–10; "Opinion of the Court," May 25, 1956, p. 4, both in *Tijerina v. Brownell.*

6. Philip Montalbo, interviews by author, Houston, Tex., Apr. 6, 1981, May 26, 1990 (telephone); Statement of Felix Tijerina, Mar. 26, 1940, *Tijerina v. Brownell.*

7. Montalbo interviews, Apr. 6, 1981, May 26, 1990; Mrs. Felix Tijerina, Sr., interviews, June 17, 1982, Aug. 7, 1990 (telephone).

8. Sammie Alderete, telephone interview by author, Houston, Tex., Aug. 8, 1990.

9. Montalbo interviews, Apr. 6, 1981, May 11, 1990 (telephone).

10. Ibid.

11. Ibid.; Ann Stangle, interview by author, Houston, Tex., Apr. 22, 1981; "Complaint for Declaratory Judgment," Mar. 25, 1954, pp. 1–3, *Tijerina v. Brownell.*

12. "Complaint for Declaratory Judgment," Mar. 25, 1954, pp. 4–8, *Tijerina v. Brownell.*

13. *Houston Post,* Mar. 26, 1954, sec. 1, p. 9; *Houston Chronicle,* Mar. 26, 1954, sec. B, p. 10; *Houston Press,* Mar. 26, 1954, p. 4; "Sues Over Citizenship," Mar. 25, 1954, unidentified Houston clipping, Tijerina Papers.

14. "Notice of Continued Preliminary Naturalization Hearing," Plaintiff's Exhibit 10; "Pre-Trial Stipulation of Facts," Feb. 14, 1956, pp. 3–4; "Second Amended Complaint for Declaratory Judgment to Establish Citizenship," June 3, 1955, pp. 6–7; "Brief of the Plaintiff On Right to Recover Judgment," Feb. 25, 1956, p. 10; "Brief in Reply to Brief of Defendant Herbert Brownell, Jr., Attorney General," Mar. 6, 1956, p. 3; "Defendant's Brief," Feb. 25, 1956, p. 7, all in *Tijerina v. Brownell.*

15."Naturalization Petitions Recommended to Be Granted," and "Order Of Court Granting Petitions For Naturalization," May 20, 1954, Plaintiff's Exhibit 18; "Pre-Trial Stipulation of Facts," Feb. 14, 1956, p. 4; "Defendant's Brief," Feb. 25, 1956, p. 7, all in *Tijerina v. Brownell.*

16. *Houston Chronicle,* May 21, 1954, sec. B, p. 12.

17. "Application for Extension of Time Within Which to Plead," May 26, 1954, *Tijerina v. Brownell.*

18. Receipt for Payment for Passport, June 3, 1954, and other travel documents Folder, Tijerina Papers; "First Amended Complaint for Declaratory Judgment to Establish Citizenship," July 20, 1954, pp. 5–6; "Answer," Feb. 6, 1956, p. 3; Taylor C. Carpenter to Felix Tijerina, Dec. 14, 1954, Plaintiff's Exhibit 11, all in *Tijerina v. Brownell;* "Restaurateur Tijerina in Houston on 'Parole,'" *Houston Chronicle,* July 13, 1954, sec. B, p. 1; "Brief in Support of Motion to Dismiss," July 25, 1955, p. 10; "Opinion of the Court," May 25, 1956, p. 5, both in *Tijerina v. Brownell.*

19. "Brief for Plaintiff upon Motion to Dismiss of the Defendants T. C. Carpenter, E. L. Brimberry, and L. D. Crossman," July 25, 1955, pp. 16–18, *Tijerina v. Brownell.*

20."Pre-Trial Stipulation of Facts," Feb. 14, 1956, p. 4, *Tijerina v. Brownell;* "Tijerina Back to Push Bid on Citizenship," unidentified Houston clipping, ca. July, 1954, Tijerina Papers; "Restaurateur Tijerina in Houston on 'Parole,'" *Houston Chronicle,* July 13, 1954, sec. B, p. 1.

21. "Restaurateur Tijerina in Houston on 'Parole'"; "Tijerina Back to Push Bid on Citizenship," unidentified Houston clipping, ca. July, 1954, Tijerina Papers; Entries dated 4/28/54 and 5/6/54, File Cards on Felix Tijerina, Price Daniel, Sr., Papers, Sam Houston Regional Library and Research Center, Liberty, Tex.(hereafter cited as Daniel Papers).

22. "Tijerina Asks Judgment on Citizenship," *Houston Post,* July 20, 1954, Clippings, Tijerina Papers; "First Amended Complaint for Declaratory Judgment to Establish Citizenship," July 20, 1954, *Tijerina v. Brownell.*

23. "Second Amended Complaint for Declaratory Judgment to Establish Citizenship," June 3, 1955, pp. 9–10, *Tijerina v. Brownell.*

24. Ibid., pp. 1–14; "Order on Motions to Dismiss," Oct. 17, 1955, *Tijerina v. Brownell.*

25. *The Log,* Aug. 19, 1948, p. 2; Feb. 10, 1955, p. 2; Carleton, *Red Scare!,* p. 273; Joe Ingraham, interview by author, Houston, Tex., Apr. 24, 1981; File on Joseph M. Ingraham (Bio.), 1937–, *Houston Chronicle* microfiche, Texas and Local History, HPL; *Houston Chronicle,* May 10, 1954; *Houston Press,* Aug. 6, 1954; and *Houston Post,* May 24, 1954, all in Joe Ingraham Folder, *Houston Press* Clipping Files, HMRC.

26. Carleton, *Red Scare!,* p. 273; *Houston Post,* May 24, 1954, Joe Ingraham Folder, *Houston Press* Clipping Files, HMRC; *Houston Chronicle,* May 28, 1990, sec. A, p. 22; Sidney Farr, interview by author, Houston, Tex., Apr. 23, 1981; Ingraham interview, Apr. 24, 1981.

27. Ingraham interview, Apr. 24, 1981; Dwight Eisenhower to Felix Tijerina, Dec. 16, 1952, Tijerina Papers; Thad Hutcheson to Wilton B. Persons, Feb. 6, 1959, President's Personal File (hereafter PPF) 47: League of United Latin American Citizens,

Records of the President, White House Central Files; and Felix Tijerina to the President, Feb. 16, 1960 (telegram), G.F. 4-D: Texas S. Dist. End. Salinas, both in Dwight D. Eisenhower Library, Abilene, Kans.; Hernández interviews, Jan. 15, 1979, Aug. 7, 1990.

28. Ingraham interview, Apr. 24, 1981.

29. *Houston Post,* Monday Aug. 8, 1955, pp. 1, 11.

30. Ibid., p. 1.

31. Ibid., p. 11.

32. Ibid., pp. 1, 11.

33. Ibid., pp. 1, 11.

34. Ibid., p. 11.

35. Ibid.

36. Ibid.

37. Ibid., p. 1; "Brief for Plaintiff upon Motion to Dismiss as to the Defendant Herbert Brownell, Jr., Attorney General of the United States," Aug. 26, 1955, p. 25, *Tijerina v. Brownell.*

38. *Houston Post,* Aug. 8, 1955, p. 1.

39. Carleton, *Red Scare!,* pp. 12–18, 100; Carleton and Kreneck, *Houston,* p. 23.

40. *Houston Post,* Oct. 10, 1952, sec. 2, p. 8; Carleton, *Red Scare!,* pp. 64–65, 68–69.

41. *Houston Post,* May 24, 1954, pp. 1, 9.

42. "Brief in Support of Motion to Dismiss," July 25, 1955; "Motion to Dismiss as to Defendant Herbert Brownell, Jr., Attorney General of the United States," July 25, 1955; "Brief in Reply to Plaintiff's Brief upon Defendants' Motion to Dismiss as To T. C. Carpenter, E. L. Brimberry, and L. D. Crossman," July 27, 1955, all in *Tijerina v. Brownell.*

43. Farr interview, Apr. 23, 1981.

44. Ibid.

45. Ibid.

46. Ibid.; "Answer," Feb. 6, 1956, *Tijerina v. Brownell.*

47. "Answer," Feb. 6, 1956; "Pre-Trial Stipulation of Facts," Feb. 14, 1956, pp. 2–4, both in *Tijerina v. Brownell.*

48. "Felix Tijerina Offers Proof of U.S. Birth," *Houston Press,* Feb. 15, 1956, Clippings, Tijerina Papers; *Houston Chronicle,* Feb. 15, 1956, sec. B, p. 9; Feb. 16, 1956, sec. E, p. 6; "Felix Tijerina Offers Proof of Citizenship," *Houston Post,* Feb. 16, 1956, Clippings, Tijerina Papers; "Pre-Trial Stipulation of Facts," Feb. 14, 1956, pp. 1–2, *Tijerina v. Brownell.* As noted in chapter 3, Victoria had obtained her delayed birth certificate in 1940, giving her place of birth as Sugar Land. Dora obtained her own delayed birth certificate in February, 1947, claiming Robstown as her birthplace. See Certificate of Birth for Isidra Dora Tijerina, No. 1378550, Filed Feb. 17, 1947, Texas Department of Health, Bureau of Vital Statistics, Austin, Tex.

49. *Houston Post,* Feb. 16, 1956, sec. 4, p. 3; *Houston Chronicle,* Feb. 16, 1956, sec. E, p. 6; "Defendant's Brief," Feb. 25, 1956, p. 2, *Tijerina v. Brownell;* Farr interview, Apr. 23, 1981; *Texas Legal Directory, 1970,* p. 143.

50. *Houston Chronicle,* Feb. 16, 1956, sec. E, p. 6; "Felix Tijerina Offers Proof of

Citizenship," *Houston Post,* Feb. 16, 1956, Clippings, Tijerina Papers; *Houston Post,* Feb. 16, 1956, sec. 4, p. 3; "Defendant's Brief," Feb. 25, 1956; "Brief of the Plaintiff on Right to Recover Judgment," Feb. 25, 1956; "Brief in Reply to Brief of Defendant Herbert Brownell, Jr., Attorney General," Mar. 6, 1956; "Defendant's Reply Brief," Mar. 6, 1956, all in *Tijerina v. Brownell.*

51. *Houston Press,* Feb. 18, 1956, p. 4.

52. Pauline L. Bogatto to Janie Tijerina, Feb. 20, 1956, Tijerina Papers.

53. *Houston Press,* Feb. 15, 1956, p. 10.

54. "Opinion of the Court," May 25, 1956, pp. 1–12, *Tijerina v. Brownell.*

55. Ibid., pp. 10–12.

56. Ibid., pp. 3–12; Ingraham interview, Apr. 24, 1981.

57. Farr interview, Apr. 23, 1981. Unfortunately, Farr's decision not to appeal the ruling meant that transcripts of the hearing were not made, thus limiting our knowledge of what transpired in the courtroom on Feb. 15, 1956. While Ingraham gave the "Opinion of the Court" on May 25, he did not file his "Final Judgment" declaring Felix a native-born citizen of the United States until June 4, 1956, which was the concluding act in Felix's long struggle.

58. "Restaurateur Felix Wins Fight Over Citizenship," *Houston Post,* May 26, 1956, p. 1; *Houston Press,* May 26, 1956, p. 3, both in Clippings, Tijerina Papers.

59. See Clippings, Tijerina Papers, for multiple copies of articles; *Houston Chronicle,* May 26, 1956, sec. A, p. 5; John Zell Gaston, M.D., to Felix Tijerina, May 28, 1956; Maurice Hirsch to Felix Tijerina, May 26, 1956; A. Pat Daniels to Felix Tijerina, May 28, 1956 (all correspondence in Tijerina Papers).

60. In my discussions with numerous Mexican Houstonians who knew Felix Tijerina and were active during this period, most confided that they knew or believed Felix was actually born in Mexico. For the sentiments of the community regarding the separate issue of Felix winning his case see Hernández interview, Aug. 31, 1991; Eguía interview, July 7, 1990; and Lorenzo Garza, interview by author, Houston, Tex., Apr. 27, 1981.

61. *LULAC News,* May, 1956, p. 8, LULAC Records, HMRC.

CHAPTER 8. THE LULAC NATIONAL PRESIDENCY,
PART I: 1956–1958

1. *LULAC News,* May, 1956, p. 5, LULAC Records, HMRC; *LULAC News,* July, 1956, pp. 6, 12, 14, Benson Collection; Irwin Ross, "Harold Medina—Judge Extraordinary," *Reader's Digest,* Feb., 1950, p. 88; *El Paso Herald-Post,* June 25, 1956, Clippings, Tijerina Papers.

2. Photographs of Felix Tijerina at the 1956 National LULAC Convention, El Paso, Photograph Box, Tijerina Papers; Salazar interview, Apr. 21, 1997; John J. Herrera to Phil Montalbo, June 14, 1957, Herrera Papers.

3. John J. Herrera to Phil Montalbo, June 14, 1957, Herrera Papers; Salazar interview, Apr. 21, 1997; Sandoval interview, June 12, 1997; Oscar M. Laurel, telephone interview by author, Laredo, Tex., June 16, 1997; *LULAC News,* July, 1956, pp. 6, 12, 13, 14, Benson

Collection. Successful in his 1956 bid for the Texas legislature, Oscar Laurel would serve two terms as state representative from Laredo.

4. *LULAC News,* July, 1956, pp. 7, 14, Benson Collection; "LULAC through the Years: Former LULAC Presidents," in *LULAC: Fifty Years of Serving Hispanics* (not paginated).

5. *LULAC News,* July, 1956, p. 12, Benson Collection.

6. Ibid.

7. Ibid., pp. 12, 17; *LULAC News,* Oct. 1956, p. 6, LULAC Records, HMRC.

8. *LULAC News,* Oct. 1956, p. 6, LULAC Records, HMRC; Alfred J. Hernández, telephone interview by author, Houston, Tex., May 16, 1992.

9. Eguía interview, July 7, 1990; "LULAC 30th National Convention" (program), n.p., Folder 6, Box 3, Cortes Papers.

10. *LULAC News,* July, 1956, pp. 12, 17; Oct., 1956, p. 6, both in Benson Collection; interviews: Hernández, May 16, 1992; Salazar, Apr. 21, 1997.

11. *LULAC News,* Oct., 1956, p. 5, LULAC Records, HMRC; Hernández interview, May 16, 1992.

12. *LULAC News,* Nov.–Dec., 1956, pp. 7, 13; Feb., 1957, p. 3; May, 1957, p. 3; June, 1957, p. 4, all in LULAC Records, HMRC; Hernández interview, May 16, 1992.

13. *LULAC News,* Sept., 1956, p. 4, Benson Collection; *LULAC News,* June, 1957, p. 4, LULAC Records, HMRC; Hernández interview, May 16, 1992.

14. *LULAC News,* Oct., 1956, p. 5, LULAC Records, HMRC; *LULAC News,* Aug., 1958, p. 11, Cortes Papers; Laurel interview, June 16, 1997; *Noticias: semanario del medio oeste* (Chicago), Sept. 29, 1956, p. 1, Clippings, Tijerina Papers.

15. Charles Toribio to Felix Tijerina, Oct. 15, 1956, Unprocessed Correspondence, Herrera Papers.

16. Roster of Councils, 1956–57; *LULAC News,* Nov.–Dec., 1956, p. 4, both in LULAC Records, HMRC.

17. *LULAC News,* Oct., 1956, pp. 5, 11; Nov.–Dec., 1956, p. 4; Mar. 1957, pp. 2, 7, all in LULAC Records, HMRC.

18. "Memoriam to Val Hernández," by Susana Pavón, in *LULAC: Leadership, Unity, Loyalty, Americanism, Citizenship, 1961,* Tony Campos Papers, HMRC; Salazar interview, Apr. 21, 1997.

19. John J. Herrera to Dear LULACs, June 12–14, 1953, Scrapbook 1.7, García Papers; *LULAC News,* July, 1956, p. 8, Benson Collection; *LULAC News,* Nov.–Dec., 1956, p. 5; May, 1957, pp. 7, 10; June, 1957, p. 4, all in LULAC Records, HMRC.

20. *LULAC News,* July, 1956, p. 8; Feb., 1957, p. 4; Mar., 1957, pp. 8–9; June, 1957, pp. 3, 5, all in LULAC Records, HMRC; Carmen Cortes, telephone interview by author, Houston, Tex., Oct. 14, 1981.

21. *LULAC News,* Sept., 1956, p. 7, Benson Collection.

22. *LULAC News,* Mar., 1957, pp. 9, 11, Benson Collection; Texas Good Neighbor Commission, *Texas: Friend and Neighbor,* pp. 98–99; *El norte,* Mar. 23, 1957, p. 11, Campos Papers; "Visita Monterrey el presidente de la institucion Lulacs de EU.," unidentified clipping, 1957, Campos Papers.

23. *LULAC News,* May, 1957, p. 4, LULAC Records, HMRC.

24. Ibid.

25. Carlos I. Calderón, "The Fewest Words to Open the Widest Doors," *Texas Outlook,* July, 1956, pp. 14–16.

26. *LULAC News,* May, 1957, p. 4, LULAC Records, HMRC.

27. Ibid.

28. Ibid., pp. 7, 9–11; LULAC Minutes, Mar. 7, 1957, LULAC Records, HMRC.

29. *LULAC News,* June, 1957, p. 9, LULAC Records, HMRC; *Forgotten Minds* (audiocassette copy of original soundtrack), Tijerina Papers; Alexander, "Texas Helps Her Little Latins," p. 54; *Texas Outlook,* Mar., 1957, p. 43; Isabel Verver, telephone interview by author, Norwalk, Calif., Apr. 30, 1997.

30. Alexander, "Texas Helps Her Little Latins," p. 54.

31. Ibid.; *LULAC News,* June, 1957, p. 9, LULAC Records, HMRC; Verver interview, Apr. 30, 1997.

32. Alexander, "Texas Helps Her Little Latins," p. 54; *LULAC News,* June, 1957, p. 9, LULAC Records, HMRC; *A Personal Message to Farsighted Texans* (pamphlet from LULAC Educational Fund), Folder 17, Box 1, Tijerina Papers; *Forgotten Minds* (audiocassette copy); Verver interview, Apr. 30, 1997. Verver recalled that May 26 was more likely the correct starting date for her initial class.

33. Elizabeth Burrus, interview by author, Houston, Tex., July 28, 1992; Quintanilla, "The 'Little School of the 400,'" pp. 38–39; Elizabeth Burrus, *Beginner's Speaking Vocabulary* (pamphlet, 1958), pp. 1–2, Folder 10, Box 2, Tijerina Papers.

34. Burrus, "Beginner's Speaking Vocabulary," pp. 1–2; Calderón, "The Fewest Words," pp. 14–16; Burrus interview, July 28, 1992.

35. Alexander, "Texas Helps Her Little Latins," p. 54.

36. Ibid.; Burrus, "Beginner's Speaking Vocabulary," pp. 1–2; Verver interview, Apr. 30, 1997.

37. Alexander, "Texas Helps Her Little Latins," p. 54; *Forgotten Minds* (audiocassette copy); Marie Dauplaise, "The 'Forgotten Minds' Are Remembered," *Houston Press,* Mar. 12, 1958, Clippings, Tijerina Papers; San Miguel, *"Let All of Them Take Heed,"* p. 145, says that there were 60 students, based on the LULAC publication of 1962 entitled *What Price Education?* I opted for 151 because it seems to have been the most contemporaneous account based on an interview with Verver herself soon after that summer. Though her memory was inconclusive on this point almost forty years later, Verver felt that she might well have instructed that many pupils (Verver interview, Apr. 30, 1997).

38. Alexander, "Texas Helps Her Little Latins," p. 54; Verver interview, Apr. 30, 1997.

39. "The Truth about Richard Nixon!"(direct mail brochure compiled by John J. Herrera, containing his letter to the *Houston Post* editor, the *Post* article on Tijerina, Oct. 15, 1956, and an Oct. 23 telegram from Danny Olivas), Oct., 1956, Folder 7, Box 6, Herrera Papers.

40. Ibid.; Herrera interview, Oct. 29, 1981.

41. John J. Herrera to Drew Pearson, Nov. 1, 1956, Unprocessed Correspondence, Herrera Papers.

42. "The Truth about Richard Nixon!"; Herrera interview, Oct. 29, 1981.

43. De León, *Ethnicity in the Sunbelt,* p. 138; John J. Herrera,"Resultan ridiculas las

declaraciones del Sr. Felix Tijerina," ca. Jan., 1957 (typescript of letter to *El norte*), translation by Manuel Zapata, Folder 8, Box 6, Herrera Papers.

44. Herrera,"Resultan ridiculas las declaraciones del Sr. Felix Tijerina."

45. Montalbo to Felix Tijerina, May 27, 1957, Incoming Correspondence and Related Documents, 1957 Folder, LULAC Records, HMRC; Herrera to Phil Montalbo, June 14, 1957, Folder 8, Box 6, Herrera Papers; Eugene Rodríguez, Jr., *Henry B. González: A Political Profile*, pp. 79–81.

46. Alfred J. Hernández, telephone interview by author, Houston, Tex., Nov. 19, 1992; *LULAC News,* May, 1957, p. 4; Montalbo to Felix Tijerina, May 27, 1957, Incoming Correspondence and Related Documents, 1957 Folder, both in LULAC Records, HMRC.

47. Speech by John J. Herrera, Past National President of LULAC at Installation LULAC Banquet, Menden [Menger?] Hotel, San Antonio, Tex., June 1, 1957, Folder 11, Box 6, Herrera Papers.

48. Herrera to Phil Montalbo, June 14, 1957; Herrera to Montalbo, Unprocessed Correspondence, García Papers.

49. Herrera to Phil Montalbo, June 14, 1957.

50. Felix Salazar to John J. Herrera [n.d.], Outgoing Correspondence and Telegrams, 1957 Folder, LULAC Records, HMRC; Salazar interview, Apr. 21, 1997.

51. *Houston Chronicle,* Dec. 8, 1958, sec. A, p. 4; Hernández interview, Nov. 19, 1992.

52. G. C. Martínez, National Chaplain, to Sister, Brother, and Junior Lulacs, "Views and Re-Views from Your National Chaplain" (n.d), Incoming Correspondence and Related Documents, 1957 Folder; Untitled Newsletter by G. C. Martínez (n.d.), both in LULAC Records, HMRC.

53. Felix Salazar to G. C. Martínez, May 21, 1957, LULAC National Office, 1956–1959, Felix Salazar, National Legal Advisor, unprocessed folder, LULAC Records, HMRC.

54. LULAC Minutes, July 11, 1957; *LULAC News,* June, 1957, pp. 1–2, both in LULAC Records, HMRC.

55. *LULAC News,* June, 1957, p. 2, LULAC Records, HMRC; *LULAC News,* July, 1957, p. 2, Benson Collection.

56. Mrs. Felix Tijerina, Sr., telephone interview, Aug. 8, 1992.

57. Disneyland Souvenir Photograph, courtesy of Janie B. Tijerina.

58. *LULAC News,* July, 1957, p. 7, Benson Collection.

59. Pete Tijerina to John J. Herrera, July 17, 1957, Folder 8, Box 6, Herrera Papers.

60. Phil Montalbo, interview by author, Houston, Tex., Jan. 14, 1982; Salazar interview, Apr. 21, 1997; Felix Tijerina to Felix Salazar, July 14, 1957, Correspondence and Documents Re National LULAC Office, 1957–1959, National Legal Advisor, Salazar Files, Unprocessed Folder, LULAC Records, HMRC; *LULAC News,* July, 1957, pp. 6–7, Benson Collection; *LULAC News,* Sept., 1957, pp. 6–7, Hernández Papers; *LULAC News,* July, 1958, p. 14, Cortes Papers.

61. L. A. Wilke to Ainsley H. Roseen, May 26, 1957; L. A. Wilke to Felix Tijerina, May 26, 1957, both in Folder 2, Box 2, Tijerina Papers; Hernández interviews, Jan. 15, 1979, May 16, 1992.

62. *LULAC News,* June, 1957, pp. 4–5, LULAC Records, HMRC; *LULAC News,* July, 1957, p. 2, Hernández Papers.

63. Alexander, "Texas Helps Her Little Latins," p. 55; *Forgotten Minds* (audiocassette copy).

64. *Forgotten Minds* (audiocassette copy); LULAC Minutes, Aug. 8, 1957, LULAC Records, HMRC.

65. *LULAC News,* Sept., 1957, pp. 3–5, Hernández Papers; Burrus interview, July 28, 1992.

66. *LULAC News,* Sept., 1957, p. 4, Hernández Papers.

67. Daniel quoted in ibid., pp. 4, 9.

68. Ibid., pp. 3, 11.

69. *Houston Post,* Sept. 15, 1957, sec. 3, p. 6.

70. *LULAC News,* Aug., 1958, p. 7, Cortes Papers; "LULAC Educational Fund, Constitution and By-Laws, 1957," Folder 18, Box 1; *A Personal Message to Farsighted Texans* (pamphlet), Folder 17, Box 1, both in Tijerina Papers.

71. *LULAC News,* Sept., 1957, p. 5, Hernández Papers; *LULAC News,* July, 1957, pp. 2, 11, Benson Collection; LULAC Code, Folder 11, Box 3, Tijerina Papers.

72. LULAC Minutes, Nov. 7, 1957; "Memorandum from the Office of the District Governor of Dist. #8," Nov. 19, 1957, Incoming Correspondence and Related Documents, 1957 Folder; Jake Rodríguez to Felix Tijerina [Salazar], Dec. 4, 1957, Salazar Files, all in LULAC Records, HMRC; 1960 LULAC Handbook by Jacob I. (Jake) Rodríguez, Folder 11, Box 3, Tijerina Papers.

73. Felix Salazar to Jake Rodríguez, Dec. 13, 1957, Salazar Files, LULAC Records, HMRC; Salazar interview, Apr. 21, 1997.

74. Jake Rodríguez to Felix Salazar, Dec. 14, 1957, Salazar Files, LULAC Records, HMRC.

75. "Report of the Committee Sent to Gateway Crystal Pool to Investigate an Act of Alleged Discrimination against Mrs. Lillie Bata, 31 Years of Age and Her Son Henry Bata Jr., 14 Years of Age, Who are Residents of Harris County and American Citizens," Aug. 23, 1957, Unprocessed Folder 1, Salazar Files, LULAC Records, HMRC.

76. Hernández interview, Aug. 11, 1993; Salazar interview, Apr. 21, 1997.

77. Dauplaise, "The 'Forgotten Minds' Are Remembered," *Houston Press,* Mar. 12, 1958, Clippings; Jake Rodríguez, *What Price Education?: What Is It Worth? Where Does It Begin? Who Does It Benefit? What Can We Do about It? 1962 Report of the Little School of 400* (Houston: LULAC, 1962), p. 4, Folder 14, Box 2, both in Tijerina Papers; Alexander, "Texas Helps Her Little Latins," p. 54.

78. Alexander, "Texas Helps Her Little Latins," p. 54.

79. Paul Andow to Felix Salazar, Jan. 17, 1958, Unprocessed Folder, Salazar Files, LULAC Records, HMRC; LULAC Minutes, Jan. 16, 1958, LULAC Records, HMRC; *LULAC News,* Mar., 1958, pp. 3, 6, 8, Folder 12, Box 3, Cortes Papers; 1958 LULAC State Convention Program, Folder 5, Box 4, Cortes Papers; Laurel interview, June 16, 1997.

80. LULAC Minutes, Mar. 6, 1958, LULAC Records, HMRC; Dauplaise, "The 'Forgotten Minds' Are Remembered," *Houston Press,* Mar. 12, 1958, Clippings, Tijerina Papers;

Houston Press, Mar. 12, 1958, p. 16; LULAC Benefit Banquet ticket, Mar. 15, 1958, Unprocessed Folder, Salazar Files, LULAC Records, HMRC.

81. *LULAC News,* July, 1958, p. 2, Cortes Papers; *Congressional Record-Appendix,* 85th Cong., 2d sess., Mar. 18, 1958, pp. A2523–24. Yarborough and Tijerina also knew one another because the restaurateur had consistently contributed money to the senator's political campaigns. See Neal C. Pickett, interview by author, Jan. 15, 1981.

82. Albert Armendariz to All Members of Lulac, Mar. 20, 1958, Unprocessed Folder, Salazar Files, LULAC Records, HMRC.

83. Ibid.

84. Albert Armendariz to Alfred J. Hernández, n.d., Salazar Files, LULAC Records, HMRC.

85. Francisco Licón to All Members of Lulacs, Apr. 16, 1958, Ibid.; Val Hernández to Felix Tijerina, June 18, 1958, Salazar Files, LULAC Records, HMRC.

86. San Miguel, *"Let All of Them Take Heed,"* p. 146; *LULAC News,* Aug., 1958, p. 7, Cortes Papers; Board of Directors Meeting, June 22, 1958 (LULAC Educational Fund, Inc.), Unprocessed Folder, Salazar Files, LULAC Records, HMRC.

87. Dauplaise, "The 'Forgotten Minds' Are Remembered," *Houston Press,* Mar. 12, 1958, Clippings, Tijerina Papers; LULAC Minutes, June 5, 1958, LULAC Records, HMRC; LULAC Educational Fund, Statistical and Financial Report, June 1, 1958, to Sept. 15, 1958, Folder 19, Box 1, Tijerina Papers. Evidence exists that LULAC-supported preschool classes may have also operated in Laredo, Houston, Freeport, and other communities during the summer of 1958, under the auspices of individual LULAC councils using local funds. The Educational Fund, however, reported direct sponsorship of only the nine.

88. Alexander, "Texas Helps Her Little Latins," p. 54; LULAC Minutes, June 5, 1958, LULAC Records, HMRC.

89. LULAC Educational Fund, Statistical and Financial Report, June 1, 1958 to Sept. 15, 1958, Tijerina Papers; Alexander, "Texas Helps Her Little Latins," p. 54; Dauplaise, "The 'Forgotten Minds' Are Remembered," *Houston Press,* Mar. 12, 1958, Clippings, Tijerina Papers; Verver interview, Apr. 30, 1997.

90. The first mention of the name "Little School of the 400" that I have found in writing is in correspondence from Fred Nahas to the governor's office about LULAC and the program. See Fred Nahas to George Christian, June 17, 1958, Folder 2, Box 2, Tijerina Papers. For earlier mention of the project by the organization as simply the "LULAC Educational Program," see *LULAC News,* Sept., 1957, pp. 1, 3–4, 9–11, Hernández Papers.

91. Telegram, Fred Nahas to Governor Price Daniel, June 19, 1958; *The Imperial Crown,* July, 1958, pp. 1, 4, both in Folder 16, Box 1, Tijerina Papers. As part of the dedication festivities, the Educational Fund's Board of Directors met at Houston's Shamrock Hilton Hotel on the previous day, June 22, where it elected Tijerina as its president. See Board of Directors Meeting, LULAC Educational Fund, Inc., June 22, 1958, LULAC Club House Board of Trustees Minutes and Correspondence, LULAC Records, HMRC.

92. *Houston Chronicle,* June 24, 1958, sec. A, p. 7; Felix Tijerina to Judge Fidencio Guerra, June 18, 1958, Folder 16, Box 1; Program "Little School of the 400," both in

Tijerina Papers; *Houston Press,* June 24, 1958, p. 4; *Houston Post,* June 24, 1958, sec. 1, p. 4.

93. Program "Little School of the 400," Folder 16, Box 1, Tijerina Papers; *Houston Post,* June 24, 1958, sec. 1, p. 4; *Houston Press,* June 24, 1958, p. 4.

94. *Houston Press,* June 24, 1958, p. 4; Remarks of Governor Price Daniel, Little School of the 400 Dedication (LULAC), Sugar Land, June 23, 1958, Folder 16, Box 1, Tijerina Papers.

95. Ibid; Fred Nahas to George Christian, June 17, 1958, Folder 2, Box 2, Tijerina Papers.

96. Remarks of Governor Price Daniel, Little School of the 400 Dedication (LULAC).

97. Program "Little School of the 400"; *Houston Post,* June 24, 1958, sec. 1, p. 4; *Houston Press,* June 24, 1958, p. 4; Felix Tijerina to Judge Fidencio Guerra, June 18, 1958.

98. Sugar Land, Tex., June 23.—(UPI) (typescript); Felix Tijerina to Judge Fidencio Guerra, June 18, 1958; *The Imperial Crown,* July, 1958, pp. 1, 4, all in Folder 16, Box 1, Tijerina Papers. The articles in the *Houston Post,* June 24, 1958, sec. 1, p. 4; *Houston Press,* June 24, 1958, p. 4; and *Houston Chronicle,* June 24, 1958, sec. A, p. 7, are just three of better examples of the event's coverage.

99. *Houston Post,* June 24, 1958, sec. 1, p. 4; Felix Tijerina to Jimmy Day (telegram), June 19, 1958; Price Daniel to Felix Tijerina, June 25, 1958, both in Folder 16, Box 1, Tijerina Papers; Mrs. Felix Tijerina, Sr., interview, Aug. 8, 1992.

100. *Corpus Christi Caller,* June 24, 1958, Unprocessed Clippings, Tijerina Papers.

101. Contact Cards on Felix Tijerina, Daniel Papers; *Houston Chronicle,* Apr. 9, 1958, sec. B, p. 1.

102. *Corpus Christi Caller,* June 24, 1958, Unprocessed Clippings, Tijerina Papers; Rodríguez, *Henry B. González,* pp. 30–31, 62–78, 85.

103. *The Harris County PASO Fact Book,* p. 8, in Alfonso Vázquez Papers, HMRC; Alfonso Vázquez, telephone interview by author, Houston, Tex., Aug. 8, 1995.

104. Interviews: Hernández, Nov. 19, 1992; Salazar, Apr. 21, 1997; Rodríguez, *Henry B. Gonzalez,* p. 32; *LULAC News,* Sept., 1956, p. 11, Benson Collection; interviews: Vázquez, Aug. 8, 1995; Laurel, June 16, 1997.

105. *Houston Chronicle,* Dec. 8, 1958, sec. A, pp. 1, 4.

106. George Christian to Tony Campos, Aug. 25, 1958, Campos Papers; *LULAC News,* July, 1958, p. 1, Cortes Papers.

107. *Houston Chronicle,* Dec. 8, 1958, sec. A, pp. 1, 4.

108. Interviews: Hernández, Apr. 5, 1979, Nov. 19, 1992, Aug. 11, 1993, Nov. 17, 1997 (telephone); Salazar, Apr. 21, 1997, Sept. 16, 1997 (telephone).

109. Interviews: Hernández, Apr. 5, 1979, Nov. 19, 1992, Aug. 11, 1993; Salazar, Apr. 21, 1997.

110. *LULAC News,* Mar., 1958, p. 4, Benson Collection; *LULAC News,* July, 1958, p. 5, Cortes Papers; José Gómez and Modesto Rivera to the Supreme Council of the League of United Latin American Citizens, Application for a Council Charter, May 13, 1958, Folder 1, Box 4, Cortes Papers; Frank Zaragoza to Carmen Cortes, Application for Council Charter, May 23, 1958, Cortes Papers; LULAC Minutes, June 5, 1958, LULAC Records, HMRC; *Houston Post,* June 24, 1958, sec. 1, p. 4; *LULAC News,* Sept., 1958, back page, Hernández Papers.

CHAPTER 9. THE LULAC NATIONAL PRESIDENCY, PART II: 1958–1960

1. 1958 LULAC National Convention program, Folder 5, Box 3, Cortes Papers.

2. G. C. (Lupe) Martínez, National Campaign Headquarters for the reelection of Don Felix Tijerina for Natl. President of Lulac in 1958–59 (n.d.), Folder 1, Box 4, Cortes Papers; *LULAC News,* July, 1958, p. 5, Cortes Papers; LULAC Minutes, June 19, 1958, LULAC Records, HMRC.

3. *Laredo Times,* June 26, 1959, p. 1; *LULAC News,* Apr., 1959, p. 3, LULAC Records, HMRC; John J. Peres to John J. Herrera, May 23, 1959, Folder 10, Box 6, Herrera Papers; *LULAC News,* July, 1958, p. 7; Aug., 1958, p. 11, Cortes Papers.

4. *Laredo Free Press,* July 3, 1958, pp. 1, 3, Clippings, Tijerina Papers; Lyndon B. Johnson to Felix Tijerina, May 10, 1958, June 6, 1958, Lyndon B. Johnson Papers, Lyndon B. Johnson Library, Austin, Tex.; *Laredo Times,* June 25, 1958, p. 1, Clippings, Tijerina Papers; *LULAC News,* Aug., 1958, p. 12, Cortes Papers.

5. *LULAC News,* July, 1958, p. 7, Cortes Papers.

6. *Laredo Free Press,* July 3, 1958, pp. 1, 3, Clippings, Tijerina Papers; Campos telephone interview, July 25, 1994.

7. Mrs. Felix Tijerina, Sr., interview, Aug. 8, 1992.

8. *LULAC News,* July, 1958, p. 7, Aug., 1959, p. 11, Cortes Papers; *Laredo Free Press,* July 3, 1958, p. 1, Clippings, Tijerina Papers; interviews: Burrus, July 28, 1992; Mrs. Felix Tijerina, Sr., Aug. 8, 1992.

9. *Laredo Free Press,* July 3, 1958, pp. 1, 3, 5; "Gonzalez Campaign Manager Here," undated clipping; "Senator Gonzalez in Laredo," all in Clippings, Tijerina Papers; interviews: Laurel, June 16, 1997; William D. Bonilla by author, Corpus Christi, Tex., Mar. 29, 1999; Salazar, Sept. 16, 1997.

10. *LULAC News,* Aug., 1958, p. 7, Cortes Papers; Burrus interview, July 28, 1992.

11. *LULAC News,* July, 1958, p. 7; Dec., 1958, p. 2, Cortes Papers; Bonilla interview, Mar. 29, 1999; "LULAC Past National Presidents and Their Administrations," by John J. Herrera, Folder 9, Box 7, Herrera Papers; "LULAC through the Years, Former LULAC Presidents," in *LULAC: Fifty Years of Serving Hispanics* (n.p.).

12. *LULAC News,* July, 1958, p. 7; 1958 LULAC National Convention program, Folder 5, Box 3, both in Cortes Papers.

13. *LULAC News,* July, 1958, pp. 2, 4–5, 13, Cortes Papers; *LULAC News,* Feb., 1959, p. 6, Hernández Papers; *LULAC News,* Oct., 1958, p. 5; Apr., 1959, p. 3, LULAC Records, HMRC; Felix Tijerina to Felix Salazar, Correspondence and Documents Re National LULAC Office, 1957–1959, National Legal Advisor, Unprocessed Folder, Salazar Files, LULAC Records, HMRC; Moses M. Sánchez to Friends and Fellow Lulac, July 8, 1958, Council No. 60 Incoming Correspondence, Flyers, and Related Documents, 1958 Folder, LULAC Records, HMRC.

14. *LULAC News,* July, 1958, pp. 4–5, 13; Aug., 1958, p. 11, Cortes Papers; *LULAC News,* Oct., 1958, p. 5, LULAC Records, HMRC; LULAC 30th National Convention (June, 1959), program, Folder 6, Box 3, LULAC Records, HMRC.

15. Lyndon B. Johnson to Felix Tijerina, July 10, 1958, Johnson Papers.

16. Alexander, "Texas Helps Her Little Latins," p. 55.

17. Felix Tijerina to Board of Directors, LULAC Educational Fund, Inc. (report), Sept. 23, 1958, pp. 1, 3, Folder 19, Box 1, Tijerina Papers; *LULAC News,* Oct., 1958, p. 8, LULAC Records, HMRC; Alexander, "Texas Helps Her Little Latins," p. 55.

18. Tijerina to Board of Directors, LULAC Educational Fund, Inc., Sept. 23, 1958.

19. Ibid.

20. Ibid.

21. Ibid.; Alfred J. Hernández, telephone interview by author, Houston, Tex., Apr. 10, 1995.

22. *LULAC News,* Aug., 1958, p. 9, Cortes Papers; *LULAC News,* Oct., 1958, pp. 2, 4, 7, LULAC Records, HMRC.

23. *LULAC News,* Oct., 1958, pp. 3, 7, LULAC Records, HMRC.

24. *LULAC News,* Nov., 1958, p. 6, Cortes Papers.

25. *LULAC News,* Oct., 1958, pp. 2–3, LULAC Records, HMRC.

26. Ibid., p. 3; *LULAC News,* Nov., 1958, pp. 3, 7, Cortes Papers.

27. *LULAC News,* Nov., 1958, p. 3, Cortes Papers; LULAC Minutes, Oct. 23, 1958, LULAC Records, HMRC.

28. *LULAC News,* Oct., 1958, p. 3, LULAC Records, HMRC.

29. L. DeWitt Hale to the Members of the House, May 8, 1957, Hale-Aikin Committee Folder, HCR 105; *Citizens of Texas Recommend . . . a Public School Program to Meet the Needs of Their Children* (pamphlet, Texas State Teachers Association, n.d.), p. 1, in Report on Education from Committee of Twenty-four Folder; *Austin Statesman,* Oct. 17, 1957, sec. A, p. 19, clipping in Hale-Aikin News Article Folder, all in L. DeWitt Hale Papers, Special Collections and Archives, TAMU-CC (hereafter cited as Hale Papers); L. DeWitt Hale, telephone interview by author, Austin, Tex., Dec. 8, 1993.

30. *Houston Chronicle,* Feb. 9, 1958, sec. 8, p. 5, Clippings, Tijerina Papers; *Texas Outlook,* Nov., 1957, pp. 26-27; *Austin Statesman,* Oct. 17, 1957, sec. A, p. 19, clipping in Hale-Aikin News Article Folder, Hale Papers.

31. Report of Sub-Committee on Program (n.d.) in Hale-Aikin Progam Folder; Summary of School Program Section from County Reports; Minutes of the Program Subcommittee Meeting, July 1, 1958; W. R. Goodson to DeWitt Hale, July 2, 1958, and Proposed Outline for Program Committee Report; *Corpus Christi Times,* Sept. 17, 1958, p. 10, clipping in Hale-Aikin General Material Folder, all in Hale Papers; Tijerina to Board of Directors, LULAC Educational Fund, Inc., Sept. 23, 1958, Folder 19, Box 1, Tijerina Papers; Hale interview, Dec. 8, 1993.

32. *Corpus Christi Caller,* Sept. 3, 1958, clipping in Hale-Aikin Program Folder, Hale Papers.

33. "School Program," revised for meeting on Oct. 15, 1958, adopted as amended, Hale-Aikin Program Folder, Hale Papers.

34. "Proposals to Improve Public Education in Texas" (report from the Hale-Aikin Committee of Twenty-four for the Study of Texas Public Schools), Dec., 1958, pp. 2, 4, Hale-Aikin Final Reports Folder, Hale Papers.

35. Hale interview, Dec. 8, 1993.

36. Tijerina to Board of Directors, LULAC Educational Fund, Inc., Sept. 23, 1958,

Folder 19, Box 1; Tijerina to Isabel P. Villanueva, Oct. 28, 1958, Folder 2, Box 2, both in Tijerina Papers.

37. *Houston Chronicle,* Oct. 26, 1958, sec. A, p. 24; Carmen Cortes to Genaro Flores, Oct. 17, 1958, Incoming Correspondence and Documents Re National LULAC Office, 1958 Folder, LULAC Records, HMRC; *LULAC News,* Dec., 1958, pp. 4–5, 8, Cortes Papers; Wm. D. Bonilla to Alfred J. Hernández, Oct. 31, 1958, Folder 2, Box 2, Tijerina Papers; *Corpus Christi Caller,* Aug. 14, 1959, sec. B, p. 4; *Summer English Classes, Pre-School English Classes, Pre-School English Classes for Non-English Speaking Children, 1956–1960* (report) and *Evaluation of Pre-School Activity, Lamar School, Room 21, Mrs. Willie Golin* (report), summer, 1956, Pre-School English Instruction Folder, Mireles Papers.

38. LULAC Educational Fund, Inc., Financial Statements, 1957–1961, Folder 19, Box 1, Tijerina Papers; *LULAC News,* Sept., 1957, p. 4, Hernández Papers.

39. *LULAC News,* Sept., 1958, p. 4; Feb., 1959, p. 6, Hernández Papers; *LULAC News,* Oct., 1958, p. 6, LULAC Records, HMRC; *LULAC News,* Jan., 1959, p. 6, Cortes Papers.

40. *Houston Post,* Nov. 27, 1958, sec. 5 and *Houston Press,* Feb. 24, 1958, p. 4, Clippings, Tijerina Papers; *LULAC News,* Jan., 1959, p. 4, Cortes Papers.

41. *Excelsior,* Nov. 29, 1958, sec. A, p. 14, Clippings, Tijerina Papers.

42. *LULAC News,* Jan., 1959, pp. 3, 12, Cortes Papers. Nor would the October, 1958, inauguration be the only time that Tijerina shook hands with López Mateos. On October 18, 1959, Felix was a guest at a barbecue at the LBJ Ranch in honor of the Mexican president. There he discussed LULAC with "Don Adolfo" and impressed upon him that the organization was working to solve the many problems of the Latin America people in the United States. See Lyndon B. Johnson to Felix Tijerina, Oct. 26, 1959, Johnson Papers; *LULAC News,* Nov., 1959, p. 3, Cortes Papers.

43. *Houston Chronicle,* Dec. 1, 1958, pp. 1, 12; Dec. 2, 1958, pp. 1–2; Dec. 3, 1958, pp. 1, 19; Dec. 4, 1958, pp. 1, 7; Dec. 5, 1958, pp. 1, 4; Dec. 5, 1958, pp. 1, 4; Dec. 6, 1958, pp. 1, 4; Dec. 7, 1958, pp. 1, 25; Dec. 8, 1958, pp. 1, 4; Dec. 9, 1958, pp. 1, 4; Dec. 10, 1958, pp. 1, 4; Dec. 11, 1958, pp. 1, 16, Clippings, Tijerina Papers.

44. Ibid., Dec. 1, 1958, pp. 1, 12.

45. Ibid.

46. Ibid., Dec. 2, 1958, pp. 1–2; Dec. 9, 1958, pp. 1, 4.

47. Ibid., Dec. 2, 1958, pp. 1–2; Dec. 8, 1958, pp. 1, 4; Dec. 10, 1958, pp. 1, 4.

48. Ibid., Dec. 8, 1958, pp. 1, 4.

49. *LULAC News,* Feb., 1959, p. 6, Hernández Papers.

50. *LULAC News,* Mar., 1959, p. 2, Cortes Papers.

51. *LULAC News,* Feb., 1959, p. 24, Hernández Papers; *LULAC News,* Mar., 1959, pp. 4, 6, 8, Cortes Papers; Thad Hutcheson to Wilton B. Persons, Feb. 6, 1959, PPF 47: League of United Latin American Citizens, Records of the President, White House Central Files, Eisenhower Library; *Houston Press,* Feb. 10, 1959, p. 2; Lyndon B. Johnson to Felix Tijerina, Mar. 9, Mar. 11, 1959, Johnson Papers; *The Log,* Feb. 26, 1959, p. 1.

52. Minutes of Meeting of the Houston Members of the Texas Committee to Plan for the 1960 White House Conference on Children and Youth, Folder 12, Box 1, Tijerina Papers.

53. *LULAC News,* Apr., 1958, pp. 2–3, LULAC Records, HMRC; George Rivera, Jr.,

and Juventino Mejía, "Más aya del ancho río: Mexicanos in Western New York," *Aztlán: International Journal of Chicano Studies Research* 7, no. 3 (fall, 1976): 500–501.

54. *The Lackawanna Leader,* Mar. 26, 1959, p. 1, Folder 2, Box 4, Cortes Papers; LULAC *News,* Apr., 1958, pp. 2–3, LULAC Records, HMRC; *LULAC News,* May 1959, p. 4, Cortes Papers.

55. *LULAC News,* Apr., 1958, pp. 2–3, LULAC Records, HMRC; *LULAC News,* May, 1959, pp. 4–5, 7, Cortes Papers; Rivera and Mejía, "Más aya del ancho río," p. 501.

56. Minutes, Third Supreme Council Meeting, Apr. 24, 1960, Albert Hotel, Albert Lea, Minn., p. 2, Unprocessed Folder, Salazar Files, LULAC Records, HMRC.

57. Rodríguez, *What Price Education?,* p. 4, Folder 14, Box 2; *Corpus Christi Caller-Times,* Mar. 8, 1959, p. 16, Clippings, both in Tijerina Papers; *LULAC News,* Apr., 1959, p. 3, LULAC Records, HMRC.

58. *LULAC News,* Apr., 1959, p. 3, LULAC Records, HMRC.

59. *LULAC News,* May, 1959, p. 8, Cortes Papers; Hale interview, Dec. 8, 1993; "A Bill to Be Entitled an Act authorizing a pre-school instructional program for non-English speaking children" (H.B. 51/S.B. 62), Hale-Aikin—Other than H.B. 22 Folder, Box 2 of 3, Hale Papers.

60. Alexander, "Texas Helps Her Little Latins," p. 55; *Corpus Christi Caller,* Aug. 14, 1959, sec. B, p. 4. Jake Rodríguez in *What Price Education?* (p. 4, Folder 14, Box 2, Tijerina Papers) notes that the Tijerina administration had gathered results from pre-school programs in Eagle Pass, Odessa, Freeport, McAllen, and Corpus Christi. Also, *LULAC in Action—Human Values, Unlimited* (Folder 13, Box 2, Tijerina Papers), an official Little School publication, reviews the work of E. E. Mireles, which no doubt had come to Tijerina's attention by this time.

61. Elliott, "Now Juanito Can Read," p. 135; Hale interview, Dec. 8, 1993.

62. *Houston Press,* Feb. 10, 1959, p. 2.

63. *Corpus Christi Caller,* Mar. 10, 1959, sec. B, p. 8.

64. Price Daniel to Felix Tijerina, Apr. 3, 1959, Folder 15, Box 2, Tijerina Papers.

65. *Journal of the House of Representatives of the Regular Session of the Fifty-sixth Legislature of the State of Texas,* pp. 1626–28, 2853–54, 3016; *Journal of the Senate of the State of Texas Regular Session of the Fifty-sixth Legislature,* pp. 1302–1303; Quintanilla, "The 'Little School of the 400,'" p. 80; *LULAC News,* May, 1959, p. 8, Cortes Papers.

66. *LULAC News,* June, 1959, p. 3, Cortes Papers; Elliott, "Now Juanito Can Read," p. 135; Felix Tijerina to DeWitt Hale, May 14, 1959, Committee of Twenty-four's Report on Education Folder, Hale Papers.

67. Status of Hale-Aikin Recommendations, May 22, 1959, Final Press Release—Hale-Aikin Folder, May 22, 1959; Statement of Representative L. DeWitt Hale Concerning a Special Session for Consideration of Hale-Aikin Committee Proposals, Hale-Aikin—General—1959 Folder, both in Hale Papers; Hale interview, Dec. 8, 1993.

68. Captioned photograph of Bill Signing, June 1, 1959, Folder 15, Box 2, Tijerina Papers; *Dallas Morning News,* June 2, 1959, Bound Newspaper Clippings, Daniel Papers.

69. San Miguel, *"Let All of Them Take Heed,"* p. 149; H.B. 51 by McGregor and Hale, Hale-Aikin Other Than H.B. 22 Folder, Hale Papers; Texas Legislature, 56th Regular

Session, H.B. 51, *Non-English Speaking Children: Pre-School Instructional Program,* General and Special Laws of the State of Texas (Austin, 1959), chap. 481, pp. 1052–1053.

70. Address of L. DeWitt Hale to Beeville Faculty Association, Nov. 18, 1958, pp. 12–13, Hale-Aikin Speech Material Folder, Hale Papers; Hale interview, Dec. 8, 1993.

71. *Corpus Christi Caller-Times,* Feb. 1, 1959, sec. B, p. 2; Feb. 15, 1959, sec. B, p. 5, Hale-Aikin Speech Material Folder, Hale Papers; author's recollections of the late 1950s and early 1960s.

72. Author's recollections of the late 1950s and early 1960s.

73. *Houston Chronicle,* Dec. 1, 1958, p. 1; author's recollections of the late 1950s and early 1960s.

74. *LULAC News,* May, 1959, p. 2, Cortes Papers.

75. Ibid., pp. 2–3.

76. Carmen Cortes interview, Nov. 1, 1981 (telephone); *LULAC News,* June, 1959, pp. 1–2, 4, 6, 8, Cortes Papers.

77. Minutes of 30th National LULAC Convention, Unprocessed Folder, Salazar Files, LULAC Records, HMRC; LULAC 30th National Convention (June, 1959) program, Folder 6, Box 3, Cortes Papers.

78. Interviews: Hernández, Aug. 11, 1993; Salazar, Apr. 21, 1997; Tony Campos by telephone with author, Houston, Tex., Sept. 21, 1997; Minutes of 30th National LULAC Convention, Salazar Files.

79. Minutes of 30th National LULAC Convention; John J. Herrera, "Felix Tijerina: 'His Work Was His Monument'" (speech), ca. 1965, Folder 21, Box 6, Herrera Papers.

80. Felix Tijerina to Felix Salazar, July 29, 1959 (with attachments), Unprocessed Folder, Salazar Files, LULAC Records, HMRC; Hernández interview, Aug. 11, 1993.

81. Hernández interview, Aug. 11, 1993; LULAC 30th National Convention (June, 1959) program.

82. LULAC 30th National Convention (June, 1959) program; Salazar interview, Apr. 21, 1997.

83. Tentative National Roster 1959–60, Unprocessed Folder, Salazar Files, LULAC Records, HMRC; *LULAC News,* Nov., 1959, pp. 2–3, Cortes Papers.

84. J. W. Edgar to the Superintendent Addressed, July 13, 1959, Unprocessed Folder, Salazar Files, LULAC Records, HMRC; San Miguel, *"Let All of Them Take Heed,"* p. 151.

85. *Corpus Christi Times,* Aug. 14, 1959, sec. B, p. 4; "Local Language Plan Used as State Model," unidentified Corpus Christi newspaper, Aug. 12, 1959, Clippings; Rodríguez, *What Price Education?,* p. 4, Folder 14, Box 2, both in Tijerina Papers.

86. Alexander, "Texas Helps Her Little Latins," p. 55; LULAC Educational Fund, Inc., Statement of Income and Expenses, 10/1/57 thru 2/28/62; LULAC Educational Fund, Inc., Financial Report, Dec. 31, 1958; To the Board of Directors, LULAC Educational Fund, Inc., ca. Feb. 28, 1959; LULAC Educational Fund, Inc., Receipts and Disbursements, June 10, 1959, to June 10, 1960, all in Folder 19, Box 1, Tijerina Papers; *Houston Press,* Jan. 23, 1960, p. 2, Folder 3, Box 4, Cortes Papers.

87. LULAC Educational Fund, Inc., Cost of the Little School of the 400 per Child Attending 1957 through 1962, Folder 19, Box 1, Tijerina Papers.

88. J. W. Edgar to the Superintendent Addressed, July 13, 1959, Salazar Files; San Miguel, *"Let All of Them Take Heed,"* p. 151.

89. "A Four-Hundred-Word Start," *Time,* Aug. 17, 1959, p. 56.

90. Ibid.

91. Ibid.; Alfred J. Hernández, telephone interview by author, Houston, Tex., Oct. 11, 1993; *LULAC News,* Nov., 1959, p. 5, Cortes Papers.

92. LULAC Minutes, Sept. 17, 1959, LULAC Records, HMRC.

93. Ibid.; LULAC Minutes, Oct. 8, 1959, LULAC Records, HMRC.

94. *Impacto* (Mexico City, international edition), Jan. 20, 1960, p. 26, Campos Papers.

95. Joseph Blank to Felix Tijerina, Aug. 25, 1959, Nov. 7, 1970, Folder 2, Box 2, Tijerina Papers.

96. Felix Tijerina to Whom This May Concern, Oct. 1, 1959, Folder 15, Box 2; J. W. Edgar to Jake Rodríguez, Oct. 14, 1959; Jake Rodríguez to Lulacs and Friends, Oct., 1959, Folder 2, Box 2; Rodríguez, *What Price Education?,* p. 5, Folder 14, Box 2, all in Tijerina Papers; *State Director Bulletin,* Dec., 1959, Unprocessed Folder, Salazar Files, LULAC Records, HMRC; LULAC Minutes, Aug. 20, 1959, LULAC Records, HMRC; *LULAC News,* Nov., 1959, p. 3, Cortes Papers; Felix Tijerina to Whom This May Concern, Dec. 22, 1959, Folder 15, Box 2, Tijerina Papers.

97. Felix Tijerina to Fellow LULACs, Jan. 13, 1960, Folder 3, Box 4, Cortes Papers; Rodríguez, *What Price Education?,* p. 4, Folder 14, Box 2; LULAC Educational Fund, Inc., Financial Statement, June 10, 1960, and LULAC Educational Fund, Inc., 2-23-60 thru 4-28-60, Folder 19, Box 1, both in Tijerina Papers; Alexander, "Texas Helps Her Little Latins," p. 54; San Miguel, *"Let All of Them Take Heed,"* pp. 152–54; interviews: Hernández, Oct. 11, 1993; Adame, Mar. 10, 1997.

98. *LULAC News,* Nov., 1959, p. 3, Cortes Papers; LULAC Minutes, Aug. 20, 1959, LULAC Records, HMRC.

99. LULAC Educational Fund, Inc., Public Contributions, June 10, 1959, to June 10, 1960; LULAC Educational Fund, Inc., Fund Raising Projects for 1960; LULAC Educational Fund, Inc., Felix Tijerina to Hon. National President, Vice Presidents, State Directors, District Directors, Council Presidents, Officers and Members of LULAC, Undated, all from Folder 19, Box 1, Tijerina Papers.

100. William H. Nims to Felix Tijerina, May 23, 1960, Folder 2, Box 2, Tijerina Papers; *The Log,* May 5, 1960, p. 1.

101. *Houston Post,* Mar. 27, 1960, sec. 1, p. 20; *Houston Chronicle,* Mar. 27, 1960, sec. 2, p. 2; Elliott, "Now Juanito Can Read," p. 135; A. F. Lorton, Jr., to Felix Tijerina, Mar. 25, 1960, Folder 1, Box 3, Tijerina Papers.

102. LULAC 31 Annual National Convention, San Antonio, Texas, Hilton Hotel (1960) program, back page, Folder 7, Box 3, Cortes Papers; San Miguel, *"Let All of Them Take Heed,"* pp. 154–55; Poster of Pre-School Instructional Classes for Non-English Speaking Children, Shelf Material; *LULAC in Action—Human Values, Unlimited,* both in Tijerina Papers; "Important Notice" regarding "Operation Little Schools," Folder 14, Box 3, Jake Rodríguez Papers, Benson Latin American Collection, University of Texas at Austin.

103. "Important Notice" regarding "Operation Little Schools"; LULAC 31 Annual

National Convention program, back page; Photograph captioned "Operation Little Schools," n.d., Clippings, Tijerina Papers; San Miguel, *"Let All of Them Take Heed,"* pp. 154–55.

104. Minutes, National Supreme Council Meeting, Dec. 6, 1959, Santa Fe, N.M.; Minutes, Third Supreme Council Meeting, Apr. 24, 1960, Albert Lea, Minn., both in Unprocessed Folder, Salazar Files, LULAC Records, HMRC.

105. Minutes, Third Supreme Council Meeting, Apr. 24, 1960, Albert Lea, Minn., Salazar Files; Minutes, National Supreme Council Meeting, Dec. 6, 1959, Santa Fe, N.M.

106. Annotated photostatic copy of Ernest Conine's article, "Cheats Death by Seconds," *Houston Chronicle,* Mar. 2, 1954, p. 1, Clippings, Tijerina Papers; Hernández interview, Aug. 11, 1993.

107. Minutes, National Supreme Council Meeting, Dec. 6, 1959, Santa Fe, N.M., p. 2; Minutes, Third Supreme Council Meeting, Apr. 24, 1960, Albert Lea, Minn., Salazar Files, p. 2.

108. *Houston Chronicle,* Apr. 22, 1990, sec. G, p. 1.

109. Ibid.; James J. Braniff, Jr., to Felix Tijerina, May 16, 1960, with attached clipping entitled "Latin Leader Urges Negroes to Be Patient," Unprocessed Correspondence, Tijerina Papers.

110. Ibid.; Untitled and unaddressed manuscript letter signed by Felix Tijerina, ca. May, 1960, Unprocessed Correspondence, Tijerina Papers.

111. James J. Braniff, Jr., to Felix Tijerina, May 16, 1960, with attached clipping; *Houston City Directory, 1960,* p. 137.

112. San Miguel, *"Let All of Them Take Heed,"* p. 151; *Preschool Instructional Program For Non-English Speaking Children* (Texas Education Agency, revised Feb., 1961), acknowledgments page, Folder 11, Box 2, Tijerina Papers.

113. San Miguel, *"Let All of Them Take Heed,"* p. 151.

114. Ibid.; Quintanilla, "The 'Little School of the 400,'" pp. 92–96.

115. *LULAC in Action—Human Values, Unlimited,* Folder 13, Box 3; Undated document on figures for summer, 1960, Preschool Program, Folder 2, Box 2; School Districts Approved to Participate in the Instructional Program for Preschool Non-English Speaking Children, 1960–61, Folder 16, Box 2, all in Tijerina Papers; Qunitanilla, "The 'Little School of the 400,'" p. 97.

116. Hernández interview, Aug. 11, 1993; Val Hernández to Carmen Cortes, Jan. 24, 1960, Folder 2, Box 4, Cortes Papers; Constitution and By-Laws of the League of United Latin American Citizens, 1960, pp. 16, 45, LULAC Folder, Mireles Papers.

117. Hernández interview, Aug. 11, 1993.

118. Ibid., Oct. 11, 1993; LULAC 31 Annual National Convention program, Cortes Papers; Minutes, LULAC National Convention, June 30–July 3, 1960, San Antonio, Tex., Folder 9, Box 3, Tijerina Papers.

119. Minutes, LULAC National Convention, June 30–July 3, 1960; LULAC 31 Annual National Convention program, Cortes Papers.

120. Minutes, LULAC National Convention, June 30–July 3, 1960, Resolution Nos. 10, 11, 12, 13, 15, and 19, Folder 9, Box 3, Tijerina Papers.

121. Ibid., Resolution No. 18; Hernández interview, Oct. 11, 1993.

122. Minutes, LULAC National Convention, June 30–July 3, 1960, Resolution No. 26.

123. *LULAC in Action—Human Values, Unlimited,* Folder 13, Box 3; *Houston Press,* July 11, 1960, p. 14, Clippings, both in Tijerina Papers.

124. Minutes, LULAC National Convention, June 30–July 3, 1960. Bitterness seems to have been a feeling shared by many of the past LULAC national presidents.

125. Hale interview, Dec. 8, 1993.

126. Map of the states within the American G.I. Forum, García Papers; *LULAC News,* Feb., 1959, p. 5, Hernández Papers.

127. League of United Latin American Citizens, 37th National Convention (program, 1966), n.p., Ernest Eguía Papers, HMRC; Hector Godínez to Carmen Cortez [*sic*], Jan. 29, 1960, Folder 2, Box 4, Cortes Papers; *LULAC: Leadership, Unity, Loyalty, Americanism, Citizenship, 1961* (newsletter-type publication), n.p., Campos Papers.

128. *Houston Chronicle,* Dec. 8, 1958, p. 4; García, *Mexican Americans,* p. 60; De León, *Ethnicity in the Sunbelt,* pp. 136–37. Herrera's criticisms of the Little School appear in the above-cited *Houston Chronicle* article. While the article does not specifically identify Herrera by name, he is most likely the source of these negative comments. Benjamin Márquez, *LULAC: The Evolution of a Mexican American Political Organization,* p. 59.

129. *LULAC: Fifty Years of Serving Hispanics* (n.p.); interviews: Hernández, Oct. 11, 1993; Salazar, Apr. 21, 1997.

130. San Miguel, *"Let All of Them Take Heed,"* pp. 158–59.

131. "LULAC National Presidents and Their Administrations," by John J. Herrera, Herrera Papers. When Tijerina turned the national office over to Hector Godínez, Felix transferred to his successor the funds in the treasury as well, amounting to a little over twenty-four hundred dollars, somewhat less than the three thousand dollars Tijerina had received from Oscar Laurel four years before. Herrera's critical assessment no doubt referred to the initial expectations among at least some LULACs that Tijerina, as a successful businessman, would bring financial solvency to the organization. See League of United Latin American Citizens Financial Statements, such as June 19, 1961, Exhibit D, Folder 8, Box 3, Tijerina Papers.

132. *Houston Chronicle,* Dec. 1, 1958, pp. 1, 12; Dec. 10, 1958, pp. 1, 4; Dec. 11, 1958, pp. 1, 16.

133. Ibid., Dec. 8, 1958, pp. 1, 4; De León, *Ethnicity in the Sunbelt,* pp. 138–39.

134. Márquez, *LULAC,* pp. 51–53, 56–58.

135. *LULAC News,* Dec., 1958, p. 3, Cortes Papers.

136. "A Four-Hundred-Word Start," *Time,* Aug. 17, 1959, p. 56.

137. Senator Carlos F. Truan, interview by author, Corpus Christi, Tex., Nov. 14, 1997.

CHAPTER 10. CITIZEN FELIX: THE FINAL YEARS, 1960–1965

1. Carl Allsup, *The American G.I. Forum: Origins and Evolution,* pp. 130–32; Card of appreciation from cochairmen of the Johnson for President Dinner, June 13, 1960,

Tijerina Papers; Alfred J. Hernández, telephone interview by author, Houston, Tex., July 19, 1994.

2. Allsup, *The American G. I. Forum,* pp. 131–32; Alfonso Vázquez, interviews by author, Houston, Tex., Sept. 26, Oct. 20, and Nov. 15, 1978, Oral History Collection, HMRC; Vázquez interview, Aug. 8, 1995; Inauguration ceremonies program, 1960, tickets, and passes to inauguration activities, Box 3, Folder 13, Tijerina Papers; Alfred J. Hernández interview, July 19, 1994.

3. Mrs. Felix Tijerina, Sr., interview by author, Houston, Tex., July 30, 1994.

4. LULAC Minutes, Sept. 8, 1960, LULAC Records, HMRC; *Houston Post,* Oct. 8, 1960, Clippings, Tijerina Papers.

5. *Houston Chronicle,* Oct. 30, 1960, sec. 1, p. 16; Carleton, *Red Scare!,* pp. 154–78.

6. Carleton, *Red Scare!,* pp. 293–94; *Houston Post,* Oct. 8, 1960, Clippings, Tijerina Papers; *Houston Chronicle,* Oct. 9, 1960, sec. 6, p. 3; Oct. 23, 1960, sec. 6, p. 2.

7. Carleton, *Red Scare!,* p. 293; *Houston Chronicle,* Oct. 21, 1960, sec. 1, p. 14; Oct. 23, sec. 6, p. 2.

8. Hernández interview, Oct. 26, 1983.

9. *Houston Press,* Feb. 9, 1960, Clippings, Tijerina Papers.

10. *Houston Chronicle,* Oct. 12, 1960, sec. 15, p. 15; Oct. 19, 1960, sec. 1, p. 9; Oct. 20, 1960, sec. 4, p. 20; Oct. 26, 1960, sec. 1, p. 9; Oct. 27, 1960, sec. 6, p. 1; Oct. 31, 1960, sec. 1, p. 8; Nov. 1, 1960, sec. 1, p. 1.

11. Ibid., Nov. 6, 1960, sec. 1, p. 1.

12. Ibid., Oct. 19, 1960, sec. 1, p. 9; Oct. 23, 1960, sec. 6, pp. 2–3; Oct. 30, 1960, sec. 1, p. 16; *Houston Press,* Nov. 2, 1960, p. 4.

13. *Houston Chronicle,* Oct. 30, 1960, sec. 1, p. 16; Oct. 23, 1960, sec. 6, p. 2.

14. Ibid., Oct. 18, 1960, sec. 2, p. 1; "Third School Election Slate Is Proposed," *Houston Chronicle;* Jim Maloney, "Middle-of-the-Roaders May Form School Slate"; *Houston Chronicle,* Oct. 16, 1960, all in Undated Clippings, Tijerina Papers.

15. *Houston Chronicle,* Nov. 5, 1960, sec. 1, p. 1; Oct. 20, 1960, sec. 4, p. 20; *Houston Press,* Nov. 1, 1960, p. 4.

16. *Houston Chronicle,* Oct. 21, 1960, sec. 1, p. 14; Carleton, *Red Scare!,* p. 293.

17. *Houston Chronicle,* Oct. 27, 1960, sec. 6, p. 1; Nov. 1, 1960, sec. 1, p. 1.

18. Ibid., Nov. 2, 1960, sec. 1, pp. 1, 7.

19. *Houston Press,* Nov. 1, 1960, p. 4.

20. *Houston Chronicle,* Nov. 3, 1960, sec. 1, p. 9; Carleton, *Red Scare!,* pp. 292–94.

21. *Houston Post,* Nov. 3, 1960, sec. 3, p. 15.

22. Hernández interview, Oct. 26, 1983; Campaign push card, bumper sticker, and postcard, n.d., Folder 14, Box 1, Tijerina Papers; *Houston Press,* Nov. 2, 1960, p. 11; *Houston Chronicle,* Oct. 21, 1960, sec. 1, p. 14; *The Informer* (Houston), Nov. 5, 1960, p. 8.

23. *Houston Chronicle,* Nov. 9, 1960, sec. 1, p. 1; *Houston Post,* Nov. 9, 1960, sec. 1, p. 8.

24. *Houston Chronicle,* Nov. 9, 1960, sec. 1, p. 9; Oct. 13, 1960, sec. 1, p. 1; *Houston Press,* Nov. 2, 1960, p. 4.

25. Ken Parker, interview by author, Houston, Tex., June 10, 1983.

26. Anonymous interviews by author, Feb. 26, 1983, Mar. 1, 1983.

27. *Houston Press,* Nov. 15, 1960, Clippings, Tijerina Papers; Mrs. Felix Tijerina, Sr., interview, July 30, 1994.

28. Carleton, *Red Scare!,* pp. 297–98.

29. Tony Campos to Price Daniel (telegram), Dec. 28, 1960, Daniel Papers; Price Daniel to Tony Campos, Jan. 3, 1961; Lyndon B. Johnson to Tony Campos, Jan. 4, 1961, both in Campos Papers; Tony Campos to President Elect John F. Kennedy (telegram), Dec. 27, 1960, White House Name File, John Fitzgerald Kennedy Library, Boston, Mass.

30. Lewis Cutrer to President Elect John F. Kennedy (telegram), Dec. 29, 1960, White House Name File, Kennedy Library. Cutrer's was the only other letter forwarding Tijerina's name found in the Kennedy Library's files dealing with this issue and time period.

31. Campos interview, July 25, 1994; "Texas Solon's Spanish Fluency Comes in Handy," undated clipping, ca. early 1961, Tijerina Papers; Hernández interview, July 19, 1994.

32. "El Paso Mayor May Get Diplomatic Post," undated clipping, Tijerina Papers; *New York Times,* Feb. 16, 1961, p. 5; Campos interview, July 25, 1994.

33. Lawrence F. O'Brien to Tony Campos, Mar. 14, 1961, Campos Papers; Lawrence F. O'Brien to Mayor Lewis Cutrer, White House Name File, Kennedy Library; *New York Times,* Mar. 31, 1961, p. 7; Apr. 1, 1961, p. 17.

34. Interviews: Mrs. Felix Tijerina, Sr., July 30, 1994; Campos, July 25, 1994; Hernández, July 19, 1994.

35. *La verdad* (Corpus Christi), Mar. 31, 1961, Campos Papers; Photograph of Tijerina with U.S. Senator Bill Blakley, Photograph Box; *Corpus Christi Caller,* Feb. 13, 1961, Clippings, both in Tijerina Papers.

36. "LULAC through the Years, Former LULAC Presidents," in *LULAC: Fifty Years of Serving Hispanics* (n.p.); Jake Rodríguez to Felix Tijerina, Nov. 7, 1961, Folder 5, Box 2; Frank M. Valdez to Felix Tijerina, May 29, 1961, Folder 10, Box 3, both in Tijerina Papers.

37. Felix Tijerina to J. W. Edgar, Sept. 24, 1960, Campos Papers; Felix Tijerina to William Bonilla, no date, Folder 3, Box 2; LULAC Educational Fund, Inc., Fund Raising Projects for 1960, Folder 19, Box 1, both in Tijerina Papers; *LULAC: Leadership, Unity Loyalty, Americanism, Citizenship, 1961* (n.p.), Campos Papers; *Houston Press,* July 15, 1960, p. 19.

38. *LULAC News* [ca. June, 1961], Folder 15, Box 3, Cortes Papers; Felix Tijerina to William Bonilla, no date; Felix Tijerina to Mamie Zisemore, July 10, 1961, both in Folder 3, Box 2, Tijerina Papers.

39. Jake Rodríguez to Felix Tijerina, July 5, 1961; Felix Tijerina to Jake Rodríguez, July 8, 1961; Hector Godínez to Felix Tijerina, July 5, 1961, all in Folder 3, Box 2, Tijerina Papers.

40. Felix Tijerina to Hector Godínez, July 8, 1961, Folder 3, Box 2, Tijerina Papers.

41. *Arizona Republic,* July 1, 1961, Clippings, Tijerina Papers; *Houston Press,* June 21, 1961, sec. 2, p. 13.

42. Elliott, "Now Juanito Can Read," pp. 132–36; *Congressional Record-Appendix,* Aug. 4, 1961, pp. A6063–A6065, Folder 1, Box 2, Tijerina Papers.

43. Alexander, "Texas Helps Her Little Latins," pp. 30–31, 54–55. Estimates of how much of his own money Tijerina ultimately spent on LULAC and the Little School program vary. Daniel Sandoval, his bookkeeper/accountant, estimated that his employer spent upwards of seventy thousand to eighty thousand dollars. Mrs. Felix, who also had reason to know, stated that it totaled a six-figure sum. Whatever the exact figure, it was substantial (Sandoval interview, June 12, 1997).

44. Louis Alexander, interview by author, Houston, Tex., May 6, 1983.

45. *Houston Post,* Aug. 1, 1961, sec. 2, p. 8; Photograph of Felix Tijerina and Dan Rather, ca. 1961, Photograph Box, Tijerina Papers; A. F. Lorton, Jr., to Felix Tijerina, Sept. 6, 1961, Folder 4, Box 4; Mrs. Charles E. Steele to Felix Tijerina, Oct. 4, 1961, Box 4, Folder 4; Frank H. Kelley to John Chancellor, Nov. 21, 1961, Folder 5, Box 2; Felix Tijerina to Jake Rodríguez, Nov. 22, 1961, all in Tijerina Papers; *Houston Press,* June 21, 1961, p. 13.

46. *Magazine reportaje del norte,* Sept.–Oct., 1961, p. 24, in Campos Papers.

47. *La prensa* (San Antonio), Aug. 16, 1962, p. 2; Aug. 23, 1962, p. 2; Rodríguez, *What Price Education?,* pp. 2, 11, 14, Folder 14, Box 2; Mexican Chamber of Commerce *Official Bulletin* (San Antonio), Aug., 1962, p. 2, all in Tijerina Papers.

48. *San Antonio Light,* Aug. 9, 1962, Clippings; Mexican Chamber of Commerce *Official Bulletin,* San Antonio, Aug., 1962, p. 2, Folder 14, Box 2; *San Antonio News,* July 9, 1963, sec. A, p. 8, Clippings, all in Tijerina Papers.

49. Letters to Felix Tijerina from: John Tower, Sept. 1, 1961, Folder 4, Box 4, Tijerina Papers; Bertha James, June 27, 1961; Sister Helen Marie, July 2, 1961; Helen Jacobstein, July 7, 1961; Melvin E. Sine, July 7, 1961; James M. Wolf, July 13, 1961; K. Frances Pendergast, July 21, 1961; Pearl Queree, July 24, 1961; Paul P. Corwin, July 24, 1961, all in Folder 3, Box 2, Tijerina Papers; Jane Montgomery, Nov. 4, [1961]; George Johnson, Nov. 27, 1961; Nell Peerson, Nov. 29, 1961, all in Folder 5, Box 2, Tijerina Papers; Clare Lee, Jan. 12, 1962, Folder 6, Box 2, Tijerina Papers; Juan D. Acevedo, Aug. 7, 1961; Phillip E. Ostroff, n.d. [ca. Aug., 1961]; Mrs. Charles E. Steele, Oct. 4, 1961; Otha E. Watts, Oct. 10, 1961; M. J. Senter, Oct. 11, 1961; Beatrice Griffith, Oct. 31, 1961, all in Folder 4, Box 4, Tijerina Papers; Campos interview, Sept. 8, 1991.

50. J. B. Casas to John J. Herrera, Aug. 4, 1961, Herrera Papers; Ernest Eguía to Dear Friend, n.d. (ca. Nov., 1961), Folder 5, Box 2, Tijerina Papers.

51. Jim Silva to Felix Tijerina, Dec. 29, 1961; Felix Tijerina to Jim Silva, Jan. 10, 1962, both in Folder 5, Box 2, Tijerina Papers; Jim Silva to Tony Campos, Jan. 11, 1962; Felix Tijerina to Frank Valdez, Jan. 18, 1962, both in Folder 6, Box 2, Tijerina Papers.

52. William Bonilla to Felix Tijerina, Feb. 20, 1962; Felix Tijerina to William Bonilla, Feb. 26, 1962, both in Folder 6, Box 2, Tijerina Papers; Minutes, Meeting of the Board of Directors of LULAC Educational Fund, Inc., Mar. 23, 1962, Folder 16, Box 2; Felix Tijerina to LULAC Members, Mar. 23, 1962, with LULAC Educational Fund, Inc., Statement of Income and Expenses, 10/1/57 thru 2/28/62, Folder 19, Box 1, both in Tijerina Papers.

53. Minutes, Meeting of the Board of Directors of LULAC Educational Fund, Inc., Mar. 23, 1962; Quintanilla, "The 'Little School of the 400,'" p. 134; Truan interview, Nov. 14, 1997.

54. Tijerina to contributors, July 27, 1962, July 31, 1962, Folder 6, Box 2; Tijerina to Sir or Madam, May, 1962, Folder 15, Box 2; Felix Tijerina to Dear Friend, Apr., 1963, Folder 7, Box 2, all in Tijerina Papers.

55. Mrs. Thomas F. Richardson to Felix Tijerina, July 30, 1962; Clarence D. Wiggam to Felix Tijerina, Apr. 18, 1962, Folder 6, Box 2, both in Tijerina Papers; Robert A. Calvert and Arnoldo De León, *The History of Texas,* p. 381; Felix Tijerina to Elizabeth Ott, Nov. 29, 1963, Folder 7, Box 2; Felix Tijerina to William Bonilla, Sept. 22, 1964, Folder 8, Box 2, both in Tijerina Papers; *Texas Outlook,* Oct., 1964, pp. 8, 32–33. Other related talks of interest which Tijerina gave during this period include an address to an assembly at Cypress-Fairbanks High School in April, 1962, for Pan American Week, where the student newspaper declared him a living example of the biblical "Good Samaritan." Tijerina delivered a "tribute" in October, 1962, at the annual Houston Journalism Assembly at the University of Houston. See *Cy-Fair Reporter,* Apr. 11, 1962, and "Latin America Focus at Journalism Meet," undated clipping, ca. Oct., 1962, both in Tijerina Papers.

56. San Miguel, *"Let All of Them Take Heed,"* p. 157; Rodríguez, *What Price Education?,* pp. 6, 11. LULAC publications show some discrepancy in the numbers of participating districts, classes, and teachers. I use those figures chosen by San Miguel as the most accurate.

57. *The Log,* Mar. 19, 1959, pp. 2–3; Mar. 26, 1959, p. 1; Apr. 2, 1959, pp. 4–5; Oct. 29, 1959, p. 2; Mar. 31, 1960, p. 3; Sept. 16, 1965, p. 2.

58. Rotary Club of Houston, Board of Directors' Meeting, Mar. 15, 1960, Tijerina Papers; *The Log,* Oct. 29, 1959, p. 2; *Pasadena Daily Citizen,* Feb. 16, 1961, p. 1, Clippings, Tijerina Papers.

59. *Houston Press,* Sept. 26, 1960, p. 4, Clippings, Tijerina Papers.

60. *The Log,* Dec. 22, 1960, p. 5; May 10, 1962, p. 2.

61. *Houston Post,* Oct. 1, 1961; *México Rotario,* Sept. 28, 1965, p. 5, both in Clippings, Tijerina Papers.

62. *El norte* (Monterrey), Dec. 9, 1961; *El porvenir* (Monterrey), Dec. 9, 1961, both in Clippings, Tijerina Papers.

63. *Houston Press,* Apr. 13, 1962, pp. 1, 7, Clippings, Tijerina Papers.

64. *The Log,* May 10, 1962, p. 2, Tijerina Papers.

65. Ibid.; *México Rotario,* Apr. 24, 1962, pp. 4, 8; Sept. 28, 1965, pp. 5–6, all in Tijerina Papers.

66. *Novedades* (Mexico City), Apr. 22, 1962, sec. 2, Tijerina Papers.

67. *Houston Press,* Apr. 25, 1962, p. 1; "Mexico Government Honors Felix Tijerina," undated clipping, both in Tijerina Papers; Mary and Charles Royds to Felix Tijerina, Apr. 27, 1962, with undated clipping, *Houston Chronicle,* sec. 3, p. 2; Unprocessed Correspondence; *The Log,* May 10, 1962, p. 2, Clippings, both in Tijerina Papers.

68. *Houston Press,* Nov. 2, 1962, p. 8; Virgil P. Lee to Ernesto S. Maurer, Oct. 18, 1962, Unprocessed Correspondence, both in Tijerina Papers; *The Log,* Nov. 1, 1962, p. 1.

69. Hubert Kanter to Felix Tijerina, June 28, 1963, Folder 23, Box 3, Tijerina Papers. Nor was Tijerina's Pan American fame limited to Mexico. Having heard of Felix's work in Texas, an Ecuadoran priest named Carlos Cuadrado G. founded and named a school

after him in Daule, Ecuador, in the early 1960s. Called Escuela de Artes y Oficios "Felix Tijerina," the school was designed to teach vocational skills to the male youth of that area. See School Named for Felix Tijerina in Ecuador, 1963, Folder 9, Box 4, Tijerina Papers.

70. *Women of Rotary Club of Houston, 1952–1953,* p. 5; *1954–1955,* p. 5; *1957–1958,* p. 8; *1958–1959,* p. 8; *1959–1960,* p. 8; *1961–1962,* p. 8, all in Tijerina Papers; *Houston Chronicle,* June 5, 1960, sec. 15, p. 7; *Houston Post,* Sept. 20, 1959, sec. 7, p. 4.

71. *The Log,* Dec. 22, 1960, p. 5; *Houston Chronicle,* Apr. 27, 1958, sec. 1, p. 6; *Houston Post,* May 28, 1960, sec. 7, p. 7; May 25, 1961, sec. 2, p. 2; *Houston Chronicle,* June 5, 1960, sec. 7, p. 17; Feb. 4, 1962, sec. 9, p. 7; *Houston Press,* Nov. 2, 1962, p. 8; Sept. 25, 1963, p. 18; *River Oaks Times* (Houston), Sept. 25, 1959, p. 10, all in Clippings, Tijerina Papers.

72. Women of Rotary Club of Houston, Texas, 1961–1962, Meeting Minutes, Folder 5, Box 6; *Houston Chronicle,* Feb. 4, 1962, sec. 9, p. 7, Clippings; Women of Rotary, cards and letters of thanks to Mrs. Felix (Janie) Tijerina, 1961–62: Ruth (Lichty), June 13, 1962; Evelyn Mergele, Feb. 26, 1962; Barbara Gayden, Apr. 26, 1962; Margaret Coleman, May 12, 1962, all in Tijerina Papers.

73. *Houston Press,* Sept. 25, 1963, p. 18, Clippings, Tijerina Papers.

74. Allan Shivers to Felix Tijerina, Sept. 27, 1956, with attachment "Harris County Parole Board Members," Folder 14, Box 3; Felix Tijerina to Jack Ross, Oct. 30, 1958, Folder 16, Box 3, both in Tijerina Papers; *LULAC News,* Nov., 1959, p. 3, Cortes Papers; Eddie Gutiérrez, interview by author, Houston, Tex., Nov. 17, 1988.

75. George Beto to Felix Tijerina, July 12, 1962; "To Those Individuals Participating in the Pre-Release Program," Aug. 19, 1963; Jerry W. Samford to Felix Tijerina, Sept. 16, 1963, all in Folder 19, Box 3, Tijerina Papers; Blas Rodríguez, Sr., telephone interview by author, Sugar Land, Tex., Jan. 18, 1985.

76. Members of the Grand Jury to Arnold H. Krichamer, Aug. 4, 1961, Folder 17, Box 3, Tijerina Papers.

77. Houston Housing Authority, *Houston Chronicle* (microfiche), Feb. 21, 1958, Mar. 12, 1958, Texas and Local History, HPL.

78. Ibid., Feb. 10, 1958, Feb. 21, 1958, Mar. 12, 1958, Mar. 13, 1958, Mar. 26, 1958, Apr. 7, 1958, Apr. 15, 1958, and Oct. 16, 1956; Housing Authority Minutes, Nos. 376–90: 1958, pp. 2457, 2487–88, 2519.

79. Housing Authority Minutes, Nos. 376–90: 1958; Nos. 391–405: 1959; Nos. 406–18: 1960; Nos. 419–28: 1961; Nos. 429–39: 1962; Nos. 440–51: 1963; Nos. 452–63: 1964; and Nos. 461–66: 1965; *Houston Chronicle* (microfiche), Jan. 13, 1960, Feb. 28, 1962, May 29, 1963, and Mar. 26, 1964, Texas and Local History, HPL; Housing Authority Minutes, Nos. 367–90: 1958, p. 2459; Nos. 391–405: 1959, p. 2667; Nos. 440–51: 1963, p. 3372; Nos. 452–63: 1964; Nos. 461–66: 1965.

80. Housing Authority Minutes, Nos. 376–90: 1958; Nos. 391–405: 1959; Nos. 406–18: 1960; Nos. 419–28: 1961; Nos. 429–39: 1962; Nos. 440–51: 1963; Nos. 452–63: 1964; Nos. 461–66: 1965; Nos. 376–90: 1958, pp. 2479–80; Nos. 452–63: 1964, p. 3630; and Nos. 461–69: 1965, pp. 3691, 3769.

81. *Houston Post,* Sept. 14, 1961, p. 1, Clippings, Tijerina Papers.

82. *Houston Post,* Sept. 7, 1962, p. 1, Clippings, Tijerina Papers.

83. "Completely Redecorated Re-Opened Today," *Houston Post,* undated clipping; *Houston,* Feb., 1958, p. 35; Notice to All Personnel, Dec. 8, 1959, Folder 4, Box 1, all in Tijerina Papers; Mrs. Felix Tijerina, Sr., interviews by author, June 17, 1982, June 10, 1995 (telephone), Aug. 11, 1995; Frank Barrera, interview by author, Houston, Tex., July 20, 1990; Sandoval interview, June 12, 1997.

84. Felix Tijerina, Jr., telephone interview, Nov. 2, 1994; Sandoval interview, June 12, 1997.

85. Felix Tijerina, Jr., interview, Nov. 2, 1994; *Houston Post,* July 27, 1961, sec. 5, p. 5, Clippings; *Houston Chronicle,* July 30, 1961, Clippings; *Houston Press,* July 28, 1961, Clippings; Photograph of Felix Mexican Restaurant on Telephone Road, ca. 1961, Photograph Box, all in Tijerina Papers.

86. *Houston Chronicle,* July 30, 1961, Clippings, Tijerina Papers.

87. *Houston Press,* July 28, 1961, p. 9; *Houston Chronicle,* Oct. 18, 1961, Peach section, p. 1, both in Clippings, Tijerina Papers; Felix Tijerina, Jr., interview, Nov. 2, 1994.

88. *Houston Chronicle,* Nov. 14, 1962, p. 4, S.W.-Village, Clippings, Tijerina Papers.

89. Mrs. Felix Tijerina, Sr., interviews, June 17, 1982, July 30, 1994; Felix Tijerina, Jr., interview, Nov. 2, 1994; *Beaumont Enterprise,* Aug. 23, 1967, p. 10, Folder 4, Box 12; *The Star News and Shopper* (Pasadena), Feb. 5, 1970, Clippings, both in Tijerina Papers.

90. Photograph of Felix Mexican Restaurant, 616 Main Street, Photograph Box, Tijerina Papers; Mrs. Felix Tijerina, Sr., interviews, June 17, 1982, July 30, 1994; Felix Tijerina, Jr., interview, Nov. 2, 1994.

91. Central National Bank file, 1955–1971, *Houston Chronicle* (microfiche), Texas and Local History, HPL.

92. Ibid.

93. Clifton C. Carter to Felix Tijerina, Jan. 3, 1962, Vice President Collection, Container No. 52, Lyndon B. Johnson Library; Surety Savings and Loan Association Clipping File, 1961-1965, *Houston Chronicle* Library; *Houston Post,* June 30, 1965, sec. 4, p. 6, Clippings, Tijerina Papers.

94. *Wall Street Journal,* Ibid.; Sandoval interview, June 12, 1997.

95. Felix Tijerina, Jr., interview, Nov. 2, 1994.

96. Ibid.; Mrs. Felix Tijerina, Sr., interview, Sept. 13, 1980.

97. Interviews: Mrs. Felix Tijerina, Sr., July 30, 1994; Felix Tijerina, Jr., Nov. 2, 1994; *Houston City Directory, 1958,* p. 249; *1959,* p. 253.

98. Felix Tijerina, Jr., interview, Nov. 2, 1994.

99. *Houston Press,* Nov. 18, 1958, p. 6, Clippings, Tijerina Papers; Felix Tijerina, Jr., interview, Nov. 2, 1994.

100. Felix Tijerina, Jr., interview, Nov. 2, 1994.

101. Ibid.

102. Ibid.

103. Ibid.

104. Ibid.

105. Jack McIntosh to Jake Rodríguez, Dec. 21, 1964; William Bonilla to Felix

Tijerina, Sept. 16, 1964; Felix Tijerina to William Bonilla, Sept. 22, 1964, all in Folder 8, Box 2, Tijerina Papers.

106. *Houston Post,* Feb. 14, 1965, sec. 1, p. 18, and Mar. 17, 1965, Clippings, Tijerina Papers.

107. U.S. Senate Committee on Labor and Public Welfare, *Elementary and Secondary Education Act of 1965: Hearings Before the Subcommittee on Education,* 89th Cong., 1st sess., S.R. 370, Jan. 26, 29, 1965, Feb. 1, 2, 4, 8, 11, 1965, Part 1, pp. 630, 639, 803–804; "Johnson's Message to Congress Outlining Broad Program of Educational Gains," *New York Times,* Jan. 13, 1965, p. 20; Edward Zigler and Jeanette Valentine, eds., *Project Head Start: A Legacy of the War on Poverty,* pp. xv–134, 163, 195; Edward Zigler and Susan Muenchow, *Head Start: The Inside Story of America's Most Successful Educational Experiment,* pp. 4–14, 18; Housing Authority Minutes, Nos. 461–469: 1965, p. 3707; Hernández, "The Little School of the 400," in *LULAC: Fifty Years of Serving Hispanics,* n.p.; Quintanilla, "The 'Little School of the 400,'" p. 136; L. DeWitt Hale, telephone interview by author, Austin, Tex., Aug. 22, 1996; Truan interview, Nov. 14, 1997. Apparently, Project Head Start had not been formulated on the national level, at least, with the Little School of the 400 or the Texas-based Preschool Instructional Classes for Non-English Speaking Children directly in mind. If, in its inception, this federal program drew directly from the Texas effort, the record does not readily indicate so. Project Head Start emerged through the efforts and under the overall direction of Sargent Shriver, head of President Johnson's Office of Economic Opportunity. Shriver's thinking in the earliest stage was principally influenced by Susan Gray's Early Training Project in Murfreesboro, Tennessee. After being given his charge by the president, Shriver convened the Head Start National Planning Committee in January, 1965, chaired by Dr. Robert Cooke of Johns Hopkins University Medical School. This committee had thirteen other members, including public health experts, physicians, social workers, psychologists, and early childhood educators. The Cooke Committee's deliberations gave intellectual shape to the program. Much broader than anything that had come before it, Project Head Start was designed to be a comprehensive intervention program covering many aspects of early-childhood development and containing five basic components: health, education, parental involvement, nutrition, and social and psychological services. Designed to be flexible, Project Head Start actually had no specific educational curriculum "model" at the national level that could be termed *the* Head Start curriculum. But, according to its founders, the first guidelines of the educational component of Head Start emerged using the model of a 1963 prekindergarten program in New Haven, Connecticut, run by Jeannette Stone. This credit to Stone's project, however, does not rule out a more indirect influence of the Texas efforts on these national developments, especially given the great amount of publicity Tijerina received; it is a subject that might bear more scholarly examination. Also of merit for future study is the influence of the Little School and Texas-financed preschool classes on local Texas/Southwestern Head Start programs, since much latitude was afforded local agencies in the design and implementation of their Head Start efforts. Clearly, people familiar with Head Start during the 1960s and Tijerina's Little School perceived a similarity between the two.

In his message to Congress on Jan. 12, 1965, presenting his elementary and secondary school legislation, President Johnson mentioned only preschool projects in Baltimore and New York as examples of successful programs he wanted to initiate through this legislation.

108. Henry J. Lacour to Chamber of Commerce, Houston, Tex., Aug. 8, 1961, Folder 1, Box 2, Tijerina Papers; Hernández interview, Apr. 10, 1995. Senator Ralph Yarborough would himself author the first federal bilingual education bill in 1968. Carlos Truan, as a member of the Texas legislature, would work with Yarborough on this act (*Corpus Christi Caller-Times,* Jan. 28, 1996, pp. 1, 9).

109. San Miguel, *"Let All Of Them Take Heed,"* p. 157; Kennon Hillyer to Felix Tijerina, July 6, 1965; William H. Rouse to Felix Tijerina, July 5, 1965, Folder 9, Box 2, both in Tijerina Papers.

110. Hernández interview, Apr. 10, 1995; "LULAC through the Years, Former LULAC Presidents," in *LULAC: 50 Years of Serving Hispanics* (n.p.).

111. Mrs. Felix Tijerina, Sr., interviews, May 31, 1983, July 30, 1994; "Han matado a mi presidente," Folder 16, Box 3, Herrera Papers.

112. Mr. and Mrs. Felix Tijerina to the President (telegram), Nov. 26, 1963, Johnson Papers.

113. *New York Times,* July 3, 1964, pp. 1, 9; Notice to Hostess, Cashiers, and Waiters, from Felix Tijerina, Owner, July 3, 1964, Folder 4, Box 1, Tijerina Papers.

114. Housing Authority Minutes, Nos. 461–69: 1965, p. 3691.

115. *Houston Chronicle,* Mar. 26, 1964, Clippings; Joan Moore to Felix Tijerina, Apr. 13, 1964, Folder 8, Box 2, both in Tijerina Papers.

116. Joan Moore to Felix Tijerina, Apr. 13, 1964; Leo Grebler, Joan W. Moore, Ralph C. Guzman, et al., *The Mexican-American People: The Nation's Second Largest Minority,* pp. vii, ix, 3, 607–608, 674.

117. *Houston Chronicle,* May 4, 1964, sec. 4, p. 1, and June 20, 1964, the Church Chronicle Section, p. 4, Clippings; *La voz* (Houston), June 19, 1964, p. 1, Clippings; Receipt from Felix H. Morales and Son Funeral Home, May 14, 1964, Unprocessed Materials, all in Tijerina Papers; Mrs. Felix Tijerina, Sr., telephone interview, Feb. 14, 1995; Francisco Peña Ayala and Francisco Peña Garza interview, Sept. 27, 1997; Mario Góngora Villarreal interview, Sept. 27, 1997.

118. Hernández interview, Apr. 10, 1995; Vázquez interview, Aug. 8, 1995.

119. Mrs. Felix Tijerina, Sr., interview, July 30, 1994.

120. *The Log,* Mar. 25, 1965, p. 1; Sept. 16, 1965, p. 2; Carleton and Kreneck, *Houston,* p. 25.

121. *Houston Post,* June 30, 1965, sec. 4, p. 6, Clippings, Tijerina Papers.

122. Interviews: Mrs. Felix Tijerina, Sr., May 31, 1983, Feb. 14, 1995; Felix Tijerina, Jr., Nov. 2, 1994; Felix Tijerina to Jake Rodríguez, Nov. 19, 1964, Folder 8, Box 2, Tijerina Papers; Hernández interview, Apr. 10, 1995.

123. Mrs. Felix Tijerina, Sr., interviews, May 31, 1983, Feb. 14, 1995; Photographs of Felix Mexican Restaurant, 105 West Bird, Pasadena, Tex., Photograph Box, Tijerina Papers.

124. Interviews: Mrs. Felix Tijerina, Sr., May 31, 1983, Feb. 14, 1995; Felix Tijerina, Jr., Nov. 2, 1994.

125. Interviews: Mrs. Felix Tijerina, Sr., Feb. 14, 1995; Felix Tijerina, Jr., Nov. 2, 1994; *Star News and Shopper* (Pasadena, Tex.), Feb. 5, 1970, Clippings; Undated Newspaper Advertisement, Clippings; *Beaumont Enterprise,* Aug. 23, 1967, p. 10, Clippings; Photographs of Felix Mexican Restaurant, Pasadena, Tex., and Billboards, Photograph Box, all in Tijerina Papers.

126. Interviews: Mrs. Felix Tijerina, Sr., May 31, 1983, Feb. 14, 1995; Felix Tijerina, Jr., Nov. 2, 1994.

127. Mrs. Felix Tijerina, Sr., interviews, Feb. 14, 1995, Aug. 11, 1995.

128. Ibid.; *Houston Chronicle,* Sept. 4, 1965, p. 1, Clippings; *Houston Post,* Sept. 5, 1965, p. 1, Clippings; Certificate of Death, Felix Tijerina, Sept. 9, 1965, Documents Dealing with Death of Felix Tijerina, all in Tijerina Papers.

129. Mrs. Felix Tijerina, Sr., interviews, Feb. 14, 1995, Aug. 11, 1995.

130. *Houston Post,* Sept. 5, 1965, pp. 1, 4; *Houston Chronicle,* Sept. 5, 1965, p. 1, both in Clippings, Tijerina Papers.

131. Interviews: Mrs. Felix Tijerina, Sr., Feb. 14, 1995; Francisco Peña Garza, Feb. 21, 1998 (telephone); "Felix Tijerina, 'His Work Was His Monument,'" ca. 1965, Folder 21, Box 6, Herrera Papers; Salazar interview, Apr. 21, 1997.

132. Interviews: Mrs. Felix Tijerina, Sr., Feb. 14, 1995; Hernández, Oct. 11, 1993, Apr. 10, 1995; "Felix Tijerina, 'His Work Was His Monument'"; "Sermon at the Funeral of Felix Tijerina," Sept. 6, 1965, Folder 10, Box 4, Tijerina Papers.

133. Mrs. Felix Tijerina, Sr., interview, Feb. 14, 1995; *Houston Post,* Sept. 5, 1965, sec. 1, pp. 1, 4; Sept. 5, 1965, sec. 5, p. 3; Sept. 6, 1965, sec. 3, p. 20; Felix Tijerina, Jr., telephone interview, Nov. 5, 1997; Larry Jasek, telephone interview by author, Houston, Tex., Feb. 26, 1998; Hernández interview, Nov. 17, 1997; "Felix Tijerina, 'His Work Was His Monument.'"

134. Richard Nixon to Mrs. Felix Tijerina, Sept. 20, 1965, Tijerina Papers; *The Log,* Sept. 16, 1965, p. 2; *México Rotario,* Sept. 28, 1965, pp. 5–6, Tijerina Papers; Fidencio M. Guerra to E. E. Mireles, Sept. 10, 1965, Unprocessed Correspondence, Mireles Papers; LULAC Correspondence, 1965, Folder 19, Box 6, Herrera Papers; "Felix Tijerina, 'His Work Was His Monument'"; *Chuck Wagon,* Oct., 1965; *Corpus Christi Caller,* sec. B, p. 2, Clippings, both in Tijerina Papers.

135. *Houston Post,* Sept. 5, 1965, p. 1, Clippings, Tijerina Papers.

BIBLIOGRAPHY

UNPUBLISHED SOURCES

Archivo de la parroquia de San Nicolás Tolentino en San Nicolás de los Garza, estado de Nuevo León. Matrimonios, bautismo de hijos legitimos, y confirmaciones. Local History Department, Corpus Christi Public Library, Corpus Christi, Tex. Microfilm.

Campos, Tony. Papers. Houston Metropolitan Research Center, Houston Public Library, Houston, Tex.

Censo del estado de Nuevo León. October 20, 1895. Local History Department, Corpus Christi Public Library, Corpus Christi, Tex.

Centro de Información de Historica Regional. Records. Hacienda San Pedro, Zuazua, Nuevo León.

Chaírez Family Collection. Houston Metropolitan Research Center, Houston Public Library, Houston, Tex.

Club México Bello Records. Houston Metropolitan Research Center, Houston Public Library, Houston, Tex.

Cortes, Carmen. Papers. Houston Metropolitan Research Center, Houston Public Library, Houston, Tex.

Daniel, Price, Sr. Papers. Sam Houston Regional Library and Research Center, Liberty, Tex.

Denison, Lynne W., and L. L. Pugh. "Houston Public School Buildings: Their History and Location." Typescript, 1936. Texas and Local History Department, Houston Public Library, Houston, Tex.

District Court of the United States for the Southern District of Texas. Houston Division Records. *Felix Tijerina, Plaintiff, v. Herbert Brownell, Jr., Attorney General of the United States, et al.,* Civil Action No. 8113, "Complaint for Declaratory Judgment to Establish Citizenship." 1954–56.

Doughty, W. D. "History of Robstown." Undated Manuscript. Kilgore Collection, Special Collections and Archives, Bell Library, Texas A&M University-Corpus Christi, Corpus Christi, Tex.

Dow School Census, 1925. Dow School, Houston Independent School District, Houston, Tex.

Eguía, Ernest. Papers. Houston Metropolitan Research Center, Houston Public Library, Houston, Tex.

Eisenhower, Dwight D. Papers. The Dwight D. Eisenhower Library, Abilene, Kans.

Frucht, Sig. Papers. Houston Metropolitan Research Center, Houston Public Library, Houston, Tex.

García, Dr. Hector P. Papers. Special Collections and Archives, Bell Library, Texas A&M University-Corpus Christi, Corpus Christi, Tex.

García, Isidro. Collection. Houston Metropolitan Research Center, Houston Public Library, Houston, Tex.

García, Mr. and Mrs. Lupe. Collection. Mexican American Small Collections, Houston Metropolitan Research Center, Houston Public Library, Houston, Tex.

General Escobedo Municipio, Nuevo León. Civil Registration. Matrimonios, 1868–1910, Nacimientos, 1896–1930, Defunciones, 1868–1916. Genealogical Department, the Church of Jesus Christ of Latter-Day Saints, Salt Lake City, Utah. Microfilm.

Gomez, Melecio. Family Collection. Houston Metropolitan Research Center, Houston Public Library, Houston, Tex.

Hale, L. DeWitt. Papers. Special Collections and Archives, Bell Library, Texas A&M University-Corpus Christi, Corpus Christi, Tex.

Harris County, Tex. Records. Office of County Clerk, Houston, Tex.

Hernández, Alfred J. Papers. Houston Metropolitan Research Center, Houston Public Library, Houston, Tex.

Herrera, John J. Papers. Houston Metropolitan Research Center, Houston Public Library, Houston, Tex.

Holcombe, Oscar. Papers. Houston Metropolitan Research Center, Houston Public Library, Houston, Tex.

Housing Authority of the City of Houston. Minutes. 1952–65. Houston Housing Authority Office, Houston, Tex.

Houston Independent School District. Board of Education. Records.

Imperial Sugar Company. Records. Houston Metropolitan Research Center, Houston Public Library, Houston, Tex.

Johnson, Lyndon B. Papers. Lyndon B. Johnson Library, Austin, Tex.

Kennedy, John F. Papers. John F. Kennedy Library, Boston, Mass.

LULAC Council No. 60. Records. Houston Metropolitan Research Center, Houston Public Library, Houston, Tex.

Mexican-American Photograph Collection. Houston Metropolitan Research Center, Houston Public Library, Houston, Tex.

Mireles, E. E., and Jovita González de Mireles. Papers. Special Collections and Archives, Bell Library, Texas A&M University-Corpus Christi, Corpus Christi, Tex.

Mora-Torres, Juan. "The Transformation of a Peripheral Society: A Social History of Nuevo León, 1848–1920." Ph.D. diss., University of Chicago, 1991.

Morales, Mr. and Mrs. Félix H. Papers. Houston Metropolitan Research Center, Houston Public Library, Houston, Tex.

Our Lady of Guadalupe Church, Houston, Tex. Records. Genealogical Department, The Church of Jesus Christ of Latter-Day Saints, Salt Lake City, Utah. Microfilm.

Quintanilla, Guadalupe Campos. "The 'Little School of the 400' and Its Impact on Education for the Spanish Dominant Bilingual Children of Texas." Ed.D. diss., University of Houston, 1976.

Rodríguez, Jake. Papers. Benson Latin American Collection, University of Texas at Austin, Austin, Tex.

Rodríguez, Juan. Family Collection. Houston Metropolitan Research Center, Houston Public Library, Houston, Tex.

Rodríguez, Juvencio. Collection. Houston Metropolitan Research Center, Houston Public Library, Houston, Tex.

Small Collections. Houston Metropolitan Research Center, Houston Public Library.

Texas Department of Health. Bureau of Vital Statistics. Certificates of Births and Deaths. Austin, Tex.

Tijerina, Mr. and Mrs. Felix, Sr. Papers. Houston Metropolitan Research Center, Houston Public Library, Houston, Tex.

U.S. Bureau of the Census. Fourteenth Census of the United States, 1920. Fort Bend County, Tex. Clayton Genealogical Library, Houston Public Library, Houston, Tex. Microfilm.

———. Thirteenth Census of the United States, 1910. Fort Bend County, Tex. Texas and Local History Department, Houston Public Library, Houston, Tex. Microfilm.

———. Thirteenth Census of the United States, 1910. Victoria County, Tex. Texas and Local History Department, Houston Public Library, Houston, Tex. Microfilm.

U.S. Department of Justice. Federal Bureau of Investigation. Records. Washington, D.C. File: Felix Tijerina, 39-2521.

Vázquez, Alfonso. Papers. Houston Metropolitan Research Center, Houston Public Library, Houston, Tex.

PUBLISHED SOURCES

Acuña, Rodolfo. *Occupied America: A History of Chicanos.* New York: Harper and Row, 1988.

Alexander, Louis. "Texas Helps Her Little Latins." *Saturday Evening Post,* August 5, 1961.

Allsup, Carl. *The American G.I. Forum: Origins and Evolution.* Austin: Center for Mexican American Studies, University of Texas, 1982.

Alvarado Segovia, Francisco Javier, Rogelio Velázquez de León, and Sandra Lara Esquivel. *Historias de nuestros barrios.* Monterrey, Mexico: Gobierno del Estado de Nuevo León, 1995.

Beaumont City Directory, 1941. Dallas and Houston: Morrison & Fourmy Directory Co., 1941.

Beaumont City Directory, 1953. Dallas: Morrison & Fourmy Directory Co., 1953.

Calderón, Carlos I. "The Fewest Words to Open the Widest Doors." *Texas Outlook,* July, 1956, pp. 14–16.

Calvert, Robert A., and Arnoldo De León. *The History of Texas*. Arlington Heights, Ill.: Harlan Davidson, 1990.

Carleton, Don E. *Red Scare!: Right-Wing Hysteria, Fifties Fanaticism, and Their Legacy in Texas*. Austin: Texas Monthly Press, 1985.

Carleton, Don E., and Thomas H. Kreneck. *Houston: Back Where We Started*. Houston: de Menil Publications, 1979.

Carrell, Theresa, and Traxel Stevens. "Leaping the Language Barrier." *Texas Outlook*, September, 1961, pp. 19–20, 44.

Cavazos, Israel. *Nuevo León: montes jovenes sobre la antigua llanura*. Mexico City: Monografía Estatal, Secretaría de Educación Pública, 1982.

Congressional Record–Appendix. 85th Cong., 2d sess., March 18, 1958.

Corpus Christi City Directory. Corpus Christi, Tex., and Asheville, N.C.: The Miller Press, 1929.

Cumberland, Charles C. *Mexican Revolution: The Constitutionalist Years*. Austin: University of Texas Press, 1972.

De León, Arnoldo. *Ethnicity in the Sunbelt: A History of Mexican Americans in Houston*. Houston: Mexican American Studies Program, University of Houston, 1989.

———. *The Tejano Community, 1836–1900*. Albuquerque: University of New Mexico Press, 1982.

Dauplaise, Marie. "They Have a Simple Dream, 400 English Words for Every Child." *Houston Press*, Mar. 12, 1958.

Elliott, Keith. "Now Juanito Can Read." *Coronet*, July, 1961, pp. 132–36.

Fiftieth Anniversary, 1912–1962: Rotary Club of Houston. N.p.: n.d.

"A Four-Hundred-Word Start." *Time*, August 17, 1959, p. 56.

Galarza, Ernesto. *Barrio Boy: The Story of a Boy's Acculturation*. South Bend, Ind.: University of Notre Dame Press, 1971.

García, Juan Ramón. *Operation Wetback: The Mass Deportation of Mexican Undocumented Workers in 1954*. Westport, Conn.: Greenwood Press, 1980.

García, Mario T. "Americans All: The Mexican-American Generation and the Politics of Wartime Los Angeles, 1941–45." *Social Science Quarterly* 65 (June, 1984): 278–89.

———. *Mexican Americans: Leadership, Ideology, and Identity, 1930–1960*. New Haven and London: Yale University Press, 1989.

———. "Mexican Americans and the Politics of Citizenship: The Case of El Paso, 1936." *New Mexico Historical Review* 59 (April, 1984): 187–204.

Garza Guajardo, Gustavo. *Testimonios de ciudad General Escobedo, N.L.* Monterrey, Mexico: Folletos de Historia del Noreste, Universidad Autonoma de Nuevo León, n.d.

Garza Guajardo, Juan Ramón. *Capilla de San Nicolás de Bari*. Mexico City: C y C Impresores, 1994.

———. *La estación del topo grande de General Escobedo, N.L.* Monterrey, Mexico: Grafo Print Editores, 1997.

———. *Municipio de General Escobedo, N.L.: historia de sus ayuntamientos (1868–1997)*. Monterrey, Mexico: Presidencia Municipal de General Escobedo, N.L., 1997.

Giles, Robert C. *125th Anniversary: Diocese of Galveston-Houston, 1847–1972*. N.p.: N.d.

Grebler, Leo, Joan W. Moore, Ralph C. Guzman, et al. *The Mexican American People: The Nation's Second Largest Minority*. New York: Free Press, 1970.

Grimes, Roy, ed. *Three Hundred Years in Victoria County*. Victoria, Tex.: Victoria Advocate Pub. Co., 1968.

Haynes, Robert V. *A Night of Violence: The Houston Riot of 1917*. Baton Rouge: Louisiana State University Press, 1976.

Hernández, Alfred J. "The Little School of the 400." In LULAC: *Fifty Years of Serving Hispanics, Golden Anniversary, 1929–1979*.

Houston City Directory (published under various titles). Houston and Galveston: Morrison & Fourmy Directory Co., 1908–55; Dallas: R. L. Polk & Co., 1958–60.

The Houston Community Chest and Its Agencies: Campaign for 1937. Pamphlet. Texas and Local History Department, Houston Public Library.

The Houston Community Chest: A Description of Nine Months' Working, with a Statement of Accounts and a List of Subscribers, with Amounts Pledged, 1925, 1928, 1930. Pamphlets. Texas and Local History Department, Houston Public Library.

Jackson, Kenneth T. *The Ku Klux Klan in the City, 1915–1930*. New York: Oxford University Press, 1967.

Johnson, William R. *A Short History of the Sugar Industry in Texas*. [Houston]: Texas Gulf Coast Historical Association, 1961.

Jones, John. *This Is the Way It Was: The Reminiscences of Sig Frucht*. Houston: N.p., 1979.

Journal of the House of Representatives of the Regular Session of the Fifty-sixth Legislature of the State of Texas. Austin, 1959.

Journal of the Senate of the State of Texas Regular Session of the Fifty-sixth Legislature. Austin, 1959.

Knight, Alan. *The Mexican Revolution*. 2 vols. Cambridge and New York: Cambridge University Press, 1986.

Kreneck, Thomas H. *Del Pueblo: A Pictorial History of Houston's Hispanic Community*. Houston: Houston International University, 1989.

Los municipios de Nuevo León. (Colección: Enciclopedia de los Municipios de México). Monterrey, Mexico: Gobierno del Estado de Nuevo León, 1988.

LULAC: *Fifty Years of Serving Hispanics, Golden Anniversary 1929–1979*. N.p.: N.d.

McComb, David G. *Houston: A History*. Austin: University of Texas Press, 1981.

McMillan, S. A., and Philip Rich. *The Book of Fort Bend County Texas*. [Richmond, Tex.]: [Fort Bend County], 1926.

Map of Houston, Harris Co., Texas. Houston: P. Whitty, Civil Engineer and Land Surveyor, 1900. Texas and Local History Department, Houston Public Library, Houston, Tex.

Map of Houston, 1928. Houston: River Oaks Corporation, 1928. Texas and Local History Department, Houston Public Library, Houston, Tex.

Márquez, Benjamin. LULAC: *The Evolution of a Mexican American Political Organization*. Austin: University of Texas Press, 1993.

Martínez, Oscar. "On the Size of the Chicano Population: New Estimates, 1850–1900." *Aztlán: International Journal of Chicano Studies Research* 6 (spring, 1975): 43–59.

Meier, Matt S., and Feliciano Rivera. *The Chicanos: A History of Mexican Americans*. New York: Hill and Wang, 1972.

———. *Dictionary of Mexican American History*. Westport, Conn.: Greenwood Press, 1981.

Montejano, David. *Anglos and Mexicans in the Making of Texas, 1836–1986*. Austin: University of Texas Press, 1987.

1923 Street Map of the City of Houston. Houston: Texas Map and Blue Printing Co., 1923. Texas and Local History Department, Houston Public Library, Houston, Tex.

Nueces County Historical Society. *The History of Nueces County*. Austin: Jenkins Publishing Company, 1972.

"An Outstanding Lulac: Felix Tijerina." *LULAC News,* February, 1954, p. 49. LULAC Council No. 60 Records, Houston Metropolitan Research Center, Houston Public Library.

Ragsdale, Silas B. "Biography: Felix Tijerina." *The Log: Weekly Bulletin of the Rotary Club of Houston,* 36, 7, August 19, 1948, p. 4.

———. "Mother-Wife-Friends Form Real Keystone of Felix's Success Story." *Houston Press,* August 26, 1948, p. 9.

Ray, Edgar W. *The Grand Huckster: Houston's Judge Roy Hofheinz, Genius of the Astrodome.* Memphis, Tenn.: Memphis State University Press, 1980.

Reisler, Mark. *By the Sweat of Their Brow: Mexican Immigrant Labor in the United States, 1900–1940.* Westport, Conn.: Greenwood Press, 1976.

Rhinehart, Marilyn D., and Thomas H. Kreneck. "'In the Shadow of Uncertainty': Texas Mexicans and Repatriation in Houston during the Great Depression." *Houston Review* 10, no. 1 (1988): 21–33.

Rivera, George, Jr., and Juventino Mejía. "Más aya del ancho río: Mexicanos in Western New York." *Aztlán: International Journal of Chicano Studies Research* 7, no. 3 (fall, 1976): 499–513.

Rodríguez, Eugene, Jr. *Henry B. González: A Political Profile.* New York: Arno Press, 1976.

Roel, Santiago. *Nuevo León: Apuntes históricos, tomo II.* Monterrey, Mexico: [J. P. Cueva], 1938.

Romo, Ricardo. "The Urbanization of Southwestern Chicanos in the Early Twentieth Century." *New Scholar* 6 (1977): 183–207.

Rosales, Francisco A. "The Mexican Immigrant Experience in Chicago, Houston, and Tucson: Comparisons and Contrasts." In *Houston: A Twentieth Century Urban Frontier,* edited by Francisco A. Rosales and Barry J. Kaplan. Port Washington, N.Y.: Associated Faculty Press, 1983.

———. "Mexicans in Houston: The Struggle to Survive." *Houston Review* 3, no. 2 (summer, 1981): 224–48.

Ross, Irwin. "Harold Medina—Judge Extraordinary." *Reader's Digest,* February, 1950, pp. 85–90.

Ruiz, Ramón Eduardo. *The Great Rebellion: Mexico, 1905–1924.* New York: Norton, 1980.

San Miguel, Guadalupe, Jr. *"Let All of Them Take Heed": Mexican Americans and the Campaign for Educational Equality in Texas, 1910–1981.* Austin: University of Texas Press, 1987.

Saragoza, Alex M. *The Monterrey Elite and the Mexican State, 1880–1940.* Austin: University of Texas Press, 1988.

Sifuentes Espinoza, Daniel. "De un rancho a otro: haciendas congregaciones y poblados en Nuevo León, siglo XIX." *Bitácora: revista trimestral de la hacienda San Pedro* (mayo, 1997, no. 1): 27–55.

Sorelle, James M. "'An de Po Cullud Man Is in de Wuss Fix uv Awl': Black Occupational Status in Houston, Texas, 1920–1940." *Houston Review* 1, no. 1 (spring, 1979): 15–26.

Taylor, Paul Schuster. *An American-Mexican Frontier: Nueces County.* Chapel Hill: University of North Carolina Press, 1934.

Texas Almanac and State Industrial Guide, 1911. Dallas and Galveston: A. H. Belo & Company, 1911.

Texas Almanac and State Industrial Guide, 1939–40. Dallas: A. H. Belo Corporation, 1939.

Texas Almanac and State Industrial Guide, 1941–42. Dallas: A. H. Belo Corporation, 1941.

Texas Good Neighbor Commission. *Texas: Friend and Neighbor.* Austin: Von Boeckmann-Jones Press, 1961.

Texas Legal Directory, 1970. Los Angeles: Legal Directories Pub. Co., 1970.

Texas Legislature. *Non-English Speaking Children: Pre-School Instructional Program.* General and Special Laws of the State of Texas, 56th Regular Session, 1959, H.B. 51.

Tijerina Cantú, Ernesto. *Apuntes genealógicos familia Tijerina, China, Gral. Bravo, y los Herreras.* Monterrey, Mexico: Grafo Print Editores, 1996.

Tsanoff, Corinne S. *Neighborhood Doorways.* Houston: Neighborhood Centers Association of Houston and Harris County, 1958.

U.S. Senate Committee on Labor and Public Welfare. *Elementary and Secondary Education Act of 1965: Hearings before the Subcommittee on Education.* 89th Cong., 1st sess., 1965, S.R. 370.

Valdez, Sister Mary Paul, M.C.D.P. *The History of the Missionary Catechists of Divine Providence.* N.p., 1978.

Walls, Eric. "Texas's 'Sugar Bowl' Heaps Three Million Pounds of Sugar Daily." *Texas Historian* 34, no. 2 (November, 1973): 2–7.

Webb, Walter Prescott, ed. *The Handbook of Texas.* Vols. 1 and 2. Austin: Texas State Historical Association, 1952.

Zamora, Emilio. *The World of the Mexican Worker in Texas.* College Station: Texas A&M University Press, 1993.

Zigler, Edward, and Susan Muenchow. *Head Start: The Inside Story of America's Most Successful Educational Experiment.* New York: Basic Books, 1992.

Zigler, Edward, and Jeanette Valentine, eds. *Project Head Start: A Legacy of the War on Poverty.* New York: Free Press, 1979.

INDEX

FT refers to Felix Tijerina. JT refers to Janie González Tijerina. Photos are indicated by *fig.*

executive director appointment, 252;
FT-Godínez correspondence, 285;
FT's ambassadorship, 282, 283;
McAllen proposal, 249; Minnesota
meeting, 260; Operation Little
Schools, 258; passive membership plan,
196; publicity director appointment,
230; resignation, 289; Verver's pre-
school classes, 201
Canales, Alejandro, 51
Canales, Henry, 112
Canales, J. T., 68
Cancer Patients' Aid, Emergency Relief
Committee for, 149–50
"Cantinflas" (comedian), 124–26
Cantú, Gregorio, 61, 65
Cantú, Reverend Toribio, 17
"Capon Dinner," 136
Cárdenas, Alfredo M., 162
Cárdenas, Leo, 199, 200
Carmack, George, 123–24, 188, 279, 294
Carpenter, T. C., 179
Carr, Waggoner, 245
Casas, David, 132
Casas, J. B., 196, 289
Casas, Raúl, 252
Castañeda, Carlos E., 102, 168
Catholic Church: FT's children, 305;
FT's rites of passage, 17, 20, 61, 315,
333–34n 42; importance to Dionicia,
27, 28, 46, 56–57; urbanization role,
44–47
Cavazos, Juan L., 17
Center Street neighborhood, 56–57,
61, 72
Central National Bank, 304
Centurioni, Father Pedro, 46
Cerda, David, 233
Chaírez, Francisco, 63–64, 75, 97, 168
Chaírez Pérez, Inocencia (Chencha), 168
Chancellor, John, 287
character (FT's): bicultural, 9–11; con-
cern for extended family, 43, 44; con-
ciliatory/diplomatic nature, 70, 97,

100, 104, 134–35, 270; courtesy, 42;
ego, 94, 104; eulogized, 316–17; family responsibilities, 29, 31, 32, 40; generosity, 28, 48, 98, 165–66, 339n 23;
media portrayal, 13, 89, 110–11; par-
enting style, 116–17, 142, 209, 274,
305–307
Chicago: Council formation, 196–97;
LULAC 1959 convention, 249–52
Chicago Tribune, 250
childhood/youth (FT's): appearance, 42,
51; birth, 17, 321–22n 7; border crossing episode, 43–44; confirmation, 20;
courtship, 49, 51; education, 22, 28,
42, 48; emigration, 21–22; Escobedo
life, 17–18, 19–21, 322n 8, 324n 17,
fig. 1; family members, 16–17;
Guadalupe Church, 44–46; Houston
community influences, 48–49, 51–52;
Houston move, 30, 327n 61; job assistance for family, 43, 44; Mexican Inn
opening, 52–53, 56; move of family to
Houston, 35–36; name change, 17,
33–35, 327–28n 65; Produce Row
job, 31–33; restaurant work, 33, 40–
42, 52; Sugar Land period, 25–30,
326n 50, 326n 51, 326n 52; Victoria
County moves, 22–24
children (FT/JT's), *fig. 14;* adoption, 89,
105, 115, 142; FT's death, 314–15;
naturalization, 172–73, 177; restaurant
operations, 113, 117; upbringing, 116–
17, 142, 209, 274, 305–307
Christian, George, 223
Christie, H. Merlyn, 107
Christmas Basket Fiesta and Dance,
163–64
Chuck Wagon (magazine), 316
Cinco de Mayo sponsorships, 58, 91, 98
Cisneros, Petra, 164
Citizens' Charter Committee, 130–32
citizenship issue: birth "affidavit" episode,
81–85; border crossing impact, 43–44,
80–81; civic memberships and, 68, 69,

141–42; media profiles, 138–39, 142–44; México Bello club, 75; parents/siblings, 49–50, 143; personality, 137–38, 144; Pilot Club, 139–40, *fig. 13;* public partnership with FT, 7, 78, 211; relationship with FT's family, 72, 117–18; Republican presidential candidates, 276, 312; restaurant operations, 73, 74, 90–91, 115, *fig. 11;* Rotary Club, 140–41, 273, 294–95, 296–98; work history, 50–51, 61. *See also* children (FT/JT's)

Tijerina, Jesús María, 322*n* 8

Tijerina, María Victoria (sister): Alba Award ceremony, 168; Artesian Place neighborhood, 39–40, 42–43; birth, 16; Center Street neighborhood, 56–57, 72; citizenship issue, 82, 187; education, 47–48, 57, 101; emigration, 21–22; Escobedo life, 17–18, 19–21, 322*n* 8, 324*n* 17, *fig. 1;* FT's death, 315; Guadalupe Church, 44–46; Houston move, 35–36, 327*n* 61; Sugar Land period, 25–29, 326*n* 52; Victoria County moves, 22–24

Tijerina, Pete, 156, 165, 209, 230

Tijerina, Trinidad (sister), 16, 21, 26–27

Tijerina, Victoria. *See* Tijerina, María Victoria (sister)

Tijerina Álvarez, Rafael (father), 16–17, 19–20, 21

Tijerina Elizondo, Rafael (grandfather), 16, 21

Los Tijerina (hacienda), 322*n* 8

Tijerina Villarreal, Felix: summarized, 3–13

Tiller, Frank M., 294

Time magazine, 254–56

Title I funding, 307–308

"tomato catsup" story, 41–42

Topo Chico, 320–21*n* 3

Topo Grande, 320–21*n* 3

Toribio, Charles, 196–97

Torres, Albino, 122, 149–50

Torres, Pascuala, 20

Tovar, Henry, 163

Tower, John, 284, 288

Trejo, Frank, 288

Treviño, Albert, 212

Truan, Carlos, 290, 308, 374*n* 108

Trujillo, Joe, 194

Twelve Year Plan, 278

"umbrella organization" effort, 150–51

United Citizens Association, 131–32

United Fund, 136

University of Texas at Austin, 198

urbanization phase: overview, 5–6, 37–38, 53–54; anti-Mexican sentiment, 33–35; church's role, 44–47; family support network, 42–43, 44; Houston's incentives, 30–33, 35

Valdez, Frank M., 284, 289

Valentine, Ann, 111

Vanderbilt Little School, 218–19

Variety Boys Club, 124–26, 154

Vaubel, E. A., 293

Vázquez, Hilda, 234, 252

Vázquez, Rosa, 50

Vela, Albert G., 81, 82, 299–300

Verges, George, 40

Verver, Isabel, 10, 200–203, 210, 215, 219, 354*n* 37

Victoria County moves, 22–24

Villa, General Francisco, 20, 59

Villarreal, Atanacio, 20

Villarreal, Aurelio (uncle): daughter, 323*n* 13; Edna to San Antonio moves, 35; emigration, 18–19; return for FT's family, 21–22; Sugar Land period, 25–27; Victoria County moves, 22–24

Villarreal, Cecilio (cousin), 57, 72

Villarreal, Concepción, 17

Villarreal, Dionicia. *See* Villarreal de Tijerina, Dionicia (mother)

Villarreal, Domingo (cousin), *fig. 9;* emigration, 44; Felix Mexican Restaurant,

ISBN 0-89096-936-1

90000

9 780890 969366